DOWN YOUR AISLES

The Diocese of Hexham and Newcastle 1850-2000

by

Michael Morris & Leo Gooch

Northern Cross
2000

First published in Great Britain 2000 by
Northern Cross, St Joseph's, St Paul's Rd., Hartlepool TS26 9EY

Copyright: The authors, photographers and the trustees of Northern Cross

ISBN 0-9538280-0-X

Cover designed by Dominic Bailey

Typesetting and printing by Edward Thompson Printers Ltd., Sunderland

Contents

Prefaces	4-5
Part 1: An Outline History of the Diocese 1850-2000	7
Index to Part 1	59
Part 2: Parishes of the Diocese	65
Index to Part 2	289
Select Bibliography	305

Bishop's House
East Denton Hall
800 West Road
Newcastle upon Tyne
NE5 2BJ

The diocese of Hexham and Newcastle has a long and distinguished history. The See of Hexham was founded in the seventh century, merged with that of Lindisfarne in the ninth century and moved to Chester-le-Street; it was then transferred to Durham in the last years of the first millennium. The old English hierarchy came to an end at the Reformation and was not restored until 1850 at which time the ancient See of Hexham was revived (Newcastle was added in 1861).

Now at the end of the second millennium we celebrate the 150th anniversary of that restoration with a book which describes how the diocese had developed over the last century and a half and it does this in two parts. Firstly, there is an outline history of the diocese as a whole, which is being published for the first time, then there are sixty-six individual parish histories which have been published separately in *Northern Cross* over the years. The two parts complement each other admirably and serve to make us realise that as members of our local churches we belong to a wider community.

I heartily commend *Down Your Aisles* and congratulate the authors and *Northern Cross* for producing such a valuable and interesting volume.

+ Ambrose Griffiths

Ambrose Griffiths O.S.B.
Bishop of Hexham and Newcastle

Boarbank Hall
Grange-over-Sands
Cumbria
LA11 7NH

I welcome this Northern Cross publication of Michael Morris' 'Down Your Aisles' articles and Leo Gooch's 'Outline History of the Diocese'. Each author has courageously undertaken a difficult task.

Michael Morris began his work many years ago when the Northern Cross began to publish his monthly 'Down Your Aisle' article, featuring photographs of one of our diocesan churches and a short history of the parish. I have read and enjoyed each of them as they appeared. They aroused interest far beyond each parish concerned, and helped us to develop a greater consciousness of our diocesan history. Inevitably, not every person and place could be mentioned, but that was far outweighed by the wide coverage given to each 'Aisle' parish.

The publication of these articles and pictures has given Leo Gooch a chance of composing his outline history of our diocese. He has undertaken an even more difficult task because inevitably, so much cannot be mentioned in an outline which has to give a good, general picture of our history. It is also extremely hard to write about recent history because readers will inevitably have their own very different opinions about some of the matters mentioned. All told, Leo has given us a useful outline, to supplement Michael's articles and also to provide us with a reliable background to them.

This book consolidates and pushes forward a good deal of work done in recent years, at parish and diocesan level, to record some of our diocesan history. I hope that someone will one day be tempted to undertake a definitive history of the diocese of Hexham and Newcastle since its foundation in 1850.

In the meantime, this book should give great pleasure in the diocese, and serve as a useful Jubilee 2000 memento as well as commemorating the 150th Anniversary of the diocese which occurs also in this year of Jubilee.

✝ Hugh Lindsay

Bishop of Hexham and Newcastle 1974-1992

Some Episcopal Coats of Arms

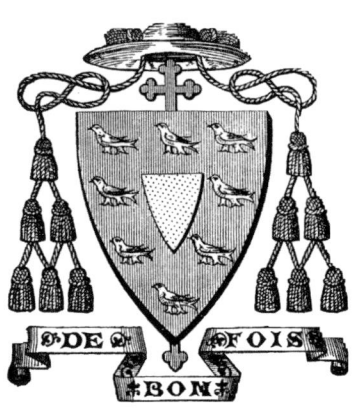

Bishop J. Chadwick

Bishop J.W. Bewick

Bishop T.W. Wilkinson

Bishop R. Collins

Bishop J. Thorman

Bishop J. McCormack

Bishop J. Cunningham

DOWN YOUR AISLES

Part 1

An Outline History of the Diocese of Hexham and Newcastle 1850-2000

by

Leo Gooch
MA, PhD, FRHist.S

Acknowledgements and Editorial Notes

This essay is based largely on the Hexham and Newcastle Diocesan Archives, the annual *Northern Catholic Calendar*, the monthly *Northern Cross* and the collection of Catholic periodicals at Ushaw College, as well as the published books and articles listed in the Bibliography. I am most grateful to the Rt. Revd. Ambrose Griffiths, MA, OSB, and the Revd. Fr. James O'Keefe, President of Ushaw College, for permission to use the materials in their care. Mr Robin Gard, MA, Diocesan Archivist, has been of inestimable help at Bishop's House; Dr Alistair McGregor, Librarian, kindly facilitated my research at Ushaw College; and Mr John Bailey, Editor of *Northern Cross*, obligingly gave access to the paper's files. I would also like to thank Mrs Averill Robson for compiling the index. The Rt. Revd. Hugh Lindsay and the Revd. Fr Michael Finnigan read the text and saved me from some howlers; they will see, however, that I have not always followed their advice on other matters. Hence none of those mentioned above is responsible for any opinion expressed here. I would especially like to thank Mr. F. S. Cronin, Mr. S. White and Mr. W. E. Boddy for shepherding the book through to publication so expertly.

It should be noted that the discussion centres on the present diocese, comprising the historic counties of Northumberland and Durham, not the diocese as erected in 1850 which included Westmorland and Cumberland. Nor does it touch on the history of Ushaw College which has already been written by the Revd. Dr. David Milburn.

Finally, it may be useful to say a word on the currency in use for much of the period covered in this book. One pound [£1] had 20 shillings [20s.] and there were twelve pence [12d.] in a shilling. £1 now has 100 pence. The Bank of England calculates that the approximate relative value of £1 in 2000 was £20 in 1950, £55 in 1900 and £48 in 1850.

On 29 September 1850, Pope Pius IX signed the Apostolic Letter *Universalis Ecclesiae* restoring the hierarchy of England and Wales which had been extinguished at the Reformation. Britain had become a missionary country at the break with Rome and, as was usual in such cases, the Holy See appointed *vicars apostolic* to govern the church in lieu of *bishops in ordinary*. A bishop in ordinary has full, personal and independent powers whereas a vicar apostolic, although he has episcopal rank, only has such limited powers as are delegated to him by the Pope. In 1688 England was divided into four vicariates or districts, and the Northern District comprised the whole country north of the Humber until 1840 when a further subdivision was made. A succession of fourteen vicars apostolic administered the Northern District before the hierarchy was restored in 1850.

A revival of English Catholicism began in the late eighteenth century: Catholic Relief Acts were passed in 1778 and 1791; the Catholic population began to grow from the end of the Napoleonic wars and Catholics were to be found at most levels of society. There were no Catholic peers resident in the north-east and only two baronets, but over twenty landed gentry families lived in Northumberland and Durham, and the heads of those families served on the bench and in other civic capacities such as lords lieutenant or sheriffs. They supported mission-stations, not just for themselves and their dependents, but for all Catholics living in their neighbourhoods, and most of their chapels were rebuilt around that time to provide for the growing congregations. The major towns of the region also had chapels, though in secluded locations. Thus the last generation of English recusants laid the foundations on which the achievements of the post-restoration Church would build. Indeed, progress was such that it was thought opportune by many to seek a restoration of the hierarchy when the Relief Acts were being negotiated. But the Holy See could not agree so long as the English Catholics lay under any form of restriction and it was not until after Catholic Emancipation had been enacted in 1829 that a restoration became possible. But then, a variety of political factors at home and abroad prevented progress for a further twenty years.

The British government raised no objections when it was told in 1847 of the planned restoration. The restoration was referred to in parliament on several occasions and the press reported it from time to time. So as not to offend Anglican sensitivities by adopting titles of existing dioceses, care had been taken to choose new or unused ancient sees for the restored hierarchy: Beverley, Hexham, Liverpool, Salford, and so on. The vicars apostolic were confident enough therefore to reassure the Holy See that the political climate was favourable for a restoration and that it would be accepted throughout the country with indifference (except, as always, by extremists). But, when Nicholas Wiseman, the newly-appointed Cardinal Archbishop of Westminster, announced the restoration from Rome in an ebullient pastoral letter *Ex Porta Flaminia*, the age-old English fears of Catholicism were reawakened and a fierce storm broke over his head. Memories of the Oxford Movement were still fresh in the public's mind, of course, and anti-Catholic prejudice had grown as migration from Ireland had increased. And now the somewhat jubilant language of Wiseman's pastoral letter was interpreted by many as insinuating papal jurisdiction over the whole country. Queen Victoria asked 'Am I Queen of England or am I not?' *The Times* felt obliged to remind its readers about the Gunpowder Plot, and the *Newcastle Guardian* prophesied that the end of the world was at hand. The outraged Bishop Edward Maltby of Durham wrote to the Prime Minister, Lord John Russell, deploring what he called this 'Papal Aggression', whereupon the premier took fright and replied with an open letter hinting at legal action against the new hierarchy. An act prohibiting the use of any English territorial title by Catholic prelates was introduced shortly afterwards and passed into law on 1 August 1851.

In the north-east, the 'no-Popery' campaign was supported mostly by the Dissenters who circulated petitions round the reading-rooms and from door-to-door. They also convened public meetings in town halls to protest against the restoration, but Catholics attended in large numbers to vote down inflammatory motions. Feelings ran high, however, and many meetings became so rowdy that violence broke out. On one occasion the preacher and his supporters had some difficulty reaching safety after causing a riot by attempting an anti-Catholic open-air sermon in Sandgate, an Irish enclave in Newcastle. (The fracas was quickly rendered by J.P. Robson into the folk-ballad *The Horrid War i' Sandgeyt*.) The Catholic clergy preached conciliatory sermons and Charles Larkin, a prominent Tyneside Catholic surgeon, gave several public lectures which helped to moderate the anti-Catholic hysteria. In any case, most people, especially, it was observed, 'the middle and trading classes', kept aloof from the agitation because they were satisfied that the restoration would make no inroads on Anglican supremacy and that it was purely an internal Catholic matter. Among others, the Town Council of Tynemouth refused to entertain a 'no-Popery' motion.

The Catholics were not substantially inconvenienced by this latest bout of hostility. Indeed, early in November at the height of the agitation, Alessandro Gavazzi, an apostate Italian priest, was lecturing against Catholicism in Sunderland, South Shields and Durham, but at the same time Fr Betham with the choir of St Andrews, all fully robed, took part in a funeral procession through Ouseburn without incident. Nor was Fr Ignatius Spencer molested as he went about in full Passionist dress, even when he was urging people to say a Hail Mary each day for the conversion of England. Public lectures on the faith given in Sunderland in 1851 were respectfully attended. Cardinal Wiseman carried out public engagements in Hartlepool, Darlington, Esh, Stella and Newcastle without interference a month after the Ecclesiastical Titles Act became law. And in 1852 a 500-ton East Indiaman named the *Cardinal Wiseman* was launched by Messrs. Austen & Mill of Sunderland. The agitation quickly subsided, then, and, though it was not repealed until 1871, the Ecclesiastical Titles Act was never invoked. But the episode led to the formation of a Catholic Defence Association in the north-east to circulate tracts and give talks explaining the faith. Similarly, the Catholic electorate of the region formed voting blocs in an effort to protect their religious interests - a strategy which many a parliamentary candidate would find disconcerting.

Bishop W. Hogarth

The first Bishop of Hexham in the restored hierarchy was the 64-year-old William Hogarth. He was born at Dodding Green in Westmorland and, in December 1809, he was ordained priest at Ushaw College, which had opened the previous year. He stayed on as a professor for some years but in 1824 he took over the mission at Darlington and he would remain there for the rest of his life. He was a highly energetic man with, as Bishop Ullathorne noted, a marked capacity for business, and it was not altogether surprising that he became vicar general to three vicars apostolic: John Briggs, Francis Mostyn and William Riddell. The latter died in November 1847, having contracted cholera while ministering to the sick in Newcastle, and Hogarth succeeded him in July 1848 thus becoming the last Vicar Apostolic of the Northern District.

The new diocese of Hexham embodied the medieval dioceses of Durham and Carlisle and comprised the counties of Northumberland, Durham, Cumberland and Westmorland, which had already been divided into four deaneries in 1849: North Northumberland; South Northumberland & North Durham; South Durham; Westmorland &

Cumberland. The name of the diocese was intended by the Roman Curia to be Newcastle but Hogarth preferred Hexham because it was

> by far the most central and easy of access by means of railroad from all parts of the District and as to the idea of gratifying the people of Newcastle, I think it of little value. A bishop may go into Newcastle occasionally on great occasions, but no one should be condemned to live there ...

It seems that he even contemplated building a cathedral at Hexham for, on 1 September 1852, two months after creating a cathedral chapter of eleven canons, headed by a Provost, he 'formally took possession of the Church of St Mary, Newcastle-on-Tyne, as his Cathedral church for the time being, until a Cathedral should be erected in the episcopal city' [Minute Book of the Cathedral Chapter]. Hogarth, however, soon came to realise the importance of Tyneside: the first Diocesan Synod was held in Newcastle in February 1854; St Mary's was consecrated as the cathedral in August 1860; and he raised no objections to the renaming of the diocese as Hexham and Newcastle in May 1861. But still he declined to live either in Hexham or in Newcastle.

*

The diocesan mission on the eastern side of the Pennines in 1850 consisted of 35 churches or chapels, many of which had been in place for over a century, served by 55 priests, the overwhelming majority of whom were secular priests, but there were Benedictines at Birtley, Cowpen, Morpeth and in a few Northumbrian chaplaincies. Alnwick was served by a Jesuit until 1856. The Dominicans took over St Andrew's in Newcastle in 1860 and moved into their own new church, St Dominic's in the eastern part of the town in 1861. The number of Catholics in the north-east at the time of the restoration can be established from the national Census of Religion which was held on Easter Sunday 1851. The clergy were required to state the number in their congregations over several months (not just on Easter Sunday) and their replies permit us to calculate the overall size of the Catholic community, especially as many of the priests in the densely populated towns took absentees into account. It was reported that only 580 of the 1,220 Catholics in Durham city went to Mass because the chapel was too small. Some 3,500 people attended Mass at the two churches in Newcastle on Easter Sunday, but Fr Cullen reckoned that there were some 10,000 in the town; Fr Smith said there were 900 Catholics in Bishop Auckland but only 240 usually attended Mass; and the priests at Gateshead and Sunderland said much the same kind of thing. Taking such remarks into account, then, the census showed that around 26,000 Catholics lived in the two north-eastern counties, representing 3.6% of the whole population of 715,000. In 1849 *The Tablet* had noted that there were 23,000 and in 1861 Bishop Hogarth would recall that there had been no more than 30,000 in all four counties of the diocese, so the census seems to have been reasonably accurate.

This was, however, a time of rapid demographic change, particularly in County Durham, and no sooner had a count been taken than it was out of date. In March 1851 Bishop Hogarth had told the census that there were 400 Catholics in Darlington; eighteen months later he said the total had tripled. Fr Wilkinson reported 150 Catholics in Weardale in 1851 but there were 700 the next year. This rapid increase in the Catholic population of the north-east was due to two factors. In 1850 the region was on the point of economic take-off. Over the previous half-century sustained investment in the technological development of coal-mining, iron- and steel-making, shipbuilding, railways, engineering, glass-making, and in the potteries and chemical works, had resulted in a phenomenal increase in production and trade which was clearly set to grow even further. These heavy industries were highly labour-intensive and it happened that large numbers of Irishmen who had been forced to leave their own land during the 1840s because of the potato famines were coming into the region looking for work. Thus, fortuitously, the shipyards on Tyneside and Wearside, the new steel-making companies in West Durham and on Teesside, and the developing coalfield of East Durham offered employment opportunities to the destitute migrants when it was most needed. In October 1850 *The Tablet* remarked that the collieries around Thornley employed 'a vast number of Irishmen, and it is an important fact that from their extensive numbers they are likely to become a very formidable and important portion of the workmen in the coalfield of Durham'. Quite so: by 1861 the Irish population (some 42,000) of Northumberland and Durham was the fourth largest in the country, and it may be doubted whether the regional industrial take-off could have been sustained without them. Nonetheless, it is emphasised that the native Catholic population had begun to grow from around the end of the eighteenth century, hence the effect of Irish migration (and the Oxford Movement) was to accelerate the rate of growth of the Catholic population, not initiate it. It should be noted, however, that the Irish became Britain's largest ethnic minority group, and remained so until migration from the 'New Commonwealth' began after the Second World War.

At any rate, in 1850 the region entered a period of unprecedented and sustained economic growth which lasted until the First World War and which wrought major change on every aspect of life. That period will be taken here, then, as a more or less coherent whole, for, in parallel with the commercial and industrial expansion of the north-east, the Church also made great progress in the second half of the nineteenth century. But it faced three key inter-related tasks from the outset: pastoral care, charitable work, and education. The ways in which these were dealt with by the bishops, the clergy and the laity working together will be explored in the paragraphs which follow.

*

As the census of 1851 had shown, large numbers of Irish migrants were non-practising Catholics but they, as well as later arrivals, could only be recovered for the Church if there was a substantial expansion of pastoral care. The first challenge, then, was to train the priests and to build the churches and schools to cope with burgeoning numbers. In point of fact, the Catholic population of the region would multiply about sevenfold between 1850 and 1914 (that is, to around 190,000). The statistics of the most obvious indicators of achievement are remarkable. On average, a new Catholic mission-station was opened every year in the period (to be precise, 71 new churches in 64 years). Similarly, the number of priests ministering in the region rose from 55 to 200. They were trained at Ushaw College and at a number of seminaries on the continent; there were also some Belgian, Dutch, French, Irish and Italian priests working in the region. By any standard that was an extraordinary achievement but it was accomplished only at great cost in human and material resources; it was also the more impressive for being made entirely voluntarily by a community which was always relatively poor and disadvantaged.

The new missions were financed in a variety of ways. A priest might place an appeal in the Catholic papers, or tour the country to beg in the wealthier localities; the northern Catholic gentry were always dunned for subscriptions; the local congregation itself was expected to make donations where possible; and a contribution from the diocese itself was usually required. As so often happens, however, in the event there is a shortfall. In his first pastoral letter, therefore, Bishop Hogarth established a Diocesan Fund to finance new missions more systematically, and he suggested that everyone in the diocese over the age of fourteen contribute one halfpenny a week to it. The idea was not universally popular, of course, but in some areas it did prove successful, especially where collectors went round the houses; in North Shields four times the congregation's previous contributions were taken. Donations to the Fund totalled more than £700 in 1854, and over the years the Fund helped to support most new missions to a greater or lesser extent. Furthermore, within five years the diocese was able to send money to Rome in support of the Pope; the revival of Peter's Pence in England began at St Andrew's, Newcastle, in 1859.

About thirty missions were created in the twenty years after the restoration and all were in places which were rapidly industrialising and experiencing a sudden increase in population, mostly to the east of a line drawn between Blyth and Bishop Auckland, half of them in County Durham. No new development was required in the rural uplands north of Hexham or in Teesdale, but missions were required in the mid-west at Blackhill, Haltwhistle, Haydon Bridge, Tow Law and Wolsingham, most of which were Victorian 'new towns'. For the most part, the acquisition of land presented few problems although a site may not have been in the best locality; indeed, it became something of a disparaging cliché that a town's Catholic church could always be found close by the railway station. In one or two cases land was hard to come by. Notoriously, the formidable dowager Marchionness of Londonderry (whom Disraeli called a 'tyrant') was twice petitioned in 1860 by Fr Robert Belaney (a Scot) for a grant of land at Seaham Harbour for a chapel but she refused, even though around 1,000 Catholics lived thereabouts, including 500 of her fellow-Irishmen employed in her collieries. She would not relent, and it was only after her death in 1865 that her successor Earl Vane agreed to a lease, and a church was opened in 1869. Difficulties were also experienced at Esh, and at Jarrow where the priest was eventually reduced to buying a disused Baptist chapel. On the other hand, Sir Hedworth Williamson gladly gave land for St Hilda's in Sunderland in 1861.

It was important for the recently emancipated church to emphasise continuity with its medieval antecedents and this was done in two ways (apart from the choice of the ancient episcopal title and the adoption in 1853 of St Cuthbert as the diocesan patron). Firstly, new and rebuilt churches were larger and more prominent, in complete contrast to the anonymous, vernacular buildings which had been usual almost up to this time. Long after the Relief Acts it was still thought prudent to make the new churches at Esh (1799) and Stella (1830) unrecognisable as such from the road; and Ushaw was chosen as the location for the new seminary in 1799 largely because it was so remote. The foundations of St Augustine's, Darlington, were sabotaged on three separate occasions, and attempts were made to stop work on St Mary's, Hartlepool, during the 'Papal Aggression' episode. But now almost every new church was professionally executed in the Gothic style of architecture (the Gothic Revival was then in full flood) by the younger Pugin and other wellknown architects, particularly Dunn and Hansom of 23 Eldon Square, Newcastle. Elaborate stained-glass windows were installed and the fixtures and fittings for the sanctuary had an appropriately neo-medieval design. When money was available, Stations of the Cross, statues, paintings and a stone font would be introduced, a pipe-organ installed, and bells might even be obtained. (Those of St Mary's, Hartlepool, were the first Catholic church-bells to be rung in England since the Reformation but in 1851 the Vicar of Hartlepool asked the magistrates to silence them because they disrupted his sermons; his request was rejected, not least because the clock on his own church-tower rang the quarters, without apparent inconvenience to him.)

The second way in which the church's antiquity was emphasised was by giving new churches traditional dedications: to Our Lady in the old English style of St. Mary, and to the popular saints of the middle ages: Andrew, Augustine, Cuthbert, Oswald, Robert, and so on. In one or two places the name of the local Anglican parish church was adopted, especially if it was a pre-Reformation building, as in the case of St Michael's at Esh Laude. As time passed, however, other dedications were adopted, notably that to The Immaculate Conception, following the proclamation of the dogma in 1854, and to St Patrick where the congregation was predominantly Irish. The foundation stone of St Patrick's in the east end of Sunderland (where 4,000 Catholics were said to live) was laid on the patron's feast day in 1860.

In such ways were the ancient and universal credentials of the north-eastern Catholics proclaimed. Furthermore, in most cases, the opening of a new church would be carried out with great public ceremony, liturgical and social, and it would be reported at some length in the local press. The High Mass, with music by Beethoven or Mozart, and often celebrated by the bishop, would be attended by large numbers of clergy and the sermon would be delivered by a well-known preacher. The Catholic gentry would turn out in force and usually civic dignitaries would be present. Afterwards, a grand banquet would be given in a hotel or the Assembly Rooms which would conclude with a series of speeches and toasts. The day would end with Vespers or Benediction.

The clergy found that their greatest missionary problem lay in the urban areas among the socially deprived and, for the most part, unschooled people living in the dreadful slums which had grown up near shipyards, coal-mines and other fast-growing industrial complexes where the ordinary decencies of life were unknown. In 1861 one official reported that Sandgate exceeded Cairo for 'filth, overcrowding and pestilential ills'. The unfortunate poor in such places were lax in more ways than religious practice and it was quite clear that they would not be won back by the provision of churches alone, recovery would be achieved only through a dedicated and wide-ranging pastoral ministry. One way of revitalising the faith of the inactive and of making conversions was to make frequent sick calls and regular pastoral visits to the disease-ridden localities. An official report of 1850 reported: 'The priest visits [the Irish families] assiduously, keeps alive religious feeling, and inspires them with veneration *and hope* [my emphasis]. In 1860 the priest at St Andrew's said that it was necessary constantly 'to visit, encourage, or reprimand' each family, 'enquiring what is to become of the children, restoring peace in families and, as it were, intervening at every moment'. Indeed, it had been as a result of such visits that in 1847 Bishop Riddell and two of his priests wrote a damning report on living conditions in Sandgate which had galvanised the city fathers of Newcastle into action by moving fever patients out of their homes and into treatment centres to prevent the spread of cholera: some 10,000 people were treated within the year. Unfortunately, the bishop and the priests, Frs Joseph Dugdale, William Fletcher and James Standon became martyrs of charity by falling victim to the cholera epidemic they were trying to halt. Bishop Bewick would later recall that the Corporation of Newcastle had placed cabs at the disposal of the clergy night and day during the cholera epidemic of 1853.

Pastoral care for the migrants depended on there being foreign-speaking missioners, but, to avoid adverse political reaction, the bishops were very cautious about employing Irish priests and only a handful of them were taken onto the diocesan strength during the century. Ralph Platt, missioner at Stella 1847-57, learned Gaelic to overcome the difficulty, and from 1851 the Irish were able to go to confession to the Gaelic-speaking priest Robert Foran at St Andrew's in Newcastle as well, and there were one or two others. An Italian priest preached and heard confessions on the first Sunday of the month at Gateshead for the growing numbers of Italian males migrating into the north-east. By the end of the century there were probably around 1,000 mixed Italian-English families in the region.

Another way of reaching the people was for the clergy to ensure that services were colourful and attractive with splendid displays of flowers, candles and vestments; to hold grand liturgical ceremonies with large choirs and rousing hymns; and to celebrate the month of May and feast days with special devotions. How far this differed from the practice of the recusants has been widely discussed. Clearly, a free and full public expression of the faith was not possible under the penal laws, but that is not to say there was an absence of devotion. The use of the Rosary persisted throughout the post-reformation period and it was recommended, together with the Angelus and the Litany of Loreto, by Bishop Richard Challoner in his manual *The Garden of the Soul* (1740) which became the primary text of English Catholic lay spirituality. The manual advocated a quiet, undemonstrative piety and taught that charity was the key attribute of the true Christian. He also recommended Benediction (a service of eucharistic adoration and blessing, but not reception) and the Stations of the Cross. Opportunities for spiritual reading were possible in the eighteenth century through an extensive Catholic publishing network as just a few examples show. Devotion to the Sacred Heart was introduced into England in 1676 and its spread during the next century was assisted by the North Yorkshireman Thomas Lawson, SJ, whose book on it went into eight editions. There were at least three collections of lives of the saints ('interspersed with suitable Reflections') in print: Charles Fell's of 1729, Richard Challoner's of 1745, and Alban Butler's of 1745 with innumerable editions since. In 1780 Charles Cordell, the priest at St Andrew's, Newcastle, published a second edition of *The Divine Office for the Use of the Laity* in English (but he attracted episcopal censure for introducing Sunday Vespers in English publicly). Choirs used Samuel Webbe's *Collection of Sacred Music* (1792) for the liturgy and vernacular hymns were the simple diatonic compositions of Samuel Webbe and Vincent Novello. Sunday missals for the use of the laity were published from 1852.

It would be incorrect, then, to suppose that extra-liturgical devotional practices were innovations in post-restoration England; it was more to do with *style*: henceforth Catholic practices would be more conspicuous and populist. Vernacular hymns, for example, were taken from Henry Hemy's *Crown of Jesus Music* (1864) which became widely popular, largely because many of its tunes were from the opera-house or concert-room and were not, of course, intended for devotional purposes at all. The more exuberant spirit which became the hallmark of the post-restoration Church was introduced to enthuse the lukewarm and the lapsed and to attract potential converts, but the devotions were familiar and remained essentially the same. Old recusants, however, like John Lingard and Mrs Barbara Charlton of Hesleyside, regretted the changes brought about by the 'influx of converts and colonists'; she thought the 'peculiar antics' of the new style made 'a caricature of Catholic religion'. It is perhaps ironic that Lingard's hymn 'Hail, Queen of Heaven', set to the tune of a Durham folk-song by Henry Hemy, the Newcastle-born Catholic organist and music-teacher, became, with 'Faith of Our Fathers', typical of the new Catholic religiosity he disliked so much.

Pious fervour was also engendered by holding special events such as retreats, pilgrimages and processions in May, on Ascension Day and on the feast of Corpus Christi but it was the *mission* that came to be seen as the most effective means of re-invigorating faith and practice. St Ninian's Diocesan Missionary Establishment, at Wooler from 1851 to 1854, provided secular priests to conduct parochial missions and conventual retreats throughout northern England, and the clerical orders - the Passionists, Redemptorists and Rosminians - gave invaluable help to the parochial clergy in this way. The missions usually lasted a week and were often spectacular evangelistic events typified by revivalist hell-fire sermons, street-preaching, out-door processions, mass confirmations and long queues at the confessionals. The mission usually culminated in an elaborate service, Solemn Benediction perhaps, at which a Papal Blessing would be imparted, the Abstinence Pledge administered, the prohibition of secret societies reiterated and a plenary indulgence granted. The Redemptorists often erected an indulgenced mission-crucifix in the church as a permanent reminder of their visit. There is little doubt that these intensely emotional missions were highly popular (one held in Hartlepool in 1851 attracted 600 people to every service), and people eagerly looked forward to the next.

Piety and commitment were also encouraged by the formation of devotional guilds and sodalities. Several confraternities had flourished before the restoration but the following were active in Newcastle in 1852: Blessed Sacrament, Sacred Heart, Most Holy Rosary, the Blessed Virgin Mary & St Joseph, Association of the Sacred Heart of Mary for the conversion of sinners, Sanctuary Guild of St Aloysius, Bona Mors, Confraternity of Our Lady of Mount Carmel, Sodality of the Living Rosary, Temperance Society of Our Lady & St John the Baptist, Society of the Blessed Virgin Mary & St Elizabeth for visiting the sick, and the Society of St Vincent de Paul. The members of these societies had spiritual obligations, such as the recitation of particular prayers, and they would make their monthly communion on a given Sunday. As their titles make clear, many of these societies had a charitable as well as a devotional purpose. The surgeon Charles Larkin was a leading advocate of medical insurance and he helped to found and promote the Catholic Medical Club of Newcastle on Tyne in 1851. Moreover, scarcely a major town in the north did not have a branch of the Catholic Benefit Society (founded in 1871), contributions to which began at five and a half pence a week. By the end of the century there were 36 branches in the north-east and they had paid out some £63,000 in sickness benefits, old-age pensions and death grants. Self-improvement was very much a Victorian ideal, and a number of Catholic literary societies as well as youth and sporting clubs were also formed. St Andrew's in Newcastle had a library and a parish reading-room attached to the church and there was an Irish Literary Institute in the town in 1877.

These organisations provided Catholics of all ages with the widest range of devotional, educational and recreational activities together with a degree of social welfare. Many of these facilities would not otherwise have been available but, regrettably, their creation has been dismissed for being instrumental in the development of a 'Catholic ghetto' (somehow unlike the Methodist enclaves of, say, Weardale, which were also essentially self-contained) and it is, of course, undeniable that Catholics did not easily mix socially with Protestants. For community to thrive, however, there has to be a unifying ethic of companionship and mutual support - which is, of course, the age-old Catholic way. It should hardly have been surprising, then, that the Church would gather its people into cohesive and supportive communities with a distinctively Catholic ethos. (A little more than a century later, it would be widely argued that society had lost its unifying sacred belief and suffered increasingly from weak community structures and a lack of companionship, or 'solidarity' to use the word by which Pope John Paul II summed up Catholic social doctrine.) In fact, the existence of all these groups shows that the Church had an extraordinary vitality and that it engendered a deep loyalty; it did not just build churches, it built communities intended to provide mutual support from the cradle to the grave. Moreover, the socially-conscious leadership of the clergy was a crucial influence in the promotion of personal pride and civic values which ultimately helped layfolk to gain substantial upward social mobility. The Catholic temperance movement was of major importance in this respect. A branch of the Catholic Young Men's Society (CYMS) was formed in Newcastle in 1881 and five years later Drysdale Hall, Marlborough Crescent, was opened as its diocesan headquarters with meeting-rooms, games-rooms, reading-room and library for the 350 members in Newcastle who attended temperance meetings, self-improvement lectures and participated in various entertainments. The society held its national AGM there in 1888.

The Society of St Vincent de Paul (SVP) was described as a 'welfare state within the state' and it became so influential that around 4,000 Catholics attended its annual general meeting in the new Town Hall, Newcastle, in 1859. It is therefore worth tracing the society's formation and progress in the region in some detail. In May 1833, the twenty-year-old Frederick Ozanam and six companions, inspired by the example of St Vincent de Paul, formed a Conference of Charity in Paris to carry out the corporal works of mercy among the poor. The new brotherhood, entirely voluntary and unpaid, quickly spread across Europe and was introduced into England in 1844. Three conferences were soon established in the north-east: at St Andrew's in Newcastle and St Cuthbert's, North Shields in 1846, and Sunderland in 1847. The number of brothers in each conference varied: by the time of the restoration there were twelve in Newcastle and eleven in North Shields, but there were seventy in Sunderland. Other conferences were established later in the century: South Shields (1855), Felling (1858), Gateshead (1859), Jarrow (1864), Barnard Castle (1872), Durham (1877), Hebburn (1882) and Darlington (1889).

Almsgiving was a major part of the Society's work, especially during times of unemployment or epidemic, and they distributed clothes, fuel and food to the poor, but help was given in other ways. Brothers would ensure that people entitled to parochial relief got it; and in appropriate cases they would provide a man with wares and send him out to earn a living. Visits to the poor in their own homes showed that many children never went to school, either because they had to earn a wage to help support the family or because they were ashamed at having no proper clothes (this was often the reason given by adults for not attending Mass). In 1849 the Sunderland conference clothed sixty to seventy children and paid the then obligatory school fees for them. In 1850 the conference started a Sunday School in North Shields and at New York north of Tynemouth; they also gave religious instruction to Catholic boys training for a maritime career on the *Wellesley* training ship in the Tyne, an institution founded in 1867 for homeless and destitute lads (unconvicted of crime) intent on a seafaring life; 114 Catholics were under training in 1879. The Society cared for the sick by paying nurses and buying medicine and, ultimately, coffins. Brothers would also arrange a funeral when the deceased had no known relatives and the body might otherwise have been taken into non-Catholic hands. Until Catholic burial places were legalised in 1880, the burial service was usually read over the body before it was taken to an Anglican cemetery. The first Catholic chapel of rest was opened in Bishop Auckland in 1881.

It is difficult to exaggerate the importance attached by the Victorians to temperance. The Catholic crusade for teetotalism became a major force; more than 400 people attended the first annual general meeting of the Catholic Total Abstinence Society of Darlington held in 1856. Cardinal Manning would address large public meetings on the evils of strong drink whenever he visited the region (a sure sign of the extent of the problem). Drunkenness was greatest in the poorer localities. In 1860 a priest at St Andrew's said that though the majority of Catholics were practising and fervent, there was also a large number who were negligent in their religious duties 'partly because of their appallingly excessive drinking'. Drink-inspired riots between English and Irish workmen of the Derwent Iron Co. at Consett were not infrequent but by 1879 it was claimed that almost all the men of the Blackhill congregation had pledged total abstinence and that 'the public houses both at Consett and Blackhill were all but deserted'; Canon Kearney of The Brooms unwisely predicted 'the speedy closing of all the public-houses of the district'. Fr Wilkinson would ride around the market-place of Crook on pay-days to ensure that no Catholic entered an inn before taking his wages home, and he was not above dismounting to drive out any who might have slipped in while his back was turned. In Washington Catholics gave up drinking during a mission and the lock-up would be empty on the pay-day whereas it was usually full. When there was trouble in east Newcastle people would fetch a priest from St Dominic's and, armed with a shelaghly, he would swiftly deal with the troublemakers. In Jarrow, Sir Charles Palmer, M.P. remarked that 'his friend Father Meynell was as good as a number of policemen'. In Felling and elsewhere the Brothers helped the clergy to promote temperance; they made it a practice to attend the funerals of the poor 'to suppress drunkenness at wakes by reciting the Rosary'; in 1877 Catholic Burial Clubs were formed for that purpose. Priests often arranged social events on St Patrick's Day to keep their people out of the public houses. The League of the Cross was founded by Cardinal Manning in 1872 and within ten years the League's Temperance Resolutions were read publicly from every pulpit on the first Sunday of every month to encourage people to take the pledge.

Much of the work of the Society and the clergy, however, had to be directed at counteracting the anti-Catholicism of officialdom and subversive Protestant philanthropy aimed at children. In 1852 the Ragged Schools authorities of Newcastle offered free flour and oatmeal as an inducement to poor Catholic children to apostatise from the faith. Permission for Catholics in workhouses to attend Sunday Mass was at the sole discretion of the Poor Law Guardians and was often refused or given only on condition that they were conducted to and fro by the Brothers. The high death-rate due to cholera and other fevers endemic in the towns meant there were as many as four hundred Catholic orphans in the workhouses of the region and worries about their faith were ever-present. The Guardians in Newcastle tried to dissuade a Catholic from employing a Catholic orphan as a servant-girl. The Guardians in Gateshead and Sunderland would not allow Catholic ladies to catechize children, and the clergy protested about children being prevented from attending Mass. The Darlington Guardians declined to allow Catholic children to attend their own school. Legislation was passed in 1866 and 1868 permitting adult Catholics in workhouses to be visited by their priests and to attend Sunday Mass freely, but some Boards continued to obstruct the practice of the faith. Non-Anglican clergy could attend the workhouses to instruct children up to the age of thirteen, but older children were allowed to decide for themselves, and for many years the Brothers took particular care to ensure that Catholic youths were not penalised for holding to their faith and that the younger children were escorted to Mass. In the long run, however, the faith of the children could be secured only if Catholic institutions were created for them. In 1869 Tudhoe Academy, the old Catholic private school, was bought by the diocese from the Salvin family for £1,000 and opened as a Catholic Poor Law School in 1872 under a Mr Bulmer. There were fifty inmates within three years and the number steadily grew.

It was not just pauper children who had to be prised from non-Catholic control, young Catholic delinquents, too, had to be cared for. Parliamentary acts were passed in the fifties permitting magistrates to commit wayward children to a residential institution - the Reformatory (a corrective institution) or Industrial School (an educational establishment) - to prevent them growing into adult criminals; all reformatories had Catholic boys (in 1881 there were 39 in Netherton Reformatory) but access by priests was denied. From 1862 Catholic children were allowed to receive religious instruction and even be boarded in denominational establishments but alternative Catholic facilities were not available locally and Catholic delinquent boys had to be sent to a Catholic Reformatory at Market Rasen and girls to one in Sheffield, but, as in the workhouses, passive resistance to the transfer of children was general among officials. Bishop Chadwick set about collecting £7,000 to build a Catholic Industrial School at Gosforth. He died before its completion but it became the Chadwick Memorial Industrial School in two sections: St James for boys (1882-1905, and then at Stanwix, Carlisle) run by the Presentation Brothers, and St Elizabeth for girls in Ashburton House, Gosforth (1884-1906) run by the Sisters of Charity. In 1893 the latter took on two more industrial schools: St Vincent's in

Bishop J. Chadwick

Elswick, Newcastle, and St Joseph's in Darlington. Vocational training was given as well as elementary education: the boys learned tailoring, shoemaking, and some of the older lads went out to do gardening and other manual labour; the girls were taught domestic skills, laundering and embroidery and, later on, shorthand. These schools were approved by the Home Office and the annual reports of inspection were almost always complimentary; they reduced juvenile crime and enabled many disadvantaged children to develop into upright citizens. Adult Catholic criminals did exist, of course; routinely a quarter of prisoners in Durham Gaol were Catholics but repeated requests to the Quarter Sessions of Durham begging that a priest be allowed to attend them were refused until 1864. Only two years later, however, the services of the Catholic chaplain of Durham Gaol were so much appreciated that he was awarded a yearly salary of £70.

It is worth noting that much anti-Catholicism originated locally and was out of step with national policy; for example, Catholic military chaplains were first commissioned in 1858 and priests always served in the armed forces thereafter.

This very brief summary of the activities of the Society of St Vincent de Paul shows that it was undoubtedly the pre-eminent lay action group in the Church. Its charitable and social work was of primary importance, but its defence of the faith was just as necessary; and through its practical Christianity this apostolic brotherhood became a pillar of the Church. Another was the apostolic sisterhood of the religious congregations. Since the Reformation, the religious life has attracted more women than men, and the Victorian period was perhaps the greatest age of the womens' orders, notwithstanding the fierce opposition

18

to convents among Protestants. The first major political campaign mounted by the Victorian Catholics took place in 1853 when in all the Tyneside towns they combined to oppose the Nunnery Inspection Bill. A petition against convents was signed by over 1,000 women in South Shields, where there was no convent, but no petition was raised in Sunderland where the Sisters of Mercy had been working for ten years. The older congregations flourished, but large numbers of new communities were founded. These accepted many working-class novices (else recruitment would have been impossible) and in that way they offered a vocational career to Catholic girls which was not otherwise available.

Several orders came into the region in the half-century after emancipation. The contemplative Carmelites were the first to arrive. They had been driven out of Lierre by the French revolutionaries and were housed temporarily in St Helen's Hall and Cocken Hall, Durham, before purchasing Cockerton Field House with twenty acres near Darlington which became their permanent home in 1830. The Poor Clares were initially given refuge in Haggerston Castle and then at Scorton but in 1857/8 they founded Clare Abbey in Darlington on land bought from the Carmelites. The Sisters of Mercy went to Sunderland in 1843; in 1854 the Sisters of Charity in Birmingham sent six sisters to Newcastle to open an orphanage in Westgate Street. The Sisters of Charity of St Paul established convents at Crook (1862), Blackhill (1869) and Stockton (1872); at the request of Mr Saville of the SVP, the Little Sisters of the Poor provided a refuge for the aged poor in Newcastle in 1866; the house was funded entirely by alms, generally collected by the sisters themselves; they opened a second refuge in Sunderland in 1882. In 1878 the Sisters of the Sacred Hearts of Jesus and Mary took charge of the Tudhoe home. The old house was demolished in 1884 and a new establishment, St Mary's, for girls only, was opened. In 1879 St Catherine's Dominican convent was opened in Newcastle and the sisters engaged firstly in education and later in nursing care. The Faithful Companions of Jesus went to Hartlepool in 1885. The Sisters of Mercy opened a house at Summerhill in Newcastle in 1886 to train poor girls of good character for domestic service; in 1888 the Sisters of the Good Shepherd opened Benton Grange as a refuge for fallen women and for the protection of endangered young women; they were employed in a laundry and within a very short time the house was full. Despite various setbacks, including a major fire, some 840 women were rescued from the streets by the end of the century.

By 1900 there were thirty female religious communities in the north-east and their contribution to the spiritual life and the development of the charitable and social institutions of the Church cannot be over-estimated. Indeed, so extensive had the work become that a diocesan Children's Homes and Care Committee was formed to supervise it and a Catholic Workhouse Children's Fund to pay for it. On Guy Fawkes Day 1895 a Grand Bazaar and Winter Fête was held in the Olympia, Newcastle, to raise money, as Canon James Rooney explained,

> for the building of homes in which to receive a further number of the destitute Catholic children from our workhouses. The importance of educating these children away from pauper surroundings and the need, in their case especially, of a practical training which shall fit them for employment afterwards, is admitted on all hands to be urgent.

The bishop appealed for £14,000 to fund the removal of 500 Catholic children aged fourteen or less from non-Catholic into Catholic institutions. St Peter's, Gainford, was then being built as another Catholic Industrial School.

It is particularly important to notice that in all this work, the Church was in the vanguard of social work. The Good Shepherd apostolate was as novel as the care of the Little Sisters of the Poor for the indigent elderly; Charles Dickens, not a pro-Catholic, wrote of the latter: 'A few women, feeble in frame but strong in heart and mind, without publicity, or subscription dinners or charity sermons ... patiently go round collecting from one house to another these scraps, wherewith, in humility and tenderness, they nourish the poor' [F. Trochu, *Jeanne Jugan* (1960) 161]. Ruskin, another anti-Catholic, remarked: 'I know well how good the Sisters of Charity are and how much we owe to them'; he nonetheless advised his correspondent not to take the veil. [*Collected Works* vol 18, p 44]. The orders were not only leaders in the development of social work but, with the nursing and teaching congregations, they were also highly important in developing professional practices and standards for women. Catholics were very fortunate to have these entrepreneurial nuns, focussed entirely on gospel imperatives, working in their localities.

Thus the work of the Church in this period was remarkable both for its quality and for its refusal to give in to the anti-Catholicism which was more or less prevalent across the region. The prejudice was as much anti-Irish as anti-Catholic. In March 1852 *The Tablet* observed, 'during the last few years in the north of England Irishmen as a body have considerably improved their condition in society and it is self-evident they are every day becoming a more influential portion of English society.' That, frankly, was an exaggeration and was probably inspired by the ostentatious events of St Patrick's Day. The Hibernian Society had attended Mass in Newcastle and then marched in procession with bands playing and banners flying to their different lodges to dine. But earlier in the month the bishop had issued a pastoral letter reminding everybody that the sacraments would be denied to members of secret societies such as the Hibernian Society, the Knights of St Patrick (which, it appears, 'passed itself off as a sick club'), the Ribbonmen (agrarian terrorists) and, of course, the Freemasons. Initially the Church was also hostile to trade unions because of their use of secret oaths but the hierarchy abandoned its stance in the mid-forties when their true nature was understood. Irish people had certainly become more prominent but it was premature to call them influential for they would represent both an ecclesiastical and a civil disciplinary problem for some time. Fighting between the Orange and the Green (not all Irish migrants were Catholics) and between the indigenous and migrant people broke out intermittently but it reached a peak between 1868 and 1873, when Fenianism was at its height, and public disorder occurred in a number of industrial centres [Neal, 61 ff.]. But these disputes should be seen in perspective: the numbers involved represented a very small minority on both sides; the English working class had nothing to learn from the Irish about drinking and fighting; and the perception of the Irish as troublemakers was partly due to the xenophobia directed at any migrant group, especially one which refused to be intimidated and always acted in unison to defend its religion and ethnicity. In fact, because there was enough unskilled labouring work in the expanding industries for all, migrants did not represent a threat to the livelihood of indigenous workers; similarly, the number of idle migrants was smaller than elsewhere in the country. For both these reasons anti-Irish prejudice was much less pronounced in the north-east than elsewhere.

Nevertheless, attempts at rabble-rousing were made by extremists. The Protestant Alliance held rallies in Morpeth with the mayor in the chair and Catholics were denied a right of reply. 'Petty Orangeism' prevailed in Darlington where Joseph Pease M.P. was wont to make anti-Catholic speeches. On the other hand, Joseph Cowen, the Radical M.P. for Newcastle, held pro-Irish meetings. William Murphy, the most vituperative of Protestant demagogues to tour the country lecturing, was refused entry to a number of towns in Northumberland in 1869; his appearance in the Oddfellows Hall at Tynemouth was disrupted by 250 Irishmen who threatened to kill him. (He would later die from injuries inflicted during a massed Irish assault at Cleator Moor.) Individual priests suffered unjustly. In 1854 Fr Richard Singleton was falsely charged with the maintenance of an illegitimate child. In 1858 Fr Hannigan was shot at in Blackhill. In 1860 Fr John Kelly, the 56-year-old Irish priest at Felling, was gaoled at Durham for refusing to break the confessional seal but the subsequent outcry led to his release within two days and the case was raised in the House of Lords. Fr Fortin of Newhouse while visiting Catholic families in Ushaw Moor in 1882 was told to leave by the colliery manager; he refused but the police declined to take the manager's part.

The northern Catholics were undeterred. For one thing, the building of churches went on apace and we shall shortly remark upon the astonishing efforts put into Catholic education. But there were other indications of self-confidence. As we have seen, Catholic devotional publishing had long flourished but now local journalism began to appear with the annual publication from 1869 of the *Northern Catholic Calendar* and from 1884 of the weekly *Newcastle Irish Tribune*, founded by the Irish Catholic journalist Charles Diamond who would go on to establish a chain of forty papers across the country. The *Tribune* belied its title by carrying general Catholic and other news and established itself as the only paper many Catholics took. It was replaced by the *Tyneside Catholic News* in 1896. Then there was the arrangement of major public events. The diocese had always been devoted to its principal saints. A pilgrimage to Finchale Abbey on St Godric's feast day in May 1859 attracted 3,000 people. In 1886 261 English martyrs were declared Venerable and 54 others were beatified. Nine more martyrs were beatified in 1895 to general approbation and the diocese proudly claimed sixteen of the *beati* for its own. In 1896 the feast of Bl. Thomas Percy was established on 14 November (the anniversary of the outbreak of the Rising of the North in 1569). The twelfth centenary of St Cuthbert (the diocesan patron whose episcopal ring is worn by the bishop when ordaining) was celebrated on Holy Island in August 1888 by some 8-10,000 people. England was re-consecrated as the Dowry of Mary and dedicated to St Peter on 29 June 1893. St. Bede, almost as popular as St Cuthbert, was created a Doctor of the Church in November 1899 and was given a universal feast day (27 May) from 1901. He was (and remains) the only Englishman to be accorded this dignity and it invested all the Catholics of north-east England with great pride.

Rallies and other public events further served to make the Catholic presence felt. Cardinal Manning, the Marquess of Ripon and other national figures would address huge audiences in Newcastle and elsewhere on the topics of the day. In 1872 the Mayor of Newcastle and his predecessor attended the formal dinner held to celebrate the completion of the spire of St Mary's cathedral. The Central Council of the SVP and the CYMS both held their annual national conference in Newcastle in 1889. Then there were large social gatherings, primarily to raise money, but which also served to demonstrate the Church's growing security. *Soirees*, at which tea was served, a concert given and speeches were delivered by prominent clerics or local dignitaries became increasingly frequent. These were not hole-in-the-corner gatherings but large and impressive affairs attracting a thousand or more people and were held in the principal venues of the major towns: the Theatre Royal or Athenaeum in Sunderland, the Central Hall in Darlington, the Assembly Rooms in Newcastle, the Town Hall in Durham. A Grand Bazaar in 1868 for St Mary's, Hartlepool, was opened by R.W. Jackson, M.P. and gained the patronage of the Mayor. A much grander bazaar held over three days in Whit Week 1876 at St Bede's, South Shields, raised £600; the patrons were several noble ladies, Bishop Chadwick, the President of the French Republic and Pope Pius IX - 'Pio Nono'. (In 1877 the diocese raised £800 for the Pope's Episcopal Jubilee Fund; he died in 1879 and was succeeded by Leo XIII.) In 1889 the first Grand Catholic Ball was held in the Assembly Rooms, Newcastle.

Much the most effective way of influencing public policy, of course, was to gain political office. The landed Catholic gentry had long been accepted as magistrates, sheriffs and lords lieutenant, and George Silvertop of Minsteracres and Henry Witham of Lartington, among others, were invited to stand for parliament, but as the period progressed increasing numbers of middle-class Catholics came forward as local councillors. Councillor Thomas Dunn (1796-1855), a glass manufacturer, was Sheriff of Newcastle in 1836 and, as the *Newcastle Journal* peevishly pointed out, he became the town's 'first popish mayor' in 1842. George Thomas Dunn (1785-1852), his older brother, was elected alderman in 1836; he was a magistrate, a chairman of the finance committee and, though he declined the mayoralty in 1847, he accepted the chairmanship of the River Tyne Commission. He was dubbed 'the Pugnacious Alderman' by the *Journal* which also invariably reported his absence from civic services held in Anglican churches. The whole Town Council, however, attended his Requiem Mass at St Mary's in 1852 and his burial in All Saints' cemetery. His eldest son, William, was also a prominent Tyneside businessman and councillor. Richard Thompson, a Catholic solicitor, was elected Mayor of Durham in 1846. More Catholics were appointed to the bench and after 1875 many Catholics, including priests, topped the polls in elections to School Boards or as Poor Law

Guardians. The Catholic Henry Thompson, Mayor of Darlington, went in civic procession to St Augustine's in 1892. At the turn of the century 158 Catholics held civic office in the two counties and there was a county court judge. Catholics also began to enter national politics. In 1881 Mr H. Jerningham of Longridge Towers was elected to the Commons for Berwick, the first Catholic to be returned for many years.

Significantly, Irishmen were taking their places in these circles. In 1872 Hugh Heinrick of the *Nation* newspaper conducted a survey to establish how influential the Irish had become in England. In Newcastle it was found that 'the great bulk of them find constant employment at good wages, and are in a condition of comparative prosperity'; some 4,000 Irishmen were in skilled occupations. Heinrick also noticed that the Irish on Tyneside generally lived in better conditions than their English counterparts and that they were more 'favourable socially, and morally even more favourable still'. Moreover, there were distinct signs of the emergence of an Irish middle class with some 400 Irish businessmen in the city. John Denvir conducted another survey of the Irish in 1891 and confirmed the upward social mobility achieved by the second-generation Irish, many of whom had 'attained to good social and public positions' and several were 'among the foremost citizens of the place' [Cf. MacRaild, pp. 65-74]. Bernard ('Barnie') McAnulty, a successful businessman on Tyneside, who, according to the *Newcastle Daily Chronicle*, was known as the 'father of the Irish in England' because of his philanthropy and deep involvement in Irish Home Rule politics, was the first Irishman to sit on an English town council (Newcastle, 1874-82); he declined Parnell's offer of a safe parliamentary seat in 1885. Stephen Quinn (son of the first President of the Irish Institute in Newcastle, 1871), already an alderman, magistrate and sheriff of Newcastle, was unanimously elected mayor in 1894. Perhaps the most eminent Tyneside Irishman was Tim Healy who came from Bantry to Newcastle in 1871 to work as a clerk with the North Eastern Railway; he became an M.P. and K.C. and was ultimately the first Governor-General of the Irish Free State in 1922.

By the end of the century, then, the diocese had enjoyed fifty years of almost uninterrupted progress. The Victorian Catholic clergy, religious and laity had won for themselves an established place in northern society. They had been determined not to allow a deeply-imbedded anti-Catholicism to impede them and, as time went by, they had found it a little easier though it is somewhat exaggerated to say that after 1868 'anti-Catholicism was never again a major issue in local politics' [McClelland & Hodgetts, 28]. In his first pastoral letter (October 1882), Bishop Bewick paid tribute to the Mayor and Corporation of Newcastle for their 'unvarying consideration and kindness' and he thanked the press which, he said, had 'always behaved generously towards us'. This was perhaps necessarily diplomatic, but certainly by his time there was greater tolerance. Catholic chaplains were routinely appointed to the various institutions: the Newcastle Guardians allowed Mass to be said weekly in the workhouse from 1882, (but it was not until 1919 that they voted a salary to the priest). The Newcastle Circle of the Catenian Association, a social organisation for professional and business men, was inaugurated in 1910 and its roll shows how far the northern Catholics had come; its early members included three Lord Mayors of Newcastle (W. Lee, Sir John Fitzgerald and J.F. Weidner), a Mayor of Gateshead (W.J. Costelloe) and the M.P. Sir N. Grattan Doyle, in addition to shipowners, members of the medical, legal and teaching professions and two names familiar to high-street shoppers: Donald and Farnon. Moreover, by this stage the substantial electoral strength of the Catholics could not be ignored. In 1908 an attempt to ban a eucharistic procession in London by the Liberal administration aroused considerable Catholic indignation. It happened that a by-election was then underway in Newcastle and both the clergy and the United Irish League unhesitatingly advised the 2,000 Irish electors to vote for the *Unionist* candidate; he gained the seat by 2,143 votes.

Bishop J. W. Bewick

The achievements of the Victorian Church were very impressive, but education was the one area in which progress was more difficult, for the status of Catholic schools was always vigorously disputed. The Church has always insisted on the principle that Catholic beliefs and morality are best taught in its own schools by teachers of the same faith, and that the state has a duty not to discriminate financially against them; furthermore, the control of religious education is an ecclesiastical not a secular matter. Governments, on the other hand, have always argued that they must have some control over how public money voted by parliament is spent. The attempt to reconcile those opposing philosophies is, in short, what the history of the Catholic schools in this country is about.

To ensure that the faith was handed on and that the next generation became practising communicants, small, clandestine 'dame schools' were kept by priests and layfolk in recusant times, and an elementary school became an integral part of all new missionary developments in the region after the Relief Acts. This emphasis on education was reinforced at the first Westminster Synod (1852) which declared that Catholic elementary education 'must become universal. No congregation should be allowed to remain without its schools, one for each sex'. The bishops also said that 'wherever there may seem to be an opening for a new mission, we should prefer the erection of a school, so arranged as to serve temporarily for a chapel, to that of a church without one'. It was for that reason that some twenty or more parishes in the north-east trace their origins to a school-chapel; some others were founded in a two-storeyed building of which the ground floor became the school and the upper floor the chapel. But while one-room schools and the monitorial system of teaching were cheap, their days were numbered because the rapidly growing population required a much greater financial outlay on new and larger schools and on formal teacher-training.

In 1833 a new school for 700 children of St Andrew's, Newcastle, cost £1,500 and in October 1840 a new school in North Shields cost £800. Such high levels of expenditure was another reason why the bishops pressed for state aid. Assistance was offered on condition that the government could inspect the schools for efficiency in all subjects, but the bishops, wishing to reserve religious instruction to their own supervision, declined, arguing that aid was both a right and a matter of equity with other denominations, not a reward for submitting to state control. The hierarchy also refused to allow the use of the Authorised Version of the Bible and virtually forbade Catholics to attend non-Catholic schools. The independent stand of the bishops meant therefore that the Catholic community had to finance its schools from voluntary contributions. Despite considerable secular opposition, the state came round in 1847 to making the Church a grant towards its building costs without strings, but since it amounted to under 1% of the money allocated to non-Catholic denominational schools and only three Catholic schools actually got a grant, voluntary contributions remained the principal source of finance. A national Catholic Poor School Committee was therefore formed to ensure that funds were raised to provide an elementary education for all Catholic children.

By the late 1840s there were fifteen Catholic elementary charity-schools in the north-east, most of them with lay teachers, who were paid around £30 a year, about a quarter of what a certificated Anglican teacher got. These schools were unable to accommodate more than a third of the 2,500 children who needed places, and the situation was becoming more urgent by the week. Some of the religious orders therefore started teaching to relieve the pressure. In Sunderland a two-storeyed school for over 300 children (including many non-Catholics) was opened in 1835 and in 1836 two Irish Christian Brothers went there to teach the boys, leaving the girls to a lay mistress until 1843 when the Sisters of Mercy arrived. The Brothers withdrew in 1847 rather than submit to government inspection and were replaced by the Presentation Brothers but they too left in 1858 and the Sisters took charge of the whole school and they would shortly open a middle school. The pace was as relentless in other towns; in Newcastle, St Andrews had day and night schools with some 800 children on the roll by 1859 and the Mercy sisters established a school for 600 children in St Mary's. Moreover, despite legislation to allow pauper Catholic children to receive Catholic instruction and even be transferred to Catholic schools, obstruction by Guardians prevented the acts being implemented fairly so that priests and layfolk had to fight cases almost one by one but they could be successful only if Catholic school-places were available. There was, however, a shortage of teachers; only certificated teachers could train pupil-teachers and, although by 1860 qualified Catholic teachers were to be found in Alnwick, Darlington, Durham, Hartlepool, Hexham, Houghton-le-Spring, Newcastle, North Shields, Stella and Sunderland, many more were needed.

The Roman Catholic Charities Act (1860) allowed schools to come under diocesan ownership and from that point Bishop Hogarth, who had already appointed diocesan inspectors of religion, took complete control of Catholic education. The religious orders were running eight schools and he asked them to provide more teachers for the new schools he was to build in the rapidly developing areas. This was partly because of the shortage of lay teachers and because the religious education delivered by nuns was thought to be more rigorous than that given by layfolk, but it was principally to consolidate his own episcopal authority. The Liverpool branch of the Mercy sisters went to Newcastle in 1855 and North Shields in 1860. The Sunderland community established daughter-houses in Hexham (1858), Durham (1860), Darlington (1862), Tow Law (1870) and Bishop Auckland (1875). By 1871 the Sisters of Charity of St Paul were established at Crook and Benfieldside. The Faithful Companions of Jesus moved from Redcar to Hartlepool in 1885. The creation of these convents and their associated schools in such a short period was remarkable, but the educational needs were great.

In 1870 the government passed an Elementary Education Act to establish 'a complete national system of education' for children aged four to thirteen, funded from the rates (local property-taxes) and managed by locally-elected School Boards. Clearly, more and better schools were required to achieve this aim but voluntary schools were in serious difficulties because their financial resources were quite inadequate to provide places for every child they would have to take. Crucially, however, the government had to concede to the secularists that doctrinal religious instruction could not be given in rate-aided Board schools; Catholic schools were therefore excluded from the new system. (Incidentally, the English bishops would make instruction in the 1876 edition of the *Catechism of Christian Doctrine* compulsory in 1880 and passed a resolution in 1888 that, as a precondition of employment, teachers should be present in church with their classes at Mass on Sundays and holydays.) Whereas Board schools enjoyed a secure income, voluntary schools continued to depend on fees (school-pence), voluntary Sunday collections, bazaars and (if the inspectors approved the secular curriculum, teaching qualifications and building standards) *per capita* maintenance grants of 60% from central government. The bishop formed a Diocesan Poor School Committee to deal with the new situation and it found that thirty new schools would be required in addition to the enlargement of existing schools, twenty of which were still doubling as chapels. Remarkably, building-work to the value of £26,684 was completed within two years, although half of the money had yet to be raised. By 1880 all but 16 of the 85 missions in the north-east had schools, almost all of which were approved for grants by the inspectors, and two-thirds of the estimated population of 23,000 children were at school (the third highest proportion among the English dioceses). There were 175 teachers and 160 pupil-teachers in the region at this time and in 1875 they formed the Schoolmasters and Schoolmistresses Benevolent Institution to provide sickness benefits and the relief of destitution in old age or widowhood; the subscription was five shillings a year.

Growth was temporarily halted in the eighties because of an economic depression. In the prosperous period up to 1883 the Diocesan Fund had reduced the diocesan debt by £13,000 by liquidating the debts of 35 missions, but then income from all sources dropped leaving many priests facing deprivation and 56 missions heavily burdened with debt. School-pence also fell markedly which further exposed the anomalies of the 1870 act. The income of Board schools was three times greater than that of voluntary schools (26s.9d. per pupil as opposed to 10s.6d.) and so they could take more pupils and employ more teachers at higher salaries. School Boards would therefore argue that an application to build a voluntary school nearby be rejected and thus compel Catholic children to attend a Board school. In any case, the better-off Board schools became more selective; they poached pupils from voluntary schools and began to exclude penniless children so that voluntary schools had four times the number of poor pupils entitled to a free education. To add further insult, voluntary schools had to pay rates and hence contribute towards Board schools. Not surprisingly, many non-Catholic voluntary schools transferred to the Boards. Self-evidently, then, the 1870 Education Act did not create an equitable system of national education. Thanks, however, to the voting system, which allowed electors as many votes as there were candidates, some fifty Catholics (including priests) secured election to the School Boards across the region, and they maintained the pressure for a fully rate-aided voluntary system.

The problem was becoming more acute; each year from 1870 to 1900 there were on average around 1,000 marriages, 6,000 baptisms and 2,500 confirmations in the diocese. In 1870 7,000 children needed school places and the school-leaving age was going up all the time - to ten in 1876, eleven in 1883 and twelve in 1899, so the facilities and the number of teachers had to rise in line with the number of pupils. In 1885 an Association for the Defence of Civil and Parental Rights was formed at a public meeting of Catholics in Newcastle to campaign for an alleviation of their increasingly onerous burden. A Commission which reviewed the working of the act in 1888 expressed sympathy with the Catholic position but the disparities remained though one or two concessions were made: elementary education was made free in 1891, and in 1897 the rating of voluntary schools was abolished and the parliamentary grant was increased. At that time the head-teacher at St Patrick's Catholic school in Sunderland got £100 a year and the other masters got £73 a year; at a comparable Board school, the head got £190 a year and the masters £100. Mistresses in all schools were paid less. As the end of the century approached, then, while it was clear that it was politically impossible to abolish voluntary schools, a complete overhaul of the system was required if they were to be saved from dissolution; in 1891 the diocese had to find £147,500 for its schools programme. There were then 83 Catholic elementary schools in the region with accommodation for 40,000 children of whom 71% attended regularly. The number of pupil-teachers had risen steadily and was 200 by 1890. The Catholic Teachers' Association was founded in 1894.

Under the Education Act of 1902, School Boards were replaced by Local Education Authorities (LEAs), responsible to County Councils. Building grants for Catholic schools were abolished but the LEA had to maintain them, meet their running-costs, and pay teachers' salaries at the county scales. The school managers (who were to include two LEA nominees) appointed the teachers, but the LEA retained a veto to ensure efficiency. The LEA set the secular syllabus but the managers were allowed to control religious education. Thus the act acknowledged the Catholic claim to a 'dual system' but it was fought bitterly by the Nonconformists under the war-cry of 'Rome on the Rates' even though full equality had not been conceded and the Church still had to build the schools and pay for any alterations and improvements. A threat to withdraw all grants from voluntary schools led to a massive public demonstration on the town moor in Newcastle in 1906. In 1912 some 31,300 children were on the books of the diocesan schools in the region but the shortfall in income (between grants and expenditure) was 13s. per pupil. There were other grounds for complaint: the number of holydays was limited to five and religious education was reduced from one hour to half an hour a day. Catholic representation on county education committees was limited and so Bishop Preston formed a Catholic Manager's Association to ensure the Catholic voice was heard. Durham County and other LEAs objected to the establishment of Catholic Pupil Training Centres (that in Sunderland was approved by only one vote) and tried to insist that pupil teachers attend the nearest training centre rather than their own at Darlington, Fenham, Hartlepool or Sunderland. The Catholic Schools Defence League mounted a demonstration in Durham at which 20,000 Catholics attended.

The Act of 1902 also sought to ensure that secondary or technical education was available up to the age of fourteen for those who could benefit from it. A Catholic system of secondary education had been in place for some time but it had to be self-supporting because the Church was fully stretched maintaining the elementary sector. There were no Catholic public schools in the diocese but Ushaw College had accepted lay pupils since its opening at the beginning of the century. The *Catholic Directory* of 1850 referred to examinations being held in August 1855 at Mr Duffy's Catholic Grammar School in Old Roman Tower, Newcastle. The date at which it closed is not known but in the late 1860s Bishop Chadwick was asked to provide a replacement. Accordingly, on 1 September 1870, a new school was opened in a house in Blackett Street, opposite Eldon Square, belonging to Bernard McAnulty. A Mr Lafferty was the first master of the school but he was succeeded by Mr J.M. Kelly in 1871 who moved the school into new premises in Westmoreland Road the following year and there were fifty pupils in 1875. The Marist Brothers opened another secondary school, St Bede's, in Jarrow in 1876. (They left in 1906 because they did not have the newly-required qualifications.) In the late 1870s it seems that Mr Kelly, who was a Fenian, was obliged to close his school and emigrate to America. The bishop took it over; he bought the adjoining house in Westmoreland Road and, in August 1881, the combined property became St Cuthbert's Grammar School under the mastership of the secular clergy. At the end of 1882, the number of students having doubled, the school moved into an old brewery, 49 Bath Lane, where it would remain for the following forty years or so. The grammar school, which took boarders from all over the region, served two purposes: to prepare boys going on to Ushaw College to become priests, and to provide the secular education needed for a professional or business career; preparation for university matriculation was added later. Science and Mathematics were the only subjects for which a government maintenance grant could be obtained and since that depended on the number of passes, the school worked hard to gain the maximum number of certificates, and Chemistry and Physical laboratories were provided. Catholic grammar schools would be opened in the other major population centres of the diocese in the half-century that followed.

Secondary education for girls was hardly considered worthwhile except by the Church. In recusant times many daughters of the better-off went abroad or to the Bar Convent school at York which had operated without interruption since the seventeenth century. When they were repatriated at the time of the French Revolution, the religious orders established boarding-schools in many parts of the country, such as the Poor Clares, firstly at Scorton in 1809, and then at Darlington from 1857 to 1887. In the mid-nineteenth century we find Miss Marsh's Seminary for Young Catholic Ladies at 1 Portland Place, Newcastle, and Mrs and Miss Mesnard kept a similar establishment in Sunderland. The newer religious orders also provided private schools, like the Assumption Sisters at Richmond in 1850. In Newcastle there were the Sisters of Mercy at St Mary's (1855) and then St Anne's (1874); and the Dominican Sisters from Stroud started a school at St Dominic's (1879) which was later called St Catherine's; the Faithful Companions of Jesus also opened a boarding-school in Hartlepool (1886). St Mary's, Fenham, in addition to being a teachers' training college from around 1902, was an independent boarding school until 1918 when it became a day-school. In 1889 the Ursulines opened a school in Berwick overlooking the Tweed. All these schools were taught by extremely capable nuns who, as well as teaching dancing, needlework and other decorative accomplishments, taught an advanced syllabus of mathematics, botany, geography, history, languages, music and, of course, religion.

The Victorian Church's determination to provide an avowedly Catholic education for its young was highly impressive given the financial sacrifice it entailed and, since the Catholic population was increasing all the time and the school-leaving age was raised to fourteen in 1914, the burden would not get any lighter. In the first quarter of the new century the number of marriages rose to 1,800 a year and the number of baptisms to 7,200 a year (and most of those children went on to be confirmed). In the same period the number of Catholic elementary schools in the region rose to 120 (with 45,000 pupils) and the number of secondary schools to 15 (with 1,550 pupils).

*

The bishops of Hexham and Newcastle who presided over the northern Church during this period were, firstly, Bishop Hogarth, who set the immediate post-restoration expansion going. He was older than many of his episcopal colleagues and somewhat bluff in manner, and he steered clear of ecclesiastical politics, preferring to concentrate on diocesan development. He died in January 1866 aged eighty at Darlington where he had lived for so long; the whole town came to a halt during his funeral and the streets were lined by respectful crowds to see his cortege leave for Ushaw. His successor was James Chadwick, 53 years old, who came from old Lancastrian Jacobite stock though he was Irish-born. He went to Ushaw College in 1825 where he was ordained in 1836. In 1850 he joined the Diocesan Missionary Establishment at St Ninian's; Fr Chadwick was gifted as a spiritual director and was generally known as a saintly man. St Ninian's was destroyed by fire in 1857 and Fr Chadwick returned to Ushaw College; he was consecrated bishop there by Archbishop Manning in October 1866 and made his first visit to Rome in 1867, accompanied, coincidentally, by his two successors: Canons Bewick and Wilkinson. He convened a special Diocesan Clergy Synod in 1869 preparatory to his departure for the First Vatican Council, which opened in Rome on 8 December, and he voted for the definition of papal infallibility the following July. In 1874 the cathedral chapter presented him with a replica of St Cuthbert's pectoral cross, made by Hardman's of Birmingham. He was the first English Catholic bishop of modern times to visit the Holy Land, which he did for his health in February 1875 before going to Rome on his *ad limina* visit in October taking £600 in Peter's Pence from the diocese. In 1877 he became the eighth President of Ushaw College but he resigned the following year because his diocesan duties were so demanding. In October 1879 the bishop made another *ad limina* visit and presented the Pope with £530 in Peter's Pence. Diocesan synods had been meeting at intervals for some time but Bishop Chadwick stipulated in 1879 (when for the first time 100 priests attended) that they would assemble triennally. The diocesan debt was reduced by £10,000 during his episcopate. Bishop Chadwick wrote the Christmas carol: 'Angels we have heard on high'. He died at Newcastle in May 1882, aged 69, and was buried at Ushaw.

The third bishop of Hexham and Newcastle was John William Bewick (1824-1886). He was born at Minsteracres, where his father was steward to the Silvertop family. At the age of fourteen he entered Ushaw College where he was said to have become both a brilliant scholar and an accomplished athlete. He was ordained in 1850 and served all his priestly life on Tyneside and became Diocesan Treasurer. He was the author of the historical accounts of the missions which were published in the *Northern Catholic Calendar*. He succeeded Bishop Chadwick, though his health was in decline (he was a diabetic). When Canon Bewick was Vicar General (from 1868), Fr J.S. Rogerson, a retired chaplain of Minsteracres, gave him a house at Tynemouth called 'The Martyr's Peace' and it became Bishop's House. Bishop Bewick held the see for almost exactly four years, during which time he confirmed nearly 10,000 people. He died on 29 October 1886, aged 63.

Bishop H. O'Callaghan

Bishop Bewick's death was followed by a nine-month period of *sede vacante*. Henry O'Callaghan (1827-1904), an Oblate of St Charles Borromeo and Rector of the English College, Rome, was nominated but he felt unsuited to the episcopal rule and tried all he could to get out of it, but the Pope stood firm. Reluctantly, then, and under obedience, he was consecrated in Rome in January 1888 and was enthroned in Newcastle in March. Bishop O'Callaghan made Canon Wilkinson his Vicar General and ten weeks later he went back to Rome to arrange for Wilkinson to be made his auxiliary-bishop and the government of the diocese was thereafter conducted wholly by Bishop Wilkinson. In September 1889 after little more than two years in office Bishop O'Callaghan resigned and Bishop Wilkinson was translated to Hexham and Newcastle in December. O'Callaghan was made titular archbishop of Nicosia and lived out the rest of his days in Italy.

Bishop T.W. Wilkinson

Thomas William Wilkinson (1825-1909), a West Durham-born Anglican convert, came from a family of lawyers and clergymen and was himself intended for holy orders. He was educated at Harrow and he matriculated at Durham University at the time of the Oxford Movement and John Henry Newman's conversion. After his graduation he went to St Saviour's, an Anglican high-church parish in Leeds, where he continued his theological studies but, on 29 December 1846, he made his submission to the Catholic Church. He was ordained at Ushaw by Bishop Hogarth in December 1848 and was sent immediately to re-evangelise Weardale; he ministered in his native West Durham for the next twenty years and was appointed to the Cathedral Chapter in 1865. During his visit to Rome with Bishop Chadwick in 1867 he came across the newly-formed Pontifical Zouaves - an international volunteer army formed to defend papal Rome. When he got back home he got six of his parishioners to enlist as Zouaves and there is a photograph of them in a very Italianate uniform in the *Ushaw Magazine* of July 1909. Canon Wilkinson went into partial retirement in 1870; he became a gentleman-farmer and gained something of a reputation as a breeder of Durham shorthorn cattle. But his peaceful retirement was brought to a close in 1888 when, as he was nearing 63 years of age, he became an auxiliary-bishop; he was elected a Freeman of Newcastle in October that year. When his subsequent appointment as Bishop of Hexham and Newcastle in 1889 was announced, he remarked to a friend:

> God help me. I have sought nothing, I wanted nothing. I have neither learning, knowledge nor virtue, so they must take what they can get. I am put under obedience to accept, so here goes. I will do my best, no-one could do more than that.

Within the year he was appointed twelfth President of Ushaw College, and he would lead both the college (where he took up residence) and the diocese into the twentieth century.

Bishop Wilkinson inherited a vigorously growing diocese which needed continuity rather than reform, which was just as well for as a north-country Tory he was disinclined to radical change. He rapidly cleared the arrears of episcopal work and soon became known as a highly efficient administrator and financial manager who would brook no secretarial prevarication, or, indeed, liturgical sloppiness. He was also 'profoundly apostolic' and at first he carried out his public duties energetically but they took their toll and in 1894 he felt obliged to submit his resignation because of failing health. Cardinal Vaughan told the Holy See that his resignation would be not only a great injury to the diocese but 'a distinct loss to the whole English episcopate' and that the appointment of an auxiliary would be the best solution. Bishop Wilkinson demurred but he eventually came round to the idea and he nominated the 44-year-old Revd Dr Richard Preston.

Dr Preston, a Lancastrian and alumnus of Ushaw College, was considered a brilliant scholar and was sent to Rome for advanced studies prior to his ordination there. He became Professor of Moral Theology at Ushaw. After his episcopal consecration at Ushaw in July 1900 he remarked to a friend: 'being a bishop even in the mitigated auxiliary form is, I assure you, very terrible'. He relieved his diocesan of the fatiguing duties of public ceremony and representation, which were described later by a colleague:

Bishop R. Preston

> On one day he may be preaching in the cathedral, on the next he is opening a bazaar amongst the Durham miners, or blessing a cemetery at the foot of the Cheviots, on a third he is lending a helping hand to the Benedictine Fathers in one or other of the great parishes that fringe our western coast.

Even allowing for poetic licence, the episcopal round obviously required energy, but these duties proved too taxing for Bishop Preston, whose constitution was already weak, and he died at Lancaster five years later. Within four months a second auxiliary was appointed: Canon Richard Collins, the 48-year-old cathedral administrator. He had been ordained in 1885 at Ushaw where he became a keen sportsman. He was first appointed to the strenuous parish of Wolsingham and Witton Park (and was the second bishop to have served in West Durham as a priest; Bishop Thorman would be a third). He was consecrated bishop in the cathedral by Cardinal Bourne in June 1905. In November that year Bishop Wilkinson was made an Assistant Prelate at the Pontifical Throne by Pope Pius X. Though he became increasingly infirm, his mental capacities were undiminished and his strong personality continued to guide his auxiliary in the executive work of the diocese. The twenty years of his combined episcopate and presidency culminated with the centenary of Ushaw College and the diamond jubilee of his priesthood in 1908, but he died four months later in April 1909 and was buried at Ushaw. He left his entire fortune of over £50,000 for the education of priests for County Durham.

*

The first World War marked the end of an era in the economic and social history of the region. The predominant heavy industries of coal, iron and steel, shipbuilding, engineering and transport on which the region's prosperity depended, interlocked so that they rose and fell in synchrony; a major fall in demand would lead to a fall in prices and rising unemployment in all sectors. When demand did fall in the post-war period the result was a 'great depression' and the consequent social and economic deprivation in the region affected the Catholic population disproportionately because of its largely working-class composition. The national rate of unemployment was never less than one million between 1920 and 1940; in June 1934 it reached 50% in Bishop Auckland and 57% in Jarrow. Recovery only came with rearmament.

Bishop Collins, the auxiliary-bishop, was translated to Hexham and Newcastle at Bishop Wilkinson's death in 1909 and he lived in the cathedral house. Two years later, by Letters Apostolic (*Si qua est*), the diocese became part of the newly constituted Province of Liverpool. In December 1922 shortly after returning from his *ad limina* visit to Rome the bishop had a stroke from which it seemed he would not recover and Mgr James Rooney VG was appointed Apostolic Administrator of the diocese by the Holy See. The bishop died in February 1924, aged 67, and was buried at Ushaw. His obituarists described him as affable and gentle but conscientious and exact in his episcopal duties. Joseph Thorman (1871-1936), a Gateshead-born Anglican convert, was consecrated in January 1925; the ceremonies at the cathedral were attended by large numbers of Tyneside's civic dignitaries and they all went on to lunch in the Old Assembly Rooms. He had been educated at St Cuthbert's Grammar School and at Ushaw; he was ordained priest in 1896 and had spent twenty years in St Andrew's parish in Newcastle. He was an active member of the city's Education Committee but he was particularly well known for his work with Belgian war refugees for which he was later decorated by the King of the Belgians. He was a small, slight figure, full of energy, with a very simple, direct and determined manner with a complete lack of ostentation. In a play on his name he adopted *Servitor Maneo* (I remain a servant) as his episcopal motto; his coat of arms depicted the lilies of St Joseph, not, as some suggested, the hand of Thor grasping thunderbolts - a reference to his firm episcopal manner.

Bishop R. Collins

In November 1924, during the period of *sede vacante*, the diocese had been divided (by the Apostolic Constitution *Universalis Ecclesiae Solicitudo*) and the new bishop's first pronouncement was that this 'hitherto almost unwieldly diocese' had given up Cumberland and Westmorland to the newly-created diocese of Lancaster. The division, he said, was long-expected and would cause no surprise. Indeed, even when the 18 parishes with 21,098 people and 32 priests were detached, Hexham and Newcastle had 220,000 people (including 40,000 children) in 130 parishes with 245 priests, and it would continue to grow; by 1937 the Catholic population of the region numbered 230,394, or about 10% of the whole. In the twenty-year inter-war period (1919-39) some 39 new missions were started, all of which, except Rothbury and Otterburn, were in the industrial belt in the east of the region. The total number of parishes rose to 145. The Gothic style was no longer the automatic choice and the new churches were more likely to be built in the Romanesque fashion in which a single wide and open main aisle provided an unimpeded view for the whole congregation.

In many ways, the inter-war period was a golden age in English Catholicism. The post-restoration Church had reached maturity: the majority of members were regular worshippers, the sense of it being an Irish institution was weakening, it had an unchallenged status as a coherent moral force, and it had gained prestige as a socially responsible and politically neutral national institution. Though its membership was predominantly working-class and left-leaning, both its principal lay organisations, the SVP and the CWL, were not class-based and the Church attracted a large number of converts of the highest social standing. This was the great period of Catholic Action, as the lay apostolate was then generally known (although a joint Pastoral Letter of the hierarchy in Advent 1936 was entitled *The Apostolate of the Laity*). The centenary of Catholic Emancipation in 1929 was celebrated widely and confidently; English Catholic writing and publishing flourished: the names of Belloc, Chesterton, D'Arcy, Dawson, Hollis, Jarrett, Martindale, McNabb, Sheed, Ward, Woodruff and Vann evoke the great literary revival of the day; these and other Catholic intellectuals commanded huge audiences wherever they appeared and their influence spread throughout the Catholic body and beyond. Annual Catholic rallies were held at Wharton Park, Durham, which combined catechetics and entertainment. The Durham University Catholic Society was formed in 1920, and there was the Alcuin Society for Catholic graduates which later became the Newcastle Circle of the Newman Association.

Bishop J. Thorman

A diocesan branch of the Catholic Truth Society (founded on Guy Fawkes Day 1884) was inaugurated in 1923 at St Mary's Newcastle and it soon had 400 members; it opened a Catholic Lending Library and in 1938 a shop in Westgate Road which sold an average of 28,000 pamphlets annually; the society also arranged a Catholic Press Exhibition in Newcastle and public lectures in Durham. The Catholic Evidence Guild (CEG) was formed in June 1925 at a meeting presided over by Bishop Thorman in the Connaught Hall, Newcastle, at which Maisie Ward (Mrs Frank Sheed) was the principal speaker. Some forty people gave in their names as speakers and the first open-air meeting in Bigg Market on 20 September attracted a crowd of around 700. The first Spiritual Director was the diocesan secretary of the CTS, and its pamphlets were distributed freely at CEG meetings. On Good Friday the Stations of the Cross were said at 3 pm and 8 pm. Pitches were also opened at Felling, South Shields and Sunderland; a pitch at Whitley Bay was well attended during the summer by holidaymakers. A praesidium of the Legion of Mary, which undertook parochial and evangelical work for the clergy, was established in Newcastle in 1929. In 1934 the first branch of the Catholic Nurses Guild was formed at St Andrews, Newcastle; by the war there were nine branches in the diocese and there were five more by 1945. The Mill Hill Fathers bought Burn Hall, Durham, from the Salvin family in 1926.

In the pre-Great War period, Fr Charles Plater, SJ, the apostle to working-men, made an annual visit to Whinney House, the Jesuit residence in Gateshead, and introduced the Catholic Social Guild (CSG) into the diocese in 1911. The Guild had been formed in Manchester two years earlier to foster study of the social teaching of the Church in the papal encyclicals issued between 1878 and 1901, most famously *Rerum Novarum* (1891). Fr Plater held a number of summer schools for the CYMS (which at its peak had 39 branches in the diocese with almost 3,000 members) out of which the Tyneside and Durham branch of the Guild soon emerged. Guild membership was small but exceptionally active; by the outbreak of the First World War there were twenty CSG study-clubs in the diocese with over two hundred members. Father, later Canon, Magill, a promoter of the CSG at Leadgate, told Fr Plater: 'Twelve to fifteen of our miners, all trade unionists and most of them married men, meet every Sunday night from 8 to 9 from October to June with myself and my curate ... the discussion is often very lively'. The long term results of the Guild's work soon appeared: visiting Leadgate a few years later Fr Plater observed, 'The Catholic men appear to run the public life of the town'. In the 1930s Catholic miners in the Deerness valley took control of their union from the Methodists. The Guild continued to flourish partly, no doubt, because Bishop Thorman became its president in 1928; it would later fund an annual Bishop Thorman Memorial Scholarship to the Catholic Worker's College, Oxford. By 1939 the diocesan membership of the Guild had grown to 3,910 in 55 study-clubs. A number of men made substantial contributions to public life in the region arising from their involvement in the Guild among whom we may note especially: Edward Colgan of Tyneside; Michael Hoey and Joseph Kirwan of Wearside; and Pat Bartley, a pitman and the first student of the college to enter parliament (he sat for Chester le Street from 1909 to 1956) [Cleary passim]. In 1913 Fr Plater had instituted lay retreats for the men of the diocese but Whinney House was taken over as a hospital during the war and sold to the town council in 1920. In August 1933, therefore, the Jesuits opened a new retreat-house in Corby Hall, Sunderland, and over 1,000 men and 200 priest made retreats there during the 1930s. The Marie Reparatrice sisters opened a retreat-house for women in 1937.

Charitable work of every kind engaged the Church at all levels as it had always done. Expenditure on the diocesan orphanages rose to almost £5,000, of which about £1,000 was raised in Advent and Lenten alms. The CWL opened a registry office to place maids in suitable Catholic homes; in 1925 a CWL Social Centre was opened in Durham. Membership of the League rose to over 3,000 in 1934. In 1917 the Poor Sisters of Nazareth set up a girl's home in Sandyford House, Newcastle, in the old surgery of the celebrated doctor in the song *Blaydon Races*: '... some went to the Dispensary, and some to Dr Gibbs ...' and there were eighty residents by 1919. Membership of the SVP at this time was 1,260 in 109 conferences and from the 1920s to 1936 the society organised the Ovingham Camp so that boys of poor families could enjoy a summer holiday. In 1921 the society opened Heddon House as a respite-home to give needy elderly people a free two-week holiday; and in 1930 the society started a Deaf Club in Summerhill Grove, Newcastle. The SVP formed a women's conference at St Edward's, Whitley Bay, in 1933. The diocese opened St John Bosco's Farm Training Centre at Hylton, Sunderland, to provide three-month courses for deprived boys aged fourteen wishing to take up agricultural work. The Sisters of Our Lady of Good & Perpetual Succour opened Strickland Hall, Ebchester, as a private school in 1935 but it became a rest home for ladies in 1937. The Little Sisters of the Poor in Sunderland continued to beg money and clothes from a horse and cart; in 1936, however, they obtained a ten-year-old green Rolls-Royce car (No. WW 4115) which they converted to a van. George Gammie drove it around the county for 22 years collecting gifts of provisions, clothes and furniture. Though it still ran smoothly after having done 145,000 miles, it had to be laid up in 1958 since it was no longer possible to get the tyres.

The diocese continued to express public devotion to its saints. In September 1924 the 1,250th anniversary of the foundation of St Peter's church in Sunderland was celebrated and Francis Cardinal Bourne led a two-mile-long procession to Cliffe Park, Roker, to the newly-erected Bede Memorial Cross. The first diocesan pilgrimage to Lourdes was organised by Fr John Jacobs in 1926 and 600 pilgrims travelled; 900 went in 1937 and one thousand got back two weeks before the outbreak of the Second World War. A major diocesan pilgrimage to Newminster at Whitsun 1927 attracted 20,000 people. The cause of the English Martyrs, which had been in abeyance since 1895, was resumed after the first world war and 136 martyrs were beatified in 1929, the centenary of Catholic Emancipation. In 1934, its jubilee year, the Catholic Truth Society arranged the first Pilgrim Walk in honour of the English Martyrs from the site of Newgate Gaol in Newcastle to St Edward's Chapel in Gateshead (now Holy Trinity church) and 200 made the pilgrimage. In 1935 John Fisher and Thomas More were canonised and the commemoration of the twelfth centenary of Bede's death at Jarrow attracted up to 50,000 people led by Archbishops Hinsley and Downey.

Bishop Thorman died at Tynemouth in October 1936. He was succeeded the following February by Joseph McCormack who was born in Worcestershire in 1887 and educated at St Cuthbert's, Newcastle, and at Ushaw. He was ordained in 1912 and went on to study at the University of Louvain. He was appointed secretary to Bishops Collins and Thorman; he became Vicar General, Cathedral Administrator, and, in 1934, Canon Theologian, making him an obvious episcopal candidate. He was consecrated by the Archbishop of Liverpool in February 1937 in the year of his priestly Silver Jubilee; the Mayor of Newcastle gave two civic banquets in the new bishop's honour; more practically the diocese gave him a motor-car.

The public life of the diocese went on beyond the outbreak of the Second World War in September 1939. The national annual conferences of the Catholic Federation of Teachers, the CYMS and the SVP were all held in Newcastle in 1939/40 but normal life was disrupted when air-raids on the industrial areas of the region began and many parochial and diocesan societies suspended operations. The diocesan school-building programme, on which around £250,000 was spent in 1936, was brought to a halt and some 15,000 schoolchildren and their teachers were evacuated into the country from the urban areas; St Cuthbert's Grammar School went to Cockermouth and St Mary's Teacher Training College moved into Swinburne Castle. St Vincent's Orphanage (in Brunel Terrace, the same street as St Michael's church in Newcastle which was bombed in Holy Week 1941) went to Cheeseburn Grange and Nazareth House moved to Carlisle. St Peter's, Gainford, was firstly given over to 350 refugees from the Spanish Civil War of 1936-9, and then to evacuees from Teesside. More than thirty Mass centres were established in the country for the evacueees. Mass attendances fell in the

Bishop J. McCormack

towns because of the evacuations and the absence of large numbers of men and women in the armed services. Sanctuary lamps were extinguished and evening services (including Midnight Mass at Christmas) were abandoned to conform with the black-out regulations. Fasting and abstinence rules were set aside and the eucharistic fast was relaxed; the Jesuit retreat-house in Corby Hall remained open. The bishop moved his residence from Tynemouth to Newcastle observing that 'It is necessary to be in a more central position' and because of the difficulty of access to the wartime defence area at the mouth of the Tyne. He went first to Sandyford Road and then in 1942 to East Denton Hall, which remains Bishop's House. The CWL re-established their Huts and Canteens for the troops and opened a hostel for Catholic servicewomen in Newcastle. Towards the end of the war the CWL became involved in helping displaced persons from Europe. The various social services provided by the church were maintained but little development could take place. In 1940 the Tyneside Catholic Youth Council was established to promote leadership through retreats, social and sporting activities, and all parish youth clubs automatically became members. Also in 1940 Tudhoe became a boy's home under the charge of the Sisters of Charity. The SVP opened Ozanam House as a probation hostel in 1941 for boys aged fifteen to eighteen, and it was recognised by the Home Office in 1943.

The number of the laymen and women who served in the Second World War is impossible to count, any more than it is easy to establish the number of all those who were decorated, or killed or injured; notably, Adam Wakenshaw, an alumnus of St Aloysius School in Newcastle and a private in the DLI, was awarded the Victoria Cross. Forty priests of the diocese served as chaplains, seven of whom were decorated for bravery. Two priests, Frs E.W. Hodgson and G.W. Forster, became prisoners of war in Italy and Germany. Fr Forster's uniform became so worn that he was loaned a Franciscan habit; his Mass kit and portable altar were destroyed in battle at Tobruk but, defying the outrage of his captors at Bari, he declined point blankly to offer Mass on the altar provided for him while it was draped with the Italian flag; he won the point. Some priests were wounded: Fr Cornelius O'Callaghan (Green Howards) was in a vehicle when it was blown up but the doctor who was sitting alongside him took the full force of the explosion. Two diocesan priests died in action: Fr James O'Callaghan, the former's brother, was killed in Burma; and Fr Gerard Nesbitt of Felling: he had been mentioned in despatches and he was awarded a posthumous Croix de Guerre.

There were some 8,700 German and Italian prisoners of war in the diocese by the end of the war, mostly in rural camps, from which they were employed in agricultural work. They were attended by local priests whenever possible and the SVP provided limited material comforts such as chocolate and cigarettes. Relations between the captives and the population seem to have been relaxed and it was not unusual for prisoners to attend local churches freely and even take Sunday lunch with parishioners. The Germans adapted well; the following exchange was overheard between two prisoners negotiating a farm-cart through a gate: "Vill it gann, Kurt?" "Nein, Fritz, its ower narra."

*

Despite the experience of the inter-war economic depression, there had been little modernisation or diversification of the region's economic base, and defence expenditure only masked its vulnerability to low productivity in a narrow range of declining industries. The adoption of new technology was fiercely resisted in places until force of circumstance compelled a greater flexibility in investment and working practices. The region's economy was slow to diversify and it was only towards the end of the century that it had modernised to the extent that a majority of people were working in high-technology industries. The reluctance to transform the industrial base of the region contrasted sharply with an enthusiasm for post-war social reconstruction. Since unemployment and low wages were the chief causes of poverty and ill-health in the pre-war years, official policy now aimed at full employment, and major reforms in social-security, health, housing and educational policy were introduced. The whole package became known as the 'welfare state'.

As we have seen, Catholics shared with their fellow-citizens the fundamental political values of democracy and allegiance to the crown; they could therefore be found in all walks of life and they willingly volunteered for armed service. But, their obedience to the Holy See marked them out as adherents of a clearly defined moral teaching, especially in the marital field, in contrast to that of their non-Catholic neighbours. Catholic social teaching laid very great stress on the family, on parental rights, on the natural right to property ownership, on the fair wage, and on the principle of subsidiarity, and was therefore at variance with most aspects of British post-war social policy. In fact, opposition had been voiced much earlier: the Education Act of 1918 and the Health Act of 1919 were held to sanction an intrusion into family life of 'godless cranks and faddists'. Similarly, the introduction of the welfare state was opposed because it seemed to enforce collectivist, bureaucratic state control in areas which were properly the province of individuals, families and voluntary associations; consequently, private rights and responsibilities, personal independence and initiative, would be diminished. Social security, the Church held, was best achieved by savings, self-help through insurance with Friendly Societies, and the payment of fair wages. State-paid allowances would not only depress wages but make people irresponsible by relieving them of the ordinary risks of daily life. The Church also feared that contraception, abortion and euthanasia would be introduced, perhaps imposed, as part of the national health service, and the Catholic doctors of the Guild of Sts. Luke, Cosmas & Damian rejected cooperation with it. A diocesan Association of Public Representatives was inaugurated in 1948 to maintain Catholic principles in political life.

These principles were promulgated widely at the time but Catholic reaction to the welfare state varied. On the one hand there were those in sympathy with Chesterton, Belloc and Gill who were opposed to modern society and all its works and wanted a return to the medieval guild system. On the other hand, many of those who remembered the privations of the inter-war period accepted the new system without demur and would have welcomed a great deal more state intervention. Between those extremes, the majority of Catholics recognised that since the society envisaged in the Church's social teaching was unattainable in the prevailing circumstances, the reforms could be accepted as a second-best solution because they did go some way to alleviating terrible social problems. The welfare reforms were introduced and Catholic opposition, such as it was, evaporated, for the British Catholics could hardly exclude themselves from the new system. In any case, of course, the Church was not in a position to provide alternative health or social security services to the same extent that it had provided its own schools, although it did maintain an extensive charitable network. Indeed, the difficulty of applying traditional teaching to modern social security systems led to a change in the Church's position [*Mater et Magistra* 1961, paras 105-7] and in later years when the British welfare state appeared to be under threat, the hierarchy was vehement in its support.

Changed conditions in the post-war years indicated that the diocesan social services needed to be reorganised. In 1945 Bishop McCormack replaced the Children's Care Committee with a Diocesan Rescue Society (Administrator Fr J.V. Smith, a former Secretary of the Children's Homes Committee). The Society's aim was

> to seek out and rescue, educate, adopt, or cause to be adopted, train, place out in life and otherwise promote the welfare of orphans and destitute children, and other persons of either sex suffering from mental or physical disability or other material or moral misfortunes.

The emphasis, unchanged from earlier days, was on *rescuing* children from unsatisfactory living conditions or from the danger of losing their Catholic faith. The bishop had complained in 1935 that requests for the transfer of Catholic children placed in non-Catholic homes were being refused, and as late as 1956 Canon Smith said that local authorities were still not transferring Catholic children into the Society's care. The Rescue Society's work in 1946 required £7,000 a year and was partly funded through a 'Good Shepherd Collection' taken in the schools of the region between Ash Wednesday and Good Shepherd Sunday; in the first ten years of its existence it raised £30,000. The first edition of *The Fold*, the monthly magazine of the Diocesan Rescue Society, appeared in June 1947. In addition to news about the society's work, it discussed a wide range of current affairs of interest to Catholics. The magazine was taken by some 4,000 households but, without explanation, it abruptly ceased publication with the twentieth edition, March 1952.

At its inception, the Rescue Society had four large orphanages caring for about 500 children: St Vincent's and Nazareth House in Newcastle; St Joseph's in Darlington, and St Mary's at Tudhoe. In the post-war years St Peter's, Gainford, became an Approved School for juvenile delinquents. The newly-formed national social services, however, were developing policies which required the professionalisation of care-workers and a gradual break-up of large institutions. Government now encouraged the adoption and fostering of children, and support for parents in difficult circumstances wishing to keep their children at home. The Rescue Society willingly complied with the new approach and in 1950 it opened the first diocesan Family Group Home in England and Wales. Two small hostels for working teenagers, St Philip's and St Philomena's, were also opened in Newcastle. In 1957 the Rescue Society took over a house in Whitley Bay to provide a holiday home for the children in all its diocesan homes. By the early sixties the number of children in the orphanages had halved and over 100 nuns had qualified for the new Certificate for Proficiency in Child Care. The diocese was able to close St Mary's, Tudhoe, in 1963, St Joseph's, Darlington, in 1968 and St Peter's, Gainford, in 1984.

There were other developments in the social field, though not all of them under the aegis of the Rescue Society. The Little Sisters of the Assumption, a nursing order, opened a house in Gateshead shortly after the war. At the same time the SVP sponsored Westoe Towers, an Apostleship of the Sea hostel in South Shields. In 1947 the Stella Maris Club with accommodation for 55 seamen opened; the Sisters of the Sacred Hearts of Jesus and Mary opened Lemmington Hall for mentally-handicapped females; and St Camillus Hospital, a nursing home for the elderly was opened at Swinburne Castle. St Cuthbert's Hospital, Hurworth, for physically and mentally-handicapped people opened in 1948. The CWL was very active at this time; there were 2,422 members in the Branch in 1946 and in 1947 it bought a house in Bentinck Road, Newcastle, for £4,000 and converted it into bed-sitting rooms to provide sheltered accommodation for elderly ladies. In 1949 the CWL supported the Diocesan Mother and Baby Hostel in Lovaine Place and in 1950 it instituted Our Lady's Catechists. In 1955 it joined the SVP to set up a Youth Camp on Holy Island, in place of Ovingham, which was still going strong at the end of the century.

Educational reform was always on the agenda and, as ever, was a matter of controversy between Church and State. The Education Act of 1936 had expressed the government's intention of making secondary education compulsory, though free, for all up to the age of fifteen in 1939; it would also introduce examinations for entry into grammar schools at the age of eleven. To the Church's partial relief, however, it empowered local authorities to make grants of 50-75% towards the cost of building the Catholic schools made necessary by the changes. The Second World War intervened before the reforms could be introduced but, looking ahead to the proposed post-war legislation which threatened the existence of Catholic schools, the Church stood by its view that parents, not the state, had the right and duty to decide how their children were to be educated and hence denominational schools had to be maintained with 100% grant-aid. Bishop McCormack, who was by this time an expert on educational law and practice and who would become a principal negotiator on the legislation, issued a number of pastorals on the topic. A massive public campaign was mounted by Catholic parents and electors from 1942, but to little avail.

Although the 1944 Education Act preserved the voluntary system, the Church was limited to 50% of construction and building maintenance costs despite being faced with an estimated expenditure of £1.5 million arising from the reorganisation of secondary education quite apart from bomb damage and slum clearance. The political campaign for larger grants was revived at subsequent elections but no political party felt inclined to amend the act although it was glaringly obvious that the burden on the Church was too great; it was not until 1959 that the grant was increased, but even then only to 75%. The Church would continue to find primary and secondary education its most expensive activity but it never doubted its value. In 1948 the Christian Brothers took over Corby Grammar School (216 pupils) in Sunderland from the Jesuits and renamed it St Aidan's. The Xaverian Brothers opened a Grammar and Technical School in Hartlepool in 1956.

Another, but less controversial, major post-war educational development was the expansion of university education. After the war 300 (or 10%) of undergraduates at King's College, Newcastle, were Catholics and, in anticipation of many more students, a house in Jesmond was opened as a new chaplaincy in 1954. By 1962 there were 400 Catholic students (including eleven nuns) and by 1970 there were 600. This was the clearest indication of the settled place of the Catholic middle class in English society. In 1963 the Catholic teacher-training college at Fenham was constituted a College of Education and a member of the Institute of Education in Newcastle University, and in 1971 the student body numbered almost 800.

Bishop McCormack became the longest serving English bishop in 1956 and his 21-year episcopate was a diocesan record. He was a meticulous and unhurried administrator who had the appearance of being cold and reserved but in private he was considerably more relaxed and jovial. He will be best remembered as a champion of Catholic education, for which he fought with skill and firm diplomacy, and which gained him and his cause considerable respect in official and political circles. He reached the age of seventy in May 1957 and in November James Cunningham was consecrated his auxiliary - the first auxiliary-bishop since Bishop Collins 48 years before. Bishop Cunningham was born in Manchester in 1910 and was ordained at Upholland in 1937. After further studies in Rome he returned to his native diocese of Salford and in due course became a canon, the cathedral administrator, and vicar general. Bishop McCormack died in March 1958 and, like the majority of his predecessors, he was buried at Ushaw. In July Bishop Cunningham was translated to the see of Hexham and Newcastle. The people of the diocese gave him a crozier, made in Newcastle, in the style of the ancient Celtic design of the Lismore crozier and the crook of St Keiran, with decorative filigree-work and bird forms taken from the Lindisfarne Gospels. His arms comprised the shells of St James of Compostella and the letter Y for the Cunningham family. (Incidentally, no later bishop of the diocese adopted a coat of arms.)

Bishop J. Cunningham

In the first ten years after the war 29 churches were built in the diocese but in 1956, with some 160 parishes and 420 priests (including 48 regulars), the bishop remarked on the shortage of priests which was slowing down further growth; he said he could employ another twenty without the least difficulty; only fifty had been ordained since 1950. In Sunderland during the suburban building boom of the mid-fifties, for example, there were 23,400 Catholics in ten parishes with two more about to be created. There were 4,000 children in church primary and secondary schools and 750 at grammar schools; there were over 200 Catholic teachers. The seventeenth diocesan synod at the cathedral in November 1961 was told that £4 million would be needed for new churches, schools and other buildings across the region. The diocesan population was still increasing year by year: in 1957 there were as many in the diocese as there had been when it was divided thirty years before, and in the first half of the 1960s it became clear that the diocese was the fastest growing in the northern province. Seven new churches were opened between 1958 and 1965 and a large week-long religious vocations exhibition was mounted on the Town Moor, Newcastle in 1963. The Catholic population reached 284,242 in 1968 (12% of the whole) in 172 parishes with 431 priests. Further growth could be expected because marriages averaged around 2,600 and baptisms 6,500 a year. In 1965 there were 65,509 children enrolled in 227 Catholic schools (of all kinds) which were staffed by 2,051 Catholic teachers. The school population would rise for several more years (it was 67,570 in 1971 when there were 6,811 confirmations).

Many longstanding lay Catholic organisations continued to be prominent in the diocese in the post-war years and the diocese hosted their major assemblies. The Knights of St Columba was the largest lay organisation in Britain; Province No. 4, in the north-east, was the second oldest in England and Wales and in 1958 the province hosted the meeting of its Supreme Council in Whitley Bay. In the same year the national AGM of the SVP returned to Newcastle after nineteen years. In 1965 there were 1,600 members in 167 SVP conferences across the diocese. The National Council of the CWL and the Catholic Pharmaceutical Guild met in Newcastle in 1960. The Tyneside Branch of the Catholic Social Guild was the largest in the country in 1960; at the same time the CTS, which was selling some 45,000 pamphlets annually, had 1,700 members in the diocese and it moved to more prominent premises in Ridley Place in 1962. The CEG, (which opened a platform at the north end of the railway station in Sunderland in 1954) held its national conference in Newcastle in 1961. The war took such a toll of the CYMS that in 1957 its combined membership in Newcastle, Durham and Sunderland was only 609 members. Nonetheless from 1958 the society went on an annual pilgrimage to Holy Island. In 1963 it reconstituted several parish branches and the national annual conference was held in Whitley Bay in 1965.

A number of other groups made their appearance or were revived in the diocese in this period. During the negotiations over the 1944 Education Act, a meeting was held at St Leonard's in Durham by Catholic trade unionists to protest about the TUCs opposition to Catholic schools and, as a result, the Association of Catholic Trade Unionists (ACTU) was formed; it spread rapidly through the country and a national committee was formed in 1946. Late in 1955 members of the writers' Guild of St Francis de Sales met in an upper room of the Bridge Hotel, Newcastle, and in January 1956 the first edition of *Northern Cross*, an independent monthly newspaper for the diocese, began publication under the editorship of Terence Wynn, a professional journalist working in the region for the *Daily Sketch*. A Polish Catholic Centre was opened in Westmorland Road in 1957; it moved to new premises in Rye Hill in 1972. The initial AGM of the Handicapped Children's Pilgrimage Trust was held in 1963 and the Trust's first diocesan pilgrimage to Lourdes took place in 1968. In 1966 a diocesan branch of the Catholic Housing Aid Society was formed. From 1972 a guild of priests' housekeepers met monthly at St Andrew's, Newcastle, and enjoyed an annual outing. In 1968 *Lampades Christi*, an association of voluntary lay missionaries with a variety of teaching and vocational skills, was formed at Corby Hall. Within two years of its formation it had forty members serving overseas. A University Catholic Society was established in Durham in 1947 and a new chaplaincy opened in 1966. A Diocesan Catechetical Centre was established at St Mary's College, Fenham in 1967.

One feature of the Catholic parochial social scene over the years was the licensed club, and in 1965 a North Eastern Association of Catholic Clubs was formed. From 1968 the CWL ran a week-long holiday and Catechism Camp for children at the Ursuline Convent, Longridge Towers, Berwick, and they have been held at various venues since then.

Continuity and development in individual and group spirituality were also features of these years. In 1951 the 13th centenary celebrations of St Aidan were held at Ushaw College and 40,000 people are said to have attended. In Marian Year, 1954, the CWL staged a pageant entitled *Ave Maria* and the medieval pilgrimage to the shrine of Our Lady of Jesmond was revived. In 1956 4,000 people went there on 29 April to pray for the conversion of Russia and in May 1958 6,000 pilgrims went - the largest number ever. The centenary in 1958 of the apparitions at Lourdes was celebrated in Sunderland with a procession of tableaux and brass bands and attracted 10,000; a pageant entitled *Mary Immaculate* was presented in Newcastle City Hall and was seen by 12,000 people. In 1960 the first CWL Family Fast Day was held. The All-Night Vigil movement grew from around 1965 and the retreat movement expanded. Minsteracres, the old residence of the Silvertop family, was taken over in 1952 as a Passionist monastery and seminary. The community soon numbered thirty and it was decided to add a retreat-house. By 1961 £3,000 was raised in the diocese; the work was undertaken by the Catholic men of Consett and the new retreat-house was opened in 1967. The retreat-centres at Minsteracres, Corby Hall and Marie Reparatrice became popular; almost 50,000 men had made retreats at Corby Hall by 1965, and in 1972 1,856 individuals and 900 parish groups made use of the facilities at Minsteracres.

The Second World War had interrupted further progress on the cause of the English martyrs, but it was resumed in 1960 with a petition to the Holy See from the hierarchy for the canonisation of forty men and women, representative of place of origin, state of life, and so on. The cause generated a great deal of interest and in 1961 a pageant about the martyrs, written by Fr Wilfrid Fee, ran at the City Hall, Newcastle, for four nights and was seen by 8,000 people. An outdoor rally at St Leonard's, Silksworth, was attended by 4,000 people and in 1962 10,000 people attended a rally at Ushaw for Martyrs Day. On 25 October 1970 the Forty Martyrs were canonised and in 1972 the pre-war annual walk in honour of the martyrs was reinstituted in Gateshead in honour of Bl. John Ingram.

Clearly, then, in the twenty years after the war the Church's spiritual and social mission flourished: the number of Catholics in the diocese increased both absolutely and proportionately; they willingly financed the Church and supported a wide range of devotional and charitable activity; and they played a major part in all aspects of life. But in the late sixties there were ominous signs that the diocesan trends were about to go into reverse. There were only 34 ordinations in the 1960s which meant that between 1939 and 1969 ordinations had fallen by half. The decline in the number of priests gathered pace: In 1972 there were 379 priests, fifty fewer than in 1968. Vocations, too, had fallen off: up to 1967 there was a yearly average of fifty applications for church-studentships; in 1970 there were twelve and there were only seventy seminarians, a third of the number in 1960. The 17th (and last) Diocesan Synod of 1961 was told that the number of convents in the diocese was below the national average and the number of female vocations was beginning to fall: in 1961 there were 46 female postulants, in 1972 there were 42. Finally, by 1972 the Catholic population had fallen by 9,000 and, although the number of marriages had kept up, the number of baptisms had decreased by 1,000. Thus the late 1960s mark a watershed in diocesan history. Until that time, gains had been recorded continuously since the restoration in 1850, but the number of priests, religious and laity fell year by year thereafter and many other participant activities were similarly affected.

It is important to recognise at once that a reverse of such proportions cannot be attributed to a single cause but to a cluster of inter-related external and internal factors. Firstly there were the external secular influences of the social upheavals of the post-war years: the break-up of old communities, the creation of a welfare state, the introduction of secondary education for all, the expansion of the universities, the impact of the mass media, upward social mobility, economic prosperity and advances in medical science, all of which exerted increasing materialistic pressures on Catholics (as on everyone else) and which served to detach those members having a weak allegiance from their faith. But the Church had also begun to experience a build-up of internal pressure from those who demanded a review of its practice and of its place in the modern world. Those concerns were addressed by the Second Vatican Council, which met from 1962 to 1965, and which introduced changes in ecclesiastical practice which amounted to nothing less than a revolution in Catholic life. Indeed, as suggestions of what the Council might do began to circulate, many Catholics, hopeful and fearful alike, began to think that the headline in *Northern Cross* of November 1961 predicting 'Another Reformation is on the way' was about to come true. The paper changed its tune in February 1962 saying: 'We need not expect anything dramatic', which was too late and too vague to reassure either party. And in later years progressives would, often erroneously, cite the Council for any change they chose to promote and conservatives would, equally wrongly, blame the Council for changes they deplored. In fact, the social and ecclesiastical way of life of the English Catholics was transformed in this period for many reasons, some of which are given above, but since this survey is concerned principally with church-history it must now examine the immediate pastoral effect of the Council.

*

Of the wide-ranging reforms introduced by the Council, perhaps those of the *Constitution on the Sacred Liturgy* (December 1963) had the most immediate impact. In fact, liturgical reform pre-dated the Council by many years. Although Britain was never in the vanguard of reform, the foundation in 1929 of the Society of St Gregory to promote greater participation in the liturgy was an important development. It used to be that most Catholics only ever attended Low Mass (that is, one celebrated by a single priest and without music) the central part of which was inaudible and invisible to the majority: a principal function of the altar-boy was to ring a bell to alert the congregation as the celebrant reached successive stages. Many people busied themselves with private devotions during Mass. Missals for the use of the laity were published from 1852 but they did not become cheap enough for all until after the First World War. Increased liturgical participation became possible with the introduction of the Dialogue Mass in 1928 in which the congregation could sing the Ordinary of the Mass with the choir at High Mass or say the responses together with the altar-server at Low Mass. The encyclical *Mediator Dei* (1947) recommended a more active participation by the laity and in 1951 the ancient liturgy of Holy Saturday was restored, partly in the vernacular. Evening Masses on holydays of obligation, with the appropriate reduction in the Eucharistic fast, were authorised from 1953 and on Sundays from 1956/7. Revised liturgies for Holy Week were introduced in 1956; the Easter Triduum could now be celebrated at times convenient for the people (the Chrism Mass on Holy Thursday morning was moved from Ushaw College to the cathedral) and everyone was permitted to receive Holy Communion on Good Friday. In 1958 lay lectors were permitted to deliver the scriptures publicly in English. Hence the provisions of the Council's *Constitution* of 1963 can be traced to developments over many years.

It is unnecessary to outline fully the provisions of the Council's document except to note that its basic purpose was to encourage an understanding of the Mass as a corporate not just a priestly act, and that the congregation should become an actively-participant worshipping community. That concept wrought the most dramatic change imaginable on the practice of Catholicism in England. From 1964 the passive liturgical life of the people came to an end and they were caught up in a seemingly endless series of alterations to their churches and piecemeal changes to the liturgy, known collectively as 'Liturgical Renewal'.

In January 1964 Bishop Cunningham began a series of diocesan consultations on proposals for liturgical change. He first asked the clergy for their opinions on the celebration of Mass in Latin. Of 345 replies, 26 were entirely opposed to any change and only 40 wished to say the Mass wholly in English. The rest suggested that if the vernacular had to come then only the public prayers should be translated, and the hierarchy agreed. From Advent 1964 English could be used up to the Secret [now the Prayer over the Offerings] and from the *Pater Noster* [Our Father] to the end of Mass. The eucharistic fast was reduced to one hour. In January 1965 an *ad clerum* asked for the views of the laity on the changes. Of 269 replies, two parishes (Croxdale and Swinburne) were entirely opposed to them while 161 approved; the others had reservations, mostly about the quality of the translations and the constant bobbing up and down, especially after Holy Communion. Thirty parishes wanted to retain a Latin Mass on Sundays; 180 would abandon it altogether. There then followed a long period of experimentation in the Mass, with Latin, a little Greek but mostly English, and a variety of movements, which most of the clergy and laity found confusing and uninspiring. A survey held in June 1967, however, showed that there was a widespread desire for a simple Mass said entirely in English: only 16 priests remained opposed to Englishing the Canon, though 30% of the laity still wished to retain Latin. A wholly vernacular Mass with simplified rubrics was authorised that year.

A comprehensive questionnaire was circulated later in 1967 about the pastoral impact of the liturgical changes and 163 parishes responded. 142 reported that the changes had been generally beneficial, only five said that the benefits had been negligible. Asked about ill-effects, ninety said there had been none, most of the others said there had been a decline in private devotion and general reverence. Almost all parishes said that attendance at Mass had increased; 52 said there had been no increase at Holy Communion; 43 said there had been no change in the numbers at Confession. The introduction of the vernacular was almost unanimously welcomed and only 22 parishes regretted the non-availability of even one Latin Mass. It is clear, then, that opinion shifted quite markedly during the trial period in which the liturgical changes were introduced. Initially most priests and laypeople wished to have a more intelligible liturgy while retaining the historical Latin Mass; but, having tried the alternatives, only a very small number held that view three years later.

Importantly, however, while it was generally agreed that the vernacular had not led to defections but rather that attendances had risen and that it had enhanced liturgical understanding and participation, the need for a better translation of the Roman Missal was widely expressed. At first, national hierarchies had used their own versions, then the hierarchies of the British Isles agreed a common translation while waiting for a universal English-language text which, it was thought, might take ten years to produce. As early as 1969, however, the International Commission on English in the Liturgy (ICEL) began to issue translations of the Roman Missal and the Sacramentary and the whole was completed in 1973. Inevitably they showed all the literary shortcomings which arise when a committee works at speed and under pressure to accommodate various national linguistic preferences, but they also attracted criticism for some unfaithful or flawed versions of the Latin texts. But subsequent, more considered, translations were well received. The new *Order of Christian Funerals* and the *Rites of Anointing and Viaticum* were beautiful, sensitive and practical (all the sick, not just those *in extremis*, could now be anointed). The revival of the catechumenate in 1971 with a carefully structured approach to the process of adult conversion and its accompanying ritual was provided for in the *Rite for the Christian Initiation of Adults* (RCIA). A reworking of the *Rite of Marriage* was underway at the time of writing and a more considered English translation of the Roman Missal was also in its final stages; having seen the latter texts, one non-Catholic liturgical scholar said that enormous efforts had clearly gone into composing beautiful and accurate English translations and into rethinking pastoral and liturgical presentation. The influence of this missal was expected to extend way beyond the Catholic communion and to put the ICEL texts into abeyance.

The Council confirmed music to be an integral part of the liturgy and almost as much attention was given to it in the conciliar document as was paid to the Eucharist. But if the quality of spoken English in the revised liturgy was found wanting, for many the standard of church-music was very much worse. Catholic singing before the Council was not invariably of a high standard, of course. As early as 1903 the prevailing theatrical style of church-music was condemned by Pope Pius X who required greater emphasis on traditional plainsong and early polyphonic music instead; the organ was to play a modest not a dominant role; only males were to form the choir. As a result many generations of Catholics learned the choral parts of the Ordinary of High Mass (*Kyrie, Gloria, Credo, Sanctus, Agnus Dei*). A number of choirs and organists had a wide repertoire and would sing the church-music of Byrd and Tallis, as well as that of Haydn, Beethoven and many other composers (Mozart was preferred to Palestrina in Durham). The setting of the Benediction hymn *Tantum Ergo* by Charles Newsham, fifth President of Ushaw College, was also popular. When visiting friends in Bishop Auckland, Sir Edward Elgar worshipped at St Wilfrid's, where there was a choir of 14 mixed voices, and he played the organ on many occasions; his settings of the motets *Ave verum corpus* and *Ave Maris Stella*, the Litany of Loreto, and the Benediction hymn *O Salutaris* were sung regularly.

The Council decree stipulated that Gregorian chant 'should be given pride of place in liturgical services' but it was in fact summarily abandoned and replaced by religious songs having cheap, trite, though catchy, tunes however unliturgical their words (such as 'Let us break bread together on our knees') or banal ('Sing a Simple Song') or even when the congregation became the voice of God ('This is my Body'). Moreover, the psalm-settings by Joseph Gelineau published by The Grail, and one of the glories of the modern liturgical renewal movement, remained unknown in most churches despite the creation of a Diocesan Liturgical Commission in 1968. Like house-masses, the Folk Mass came and went; a guitar accompaniment to congregational worship having been quickly found to be better suited to the convent or school-chapel than to the church itself, but matters were not improved when electronic instruments replaced pipe-organs (despite official encouragement of the latter). Thus music often seemed to detract from, if not displace, the liturgy rather as it had done in the late 19th century. Organists were either made redundant or declined to perform the new repertoire and serious composers began to complain that liturgical music was no longer commissioned for general use. Towards the end of the century, however, the treasury of church-music was re-examined and found to have a perennial relevance, and signs of a revival was discernible. Many older people relished the opportunity to sing the *Credo* from the *Missa de Angelis* and the marian motet *Salve Regina*. Dom Joseph E. Turner's Latin mass in honour of St Cecilia (1892) was revived at St Cuthbert's, Durham, in 1980 and was 'much appreciated' [Tweedy, II, 18]. The Schola Gregoriana of Northumbria was formed in 1993 to sing and promote interest in Gregorian chant and soon found itself increasingly in demand.

The aesthetics of liturgy are as susceptible to the physical environment as they are to linguistic or musical influences, and the Council had much to say about the construction and internal arrangements of churches but it came too late to influence immediate post-war building-styles. In the twenty years between the end of the war and the end of the Council, some 45 new suburban missions were created across the region to serve the housing estates built to replace devastated town-centres. Money was not available to build a church in every place, but in two-thirds of them churches were erected and all, necessarily, were built in accordance with pre-conciliar norms. Fortunately, however, the modern, open architectural style in which these churches were designed permitted alterations to be made to accommodate the new liturgy without difficulty. But the adaptation of Gothic-style churches to conciliar norms was more problematical. Two principles governed church-architecture until the Council: the sanctuary was separated from the nave by a chancel-arch, and usually by altar rails, to create a clearly-defined sacred space; a church had to be oriented more or less on an east-west axis and the celebrant and the congregation were all to face east, that is, the priest had his back to the people when at the altar, which was on the east wall. The Council, however, permitted the celebration of Mass by the priest with his face to the people but, since the altar was fixed to the reredos on the east wall, it became necessary to provide an alternative. In general a temporary altar (usually a wooden table) was placed in a prominent forward position in the sanctuary until a permanent altar could be afforded. (Altar-rails were usually retained until the practice of receiving Holy Communion standing became general.) Two other centres of attention were created: the *ambo*, or lectern, and the 'president's' chair. The *ambo* presented few problems, indeed the removal of an intimidating pulpit was often quietly welcomed, but the chair was sometimes placed, confusingly, in front of or behind the altar and remains there to this day in many churches.

These were but the preliminaries to a wide-ranging process called 're-ordering' (approval for which, it is emphasised, was always given by the diocesan authorities). For traditionalists re-ordering was a euphemism for the stripping of the sanctuaries in a process many regarded as iconoclastic as the stripping of the altars at the time of the Reformation, whereas for progressives it was the elimination of decorative or distracting clutter. Statues and pictures were discarded or removed to less prominent positions. In some churches the font was given the prominence hitherto accorded to the pulpit; in other cases the tabernacle was moved to a side-chapel; and in one or two churches the altar was removed entirely from what had been the sanctuary and placed half-way down the nave so that the congregation could surround it. Fortunately, many of these alterations could be described as 'experimental' and be reversed after a discreet, face-saving interval. Famously, the crucifix which hung over the nave of the cathedral fully visible to everyone was rehung to face south, out of view except to those leaving the sacristy. At the same time the statue of Our Lady was removed to the back of the church. Neither was restored to its original position until seventeen years had passed.

A large number of related innovations were introduced piecemeal in the years that followed: concelebrated Masses; Sunday Mass on Saturday evening; Holy Communion received under both kinds, the host being received in the hand and standing, instead of on the tongue and kneeling, and distributed by layfolk, including women (not just in church but to the housebound); female altar-servers; lay-led Communion services when priests were not available to offer Mass; face-to-face Confession and the occasional Penitential Service. At the same time, a number of old services were abruptly discontinued such as Benediction, May and October Devotions, and the public recitation of the Rosary. On the other hand, prayer groups were formed around the diocese and the revised breviary, published in English as the *Liturgy of the Hours*, was taken up by the laity although they usually recited it privately.

Mary Douglas, the well known Catholic anthropolgist and sociologist, described the liturgical innovators as 'colour-blind signalmen' for ignoring the fundamental importance of continuity in the use of symbols. In 1980 the Pope had to issue instructions reminding the clergy of the proper interpretation of the liturgical reforms introduced by the Council. In 1983 clerical unease was expressed locally that liturgical change had failed to revitalise parishes as had been promised; that temporary and inadequate liturgical arrangements had prevented the fullness of the reforms being fully appreciated; and that architects involved in the reconstruction of internal arrangements had not been given a sound liturgical brief. The eighty churches which had been re-ordered by 1983 made this clear. Though some re-orderings were welcomed, in other cases objections were voiced and well-publicised rows erupted and statutory preservation groups were able to prevent some insensitive alterations to buildings listed as having particular architectural merit. Nonetheless, by the end of the century virtually every church had been altered to a greater or lesser extent.

Readers for whom these changes have long ceased to have any novelty may be surprised that most of them were deplored by one section of a congregation for going too far and by another for not going far enough. It should be remembered, however, that at the time of the Second Vatican Council any Catholic over the age of consent had been raised during an era of an unchanging liturgy, in which the old ways were sanctioned by custom and tradition and for whom change, especially in the Mass, was unthinkable. On the other hand, progressive Catholics saw in the Council the opportunity to effect a radical overhaul of the liturgy together with, as we shall see, other practices. Controversy was bound to result.

The Second Vatican Council was perceived by many as a liberalising force corresponding with the secular liberalisation which was taking place at the same time. Some progressives thought that liturgical change implied a change in doctrine, a conflation of ideas which would be reflected in their response to papal teaching in the years which followed.

Certainly, the Council marked the end of the post-reformation period of 'closed' Catholicism and served to reduce that separateness which had been encouraged throughout the post-restoration period. This development led Mary Douglas to observe in the late sixties: 'Now the English Catholics are like everyone else'. One example was the abolition in 1966 of that quintessential Catholic practice by which the faithful abstained from eating meat on Fridays. And it did not stop there. The 1983 Code of Canon Law reduced the requirement for fasting and abstinence to Ash Wednesday and Good Friday and suggested some act of self-denial, such as almsgiving, prayer or 'abstinence from meat or some other food' on other Fridays. An accommodating process could also be discerned in the Church's external relationships. To the surprise of many outside the Church, and the regret of some in it, the general trend was to promote interdenominational cooperation wherever possible in an increasingly irreligious society. Indications of convergence included the abolition in 1969 of the promises required from non-Catholic spouses about the Catholic upbringing of their children, and the mutual recognition of the baptism of the main denominations in 1971. A sharp rise in the number of mixed marriages followed. Inter-church relations became more openly friendly and 'ecumenical' events became commonplace. The Unity Octave in January was more frequently observed, and Catholic participation in the Women's World Day of Prayer began in 1968. The presence of Pope John Paul II together with the Anglican Primate in Canterbury Cathedral during the papal visit of 1982 marked the high point of the ecumenical process; but it declined thereafter following the departure of the Anglican Church from some commonly-held practices, chiefly the ordination of women (over which, incidentally, only a dozen clergymen in the region became Catholics despite claims that the Anglican community would be split in two).

Internally, a recognition that the fully-educated new middle-class Catholics required a less patronising approach led to a softening of lay-clerical relationships. The more collegial concept of the Church as the 'People of God' was preferred to the hierarchical model, though lay participation in the national, diocesan and parochial councils of the Church spread but slowly (and never, never with decision-making powers or financial responsibility). Moreover, in the wake of the Council the validity of different components of Catholic social teaching came under scrutiny in a debate which, taken as a whole, amounted to a wide-ranging challenge to papal authority. It was argued that principles of subsidiarity and widespread property ownership were extremely difficult to implement by remotely-managed large-scale companies; multi-national corporations were, in any case, unsympathetic to the concept of a fair wage. The paternalistic tenor of the Church's teaching deprecating the employment of married women outside the home was deplored just as its teaching on artificial contraception was questioned in view of over-population. In short, the laity became more independently-minded. Perhaps the last occasion when the Catholic hierarchy was able to mobilise Catholic electors in large numbers was in the early 1950s when they lobbied for the preservation of Catholic schools. On no occasion since, not even when major issues of morality, such as the legalisation of abortion, have Catholics demonstrated *en masse* to prevent the passage of legislation inimical to Catholic teaching, and most parliamentary bills on such matters have been enacted without substantial amendment. (It is worth noting, in passing, that the English Catholics have never sought to establish a Catholic political party on the continental model, preferring to work within existing mass parties. In any event, in view of their full social integration it is doubtful whether a 'Catholic vote' can now be identified or its influence measured.)

The most important example of the decline in ecclesiastical obedience can be demonstrated by the history of Catholic education in the last quarter of the century. Throughout the post-restoration period the Church devoted a large proportion of its human and financial resources to the protection of the religious upbringing of its youth and Catholic schools had flourished despite much opposition, numerous organisational changes and a heavy financial commitment. Rising school rolls, a plentiful supply of Catholic teachers and a loyal, compliant laity ensured widespread support for the voluntary system. But, for a number of reasons, the Catholic educational system was on the point of radical change.

Firstly, there was yet another major reorganisation of the national educational system only twenty years after that of 1944. Examination at the age of eleven to qualify for a superior education at a grammar school was now deemed both socially divisive and unfair. Instead, secondary education would be given to all children aged eleven to sixteen at a school in which all subjects would be available to them, that is, selective education was to be replaced by a comprehensive system. Philosophically the diocese welcomed the change and, despite fears of another massive financial imposition so soon after the previous reorganisation, agreed to cooperate in its introduction with the LEAs (and there were nine of them to deal with in the region). Mercifully, however, in 1967 capital grants were increased to 80% and there were soon 25 diocesan comprehensive schools; the diocese would spend an average of £500,000 a year on school-building or renovation work in the quarter-century after 1970. The private sector found greatest difficulty in coming to terms with the comprehensive system and in 1973 after prolonged negotiations La Sagesse in Newcastle decided to retain its independent status outside the system. Secondly, a fall in the birth-rate became apparent from the mid-sixties and, while it is important to note that this pre-dated the promulgation of the encyclical *Humanae Vitae* (1968) which reaffirmed the Church's prohibition of artificial contraception, the Catholic birth-rate would shortly fall by almost three times the national average. A Diocesan Schools Commission was set up in 1968 to plan for the long term implications of the decline in the number of school-children. It was quickly realised that hard decisions would be required on the amalgamation or perhaps closure of existing schools and the redundancy or redeployment of teachers. These were frequent topics of discussion at the annual Diocesan Catholic Teachers Education Days held after 1973.

Other questions were raised about Catholic schools. It was increasingly held that they were less efficient in preparing children for the contemporary world, hence religious formation should be dissociated from secular education; indeed, many had come to see Catholic schools as merely state schools with statues. In view of the high rate of lapsation, criticism was also expressed about the efficiency of religious education, which was based largely on the *Catechism* introduced in 1880 and not revised until 1971. In June 1975 *Northern Cross* quoted a diocesan priest's opinion that 'some 75% of [Catholic] children leaving school eventually fall away from the faith'. When it was countered that domestic or other socio-economic conditions were the real causes of lapsation, some argued that if that was the case the Church should divert its resources from schools to housing and other environmental projects. Catholic schools were also perceived to be divisive in a pluralistic society - relics of the fortress church of the pre-ecumenical era. Moreover, the Church appeared to lack a persuasive defence of the ideals of Catholic education in a fast-changing and highly competitive world. Similarly, clerical trustees tended to be unresponsive to lay concerns: in January 1969 an attempt by a group of parents to form 'an association that would have a say in the education of their children' was opposed by the Diocesan Schools Commission and by Bishop Cunningham [*Catholic Education Today* March-April 1969, p23]. This clerical dominance of the Catholic educational system was progressively eroded, particularly during the 1980s, both by legislation and legal decisions affecting school-management and the rights of governors and parents, just as directives on admissions policy, parental choice, teacher-training and the nationalisation of the curriculum, reduced the distinction between Catholic and other schools.

While these trends were resisted by the hierarchy, Catholic parents were less certain and school-rolls began to fall. It emerged that a significant number (one national survey said almost half) of English Catholics had ceased to attach importance to separate educational provision. At any rate, so little did the schools instil a commitment to Catholic education that no more than 60% of those baptised in the diocese in the late seventies subsequently appeared at a Catholic primary school, and even when they did so, many did not go on to a Catholic secondary school; the proportion was less than 50% by the nineties by which point 10% of Catholic schools had amalgamated or closed. There was a shortage of two thousand Catholic teachers, but in 1984 St Mary's College of Education, Fenham, the only Catholic teacher-training college in the diocese was closed by the Department of Education after eighty years; in its heyday in the post-war years the number of students had peaked at 800, and in 1956 the college produced nearly 200 graduates. Thus whereas at the end of the nineteenth century Catholic schools enjoyed unquestioned support, at the end of the twentieth century commitment had so atrophied that Catholic education was in danger of extinction, for, in addition to the perennial hostility of the secular authorities, it had to contend with the indifference of those it was meant to serve. In 1990, addressing the 77th North of England Education Conference in Newcastle, Cardinal Hume reiterated the Church's holistic approach: 'Education in its broadest sense is concerned with lifelong inner growth, with the achieving of personal wholeness and integrity, with the development to the utmost of personal gifts and creativity'. Many parents, however, had succumbed to the secular cultural influences which side-lined that Catholic ethos as inappropriate to the highly competitive economic and social environment of the day. Yet an extensively researched report entitled *The Struggle for Excellence: Catholic Secondary Schools in Urban Poverty Areas* (1997) concluded that, like the Church's poor schools of 150 years earlier, Catholic schools had maintained standards against all the odds.

A fall in commitment towards various Catholic societies and organisations could also be detected. By the late 1960s membership of ACTU fell away because of apathy, but also because of an inability to moderate the extremism of some unions. The CTS had opened a second shop in the Grainger Market in 1965 and by 1967 revenue had doubled; membership increased to over 2,000 by 1969. The growth in sales was partly due to the new publications associated with the Council and its liturgical reforms but once they had worked through sales inevitably fell back. Nonetheless the Society was selling some 30,000 pamphlets annually until 1970. But the outlet in the Grainger Market was closed in 1972 and five years later its main shop moved into new, and less prominent premises in Princess Square. The Catholic Marriage Advisory Council launched talks for engaged couples in 1963 but they were not universally popular; in 1969 only 186 couples sought counselling. The Jesuits left Sunderland and in 1973 the Friends of Corby Hall was established to preserve the hall for a pastoral use while developing the surrounds as a housing estate but nothing came of the project and the whole property was sold later. The Medical Mission Sisters who had opened their novitiate in South Shields in 1952 closed it in 1968.

*

The cumulative effects of post-war social developments together with post-conciliar ecclesiastical change can be traced in each successive Quinquennial Report (*Relatio*) presented to the Holy Father during the bishop's *ad limina* visit to Rome and much of what follows is abstracted from them. Bishop Cunningham's *Relatio* of 1971 was the first to be written after the Second Vatican Council which had closed some six years before. Having previously noted the overall statistics at this date, we can turn to other matters. A Diocesan Council of Priests was established in 1967; two priests from each of the 25 deaneries met twice yearly and the bishop said it had proved to be a valuable forum for advising him as well as for effecting a spirit of cooperation throughout the diocese. At the same time, however, only about forty parishes had set up a Parish Council. The bishop remarked on the decline in religious practice among the laity: Sunday Mass attendance was 116,320 (42%). On the other hand, membership of lay confraternities totalled 7,592 and he had noted a strengthening of such groups as Family and Social Action, The Grail and Teams of Our Lady. Most groups had chaplains and they met for prayer, discussion and mutual support in their apostolate. He said there was little enthusiasm for ecumenism, although Catholics did attend formal inter-church meetings. He also said that the introduction of the vernacular liturgy had been accepted 'smoothly and with little difficulty' and that most people showed a marked preference for the English rites. The re-ordering of existing churches was proceeding slowly for financial reasons but new churches were designed to meet the new liturgical requirements.

The Diocesan Rescue Society had continued to develop its working practices in accordance with national social policy and had become an increasingly respected professional organisation. It had broken up its large institutions to comply with modern social-work practice for care to be given in small units. In 1971/2 the Society had forty children in foster homes, ten family group homes accommodating 126 children, two hostels with 24 working teenagers in Newcastle and an approved school for 125 children at Gainford. The Society received the bulk of its income in government maintenance grants but it still needed some £35,000 a year in charitable donations. The Little Sisters of the Poor maintained 264 old people in their two houses in Sunderland and Newcastle and 46 elderly ladies were looked after by the Sisters of Our Lady of Good and Perpetual Succour at Ebchester. The Brothers of St John of God cared for 110 handicapped people; some 60 mentally-retarded girls were looked after in Alnwick.

The SVP, meanwhile, maintained its position as the pre-eminent parochially-based voluntary society. In addition to its usual activity, and in conjunction with the Rescue Society and the local authority, it reinstituted the diocesan Deaf Service in Our Lady of Lourdes Club in Newcastle in 1973; the Catholic Deaf Club had 200 members. The SVP-sponsored Westoe Towers closed in 1988 but the society sponsored St Christopher's House, a hostel for the care and resettlement of offenders and Ozanam House, a hostel for homeless Catholic working teenage boys.

The latter was refurbished in 1965 to take 22 occupants and reopened in 1967. The CWL had 2,213 members in the six areas of the Hexham and Newcastle Branch in 1973 (membership had been around 3,300 in 1960), and, although its Nursing Service closed in 1966 and its house in Bentinck Rd was sold in 1976, the branch was fully engaged in running catechism camps, Our Lady's catechists and various other parochial and local charitable activities.

Bishop Cunningham resigned in ill-health in May 1974; he died on 10 July after a seventeen-year episcopate and was buried at Ushaw. He had administered the diocese during the particularly difficult period which preceded and followed the Second Vatican Council. Some fifty new churches and eighty new schools were built during his time. His successors would not have to cope with the massive social change and demographic upheaval that took place during his episcopate and, to that extent, he was the last in the line of expansionist bishops; they would be faced with different problems. In 1969 Hugh Lindsay had been consecrated Bishop of Chester-le-Street and appointed auxiliary. He was born in Jesmond, Newcastle, and was educated at St Cuthbert's Grammar School and Ushaw College. At 42 years of age he became the youngest of the English bishops. His episcopal ordination was the first to be conducted in English in the diocese and the occasion was a major civic and inter-church event; 500 sat down to lunch in the Newcastle Civic Centre. Bishop Lindsay succeeded Bishop Cunningham as diocesan and he took his chair in February 1975.

It had been thought for some time that the diocese was becoming unwieldy and a survey undertaken for the English and Welsh Bishops' Conference entitled *Groundplan* (1974) had proposed a revision of the diocesan structure in the region. It was suggested that a new diocese combining the county of Cleveland with Hartlepool and Stockton be created and the remainder of Hexham and Newcastle be divided into two: Northumberland with Tyneside, and County Durham with Wearside but the Holy See declined to create the new diocese. In July 1977 the 49-year-old Owen Swindlehurst, a canon lawyer and moral theologian, was appointed auxiliary bishop. Bishop Lindsay lived in Newcastle as diocesan and with particular care for the northern part of the diocese while Bishop Swindlehurst lived in Sunderland and looked after the southern part of the diocese. Together they would administer the diocese during the next two decades.

Public acts of faith, which had always been characteristic of the northern Church, were maintained. The diocesan pilgrimage to Lourdes which always took large numbers of the sick remained popular; in 1973 some 1,400 pilgrims filled 14 coaches and 3 aircraft. In 1971 Mass was offered in Tynemouth Priory for the first time since the Reformation. The 1300th anniversary of St Bede's birth was celebrated on 20 May 1973 at Jarrow. Some 5,000 people attended the ceremonies which were presided over by John Carmel, Cardinal Heenan. Holy Mass was also celebrated in St Paul's, Jarrow, by thirty Benedictine monks including Abbot Basil Hume and Dom Ambrose Griffiths of Ampleforth Abbey. George Basil Hume, son of Sir William Hume, a Professor of Medicine at Durham University, was born in Newcastle in 1923. He took solemn vows as a Benedictine monk in 1945 and read for a master's degree in history at Oxford and the licentiate in theology at Fribourg; he was ordained in 1950. He was elected fourth (and youngest) Abbot of Ampleforth in 1963 from which post he went as Archbishop of Westminster in March 1976 and was raised to the Sacred College two months later. The cardinal was often spoken of as *papabile* but in fact his next promotion came in 1980 when he was made a Freeman of Newcastle. In 1987 he was awarded an honorary doctorate of divinity by the University of Durham, on which occasion the cardinal's merits were declaimed by the Revd Dr Patrick FitzPatrick, the University Public Orator, who for many years lectured on philosophy in the university and was chaplain at the Little Sisters' Home in Sunderland. Cardinal Hume died in June 1999 shortly after receiving the Order of Merit from Her Majesty Queen Elizabeth II.

Bishop Hugh Lindsay; Archbishop Derek Worlock; Bishop Ambrose Griffiths, OSB; Cardinal Basil Hume OSB, OM; Bishop Owen Swindlehurst at the consecration of Bishop Griffiths on 20th March 1992 (Feast of the diocesan patron: St. Cuthbert)

In his *Relatio* of 1976 Bishop Lindsay reported that the Catholic population had risen by a little over two thousand in the previous five years and comprised about 12% of the regional population. The number of baptisms, however, had fallen: in 1967 there had been 6,834 but in 1976 there were 4,088. Only two-thirds of those baptised entered Catholic schools; Confirmation was usual at the age of nine but as the age increased so the number coming forward to be confirmed declined. Some threequarters of marriages were mixed, which was not a noticeable change but the number marrying in church had fallen. A change in the law allowing divorce after two years by mutual consent had had a devastating effect on the institution of marriage and the family. The practice of monthly confession had declined; questions arose about the Church's teaching on contraception, and admission to the sacraments of non-Catholics or divorced and remarried people without a decree of nullity. The bishop thought that the older generation missed the security of the pre-conciliar Church; many people had reservations about the style of English in the liturgy and attendance at Mass had declined. There was a small group of Lefebvrists (followers of Archbishop Marcel Lefebvre who rejected the liturgical reforms of the Council) in the diocese who gathered for Mass said 'in the former rite unlawfully by priests without faculties'; there were still around 100 Lefebvrists in the diocese in 1988. In general, however, the bishop said, the liturgical reforms had been introduced 'smoothly' but there had been a diminution in the public services of Benediction, the Rosary, October Devotions and processions. Devotion to the saints, which he said was never strong, was also declining. Although the diocesan Council of Priests met twice yearly, the tradition of parochial independence and the reluctance of the clergy to involve the laity was but slowly changing and diocesan lay structures were in their infancy; only about half of parishes had a parish council. The lay apostolate was generally based on associations such as the SVP or the CWL but they were beginning to find difficulty recruiting new members. The revival of the hospice movement from about 1980 attracted considerable interest among Catholics. The Society for the Protection of the Unborn Child was another socio-religious organisation to emerge at this time.

There was one priest to 837 people (there had been 1 to 1,000 a century earlier), which compared unfavourably with the neighbouring dioceses of Lancaster and Middlesbrough which had one priest for 600 people. 35 priests had died and of the 31 who had left the priesthood since the Council, some had sought independence, others had become dissatisfied with pastoral work, but about half had found difficulty with celibacy. Most had left the diocese and were settled in marriage and secular work. There were no permanent deacons in the diocese. There were unmistakable signs of the growing shortage of priests and a grouping or merging of parishes would shortly become necessary. Other steps were being taken to cope with the shortage; Saturday evening Mass was available in some places but it was 'used very discreetly' and preparations to introduce Extraordinary Ministers of the Eucharist were in hand. Mass was occasionally broadcast on the radio or television. The frequency of concelebrated Masses had increased. There had been a slow movement towards the re-modelling of sanctuaries and the introduction of face-to-face confessionals.

The finances of the diocese were most satisfactory ('planned giving' had spread from 1967); and were managed by a Diocesan Trust of six trustees. The only major debt outstanding was £340,000 borrowed from the government for educational purposes. In the five years up to 1976 the diocese had undertaken major works with a value of £2.023 million which included new churches and presbyteries, parochial social facilities, a number of schools and the chaplaincy at Newcastle University. A diocesan Small Parishes Fund account was created so that those parishes which needed loans could have them at low interest. The clergy had their board and lodging paid by the parish and they retained Mass stipends and stole fees; in 1971 a parish priest's annual salary was £310 and an assistant priest got £260. In 1975 retired priests had £780 a year from the diocese in addition to their national insurance pensions but they had to find their own accommodation.

A National Pastoral Congress held in Liverpool in 1980 was preceded by two years preparation. The congress was intended to 'renew the English Church' and each diocese prepared a discussion document on key contemporary problems, and the submissions give a useful insight into opinion within the Church at that time. Hexham and Newcastle noted firstly that in the prevailing circumstances it was usual to attach more importance to science than to religious belief and that Catholics did not witness to their faith. The Church ought to be more outspoken on social issues and give support to ethical investment plans, CAFOD and Justice and Peace groups. Although there was no undue economic hardship among Catholics, other problems had arisen. Due to the dispersal of the extended family there had been a decline in mutual support and that modern marriages seemed prone to earlier breakdown because individuals were unable to appreciate that relationships were not ready-formed but had to be given an opportunity to develop and mature. The Catholic birth-rate had fallen to the point that it was no different to that of any other group and showed that Church teaching was not being followed or, perhaps, not understood. It was concluded that education on family life be included in school syllabi; that the Church should relax its approach to mixed marriages; that there should be a longer preparation for marriage; and that there ought to be a major review of the theology of marriage. There was general support for Catholic schools and a desire for more parental involvement in them, though a more rigorous approach to religious education was recommended. It was observed that although the new liturgical practices were generally welcome, the peremptory abolition of the old rite was deplorable and it was recommended that 'the riches of the Tridentine-inspired [musical] compositions be reintroduced'. There was also a need for educational programmes to develop individual prayer-lives. No solution to the crisis of priestly vocations was offered, but there was some support for a married priesthood; doubts were expressed about the introduction of permanent deacons and extraordinary ministers of the Eucharist. Although the place of women in the Church should be reconsidered, it was unclear in which new capacity they could act given that they already played an invaluable part in the Church's life. Properly constituted, responsible and accountable parish councils were required to free the clergy for their missionary vocation. Little enthusiasm for ecumenical progress was felt, although much common ground was acknowledged.

The 2,000 delegates to the National Pastoral Congress were largely from the 'new' Catholic middle-class: articulate, non-deferential and well-educated. After wide-ranging and open discussion they recommended that consideration be given to inter-communion with non-Catholics, the ordination of women, and a review of the Church's teaching on sexuality. They also urged that the Church become more socially-concerned and they asked for a recognition of the laity's capacity to carry out a more participant role in the Church. Importantly, voting in the Congress generally went on progressive versus traditionalist lines, showing that there was no deep-seated antagonism between the laity and the clergy (the delegates included some 400 priests and religious). The bishops replied to the Congress report in 1981 with the paper *The Easter People* in which they sought to take into account the progressive conclusions of the congress while bearing in mind the traditional outlook of the ordinary Catholic and at the same time being aware of the likely reaction of the Holy See (the paper was to be sent to Rome with an invitation to the Pope to visit Britain). Not surprisingly, then, the paper was widely seen as defensive and timid and written so as not to prejudice a papal visit. Pope John Paul II came in May 1982. He offered Mass on the Knavesmire in York where some 210,000 people from the northern dioceses had gathered, and his address referred to Cuthbert, Aidan, Bede, Margaret Clitheroe and Nicholas Postgate. The Holy Father's charismatic presence was highly impressive and the visit was a public-relations triumph, especially for Anglican-Catholic relations, but the Catholic laity were not given an opportunity to present their concerns to him and they remained unpersuaded that they were being considered. Little of substance resulted from either the Congress or the visit.

The modest rise in the Catholic population Bishop Lindsay had reported in 1976 turned into a loss of 12,469 by the date of his next *Relatio* in 1981. Baptisms had, however, increased by around four hundred, although attendance at Confession and at Mass continued to decline and was then around 38%. Extraordinary Ministers of the Eucharist had been introduced but not the permanent diaconate. The post-conciliar re-ordering of churches was still in progress. Lay participation in parochial affairs was by no means universally accepted: no more than half of parishes had a parish council. The accounts, which had been published and widely circulated since 1977, showed that the financial condition of the diocese was still in a healthy condition. Parochial collections amounted to £2.55 million and there were no major debts. Some £2 million had been spent on school-building work but church-building virtually ceased in 1980. There were, however, some innovative developments such as the agreement reached between the Catholic and the United Reform Church in Haltwhistle for the joint ownership of the church building. Another was the decision of the Catholics of Alnwick to take over a redundant Anglican church rather than build an expensive new church. An earlier transfer of this kind took place in 1912 when Bishop Collins took over an Anglican church in North Gosforth to become the church of The Sacred Heart.

Bishop Lindsay compiled a *Relatio* for the *ad limina* visit to Rome he made with Bishop Swindlehurst in 1987, the 1,300th anniversary of St Cuthbert's death. On this occasion he reported a further drop of 11,646 in the Catholic population. Collections amounted to £2.8 million, the diocese had investments of £2.5 million, and £1.9 million had been spent on school-building work since the last report. He had sanctioned expenditure £870,000 for new work on schools which was much less than in recent years and reflected the fall in the birth-rate. A simplification of tax law in 1973 permitted the Church to recover income tax on covenanted donations and in ten years some £2.5 million had been recovered, but in 1988 it was estimated that a levy of £6.50 for every Catholic in the diocese was necessary to cover a shortfall of income over expenditure.

A great deal of anxiety had been apparent in clerical circles for some time about the significant downturn in most ecclesiastical statistics. In 1985, twenty years after the Council, and after widespread consultation on a set of questions posed by the Holy See on opinion in the diocese, the bishop compiled a report in which it is difficult to discern any consistent conclusions. While there had been a decrease in vocations and the size of congregations, at the same time increased liturgical, spiritual and catechetical renewal was reported among those who remained, but a need for more adult education and youth programmes was expressed. Some priests had blocked the introduction of Extraordinary Ministers of the Eucharist; nonetheless 1,327 had been commissioned (and at an average of seven to a parish they were surely no longer *Extraordinary* Ministers). Tensions persisted arising from different interpretations of the Church as a community or as a hierarchy; consultation was taking a long time to become established despite improved communications within the diocese. The only unambiguous conclusions were that there had been a decline in reverence, that there was a diminishing respect for the Church's teaching authority, and that morality was increasingly subjective in a powerfully secularist and materialist world.

Diocesan structures had been developing around this time. A Youth Officer was appointed in 1981 and a Diocesan Youth Service was created two years later; retreats for young people soon began at a centre in Seaham Harbour and the service grew rapidly. In December 1984 the bishop instituted a Diocesan Pastoral Council, comprising two representatives from each deanery. RCIA was launched in the diocese in 1985 at the Diocesan Religious Education Centre. In May 1987, a major conference entitled *Pilgrim Church North-East* was held at Ushaw College to examine the place of the Church in the region as well as evangelism and ecumenism; no concrete proposals appear to have resulted. The numerical decline showed no signs of improvement: the annual average of marriages was 1,715, baptisms 4,280 and confirmations 2,613; Mass attendance was 34% in 1985. Of the 303 priests working in 190 parishes in 1983, 172 were over sixty years of age; in 1990 there were 223 active priests in the diocese and 23 church-students. Bishop Lindsay noted in 1991 that there were 94 active priests and 20 seminarians fewer than there had been when he took office. The cost of supporting sick and retired priests fell largely on the diocese though contributions to their support were also available from the Northern Brethren's Fund, a charitable society which traces its origins to the seventeenth century to which the laity were the principal donors.

Changing secular conditions in their traditional areas of activity (especially teaching and nursing) and the results of the renewal, or back-to-basics, process required by the Vatican Council brought about alterations in the lives of the religious orders. In 1965 the Society of the Sacred Heart decided it should no longer be an enclosed order. Religious habits were up-dated; the traditional dress of a Breton widow worn by the Little Sisters, for example, was adapted to be more practical; and the highly distinctive head-dress worn by the Sisters of Charity was abandoned (early in the century the Chief Constable had complained to the parish priest of Darlington that it frightened the horses). Many institutions closed and communities, now much reduced in numbers and ageing, moved into smaller houses and undertook care-work or parochial work. The convent of Marie Reparatrice closed in 1982 and the building was sold; the Christian Brothers left St Bede's, Stockton, in 1967; the Dominican sisters left Newcastle; the Ursulines left Berwick in 1983; St Cuthbert's hospital at Hurworth closed in 1991 as did St Camillus' hospital in 1989; the Camillans sold their property and left the diocese in 1999. The seminary of the Mill Fathers at Burn Hall closed in 1971 and the House of Prayer which opened at Burn Hall in 1983 with a poustinia for 24-hour personal vigils closed in 1992; in 1996 the community moved into a house in Durham. The number of Benedictine parishes gradually fell so that in the 1990s the order was represented in the diocese only by the bishop. The Sisters of Charity in Darlington moved into smaller premises alongside the Poor Clares.

On the other hand, small groups from other orders came into the diocese to do both parochial and specialised work with the socially marginalised: an Emmaus Community was formed by two Jesuits, a Sister of St Joseph of Peace and a Daughter of Charity for 'non-church-based social ministries' in the otherwise 'unchurched' east end of Sunderland; the Claretians went to Esh Laude; the Salesians to Durham and Stockton; the Rosminians to Durham; the Franciscans and the Blessed Sacrament Fathers to Newcastle; and at the end of the century attempts were being made to establish an Albertine eremitical monastery in Northumberland. Nonetheless, in 1997/8 there were only 48 regular clergy and religious men in thirteen houses and around 230 women religious in 44 communities, only five of which had more than ten professed nuns. In earlier days the professed nuns in the Mercy convent in Sunderland had numbered 117 and in the 1950s a noviciate of twenty was common, but by the 1990s the total community was 56.

Whereas weekly church attendance was falling, diocesan events remained popular (although, following a rally at Ushaw at Whitsuntide in 1979, the *Northern Catholic Calendar* [1980, p 133] wondered if such events were still relevant). Vespers in Latin were sung by the monks of Ampleforth in Durham Cathedral on the 15th centenary of St Benedict in April 1980. The tenth walk in honour of Bl. John Ingram took place in 1982; A Holy Year was celebrated with the customary devotions and pilgrimages in 1983, and in 1984 2,000 people made an ecumencial pilgrimage to Alnmouth to mark 1,300th anniversary of St Cuthbert's election as a bishop. In 1985 an annual procession through the town in honour of Our Lady of Walsingham was instituted in Newton Aycliffe. The diocesan pilgrimage to Lourdes that year was undertaken by both bishops, 25 priests and 1,100 lay people. Of the remaining Venerable martyrs, 85 were beatified in 1987 including a dozen who were particularly associated with the north-east. In all, Hexham and Newcastle claims 29 of the canonised and beatified English martyrs, chief among them Sts. John Boste and Henry Morse. In the summer of 1987 a Rosary Rally was held on Newcastle Racecourse and pilgrimage to Jesmond was again revived in 1991. In 1982 the Catholic Teachers Federation celebrated its 75th anniversary; north-east members had provided five national Presidents and two National Treasurers in its history. The Silver Jubilee of the Junior Legion of Mary in the diocese was celebrated in 1985. In 1987 400 pilgrims attended Mass in the ruins of Holy Island priory to celebrate the 1300th anniversary of the death of St Cuthbert. These activities, however, were all undertaken by committed Catholics and it is salutary to compare the numbers in attendance with those at similar events earlier in the century; two-thirds of nominal Catholics were almost wholly inactive in the Church.

In 1986, forty years after its creation, the Diocesan Rescue Society was re-named *Catholic Care - North East* [CC-NE] to reflect contemporary thought that the concept of *rescuing* children was outmoded in a fully democratic and welfare-oriented social environment. There would always be a residual need for long-term residential homes for the most difficult cases (and the diocese had seven Family Group Homes with nine youngsters in each), but in general the emphasis was to be placed on helping families to cope with problems in their own situations thus preserving family units instead of breaking them up. Acting on referrals from the parochial clergy, charities, schools and social-work agencies, and in conjunction with eight local government social services departments, then, the diocese provided a counselling service for people in difficulty from its offices in Newcastle, Sunderland and Darlington, and accommodation for those in need of short-term care: homeless mothers and babies, pregnant young girls expelled from their own homes, students, people needing respite breaks. Reporting the 1985/6 accounts, Fr Dennis Tindall, the Administrator, said that the agency had a staff of ninety (both professional and part-time) who managed seventeen establishments of various kinds, and twenty vehicles. Turnover was £794,000, and about half of its expenditure went towards maintaining the group homes, and another quarter on its social work; there was, however, an accumulated deficit of £131,000. The vastly increased scale of its operations since the war can be judged by comparing, at mid-1980s values, the equivalent weekly cost of maintaining a child: around 1946 it was about £14, by 1966 it had risen to £42 and in 1986 it amounted to £174. Under ten percent of income came from grants but twice that was received in voluntary donations, partly from the Annual Charity Ball, which had been held for 35 years, the Good Shepherd Collection in schools, and almsgiving in parishes. Additionally, in 1989 CC-NE took over the home for mentally-handicapped in Lemmington Hall, Alnwick, from the Sacred Heart Sisters who were suffering a fall in the number of their vocations.

Normally, Bishop Lindsay would have made another *ad limina* visit to Rome but he retired because of ill-health, aged 65, in January 1992. On St Cuthbert's feast-day the 64-year-old Dom Ambrose Griffiths, OSB, was consecrated Bishop of Hexham and Newcastle by Archbishop Derek Worlock. He had gained a first-class degree in natural sciences at Oxford and proceeded to M.A. He was titular Abbot of Westminster until his episcopal consecration and was the first regular to be appointed to the see since the early 18th century (Bishop O'Callaghan, an Oblate of St Charles, was a secular priest who lived in community). Bishop Griffiths' *Relatio* covering the period 1992-6, the last to be considered here, contained some startling facts. In 1996 the Catholic population of the diocese was 235,000 (10%). The numbers of baptisms and funerals were about equal. But the greatest problem was the religious apathy and indifference of those who had been baptised and had attended a Catholic school: threequarters of Catholics did not attend Mass and young people were largely absent. The Council decrees had been well-accepted though they had yet to be fully implemented, except that virtually all churches had been re-ordered. Confessions were much less frequently made. He permitted the celebration of Mass in Latin in accordance with the rite of 1962 in one church and occasionally at other times. Confirmation was usually administered by one of the vicars general in a three-yearly cycle and given to those aged twelve to fourteen; in 1996 1,596 individuals had been confirmed. The number of marriages (827) had fallen by over a third in five years and threequarters (606) of those solemnised by the Church were mixed; more than one in three ended in divorce, and one in four children were born to single parents.

There were 227 priests working in the diocese (and paid £160 a month); the incumbents of five of the 180 parishes were regulars. Over the period 41 priests had died, twenty had retired and seven had been laicised, and since there had been only eighteen ordinations, there had been a net loss of fifty working priests since 1987. The bishop had therefore been obliged to revise parochial management. In twenty cases one priest was responsible for two parishes and there had been an increase in the number of lay-led Eucharistic Services. The Diocesan Religious Education Centre had provided courses in lay ministry from 1987 and they were helping to extend the practice of joint or collaborative ministry between priests and layfolk (but only where the clergy were amenable to the episcopal will in the matter). In 1999 eighteen laypeople received degrees or diplomas in church ministry validated by Loyola University, New Orleans. The finances of the diocese, managed by a Diocesan Trust with charitable status, continued to be healthy; no major loan was outstanding and there were about £4.4 million in investments, though expenditure of £5.2 million had been authorised. Collections in the churches had been £3.6 million in 1990 and £4.4 million in 1995. The Diocesan Youth Service was reorganised in 1994 as the Diocesan Youth Mission Team to work in both schools and parishes. Its first group of young volunteers was formed at Heddon House in September 1995. A second base was established in 1997 in St Mary's presbytery, Stockton, and the old convent of the Sacred Heart in Blyth was taken over as a third in 1998.

In 1996 Bishop Griffiths said that the Liturgy of the Hours was not popular and that the introduction of evening Mass had seen a corresponding decline of eucharistic exposition. The level of devotional practice in the diocese toward the end of the century can be assessed by reference to the *Northern Catholic Calendar* for 1999. Many services, however, are listed as 'as announced' and so their regularity or frequency cannot be given accurately; others, such as lenten devotions, are not listed at all, yet anecdotal evidence suggests that they were widely available. At any rate, only 13 parishes were stated as publicly celebrating Morning or Evening Prayer of the Church; ten parishes advertised 'Devotions' on a weekday evening, twenty others specified these as the Rosary, or a Novena. Only one parish offered *Bona Mors*. More impressively, a weekly eucharistic devotion, either Exposition or Benediction of the Blessed Sacrament, was available in 100 parishes. The creation in 1998 of a chapel in the Metro-Centre, the largest shopping complex of the region, in which Mass was offered on most weekdays was an unusual development.

The bishop revised parts of the diocesan administration. Auxiliary Bishop Swindlehurst died in August 1995, aged 67, and was buried in Washington. It soon became known that the Holy See would not appoint another auxiliary and so, in January 1996, the bishop appointed four vicars general (the Rev. A. Barrass, J. Coyle, W. O'Gorman and R. Spence) to share some of his episcopal duties. The bishop also sub-divided the 21 rural deaneries into 41 pastoral areas so as to facilitate a sharing between contiguous parishes of those facilities and services which would be increasingly difficult to provide on a parochial basis. He also reconstituted the diocesan consultative bodies. A new Council of the Laity of 55 members, comprising a representative from each pastoral area, six religious and eight youth representatives, convened in February 1995. The large and unwieldy Diocesan Pastoral Council was reduced to six laypeople, four priests and two religious, all elected from the Council of Priests and the Council of the Laity. In 1999 the smaller Council, then chaired by a layman, instituted the widest possible consultation in the diocese on a document issued by the bishop entitled *A Diocesan Vision - Our Future Together*, to secure general agreement on the principles which should inform a projected Diocesan Pastoral Plan.

In October 1998 a survey was undertaken of the Laity Council's composition and opinions. Two-thirds of members responded, and the replies to a number of questions on topics which had been addressed at the National Pastoral Congress in 1980 gave some idea of developments in lay opinion. Women outnumbered men on the Council by two to one; most members were of working-age, one third were aged sixty or more, but only two members were under thirty. Only three members of the Council held public office. Surprisingly only 40% of the Council belonged to a Catholic voluntary organisation, though all of those who did so held office; only five members did not take a Catholic periodical. All but five members performed some function in their parish churches. About half of members thought that their own parish councils and the diocesan council were generally effective but that their pastoral area councils were ineffective. The opinion of the Laity Council on the clergy was favourable; priests were thought to have more to contribute to society than, say, scientists, and they ought not have to retire automatically. Almost everyone thought that Church leaders were entitled to and should speak out on social and political issues, but that they were insufficiently vigorous in combatting racism. About threequarters of members were dissatisfied with press-reports of Church affairs. On ordination to the priesthood, opinion was evenly divided about maintaining the present practice. Of the alternatives to the ordination only of single men, most would accept married men, some fewer would favour single women but by substantial majorities the ordination of nuns or married women was least popular. The Council was a highly ecumenical body; well over threequarters attended inter-church events and thought that Christian unity could be achieved within the next century; a third thought unity was realisable within fifty years. Most of the Council was satisfied with contemporary liturgical practice and standards. Half the Council thought that the Sunday Mass obligation should begin at noon on Saturday. The Council was evenly divided about allowing the annulment of a marriage when both partners agreed that it had broken down irretrievably. Most members of the Council thought Catholics were no different to anyone else socially, though half thought they were in general less well-off. The Council divided evenly on whether Catholics were more left-wing than other people. Most members thought that Catholics were community-minded and generous to charitable causes. On one other potentially contentious matter (especially in view of trends described earlier) almost the whole Council wanted to preserve Catholic schools.

A comparison between the opinions of the diocesan delegates to the National Pastoral Congress in 1980 and the Council of Laity in 1998 is instructive although it must be borne in mind that threequarters of Council members were nominated (by the clergy), not elected, whereas in 1980 opinion was widely canvassed in the diocese, ostensibly at least. The same analysis of social ills was made on both occasions and there was similar support for the clergy, for Catholic schools, for international aid organisations; it was also felt that Church was too reticent in public affairs. On the earlier occasion, however, ecumenism was lukewarm whereas in 1998 it was hotly supported. In 1980 the ordination of women was only hinted at and the permanent diaconate was disliked; there were misgivings about the loss of the old liturgy and about the possibility of extraordinary ministers. In 1998 the ordination of women was still supported by a small minority and a proposal to introduce the permanent diaconate was voted down, but neither the liturgical changes or the creation of extraordinary ministers was controversial. The laity was broadly satisfied with things as they were in 1998 - there were no large majorities for substantial change in the way the Church in the diocese operated. That was probably because insofar as those matters which lay within the bishop's competence were concerned, the laity had a much greater practical and consultative role in the diocese than it had in 1980. In particular, given that the Council was the principal consultative lay body in the diocese and threequarters of its members were women, they could no longer claim that their voice went unheard.

The 1999 *Northern Catholic Calendar* listed fifty voluntary associations with an address in the diocese. Two-thirds of them were clearly identifiable as Catholic societies with traditional social, charitable, occupational, devotional or educational functions. Significantly, however, whereas in earlier days such bodies had branches in a large number of parishes, there were now one or perhaps a handful of branches in the diocese and membership was small. The Catholic Evidence Guild which had been revived in the post-war period steadily declined: the Sunderland Guild closed in the 1980s and the Newcastle Guild was gone by the early 1990s. The Tyneside Branch of the Catholic Social Guild had been the largest in the country in 1960 no longer existed. The priests' housekeepers guild was wound up after only twelve years. In 1969 the Catholic Writers' Guild convened a meeting of some twenty societies to find ways of improving communications but thirty years later the bishop noted that recruitment was still difficult, partly because existing members could be inflexible and resistant to new ideas. Indeed, the old societies were sidelined by younger Catholics who preferred new single-interest groups which supported people in a variety of social or medical conditions regardless of ecclesiastical affiliation. These groups flourished because they were open, non-denominational in title, progressive in outlook and highly imaginative in their fund-raising and other activities.

Paradoxically, in view of the growth in the nation's wealth, the diocesan agencies caring for deprived and vulnerable people, continued to grow, but there was a major change in their outlook, typified by a project set up in the deprived west end of Newcastle by the Good Shepherd Sisters in January 1985. Their aim was to provide a welcoming and confidential crisis intervention facility, with advice and information on benefits and other practical matters, as well as the provision of material help including food, clothing and furniture. Unlike previous Catholic ventures, however, this project supported families and individuals without regard to age, gender, religion or ethnicity. Some six laypersons were trained for the work in premises rented from the local authority and the project was funded initially by the government. When public funds ran out the project became dependent on a number of charitable trusts and individual donations, but it was still working at the end of the century. In 1997 Catholic Care - North East also reviewed its priorities. The name was changed to *St Cuthberts Care* [*sic*] and it adopted a 'mission to work with and for people with special needs regardless of race or religion'. The agency maintained three small children's homes, recruited foster-parents and provided accommodation for young single parents and the elderly with mental problems, but it would now develop services for people of all ages with learning disabilities who were excluded from an increasingly complex and diverse social environment and required considerable practical help to expand their employment opportunities so as to live fuller and more socially-integrated lives. Means to achieve these aims included the provision for sixty adults of residential accommodation in six group homes, and two support schemes for independent living; day resource-centres in Ashington, Gateshead and Sunderland; drop-in facilities and coffee rooms; respite services and charity shops. Seven school-based social workers were appointed and a Community Development Team project was formed to provide support and advice on the creation of various projects around the diocese such as rent guarantee schemes, classes on parenting skills, credit unions (in 1988 a union was established in Newton Aycliffe parish to provide cheap loans and to fund local community projects), and so on. In 1995 it took over the work of the Sisters of Nazareth who withdrew from Newcastle when the community fell to five members. In 1998/9 St Cuthberts Care had a turnover of £4.3 million and employed some 250 people in 24 different locations in the diocese, and was clearly a vitally important social welfare agency, not just for the Catholic community, and obtained funding for its work from several other charitable trusts and from statutory authorities. This scale of operations could not have been envisaged by its predecessor, but St Cuthberts Care shared an important characteristic with the old Diocesan Rescue Society - an openness to change and a readiness to develop new strategies for contemporary social needs.

The voluntary charitable society which was working at the beginning of the period was still going strong at the end. In the late 1990s the SVP had around one thousand members (about a third of whom were women) in 163 adult and 12 youth conferences. Some 130,000 visits a year were being made to the old, lonely and deprived people in their homes, in residential care or in hospital. Members were engaged in probation work, prison visiting and dealing with those recovering from alcohol and drug abuse; they were running holiday camps for children as well as providing holidays and pilgrimages for elderly and sick poor people; and they were providing services for the deaf; in 1990 the Summerhill Grove Deaf Centre was refurbished. The Vincentian Care Services had several establishments: Ozanam House, St Christopher's House, Blackfriars' Care Centre, Leo Edgar Group Homes and Matt Talbot House in Newcastle; Rosalie House in Sunderland; and St Anthony Claret House in South Shields. The Society was twinned with SVP conferences in India, exemplifying the support increasingly given after the 1960s by the Church in the 'first world' to the people of the developing countries of the 'third world'. The Catholic Fund for Overseas Development (CAFOD), founded by the post-Council justice and peace movement, had become the principal means by which foreign-aid from the Church was distributed. A diocesan Justice and Peace Committee was created in 1983; it later became the Diocesan Justice and Peace Co-ordinating Council, and a full-time diocesan Justice and Peace Field Worker was appointed in 1998 to promote and develop its work. Some thirty Justice and Peace groups were operating in the diocese in 1999. A Diocesan Ecumenical Officer was also appointed in 1998 to follow up existing contacts and to develop new local ecumenical partnerships such as sharing buildings, and establishing joint chaplaincies or social-work projects.

*

In January 1998 Bishop Griffiths was quoted by the *Universe* as saying: 'In our diocese Church attendance has been going down on a straight-line graph for the last 25 years ... extrapolating from that line, the Catholic Church in Hexham and Newcastle will cease to exist in the year 2028' and his startling analysis was certainly borne out by the statistical trends. But figures given in the *Northern Catholic Calendar* at the end of the century suggested that the decline might perhaps have been arrested. The diocesan Catholic population stood at 238,755 (10.3%) which was about 85% both absolutely and proportionately of what it had been at the time of the Vatican Council some 35 years earlier. Mass attendance had levelled out at around 60,000 (25%) and the number of baptisms, confirmations and convert-receptions was maintained. There were 191 diocesan secular priests and 31 regular priests living in the diocese and although the ratio of priests to *nominal* Catholics had widened from 1 to 850 to 1 to 1,000 over the preceding twenty years, there were still 177 priests working in the parishes of the diocese, which worked out at 1 to 340 *practising* Catholics. Nonetheless, a diocesan study was published in 1999 showing that if current trends continued only 50 active priests could be left in the diocese by 2030. In October 1998 speaking to the *Newcastle Journal* after it had been announced that for the first time in the history of the diocese no new student had entered Ushaw College at the start of the academic year as a candidate for the priesthood, Bishop Griffiths said that fresh initiatives would be required to increase vocations: there were only nine diocesan candidates for the priesthood in 1999. He also said that if the Church did not have enough priests under the present system then it would have to ordain married men; although Rome was reluctant to consider the matter, discussions *were* taking place and the recent intake of married Anglican clergymen had opened minds to the possibility. The first married Anglican convert-clergyman was ordained for the diocese in July 1996.

Meanwhile, the necessity for parishes to share priests which had begun in the early 1990s was increasing. Some 70 parishes were already doing so but that number would increase to such an extent that it would become exceptional for a priest to be in charge of a single parish - within ten years only 25 parishes would be standing alone. In the long term it might be that most priests would be serving three parishes rather than two. Thus, three of the parishes of Durham would be grouped together as would all those in Bishop Auckland; the 11 parishes in Sunderland could reduce to 3 independents and 3 groups; the 11 parishes in north-west Durham might become 4 groups. Ultimately the 19 Newcastle parishes could reduce to 5 independents and 9 groups. The bishop said, however, that parishes 'will not be closed unless, after wide consultation, they are agreed to be unviable'. In 1999, in a related development to widen the scope of the lay apostolate as well as cater for the reduction in the number of priests, it was decided to introduce the permanent diaconate into the diocese; deacons would do full-time pastoral and community work in such specialised roles as prison, school or hospital chaplains and undertake limited parochial functions. The diaconate was, of course, reserved by Canon Law to men, but the bishop pointed out that in several cases women were already doing equivalent work: Youth Mission Team Leader, Adult Education Officer, Diocesan Ecumenical Officer and school chaplains.

The Church was obviously right to be concerned that the number of practising Catholics had fallen not risen over the last quarter of the century, especially as the renewal process which began in the 1960s was intended to revivify the faithful. But leakage has always been a problem and, though the causes differ, throughout the ages many Catholics have called on the Church only for the rites of passage. Even in its Victorian heyday the Church did not attract all its members to Sunday Mass when the obligation to attend was heavily stressed: only 31.1% of Catholics in Newcastle made their Easter Communion in 1882. Religious practice was put under strain during the latter part of the twentieth century partly by an easing of ecclesiastical discipline and partly by changing social conditions. The obligation to attend Mass or to make one's Easter duty was never mentioned and a priest in the diocese remarked on 'the clergy's singular failure to evangelize' at this time [Archer, p.160]. The corollary of the high level of social assimilation was that losses were higher in mixed marriages when the duty to raise children in the faith was regarded as divisive. And then, legal reforms, by directly contradicting the traditional religious teaching on which civil law was based, effectively secularised social life, and many Catholics adopted the new norms. There was also a privatisation of cultural habits. People stopped going to church for much the same reason that they no longer joined political parties, trade unions or societies, that is, they chose to lead more individualistic than communal lives. Losses were fewer among the working-class, the women and the old than among the bourgeoisie, the men and the young. Women were slower to disaffiliate from the Church only because they hardly ever joined parties or unions; indeed the general decline in church-attendance would have been much greater if they had, because it was the women who sustained religious practice in their families. The fragmentation of family life inevitably reduced the influence of women, and hence, among many other things, the practice of churchgoing. Moreover, sociological studies of the English Catholics at the end of the century concluded that the fall in Sunday Mass attendance and other indicators of practice did not necessarily prove that the Church was in decline only that there had been a major transformation in the style of 'belonging'. Thus 'evident signs of new life and vitality in some parts of contemporary Catholicism' seemed to show that there had been a shift from the traditional, compulsory and communal norms to modern, voluntary and individual activities, such as prayer-groups, support for charities, social work, and so on; the parish had become not so much a community as a catchment area. [Hornsby-Smith 1991; Ryan 1996]

The first age of the English post-reformation Catholic Church is represented by the three centuries of recusancy which culminated in emancipation in 1829 and the restoration of the hierarchy in 1850. Its second, expansionist and triumphalist age, lasted until the Second Vatican Council of 1962-5. The momentous changes which came about at that time opened its third age, one of retrenchment and reticence. It may well prove, however, that after only 35 years we have not had sufficient time to gain a reliable perspective of the post-conciliar Church, hence over-optimism about a revival or excessive pessimism at the prospect of continued decline would be misplaced. It has to be left to the writers of the diocesan history on the bicentenary of the restoration of the hierarchy, or at the start of the next Christian Millennium, or, perhaps, on the occasion of the Third Vatican Council, to evaluate the historical character of the northern Catholics of the late twentieth century.

*

INDEX TO PART 1

A Diocesan Vision - Our Future Together	54
Abortion	35, 44
Abstinence pledge	15
Aidan, St	39, 50
Albertine eremitical monastery	52
Alcuin Society	31
All-Night Vigil movement	39
Alnmouth	52
Ampleforth Abbey	48, 52
Angels we have heard on high	27
Angelus	14
Anglican convert-clergyman	57
Anglican Primate	44
Anti-Catholicism, no-popery	9, 10, 22
Apostolate of the Laity	31
Approved or industrial school	18, 36
Association for the Defence of Civil and Parental Rights	25
Association of Catholic Trade Unionists (ACTU)	38, 46
Association of Public Representatives	35
Association of the Sacred Heart of Mary	15
Assumption Sisters, Richmond	26
Bar Convent, York	26
Barnard Castle	16
Barras, A. Rev	54
Bartley, Pat	32
Bede, St.	21, 32/3, 48, 50
Belaney, Robert	13
Belgians, King of	30
Belloc, H.	31, 35
Benedict, St., Benedictine(s)	11, 48, 52
Benediction	13-5, 43, 49, 54
Berwick: Ursuline Convent, Longridge Towers	26, 39, 52
Betham, Fr.	10
Bewick, Bishop John William	14, 22, 27
Bishop Auckland	17, 42
Bishop's House, Tynemouth, Newcastle	27, 34
Blackfriars' Care Centre	56
Blackhill	17, 20
Blyth	54
Bona Mors	15, 54
Boste, John, St.	52
Bourne, Cardinal Francis	29, 32
Briggs, Bishop John,	10
Bulmer, Mr.	17
Burn Hall, Durham	31, 52
Butler, Alban	14
Canterbury, cathedral	44
Carlisle	33
Carmelites	19
Catechism, catechist camp	24, 39, 45
Catenian Association	22
Catholic Action	31
Catholic Benefit Society	15
Catholic Burial Clubs	17
Catholic Care - North East (St. Cuthbert's Care)	53, 56
Catholic chaplains: prison, armed forces	22
Catholic Charity Ball, Grand Ball	21, 53
Catholic Deaf Club; service	32, 47
Catholic Defence Association	10, 11
Catholic Directory (1850)	26
Catholic education	17, 23-6, 36-8, 40, 44/5, 55
Catholic Emancipation	9, 31, 33
Catholic Evidence Guild (CEG)	31, 38, 55
Catholic Federation of Teachers	33, 52
Catholic Fund for Overseas Development (CAFOD)	50, 56
Catholic Housing Aid Society	38
Catholic Lending Library	31
Catholic Manager's Association	25
Catholic Marriage Advisory Council	46
Catholic Medical Club, Newcastle	15
Catholic Nurses Guild	31
Catholic Pharmaceutical Guild	38
Catholic Press Exhibition	31
Catholic Relief Acts	9, 13, 23
Catholic Schools Defence League	25
Catholic Social Guild (CSG)	32, 38, 55
Catholic Teachers' Association	25, 45
Catholic Total Abstinence Society, Darlington	17
Catholic Truth Society (CTS)	31, 33, 38, 46
Catholic Writers' Guild	38, 55
Catholic Young Men's Society (CYMS)	16, 32, 33, 38
Census (1851)	11, 12
Chadwick, Bishop James	18, 21, 26, 27
Challoner, Bishop Richard	14
Charlton, Mrs. Barbara	15
Cheeseburn Grange	33
Chesterton, G.K.	31, 35
Children's Care/Homes Committee	35
Cholera epidemic	14
Christian Brothers	37, 52
Cleator Moor	20
Cleveland	47
Clitheroe, Margaret	50
Cockermouth	33
Code of Canon Law	44, 57
Colgan, Edward	32
Collins, Bishop Richard	29, 30, 33, 51
Community Development Team	56
Confession	43
Confraternities, guilds, sodalities	15
Constitution on the Sacred Liturgy	40
Contraception	35, 49
Consett	17
Corby Hall, Sunderland	32, 34, 38, 39, 46
Cordell, Rev. Charles	14
Costelloe, W.J.	22

Council of the Laity	54/5	Family & Social Action	46
Cowen, Joseph, M.P.	20	Family Group Home(s)	36, 53
Coyle, J. Rev.	54	Farm Training Centre	32
Cullen, Fr.	11	Fee, Rev. Wilfrid	39
Cunningham, Bishop James	37, 40, 45-7	Fell, Charles	14
Cuthbert, St.	13, 21, 50-2	Felling	16, 20
CWL	31/2, 34, 36, 38, 39, 47, 49	Fenham, St. Mary's School, (College)	26, 38, 46
		Fenianism	20, 26
D'Arcy, Martin	31	Finchale Abbey	21
Darlington;	10/11, 16, 19, 26/7, 36, 53	Fisher, John, St.	33
		Fitzgerald, John, Sir	22
Dawson, C.	31	FitzPatrick, P., Revd. Dr.	48
Denvir, John	22	Fletcher, William	14
Diaconate	55, 57	Foran, Robert	14
Diamond, Charles	21	Forster, G.W.	34
Diocesan Catechetical Centre	38	Fortin, Fr.	20
Diocesan Catholic Teachers Education Days	45	Forty Martyrs	39
Diocesan Council of Priests	46, 49, 54	Freemasons	20
Diocesan Ecumenical Officer	56	French Revolution	26
Diocesan Fund	12, 24	Fribourg	48
Diocesan Liturgical Commission	42	Friendly Societies	35
Diocesan Missionary Establishment, Wooler	15, 27	Gainford	33, 36
Diocesan Mother and Baby Hostel	36	Gammie, George	32
Diocesan Pastoral Council; Plan	51, 54	*Garden of the Soul* (1740)	14
Diocesan Religious Education Centre	51, 53	Gateshead	33, 36
Diocesan Rescue Society	35/6, 47, 53, 56	Gavazzi, Alessandro	10
Diocesan Schools Commission	45	Gelineau, Joseph	42
Diocesan Small Parishes Fund	49	Germans	34
Diocesan synods	11, 27, 38, 39	Gill, Eric	35
Diocesan Trust	54	Good Shepherd Sunday; Collection	35, 53
Diocesan Youth Mission & Service	51, 54	Gothic, -style	13, 30, 42
Dominicans; Dominican Sisters	11, 26, 52	Grail, The	46
Douglas, Mary	43, 44	Gratton Doyle, Sir N.	22
Downey, Archbishop Richard	33	Gregorian chant	42
Dowry of Mary	21	Griffiths, Bishop Ambrose (OSB)	48, 53/4, 57
Dual system	25	*Groundplan*	47
Duffy, Mr.	26	Guild of Ss. Luke, Cosmas & Damian	35
Dugdale, Joseph	14	Gunpowder Plot	9
Dunn, George Thomas; Thomas	21	Haggerston Castle	19
Dunn & Hansom (architects)	13	*Hail Queen of Heaven*	15
Durham: cathedral; gaol; university	9-12, 16, 18, 28, 31, 38, 48, 52	Haltwhistle	51
		Handicapped Children's Pilgrimage Trust	38
Easter Communion	57	Hannigan, Fr.	20
Ecclesiastical Titles Act	10	Hartlepool	10, 13, 21, 26, 47
Ecumenism, church unity	44, 55		
Ebchester, Strickland Hall	32	Health Act (1919)	35
Education Act(s)	24/5, 35/6, 38	Healy, Tim M.P. K.C.	22
Education Committee	30	Hebburn	16
Elgar, Edward, Sir	42	Heddon House	32, 54
Elizabeth II, Queen	48	Heenan, Cardinal John Carmel	48
Emmaus Community	52	Heinrick, Hugh	22
English Martyrs	33, 39	Hemy, Henry (*Crown of Jesus Music*)	15
Esh; Esh Laude	10, 13	Hexham; Hexham & Newcastle	10, 28, 30, 37, 47, 50, 52/3, 57
Eucharistic fast; services, ministers	40, 43, 49, 51, 53-5		
		Hibernian Society	20
Euthanasia	35	Hinsley, Archbishop Arthur	33
Evacuations	34	Hodgson, E.W.	34
Ex Porta Flaminia	9	Hoey, Michael	32
Faithful Companions of Jesus	19, 24, 26	Hogarth, Bishop William	10, 11, 24, 27/8
Faith of Our Fathers	15	Hollis, C.	31

Holy Island	21, 36, 38, 52
Holy Land	27
Holy See	9, 30, 35, 39, 46/7, 50/1, 54
Holy Week, Easter Triduum	40, 44
Holy Year, 1983	52
Holydays of obligation	25, 40
Humanae Vitae	45
Hume, Cardinal Basil; Sir William	46, 48
Hurworth	36, 52
Ingram, Bl. John	39, 52
International aid organisations	55
International Commission on English in the Liturgy (ICEL)	41
Irish Home Rule politics; Irish Free State	11, 12, 22
Irish Literary Institute	15
Italians	34
Jackson, R.W.	21
Jacobs, John	32
Jarrett, Bede	31
Jarrow	16, 33, 48
Jerningham, H.	22
Jesmond; Shrine of Our Lady	39, 52
Jesuit(s)	11, 32, 34, 37, 46
John Paul II, Pope	16, 50, 44
Justice & Peace	50, 56
Kearney, Canon	17
Kelly, J.M.	26
Kelly, John	20
Kirwan, Joseph	32
Knights of St Columba	38
Knights of St. Patrick	20
La Sagesse	45
Lafferty, Mr.	26
Lampades Christi	38
Larkin, Charles	10, 15
Lawson, Revd. Thomas (S.J.)	14
League of the Cross	17
Lee, W. (Lord Mayor of Newcastle)	22
Lefebvre, Archbishop Marcel; Lefebvrists	49
Legion of Mary	31, 52
Lemington Hall	36, 53
Lent	14, 54
Leo Edgar Group Homes	56
Lindisfarne Gospels	37
Lindsay, Bishop Hugh	47, 49-51, 53
Lingard, John	15
Litany of Loreto	14
Little Sisters of the Poor	32, 47
Liturgy: Latin, liturgical renewal, missal, *Liturgy of the Hours, Divine Office*	13/4, 40-3, 53/4
Local Education Authorities (LEAs)	25, 45
Londonderry, Marchioness of	13
Lourdes, diocesan pilgrimage	32, 38/9, 48, 52
Loyola University	54
Magill, Canon	32
Maltby, Edward, Bishop of Durham	9
Manning, Cardinal Henry Edward	17, 21, 27
Marian Year (1954)	39
Marie Reparatrice, (Sisters)	32, 39, 52
Marist Brothers	26
Marsh's Seminary for Young Catholic Ladies	26
Martindale, C.	31
Mass media	40
Mater et Magistra (1961)	35
Matt Talbot House	56
May Devotions	43
McAnulty, Bernard ('Barnie')	22, 26
McCormack, Bishop Joseph	33, 35-7
McNabb, V.	31
Mediator Dei	40
Medical Mission Sisters	46
Mesnard, Mrs & Miss	26
Metro-Centre Chapel	54
Mill Hill Fathers	31, 52
Minsteracres	27, 39
Missions	15
More, St. Thomas	33
Morse, Bl. Henry	52
Mostyn, Bishop Francis	10
Murphy, William	20
Napoleonic wars	9
Nation	22
National Health Service	35
National Pastoral Congress (1980)	50, 54/5
Nazareth House	33
Nesbitt, Gerard	34
Netherton Reformatory	18
New York, (Tynemouth)	16
Newcastle	10, 11, 14/5, 17, 19, 21/2, 24/5, 28, 30, 33/4, 36, 38/9, 47/8, 52/3
Newcastle, Cathedral of St Mary; chapter	11, 21, 28, 31
Newcastle Daily Chronicle	22
Newcastle Guardian	9
Newcastle Irish Tribune	21
Newcastle Journal	21, 57
Newcastle, St. Aloysius School	34
Newcastle, St. Andrew's,	10-12, 14-16, 23, 30/1, 38
Newcastle, St. Cuthbert's Grammar School	26, 30, 33, 47
Newcastle, St. Dominic's	11, 17
Newcastle, King's College; University	37, 49
Newcastle, Nazareth House; St. Vincent's; St. Philip's; St. Philomena's	36
Newgate Gaol	33
Newhouse	20
Newman, J.H.; Newman Association	28, 31
Newminster	33
Newsham, Charles	42
North Eastern Association of Catholic Clubs	39
North Eastern Railway	22
North Gosforth, Sacred Heart	51
North of England Education Conference	46
North Shields	12, 16, 23
Northern Brethren's Fund	52
Northern Catholic Calendar	21, 27, 52, 54/5, 57

61

Northern Cross	38, 40, 45	Roman Catholic Charities Act (1860)	24
Northumberland	9, 47	Roman Curia	11
Nunnery Inspection Bill	19	Romanesque	30
O'Callaghan, Cornelius; James	34	'Rome on the Rates'	25
O'Callaghan, Bishop Henry,	28, 53	Rooney, James	19, 30
O'Gorman, W. Rev.	54	Rosalie House	56
October Devotions	43, 49	Rosary; Rosary Rally	14/5, 43, 49, 52
Order of Christian Funerals	41	Rosminians	15
Ordination of women	50	Russell, John, Lord	9
Our Lady of Lourdes Club	47	Sacred Heart, devotions	14, 15
Our Lady of Walsingham	52	Salvin Family	17, 31
Our Lady's Catechists	36	Sanctuary Guild of St. Aloysius	15
Ouseburn	10	Saville, Mr.	19
Ovingham Camp	32	Schola Gregoriana of Northumbria	42
Oxford Movement	9, 12, 28	School Boards, board schools	21, 24, 25
Oxford; Catholic Worker's College	32	School-chapel, school-pence	23-5
Ozanam, Frederick; House	16, 34, 47, 56	Schoolmasters and Schoolmistresses Benevolent Institution	24
Palmer, Sir Charles	17	Scorton	19, 26, 47
Papal: 'aggression', blessing, infallibility	13, 15, 27	Seaham Harbour	51
Paris	16	Sheed, F.	31
Parish council(s)	46, 49, 51, 54	Silksworth	39
Parliamentary acts	20	Silvertops of Minsteracres	21, 27, 39
Passionist(s)	10, 15, 39	Singleton, Richard	20
Pease, Joseph, M.P.	20	Sisters of Charity	18, 34, 52
Pectoral cross	27	Sisters of Charity of St Paul	19, 24
Penitential service	43	Sisters of the Good Shepherd	19, 55
Percy, Bl. Thomas	21	Sisters of Mercy	19, 23, 26
Peter, St.; Peter's Pence	12, 21, 27	Sisters of Our Lady of Good and Perpetual Succour	32, 47
Pilgrim Church North-East	51	Sisters of the Sacred Hearts of Jesus and Mary	19, 36
Pius IX, Pope	9		
Pius X, Pope	29, 42		
Plater, Charles, SJ	32	Smith, Fr.	11
Platt, Ralph	14	Smith, J.V., Canon	35
Polish Catholic Centre	38	Society for the Protection of the Unborn Child (SPUC)	49
Pontifical Zouaves	28		
Poor Clares	19, 26, 52	Society of St Gregory	40
Poor Law Guardians	17, 21/2, 24	Society of St Vincent de Paul (SVP)	15, 18, 31-4, 36, 38, 47, 49, 56
Poor Sisters of Nazareth	32, 56		
Postgate, Nicholas	50	Society of the BVM & St. Elizabeth	15
Potato famine	11	Society of the Sacred Heart	52
Prayer-groups	58	Socio-economics	24, 30, 40
Presentation Brothers	18, 23	Sodality of the Living Rosary	15
Preston, Bishop Richard	25, 29	South Shields; Westoe Towers	10, 16, 36, 47
Protestant Alliance	20	Spanish Civil War	33
Pugin A.W.	13	Spence, R. Rev.	54
Quinn, Stephen	22	Spencer, Ignatius	10
Quinquennial reports (*Relatio*)	46	St Camillus Hospital	36, 52
Redemptorists	15	St Christopher's House	47, 56
Reformation	9, 43, 48	St. Mary's Teacher Training College	33
Religious instruction	23	St. Vincent's Orphanage	33
Rerum Novarum	32	Standon, James	14
Ribbonmen	20	Stella Maris Club	36
Riddell, Bishop William	10, 14	Stella	10
Ripon, Marquess of	21	Stockton	47, 52
Rising of the North	21	Summerhill Grove Deaf Centre	56
Rite for the Christian Initiation of Adults (RCIA)	41, 51	Sunderland	10, 11, 13, 16, 26, 32, 37-9, 53, 55
Rite of Marriage; of Anointing & Viaticum	41		
Robson, J.P.	10		
Rogerson, J.S.	27	Swinburne Castle	33, 36

Swindlehurst, Bishop Owen	47, 51, 54
Tantum Ergo	42
Teacher-training colleges	25/6, 37
Teams of Our Lady	46
Teesside	11
Temperance Society of Our Lady & St John the Baptist	15
The Easter People	50
The Fold	36
The Horrid War i Sandgeyt, (ballad)	10
The Tablet	11, 12, 20
The Times	9
Third world	56
Thompson, Richard; Henry	21, 22
Thorman, Bishop Joseph	29-33
Tindall, Rev. D.	53
Tobruk	34
Trades Union Council	38
Tudhoe	34, 36
Tynemouth; Priory	10, 20, 27, 33/4, 48
Tyneside Catholic News	21
Tyneside; Catholic Youth Council	11, 34, 47
Ullathorne, Bishop William Bernard	10
Unionist	22
United Irish League	22
Unity Octave	44
Universalis Ecclesiae	9
Universalis Ecclesiae Solicitudo	30
Universe	57
University of Louvain	33
Ursulines	26, 52
Ushaw Magazine	28
Ushaw College; Ushaw Moor	10-13, 20, 26/7 29/30, 33, 37, 39, 40, 42, 47, 51/2, 57
Vane, Earl	13
Vann, G.	31
Vatican Councils	27, 40, 43/4, 46/7, 52, 57/8
Vaughan, Cardinal Herbert	28
Victoria Cross	34
Victoria, Queen	9
Vincentian Care Services	56
Vocations exhibition	38
Wakenshaw, Adam	34
Ward, Maisie	31
Washington	17
Webbe, Samuel (*Collection of Sacred Music*, 1792)	14
Weidner, J.F. (Lord Mayor of Newcastle)	22
Welfare state	34/5, 40
Wellesley (training ship)	16
Westminster Synod (1852)	23
Westminster, Archbishop; Abbot	48, 53
Whinney House	32
Wilkinson, Bishop William	27/8
Wilkinson, Fr.	11, 17
Williamson, Hedworth	13
Wiseman, Cardinal Nicholas	9, 10
Witham, Henry,	21
Wolsingham and Witton Park	29
Women's World Day of Prayer	44
Woodruff, D.	31
World Wars	12, 30-4, 36, 39, 40
Worlock, Archbishop Derek	53
Wynn, Terence	38
Xaverian Brothers	37

DOWN YOUR AISLES

Part 2

Parishes of the Diocese

by

Michael Morris

In memory of my deceased father and mother, Peter and Norah Morris, and my late brother Philip, who kept the Faith and passed it on.

INTRODUCTION

The following articles were published in the *Northern Cross* newspaper between the years 1983 and 1999. They are re-issued in their present form to commemorate the 150th Anniversary of the Hexham and Newcastle Diocese.

In publishing this series of 'parish profiles' we hoped that they would tell the reader something about the strong faith and commitment of our ancestors and portray something of parish life today.

I owe a debt of gratitude to the many people who assisted and encouraged me in this task. I would like to thank members of the *Northern Cross* Board and in particular, the chairman, Father Dennis Tindall, for their whole-hearted support; the editor, John Bailey, who provided me with good advice and offered his professional acumen to an amateur; Robin Gard, Diocesan Archivist, and Philip Hall of Sunderland Libraries who often went beyond the call of duty to supply me with material and point me in the right direction; and the late Father W. Nicholson who, in the early days, was most helpful and supportive.

In the course of writing these articles many journeys were made and many photographs were taken. My thanks to Tom Mackin who helped to initiate the series, ferry me around and took most of the earliest pictures; to Father Eamonn Croghan for his many colour photographs and his jovial company as we journeyed round the diocese; to Joe Aiken of St. Cecilia's, Sunderland, who was always ready with his camera when asked to cover an assignment.

When it was decided to publish the articles in book form more people became involved. The daunting task of putting this section of the book together was made a lot easier for me by the expertise, in the world of writing and publishing, offered by Dr Leo Gooch.

The rather dreary and exacting exercise of typing and later word-processing the original articles was undertaken by my sister, Susan, to whom I am most grateful. Recently when it came to putting them into book form she and Sister Raphael - and some of her pupils - set to work and copied every one on to the disks with an enthusiasm and rapidity that was commendable. Without their help the book would never have been published.

When writing the articles I relied heavily (in some cases totally) on the parish histories written by dedicated parishioners who desired that the story of their parish be told. Without their original research my task would have been impossible (see Bibliography). Our visits to the many parishes, scattered as far afield as Berwick in the north and Barnard Castle in the south, were made enjoyable and worthwhile by the priests and people whose welcoming hospitality and co-operation were magnanimous.

We record our thanks to:
Bishop Ambrose Griffiths O.S.B., and Bishop Hugh Lindsay; Rev. Canons W. Fee, F. Kearney, P. McKenna*, C. O'Callaghan, R.Spence; Rev. Fathers R. Appleyard, C.P. and Minsteracres Community, P. Blandford CMF, G. Bryce*, T. Buckley(CSSR), G. Carey*, T. Cass. N. Colahan, J. Connolly*, J. Costello, K. Cummins, T. Cunningham, A. Cunningham*, F. Daley, T. Dollard*, A. Donoghue, A. Duffy, M. Deegan, F. Ellis, A. Faley, J. Galletly*, J. Gibbons, M. Griffiths, J. Gunning*, J. Hughes, W. Jacks, D. Kellett, M. Keoghan, J. Kennedy*, John & Joseph Lennon, W. Lowrie*, E.V. Marron, D. Meagher, T. McCormack, P. McDermott, C. McDonnell, B. McNamara, V. & M. Melia, G. Monaghan, P. O'Connell, J. O'Keefe, W. O'Gorman, E. Ord*, A. Owens, A. Pickering, T. Power, M. Purtill, L. Pyle, J. Reid, R. Richmond, G. Scott O.S.B., M. Sharratt, T.V. Sheehan*, J. Skivington, B.Stronge*, M. Sweeney, D. Tanner, J. Timney, D. Treacy, J. Walsh*, S. Wetherall(CSSR). (*Deceased).
Sister Brigid (Alnwick), Major and Mrs John Charlton (Hesleyside), Sister M. Aelred (Blackhill), Mrs R. Rowell (Blyth), E. Kennedy (Felling), Rev. Mother and Sister Catherine (La Sagesse), Mr Reilly (Widdrington), Sheila Ward (Murton), A. Morley (Gosforth),
Mrs J. Shepherd, R. Pattison (North Gosforth), Sister M. Benedict (Seaham), Mrs V. Grant (Seaham), Jim Doherty (Stockton), Mother Martina and Mercy Community (Sunderland), K. Finn (Sunderland), Mr J. Cummings (Esh Laude), Sister Christopher and J. Herbert (Berwick), Sister Margaret and Carmel (Darlington), Mrs Dobson (Brancepeth Castle), J. Hirst, D. Callanan and Sister Catherine, Staff of Seaton Holme Visitors' Centre (Easington), F. Hurst (Sunderland), Mrs B. Lawson (Sunderland).
Finally, my thanks to Kevin Finn and Bernadette Lawson who read over the final script.

M. Morris January 2000.

1. ALNWICK   St. Paul   *(September, October 1997)*

The Northumbrian market-town of Alnwick, centred around the castle of the Percys, offers the student of Christian history a heritage which, we believe, goes back to Saxon times.

Perhaps the place to start is in the parish church of St. Mary and St. Michael - mainly of the Perpendicular period of architecture - built on, it is conjectured, an earlier Norman site and possibly an earlier Saxon one. Whatever the theories regarding the church's evolution, we can say with certainty that here Mass was celebrated regularly for our Christian forefathers in pre-Reformation times.

Thompson in his *Guide to Northumberland,* written in 1888, mentions that there were two bells in the tower: the first one inscribed with the words - 'Michael the Archangel come to the help of the people of God' and is of the 13th century; the second bell, of a later century has the words 'Hail Mary, full of grace, pray ye for the soul of John Valka'.

After leaving the town centre along the Wooler road one cannot but notice an imposing medieval gateway, the sole reminder that here once stood the Abbey of the Blessed Mary built for the Premonstratensian Canons, or Norbertines, in the 12th century. Their other foundation in the north was at Blanchland much of which, now incorporated into the village, is still preserved.

The 'White Canons' of Alnwick Abbey ministered to the people of Alnwick and the surrounding district until they were dispersed in 1539 at the Dissolution - a faithful record of service of almost 400 years to this area, now almost forgotten, yet a vital part of the Christian story here.

Within the castle park is a further reminder of the Faith: Hulne Priory where Carmelite friars settled round about 1242. The story of how they came here is an interesting one although the details are somewhat obscure. A traditional tale relates that a Ralph Fresburn, possibly of Northumbrian origin, had been a crusading knight in the Holy Land who, attracted to the Carmelite way of life, had settled with the hermit community on Mount Carmel. Because of the unsettled state of Palestine at that time the Carmelites dispersed to various parts of Europe; some, including Ralph, came to Alnwick and founded Hulne Priory on land granted by William de Vesci, Baron of Alnwick. The de Vescis and Percys were to be the major benefactors of these hermit friars who led a secluded life of prayer and penance within the priory walls.

Another reason why this particular site may have been chosen is that nearby Brizlee Hill, it is said, bore a resemblance to Mount Carmel. On January 24th, 1954, the Prior of Aylesford, (a re-occupied Carmelite priory in Kent), the late Father Malachy Lynch preached at Benediction in St. Mary's Church. The purpose of his visit was to discuss Hulne Priory and over dinner with the Duke he was told that small groups could visit the priory on special occasions - the priory stands within the Duke's Park. A further reminder of our Christian past would have been the ancient chantry chapel in the castle which disappeared in 1780 with the restoration of the castle. And still visible in Walkergate is the wall of St. Mary's chantry chapel where two priests lived who served St. Mary's parish church and taught 'poor boys in the art of Grammar gratis'.

The name Percy will be forever associated with Alnwick Castle and the resistance of some of them to the religious changes of the 16th century. One of the leaders of the Pilgrimage of Grace of 1536-7 was Thomas Percy; its purpose was to restore the monks to their monasteries and the practice of the Catholic Faith. Its failure led to the execution of Thomas who, it has been claimed, could have saved his life had he consented to take the Oath of Supremacy. Better known is his son, the Blessed Thomas Percy, who had the earldom restored when Mary Tudor became queen. Unfortunately the accession of Elizabeth in 1558 was to create further problems for those who wished to preserve the Catholic Faith. When the Rising of the North of 1569 - a further attempt to restore Catholicism - failed, Thomas who like his father had desired to follow the Church of Rome refused to conform and was beheaded at York in 1572.

October 15th, 1972, was another significant date in Alnwick's Catholic history. Special celebrations were held in honour of Blessed Thomas Percy, 400 years after his martyrdom. During the Solemn High Mass, Father Clement Tigar S.J., preached 'a vivid and moving sermon' on the martyr and his family. The Duke of Northumberland sat in a place of honour on the sanctuary and afterwards invited the clergy to the castle for sherry and showed them a missal used by Thomas Percy and a commentary in Thomas's own hand on the *Imitation of Christ*. Father Tigar, also, brought some relics of the martyr with him for this special occasion.

The Catholics in and around Alnwick during the penal days were fortunate in that they were able to maintain contact with priests who secretly served the chaplaincies in the homes of the Northumbrian Catholic gentry. Written records of their activities are limited as the penalties for recusancy were punitive. Quietly and unobtrusively they practised their Faith and the advice to 'Read and Burn' written communications, whilst reducing the risk of prosecution, has deprived us of much that would have given us a fascinating account of their daily lives. Although Mass would have been said at irregular intervals in the homes of Alnwick Catholics, the first record we have of a regular place of worship in post-Reformation times is the home of the Coates (or Cotes) family next to the Plough Inn in Bondgate Without. Here in 1700 was born Father John Coates whose grandfather, Edward Strother, a Catholic doctor, had left the house to Father John's mother, Winifred. 'At the beginning of the 18th century', according to one source, 'Father Robert Widdrington S.J., who resided at Widdrington Castle, said Mass once a month on weekdays at Mr. Cotes' father's house in Bondgate'. Father Coates' grandmother, Mary Coates of Morpeth, was accused in 1681 of sending her son to be educated abroad at St. Omer's - a punishable offence then. This family typify the fervour of the Catholic recusants who were determined to cling to the 'Faith of Our Fathers' come what may.

There had been a Jesuit presence in the North of England even in Elizabethan times. The young heirs of Catholic gentry educated abroad in Jesuit schools tended to have Jesuit chaplains in their homes before going abroad or on succeeding to the family estates. It is not surprising then to find a Mary Butler, a relative of the old Northumbrian Ord family, making provision for a fund to be administered by the Jesuit Provincial, Father Henry Sheldon, to maintain a priest at Sturton Grange or near it for the benefit of local Catholics. She further stipulated that a monthly Mass be said for herself and her relatives; an obligation fulfilled even to this day by Father John Skivington, the present parish priest.

Sturton Grange, six miles from Alnwick, was not the most convenient place to have a resident priest, so meeting the broad terms of Mary Butler's will the Jesuits decided to use the fund to support a resident priest in Alnwick town. Father John Parker, who arrived in 1756 dying here in 1770, appears to have been the first. He is mentioned in the Papist Returns of 1767 as George Parker along with 70 other named recusants of the Alnwick Deanery.

A house in Bailiffgate, in which Mass was said, was likely, at first to have been rented and later purchased and it was on the site of the old house that the Catholic Church of St. Mary was built in 1836. A written source of 1822 states that the house 'is situated about the middle of Bailiffgate on the north side. It belongs to the Society of Jesuits who assembled for some time in a small room appropriated to their religious services and ceremonies till, their numbers increasing, the Rev. W. Strickland built the present chapel in which he placed an altar piece of exquisite workmanship'. Over the years extensions and alterations were made to the small room which appears to have been extended to form a chapel. Father Howard remarks in an old register: 'I introduced my people into my new chapel in Alnwick the 14th August, 1796, and on the 21st of the same month were confirmed by Bishop William Gibson, 27 people'.

It was during Father John Fishwick's pastorate (1832-53) that the church of St. Mary in Bailiffgate was built and opened in 1836 and was to serve the Catholics of Alnwick until 1982 when the former Anglican church of St. Paul's was purchased; it is hoped that the old Bailiffgate church will become a museum of local history.

St. Mary's church costing about £2,100 and designed by Mr. J. Green Jnr., of Newcastle, was officially opened and blessed on September 8th, 1836, by Father Fishwick during a Mozart Mass sung by the combined choirs of St. Andrew's, Newcastle, and St. Cuthbert's, North Shields. The preacher was Father Philip Kearney who the year before had seen his own church of St. Mary's in Sunderland opened. Both churches fronted main streets - a sign that Catholicism was emerging from the obscurity it had been forced to seek before the granting of Catholic Emancipation.

Alnwick's Catholics were faithfully served by the Jesuits until 1855 when they formally handed over the parish to the diocese, the first secular priest being Father Joseph Gibson, a member of the old Northumbrian family which gave two bishops to the Northern District; he was to minister here for 35 years. A reminder of the pioneering work of the Jesuit Order here is the fact that five of their brethren are buried in St. Michael's churchyard.

One of the most interesting Jesuits, who was at Alnwick from 1853 to 1855, was Father Joseph Sydney Woollett. Educated at Stonyhurst his youthful intention was to study for the priesthood. However, a change of direction saw him studying medicine in London and qualifying as a doctor. A year after his wife died he joined the Jesuits and was ordained in 1853 coming to Alnwick that same year. He then went to the Crimea serving in the French hospitals. For 35 years he served the West Indian Mission becoming Pro-Vicar Apostolic; he retired to Stonyhurst where he ended his days.

To provide an education for the parish children - and even those further afield - the Sisters of Mercy came here in 1890, during the time of the Belgian priest, Father Robert, starting a Convent High School and assisting in the parochial school. Some of the Sisters continue to live in the convent adjacent to the former church, assisting in the parish but are no longer involved in the schools where in the past they figured so prominently in educating young people in the Faith. St. Johns's First School and Thomas Percy Middle School continue to provide the Catholic education in this area before the children are transferred to the High School. St. Oswald's School, formerly Our Lady's Convent High School, is now under lay control.

It is unusual for a Catholic congregation to worship permanently in what was a former Anglican church as is the case in Alnwick. This unusual transfer occurred in 1982 when Father Joseph Marren (1978-1991) was the parish priest. Much needed to be done to the old church of St. Mary and by a happy coincidence the church of St. Paul's was no longer needed.

At the dedication ceremony, which took place on December 11th, 1982, the walls and altar were anointed with oil during the celebratory Mass. Bishop Hugh Lindsay comments in the dedication brochure: 'I hope that our first celebration in this church will make us all more ready to serve God and serve others for his sake; and that it will help our divided churches to draw more closely to each other'. A symbolic handing over of the keys took place between the Rev. Sadgrove, the vicar of Alnwick, and Bishop Lindsay. It was truly an ecumenical occasion watched by civic dignitaries and members of other religious denominations. Also present was Father Leo Maday, parish priest of St. Paul's in Voerde (Alnwick's twin town in Germany) along with three members of his congregation who presented a Mass vestment to the new parishioners of St. Paul's.

St. Paul's in the Decorated style, was built in 1846 to a design of the architect, Anthony Salvin, the founder being Hugh, third Duke of Northumberland, whose memory is preserved in the Caen stone effigy in the north aisle. The church, a very imposing building, is over 120 feet long and almost 60 feet wide with side aisles, a large deep chancel, and is capable of seating a congregation of 1,000 on its solid English oak benches.

Perhaps the most outstanding feature is the great East window designed by a Mr. William Dyce and executed in Munich by Max Aimuller, the total cost being £1,639. The window depicts Paul and Barnabas preaching the gospel at Antioch; on the lower section can be seen the coat of arms of the founder.

Memories of the old Bailiffgate church are re-kindled for older parishioners where in the north aisle stands the Lady Altar with statue, and the reredos with paintings of the Northern saints brought here in 1982.

We conclude the article almost verbatim, with an account of parish life today written by Father John Skivington in his own inimitable style:

'Yes, Alnwick has a history, but it's living history. Living people, warm, secure. You maybe think it's 'County' - classy. In reality it's ordinary, decent Northumbrian folk, with delightful lilt jargon: *'Barry pope'* (to rhyme with 'tarry rope') = 'good'. A *'jougle'* = a 'dog'. *'Clash'* = 'gossip'. There's a lot of Catholics in Alnwick and they'll greet you in the street ... Father. But maybe centuries of district missioners have made them ... less than active. 'Hatch, match, despatch' as true here as anywhere. There's a core, of course, as in every parish, who know each other and are part related. ('She's Andy's girl - Married that farmer from Felton.') Faithful too, and practised prayers. Our weekly liturgies salted with song and variety, good people, generous, caring, and careful to find God in living. Overseen by picture window, in sanctuary, of Paul and Barnabas preaching at Antioch (Acts 13). For weekday Mass we meet in quondam choir stalls, grouped prayerfully round lectern and altar; and when the priest is absent there's daily Word and Eucharist led by lay leaders of special quality. At a most recent count, we'd 30 parish groups, to pray and plan, to build and recreate. Care group, catechists or choir, flowers and finances, marriage and meditation ... All led and directed by an excelling parish council who proved that they are church when the parish priest was on sabbatical. The nuns are precious and have served so well. We've our hospitals, general and maternity and the rest homes; our schools (Infant and Middle; Northumbria's 3-tier sends our teens to good State Comp); RAF Camp, Boulmer, with radar tracking bunkers and the air/sea rescue yellow helicopter. The airmen billet in Longhoughton: a frequent prelude to retirement posting here. There's miles of coast from Alnmouth Priory in the South to Craster Kippers in the North and Dunstanburgh castle. (we're well endowed with those. King Malcolm fell at Alnwick's). The coalfield's dead now; Shilbottle closed, so too the tiny private pit at Hampeth. So we farm and we fish, we clean and commute. Some small industry and shopping (hosting crafts and boutiques in the tourist lanes and alleyways) and we try to raise our children in the love of God and others. We worship our God, with lights and with incense, with flowers and with silence. Is not that *all* our lives' task and triumph? We're parish, we're a people of God. We're Christian babies, girls and boys, women and men, ... or *'manishes'* and *'gadgies'*, as they say in Alnwick.'

2. AMBLE   The Sacred Heart & St. Cuthbert   *(December 1988)*

Few, if any, Catholic churches today stand on a site which has a pre-Reformation foundation. Such is the case, however, in Amble where next to the church are the remains of a manor house which belonged to the monks of Tynemouth Priory. If, as one writer suggests, a priest-monk lived in the manor house with the lay brothers, whose duty it was to attend to the priory business here, then Mass was celebrated on this spot more than 400 years ago.

This whole area is rich in Catholic history traceable to Northumbria's earliest Christian era. Coquet Island, just off the coast from Amble, provided a monastic cell - possibly in St. Cuthbert's time - on a site where now stands the present lighthouse. According to one source, there dwelt here a little-known Northumbrian saint, Henry, said to be of 'honourable parentage', who forsook the world and gave his days to the hermit way of life, dying on January 16th, 1127, in his hermitage; he was buried at Tynemouth Priory near the body of St. Oswin.

Within the boundaries of the present Catholic parish lies the village of Warkworth dominated by the castle (with its medieval chapel) and popular among visitors touring Northumberland. Here, too, our Christian links with the past go back to Saxon days when King Ceowulf granted lands and gave the church he had built to the monks of Lindisfarne whose monastery he himself entered in 737 A.D. The church of St. Lawrence was later rebuilt in the Norman style. Bishop Flambard of Durham also founded a chantry here in the reign of Henry III.

Near Warkworth is the famous hermitage hewn out of a cliff face and situated above the Coquet river; it can be reached by a riverside path or ferry. Inside may be seen 'the inner chapel, its altar, its piscina, its hagioscope, its cell, its niche, its columns, its groined roof and bosses richly carved'. A Latin inscription on the inner wall over the entrance reads: 'My tears have been my bread day and night' (Psalm XII.4).

This implies - as does the name and location - that the Warkworth hermitage was a place inhabited by a succession of hermits who over a period of years, spent their days atoning for their sins and those of the world. Its spaciousness and style suggest to other writers that it may have been the abode of a chaplain or chantry priest maintained by the Percy family.

A fine view of the Coquet river, where it meets the sea, is obtainable from the present sacristy window which also overlooks the old course of the river - altered in the last century - and indicates why the original manor house was built on this eminence. Amble was one of a number of manors granted by the powerful noble Robert de Mowbray in 1090 to the Tynemouth monks. They held rights to salt pans, coal mines, coney (rabbit) warrens, fishing and, possibly, the right to levy tolls on ships entering the river.

At the end of the Civil War, Sir William Fenwick, who had espoused the Royalist cause forfeited his estates in Amble although his daughter was able to retain some of the land in this area. These lands were to remain in the hands of the Radcliffe family - the first Earl of Derwentwater had married the daughter of Sir William - until 1715 when after the failure of the Stuart attempt to regain the throne, James, the Third Earl of Derwentwater and his brother, Charles, were executed and their property confiscated.

Charles had been married to the Countess of Newburgh and provision was made for their descendants. By an act of 1798, in the reign of George III, the Amble estates passed to Anthony James, Earl of Newburgh.

The Countess of Newburgh contributed regularly to the upkeep of the Amble Mission until her death in 1853 when her estates became the property of her husband, Lieutenant-Colonel Charles Leslie. Both husband and wife hoped that one day a permanent mission would be established here; the family left a legacy of £200 for this purpose.

The re-birth of a Catholic community here can be traced back to round about 1840 when a new harbour was being built to provide an outlet for coal from the new pits recently sunk, particularly the Radcliffe mine. Many Irish immigrant workers came to the area to work on the new harbour and the Rev. William Fletcher ministered to their spiritual needs on alternate Sundays and occasionally on weekdays at the Hope Farm, on the Links, until his death from fever in 1847. One source claims that the first Mass centre was at Cliff House. The Longhorsley priests continued this service for a number of years, but with the completion of the harbour the flock diminished and Amble was served monthly.

By 1859 the Amble Mission was the responsibility of the Rev. Joseph Gibson of Alnwick who was able on occasions to say Mass here. After 1868 Amble ceased to be a mission of the diocese but a resurgence in the Catholic population came in 1877 with the development of Broomhill Colliery; this increased congregation was ministered to by Father Gregory Smith O.S.B., of Felton. Father Smith was able to celebrate Mass regularly in the home of the parents of Father John Murphy. Bishop Chadwick and Father Smith, seeing the necessity of a permanent mission in Amble, were able with the goodwill of Mr. C. L. Leslie of Hassock Hall, Derbyshire - and other friends - to acquire the site of the ruined manor house for the erection of a school-chapel which was opened by the Bishop on June 22nd, 1879, the feast of the Sacred Heart.

It was almost eight years later that the parish was formally established with the appointment of its first parish priest, Father Edward Robert, in 1887. It was during Father J. Walmsley's incumbency that the present church was erected in 1913. Father Leo Hart extended the church in 1952 with the addition of a new sanctuary; and in 1977 Father Brian Malia, assisted by the men of the parish, added side aisles to the present structure and carried out a general renovation. A Mass Centre was established at Red Row in November 1946 and the church of St. Paul's was opened there in 1948. Sadly, due to the shortage of priests, the last Mass was celebrated in Red Row at Christmas (1988); parishioners, however, will have transport provided after that date to enable them to attend Mass in Amble.

Last year Father Kevin Cummins, the present parish priest, and the parishioners had the joy of celebrating the parish centenary. Naturally, the highlight of the anniversary was a concelebrated Mass celebrated by Bishop Lindsay and 22 priests on June 12th, 1987. Bishop Lindsay, whilst here for the occasion, consecrated the church and the new altar. Mr. Vincent Davis was responsible for constructing the latter and Mr. Andy Simm did much good work on the restoration of the reredos; both craftsmen were assisted by men of the parish.

In an extensive rural parish with a Catholic population of approximately 900 much is being achieved in building a community of involved parishioners who, with the assistance of Father Cummins, minister to each other and the wider community. Evidence of this was shown in June this year when a parish mission led by Father Paul Cannon of the Catholic Missionary Society prompted the formation of 12 core groups of laity to prepare and co-ordinate the parish strategy prior to and during Mission Week; they were assisted by the Legion of Mary from Ireland and Newcastle in the initial door-to-door visitation.

These lay groups - formed to organise the Mission - continue, alongside other parish organisations, to invigorate the life of the parish at the centre of which is the Eucharist. Thirteen lay ministers of the Eucharist take communion after the Sunday Mass to the sick and housebound - and more frequently, if so desired; parishioners are encouraged to share a Holy Hour each week with Christ and with each other; each day the Prayer of the Church is recited before Mass; a liturgy group and the choir assist the priest in the performance of the sacred liturgy; and frequent efforts are made for charitable appeals and the Third World - Sudan is a recent example. Adult Christian Education classes are held weekly during Lent.

Socially the parish tries to cater for as many needs as are perceived: a play group meets weekly in St. Cuthbert's First School; a Mother and Toddler group holds regular sessions; a youth group - much involved in the Mission - provides for the needs of the older children; and a Tuesday group of 20 ladies organises social events and sees to the cleaning of the church.

Many parish activities occur in the Church Hall adjacent to the church; and here on the same site the Diocesan Youth Service has extended its arm to provide a self-catering hostel for youth groups who wish to use this picturesque part of Northumberland as a place of recreation. This year, in addition to diocesan groups, youth parties have used the hostel for holidays from as far afield as Birmingham and Carluke in Scotland.

In addition to his work as parish priest Father Cummins is, also, the Catholic Chaplain to H.M. Prison at Acklington and H.M. Youth Custody Centre at Castington. At both these centres he is able to say a weekly Mass and is heavily committed to providing regular spiritual help and counselling to those who ask for it; in the latter sphere he is helped by an assistant chaplain, Sister Andrea, of the Convent of Mercy in Alnwick. Both chaplains appreciate the work of the local S.V.P. Conference who consider it one of their special works to visit regularly the inmates in these custodial centres.

Ecumenical activity is not lacking either; parishioners assist in the parish hall where Age Concern meets every Wednesday morning; the Catholics of Amble co-operate with other denominations raising funds to finance a Christmas meal for senior citizens which, because of the large numbers, takes place on three separate evenings in late November.

Three members of the Amble parish are in the lifeboat crew - a charity supported socially and financially by the Catholics of Amble whose parish priest is one of the denominational chaplains. On more than one occasion Father Cummins has had the honour of blessing the rescue vessel on Lifeboat Day, August 28th.

This energetic rural parish in Northumberland has much to be proud of in the past and present and is continuing to build a community that can look forward confidently to the future.

3. ANNITSFORD   St. John The Baptist   *(June, 1985)*

Surrounded by a modern network of roads the church at Annitsford stands, surprisingly, in a secluded spot offering peace and solitude to those who seek it. A short distance away to the south is Annitsford village and to the north the new town of Cramlington with its modern Catholic church. The name Cramlington is an old one, possibly Anglo-Saxon, and has links with the ancient faith going back to the 14th century if not earlier - a chapelry of St. Nicholas, Newcastle, probably founded by the Grenville family is recorded as being there in 1323. The present Anglican church, completed in 1868, stands on a site a little to the north of where this medieval chapel was built. More time and research would, no doubt, reveal more evidence of the Catholic Faith in and around Annitsford of long ago.

Annitsford's name is derived from the ford over the Seaton Burn which passes through the area. Its derivation is obvious from a description given in 1825: 'Annitsford at the northern extremity of the parish (of Long Benton) is a dangerous passage after heavy rains and where a bridge is much wanted'. Hardly more dangerous, one would guess, than parishioners on foot find today wending their way to their local

Annitsford, St. John The Baptist   *Photo: M. Morris*

church via the hazards of the spine roads!

There were sufficient Catholics living in the area of Seghill, Dudley, Burradon and elsewhere to warrant in 1828 a Dominican priest, Father Weldon, driving in his trap to say Mass at the Blake Arms in Seghill. The development of the mining industry in the area and the arrival of the Irish looking for employment in the pits made Annitsford a suitable central location for the formation of a parish. Father O'Dwyer was the first resident priest and it is thought he arrived here in 1858.

With the help of the Lamb family of Carlisle, who had mining interests in the area, a brick school-chapel was erected in the village in 1866; it remains today - in the hands of a local builder - virtually intact with the semi-circular sanctuary at the north end and the headmaster's house adjoining the west wall. From the outset, places were available for non-Catholic children if there was spare capacity - an early ecumenical gesture.

More details of parish life are available with the arrival from Jarrow in 1881 of Father Henry Walmsley, a member of a faithful Lancashire Catholic family, who had four priest uncles and two nun aunts. In an article in *The Lamp Magazine, Vol.III*, he gives an account of his life here in the parish and in particular the rigours endured during a Northumbrian winter: 'Annitsford is not a rich place, but it is one that would seriously impair any but a healthy constitution. Taking a circuit all round it would measure forty miles, with a diameter of seventeen miles. Imagine a scattered population of 700 people and then you may ask yourself the question, where are they?' And to that Father Walmsley would simply answer, 'you must go and look for them.' And that is just what he has been doing all these seventeen years... In summer it is his continuous recreation, but in winter often after a storm, attempts must be made to force the roads to reach the sick or celebrate Mass for an expectant congregation in an outlying district; and it is amusing, though sometimes a little anxious, to encourage your horse through snow wreaths or over flooded roads, which would be totally impassable to an ordinary pedestrian. 'But the joy of it all when you get there at last and are welcomed as one lost! Certainly much discomfort is a sure attendant in these circumstances; your horse falls or refuses the road, and you are left for an hour to stand at his head to warm your hands under his collar, and to ponder regretfully over the nice parlour fire you left behind, and all the while your feet long ago past feeling, registering several degrees of acute frost... But who would not work for the poor who love you, and who are always so generous to realise the sacrifice made for them; a single kind word is worth all the gold of the world'.

This graphic description may include experiences of his journey to and from Backworth where he opened a chapel in 1883 and which he served along with Annitsford until his retirement in 1896.

His successor was Father Scott, a theologian of some standing, who in 1902 was faced with a debt of £473 - a considerable sum in those days. Fortunately for the parish a Mrs. Shawe-Storey, who spent part of the year at her country residence at Arcot Hall - now a golf club - became a Catholic in 1900 and from that date regularly attended Mass in the school-chapel at Annitsford. One day she called on Father Scott offering him a cheque to cover the debt and a further cheque of £7,000 (who can estimate its value today?) and told him, 'Take the field on the north side of the reservoir - some half mile north of the village - and build a church where people can pray in peace and quiet'.

Soon after this, Father Scott was assigned to Rome and the task and honour of building the church fell to Father Chapman. A Mr. Parkous from Newcastle was employed as the architect. He accompanied Father Chapman to Ostend to view the Belgian cathedral and was requested to design a small-scale replica at Annitsford. Because of the danger of mining subsidence a concrete raft was laid down first and the Gothic style mini-cathedral of local stone was built on this secure foundation.

One of the few churches to have no debt on its completion, it was consecrated and opened, in 1906 presumably by Bishop Wilkinson, as the late Father Marron's parish history notes that at the ceremony the Bishop, preacher and ministers were all converts.

St. John the Baptist's church is sometimes referred to as 'The church amongst the trees', and not without reason. Almost a two acre site had been donated by Mrs Shawe-Storey who directed her gardener to landscape the site, planting hedges of beech and fir as well as a copious sprinkling of willow, elm, chestnut and poplar. This lady's ancestor had purchased East Cramlington from Sir John Lawson in 1791. Some branches of this family had tenaciously kept the faith in penal times one of whom was Dorothy Lawson whose house at St. Anthony's on the north bank of the Tyne was a centre of catholicity and a place of refuge for the persecuted.

Within the extensive grounds at Annitsford lies the cemetery which was in use before the church was built. Amongst the former parishioners lying here is Annitsford's most famous son, the international bass singer, Owen Brannigan, who in his lifetime was honoured by both pope and queen. His father became the organist here at the age of 17 and, here too, young Owen pumped the organ for him and began his singing career as a boy soprano. For years Mr Brannigan, senior, played at the first Mass in Annitsford and then journeyed by pony and trap to Backworth to play at the Mass there. The Brannigan connection with St. John's is still maintained today by the present organist, Mrs Mary Rickard, sister of the late Owen.

In a short article such as this it is impossible to even outline the work and careers of the priests who served the parish; only a brief mention of some can be made here. Father Leo Jackson was parish priest here for 43 years, assisted in his latter years by Father Philip McBrien. Father Forster succeeded him from 1955 until 1962 when Father Marron came; he remained in the parish until 1981. In that year Father Austin Tomaney, the present parish priest, was appointed after spending the previous 20 years working with the Diocesan Rescue Society and as chaplain to the deaf - this latter work he is still involved with. For six years he was national chaplain to the deaf and for five years spiritual director of the S.V.P. National Council of England and Wales. He was, also, the first Catholic chaplain to be appointed to the Industrial Mission on Tyneside.

Since 1931, the S.V.P. has carried out its charitable work in the parish and this continues today with the conference of seven members. Surely unique in England is the fact that a street in Annitsford bears the name of Ozanam (mis-spelt, however, Ozanan), the French student, who founded the S.V.P. more than 150 years ago in Paris.

A small parish hall is the meeting place for the Ladies' Group, Keep Fit classes, Irish Dancing and a Mother and Toddler Group. For larger functions the church grounds - where the annual Garden Fete on July 7th of this year hopes to raise £2,000 approx - and the Benedictine Social Club are always available.

Greater involvement by parents and families in the preparation of the children for First Communion is encouraged by means of the *Brusselmanns* programme. Another recent innovation in the spiritual development of the parish is the Care Group of about 15 people who meet regularly together and attempt to renew their lives to serve the needs of the local church and community.

One task facing Father Tomaney and his parishioners is how to re-order the sanctuary to conform with the new liturgical rules and, at the same time, preserve the original design and furnishings with which all the people are familiar. Two stained-glass windows at the rear of the sanctuary - commemorating Robert and Richard Lamb - are, we think, from the first school-chapel and they are a useful reminder of the parish's origins.

Annitsford's St. John the Baptist's parish is still a scattered one comprising the villages of Seghill, Burradon, Fordley, Dudley and parts of Cramlington New Town. The road network which confounded the present writer - and showed his lack of navigational skills - is the means today whereby the church, priest and people are more closely united and Father Tomaney does not have to warm his hands under the horse's collar in mid-winter.

4. BARNARD CASTLE   St. Mary   *(February, March 1991)*

Along the upper reaches of the Tees from Darlington to Barnard Castle, and beyond, can be found evidence of our early Christian heritage continuing through the penal times - probably without an interruption - to the present day. It is said that as early as the ninth century, Egred, Bishop of Lindisfarne gave lands here - the Barony of Gainford - to his own church of St. Cuthbert.

Barnard Castle, as a place of some importance, can be dated to Norman times when William Rufus granted lands in Teesdale to Guy Baliol who had come to England with his father, the Conqueror. Guy's son, Barnard - hence the town's name - built the castle here between the years 1112 and 1132 and within its grounds there was a chapel (little of which remains today); probably the earliest place of worship. The Anglican church of St. Mary in the town centre is, also, of Norman origin and once contained chantries dedicated to the Blessed Trinity, Our Lady, St. Margaret and St. Catherine.

A later Barnard Baliol, son of the castle builder, confirmed the grant of the churches of Gainford, Barnard Castle and Middleton to St. Mary's Abbey, York, and allotted land in Teesdale to the monks of Rievaulx Abbey. Synonymous with the name Baliol is the college in Oxford; no mere coincidence as a writer in the *Northern Catholic Calendar* of 1881 explains: 'Baliol College was founded by the widow of John Baliol ... John himself had, previously, out of a love of learning and as a condition of sacramental absolution for a personal assault upon the Bishop of Durham (Kirkham) and a sacrilegious invasion of the church of Long Newton, halfway between Darlington and Stockton, founded certain scholarships, in number sixteen at Oxford. He is also reputed to have founded and endowed the Hospital of St. John the Baptist at Barnard Castle now the property of the University of Cambridge'. This hospital, once stood in Newgate.

Another Christian relic of the past - now demolished - was Bedekirk in Galgate said to have been a chapel or chantry, whilst in Thorngate tradition claims there was once an Austin Friars' foundation. More than a century ago the writer in the *Northern Catholic Calendar* suggested this site to be near a wall in which was a large stone bearing the inscription: *Soli Deo honor et gloria*.

West of Barnard Castle at Middleton-in-Teesdale is the fairly modern stone church of St. Aidan wherein every Sunday, Father Barker, the present parish priest of St. Mary's, celebrates Mass for the

Catholics of the dale and holiday makers. But the Faith was here, too, in very early days - possibly the 11th century - as the stone piscina (extant in 1881) and a 13th century window in the vicarage garden testify. So many reminders of the ancient Faith abound in this area such as the ruined 12th century Premonstratensian Abbey of the Blessed Virgin Mary and St. John the Baptist at Egglestone lamented by Sir Walter Scott as 'the reverend pile ... wild and waste, profaned, dishonoured and defaced by dark fanaticism'. Staindrop boasts of its ancient church of St. Mary too, described by Pevsner as 'one of the most interesting parish churches in the county,' and containing visible proof of an earlier Saxon foundation. Raby Castle, a dominant feature of the south west Durham landscape, houses a chapel of some note.

In spite of the risks of fines, imprisonment and sometimes execution some of the old Catholic families continued to harbour seminary priests trained abroad. Perhaps, the seclusion of the Tees Valley lessened the risks of non-conformity whilst not removing them entirely. Enshrined in the history of these parts, and resolute in their devotion to the Faith, were the Withams of Cliffe Hall, near Piercebridge, the Maires of Lartington, the Tunstalls of Wycliffe and the Warcops of Winston, near Whorlton.

The latter family were to suffer severely for their beliefs. A Mr. Thomas Warcop, during Elizabeth's reign, was arrested for hiding the priest, Alexander Rawlins, who after an earlier imprisonment had been ordained at Soissons in 1590. His arrest occurred in 1594 on Christmas Day when 'several pursuivants searched the house of Mr Thomas Warcop called Winston (Durham) and after a long search in vain, advertised by a woman, a neighbour, renewed their search and found Mr Alexander Rawlins, a priest in a secret place whom they carried prisoner to York with Mr Warcop and some others of the house.' The Blessed Alexander Rawlins suffered martyrdom at York in 1595. Thomas, however, managed to escape with his resolution unshaken for he was again arrested a second time for harbouring the Blessed William Anlaby; both were martyred for their faith at York on July 4th, 1597.

With the accession of James II in 1685 life for Catholics was eased and when the penal laws were suspended in 1688 Rome appointed four vicars-apostolic. Bishop James Smith, consecrated publicly at Somerset House in 1688, was assigned the Northern District. This brief respite for Catholics ended when the King fled abroad and the penal laws were once more enforced. Of the four bishops recently appointed, Bishop Smith alone escaped imprisonment retiring, we think, to the safer refuge of the Tunstall home at Wycliffe from where he continued 'ministering to his subdued and dwindling flock.' Weakened by an arduous tour of the East Riding the previous summer he died at Wycliffe on May 13th, 1711, 23 years to the day of his consecration as bishop; his body was laid to rest there.

Another recusant household, who played an important role in maintaining the Faith, were the Withams of Cliffe Hall. Originally a Lincolnshire family they appear on the northern scene when George Witham married Margaret, daughter and co-heiress of John Wawton of Cliffe, in the 15th century.

A much later George Witham had seven sons and two daughters. One of the daughters became a nun, and Christopher, the fourth son became a priest. George, the second son, was to become Vicar-Apostolic of the Northern District in 1716 residing at the family mansion where he died in 1725; he was buried at Manfield church and a memorial inscription can be seen in the family mortuary chapel at Lartington. The seventh son, Robert, was to honour further the family name by becoming president of Douay between the years 1715 and 1738.

In the papist returns of 1767 there were 37 Catholics listed within the Barnard Castle chapelry. T. Heyrick, the vicar of Gainford in his report makes a specific reference to 'Piercebridge which is but a stone's cast from Cliff (the mansion house of Mr Witham) who has a priest in his house and a chapel where Mass is regularly performed, and their votaries come several miles around to attend the Service'. It was from the chaplaincy at Cliffe Hall that Father Hogarth (later bishop) was to move to Darlington in 1824 to build the church of St. Augustine's above the door of which is the crest of the Witham family.

Three miles east of Barnard Castle is yet another former recusant stronghold - Sledwich Hall, once the home of the Clopton family who were known as 'receivers of priests' and were 'greatly troubled' with pursuivants. A hiding hole under part of the garden still exists today. A member of this family, Cuthbert Clopton, was ordained in 1636 and became Chaplain to the Venetian ambassador in London. He was captured and sentenced to death in 1641 along with the martyr William Webster; his life was spared, however, through the intervention of his master. From the records of the convent of St. Monica at Louvain where, at one time four Clopton daughters became nuns, comes an account (quoted by Dr. Howard) of a search at Sledwich. The pursuivants 'came on a sudden at the stairs foot, which went up to the chapel, where they had found all, but as God would, they chose another door to go in first, which had a leaden pulley so that it shut-to presently after them, and they could not possibly open it again unless they had the trick how to do it ... but they let them knock on, till all things were put safe, so they found nothing. They had an excellent place which was made all the length of a little garden underground and could have held a dozen priests. The going into it was by a device in the parlour, and it had another going forth beyond the said little garden where, if the secret place should be descried on the inside they might get forth on the outside, and make haste to step into great woods or copses.'

Another family strong in the Faith throughout the penal days were the Maires of Lartington Hall - situated a few miles west of Barnard Castle - who were related to the Maires of Hardwick Hall near Castle Eden. Here the Mass was said secretly in the family chapel by the Douay seminary priests, who acted as chaplains to the family and the neighbouring Catholics. We know the names of a considerable number of these priests; two are said to have each served the Lartington Mission for 50 years. The first was Lancelot Pickering who died in 1763; the second was the Rev. Michael Ellis who on his death in 1861 was, along with the Rev. George Caley of the Gainford Mission, buried in the Catholic cemetery at Barnard Castle purchased from the Duke of Cleveland; the generous vendor returned the purchase price of £100 to meet the expenses entailed in preparing the land as a place of burial.

The Maires, too, gave sons to the church. One of them, William Maire, was the year before his death consecrated Bishop of Cinna and coadjutor to Bishop Petre of the Northern District. His poor health, however, brought about his return to the family home; he died there and was interred in 1769 in Romaldkirk village church.

Barnard Castle, St. Mary — Photo: A. Barker

When Henry Silvertop married Eliza Witham, heiress to the Cliffe estate round about 1800, he assumed the name of Witham - not an uncommon occurrence amongst the gentry when the family name was likely to die out. They had eleven children. When their fourth son Thomas Edward became a priest (later Monsignor) it seemed unlikely that he would have much to do with the Lartington estates. It was, however, to be otherwise as his three older brothers predeceased him and he inherited his father's lands remaining as squire there until his death in 1897 at the age of 90; his grave is at the entrance to the Lartington estate cemetery.

Thomas Edward's munificence made possible the building of the church of St Osmund's at Gainford opened in 1852.

Standing in the main street of Barnard Castle is Witham Hall with its Grecian columns - a testimony to the family's concern for others which extended beyond their estate and village. Mr H. T. M. Witham (mentioned above) with other gentlemen of the district founded the Mechanics' Institute in 1832 in order 'to afford to the working classes of Barnard Castle access to a good library at an easy rate, and to give all members of the community an opportunity of improving themselves in those sciences more immediately connected with the different arts they respectfully practise.'

It was Henry Witham's wish that the Institute should have its own purpose-built accommodation but he died before seeing its realisation. Some members of the Institute decided to erect a memorial to him but having a utilitarian purpose, so Witham Hall was built. Within the building were a library, lecture room, a surgery and dispensary.

The present parish of St. Mary's, Barnard Castle, can be said to have been founded in 1847 with the appointment of the Rev. William Allen as the first resident priest who remained in charge here until 1856. During his incumbency the Union Hall in Ware Street (still standing today) was purchased through the generosity of a local flax-mill owner, Mr Owen Longstaff; this was the first post-Reformation chapel in Barnard Castle and was capable of accommodating a congregation of 300. A local artist, Mr Harvey (later curator of Bowes Museum) painted above the altar a fresco of the crucifixion similar to the much admired one in the Lartington chapel. Within the martyr's chapel of the present parish church of St. Mary's is an old altar from the Ware Street chapel - a reminder of those earlier days.

Mrs Verna Kelly, who was born in the town and taught in the parish school, remembers well in her childhood attending the chapel: 'I remember it as quite a large church with stained-glass windows at either end and leaded windows at the sides.' There were two Sunday Masses 'and in the afternoon there was a Sunday School for the children, and Benediction in the evening when we enjoyed singing.' She recalls the dismantling of the interior and the transfer of the altars. The second altar of carved oak may be the one in the Lady Chapel which was designed by Mr E. J. Hansom in memory of Father John Dunderdale who succeeded Father Meynell in 1860.

Owen Longstaff's benevolence did not end with the purchase of the Union Hall; he continued to give financial support for the maintenance of the priest here and in his mill set aside a room for a Catholic school. When later this accommodation was found to be inadequate he donated a piece of land and financed the building of a small Catholic school thereon. This is the old Gothic-style building still in use today across the playground from the modern primary school opened in the mid-1950s.

How the present church of St. Mary's in Barnard Castle came to be, is an interesting and unusual story. Few visitors to the town will be unaware of 'the sudden apparition of that big, bold incongruity, the Bowes Museum, looking exactly like the town hall of a major provincial town in France' (Pevsner). Whether or not one agrees with this description it is undoubtedly French in style and was designed by Jules Pellechet to house the art collection of John Bowes and his Catholic wife, the Countess de Montalbo, who lived not far away at Streatlam Castle.

When John's wife, the countess, died in 1874 - a few years after, the building of the museum began - he decided to build a memorial chapel within the grounds under the chancel of which was to be a crypt where he and his wife could be laid to rest. The museum was almost finished in 1885 when John died and the walls of the large church had risen to the eaves.

John in his will had appointed two boards of trustees: one to administer and maintain the museum and a second, similarly, for the church. He was generous in his financial provisions for both, but due to his financial affairs being confused it was not until 1905 that the legacies were handed over to the two responsible bodies.

The problem facing the Church Trustees of how to fulfil the wishes of the testator when the designated sum had depreciated was solved by accumulating the income for about twenty years until there was a sufficiency. This being achieved, negotiations began between the two boards of trustees and a new church site was agreed on the corner of Newgate and Birch Road; this was necessary as to complete the original church would have been too expensive and, in addition, access would have been difficult when the museum gates were closed.

A small railway was constructed to convey some of the stone from the original church to the new location. Work progressed steadily and Bishop Thorman was able to lay the foundation stone on October 30th, 1926.

Designed in the Gothic style by Dunn, Hansom and Fenwicke of Newcastle and built by Pringle & Co of Gateshead, with accommodation for a congregation of 300, the church was consecrated by Bishop Thorman on September 29th, 1928; the cost including the presbytery was about £25,000. Having no debt on the church the Bishop was able to consecrate it on its completion.

A reporter in the local paper went to some length describing the consecration ceremony which is rich in early Christian symbolism. He described how: 'The procession began from the presbytery close at hand and the Bishop and clergy preceded by cross bearer and acolytes perambulated the exterior of the Church three times, the Bishop each time the door was reached tapping it, and at the third arrival entering. Within the Church the ceremony occupied nearly an hour ... Then followed a procession which included the bier on which the relics of the martyrs or saints were borne by two priests. This went right round the Church and entered by the front door, the arrival of the procession at the altar being the signal for the admittance of the laity ... The founders of the Church were well remembered for on their tomb ... two wreaths of evergreens from the Trustees of the Bowes Museum were reverently laid.'

The church was officially opened on Thursday, October 4th, when the Bishop celebrated High Mass. Shortly after the completion of the church the remains of John Bowes and his wife were transferred from the mausoleum of the Bowes-Lyon family at Gibside Chapel, near Rowlands Gill, and interred outside the sanctuary wall; few visitors to Bowes Museum are perhaps aware that the founder of the church and museum lies buried so near his creation.

So Barnard Castle's Catholic Church is possibly unique in our diocese as its maintenance is regulated under the terms of the John Bowes' will by the trustees (five to twelve in number) who must be professed Catholic laymen. Here the Witham influence is also manifest in that the Monsignor assisted John Bowes in drawing up the Church Trustees' regulations.

Many other people, of course, have played their part in the development of the parish; other benefactors about the time of Mr Owen Longstaff were Miss Martha Lamb and Mr John Swales. People's roots run deep here and their memories could have furnished us with much more information. One of them, Mr Dominic Rutter, a church trustee - who so kindly gave of his time, knowledge and expertise when the *Northern Cross* team visited the parish last summer - told us that his grandfather, Mr William Horner Scarre, was land agent to Mgr. Witham for over 20 years and before the opening of the Ware Street chapel walked regularly from Stainton on a Sunday to Holy Mass at Lartington Chapel. Although the Hall passed out of Catholic hands in 1917 the Gothic-style chapel of the 18th century remains with its decorated ceilings and stained-glass windows protected by netting of what is now a squash court.

We have not at hand a list of all the priests who ministered so faithfully over the years in St. Mary's parish. Mrs Verna Kelly remembers in her youth Father Bernard Darley, 'a saintly caring man who enjoyed a game of golf and was a skilled figure skater' - a skill, no doubt, acquired at Ushaw College. A considerable number of parishioners, today, will remember Father Ernest Plowman, who during a ministry of more than 30 years here, built the modern primary school and the chapel at Middleton, to serve the spiritual needs of the large number of Irish workers who were building the reservoirs in the area at that time.

When Father Plowman retired in 1980 he was succeeded by Mgr. Kevin Nichols who had spent some years with the Catholic Education Council in London. When Mgr. Nichols moved to Darlington in 1986 he was replaced by the present parish priest, Fr. Anthony Barker.

Although numerically small in terms of parishioners - the Sunday Mass attendance averages 150 - this rural parish has extensive boundaries. Earlier places of Catholic interest, mentioned previously, such as Cliffe Hall, Lartington and Wycliffe are now in the Middlesbrough Diocese. Nevertheless, this still leaves a considerable district with a scattered congregation for Father Barker to serve. He is assisted by a goodly number of parishioners who frequently visit the old, sick and housebound with Holy Communion.

Not having a parish hall makes it more difficult to organise social events; they do occur, however. Fairs and barbecues - sometimes in co-operation with the school - give the opportunity for parishioners to socialize and, also, help to raise much needed funds.

St Mary's are wholeheartedly involved in the local inter-denominational Christian Council. 'This is a very active body.' states Father Barker, 'devoted to bringing Christ to all people.' Its concerns include counselling the bereaved and offering support to various charities such as Catholic Care North East.

The main pre-occupation of Father Barker, the parishioners and the church trustees at the moment, is the re-ordering of the sanctuary (on a permanent basis) to meet the requirements of the liturgical reforms. During September and October enthusiastic volunteers in the parish have re-decorated the church. Much discussion and consultation has taken place regarding the re-ordering and it is hoped that in the not too distant future work will begin.

Perhaps the dominant thread in this story of Catholicism along the banks of the Tees, from Darlington to Lartington, has been the influence of the Witham family, but there are many nameless ones, of yesterday and today, who have made and continue to make the light of Faith shine here.

5. BELLINGHAM & OTTERBURN   St. Oswald   *(October, November 1989)*

As reported in the August edition of the *Northern Cross* St. Oswald's at Bellingham celebrated on June 26th, 1989, the 150th anniversary of the church's opening. To commemorate this great occasion Father J. Costello, parish priest, and 19 priests concelebrated a Thanksgiving Mass before an overflow congregation. To surmise, however, that the Faith has only a century and a half of existence here would be wrong; the Christian Faith was brought here, we believe, in the 6th century by our Celtic and Anglo-Saxon forebears. The Catholic parish of Bellingham encompasses a wide, unspoiled rural area stretching to the Scottish Borders and is probably one of the largest parishes geographically in our diocese. Within its extensive boundaries there is much to see and explore and much evidence of the early days of Christianity, a few references only of which we can record here.

Perhaps, the earliest piece of evidence unearthed so far is to be found in the 13th century St. Mungo's (Kentigern) church at Simonburn which contains fragments of Anglo-Saxon stonework; the most interesting is the shaft of a stone cross of the 8th or 9th century said to be the work of the Tyne Valley School of Italian workmen brought to Hexham by St. Wilfrid round about 690 A.D.

Holy wells abound in this northern region and not far from the Simonburn church is St. Mungo's Well where the saint is supposed to have baptised some early Northumbrian converts in the 6th century. Behind the Anglican parish church at Bellingham can be seen St. Cuthbert's Well now covered by a stone capping but still issuing water. Here our diocesan patron more than likely baptised his early converts. The church of St. Cuthbert, built in 1180 A.D., has the unusual feature of a stone roof necessary in an area where border warfare was not infrequent.

One of the earliest references to Bellingham church and well is an account of a miracle recorded by Reginald of Durham (c.1140). Apparently a young girl, named Edda Brown, whose hand had contracted after sewing a dress was cured when she drank from the well and recited nine *Paters* at Mass after the reading of the Gospel.

On the way to Kielder Forest is Falstone, a small village, where there is evidence of a chapel here in 1541 and some years ago a Runic cross was found at Falstone with an Anglo-Saxon inscription. Beyond this village on Plashett's Moor there once stood a cross which it has been conjectured, though never proved conclusively, was a Papist's cross; the stone socket is still extant and in 1983 was in the care of the Forestry Commission who hoped to return it complete with wooden cross to the original position.

During the days of persecution following Henry's break with Rome the Catholic Faith was often kept alive secretly by the landed gentry who provided, within their homes, a chapel and a priest to minister to neighbouring Catholics. Synonymous with Bellingham is the Charlton family of Hesleyside Hall who have inhabited this area since the twelfth century; the first recorded one was Edward Charlton c.1341. A later Edward Charlton joined other northern leaders in the Pilgrimage of Grace in 1536 in an attempt to arrest the changes of the Reformation. One remarkable fact of this period is that the rector of Simonburn, Nicholas Harborn, remained in charge here throughout the religious changes of Henry, Edward VI, Mary and Elizabeth.

Many of these ancient Catholic families can claim a relationship with one of the English martyrs and the Charltons are no exception. The present owners of Hesleyside are closely related to the Anne family of Yorkshire; in fact Major Charlton had, before his marriage, the surname Anne. The relationship claimed is to John Anne of Wakefield who on the death of his wife divided his wealth among his children and, although elderly, decided to study for the priesthood. He was ordained at Rheims in 1581 and served as a priest in the Lancashire area until his arrest in 1588 and subsequent martyrdom at York the following year. A later descendant of the martyr, Elizabeth Anne of Frickley, established a fund in 1750 for the education of two Douay students; this benefaction was later transferred to Ushaw College.

Vocations to the priesthood and religious life over the years have not been wanting in these old Catholic families. Gilbert Talbot, the son of John Talbot, an Irish gentleman, and Christian Charlton, was ordained in Rome in 1711. On the death of his brother John, in 1734, he inherited an estate at Cartington and served for a time on the Thropton Mission. Today this vocations' tradition is maintained by Father Oswald Charlton who is serving in the south of England and Father Miles Belassis O.S.B. of Ampleforth now living at St. Louis Priory, Missouri.

Records and details of the lives of our Catholic ancestors are not always easy to discover. What we do know is that in this part of Northumberland - perhaps because of its remoteness from central authority - the Faith was kept alive through the benevolence of such families as the Swinburnes, Radcliffes, Erringtons, Hodgsons and Charltons. Hesleyside seems to have been supplied for many years by priests of the Benedictine order, possibly because their children were educated by them in their continental schools. During alterations in 1713 at the Hall a hiding hole was found in a chimney breast which may date back to 1631. The present chapel (circa 1850) has replaced an older one built probably around 1760. The names of the earliest chaplains are not known; the first recorded one being that of the Rev. John Donohough in 1741. William Bede Hutton O.S.B., who served here for nine years until 1756, was the first recorded Benedictine and he, with his successor Father Turner, lies buried in the old churchyard of Bellingham. One Benedictine chaplain's name, Father Thomas Anselm Bolus, is perpetuated in a wood named after him on the Hesleyside Estate - Bolus Wood.

Too long to list here are the names of the many priests who served Bellingham and the surrounding area so faithfully over the centuries. When no priest was resident at the Charlton's home tradition says one could always be found at Tone Hall.

As a separate mission, distinct from Hesleyside, Bellingham can be said to have had its beginning in 1793 when 'at last after two hundred years or more a priest again took up his residence in Bellingham and officiated for the little household of the faith... in a loft or upper chamber formed out of two or three dwelling houses.' The old presbytery still stands in Bellingham today. The financial security of the mission was guaranteed through the generosity of William Charlton of Hesleyside and Edward Charlton of Sandhoe. The first parish priest was John Dunstan Sharrock O.S.B., who was followed a few months later by Father J.A. Pope, O.S.B., who began the parish register signing himself, 'Mr Pope, Bellingham'.

For some unknown reason the small chapel at Bellingham was not considered suitable so after 1808 the centre of Catholic life reverted to Hesleyside Hall until 1839 when the present church was built during the incumbency of Father Nicholas Brown, a secular priest. The land for the church and presbytery was donated by William John Charlton. Built in the Early English style and designed by Ignatius Bonomi, the church, capable of seating 125 people, was officially opened and blessed by Bishop Briggs on June 26th, 1839 and was of adequate size for a congregation then estimated to be about 100. Above the church entrance is the coat of arms of Pope Gregory XVI during whose pontificate the church was built. Various members of the Charlton family made donations towards the cost of £1,250 and Father Brown raised £300 by public subscription.

It has always been the aim of the Church to provide a school as well as a church for its people. Often when a parish is started, a building is erected to meet this dual purpose. Bellingham Catholic school was built separately behind the church and opened in 1849; the cost was met by William John's son, Francis Charlton. It served well the educational needs of the parish for about 100 years closing 40 years ago; it now operates as a parish centre and a play group centre.

Father Costello, like his predecessor, serves a widely scattered flock of about 310 souls. To make it easier for some to attend church a Mass Centre was started at Otterburn in 1934; a permanent chapel was formally opened and blessed there by Bishop McCormack on June 4th, 1953. Before the erection of the present chapel parishioners in this rather remote area co-operated to the full in assisting each other to attend Mass.

Michael Spencer and his wife of Monkridge Farm bought an 'especially large car' to carry other Catholics to church in Bellingham. On December 2nd, 1934, the Rev. Dr. J. Murphy celebrated the first Mass at the Spencer home and after this for a few months in a granary in Townend. By 1935 it was possible to attend Mass in another granary belonging to Mr. and Mrs Denis Towers in Otterburn which, through their kindness, continued to be used until the present chapel was built. The Rev. Doctor Delaney, who was responsible for the building of the Otterburn chapel describes a scene in the granary, almost akin to Bethlehem: 'The byre was below and confessions were heard in the implement room which generally had a number of calves penned up'.

Many priests, over many years, have served the Bellingham congregation, the longest serving of which was Father John George Flint who was here for 42 years from 1858 to 1900. Father James Costello continues this long succession of pastors who have worked with the people keeping the Faith alive here through quiet and turbulent days. Since his arrival in 1978 he has witnessed some milestones in the parish's history; he was responsible for the re-ordering of St.Oswald's in 1981, the new altar being consecrated by Bishop Lindsay in 1982; the re-ordering of and consecration of the Otterburn chapel in 1980; and more recently the 150th anniversary celebration of the Bellingham church.

At the latter celebrations the Huddleston chalice (dated 1620) was used during the Mass; this relic of the penal days came into the possession of the Charlton family when Edward Charlton married Margaret Salkeld of Whitehall, Cumbria where Dom. Richard Huddleston had been a resident chaplain. There may be a relationship with Father John Huddleston O.S.B, who saved Charles II at Worcester and secretly received him into the church on his deathbed.

Organising the spiritual and social life of an extensive rural parish has difficulties not always met within a more compact, urban one. However, Father Costello and his people work closely together in the spreading of the Gospel and the development of a community spirit.

With the help and co-operation of parents, children are instructed and prepared for the reception of the sacraments; six Lay Ministers of the Eucharist distribute Holy Communion at Mass and take the sacrament to the sick and housebound when necessary; choirs, including cantors, sing at both churches and are much appreciated by all; a Bible Study group meets fortnightly in the presbytery; and the parish co-operates wholeheartedly in appeals for those in need such as Family Fast Days etc.

The various social activities undertaken help to create a community spirit by bringing the people together informally. A Summer Barbecue is held annually in the church grounds in June; Christmas Fairs in

Bellingham and Otterburn create extra funding for the parish; and Whist Drives are always very popular social gatherings.

Bellingham with Hesleyside can be grateful for its long and faithful adherence to the Faith over many centuries - a sentiment expressed by Father Costello in the preface to the parish history where he writes: 'In the present we thank God for the past and all those good people and priests who handed on the Faith. Our Jubilee, therefore, must be a time of resolve and renewal of life in order that we may become more worthy instruments of God for the welfare of future generations.'

6. BERWICK   Our Lady and St. Cuthbert   *(December 1993, January 1994)*

In the introduction to the parish history, written by J.M. Rowley, Father Michael Melia, parish priest of Berwick, comments on the strong bond of loyalty of people of all classes to the Church and its beliefs: 'But the most important actors in this story are ordinary Catholics who kept their faith through very hard times and who passed that faith on to their children.'

This, then, is a brief account highlighting those events in the history of the most northerly parish of our diocese - events which began more than a thousand years ago.

Being about 10 miles north of Holy Island it was inevitable that the early influence of monastic faith and culture should spread from there. When King Oswald invited Aidan from Iona in 635 A.D. to become Bishop of Lindisfarne he appears to have granted him additional land to the west of Berwick which came to be called Norhamshire. Bishop Egred is believed to have built a Saxon church at Norham in 830 A.D. in which the bodies of St. Ceolwulph and St. Oswald were interred; a stone church (still standing but much altered) was constructed near the original one, in Norman times, and is dedicated to St. Peter, St. Cuthbert and St. Ceolwulph.

Norhamshire, bordering Scotland to the north and Northumberland to the south, was a peculiar entity in that it belonged to neither, but was part of the County Palatine of Durham which after the Conquest came to be ruled by the Bishop of Durham who not only held spiritual sway here, but also a temporal one on behalf of the King.

The Border was a contentious one for many years, being ill-defined and in Bishop Pudsey's time a stone castle was erected at Norham and a bishop's palace which would have contained at least one chapel. On Norham's village green stands a stone cross said to be of the medieval period.

Berwick, Our Lady & St. Cuthbert; Lady Hubert Jerningham, an early benefactress of the church   Photo: E. Croghan

83

Little remains in and around Berwick of our early Christian past. As Tomlinson remarks: 'Not a trace remains of the four convents belonging to the Red, the Black, the Grey and the White Friars nor of the three ancient hospitals and churches of Saint Nicholas, Saint Lawrence, and Saint Mary. The site of the Hospital of St. Mary is preserved by the name - Magdalen Fields.' At Spittal (from the word hospital) there was, we are told, a leper hospital named after St. Bartholomew; while at Tweedmouth, tradition claims, is St. Cuthbert's Well where the saint baptised a number of pagans.

South of Berwick lies Ancroft where, sometime before 1145, the monks of Holy Island built the church; a little further on to the East is Cheswick beach where the stone was quarried for the building of Lindisfarne Priory.

Within Ancroft churchyard is a reminder of our not too distant past where a gravestone carries the following inscription: 'To the memory of Mary Catherine Smith, deceased the 20th Jan. 1799... superior of the religious community who by the bounty of Sir Carnaby Haggerston Bart, were received and lodged at his castle during 12 years after the French Revolution'. The stone, also, records the names of nine other nuns buried there. These were the Poor Clare sisters who had to leave their convent in Rouen seeking a temporary refuge in Northumberland; their successors continue the contemplative vocation today at Clare Abbey in Darlington.

One could mention other places in this area of Northumberland with strong Christian associations; the name, Haggerston, is however, a suitable link with the pre-Reformation and post-Reformation past. One of the earliest references to Haggerston is the recorded visit of Edward II, in 1311, when it existed as a manor house. Nothing remains of the castle of the penal days wherein the Faith was sustained and strengthened by the family and the chaplains who offered spiritual solace to those Catholics who continued to practise their Faith.

The remaining tower is a remnant of the re-building of an earlier dwelling of the 1770s, executed by Norman Shaw between 1893 and 1897. The private family chapel dedicated to Our Lady and St. Cuthbert was attached to the house. What is of considerable Catholic interest is the late 18th century priest's house (now privately owned) 200 yards north of the castle site.

Although we cannot be certain, it is at least probable, that one or more of our northern martyrs sought refuge and celebrated the sacraments here. Evidence for the tenacity with which this family clung to their faith is given in a list of Northumberland Recusants for 1597: 'Henrie Haggerston of Haggerston esquier. Imprisoned at Berwicke in Januarie last and standeth indycted.'

Sometime before this the Gateshead martyr, John Ingram, 'upon some urgent occasion had been in England, and returning back again and entered into a boat to pass over the river of Tweed into Scotland (25 November, 1593) was stayed by the keepers of Norham Castle, apprehended, and carried to Berwick, there being kept under the safe custody of Mr John Carew, governor of the town, and used very courteously...'

During his imprisonment in Newcastle he was said to have been visited by the wife of one of his captors in Berwick; he thanked her 'for having made his stay there more comfortable than his subsequent incarcerations.' Tried at Durham, along with John Boste (who may also have done missionary work in this part of Northumberland), he was executed at Gateshead on July 26th, 1594.

In spite of the fear and risk of imprisonment and possibly death for harbouring a priest, certain Catholic gentry persisted in offering a home to these priests without whose ministrations the faith of the household, tenants and neighbours would have weakened and probably died. From the evidence available the Haggerstons were one of these families.

A Catholic education was important to them in the preservation of their Faith, but penal legislation forbade this so they resorted to sending their children to the schools on the continent - but even this was an offence!

Serving as a typical example of steadfastness in the Faith was Sir Thomas Haggerston (died c.1710) who reputedly had nine sons, three of whom became priests: Henry and John were Jesuits and Francis, a Franciscan. Sir Carnaby Haggerston had as his chaplain a Jesuit priest, Father John Thornton, for probably 40 years.

William, a brother of the priests mentioned above, came to live in Berwick with Anne, his wife, in the early years of the 18th century. Here, no doubt, Mass would be celebrated regularly for those who had persevered in their beliefs. Two years after her husband's death in 1708 she moved to Haggerston Castle leaving there, about 1720, to live at her Gateshead residence, eventually settling at Pontoise until 1735 where two of her daughters were nuns; she died and was buried at St. Omer in 1740.

In her will she left money to the Jesuits 'with the obligation of serving Berwick unless otherwise apply'd in urgent necessity' For 40 years the chaplains at Berrington and Haggerston attempted to carry out her wishes saying Mass either in the Haggerston house or some other Catholic household.

Berwick, also, provided priests from its own small congregation during the penal days. Robert Walker, a native, was educated at York and Carlisle being ordained in Rome in 1601.

An interesting character is Francis Walsingham, related to one of Elizabeth's secretaries who, although not a Catholic at the time, was baptised here in 1576. He studied at All Souls, Oxford, but began to have doubts about his position in the Church of England. His meeting with Edward Tempest, a priest under sentence of death, seems to have strengthened his resolve to become a Catholic. He was reconciled to the church and ordained priest in 1608 and appears to have spent part of his priestly life in the Derbyshire area. Later we hear of another Berwick son, Henry Smith, who was born in 1699, educated at Valladolid and following a Jesuit vocation.

France, which had once been a haven for persecuted English Catholics, was no longer so after the French Revolution. England became what France had been - a place where those persecuted for their religion could seek refuge and freedom for their beliefs. English students, priests and nuns returned to their homeland for safety and with them came 5,000 French priests over 100 of whom were received hospitably by the people of Berwick.

About this time a Father Tidyman - a secular priest and Newcastle born - had been appointed to Haggerston to replace 'Mr Hanne borne down by infirmities and years (is) charged with a large diffused congregation which he cannot possibly serve'.

His task was no less easy but he had the advantage of being younger. By November 1799 he had acquired a property off Church Street as a place of worship (partly paid for by the Haggerston family) - the first Catholic chapel in Berwick since the Reformation. He served the Catholics here for four years, but with such an extensive mission he looked around for a resident priest to share the responsibility. The advent of the French emigre clergy eased the problem for a number of years. Two priests, M. Bigot and Philip Besnier, assisted where they could from 1797 until 1810. Of the latter he appears to have shared the poverty of some of his flock remarking in 1810: 'The people are so poor they are more fit to receive than to give' and on another occasion he comments on the extent of his work: 'during the last 12 months I have walked no less than a 1,000 miles'. Father Tidyman wrote of him: 'His purse is emptied, his clothes are worn out, shoes are very dear etc. And yet he will not take a shilling as a consideration for his necessary expenses.' A year after Fr. Besnier's death the Catholics of Berwick were requesting a resident priest saying: 'When we get back from Haggerston (a 6 mile journey) we are so tired we fall asleep and cannot eat our dinners.'

In the early years of the 19th century the Catholic population was rising. A petition sent in 1811 to the Vicar-Apostolic requesting a permanent priest was 'signed by 136 Catholics and their children of Berwick-upon-Tweed and its vicinity (besides which they say there were Catholic Officers, about 40 privates, and the wives and children of several of the Aberdeenshire militia).' Fr. William Pepper, a Scottish Benedictine, seems to have taken up residence here in 1816 but could not have been a young man when he wrote: 'my memory and faculties much failing and living like a hermit.'

On his death in 1824 he was succeeded by Father William Birdsall from the Ellingham Mission where he had ministered over an area of 400 square miles. He was able to obtain land in Ravensdowne, building and opening the present church of Our Lady and St. Cuthbert (named after the Haggerston chapel) in 1829. Again the Haggerston family's generosity, through the goodness of Lady Mary Stanley, a daughter of Sir Carnaby, provided much of the money needed for the foundation. It must have been with a great sense of achievement and pride that the Berwick congregation, including a number of Protestant friends, on June 25th, 1829, joined Fr. Birdsall and other clergy in celebrating a Solemn High Mass during which the sermon was preached by Fr. Gillow of North Shields.

The growth of the Catholic community in Berwick appears to have been a steady one throughout the 19th century. Father Besnier, in 1810, estimated his congregation at around 110, but by 1851 it was reckoned to be nearer 600; this increase was partly due to the arrival of Irish people seeking employment here.

In the centenary year the Catholic population was about 900. The estimated parish population today is reckoned to be 1,000.

The Church has always valued highly the importance of a Catholic school for deepening and developing the Faith of its young people. Some time after the vacation of the first Berwick chapel it came into use as the parish school and served its purpose until the erection of St. Cuthbert's School in Walkergate in 1884. This served the needs of the children until 1935 when the present school was opened in Tweedmouth. This First School and Nursery has 133 on its roll under the care of the headteacher, Mr J. Smith.

Provision for girls' secondary education was made possible in 1889 with the arrival of the Ursuline sisters from Edinburgh who established their first convent and school in Tweed Street for day-pupils and boarders. For 60 years they remained here until their move to Longridge Towers - the former residence of Sir Hubert and Lady Jerningham - in 1949 where they remained serving the community well, until 1983, when a shortage of vocations and rising costs led to their departure. The Ursulines, also, taught in St. Cuthbert's School and assisted in the parish.

Berwick was not long without the presence of sisters, for a year later four Sisters of Mercy opened their convent at 72, Ravensdowne, from where two pursued their vocation as nurses in Berwick Infirmary. Today three sisters: Sister Christopher, Sister Hilda and Sister Mary Lourdes are much involved in parish life. They are frequent visitors around the parish taking communion to the housebound and giving instructions in the Faith; their convent is ever open for those seeking counselling or just a chat; they invite others to join them for Exposition in the chapel every Thursday and their weekly Rosary Group meeting; and here every fortnight the Padre Pio Prayer Group of eight members meets. A parishioner, Mr Basil Coxon, has done much to promote the latter devotion.

Much could be written about the grey stone church of Our Lady and St. Cuthbert, now more than 160 years old, approached through an archway in Ravensdowne.

On entering the church and looking down the aisle one's eye is immediately drawn to the three-sided wall of the sanctuary where three beautiful stained-glass windows (floodlit at night), each with three lights, contain pictures of saints each with a commemoration underneath. The central window portrays Our Lady, the Sacred Heart and the patron St. Cuthbert. The commemorative windows remind the viewer mainly of the role played by the Jerningham and Liddell-Grainger families who, over many years, were generous benefactors to the church, school and parish. A tastefully re-ordered marble altar and lectern sit nicely with the sanctuary background of coloured light. At the front of the nave the work of the Ursuline sisters is remembered on a brass plaque affixed to the wall: 'With affection and gratitude the parishioners erected this plaque to the memory of the Ursulines of Jesus who taught in the parish 1889-1983.'

Around the walls are oil-painted Stations of the Cross donated in 1910 in memory of Henry Liddell-Grainger. To the right of the nave is the chapel of the Sacred Heart of 1925 paid for by the same family in memory of Alice Paton; a crucifix on the wall once graced the chapel at Longridge Towers. Placed on the ceiling of the nave is a picture of 'Christ's Agony in the Garden' presented to the church in 1852 by James Grieve of Ord House who, it is claimed, received it as a gift from King Charles X of France and Navarre.

In an area where the Catholic Faith has been sustained for hundreds of years, in spite of many hardships, it is not surprising that Father Melia and his parishioners are proud of their rich heritage. This is a cause for celebration but, also, a stimulus to pass on this inheritance to their contemporaries and future generations. The parish priest, the school, the Sisters of Mercy, committed families and individuals are endeavouring to achieve this objective.

By means of the liturgy - the most important aspect of parish life - many opportunities are provided for lay participation through the Liturgy Group, Welcomers, five Lay Eucharistic Ministers and parents who assist at the Children's Liturgy during Sunday Mass.

No parish can function effectively without financial and maintenance provision. Father Melia is assisted in these tasks by a Finance Committee and a Fabric Committee which raises funds for the upkeep of church and presbytery. The St. Vincent de Paul Conference - although a small group - is dedicated to regular visitation and assistance to those in need.

Our Lady and St. Cuthbert's parish - in spite of its remoteness - seems to be a place where its priests have enjoyed a long and fruitful service here; there have been only four incumbents since 1884. Father Melia spent ten years here as a curate before he moved to Esh Winning for a further ten years. He returned here in 1976 as parish priest - so, altogether, he has spent 27 happy years in Berwick.

In 1979 Berwick Catholic Church celebrated its 150th Anniversary. Bishop Hugh Lindsay was the chief celebrant at the Mass and the homily was preached by Father Osmund Curry, Father Melia's predecessor. Among the congregation were members of Berwick Borough Council, a Jesuit priest, Mr Alan Beith, M.P. and ministers of other denominations. A far cry and a pleasing contrast to the harsh penal days of old. A year that our most northerly parish can be justly proud of and continues to be so.

POSTSCRIPT

In September, 1997, Father Michael Melia left Berwick for St. Osmund's, Gainford.
Father Francis McCullagh came to Berwick from St. Patrick's, Stockton.

7. BIDDLESTONE *(September, 1983)*

'A well-kept private road, about two miles in length, leads from the village (Netherton) to Biddlestone Hall, the stately mansion of the Selbys, which is built on the top of a gradual slope, and commands a fine prospect of the vale of Coquet and the hills beyond. Behind it rise the stern, dark hills of Harden and Silverton, separated from the house by a deep wooded dell, through which a moorland stream tumbles in a succession of pretty falls. Flourishing groves of oak and pine add to the picturesque surroundings of the place' - so runs a description, written almost 100 years ago, of one of the most northerly Catholic outposts of our diocese.

With the help of Fr. Thomas Sheehan of Thropton and the Netherton village post office we eventually arrived at the place described above. Much of the way from Netherton Village is no longer private; overhanging pine branches have narrowed what remains of a gravelled drive which wends its way for the last few hundred yards before the chapel comes into view; the mansion has been pulled down and it is difficult to discern amongst the long grass where the foundations are and still more difficult to imagine what the gardens must have looked like in their prime.

It would appear that Biddlestone Hall and the surrounding lands had been in the hands of the Selby family for over 600 years since the time of Edward I when he granted the lands to Sir Walter de Selby. In those turbulent days when the border between England and Scotland was ill-defined the inhabitants found it necessary to build strong fortified towers for protection against the marauding Scots. A later Sir Walter was killed in 1346 at Liddel Castle along with his garrison after holding out for six days against Robert Bruce and a 40,000 strong army.

It was probably, then, as a fortified tower residence that Biddlestone Hall first came into existence. Later, in the more settled times of the late 18th century, it was rebuilt with certain earlier Tudor and Jacobean features incorporated. What is of interest to Catholics is that the first floor of the tower house was converted into a chapel in the mid-19th century for the use of the Selby family and local Catholics; the existing building measures 42 feet by 32 feet and when further alterations were made in 1879 a secret passage was discovered in the six-foot-thick walls - could this have been a hiding hole from penal days?

Access to the chapel is restricted to those few occasions (about four times a year) when Mass is

Biddlestone Hall chapel   Photo: T. Mackin

celebrated there. Fr. Sheehan of Thropton was to celebrate an evening Mass there on August 10th, two days after we visited it when an attendance of 40 people from the parish of Thropton was expected. To reach the chapel one has to climb an inner stone stairway and on entering one notices the windows - incorporating some stained-glass memorials to the Selby family - are positioned behind the altar and in the right hand wall; there are no windows at the rear or the left-hand side. Above the entrance is the gallery which, if like Croxdale, would be used by the family who could come directly into the chapel from the house through a now blocked-up doorway.

Many priests must have served Biddlestone and the neighbouring Catholics over those 600 years of Selby occupation. Few of them we know. However, the first recorded name we have of a chaplain there appears in a brief entry of the Alwinton parish register: '6th July, 1725, Mr Thomas Durham, alias Collingwood, priest, Biddlestone, buried.'

Bishop Chandler reporting in 1736 notes: '28 papists meet at Biddlestone, a mile from the church at Mr Selby's. Robert Widdrington, priest.'

A Jesuit presence was also known in this place being part of the much larger northern area of England covered by the Jesuit mission of St. John's. Father William Newton reporting to his superiors in 1750 states briefly in veiled language: 'Customers here between 50 and 60, salary £10 and diet'. Customers, of course, refers to parishioners, but as some of the penal laws were still in operation and as such reports could get into the wrong hands it was considered necessary to couch such facts in business terms.

One other chaplain can be mentioned here: he was Dom. John Anselm Bolton, O.S.B., who was at

Biddlestone in 1764. Later he moved to Gilling Castle as chaplain to Lady Anne Fairfax. Not far from her home she had built Ampleforth Lodge as a residence for him. It was to this house that the English Benedictine community of monks, hounded out of Dieulouard by French revolutionaries, came in 1802 and from which developed the now famous abbey.

The last parish priest of Biddlestone was Father Francis Hutchinson who resided in the presbytery some distance from the Hall and left there to go to Wolsingham in 1944. After this it was served and continues to be served from Thropton.

Part of an obituary notice concerning Walter Selby Esq., who was buried at Alwinton on September 9th, 1868, helps to illustrate the strong Faith of these ancient Catholic families of Northumberland and their determination to preserve it: 'Like many of the old families in the North, he adhered to the Roman Catholic Church - the traditional Faith of his forefathers - but he was truly Catholic in all his sympathies and nobly supported the character of an English country gentleman. In him his family lost their best friend, his tenantry a kind and considerate landlord, and the poor the ever-ready hand of charity.'

Further confirmation of the Selby family's strong adherence to the Faith comes from the *Northern Catholic Calendar* of 1884: 'It is as far as is known the oldest mission in the Diocese, dating at least as far back as the 13th century - three hundred years before the fatal reformation. There has been no 'reformation' here, no change of creed, no interruption of the perpetual sacrifice. The family has kept the Faith as well as its name and estates through ages of persecution. It was Catholic in the 13th century - it is Catholic in the 19th.'

8. BILLINGHAM   St John The Evangelist and Holy Rosary   *(October, 1985)*

This year two parishes in Billingham celebrated - within three months of each other- the silver jubilees of the opening of their churches: St. John's on June 7th and Holy Rosary on September 22nd.

Billingham might appear to a stranger as a new town without a history and as a place where the Faith is of recent origin. Neither observation would be correct for Billingham has developed around a former Anglo-Saxon village which more than a 1000 years ago included the ancient church of St. Cuthbert. Fragments of Saxon cross-shafts in the present Anglican church suggest a Christian presence here, possibly as early as the 8th century.

From Norman times until the Reformation much of the land in the Billingham area was owned by the monks of Durham whose prior held a manor at Beaulieu, the site of which is in the middle of the Low Grange Housing Estate now part of the third parish in Billingham - St. Joseph's. Beaulieu, it is believed, was also a place of convalescence for sick monks needing rest and relaxation. At nearby Wolviston we know that a chapel was erected and named after St. Mary Magdalene in the late 12th century.

The religious changes which occurred during the Reformation era do not appear to have been acceptable to many of the inhabitants of the area. In the North a rising led by the Earls of Northumberland and Westmorland in 1569, to restore the ancient practices of the Faith, was joined by 22 men from Billingham, 10 from Cowpen, 19 from Wolviston and 10 from Bewley. After its failure retribution was swift and harsh; five men from Billingham were executed; two from Cowpen; four from Wolviston and three from Bewley. Thomas Watson, a Billingham yeoman, who was questioned after the event claimed he knew of a priest called Hartborn who had said an illegal Mass at Long Newton and Sedgefield and had re-erected some altars for the Sacrifice of the Mass. He is recorded as saying that the Billingham altar stone was hidden in the church choir and one red cope was still there.

Today, thank God, Christians - through the ecumenical movement - work peacefully and with brotherly love to further the cause of Christian Unity.

From the late 16th century until the relaxation of the penal laws in the late 18th century little is known about the activities of Catholics in the area. The re-birth of Catholicism in this corner of the diocese can be traced to the Haverton Hill and Port Clarence districts where in the latter half of the 19th century the railways, iron-works and coal-shipping staithes encouraged migration from the rural areas and from Ireland.

A Catholic nucleus was sufficiently well established to warrant Father Michael Bourke in 1879 providing a school-chapel for his expanding congregation in Port Clarence. Through the generosity of his people he was able by 1900 to have his Pugin-designed church, dedicated to St. Thomas of Canterbury, opened and blessed by Bishop Preston - the mother church of the present Billingham parishes. Alas since 1978 due to redevelopment and the consequent movement of population, parish and church no longer exist although the priests of Holy Rosary regularly celebrate Mass in the Community Centre for the few remaining Catholics - the mother church is now supported by her children.

Billingham, in the twentieth century, has always been associated with the chemical works of I.C.I. and there is no denying the part they have played in the growth of the town. In 1821 it has been estimated that Billingham and its neighbouring villages contained 1,154 people. By 1925, 600 workers were employed in the chemical works; this number rose to 12,500 by 1939. Proportionately the Catholic population was bound to increase resulting in the founding of a Mass centre in the Memorial Hall in 1929 - an historic event as this was probably the first occasion since the Reformation when the Mass was once again celebrated publicly here.

With the arrival, in 1931, of Father Eric Connell, St. John the Evangelist parish came into existence. The corner site on which the present church is situated - surrounded by a well-kept colourful garden - faces diagonally the Agricultural Division of I.C.I. and reminds the observer how industry, generating employment, has helped to form communities in which the church has an important role to play. The first building to rise - a common practice in the early days of a parish - was a school-chapel which now stands, as part of the primary school, adjacent to the present church. When Father Connell left in 1954 the school-chapel was still in use. His successor, Father Patrick Kerwick, was responsible for the building of the fine red-brick church which was designed by Crawford and Spenser and built by Hudson Bros - two Middlesbrough firms. It was opened and blessed by Bishop Cunningham on June 7th, 1960, which coincidentally was the silver jubilee of Father Kerwick's ordination. Father Kerwick who retired in 1982, and continues to live in the area, celebrated this year his golden jubilee.

Father Thomas McCormack, the present parish priest, succeeded him and last year saw through the completion of the re-ordered sanctuary. The original altar of Connemara marble has been re-fashioned by Brian Morris of Morris Marbleworks, the spare marble being utilised to make the ambo and part of the pedestal on which rests the tabernacle in the Blessed Sacrament chapel. The re-decoration of the church was undertaken by the parishioners who gave their time and energy in creating a most pleasing effect which emphasises the bright and airy appearance of the interior and blends with the altered sanctuary on whose rear wall is a splendid resurrection crucifix.

The silver jubilee was marked this year on June 7th, with a concelebrated Mass followed by a parish barbecue. Today the efforts of parishioners are channelled into various activities: the S.V.P., the Ladies' Group, the Mother and Toddler Group, a Bible and Prayer Group, a Junior Legion of Mary and Lay Ministers are some outlets for parochial community involvement. This will be further enhanced with the formation of a Parish Council in the near future.

Billingham continued to expand in the 1940s and continues to expand even today. Father Connell of St. John's saw the need, at this time for a Mass centre west of the railway line and in due course he was able to provide for this by having a Mass said every Sunday in the Swan Hotel beginning in June, 1947. By November of 1949, Father Eoghan Brady was appointed the first parish priest of the Holy Rosary parish. Post-war building restrictions prevented the immediate building of the church and it was not until October, 1958, that work could begin. Father Brady had taken ill in the previous year and he died in October, 1957. Until the appointment of a successor, Father Lawrence Deegan, the parish was in the capable hands of Father J.V. Marron who was responsible for commissioning the Middlesbrough architect, Mr. Thomas A. Crawford to design the church and Mr Frank Keelan of Thornaby to build it.

It is not difficult to perceive the exterior and interior similarities - although not identical - in the two churches which were designed by the same firm of architects.

Billingham, Our Lady of the Most Holy Rosary   Photo: T. Mackin

Holy Rosary church was blessed and opened by Bishop Cunningham on September 22nd, 1960: 'With a white stone cross on its roof standing high among the thousands of brick built homes of North Billingham ... and as the Bishop later stood at the altar of Cornish grey stone and said the first Mass, the central act of the practice of the Roman Catholic Faith, the new building which has cost £40,000 took its place with the church throughout the world'. *(Evening Gazette)*

Three of the four parish priests at Holy Rosary have celebrated their silver jubilees in the parish: Father Brady in 1955; Father David Head in 1973; and Father Michael Keoghan in 1980. Father Head is now parish priest of St. Joseph's - the third Billingham parish - and it is hoped, sometime in the future, an article will outline its contribution to Billingham Catholicism.

It was Father Keoghan's responsibility to supervise the re-ordering of the sanctuary to conform with the new liturgical norms. In 1977 the original stone altar was brought forward and the new crucifix - the wooden cross being made by a local firm, McLean, Fox, Plant & Co. - was placed on the sanctuary rear wall. Further changes occurred in 1984 when the altar rails were removed, the baptismal font was re-sited to the right of the altar and the new stone lectern was placed to the left; these alterations were carried out by Mr Norman Thurlwell of Lord Monumental Works, Middlesbrough.

Parish activities in the Holy Rosary are many and varied; among the many the following will serve as a sample: the S.V.P., the C.W.L., the Legion of Mary, Lay Ministers, a Youth Club, a Lending Library, a Prayer Group and since 1969 a Parish Council.

Father Keoghan, Father David Coxon, the present curate, and the people of Holy Rosary parish have been preparing spiritually for their silver jubilee as long ago as January. Every First Friday the evening Mass has been followed by an hour of prayer in the presence of the Blessed Sacrament. Each month has had a special theme for meditation; in January Baptism was considered whilst later monthly meditations have included among others, Confirmation, Marriage, and Youth.

The highlight of the silver jubilee feastday was a concelebrated Mass in the church on Friday evening,

September 20th, during which the homily was preached by a parishioner, Father Gerard Burns, S.M. Afterwards a social evening was held in the nearby Swan Hotel where Mass had been celebrated for the first time in the parish 38 years ago. Further spiritual celebrations continued on the Saturday and Sunday. A Flower Festival was incorporated into the celebrations organised by parishioners and friends who decorated the aisles and sanctuary with artistic arrangements expressing various spiritual ideas.

Congratulations to both parishes from the *Northern Cross*. Although comparatively young as far as parishes go they have built on a long tradition of Catholicism and will continue to do so in the future.

9. BIRTLEY   St. Joseph   *(September, October 1996)*

On September 28th Bishop Ambrose will be the chief concelebrant at a Tercentenary Mass in the parish church celebrating 300 years of a Catholic mission to this area, in and around Birtley and Chester-le-Street.

It is a remarkable occurrence that our bishop, a Benedictine monk of Ampleforth, should be leading the festival three centuries after the first Benedictine mission was established here in 1696.

The appointment of a Benedictine priest was made possible by William Tempest, an agent of the Lumley family, who left in 1696, £300 to the Benedictines to support a priest to minister to the Catholics in the area of Lumley and Chester-le-Street. Until 1687 when Richard Lumley became an Anglican the small number of Catholics probably worshipped in the castle or a building thereabouts. It is likely that the Benedictine Missioner, Father Edward Bulmer O.S.B., professed at Lambspring in Germany, (and some of his successors after 1696) celebrated Mass in the Lumley district in the home of one of the local Catholics. One reminder of those days is a small silver chalice, believed to be of the late 17th century, and still used in the parish today.

In 1746 Father Leander Raffa centred his activities at Birtley rather than at Chester-le-Street; this move may have been occasioned by the anti-popery feeling that flared up after the Jacobite rebellion of 1745 - Birtley, then a small village, would have been a safer place to base his ministry. Father Raffa was also chaplain to the Riddells of Gateshead.

Amongst the Douai archives are the memoirs of Father Wilfrid Phillipson who served St. Joseph's from 1884 to 1891. Whatever the uncertain reasons were for the move to Birtley he reminds us that the first post-Reformation 'chapel' once stood in the eastern part of the village, 'a small unlighted chamber' where the forefathers of the Birtley congregation worshipped secretly; it is said to have been in Atkinson's buildings opposite the Rose and Shamrock public house. The priest lived with a 'pious catholic family' and in order to avert suspicion and continue his ministry to his scattered flock he would travel the district disguised as a pedlar selling small wares.

Various benefactors helped to finance the expanding mission. Ralph Brandling, who had probably been taught as a boy at the Benedictine college in Douai, left £500 in 1751 for the Chester-le-Street Mission. The Brandlings were important coalowners; their agents in this area were the Humbles who lived in the White House and who played an important part in the foundation and subsequent development of the parish. A reminder of their many acts of generosity is the stained-glass window, at the rear of the sanctuary, presented by Mrs A. Humble, a sister of Bishop Hedley O.S.B.

A predecessor of hers, a Mr C.J. Humble, gave a piece of land (opposite the present church) on which Father Raffa around 1745 erected a small chapel and presbytery which served the parish for almost a hundred years until the existing church was built. By 1767 there were 172 Catholics listed in the Chester-le-Street area; by 1837 it was believed the majority resided in or near Birtley.

Father Phillipson regretted in later years that he had not taken possession of the 'unlit chamber' and the chapel of Father Raffa's time. He noted that when Sir John Bede Swale, Bart, O.S.B., served the parish from 1850 to 1879 he 'at his own expense always kept the little windowless apartment whitewashed and clean, out of reverence for the hallowed purpose it had once served'. A Miss Anne Humble who died in 1888 had once recalled to Father Phillipson a family memory of a forebear who had been married in this secret chapel in 1793. She was to give to this priest an altar-stone from the second chapel which he took to Wrekenton in 1884 when the parish of St. Oswald's was founded. He believed it was a relic of the days of persecution so possibly it had been used in the 'unlit chamber' during the penal days.

With the easing of the penal restrictions towards the end of the 18th century, Catholicism achieved a measure of tolerance. A letter is still extant in which Father John Slater applied to the Durham Quarter Sessions for the registration of himself as a Roman Catholic minister and of his Birtley chapel as a legal place of worship. During Father Slater's incumbency he was assisted for a time by a retired monk, Dom. Anselm Bolton, whose house at Ampleforth was to become the genesis of Ampleforth Abbey when the monks from Dieulouard came here during the years following the French Revolution.

There appears to have been some discussion round about 1837 whether or not to continue to use the chapel at Birtley and, if not, to transfer the priest to Chester-le-Street. The matter was eventually resolved and it was decided to replace the 'exceedingly damp chapel' with a more substantial structure. In 1842 Father James Sheridan purchased a site from the Maddison family and the present church was erected in the Gothic style to a design of Mr. John Dobson, the Newcastle architect, at a cost of £1,500 with accommodation for 400 worshippers. When the church was formally opened on August 18th, 1843, by Bishop Mostyn of the Northern District 'the company walked in procession to the church headed by the Newcastle and Sunderland Guilds...(and) the choir from Sunderland sang the Mass in their usual good style; the celebrant was the Rev. William Riddell and Father H. Brewer O.S.B., preached on the Sacrifice of the Mass'.

Almost 20 years later, as the number of Catholics had increased, it was decided to extend the nave; a separate sanctuary was added and also the sacristy. This occasioned a special Mass of celebration sung by the Prior of Ampleforth. The music for the Mass was composed by the Swinburne brothers, great benefactors to the parish. In the middle of the last century the parish was much more extensive containing over 1,000 souls. As a result of this increase, six separate parishes were created by 1896 contiguous to St. Joseph's much contracted boundaries.

When Father Phillipson arrived in Birtley in 1884 he describes a place markedly different from the Birtley of today: 'It was quite dark when the train by which I travelled from Newcastle stopped at Birtley and the solitary porter on the dimly lighted platform called out the name of the station ... I enquired the way to the presbytery ... and went as directed along a cinder path with fields on the left, and a few cottages on the right ...There was not a sound and I met nobody...I came to a road running at right angles to it - the high road from Newcastle to Durham, which passes through the heart of Birtley ...The population could not be less than 1500 to 2000 souls yet the village or township had not an inch of pavement or a solitary street lamp. There was no drainage system and no water supply! It could not boast of a single pillar box ...'

He tells of the trials and tribulations of the community when a mining disaster occurred and also a smallpox epidemic in which he played a vital part in its control by setting up a temporary isolation hospital. He describes an incident to show the fear engendered in those days when epidemics struck a community: '... another young man - a Wesleyan - fell a victim. So great was the fear of infection that when he was to have been buried, no one could be found to carry the coffin to the churchyard. To deal with panic immediate action is necessary. I sent word to the house that I would come and be one of the bearers! My message had the desired effect. Several of the co-religionists of the deceased at once volunteered lest it should be said that the Catholic priest had done what they were afraid to do. During the visitation I buried our Catholic dead at night. It was weird and impressive. I met the coffins at the church gate and went straight to the grave where, by the dim light of a lantern, the whole service was performed. Once the night was wild and stormy, and snow was falling heavily as I read the prayers for the burial of the dead. The epidemic lasted three months'.

Birtley's first Catholic School was built in the same year as the church was opened. Over the years a number of schools have been built to meet the spiritual and educational needs of the children.

Too long to list here in detail are the many spiritual and social activities that were part of parish life in those days. One from the past which is not heard of to-day is the League of the Cross (an association of

Catholic laymen committed to temperance) started in 1895. The old school became their League Hall where recreational and educational facilities were provided; they had their own brass band which won honours at more than one band contest in the North of England.

Father Benedict Scannell, who had started it, praised its effects on its members at the opening of their hall. They were men who were willing to offer their services to the parish. 'It had brought comfort in the houses of the people and happiness into once desolate homes. It had clothed the poor children and had fed the destitute and hungry. It had raised up a body of men as respectable and well-educated as any priest could wish to have in his parish'.

Although the League of the Cross ceased to exist in 1930 other groups were flourishing some of which are still part of the parish life today. The year 1933 saw the beginnings of the C.Y.M.S. (now C.M.S.) with an inaugural membership of 50. Presently its membership is about 40 very active members who assist in running the parish centre, a much improved facility compared with their first hall, an old army hut, erected on cleared ground opposite the church by the diligent and enthusiastic founder-members.

The oldest existing society in the parish is the S.V.P. started in 1914 and still continuing as a small group ministering to the needy. Equally strong in membership as the C.M.S. is the C.W.L. of 40 members, begun in 1948; one of their more recent ventures is the provision of a Thursday Lunch Club for older parishioners. In 1947 the Y.C.W. was founded and still maintains an influence here in the formation of young people.

St. Joseph's is certainly a vibrant parish providing many opportunities for lay ministry and involvement, such as the Parish Council, R.C.I.A., a Children's Liturgy Group, a Men's Choir of 15, music groups for liturgy at Birtley and Ouston, Teams of Our Lady, 40 Lay Ministers of the Eucharist, a Young Mothers' Group, ecumenical co-operation, and last but by no means least the Brownies. Alas, the Scouts and Guides, started in 1932, no longer exist, nor the Literary Society nor the Operatic Society; the latter, however, may be said to have had something of a revival with the recent production of 'Tom and the Beanstalk'. Two sisters, of the Daughters of Jesus Order, do valuable work here too; one is teaching and the other visits people in the parish. By 1935, it was decided to provide a Mass Centre at Ouston in which area about 180 parishioners lived. It is believed that the first Mass to be celebrated there by Father P. Mullarkey O.S.B., was on April 21st in the Temperance Hall before a congregation of 147 people. A regular Sunday Mass does not seem to have occurred until Passion Sunday, 1936, when the local council school was used and later a former Methodist Hall. What was once a former miners' lecture hall, opened in 1960 and named St. Benet's, is now the regular place of worship for Ouston Catholics.

At least two former priests who served at Birtley became abbots of Douai Abbey: the first was the Rev. H.L. Larkin who received the honour at the turn of the century; and the second was the Rev. D. Hurley who was responsible in 1910 for the addition of the north aisle at a cost of £1,500. A number of Benedictine vocations have come from the parish; the most recent is Father Geoffrey Scott O.S.B. of Douai Abbey in Berkshire. For more than 200 years the Benedictines supplied priests to the Birtley Mission until the year 1977, playing a vital role in maintaining the Faith here. They are still remembered by some of the older parishioners and inside and outside the church are visible reminders of their achievements. In the churchyard can be seen a memorial statue of Our Lady with some of their names on the plinth; inside on the sanctuary ceiling are painted the crests of some of their Benedictine abbeys.

With the departure of the Benedictines the parish was handed over to the diocese and Canon Henry Olsen, who died this year in retirement, became its first secular parish priest. He continued to be chairman of the Diocesan Schools' Commission overseeing, for almost 25 years, the many changes that have occurred in the re-structuring of the Catholic Schools' system in our diocese.

Celebrations for the Tercentenary year are already underway. Father Tony Duffy, parish priest - who taught at St. Cuthbert's in Newcastle for 25 years and is at present Senior Assistant Director of Schools in the diocese - and his assistant, Father Ronnie Rowbotham, assisted by many parishioners, have already organised celebratory events, one of which was a parish pilgrimage to Walsingham.

Three primary schools serve the children of the parish and they have been involved in learning more about their parish and have also been participating in various projects to commemorate the great occasion. An exhibition of photographs portraying the parish history will, as well as the church itself, remind anyone who visits or worships here of its long Catholic past kept alive in these parts for three centuries by dedicated priests and people - a record of which they can be proud.

The old chalice to be used at the Tercentenary Mass will - after the primary importance of the Mass - be a potent reminder of this parish's remarkable story.

10. BISHOP AUCKLAND   St. Wilfrid   *(November, December 1996)*

When one leaves the porch of St. Wilfrid's Church and looks west down the Wear Valley, it is possible to see in the distance the village of Escomb in which stands the ancient Saxon church of St. John the Evangelist described by Nicholas Pevsner as 'one of the most important and moving survivals of the architecture of the times of Bede' Did St. Wilfrid, in his travels through Northern England, pass through Escomb and celebrate the Holy Mass in this ancient place? The oldest church today in Bishop Auckland is the Catholic one, preceding by two years the Anglican church of St. Anne, which stands on the site of a much older pre-Reformation chapel erected before the year 1391 when known alterations were made to it.

Very near St. Wilfrid's is the Bishop of Durham's Palace whose origins can be traced to the twelfth century and wherein there must have existed a chapel in pre-Reformation days in which the Holy Sacrifice was offered; the Great Hall, now the present chapel, was converted for worship after 1660. Within the grounds of the Palace lived the famous convert, William Frederick Faber who is, perhaps, best known to an older generation of Catholics for his hymns, 'Sweet Saviour Bless Us Ere we Go', and, 'Faith Of Our Fathers'. His father was secretary to Bishop Barrington; the young Faber studied at the local King James I Grammar School and later proceeded to Oxford. Having been influenced by Newman, he became a Catholic and started a community called the Wilfridians. Soon, however, he and his friends joined Newman's Oratory in Birmingham, and later he, with other Oratorians, established Brompton Oratory in London.

St. Wilfrid's formally became a parish in 1846, although long before this there was a mission in the area served by the Jesuits from Durham. Fr Waterton, S.J., who spent his priestly life on the Durham Mission from 1731 to 1766, makes a brief reference to Bishop Auckland in his financial report of 1752: '... for assisting at Bishop Auckland £2.2s and a guinea. Mrs Durham (code name for residence) pays for my shop (chapel) there'. The Jesuit Durham register of baptisms includes four baptisms from Bishop Auckland between 1768 and 1772 and a dozen more in the neighbouring area. In the Papist Returns for 1767, the curate of Auckland St. Andrew states that there were 31 papists in the area and that they 'assemble for worship at the house of Lancelot Bradford in Bishop Auckland'. One other Jesuit, a Father Edward Walshe, is said to have helped out here, probably until 1796. Fleeing the French Revolution, three French priests are known to have stayed in the town for about six years after disembarking in the Tyne, along with many others, towards the end of the 18th century.

A further casualty of the French Revolution was a group of English Carmelite nuns who sought refuge in England, eventually arriving at St. Helen's in 1794 where they remained ten years until they moved to Cocken Hall, near Durham. They left there in 1830 for Darlington where they reside today. During their stay at St. Helen's they were shown much kindness and consideration by the Anglican bishop and his wife, Mrs Shute Barrington. The nun's chaplain was the Rev. James Roby who was able to extend his ministry to the nearby Catholic community.

From 1804 to 1825 there was no priest to serve their needs, so it was necessary for the local Catholics to journey to Croxdale as the parish history relates: 'Those in whom the faith was firmly implanted (and this was particularly so of Irish people who had settled in the town) could be seen Sunday after Sunday setting out on foot to journey those seven miles to Croxdale, there to assist at the Holy Sacrifice of the Mass and to fortify their souls with the Bread of Life'.

In order to keep the light of faith alive in the area the Rev. William Hogarth (first Bishop of our diocese) travelled when he could, from Darlington on Sundays, in the early 1840s, to the home of Mrs Elizabeth Newton in which the small Catholic flock gathered to be instructed and to recite evening prayers. Later these meetings were held in the Old Assembly Room of the Shepherd's Inn in Bondgate which is now the cafe and house of Mr Julio Zair, a parishioner. A Mr Thomas Peacock, in 1841, allowed a room to be used, free of charge, in High Bondgate for the celebration of Mass. By 1842 the Rev. Luke Curry was appointed to the Mission and was succeeded by the Rev. James Gibson who purchased the land for the church from the same Mr Peacock. In that year of 1842 an appeal in the *Catholic Directory* was made for funds to establish the new mission: 'In consequence of the numerous coalmines opened in the neighbourhood, and the establishment of several public works, the influx of population has been very great, and many of the new residents are Catholics. These, with the Catholics who for years have been scattered among the villages of the mining district, amount to not less than 400 souls ... There is no provision for the priest, except what may arise from the contributions of these poor people... '

Three years after the appeal Dr. Hogarth was able to lay the foundation stone of the church designed in the Early English style by Mr Thomas Gibson of Newcastle at a cost of £1,000 approximately; it was opened on October 13th, 1846, by Bishop Riddell and the sermon was preached by the Rev. Richard Gillow of North Shields. The first residence of the parish priest was in Tenter Street followed in 1851 by a move to the only house then in Hexham Street. It was not until 1869 that the present presbytery was built adjoining the church and to the rear there remain the outbuildings which once housed the priest's horse and carriage.

The opening of new collieries nearby and the iron works at Witton Park brought an increase in the population many of whom were Catholic; it was necessary, therefore, to enlarge the church in 1857 at a cost of £500. The building was extended 40 feet at the west end, the gallery was re-constructed and a new south porch added.

Education has always had an important part to play in the development of the Faith and this important aspect of the church's work was met in Bishop Auckland in 1861 when a school was built and opened costing £900. After 1875 the Sisters of Mercy were mainly responsible for staffing the school. This was not the first Catholic school in the area, however, as there is a record that a school existed at Bishop Middleham, a few miles away, about 1700, in the home of Mr Joseph Hildridge where 26 boys were being educated. This same source, listing popish chapels, mentions a chapel at Mr Suttons in Coundon.

After 1880 the Mustard Tree spread its branches along the Wear Valley; in 1881 Witton Park and Shildon became a separate parish in the care of Father Francis Kuyte; in 1897 Mass was being said regularly at Coundon (established as a parish in 1926) where in 1907 a school was opened; and in 1938 Father Bede Tuohey of St. Wilfrid's purchased an old Bethel chapel at West Auckland where Mass was said by him and his curates. His successor in the 1950s was Father William Malone who purchased an old school and house in St. Helen's and converted them into the present church of St. Philomena's, a name soon to be changed to St. Paulinus - another apostle of the North.

In an interesting bazaar brochure preserved in the parish, mention is made of further alterations to St. Wilfrid's and the school in 1890, incurring a debt which Bishop Thomas Wilkinson urged should be cleared quickly. To this end the bazaar was organised, lasting four days, and among the eminent patrons was Pope Leo XIII who sent a gift and a special blessing. A humorous definition of a bazaar is given in the brochure: 'a modern institution where people pay so much to go in, and a good deal more to get out'.

Today the parish of St. Wilfrid's is much reduced in size as other parishes in the surrounding districts have been established; and with the demolition of older properties in the town centre there has been a drift of population reducing the parish numbers of 1,300, some years ago, to approximately 500 now. The old school has been demolished and a residential home built on the site; primary children attend St. Wilfrid's School in neighbouring St. Mary's parish while the older children travel to St. John's Comprehensive School.

For 32 years the parish was in the care of Father Anthony Cunningham - one time teacher at St. Cuthbert's School, Newcastle, and later headmaster of St. Mary's Grammar School, Darlington - who continued the work of so many dedicated priests who have served in this area for 150 years.

The celebration of some weekday Masses in a room in the presbytery reminds us of the days, 200 years ago and more in Bishop Auckland, when a room was the only place they had for worship.

Father Anthony Cunningham, who served St. Wilfrid's for more than half of his priestly life, was buried recently in the parish churchyard. In 1991 he moved to the neighbouring parish of St. Paulinus where he died on June 27th, 1996, suffering a heart attack while preparing to take communion to a sick parishioner - a month before he was due to celebrate his diamond jubilee in the priesthood.

Father Ciaran McDonnell, the present parish priest since 1991, comes from Strabane in Co. Tyrone, Northern Ireland, and is one of a family of three girls and ten boys; he has a brother in the Franciscan Order, Fr Paschal O.F.M., and another brother a Salesian, Fr Eunan, who has recently been appointed to lecture in moral theology in Maynooth. Since Fr Ciaran's arrival the Church has been re-roofed, rewired, decorated and a new heating system installed; strong perspex now protects the old stained-glass windows. Various groups of dedicated parishioners have been fundraising to pay for these expensive refurbishments.

As with all other parishes to-day, St. Wilfrid's has to meet the challenges of the times in a rapidly changing world. Having fewer priests has led to much more lay responsibility and participation in the life of the parish. The oldest group, the S.V.P., continues its mission to the needy. Within the presbytery is preserved a memento of those harsh economic days; it is a die which can be used to stamp tokens worth sixpence which - presumably with the co-operation of local shopkeepers - enabled those in need to supplement their meagre diet.

Lay Ministers of the Eucharist visiting the sick at home and the local hospital, and other committed groups such as the Children's Liturgy Group, and Catechists preparing children and others for First Holy Communion and Confirmation, are outward manifestations of the priest and the people meeting the social and spiritual needs of the community.

Father McDonnell is keen to stress the vital importance of action based on prayer and liturgy. Already six days a week a Holy Hour of Eucharistic Adoration, which includes Morning or Evening Prayer of the Church, is available to worshippers before the celebration of daily Mass. Eucharistic Lay Leaders have been commissioned to conduct services when no priest is available. This has proved very necessary and helpful when Fr McDonnell was asked, with the full support and backing of Bishop Ambrose, to give retreats during the last three years, to priests in the diocese of Kampala, Mbarara and Kilbali in Uganda.

This, for him, was a very demanding but rewarding and enriching experience. He firmly believes that in giving to others, especially in under-developed countries, we grow in happiness and receive more from our Blessed Lord than we ever imagined. Much has been achieved and much more is planned, building on the foundations of parish life already well established, as Fr McDonnell and the parishioners prepared for the sesquicentennial celebrations in October.

He sees the anniversary as an opportunity not only to look back and see where we have come from, but to build on the good that has been done over the past 150 years and to discern where God's Spirit is leading us today. To focus mind and spirit for the task ahead a mission was given by Fr John McCaffery O.F.M. from Stratford, London, during the week beginning on Home Mission Sunday. 'It has been', says Fr Ciaran, 'another opportunity to deepen the spiritual life of the parish and help our collaborative ministry with our Bishop and priest, and to make prayer and evangelisation (reaching especially to the unchurched) our priority'.

Since the mission, there has been formed a prayer group for all ages, but especially to help the youth of the parish. This prayer group will have special training for evangelising others to the Lord Jesus, on what it means to become disciples and make disciples for the Lord Jesus, with then, hopefully, a deeper understanding and appreciation of what we mean by belonging to the church as the Body of Christ.

Father Ciaran informs us that: 'There are also plans to look at ways how best to prepare young people for marriage. We have some very qualified people in our parish whose talents and gifts are available for service. It may be a small parish, but God has truly blessed us with many wonderful people and their gifts which need more and more to be used in this day. Priests can then become more free from administration to be free for the Lord and the real work they are called to do in collaboration with their Bishop and people. To help us make the parish more collaborative we are at present establishing a Parish Pastoral Council. The most important element is probably a shared vision of what the parish can be if all the members realise to the full their baptismal vocation and mission'.

St. Wilfrid's has also become a centre of devotion to Our Lady, where monthly Medjugorje afternoons are held when from 80 to 130 people attend.

Saturday, October 12th, the feast of St. Wilfrid, was the highlight of the anniversary celebrations when the local Vicar General, Canon Robert Spence, was the chief concelebrant and preacher at the Mass celebrating 150 years of a Faith Community's history. Guests at the Mass included members of the Bishop Auckland Fellowship of Churches, another sign of our changing times.

Fr Ciaran concludes: 'As we approach the Third Millennium, my prayer and deepest desire is for this parish, and indeed for all the nations, to return to a loving sense of God's presence and respect for his will, with one flock, and one Shepherd'.

POSTSCRIPT   (F.G. Hickey, 1998)

After 35 years at St. Wilfrid's, Father Cunningham moved to the smaller parish of St. Paulinus at St. Helen's Auckland. He died on 27th June, 1996, just 4 weeks before the Diamond Jubilee of his ordination to the priesthood.

He was succeeded in November 1991 by Father Ciaran McDonnell, a zealous and caring priest, whose constant aim is to promote devotion to the Blessed Sacrament. Extensive repairs and alterations to the church and the presbytery have been carried out under his direction. These include new roofing and new lighting and the transformation of the presbytery into a parish centre with upstairs living quarters for the priest.

11. BLACKHILL   Our Blessed Lady Immaculate   (December, 1987)

This district of North West Durham, unlike many other areas of the diocese, does not have a detailed Christian history until the coming of the Industrial Revolution in the late 18th and early 19th centuries. It was this radical economic change which opened up this sparsely populated area hitherto not easily accessible.

Developing coal mines and in particular the iron works at Consett attracted many workers and their families amongst whom were many Irish seeking employment in a new land. Before the building of St. Mary's at Blackhill the increasing Catholic congregation had used the small chapel at Brooms and it was the parish priest there, Father Francis Kearney, who was responsible for the building of the first Catholic church at Blackhill.

Intolerance was one of the obstacles he had to overcome as *The Tablet* of 1854 records that, 'not a piece of land could be purchased, even by a Protestant, without allowing the insertion in the deeds of a clause preventing the alienation of any portion of it to a Catholic.' However this was only to be a temporary setback and a beginning was made when Father Kearney managed to purchase a plot of land on an eminence overlooking the Derwent Valley.

By late August, 1854, Bishop Hogarth had laid the foundation stone and later on that same day journeyed to Minsteracres to open the new chapel there. The account in *The Tablet* refers to the church at Blackhill as the Shotley Bridge Roman Catholic Church. To the great disappointment of priest and people the church when almost nearing completion was destroyed by 'violent storms of wind and rain.'

Undeterred Canon Kearney and his flock - who contributed generously from their meagre earnings - began again and by 1857 a much stronger structure was completed, to the designs of a Newcastle architect, a Mr. A.M. Dunn; the church was officially opened on July 24th by Bishop Hogarth in the presence of Cardinal Wiseman who preached the inaugural sermon. Once described as 'cathedral-like in proportions', the stone building is 105 feet long and 54 feet wide with a high tower containing a peal of eight bells and a fine clock.

For three years the parish was in the care of Father Hannigan until the appointment of the first parish priest, a Father Thomas Smith, who ministered here until his death in 1885. His concern for the Catholic education of his young parishioners resulted in the building of an infant school in 1862 and the first school at Consett in 1870; he, also, purchased a property in Durham Road from the Master and Brethren of Sherburn Hospital which he had converted to another infant school in 1880.

He was fortunate in procuring the services of the Sisters of Charity of St. Paul who established a convent here in 1869 with a convert Anglican nun as their first superior. This same order still teaches and does parish work today - a fine record of continuity and achievement.

When Father Smith arrived at Blackhill it is said that he made the journey on foot from Riding Mill Station. At his silver jubilee his parishioners purchased for him a horse and carriage which must have made parochial duties much easier.

The *Consett Guardian* of 1885 records the affection and esteem of Catholic and non-Catholic alike towards a priest who 'was of a humble and unassuming disposition and somewhat reticent and reserved in his demeanour. He was of a pleasant and genial temperament having a loving word and an encouraging smile for everyone who were lucky enough to meet him during his almost daily perambulations of this large and populous parish.' His charitable character and manner had overcome the bigotry and intolerance that had once existed for, 'During his protracted suffering Father Smith had been visited almost daily by nearly all the local clergymen of the Church of England and non-conformist ministers, priests of the Catholic church as well as Protestant and Catholic laymen all of whom expressed deep sympathy and regard for him.'

Not far from the church entrance lies a small burial plot containing the remains of three former parish priests of Blackhill. On one of the stones can be seen the name of Father James Foran who died there in 1900 at the age of 76 after 44 years in the priesthood. Fortunately his obituary was printed in the *Northern Catholic Calendar* in 1901 (reprinted in *Northern Catholic History,* Vol. 16, 1982) and provides us with a short life of a most remarkable priest.

He was born in County Waterford in 1823 and after ordination proceeded to England where he joined his brother, Robert, at St. Andrew's, Newcastle. St. Andrew's parish then stretched to North Shields and 'Many a weary tramp had Father Foran up and down through Walker to Wallsend and away out to Benton on sick calls and in pursuit of the wandering sheep.' He was a well-liked confessor especially amongst the Irish immigrants partly because he 'had the Gaelic'.

Bishop Hogarth, in 1860, appointed Father Foran to open a new mission in Walker where he won the respect of Catholic and non-Catholic alike - as his Blackhill predecessor was doing - during his 15 years ministry there leaving behind a fine church, schools and presbytery. Within him, since boyhood, had burned a strong desire to labour on the foreign missions. He had read, whilst at Walker, of the sad plight of Catholics in the Falkland Islands who were without a priest so he sought permission from Bishop Chadwick to be allowed to go there. This was granted and his missionary adventure was about to begin.

Writing in his journal on arrival in Port Stanley he describes his departure from Tyneside: 'I left Walker at 12.30 on Friday, the 17th September, 1875, on my journey to the Falkland Islands. The night was very bright and a placid moon lighted our path as I, in company with my old and valued friends, James Frazer and Michael Ryan, passed along the Byker path to Newcastle. I left in my house another dear little friend, Samuel Hawkins, to keep company with his sisters J. and Margaret who had hitherto been my servants. My poor little black dog, Prince, ran out as usual with his master, but was driven back, never perhaps to see his master again. I have often wondered how coolly and quietly I took my departure, fully aware of the 'breakers ahead' which at that distance seemed to have no terror for me. I am full of sadness now that I have just arrived at my destination.'

On November 3rd, 1875, after a prolonged voyage via Lisbon, Rio de Janerio and Montevideo he sighted the Falkland Islands for the first time: 'The desires of past years are now accomplished ... It is the will of God ... and may he grant that my arrival and ministration here may be for his honour and glory, and the salvation of my own soul and the souls of others. *Deo Gratias*'.

He wasted no time, 'saying Mass the day after landing, preaching, forming a communion class, baptizing the neglected children, and opening a Sunday school in Stanley. Soon on horseback and by schooner he set out on missionary journeys through the islands, administering the sacraments and celebrating Holy Mass in the farmhouses and winning back souls to his Master.'

Many Irish had settled in the Plate area of the Argentine and a number of Irish clergy tried to meet their spiritual needs. With Rome's permission he divided his ministry between the Argentine and the Falklands. A fifty-mile ride to and from a sick call was not uncommon for him in the Argentine. Here within six months (1884) he gave 434 communions in the Plate area and confirmed 100 Irish children.

In the course of his many sea journeys he landed and camped on the islands of Tierra del Fuego; here he celebrated on the sea shore what was probably the first Mass ever said on this southernmost tip of the American continent.

The year 1886 was a memorable year for him and his parishioners at Port Stanley when he was able to open his new church; the Bishop of Hexham and Newcastle was appointed trustee to the property of the Catholics in the Falklands. A native of our diocese, Father Austin Monaghan M.H.M ministered there until very recently as did another, Mgr. David Spraggon M.H.M until his death in September, 1985.

By the time he was 62 and feeling his age, Father Foran applied to Rome for a replacement and before his return to England he decided to see something of the South American continent. Sailing by way of the Straits of Magellan he visited Coronel, Santiago and Valparaiso feeling very much at home in the latter place with 'the soft Irish brogue' of the Little Sisters. At Lota he met an Irish gardener, named Reilly, who had trained at Kew Gardens and had worked for a time in the gardens of the Czar of Russia in Moscow.

One hundred years ago (1887) he was appointed as rector of Blackhill where he continued to serve his Lord in a Parish where he was 'loved and respected by all'. He had once remarked, 'If I cannot do my work, I'll retire'; he was able to do his work until January 29th, 1900, when after a short illness he died at St. Mary's where he is now buried. More details of his life can be found in *Northern Catholic History,* Vol. 16.

His successor was Canon Gillow, a former professor at Ushaw, who during his 16 years tenure reorganized the existing schools; the old parish school became an infant school whilst a new school was built for the older children on the Durham Road site acquired by Father Smith in 1880.

A former curate at Blackhill, Father O'Donoghue, followed Canon Gillow as parish priest. Since 1909 Mass had been said at Consett every Sunday. It was evident that a separate parish was needed here which was duly founded by Canon O'Donoghue when he left St. Mary's and became the first parish priest in 1926.

Father Kay replaced Canon O'Donoghue at St. Mary's but was to die 12 months later to be succeeded by Father John Holiday who ministered to the people during the depression years of the 1920s and 1930s. Many of the men who were unemployed occupied their time in improving the church; a new floor was laid; the stonework was repointed and electric lighting fitted. Bishop Thorman was able to consecrate the church on July 11th, 1934.

Appointed as successor to Father Holiday in 1943 was Canon Hugh McCartan who served the parish here for 40 years until his death in 1983. It is impossible in the space available to do justice to his long incumbency which saw amongst many things: the re-casting of the bells and the addition of two more bells to complete the peal; the extension of the sanctuary; the renewal of the Lady Altar; the implementation of the Vatican decrees; his devoted work as diocesan chaplain to the Legion of Mary; and the part he played in the re-organisation of Catholic secondary education in North West Durham. His memory remains fresh in the minds of many of today's parishioners in Blackhill.

September, 1957, saw the centenary of the parish; a Solemn High Mass celebrated by Mgr. Cunningham V.G. was the highlight of the occasion. A special children's Mass was, also, said; there were social functions too, including a concert, a carnival dance, a garden fete and an Old Folks' Supper Concert.

Father John Kennedy was appointed to St. Mary's in March, 1983, and after the death of Canon McCartan was made parish priest; he is assisted today by Father David Hewitt.

Together with his parishioners much is being attempted and achieved in the spiritual and social fields. A daily morning Mass attendance of about 70 parishioners is an indication of the spiritual vitality of the parish.

Various organisations and groups exist to meet the needs of the people in today's world. Probably the oldest surviving organisation within the parish is the S.V.P which is 75 years-old this year. Two praesidia of the Legion of Mary - much encouraged by the late Canon McCartan - continue with their good works under the patronage of Our Lady.

Fifteen lay ministers help in the distribution of Holy Communion during Masses and to the sick and housebound. Other groups of dedicated parishioners include: a parish adult choir of 30 members who sing each Sunday at the 11.00 a.m. Mass; a youth choir of ten members providing the music at the Sunday evening Mass: a Caritas Folk group providing the music at social evenings; two Bible study groups and a prayer group led by the Sisters of Charity; a Padre Pio prayer group; a Cafod Friday Fast group and an A.P.F. group; and a youth club providing recreation for the children in Christian surroundings. Faith, Pre-Baptism courses are held to help parents and sponsors to a deeper understanding of the Sacrament.

As with many other parish halls today St. Mary's use theirs to offer a service to the community in many different forms - some have already been mentioned above. One interesting innovation is the withdrawal of the children from the Sunday Masses during the readings and homily when a children's liturgy is offered at a level they understand and can benefit from. Here, too, every Tuesday evening a R.C.I.A. course gives an opportunity to more than 30 people to study and enrich their Faith.

Recent alterations to the church to meet the requirements of a changed liturgy have been completed under the supervision of the architect Mr. Jack Lynn; the main contractors were Messrs. J. & W. Lowry Ltd.

To incorporate the structural changes necessary in an old church is difficult; the transition has been accomplished tastefully without destroying the former character of the building. The moving of the altar from the rear of a deep sanctuary almost into the nave has brought the Eucharistic Celebration much nearer to the people.

This part of the diocese has provided a goodly number of vocations to the priesthood and religious life and St. Mary's, Blackhill has much to be proud of in this respect. Canon Francis Kearney, Father Anthony Duffy, Father James Donnelly, Father John McElhone are serving in our diocese and Father W. O'Neill is with the diocese of Nottingham. Three Holy Ghost Fathers hail from this parish; Fathers Anthony Kenny and Paul Hopper are both serving in Nigeria while Father Austin Arthurs is in Canada. Two other vocations from the parish are Father Gervase Duffy, who is a Rosminian Father working in Leicester, and Father Thomas Hillas who is a White Father working in the Sudan.

Many sisters, born here, serve the church too: Sister Genevieve Gordon, a Sister of Charity of St. Paul the Apostle, now working in Birmingham; Sister Brendan Page, a Holy Family sister, now working in Bristol while Sister Marie Joseph, a Mill Hill sister, is in London. Sister Anne Mary Parisi, a Sister of Mercy, is working in Doncaster, Sister Winefride Williams, a Sister of Our Lady of Good and Perpetual Succour is at Ebchester and Sister Stella Quinn, a Sister of Our Lady, Mother of the Church, is serving in Ireland. The two religious brothers from the parish are Brother Gerard Grant O.P. now serving in Newcastle and Brother Mark Boyle, a de la Salle Brother, now in Bournemouth.

The latest milestone in the parish's varied history was the re-opening of the church and the dedication of the altar by Bishop Swindlehurst at a concelebrated Mass held on December 11th, 1986. It was an opportunity said Father Kennedy to 'express gratitude to God for all the graces bestowed upon their parish during 130 years of its existence.'

12. BLYTH   Our Lady and St. Wilfrid   *(December 1986, January1987)*

Blyth's rise to prominence as a major coal-shipping port can be directly attributed to the development and expansion of the South East Northumberland coalfield in the 19th century. The consequent employment prospects attracted many workers to this area of the county, including a considerable number of Catholics.

As elsewhere, the Diocese accepted the challenge of providing churches and schools to nourish and develop the Faith of the newcomers. The first post-Reformation church built in the Blyth district was St. Cuthbert's at Cowpen in 1836 followed by the building of Our Lady and St. Wilfrid's in Blyth in 1861 and the church of Our Lady and St. Joseph in New Hartley in 1895: all three churches were staffed for many years by the Benedictine monks of Douai Abbey in Berkshire. Only recently has New Hartley been handed over to the Diocese leaving St. Cuthbert's at Cowpen as the sole Benedictine parish, at present in the care of the Father John Gibbons O.S.B.

This area of Northumberland around Blyth, like so many other places in the Diocese, had the Faith long before the resurgence of Catholicism in the mid-19th century. When Blyth was not much more than a medieval muddy creek records show that at nearby Newsham was a mansion house containing a pre-Reformation chapel. The Cistercian monks of Newminster Abbey (near Morpeth) owned saltpans in the Blyth area round about 1140 and a granary on Cambois links where grain was stored prior to shipment. Another order, the Augustinian Canons of Brinkburn, held land at Aynewick on the Cowpen shore. Bebside once belonged to the prior of Tynemouth; whilst at Horton an ancient chapel once stood on the site where St. Mary's church was built in 1827.

Not surprisingly after the religious changes of the 16th century the Faith continued in these parts sustained with the help of the Catholic gentry and their chaplains. In the will of Sir John Delaval made in 1655 financial provision was made for his chaplain, Sir William Anderson, to continue his ministry in the locality.

Many of those who refused to conform to the state religion were listed as recusants and their names bear witness to their fidelity to the ancient Faith. Among them in 1663, were Philip and Thomas Cramlington of Newsham and Edward Jubb of Blyth who were known to be papist. George and Madame Errington's names, along with a Philip Jubb, amongst others occur in 1706 and in the non-jurors' list of 1715 appears the well-known Catholic name of William Silvertop, gentlemen, of South Blyth.

In 1696 Newsham became the property of Colonel Thomas Ratcliffe, brother of Francis, the first Earl of Derwentwater. He did not reside here and the property was leased to the Erringtons who, it is likely, provided a place of worship in the manor house for neighbouring Catholics. Likewise it is a reasonable assumption that William Silvertop of Blyth Nook Farm, who was the son of William Silvertop of Stella and a younger brother of Albert the ancestor of the Silvertops of Ministeracres, also provided facilities for worship. Quietly and unobtrusively it can be assumed these Catholic landowners kept the Faith alive for their families, servants and neighbours in spite of the problems this entailed. With the execution of the Earl of Derwentwater in 1716 and the forfeiture of some of his lands, Newsham passed into the hands of Matthew White of Blagdon.

An extract from *The Lamp* article concerning Blyth and Dom. Boniface McKinlay (parish priest at Blyth from 1892 to 1905) provides us with some details of how the Faith survived in the locality.

'For a century and a half after 1716 the Catholics of Blyth and its neighbourhood struggled on as best they could. An old lady, Mrs Taylor, still living at Blyth at the age of ninety-two, has often related what she herself heard and afterwards experienced during those years (1715-1786). The Catholics went secretly to hear Mass at a private house in Bowle's or Buller's Green, Morpeth, a distance of nine miles where Mass was celebrated once a week by a priest from Longhorsley. Afterwards in1788, they assembled more openly in a building adapted for the purpose in Oldgate, Morpeth, till in 1850 the Rev. Father Lowe O.S.B. purchased Admiral Collingwood's property opposite the old chapel and raised the present handsome Catholic church of Morpeth'.

Oral tradition in Blyth St. Wilfrid's has preserved the story of a Catholic man from the parish who heroically walked every Sunday for Mass to Morpeth and back for 20 years missing only once because of snowdrifts near Netherton.

The role of the Catholic gentry in their support of the Faith, preceding and following Catholic Emancipation, is evident in more than a few parishes of the Hexham and Newcastle Diocese. In this part of Northumberland it was a convert Catholic family, the Sidneys of Cowpen Hall, who provided a Catholic chapel - still in use today and still in the care of the Benedictines - in the village of Cowpen in 1836; the founder Marlow John Francis Sidney was laid to rest in his church in 1859.

Before the building of St. Cuthbert's the few Catholics - said to number about one dozen people - heard Mass in a house, now the Sidney Arms, and afterwards in a neighbouring house in Cowpen Grove.

A Mrs Sidney continued the generous benefactions of the family by providing much of the money needed for building the present church and presbytery in Blyth.

This spacious, imposing grey-stone church - designed by A.M. Dunn in the Early Pointed style - was begun in 1859 and ready for services in 1861. In October, 1862, Bishop Hogarth solemnly opened the church which had been given into the care of Dom. Wilfrid Dromgoole (1861-92), the first parish priest. The total cost of the church, presbytery, adjacent school and teacher's house has been estimated at around £7,000.

The parish population in 1861 was in the region of 550 and by 1886 it had risen to more than 800.

No written record appears to exist - apart from the list of priests - of the magnificent work done by the Benedictine Order here in Blyth. For over a century they supplied priests for the parish enabling it to quietly and effectively promote the spiritual mission of the church. Perhaps future research will unearth in detail their committed role as individuals. One individual Benedictine, Father Oswald Hall O.S.B., will have to speak for them all. Father Hall served as a curate at St. Wilfrid's From 1899 to 1901; he then moved on to Liverpool returning to the Diocese as parish priest of St. Oswald's, Wrekenton.

He retired to Blyth and when interviewed on the 70th anniversary of his ordination he remarked that his ministry was nothing to brag about: 'I'm only a priest who has done his duty.' He went on to say, 'I don't care much for Blyth. It's too cold and bleak but I LOVE THE PEOPLE and it is here that I wish to spend the rest of my days.' He did - and long enough to say Mass on his hundredth birthday.

After 109 years ministry to the spiritual needs of the Blyth Catholics the Benedictines handed over the parish to the Diocese in September 1970. 'In many ways, it is sad that the Benedictines should be leaving Blyth after so many years. We have certainly been very happy here', remarked the last Benedictine parish priest, Father John Eckersley O.S.B., when speaking to a reporter of the *Blyth News*.

Father Thomas Power, a diocesan priest, took over from Father Eckersley and was to remain at Blyth for 12 years when because of ill-health he moved to Haydon Bridge in 1982.

Fortunately for the record Father Power kept a scrap book which includes the highlights of his ministry here. He was responsible in 1972 for restoring the original aspect of the church exterior. The blackened stone was cleaned and now looks as new as it did on the day it opened in 1861.

Innovative is the way to describe the incumbency of Father Power. 'Power to all our friends' is the message carried on the banner of St. Wilfrid's Juvenile Jazz Band; it was their way of thanking and publicly acknowledging their parish priest who had been responsible for its formation in 1973.

During his time here he had the honour of being chaplain to two Catholic mayors of Blyth Valley District Council; he formed a scout troop and had a team of 35 teenage altar servers; a mini-bus service was inaugurated to transport the infirm and elderly to Mass; and special bulletins were printed and distributed at regular intervals to inform and to make feel part of the parish community those who could not attend church regularly.

A Saturday Vigil Mass - a rarity then - was celebrated at St. Wilfrid's as early as 1976, during the summer months, to cater for holiday makers. Father Power solved the problem of unattended churches at risk to vandals by organising a rota of parishioners to watch and pray during the daylight hours.

Father Power had the task in 1978 of disposing of the church of St. Patrick's at Cambois on the other side of the river. This church had a very short life span; it was built in 1958 with the voluntary labour of the Irishmen who arrived here to erect Blyth power station. Redevelopment of the area for industrial purposes meant a drift of population till by 1971, when the church was closed, the congregation had dwindled to a mere 13.

Complex and time-consuming were the efforts he expended, along with other priests in the area, overseeing the reorganisation of Catholic education. September 30th, 1976, saw the closure of St. Wilfrid's Junior School in Lynn Street and St. Wilfrid's Infants School in High Street (the parish's earliest school converted by Father Power to a parish centre in 1977) the children moving a few days later on October 4th to their new St. Andrew's First School, built by Father Power. He was, also, responsible for the conversion of part of the old school building in Lynn Street into a very fine Youth Centre - it is still flourishing.

St, Wilfrid's Middle School, opened in September 1976, caters for the over 9's who proceed to St. Benet Biscop High School at Bedlington when they reach the age of 14. When the Catholic Junior School was demolished in Lynn Street in November, 1980, demolition workers discovered beneath the foundation stone a bottle containing a copy of the local paper and the *Catholic News*, a Benedictine bronze medallion, an 1894 silver shilling, a miraculous medal and a handwritten Latin document listing the principals who had attended the dedication ceremony performed by Bishop Hedley, O.S.B. of Menevia who either served at Morpeth for a time or who was a native of that place. These artefacts are now treasured possessions of the parish and a reminder of their heritage.

Father Power, helped by his curates, achieved much in his 12 years in Blyth as many newspaper cuttings testify - not only for his parish but for the community at large. The esteem in which he was held in the local community is clearly shown in a letter he received in December 1982 from the Mayor of the Borough of Blyth Valley, Councillor G.W. Barker J.P: 'I have heard of your imminent departure in order to take up an appointment in Haydon Bridge and I feel it would be very remiss of me not to give recognition to and thanks for the tremendous work which you have achieved within the Borough and adjoining districts over the years...' A year before he left he re-ordered the sanctuary and church and was able to participate in the consecration of the church and altar by Bishop Lindsay on October 20th, 1981 - 120 years after its opening. Prior to the consecration, much work had been done in the church to meet the requirements of the changed liturgy: a new altar (designed by Mr J. Lynn) facing the people had been erected and a lectern and baptismal font placed nearby. The finely carved stone reredos was retained and a new central aisle in the nave was created - altogether a happy blending of the old with the new.

Father Power was responsible for inviting the nuns of the Sacred Heart Order from Fenham to occupy the old large presbytery when he purchased a house opposite the church for use as a new and more convenient presbytery. On December 8th, 1982, the day before his departure, he blessed the beautiful Lourdes Grotto which he had had erected. It was Father Lennon's privilege to welcome the nuns and enter the new presbytery a few months later.

To narrate the history of the parish is in no way to diminish the recognition due to those who are deeply involved in the parochial life of St. Wilfrid's today. Rather it would seem to act as a stimulus and encouragement for those whose task it is to continue and strengthen the development of the strong Faith here.

Father James Lennon, who came here as parish priest in 1982 after six years with the Catholic Missionary Society, is the first to acknowledge the achievements of past priests and parishioners who have together established here a parish of which all can be proud. One of the features - emphasised by Father Lennon - which would seem to indicate the parish's spiritual well-being is the daily Mass attendance at Blyth which can number from 80 to 100 people.

Building on this firm foundation, a vibrant parish community attempts to cater for the spiritual and social needs of the youngest to the oldest. The two senior organisations in the parish are still thriving: the S.V.P. (founded in 1915) continues to assist the needy, the infirm, the old and housebound; and the C.W.L. now over 50 years old - two of its founder members still live in the parish - has also done tremendous work here.

Fourteen Lay Ministers of the Eucharist make it possible for the sick and housebound to feel part of the Sunday celebration by taking to them Communion immediately after the two Sunday morning Masses. A parish committee assists Father Lennon in the consultative process - now necessary in parish affairs - and co-ordinates the many activities that occur here.

Other groups which cover a wide range and satisfy various needs are plentiful: the Youth Club meets every Friday in its Lynn Street premises; a female Youth Choir of 30 young ladies sings regularly at the Sunday Masses; an ecumenical over 50's Club meets every Wednesday afternoon; a Ladies' Club of 30 members meets every Monday; and a Lourdes Group has regular fund raising schemes to send the handicapped to the French shrine.

Another healthy sign of growth is the successful R.C.I.A. Course now in its fourth year; this Easter a number of non-Catholics were received into the Church. The present course got underway last September. Mention has already been made of the nuns now resident in the parish; they are part of the St. Wilfrid's community sharing their worship and prayer, particularly each Monday when parishioners are invited to join their prayer group.

Regular fund-raising for the Third World - two examples of which are the concerts by the parish youth and the proceeds of the Harvest Festival - keeps before the minds of all the urgent needs of their brothers and sisters overseas.

Participation in the ecumenical services of Christian Unity Week and the Good Friday joint services further underline the commitment of St. Wilfrid's to recent developments.

In conclusion the Sunday High Mass attendance of 950 people says all that needs to be said about this strong Catholic community based at the port of Blyth.

13. BROOMS   Our Blessed Lady and St. Joseph   *(December 1985, February 1986)*

Brooms church stands in a secluded spot surrounded by trees on the outskirts of Leadgate. Its position, although remote, is in complete contrast to its importance as a centre for the development of Catholicism in North West Durham over the last 200 years. It is a direct descendant of the mission at Pontop Hall; it offered a home to French refugee priests; Crook Hall, nearby, became a diocesan seminary prior to Ushaw; and it provided for many years in its school, a secondary education of a high standard for its children when a Grammar School education was not easily available to the area.

Within its boundaries and beyond stretches the old Roman road from York to the Roman Wall along which many Saxon missionaries may have trodden bringing the gospel message to West Durham; it is, also, possible that St. Cuthbert's body was borne this way on its journey to Chester-le-Street and finally to Durham.

Medieval chapels once stood at Collierly, Tanfield, Consett, Lintz Green, Holmside, Loft House and Esp Green - ample evidence of the Faith's existence here in pre-Reformation times.

The years of persecution and hardship following the Reformation did not see the end of the 'Old Faith' in the area. Perhaps because of its remoteness, and certainly through the efforts of the local gentry adhering to the Faith, it was possible for priests on the mission to find havens where they could strengthen the resolve of those who wished to hold on to their Catholicism. Such an existence, however, was not without its hazards and trials as a report of Toby Matthews, Bishop of Durham, to Lord Burghley in 1598 demonstrates: 'May it please your Lordship to be advertised that I have lately caused the Lady Katherine Neville, widow... to be apprehended by Mr. John Conyers, the sheriff of the county and Mr. Tailboys (sic) one of the Justices of the Peace and have admitted her to the safe custody of... the gaoler of Durham Castle... She was discovered to be receiving and relieving sundry seminary priests, such as Stafferton with the flesh mark on his face; Boste who has since been executed... Sometime after Martinmas last she took to farming a house and land called Greencroft... rented to her by Mrs. Hall, a widow, and sister of Nicholas Tempest of Stella... and at Stella, if I am rightly informed, they keep up a Popish spiritual service.'

Pontop Pike, famous for its television transmitter, has - as far as Catholics are concerned - a much older claim to fame for not far from it is Pontop Hall, the estate of which dates back to the 14th century. The lands came to be owned by the Meabornes in 1600 and like many other recusant families they suffered fines and sequestrations as they continued to cling to their beliefs.

Supplementing the missionary work of the secular priests were the religious orders; a Benedictine chaplain was resident at Lintz Hall, home of Mr. Hodgson in 1698 and a Jesuit, Father Howe, lived at Stanley Hall, the seat of Sir Nicholas Tempest. In 1733 Anthony Meaborne left £500 to the Jesuits to provide a monthly Mass at Pontop. Father Thomas Leckonby S.J. reporting to his superiors in 1750 and using the veiled language of the time furnishes us with some interesting information: 'My salary from factory (chaplaincy) £33..3..0; contributions £4 and coals free; other helps about 30 shillings, customers (parishioners) to shop 145.'

Between 1778 and 1806 the baptismal registers - now preserved in the Brooms' sacristy - show a succession of priests serving the Pontop Mission including Father Worswick of Newcastle fame and a Father Johnson who started a Mass centre in North Shields journeying there eight times annually; the number of baptisms in these years was 150. For a considerable period Pontop fulfilled its missionary role; an upper room was used as a chapel, the altar rails of which are now at Ushaw College. A further reminder of these days is a chalice - similar to one at Ushaw - preserved in the parish sacristy and possibly a relic of the penal days.

Few people probably realised at the time the effects the French Revolution of 1789 were to have not only on the French Church but, also, on the Church in England and in our own Diocese. When the French armies invaded Flanders the English seminary at Douai, which had supplied the English mission with priests for over two hundred years, was closed and some of the students were imprisoned. They eventually made their way to England and those from the North were accommodated temporarily at Tudhoe. Their next move was to Pontop Hall where they came under the care of Father Thomas Eyre, the chaplain. Crook Hall, one mile from Brooms - the site is now occupied by a farmhouse - was acquired as a seminary and was ready for occupation by the 28 students and professors in October 1794; the number of students was to double in a very short time. Pontop's chaplain, Father Eyre, was appointed president and continued in this office when the community moved to Ushaw College in 1808.

Amongst those pioneering students was the illustrious church historian, Doctor John Lingard, who received the diaconate at Crook Hall, became the first vice-president of Ushaw, and midst his many duties found time to write his *Antiquities of the Anglo-Saxon Church*.

His spirit was moved to write some Latin verses (two are given below) in the style of Horace in which he praised - perhaps lightheartedly - Crook Hall, and its environment:

'May Crook's blest soil and verdant plains
 Be my retreat in trembling age
 When warned by death's approaching pains
 To quit the world's tumultuous stage'

'Pontop! With thee what clime can vie
 Where joyous whins spontaneous grow
 Where not a tree obstructs the eye
  and muddy torrents sweetly flow!'

The persecution of the French Church by the revolutionaries resulted in an exodus of many priests and nuns from their native land. Two hundred and ninety five of them landed in three ships at North Shields in October, 1796, and were dispersed throughout the Northern region into the care of Catholics and Protestant hosts. Fifteen of them were offered hospitality by Father Eyre and were allowed to occupy the unfinished presbytery making, with the help of friends in the area - including Sir John Lawson - the presbytery habitable and the chapel fit for services. They remained at Brooms six years, 'to the edification of the countryside'; some eventually returned to France when the persecution had ceased; five from Brooms remained in England and two lie buried in Lanchester churchyard.

It was the relaxation of the penal laws towards the end of the 18th century which allowed Catholics to build public chapels and one of the earliest in the diocese was the Brooms chapel, opened in 1802 (now the present sacristy). A letter from the Reverend Thomas Eyre to Mr. John Smith, written in 1793, illustrates, once again, the generosity of these old Catholic families who were liberal with their wealth and land for the re-establishing of the Faith in England: 'I am happy to inform you that, upon my reporting to Mr. Silvertop that your family was willing to make over to the clergy a plot of freehold ground containing between four and five acres, immediately adjoining onto the Pontop estate, with a view to a house and a chapel being built there for the benefit of the Pontop congregation, he expressed his approbation and consent to accept of your generous offer.' It would seem that the Silvertops of Minsteracres and the Lawsons of Brough Hall were, also, generous benefactors.

A further letter written by Mr. John Smith of Brooms to Father Eyre would indicate his direct involvement in the building of chapel and presbytery. He says that they 'had cut and led many stones and quoins for the windows, and doors were hewn, and 770 feet of timber were laid upon the spot'. His son, John, left in his will dated December 7th, 1837, more land for the Brooms Mission.

Thomas Smith, the second son of the original benefactor, was the first of two bishops to be born in the parish. He was educated at Sedgley Park School and later crossed the seas to Douai where he was ordained in 1778; he taught philosophy there until 1793 when he was imprisoned by the French for 16 months. When released he returned to England and spent his priestly life in Durham City; in 1810 he was consecrated Bishop of Bolino and was made coadjutor to Bishop Gibson whom he succeeded in 1821 as Vicar-Apostolic of the Northern District which he ruled for ten years; he lies buried at Ushaw College.

During the early years of the 19th century two priests served the Brooms Mission in succession; the Reverend John Bell resided there from 1802 until 1815 when he was followed by the Reverend John Jones from 1816 to 1819. With the departure of the latter, the parish - either because of a shortage of priests or a lack of money to support them - was without a permanent minister until Father William Fletcher took up residence in 1837.

Although the parish had no permanent priest for those 18 years, priests from Esh came to minister monthly (and later fortnightly) to the Brooms congregation. One of them was the previously mentioned Father Fletcher whom one writer described as an 'indefatigable missioner', whilst another source notes that he 'is constantly on the move attending sick persons at Wolsingham and Pontop'. In December, 1834, he had started a Sunday School at Brooms and one Sunday in March, 1836, Mr John Smith, observed, 54 children at communion of which 'a third at least... are of Protestant parents, yet voluntarily send and seem quite pleased that Mr Fletcher should teach their children.' A further observation of Mr Smith's shows the apostolic labours of the priest bearing fruit: 'It is becoming so fashionable to attend the chapel that we are never without some of the neighbouring Protestants with all of whom, so far as I can learn, Mr Fletcher is in high favour... He is just now attending two persons on their deathbeds, neither of whom, I think, have ever been in a Catholic chapel, yet they or their friends have sent for Mr Fletcher.'

When Father Fletcher left Brooms in 1838 the parish was served for eleven years by a succession of five priests until the arrival in 1849 of Father Francis Kearney, an Irishman from Co. Meath, who was ordained at Ushaw in 1848. He was to remain in the parish for 41 years and during this long period he did much for the development and consolidation of the Faith in this area.

When he arrived the parish was much more extensive than it is today; the boundaries encompassed Stanley, Blackhill, Lanchester and Chopwell. The increasing demands for coal and iron - the raw materials of the Industrial Revolution - meant the opening of new collieries and the ironworks at Consett with a significant rise in the area's population as workers, many of whom were Irish, flocked here seeking employment.

By now the chapel was too small for the numbers wishing to use it and the scattered congregation must have found it difficult to reach Brooms, particularly in the winter. The latter difficulty was eased somewhat with the building of St. Mary's, Blackhill by Father Kearney in 1857, but the problem at Brooms could only be solved with the building of a much larger church.

The present church standing at the end of a tree-lined avenue was built, adjoining the original chapel (now the vestry), to an Early English design of E. W. Pugin, a famous Catholic architect, and was opened by Bishop Chadwick on October 25th, 1869, with Pontifical High Mass. Father Kearney, who became a canon in 1881, fittingly lies buried near the church which he had built. His long ministry at Brooms saw him much involved in the public life of the area as a member of the Leadgate Local Board and the

Lanchester Board of Guardians. He established in the parish the 'League of the Cross', a temperance society, to prevent the dangers of excessive drinking and provide the men of the parish with a social, cultural and educational centre in days when the term ' Adult Education' was not commonly in vogue.

Another long-serving parish priest was Father Augustine Magill who came here in July 1892 after a period as headmaster of St. Cuthbert's Grammar School in Newcastle. A *Northern Catholic Calendar* extract of 1920 illustrates the onerous responsibilities he faced: 'Father Magill set himself to provide the advantages of religion to his widely-flung, ever-growing district, which still comprised Leadgate, Iveston, Crookhall, Annfield Plain, Dipton, Medomsley, Westwood and Ebchester. In 1897 Westwood school-chapel was opened and in 1901 became the centre of a separate parish under the Reverend W. Rickaby who developed Chopwell and Highfield in 1914. At Dipton an iron church was opened in 1907 and a school and convent in 1908.'

Catholic schools have always played an important part in the development of the Faith in any parish and Brooms was no exception. The school was operating by 1863 and had then on its roll 400 children who by 1880 were under the care of the Sisters of St. Paul. A pupil-teacher training system was developed here meeting the school's demand for teachers but following the Balfour Act of 1902, which contributed to the extension of secondary education in England and Wales, Canon Magill was determined, when possible, to provide a grammar school education for those of his young parishioners who would benefit from it; this meant the payment of fees and much travelling by the pupils to Newcastle, Sunderland and Darlington.

An unusual feature of educational provision after 1918 was the commencement of 'Central Classes' at Brooms School under the direction of Mother Benedict which enabled more of the Catholic children in the area to receive an education to Oxford School Certificate standard; this facility opened the door for many pupils to higher education between the years 1919 and 1965.

Much has changed in the field of education since then; senior pupils were transferred round about 1965 from the Brooms School and from Consett and Blackhill to the new English Martyrs Secondary Modern School. With the changeover to comprehensive education in 1974 English Martyrs became a Lower School for pupils aged 11 to 13 who, at the latter age transfer to St. Bede's Upper School (a former grammar school) at Lanchester. However, Brooms Junior and Infant School in St. Ives Road remains, retaining a link in the locality with its educational past.

Brooms parish has been fertile ground for the growth and fulfilment of vocations to the priesthood and the religious life not only in the diocese but abroad on the missions too. More than 30 men and women, who were born or educated in the parish, are mentioned in its history - unfortunately they cannot all be listed here, nor can the priests who faithfully served the parish.

We referred earlier to Bishop Smith; the second bishop, born in the parish, was the Rt. Rev. James Hagan of the Holy Ghost Fathers who was ordained in 1928 and who became Bishop of Makurdi, Nigeria. He had the honour of being consecrated bishop in 1960 by Pope John XXIII and of being present at the historic Second Vatican Council. He spent his latter years at the Little Sisters' Home in Sunderland and on his death in 1976 he was buried near the Brooms church where he had begun his service as a young altar boy.

Although today much smaller in extent and population than it was before the foundation of neighbouring parishes, Brooms continues under its present parish priest, Father Ronald Richmond - who is, also, secretary to the Diocesan Schools Commission - and his assistant Father John Reid, the nourishing of the Faith established here many centuries ago. The participation of the laity in this task is obvious when one looks at the many activities in the parish; Lay Ministers take Communion every Sunday to the sick; a parish council has been established; besides the traditional choir a youth group provides music and song for a regular Folk Mass; a Little Way Association and the Justice and Peace Group keep before the minds of the people the necessity of helping our less fortunate brothers and sisters: the prayer life of the parish is intensified through the Padre Pio prayer groups and regular recitation of the Rosary in parishioners' homes; a Senior Citizens' Club caters for the needs of the older members of the parish; and one cannot omit to mention the valuable work done over the years by the S.V.P. (established in 1912), the Women's Guild and the Legion of Mary.

Ecumenical activities include parish involvement in the Good Friday March and participation by the primary schools in joint services at Easter and Christmas. As well as the normal parish duties and the frequent hospital visitations at Shotley Bridge, Father Reid is chairman of the Consett Churches Detached Youth Project which seeks to provide useful activities for the unemployed and a 'listening ear', with advice when requested, at the Drop - In Centre in Leadgate.

Brooms parish has a long and proud history; the present church is a reminder, to parishioners and strangers alike, of the historic and continuing presence of the Faith in this north western part of our diocese.

14. BYERMOOR   The Sacred Heart   *(December 1995, January 1996)*

Once described as lying within 'the heart of the Durham coalfield' the parish of the Sacred Heart at Byermoor (founded in 1869), a few miles south west of Gateshead, is only part of the much larger ancient parish of Tanfield within which and around it are many reminders of how long the Faith has existed here.

One of the earliest remains is at Friarside in the form of a ruined chapel where, it is claimed, on the advice of St. Godric, a hermit named John settled here to lead a solitary life of prayer and contemplation. A later record of 1312 states that Bishop Kellaw gave the chaplaincy of 'the House and chapel or chantry of "Frere - Johan - side" to Sir John Eyrum.' In 1439 it was united with another chantry at Farnacres founded and endowed by Sir Robert Umfrevill who ten years earlier had stipulated that 'the chaplains shall sing according to the use of Sarum and shall celebrate regularly vespers, matins and all canonical hours and on the day of the founder's obit. Placebo, Dirige and Mass...'

The present Anglican church of St. Margaret's at Tanfield - much altered in the last 200 years - has reminders of its earlier Catholic heritage to be seen in the tower foundations possibly of the 13th century and a piscina in the north wall of the chancel; the original church may be of the Norman period or even earlier.

Lintz Hall, once the seat of the Hodgson family, related to the staunch Catholic family of Hebburn was, we are told, a place where a priest resided in the penal days ministering to the surrounding area. This chaplaincy was served for a period by the Benedictines and a Jesuit chaplain ministered at Stanley Hall for some years.

Perhaps, one of the most interesting aspects of this neighbourhood is the connection with the period of the English Martyrs. Eleanor, daughter of Sir Guiscard Harbotel, Lord of Beamish, married Sir Thomas Percy, the 5th Earl of Northumberland who was executed at Tyburn in 1537. Their son, Blessed Thomas Percy, was also executed at York in 1572 after the failure of the Rising of the North to restore the ancient Faith; a further blow was the confiscation of Percy lands in Tanfield.

Persistent recusancy in the years following is further proved for it was at, it is thought, Hamsterley Hall, the home of the Swinburne Family, that the Jesuit martyr Ralph Corby was apprehended.

One account relates his capture on July 8th, 1644, a few days after the Royalist defeat at Marston Moor: 'Father Ralph had just finished reading the Epistle when a party of Puritan soldiers burst into the house. Quick as lightning he was out of his vestments, but had not time to reach a hiding place before they were upon him. As the altar, dressed for Mass, would have convicted him in any case, he readily admitted his priesthood and thereupon was led away in triumph to Sunderland where a branch of the Grand Committee for Religion set up by parliament held its sessions'.

Born in Ireland where his parents, of Durham ancestry, had gone to escape persecution he returned to England at the age of five and when 15 proceeded to St. Omer eventually being ordained at Valladolid. After ordination he joined the Society of Jesus and laboured for 12 years on the Durham Mission. A contemporary, Father Thomas Whitfield, remarks how he was in his paradise when with the poor Durham Catholics. Many were so poor they could not support a priest as the gentry could. 'These Ralph always thought it his special province to console, help in every way, provide with the sacraments and visit their homes in the villages ... That he might more freely visit the cottages of the poor without arousing suspicion, he used to go in a very humble guise, wearing no tunic or cloak, so that he might have been taken for a common servant, or farm-hand, or letter carrier.'

Ralph, who died at Tyburn on September 7th, 1644, along with Father John Duckett, came from a remarkably devout family: his two sisters became Benedictine nuns; two brothers became Jesuits, a third dying before completing his studies; and their father ended his days as a Jesuit lay brother and their mother as a Benedictine nun.

Less well-known is Dom. George Augustine Walker, a Benedictine priest, who was incarcerated at Compiegne during the Revolution and died whilst imprisoned there in 1794. He was professed at St. Edmund's in Paris in 1743 and served the mission at Tanfield from 1750 until 1753. Whilst here he wrote an interesting account of the coal trade in this area for his confreres in Paris (see Dom. G. Scott's account in *Northern Catholic History* No.15). On leaving Tanfield he became prior of St. Edmund's and later President-General of the Benedictines.

From the foregoing it is obvious that small groups of Catholics clung tenaciously to their Faith in spite of the hardships involved. The degree of discrimination was to lessen as the 18th century wore on. In 1767 when a count of papists was made we know that there were over 70 of them living within the Tanfield parish boundaries. A Ralph Hodgson is named who was probably living at Lintz Hall. The longest residing papist was Elizabeth Tinn, aged 65, a midwife who had been there for 50 years.

So often do we see in the growth of the diocese - in the second half of the 19th century - the building of churches and schools in the coal-mining communities where the Catholic population, many of whom were Irish, was increasing. Before the appointment of the first priest to Burnopfield, a Father Patrick Thomas Mathews - the founder of the Sacriston parish - journeyed on horseback to say Mass in the house of Doctor Grensill opposite the Sun Inn.

By 1869 Father Mathews became responsible for the community here, continuing to serve Stanley until 1878; the first place of worship was a wooden building (where the garage and filling station now stand) which served later, also, as a school.

It says much for the generosity of the congregation of those times and the generous benefactors in the locality that within six years of the parish priest's appointment the foundation stone of the church was laid by Bishop James Chadwick. A lease of land at Byermoor had earlier been obtained from the Earl of Strathmore (Claude Bowes) whose family resided for many years at Gibside Hall. The owner of nearby Byermoor Colliery graciously diverted a working coal seam so that the church would not be imperilled by subsidence. On October 8th, 1876, the church of the Sacred Heart was opened, built to an Early English design of Dunn and Hansom.

'The Bishop - Right Rev. Dr. Chadwick - preached on the occasion. Mass was sung by the Rev. Henry Riley who also preached in the evening at the blessing of the bell. The Marquess of Bute who owns extensive estates and royalties in the neighbourhood and Messrs Bowes and Partners, who are lessees and workers of coal under the Marquess, and also the Earl of Ravensworth have been most generous benefactors both to the Church and Schools' Building Fund. Nor do they stand alone. Miss Surtees of Hamsterley Hall contributed upwards of £500 and presented the statue of the Sacred Heart and costly Stations of the Cross. Miss Blanche Lamb bore the cost of the altar and of the statues of Our Lady and St. Joseph' (by Meyer of Munich).

Stained-glass windows adorn the church reminding us not just of the generous people and benefactors but also of the communion of saints. The windows of the sanctuary wall are of particular interest. A St. John the Evangelist window is in memory of Canon Wilson (appointed to Byermoor in 1879); Father Mathews, the first parish priest here, is remembered in the St. Thomas of Canterbury window. Other colourful windows are of St. Patrick, the Sacred Heart, Our Lady Queen of Heaven, St. Joseph and St. Elizabeth of Hungary (given in memory of Elizabeth Surtees by parishioners). Miss Surtees was related to the Durham historian, Robert Surtees, and was a sister-in-law of Viscount Gort of Hamsterley Hall where she lived with her sister. She also paid for the wainscoting around the sanctuary wall.

The ornate carved altar in Caen stone was a further gift of Miss Blanche Lamb of Gibside Hall in memory of her mother. In 1882 at the age of 38 she joined the Sisters of Charity, dying in London at the age of 76.

When Father Mathews transferred to Gateshead he was succeeded by Father John Wilson in 1879. The priest's house was still at Lintz Green until he had the presbytery built in 1882. A year later he had a new school built. Miss Surtees gave a generous donation for the presbytery and the Marquess of Bute paid half the cost.

The fruitful years of Father Wilson's ministry can be seen in the proliferation of societies which provided for the spiritual and social needs of his people. Among them were the Children of Mary, the S.V.P., the Rosary Society, the Apostolate of Prayer and the Society of Our Lady of Compassion. In 1912 he was made a canon of the Church of St. Maria in Monte Santo, Rome, to honour his propagation of a French Association (Euvre Expiatoire) to pray and have masses said for the Holy Souls.

We are fortunate that during the incumbency of Father Alfred Chadwick (1914-25) - until his move to Alnwick - he related the main events of the parish's life in a diary. An entry for December, 1915, notes he sold the sleigh, bought by Canon Wilson for £7 to a milkman, near Tanfield, for £2-10-0d (£2.50). In a later entry he remarks: 'In view of the forthcoming Military Service of my man, John Regan, I sold today to Mr Cook of Tanfield Lane Farm, my little mare, my one and only Polly, for £25, with her harness, a heart-breaking job but good for business.'

The following piece is typical of how Catholic parishes attempted to help those in need during periods of economic recession and, in this particular case, a two week strike in April, 1921: 'Commenced feeding the children. Army cooks rigged up furnace in Boys' yard and pots borrowed, made stew etc and about 120 for Breakfast and Dinner. A plentiful supply of willing men and women workers.'

As a memorial to Canon Wilson an organ costing £327 was purchased and 'was blessed before the Second Mass (November, 1921) and broke forth at once with a joyful sound of pipes. Mr Lindsay, (Bishop Lindsay's father) assistant organist at St. Mary's Cathedral, Newcastle presided at the Instrument.'

Father Austin Pickering, who served Byermoor from 1925 until 1968, was keen to continue and develop the opportunities for lay involvement in parish life. How many still remember with affection the church processions which made a lasting impression on the young as they publicly demonstrated their Faith. Opportunities abounded in those days to satisfy the spiritual and social needs of the parishioners, old and young alike. The S.V.P. and C.W.L. are two exceptions in a list of organisations which no longer exist: for example, the Boy Scouts and Girl Guides, the Children of Mary, the Knights of St. Columba, the C.Y.M.S., and the Legion of Mary once provided much support to a variety of people and an allegiance to the parish.

Most parishes, particularly in the mining areas, were hit hard by the General Strike of 1926. Often its harsher effects were ameliorated by the village or parish soup kitchen. The Sacred Heart parish had one financed by fundraising which also enabled leather to be purchased to repair children's footwear.

A more commodious hall was built and opened in 1930 which contained a small shop, kitchen and cloakrooms with the main area suitable for dancing, concerts, receptions, parties etc. Here the Sunday evening dances and ceilidhs were held and patronised by many from the surrounding and distant parts; an additional hut was purchased in 1941 which became a Youth Centre. Much of the church's land was leased but came into parish ownership when the Earl of Strathmore in 1948 kindly donated the land to the church.

Father Pickering served here for 43 years dying in April, 1968, aged 87; he was popular not only with his parishioners but many non-Catholics also. 'Every Christmas a tree for the church arrived as a gift from Lord Gort of Hamsterley, a good friend of Father Pickering.' A glass-panelled screen was erected at the rear of the church in his memory.

His successor was Canon Lawrence Hollis who had been vice-president of Ushaw College. For 24 years he served the Byermoor parish implementing the reforms decreed by Vatican II. He served on the National Liturgy Commission and also the International Commission for English in the Liturgy. A noted musician - he had once been in charge of the music at Ushaw - Sacred Heart Church at Byermoor, through his efforts, became known much further afield when broadcasts were made from here in 1970 and later in 1980. Ill-health forced his retirement in 1992 - again a priest who 'was greatly respected and popular in the local community.'

Father Andrew Faley came from Our Lady Queen of Martyrs Parish, Esh Winning, to take up his appointment as parish priest on March 18th, 1992. In addition to his parochial duties he was involved in the work of the Diocesan Religious Education Centre, Newcastle, since 1984 and took over as Director from Father Philip Carroll. He promoted the lay formation course entitled 'Labourers in the Lord's Vineyard' and in January 1994 took up a half-time post as National Co-ordinator of Catechesis and Religious Education. This took him to London every week to work in the Catholic Education Service. Recently he has been asked to work full-time in this capacity which has necessitated his resignation as parish priest of Byermoor.

Assisting Father Faley for the last 18 months has been Father James Conway, a Salesian priest, who spent some of his time as a member of the Salesian Community at Ushaw College and before that as rector of the Salesian Community in Bolton, Lancashire. Both Father Faley and Father Conway left Byermoor early in September and Father John Taggart moved here from Whickham as the new parish priest.

Although a scattered rural parish covering the several villages of Burnopfield, Marley Hill, Sunniside and Byermoor itself - with the attendant problems of communication and travel - the priests and people continue to serve each other and the surrounding community. The SVP and CWL - two of the oldest societies in the parish - and the youth group which is one of the youngest, pursue their useful work for which they are well-known. The CWL also raises funds for the parish, various charities and overseas aid and especially for Sister Helen, SND, who is a former parishioner and who works in a school in Africa. There is a parish council of 15 members, and a finance committee both of which represent the opinions of parishioners. Special ministers take Holy Communion to the sick and the housebound on a regular basis; there is a strong group of altar servers and girls have recently begun to serve as well; and a thriving children's Liturgy of the Word, known as the Little Church has been most helpful during Sunday Mass. Ecumenical links are being strengthened, especially during Church Unity Octave Week, Advent and Lent.

Father Faley expressed the wish for the future (before his move to London) that prayer and scripture reflection groups should be formed in the different parts of the parish; such groups could visit the sick, the elderly and the housebound who live around them. Some parish social functions are organised on a regional basis at the Victory Social Club, in St. James's Church of England Hall in Burnopfield, and in Marley Hill Community Centre and Sunniside Social Club.

There has been a school in Byermoor parish for 112 years, but it was threatened with closure two years ago. However, with the continued support of parents, teachers, governors and parishioners, the school was saved.

Maintenance of our older churches presents parishes with considerable expense and in 1993 both Sacred Heart Church and presbytery were re-roofed at a cost of £48,000. The church has also been re-decorated and lighting renewed over the past three years. Unfortunately, only a few months ago, the well-known parish hall was demolished because of serious building defects. We could not conclude this article without mentioning the late Jim Dollan who lies buried in Byermoor churchyard; he faithfully edited the *Northern Cross* for many years and was associated with the paper since it was launched 40 years ago this month.

Much still needs to be researched on the part played by the ordinary Catholics and the Catholic gentry who maintained the Faith in these parts throughout the centuries - the Sacred Heart Church at Byermoor is a reminder of this tradition and fidelity.

15. CRAWCROOK   St. Agnes   *(October, November 1992)*

To celebrate a parish centenary worthily much preparation is required and this has certainly been the case in Crawcrook where Canon Francis Kearney, his parish committee and numerous parishioners have been hard at work for many months.

The first planned event in the celebratory calendar was a service for the sick of the parish held on September 22nd last year, followed a week later by a CAFOD Barbecue - two good examples of remembering our neighbour in need.

A special Youth Service took place in November, a Holy Week Ecumenical Service in April and on June 14th the St. Agnes' parishioners joined with other local Christians in their own church for an ecumenical 'Songs of Praise'. A mission given by the Catholic Missionary Society from September 12th to September 22nd afforded an opportunity for everyone to deepen and strengthen their Faith during this important year in the Parish.

The highlight of the celebrations will be a concelebrated Mass on October 7th, the chief celebrant at which will be Bishop Ambrose Griffiths; this will be followed by the concluding centenary event on October 10th, a dinner dance in the Novotel, Newcastle.

A retrospective look over the last hundred years has been made possible through the diligence and enthusiasm of Mr. Aidan Harrison who has written an interesting and detailed history of the parish. Without this work and his earlier publication, *A History of Ryton,* this article would not have been possible.

As with most Catholic parishes in our diocese St. Agnes' can claim links with a pre-Reformation past. Standing as witness to this early tradition of our Faith is the church of the Holy Cross, Ryton, (now Anglican) built in the Early English style which can be dated to the 13th century with the possibility of an original foundation in Anglo-Saxon days. Within this ancient place of worship, where our ancestors would have attended Mass before the 16th century religious changes, are two stone carvings with which they would have been familiar: an effigy of a 13th century deacon robed in a dalmatic; and a sculpture of two apostles on the communion rail reckoned to be of the year 1500 or thereabouts.

In the days of persecution following Henry VIII's break with the universal church, the ancient Faith was preserved in the locality at Stella, a few miles east of Ryton, by the Tempest and Widdrington families who maintained priests there in their home which had its own private chapel. It would be to this refuge that local Catholics would resort to sustain the practice of their religion.

Listed in the Returns of Papists for 1767 for the, then, extensive ancient parish of Ryton were 447 Catholics, three of whom are shown to be living at Crawcrook: Mary Reay, a widow, aged 51; Elizabeth, the wife of Joseph Birkley, and John Foes, servant of the latter.

Nineteenth century expansion of the Catholic population in the north east is directly attributable to the growth of industry and Irish immigration. More priests were needed, more churches and schools had to be built. This challenge at Stella was a formidable one which was met by Canon Wrennall who during his long incumbency founded four daughter parishes one of which was St. Agnes'.

No one questions the important role played by the Catholic gentry in supporting the Faith during the penal days. What may not be so well-known is the importance of their contribution to its subsequent development in some of the new missions established in the 19th century.

The Dunn family of Castle Hill was one of them. Crawcrook Catholics were fortunate in that Archibald Dunn of Castle Hill - son of Mrs Bridget Dunn of Stella Hall and a partner in the architectural firm of Dunn and Hansom - with his wife, Sarah, donated a piece of land on which they had built a small Catholic school in 1886: it was named after St. Agnes because Sarah had a special devotion to this saint. Six years later - again through their generosity - a small chapel was added, in 1892, and that same year the first parish priest, Fr. Fitzgerald (on loan from Ireland) was appointed saying his first Mass there on September 18th, 1892. It is believed he stayed about a year residing in Crawcrook House, a rented property, which became the first presbytery.

His successor was Father Edward Beech who arrived from New Tunstall in October, 1893. He was keen to have his own presbytery, remarking on one occasion that he paid £20 a year rent and had nothing to show for it. Mention has been made earlier of the contribution made by the Catholic gentry to the development of the Church, but one must not forget that the continued maintenance of priests, churches and schools was only possible through the generosity of ordinary working parishioners who, by today's standard, we would consider as living on the poverty line.

Father Beech asked his parishioners to be generous if the new presbytery was to be built. On one occasion he reminded them that 'a good number of you have not given your Day's Wage for the new

Presbytery - please try and do so before Easter.' This would have been a considerable sacrifice for many families. By 1898 the presbytery was ready for occupation and remained in use until the new church and presbytery were built in 1959 when it was converted to a Catholic Club.

Before the days of parish bulletins the congregation was informed by means of announcements read by the priest from a Notice Book usually before the sermon was preached. In Father Beech's day, at the turn of the century, we can catch a glimpse, from his notes, of some of the matters that preoccupied people at that time. He reminds the congregation of the Apostleship of Prayer (an early prayer group?); a collection for the diocesan orphanage; the strict fasting laws; the necessity of children being on time for school when religious instruction was always given at the start of each day; and the campaign nationwide to obtain equable funding for our schools.

Father Beech was to remain at Crawcrook for about seven and a half years when he was replaced by Father Mark Habell who had taught at St. Cuthbert's Grammar School. The latter's successor was Father Francis Holmes who arrived in the parish on June 14th, 1902. One of his immediate concerns was the inadequacy of the school-chapel for public worship so extra fundraising events were organised to meet the cost. A Tea Party, various concerts and a year's preparation for a Bazaar held in September, 1904, were some of the additional methods used to increase the parish income. The Bazaar realized £171 which Aidan Harrison calculates, would by today's values, be equivalent to £17,000. After this event a Sale of Work was planned as a further fund-raiser.

A permanent stone or brick church was not considered financially possible at this time so, as with a number of other parishes in our diocese, recourse was had to the construction of a temporary building of wood and corrugated iron - referred to as a 'tin church.'

No doubt it was with some satisfaction that Father Holmes was able to announce on May 21st, 1905, that 'We have made commencement with our new church. Great praise is due to those men and boys who have worked so hard during the last three days at preparing the site. The contractor will start work with the foundations... still need of much voluntary help if we are to save money and make a neat job. ... We hope to open the church on August Bank Holiday, August 7th, with Solemn High Mass by the new Bishop (Auxiliary Bishop Collins) with clergy in attendance and special choir. (There will be) a Tea Party and concert in the evening.'

The church, duly completed and opened as announced, was estimated to cost around £1,000 - a substantial sum at that time, and was to serve as the main place of worship until the present church was opened in 1959. Many older parishioners will remember with affection the 'tin church' where they grew up in the Faith.

In order to staff the expanding number of parishes in the diocese of those days the recruitment net was cast not only in Ireland but also in Holland and Belgium. A number of priests from the Low Countries offered their services to the diocese amongst whom was Father Francis James Arcadius Kuyte who was ordained at Ushaw in 1877 coming as parish priest here from Longhorsley in 1912 where he was to remain for almost 24 years. Many memories of him still linger here and much more can be learnt about him from his meticulous notes in the parish notice books which are still extant. Various tales have been told of him - perhaps, some exaggerated in the telling - such as the occasion when a deputation plucked up sufficient courage to ask permission to hold a parish dance in order to supplement the parish income.

His dislike of dances was well known so it came as something of a surprise when he agreed adding 'You may have two dances - one, one week for the men, and another, another week for the women.' On another occasion he berated his parishioners for not paying attention to his notices: 'Never knew a parish where so little notice was taken of what was announced.'

He was a noted naturalist and ornithologist contributing to learned journals and even the *Encyclopaedia Britannica*. It is, also, believed that he was the first and only person to breed the nightingale in captivity.

However, it would be unfair to Father Kuyte if one did not mention his role as pastor of souls. His frequent exhortations to his parishioners to advance in virtue and matters spiritual, his love and care for the children of his parish, his deep interest in education as a member of the local school board, show us a man who tried throughout his whole life to love Christ and his neighbour. That the road from the church to Ryton cemetery, after his requiem was lined with people, many of whom were non-Catholic, demonstrates how he had gained the respect and admiration of his flock and those of other denominations. It is a fitting tribute that Father Kuyte's chalice (probably presented to him at his ordination) was used by Bishop Ambrose at the Centenary Mass on October 7th.

When Father Kuyte died on January 5th, 1935, after 58 years as a priest he was followed by Dr. Wheatley who served St. Agnes' parish until his death in 1944. Dr. Wheatley was a man of many talents which he used to the full in his ministry; he was a fine preacher, a competent musician, and one of the first Catholic priests to broadcast on local radio. A great parish visitor of home and school he endeared himself to all, especially the children. As an administrator he saw the need for an increased parish income if the new church was to be built, so he inaugurated the 'Million Penny Fund'. Unfortunately a start on the building of a new church was delayed with the onset of war.

Many parish organisations, some of which still exist today, were started in his time: the CWL, the SVP, the CYMS, the Children of Mary, the Guild of St. Agnes, a Boys' Club as well as Scouts, Cubs and Guides indicate a vitality and variety in parish life at that time.

Father Henry succeeded Dr. Wheatley in August, 1944, just one month after the latter's death. With the help of parishioners he undertook the refurbishment of the church. Overhead gas heaters were put in and rather surprisingly, for the first time, electricity was installed providing a new lighting system and power to the pipe organ.

Towards the end of the war POWs were interned at a nearby camp at Wylam and it became a common sight to see Germans and Italians marching to St. Agnes' for Sunday Mass. Under the circumstances the priests and people did their best to show hospitality to their visitors; the Italians reciprocated by presenting a crib, which they had made, to the parish. Later the camp came to be used for Displaced Persons among whom were Latvians, Lithuanians, Estonians and Ukrainians who were also made to feel at home in the parish of St. Agnes.

The Bishop decided in 1950 that a mutual exchange of parish priests should take place between Father Henry and Father Aherne of Holy Name, Jesmond.

Two major problems faced the incoming parish priest: the improvement of educational facilities, particularly at secondary level, and the building of the new church. The first was partially solved through the efforts of Father Aherne and Mr. Maurice Fortune, head of St. Agnes' All-Age school, who arranged for some of the secondary school children to be educated in grammar schools as far away as Hebburn and Sunderland. This, however, could only be a temporary solution which was resolved when St. Thomas More's at Blaydon was opened allowing St. Agnes' School to become a primary school.

The dream of a long-awaited church was realised during Father Aherne's incumbency. It had been originally proposed to build the new church around the old tin one but a further play area was required for the school on what would have become a cramped site.

Another site had to be found and it was providential when a new location - suggested by Tommy Charlton, Surveyor of Ryton Urban District Council, whose father had built the school - turned out to be owned by Commander Dunn, grandson of Archibald, who had founded the first school and chapel. The piece of land in mind was 'Sheep Hill' (The Ridings) which the owner graciously sold at a reasonable price.

When the plans for the church were submitted to Bishop Joseph McCormack he felt that the tower was unnecessary and costly so Father Aherne was asked to think again. After discussion with his parishioners, who were keen to retain the tower, he returned to the bishop with their request to which he acceded.

One can imagine the great joy in Crawcrook when Bishop James Cunningham officially opened and blessed the new church in July, 1959. This Romanesque-style church, in grey mixed facing bricks, with its Italianate tower was built to seat a congregation of 375 by J. W. Lowry of Newcastle to the design of architects, Pascal J. Steinlet and Son and cost £60,000 (inclusive of land, furnishings and presbytery).

It was not long after the building of the church that the Vatican Council began sitting. Its liturgical reforms were to have a world-wide effect and were eventually implemented in St. Agnes' by Father Peter Callaghan, then parish priest. The work of re-ordering the sanctuary was entrusted to a parishioner, Mr Alan Greenall of Wylam, who managed successfully to re-plan the sanctuary bringing forward the high altar of Connemara marble and removing the altar rails of a similar material. Much of the surplus marble was re-used to construct the lectern, baptismal font and presidential chair.

Father Callaghan, now living in retirement at the Little Sisters' Home in Newcastle, was followed, in 1987, as parish priest by Canon Francis Kearney who for the preceding ten years had been administrator of St. Mary's Cathedral.

The centenary celebrations, mentioned at the beginning of the article, have become a stimulus for the spiritual and social enrichment of the parish which has, since its inception, always had organisations to enliven and renew the Faith.

This continuing renewal is already being fulfilled through the commitment of different groups in St. Agnes' today. The parish committee, working closely with Canon Kearney, co-ordinates the social life of the parish; they have, this year, raised £4,000 for parish funds.

Much could be written about the SVP of eight members (founded in 1936) and the CWL of 20 members whose work is much appreciated by all in Crawcrook.

Of more recent origin is the advent of 18 Lay Ministers of the Eucharist who through their devotion enable the sick and housebound to receive Communion more frequently. The Journey in Faith talks and the Bible Study Group have provided an opportunity, to those who so wish, to come to a greater understanding and appreciation of the Good News.

Castle Hill - the former home of the Dunn Family, the founders of the parish - still maintains links with the parish for as a community care home it is visited regularly by Canon Kearney.

In the foreword to the parish history Canon Kearney asks the question, 'But what is a Church?' and replies 'The Church is never a place, but always people; never a fold but always a flock.' He reminds us of the debt we owe to our forefathers who strove so hard to pass on the inheritance of our Faith. In the centenary brochure he invites us to look forward and 'Help individuals grow in the Faith, help the parish grow together as a family and help them to reach out to other people.' After 100 years of attempting to do this Canon Kearney exhorts his people to make sure it continues.

16. CROOK   Our Lady Immaculate and St. Cuthbert   *(February, March. 1984)*

It was in 1849 that Pope Pius IX began asking the Catholic bishops of the world for their opinions on the possibility of defining the Dogma of the Immaculate Conception of Our Lady and in 1853, the year before the papal definition was promulgated, Bishop Hogarth laid the foundation stone of the Catholic church at Crook dedicated to Our Lady Immaculate and St. Cuthbert. This must rank as one of the first churches in the diocese to be dedicated to Our Lady Immaculate anticipating the pope's declaration by 15 months.

As with many other churches built in the diocese during the 19th century Crook has within its present parish boundaries reminders of its strong Catholic past. The parish history tells of a tithe barn at High Woodifield which at one time had a cross on the external wall and also a belfry suggesting it was once a place of worship dating back to the 12th century. We know that the Amundeville family of Witton gave the land and buildings to the monks of Durham who rented it to the 'White Canons' (Premonstratensians) of Blanchland who appear to have used it as a rest house rather as Finchale was used by the Durham Benedictines.

The severity of the penal laws drove, as elsewhere, the Faith underground; yet a Catholic presence and practice are evident when we read of the arrest of Father John Duckett on the Tow Law to Wolsingham Road - the place of the arrest today being marked with a stone cross.

Father Duckett, a secular priest, was born at Underwinter, Sedbergh, Westmorland in 1613. He crossed the seas as a very young man to Douai where he remained for eight years followed by three more years at the College of Arras in Paris. Ordained at Douai in 1639 he returned to the Durham mission in 1643 remaining free for about a year. He is believed to have been arrested on July 2nd, 1644 by a band of Roundhead soldiers who mistook him for a Royalist refugee; in fact, he was on his way to baptize two children and the holy oils he was carrying made his captors suspicious. They pressed him to admit he was a Catholic priest but this he only consented to do after he received an assurance that the Catholic laymen accompanying him would be released. He was taken to Sunderland and a few days later was shipped, along with Blessed Ralph Corby, to London where they were both tried and executed at Tyburn on September 7th, 1644. At the place of execution he was approached by a non-Catholic minister who tried to reason with him. His reply was: 'I have not come here to have my religion explained to me, I have come to die for it.'

One of the outstanding personalities connected with the development of the Catholic church in the north east in the latter half of the

Crook, Our Lady Immaculate & St. Cuthbert *Photo: T. Mackin*

19th century was Bishop Thomas Wilkinson. He was born into a Protestant family of 11 children whose father, George Hutton Wilkinson, a prominent lawyer resided at Harperley Hall in Weardale. Educated at Harrow, the youthful Thomas went from there to Durham University where he gained a degree and a licentiate in theology. He was deeply affected by the Oxford Movement within the Anglican Church and having got his father's permission joined a semi-monastic community at St. Saviour's in Leeds. Eighteen months later he made his submission to the Catholic Church and proceeded to Oscott to study for the priesthood. In 1848 he was ordained priest at Ushaw College by Bishop Hogarth.

His first task was to take care of the mission at Wolsingham, not far from his birthplace, which at that time was extensive and where the Catholic population was rising rapidly as new coalmines were opened in which many Irish sought employment. Every Tuesday he journeyed to Crook for evening confessions and remained overnight to say Mass the following morning. By 1851 he was asking his father for land on which to build a church and school; a site at the top of Dowfold was agreed, but later exchanged for a more suitable one in Hope Street where two houses were converted for use there.

Two of his companions at Leeds, Father Ward and Father Rooke, who were now Catholic priests, came to assist here: it was the former who arranged the purchase of the site of the present church on Church Hill and the latter who requested the famous architect E.W. Pugin to design the church which was opened on

October 25th, 1854. Father Rooke was also responsible for the building of the school and presbytery but shortly after the opening of the church at Tow Law he left the parish to join the Dominicans. The Bishop now thought it desirable that Father Wilkinson should move from the less demanding parish of Wolsingham to meet the needs of the expanding Crook parish. 'Father Tom' as he became affectionately known, accepted the change remarking, 'God grant that it will be for the good of souls, both my own and theirs.'

It was a fairly demanding routine - but perhaps, no more so than some of our priests on their own find today - to which he found himself bound. There was daily Mass at 8 a.m.; the Angelus was rung out three times a day; and prayers were said in church each night followed by a spiritual reading. Before and after Benediction on Thursday there were confessions; and according to the parish history further confessions were heard on Fridays from midday to midnight and for much of Saturday too! A typical Sunday would include Mass at 8 a.m. when there would normally be 300 communicants; a sung Mass at 10.30 a.m.: a Sunday school from 3 p.m. to 4 p.m. during which the rosary was recited; and his day would close with Evening Devotions and Benediction at 6 p.m.

Through his sister, also a convert, who had been an Anglican nun, he was introduced to the Sisters of Charity of St. Paul whom he asked to staff the school at Crook as well as instructing the women and girls in the parish Sunday school and performing works of mercy in the area. This Catholic order of nuns remained here until 1910 when their work was continued by the Sisters of Mercy from Alnwick whose successors are still living in the convent near the church and who are still very active in the parish and school.

In 1865 Father Wilkinson was made a canon and two years later he accompanied Bishop Chadwick on a visit to Rome where he saw firsthand the problems faced by Pope Pius IX as the movement for Italian Unification seemed to threaten the temporal and spiritual authority of the Pope. On his return he encouraged some of his parishioners to join the Papal Zouaves, a group of volunteers enlisted to protect the Pope, meeting their expenses from his own pocket; two of them are buried near the church tower. He was able in 1869 to see his Zouaves in Rome when, because of poor health, he returned to Italy to recuperate. Shortly after his return, and still in poor health, he requested the bishop for permission to retire; this he did in 1870 moving to a farm he had bought at Thistleflatt. One might have thought his active role in diocesan and parish affairs was now over but he continued, when strong enough, to visit Crook and say the Sunday Mass. What is even more surprising is that with an obvious improvement in his health, he was consecrated auxiliary Bishop of Hexham and Newcastle in 1888 and was also president of Ushaw College from 1890 until his death in 1909, at the age of 84 years. Further details of his life can be found in Father David Milburn's, *A History of Ushaw College*.

His successor at Crook was Father Pippet who was appointed in October, 1869; stained-glass windows in the church perpetuate his memory and that of Bishop Wilkinson. Another stained-glass window commemorates the arrival of the Sisters in 1862. Father Pippet developed the parish further; he was responsible for the opening of a school-chapel and presbytery at Willington in 1873, costing £1,200; and he made further improvements at Crook with the building of the convent, the lodge, school extensions and a parish recreation room and library.

Once again the problem arises of trying to do justice in a short article to all the priests and people who contributed to the growth of the parish. The tribute paid to Father Hayes, a much-loved priest, who died in 1932, may serve as a testimony to a caring community: 'The ill-famed 1926 strike was in progress and more than half of Father Hayes' men parishioners were out of work. He did all he could to alleviate the suffering and near starvation of the women and children... often it meant the bread from his own meagre table... To the children he was really a 'father'... Frequently he arranged trips to the seaside and went with the children taking part in their games… Many did not know it then but most of these trips were paid for out of his own pocket. Not only this but he arranged transport for the children of Stanley to come to school during the winter... The news (of his death) cast a deep gloom over the whole town for Father Hayes was not only popular with his own people but with the entire town.'

Reconciliation is a theme much heard of in the church today and a striking example of this can be found in the parish in the year 1945 when with the ending of the war it was possible to celebrate Midnight Mass. During the war a prisoner-of-war camp had been established near Stanley mainly for Italian P.O.Ws and it was regularly visited by Fathers Lamb and Durnin for the celebration of Mass. Later German prisoners were interned there and they too had their spiritual needs met. They were able to attend the Midnight Mass of 1945 and show their gratitude to the parish: 'That night the church stilled to the beauty of the electrified organ played by a P.O.W. who had been an assistant organist at the great cathedral in Cologne. The mingled voices of our own parish priest and curate were joined by a powerful third - that of a German chaplain who assisted as Deacon. Our own choir alternated with a German choir as High Mass rang through the church... Our own little parish was sharing manifestly the Catholicity of the church.'

The church at Crook is of great architectural interest being designed by E.W. Pugin in the Gothic style; the church tower, a later addition built in 1897, the year of Queen Victoria's Diamond Jubilee, was designed by Dunn, Hansom and Fenwick of Newcastle. Few people, it appears, are aware that the original high altar was constructed from plans made by John Francis Bentley who was later to achieve international fame as the architect of Westminster Cathedral. One can imagine, therefore, the formidable task faced by Fr. William Lowrie and his architects, after consultation with parishioners, when it was decided to make alterations in order to conform with the new liturgical rules. The harmonious blend of the old and new accomplished by the architects and builders is well worth seeing. Without spoiling the original Bentley design the high altar has been moved forward allowing the former sanctuary area to be used as a more intimate day chapel. The Bentley reredos is now situated to the left of the high altar and forms the main part of the Blessed Sacrament chapel. A new organ gallery at the rear of the church has also been constructed using the organ, screens and the altar rails form the demolished church of St. Thomas at Port Clarence.

Those early convert Anglican founding-fathers would still see in the church much that they would recognise. For the past 34 years Father William Lowrie has served the parish, first as curate and later as parish priest and in 1981 celebrated his Golden Jubilee; he hopes now to retire and live in a house within the parish grounds. A good community spirit exists here and in addition to the fruitful work done by the S.V.P. and C.W.L. the commissioning of 16 Lay Ministers of the Eucharist has enabled the sick and housebound to receive Communion weekly when it is taken to them after the Sunday Masses.

In a parish of a 1000 souls with a Sunday Mass attendance of 520 and a daily evening Mass attendance of 40 to 50 the institution of this new ministry is of considerable help to Father Lowrie who has to minister on his own.

An interesting custom of the days of Father Peyton's Rosary Crusade of the 1950s is still thriving here: a statue of Our Lady of Fatima is taken round the parish and remains with each family for a week. The parish income has been enhanced with the covenant scheme which provides an extra £3,000 per year and a further supplement of £2,800 was raised at last year's Garden Fete. All very necessary when one considers the £40,000 spent on renewing the church roof plus the cost of the recent re-ordering of the church and the part payment of £120,000 spent on the modernising of the Primary School.

17. CROXDALE   St. Herbert   *(May, 1983)*

St. Herbert's at Croxdale is one of the lesser-known parishes in the diocese with an estimated Catholic population of 81 parishioners. The parish itself straddles the old A.1 (now the A.167) three miles south of Durham City and because of its long association with the Salvin family of Croxdale Hall the chapel is to be found not in the villages within the parish boundaries but at Croxdale Hall itself. The family chapel is housed within the east wing of the Hall and it is here that the parishioners are able to attend Mass on Sundays and weekdays. To tell the full story of this area and its strong Catholic links with this old Catholic family of the north would require a lot more research and a much longer article than is possible here.

The early history of St. Herbert's chapel, unless assiduous research unearths further information, is almost as obscure as the patron saint himself. What little we know of Herbert is contained in St. Bede's

Ecclesiastical History of the English Nation ; therein it is related that Herbert lived the life of a hermit on an island in Lake Derwentwater and relied for spiritual counsel on St. Cuthbert. On one occasion whilst Cuthbert was visiting Lugubalia in Cumberland, Herbert sought out the saintly bishop who informed him that he, Cuthbert, felt his life was drawing to a close. Herbert, on hearing this, became very sad but St. Cuthbert after much prayer prophesied that they would leave this earthly life together. According to Bede their deaths occurred on March 20th, 687 A.D. Recently in the Catholic press it was announced that a Mass was to be celebrated on April 9th, the feast of St. Herbert, on his island in Derwentwater by Mgr. Wilfrid Buxton, parish priest of Our Lady and St. Charles, Keswick.

Synonymous with the name Croxdale is the name of the Salvin family whose ancestors have inhabited the area for almost 600 years, although their earliest forefathers owned estates in Norman times near Sherwood Forest. The origin of the word Croxdale is possibly derived from the latin word Crux, meaning a cross ; and the ancient wooden cross near the old chapel may have some connection here with the name, the earliest spelling of which is Croxsteyl - the place of the cross.

Walter de Routhbury is the earliest recorded owner of the Croxdale lands in 1291; later, round about 1350 Robert de Whalton (Treasurer of Brittany in 1359) owned the estate which came into the possession of the Salvin family when Gerard, a younger son of the Salvins of Herswell in Yorkshire, married Robert's grand-daughter, Agnes.

Croxdale, St. Herbert (drawn by Peter Anson, 1934, courtesy of Northern Catholic History)

By 1840, according to Surtees, the Durham historian, fourteen generations of Salvins had held Croxdale of which the first ten successive owners were called Gerard. Croxdale was a stronghold of Catholicism for hundreds of years and the religious changes of the 16th and 17th centuries did not lessen the Faith of this ancient Durham family; Gerard Salvin participated in the Rebellion of the Northern Earls in 1569 which attempted unsuccessfully to restore Catholicism in England. During this rising Durham was occupied for a short time and High Mass was sung once again in Durham Cathedral. Later during the Civil War, fought between King and Parliament, Gerard Salvin (the 10th) was slain in a skirmish at Northallerton, whilst Colonel Francis, his uncle, also a Royalist, fell at Marston Moor in July, 1644. Fortunately the head of the family at that time, Gerard Salvin, (the 9th) had not been directly involved so his estates were not sequestered and he remained owner of the estates for 60 years and lived to see the Restoration of the monarchy.

The present Croxdale Hall was built for General Salvin about 1760 and within the east wing is contained the present chapel used for the first time in 1807. Perhaps, the most interesting part of the estate historically, lies to the north of the present hall. Surrounded by a stone wall is a piece of land on which stands the medieval chapel of St. Herbert and here were nourished the roots of Faith in Croxdale many hundreds of years ago. A south-facing Norman doorway above which is a well-worn tympanum, possibly illustrating the Tree of Life, (or could it be the Vine and the Branches ?) and a now blocked up north facing doorway, reputedly of the 12th century, bear witness to its antiquity in the Faith and are a small reminder of those great builders in stone whose greatest monument is nearby Durham Cathedral. This chapel - one of the few pre-Reformation buildings now in Catholic hands - was for many years after the religious changes of the 16th century a Protestant chapel until 1848 when the Salvin family brought it back to use as a mortuary. The Church of England congregation moved, about this time, to their new church, St. Bartholomew's, in the nearby village of Sunderland Bridge; and it is in this same village today that the Catholic presbytery of St. Herbert's stands and where the present parish priest, Father Michael Devlin, continues the work of that long line of priests who have kept the light of Faith alive in this area of Durham. It is a possibility - and only further research would reveal this - that the celebration of the Holy Sacrifice of the Mass and the Catholic Faith have continued almost without a break in this corner of our Diocese since medieval days. If this is so, then it is indeed a proud and noble record.

18. DARLINGTON   St. Augustine   *(January, 1983)*

The late 18th and early 19th centuries were an important time in the history of Catholicism in England. During that period there was a growing spirit of toleration towards religious minorities culminating in the Catholic Emancipation Act of 1829 which, more or less, restored full civil liberties to Catholics. The year 1783 was a significant year for the Catholics of Darlington for in that year the parish of St. Augustine's was formally established; and it was a significant year too for a certain Ann Kipling, who holds the honour of being the first person to have her name entered in the Baptismal Register by the Rev. John Daniel. It is interesting to speculate that if she lived to see the opening of the church in 1827 she would have been 44 years old.

The first resident priest appears to have settled in Darlington in 1804 at a house in Bondgate bought from Jonathan Backhouse, a Quaker banker, who later assisted in the purchase of a plot of land in Paradise Row on which the present church is sited. Previous to this date various priests based at Stockton and Durham had ministered to the small flock; one of the earliest we know by name being Father Luke Whitson, who visited the town in 1741 and subsequently until 1744.

The help of a notable Catholic family, the Ridsdales, who are commemorated in a stained-glass window, was invaluable in those days before the church was built, as they graciously allowed the use of their business premises for the celebration of Mass.

The outstanding figure in the history of Darlington Catholicism was Father William Hogarth, a Westmorland man, who was not only parish priest at St. Augustine's for 42 years, but in 1848 was appointed Vicar-Apostolic of the Northern District and at the Restoration of the Hierarchy in 1850 became the first bishop of what is now the Diocese of Hexham and Newcastle - truly the Father of our diocese.

He appears to have been a 'human dynamo', and his many activities deserve a history of their own. As Father Hogarth, he was responsible for the building of the original church in 1827 as well as the extensions to the nave and sanctuary added in 1865. The Bishop's House, which still stands at the corner of the lane leading to the church, was his place of residence even after his appointment as bishop of the diocese.

In addition to his priestly role, to which were later added episcopal responsibilities, he appears to have found time for ecumenical activity, particularly with the Quakers, one of whom Francis Mewburn, solicitor to the Stockton and Darlington Railway compliments him as, 'the most perfect gentleman of my acquaintance'.

The impression he left in Darlington is best shown by the esteem and public recognition manifested at his funeral. Thousands of Darlington's citizens filed past his coffin in the church and as his funeral procession passed through Darlington on its way to Ushaw College, the Church of England parish of St.

Cuthbert's paid their kindly respects by the tolling of bells. Further ecumenical recognition came when, after a public meeting, it was decided to erect a granite memorial to him in the West Cemetery. On it he is described as 'Father of the Poor'.

The visitor to Darlington is not likely to find this church easily, but should he find it, a pleasant surprise awaits him. Hidden behind some old houses on Coniscliffe Road, stands the Catholic mother church of Darlington in a quiet square away from traffic giving the appearance and atmosphere almost of a monastic cloister.

The original Gothic-style church, opened on May 29, 1827, which could accommodate 500 people, was designed by Ignatius Bonomi, whose talents are visibly demonstrated today in other parts of the diocese by buildings such as Burn Hall and St. Mary's, Sunderland.

On entering the church for the first time one is immediately impressed by its spaciousness - it can seat 700 parishioners - and one's eye is soon drawn to the carved Austrian oak reredos at the rear of the sanctuary which was erected at a cost of £800 in 1899 when Canon Rooney was parish priest (1876-1931). The four painted panels, depicted in a medieval art style, surround an exposition throne above the tabernacle and portray: the sending of St. Augustine by Pope Gregory to the English; the Resurrection; the Last Supper; and Our Lady with the Infant Jesus surrounded by English saints and martyrs.

Although steeped in history, and proud of it, the parish of St. Augustine's does not live in the past having a vibrant community life guided by its parish priest, Father Robert Spence, and his assistants, Father Wilfrid McConnell and Father Paul Southgate. The new parish centre, opened in 1979, provides a modern meeting place for the various groups and societies that are common nowadays to most parishes. Has your parish got a Mother and Toddler Group? Recently it has become a venue for parishioners to study and discuss in detail a series of talks on the Pope's addresses in England.

The ecumenical dialogue fostered by Bishop Hogarth is still in evidence; before the arrival of the Pope in Britain a joint ecumenical service of reconciliation was held in St. Augustine's and this link has been further forged by inviting the Rev. L. Gready, vicar of St. Cuthbert's (where the bells were tolled at Bishop Hogarth's funeral) and a member of the General Synod, to lead the discussion in the parish centre on the Pope's address at Canterbury.

Few parishes can claim such a variety of history and Catholic life within its boundaries. Not far from the church is Darlington market place where Blessed George Swallowell, born at Houghton-le-Spring, was martyred for the Faith in 1594.

Today four religious orders are active in the parish: the Sisters of Charity help in the schools and with social work; the Brothers of St. John of God maintain and run their hospital for the sick; and two contemplative orders - the Poor Clares and the Carmelites - continue their work of prayer for the diocese and the world. Few parishes also, can claim to have had only six parish priests in 150 years - perhaps the Darlington air has something to do with this!

Concern and care for the handicapped are very much in the minds of people today and no less so than in St. Augustine's where it is hoped in the not too distant future - with the advice of the St. John of God Brothers, the local Memorial Hospital and a Housing Association - to build flats for the handicapped on church land fronting Coniscliffe Road.

The year 1983 will see the Bicentenary of this parish when a comprehensive history of the parish written by Mr. Gerry Wild, whose notes have been invaluable in the writing of this short article, will be available.

It is surely no coincidence that the parish named after St. Augustine, the missionary of England, should have played an important part, through Bishop Hogarth in spreading the Good News throughout North Eastern England.

POSTSCRIPT *(Canon R. Spence, 1998)*

In October 1997 Bishop Ambrose opened a Housing Association development on the site of the former St. Augustine's School. There is now an attractive piazza outside the new West Door which was created at the time of the refurbishment and reordering of the church in 1993. A statue in oak of St. Augustine by Fenwick Lawson has been placed in the niche above the door to mark the 14th centenary of St. Augustine's arrival in England.

The reordering of the church included a new altar, lectern, chair and font done in oak by Fenwick Lawson.

19. DARLINGTON   Carmel Convent   *(December 1994, January 1995)*

Two hundred years ago, in 1794, Bishop William Gibson, Vicar-Apostolic of the Northern District, welcomed to the North East a small group of Carmelite nuns who had fled their convent of Lierre in Brabant when the Low Countries were invaded by the French Revolutionary Army. Bishop Gibson, in his letter to them, remarked: 'I have just received your favour of the eleventh informing me of your safe arrival at Brough and your wish to settle your Community at St. Helen's, Auckland. I most sincerely congratulate you on your escape and on your arrival in this district and neighbourhood, and it gives me great pleasure to hear of it, particularly as I have always had the greatest esteem of your Order; and I hope your prayers will be of great service to me and this District...'

The origin of this group of English Carmelites, whose successors live in the Darlington Carmel, can be traced back to the penal days when religious orders were proscribed in our country after the Reformation. But the Carmelite way of spirituality was developed much earlier by a group of hermits who inhabited the region of Mount Carmel in the Holy Land; they became dispersed in the 13th century and began to make foundations in Europe. One of their earliest was Hulne Priory, near Alnwick Castle, where a community of friars established themselves in 1242.

Later women were to form communities modelled on the rule of the Carmelite friars, and convents sprang up to provide a contemplative setting for would-be aspirants. Perhaps, the most famous Carmelite is the Spanish nun and saint, Teresa of Avila, who in middle life decided to set up a reformed convent of the Order - the Discalced (bare-footed) Carmelites - in 1562. She was assisted and advised by St. Peter of Alcantara and in the reform of the friars, some years later, her co-worker was the mystic, St. John of the Cross. Her reformed rule appealed to many women and she made further foundations in Spain. She was to die in 1582 and was canonised in 1622. Her autobiography and treatises on prayer have appealed to many people throughout the world and she is one of the few women who has been made a doctor of the church.

Her infectious spirituality and zeal for reform could not be contained in her native land. Two of her contemporaries, Blessed Anne of St. Bartholomew and the Venerable Anne of Jesus, brought the first Carmel to France in 1604; the latter was to make another foundation in Flanders.

An English connection with these holy women occurred when an English girl, Anne Worsley, born in Antwerp, entered the Mons convent in 1608 where she began to imbibe the Carmelite spirit from the sister who had known St. Teresa. Anne, on her profession, was to be known as Anne of the Ascension and she was to play an important role in passing on the Teresian tradition to later English entrants to the order.

In 1611, she and a few sisters were led by Blessed Anne of St. Bartholomew to begin a convent in Antwerp. Five years later she helped to found yet another at Mechlin.

About this time a Lady Lovel, an English exile, decided to devote her considerable fortune to the foundation of an English Carmel which, unfortunately, at that time could not be established in England. It was therefore decided to establish it in Antwerp in 1619.

Anne Worsley was elected prioress and in her community were two other English women: Sister Clare of Jesus and Sister Teresa of Jesus (a sister of Mary Ward, foundress of the Institute of the Blessed Virgin Mary). Anne Worsley is recorded as ruling the community for 25 years making 'a nursery of saints and of the true Teresian spirit.' Many young women, following Anne Worsley's example, were to find their spiritual home in this English Carmel.

They obviously had contacts with missionary priests who risked all to keep the Faith alive in their homeland. Chaplain, for a time, to the Antwerp Carmel was the martyr St. Henry Morse, who ministered, also, to the plague victims in London and Newcastle. Shortly before his execution at Tyburn he gave his friend, Father Thomas Harvey, a holy picture asking that it be given to Anne Worsley (a sister of Father Harvey) in thanks for her prayers. This relic has been preserved at the Lanherne Carmel in Cornwall (an Antwerp foundation).

Lierre, a small town south of Antwerp, was to be the place where a second English Carmel was founded in 1648 on the initiative of Mother Teresa of Jesus (Ward) then prioress at Antwerp. Here the sisters were to remain until 1794 when they returned to England. Their first chaplain was Father Edmund Bedingfield, son of Sir Henry Bedingfield, who was to be 'a devoted friend and father' to the sisters until his death in 1680. Together with the founding sisters was a Durham woman, Sister Margaret of St. Francis (Johnson) who in the order's necrology is described as one whom 'Our Lord endowed with a singular love of holy poverty... in her, the truth is exemplified that Our Lord reveals his secrets to the humble...'

Amongst the families who gave daughters to the Carmel Order was the Mostyn family of Flintshire in North Wales. Sister Margaret of Jesus of this family was prioress of the Lierre Convent for 25 years. Within living memory there has been a member of the Mostyn family in the Darlington Carmel.

A Margaret Mostyn, widowed and having tried her vocation with the Poor Clares and the Benedictines, finally settled at Lierre and when prioress was responsible for the building of a new convent. Visitors to Lierre today can still see the old convent chapel which now houses a parochial library and the offices of the St. Vincent de Paul Society. The 'new' convent is now subdivided into private apartments.

There was much persecution in France after 1789 and the religious orders were not exempt. The story of the French emigre priests who sought refuge in England is already well-known. Less well-known, perhaps, is the suffering endured by the religious orders. The Carmelite Order claims its martyrs during this period when sixteen of them were executed at Compiegne on July 17th, 1794. They were not alone: Sisters of Charity were executed at Arras and Ursulines at Valenciennes - to name but a few of those religious and layfolk who made the heroic sacrifice.

About a fortnight before the Compiegne Carmelites were guillotined, the English sisters at Lierre found it necessary to leave as the French Revolutionary Army overran the Low Countries. Earlier that same year the Duke of Cambridge and his brother, the Duke of York, had visited some of the religious houses in Flanders promising a safe haven in England if they found it necessary to leave. The Carmelite Annals record: 'It was at the suggestion of the royal family that the many English nuns on the Continent came home to their native land.'

Sister Euphrasia Ignatius of the Holy Angels was the last to be professed at Lierre shortly before their departure; she was much loved by the Darlington Carmelites being 'a living link between Lierre and Darlington' until her death in 1848. Their chaplain, who followed them to England, was Father Roby who was to devote 51 years of his life to the spiritual needs of the community until his death in Darlington in 1841.

Their history describes in a very matter-of-fact way their hurried departure from Lierre: 'On 2nd July we proceeded to Breda and thence to Rotterdam. Here we beheld a moving sight: several different communities, all on their way to England, among them the Carmelite community of Antwerp. On the 4th we took shipping to England'.

Dressed in secular clothes they arrived in London where they were hospitably sheltered, some by a Mrs Cater and the remainder by Mr Charles Butler. In the search for a permanent abode help was to come in the person of Sir John Lawson of Brough Hall, Yorkshire, who invited them to the North promising to be their protector 'which kind promise he performed until death deprived us of so valuable a benefactor'.

Early in September they journeyed North and were welcomed by the sisters of the Bar Convent in York who described the 'smiling Carmelites ... for clothing they had picked up whatever they could beg: one wore a man's hat, another had on a pair of priest's shoes. In their dresses were seen all the colours of the rainbow!' They continued to Brough Hall staying there for about a fortnight before proceeding to St. Helen Hall, near Bishop Auckland, the lease of which had been arranged by Sir John. On the feast of Our

Lady of Mercy, September 24th, the whole community were joyfully established in their new convent.

The first postulant to enter St. Helen's was a dairy maid from Brough Hall, Sister Mary Bridget of the Passion. In 1862, Grace Lawson, a granddaughter of Sir John, entered the Darlington Carmel. One other interesting point worthy of note is the kindness shown to the sisters by the Anglican Bishop of Durham, Lord Barrington, who gave them financial assistance and 'insisted on their driving through his grounds when they left Bishop Auckland ten years later, a privilege he reserved for his friends, he said, among whom he counted them.'

Due to the inadequate accommodation at St. Helen's the sisters decided to move in 1804, to Cocken Hall near Finchale Abbey; this move may have been facilitated by the Carr family who owned St. Helen's and property in the Cocken area. Their new home was described 'as a beautiful mansion with clock-tower, large gardens and woodland, ideal for a monastery'. They could not have been far from the spot where St. Godric, the hermit of Finchale, had dwelt.

The Carmelites would have liked to have remained at Cocken Hall but the rising rent made them feel insecure, so with the aid of generous benefactors they were able to procure the present site of Cockerton Field House, which then stood on the outskirts of a much smaller Darlington and to which they moved in 1830.

Field House - first mentioned in documents in 1704 - has been the Darlington Carmel for more than 100 years. Extensions were added and alterations made so that it would resemble a typical Carmel with all the requisite buildings.

On August 5th, 1848 (the Bicentenary year of the Lierre foundation), the foundation stone of a new chapel was laid; it was consecrated by Bishop William Hogarth in 1859.

There are many treasured memories of those early pioneering sisters preserved at Darlington: Mother Mary Anne Bernard, who died at Cocken Hall, in 1827, guided the community in their transition from Lierre to England; and Mother Francis Xavier Jesson, buried at Darlington, who was the 'last relic of Lierre'. One sister is buried at Bishop Auckland, 15 at Houghton-le-Spring and two at Ushaw.

Under the guidance and care of their prioress, Sister Margaret, the Darlington sisters continue the reformed Carmelite tradition inspired by St. Teresa of Avila.

Their daily life based on their love of God, contemplation and the total offering of their life to Christ through the vows of poverty, chastity and obedience, has altered little throughout the last 300 years.

The community numbers at present 26 members; 21 sisters are fully professed; there are two novices; two have made their first profession and there is one pre-postulant. Their backgrounds are varied: among them are former teachers, nurses, business people and one professional singer; quite a number hail from the North East.

Interspersed with their daily worship are the various works performed by the sisters to support themselves. The printing of books and cards, the making of icons, toy-making, knitting, gardening, candle-making all help to provide the necessary income they need to survive.

In the early 1970s it was realised that there were too many Carmels on the mainland of Britain, some of which had depleted communities. It was decided that some amalgamations were necessary and after due prayer and discussion the Wells Community in Somerset (founded from Lanherne which had its roots in Antwerp) in 1972 came to reside at Darlington.

Whilst in some parts of the world there was contraction, in others there was expansion. As early as 1931 seven Darlington sisters had gone to Rivonia, Johannesburg, to found a new Carmel; it closed fairly recently, but has a daughter-house in Wynberg, Capetown. In February, 1992, four sisters from Darlington, three from Germany and one from South Africa 'set sail from Tilbury' to begin a new foundation in Mafeking; their hope is that it will become a native African community of Teresian sisters.

Today the sisters of Darlington in their life of prayer based on the Gospel try to follow in the footsteps of Christ. Following the wise counsels of their founder, St. Teresa of Avila, their life of prayer is not just for themselves but the whole world. She encourages all those who pray to remember that: Mental prayer, in my opinion, is nothing else but falling in love with Christ, frequently conversing with him who we know loves us ... Do not be afraid that the Lord who has called us to drink of this spring will allow you to die of thirst.

Pope John XXIII stated that the contemplative life is precious in God's eyes and to the church: '... a silent reminder of the fundamentals of the spiritual life: prayer, contemplation, silent labour, sacrifice. A life of intimate union with God through love.' The words of Pope John are borne out in the testimony given below by some of the present community in Darlington.

A sister in her fifties looking back on her choice of vocation remembers asking herself the question: 'What do you want of me Lord? which for me was the essence of prayer, and then not give Him what I knew deep in my heart He was asking. There have been many surprises, at times painful, since I said, "Yes" to the Lord and entered Carmel at the age of 24, but I have never regretted entrusting my life to his unfailing love.'

Another writes: 'It is love that brought me into the cloister and it is love that keeps me here.'

A young sister recently entered finds 'that a life that is structured yet without rigidity enables my relationship with Christ and my neighbour to grow, and so is of benefit to my brothers and sisters everywhere.'

A sister in her seventies can look back over a long life spent here and rejoices that 'my love for God is lived out in silent prayer and work and in fidelity to this I discovered the secret of a happiness I cannot keep to myself.'

POSTSCRIPT   *(Sister Francis Therese, 1998)*
Love brought her to Carmel and love keeps her in Darlington.

In January, 1995, Sister Annunciata of Darlington volunteered to join the foundation of a Carmel in Nigeria. It was being founded by the Carmelites of New Ross, County Wexford, Ireland. Established at Zing, in the diocese of Jalingo, it now has a flourishing community with native vocations.

20. EASINGTON COLLIERY   Our Lady   *(January, February 1997)*

The red-brick modern church of Our Lady in Easington Colliery is the third Catholic church built for the Catholics here in the past 100 and more years. Designed and built after the reforms of Vatican II, its interior plan and seating arrangements allow the worshippers to gather more closely to the altar. During the week, with the use of a partition, a smaller chapel can be created near the sanctuary where a smaller congregation can worship more intimately.

Delving into the past history of this area, one soon becomes aware of its ancient Christian tradition going back for over a 1,000 years. Early records tells us that when Cutheard was Bishop of Chester-le-Street (900-915) the land was leased to Ealfred. The later *Boldon Book* (our northern Doomsday Book) compiled in 1183, lists Easington as a manor owned by the Bishopric of Durham and was to give its name to the administrative ward which stretched from the Wear almost to the Tees.

Prominent for miles around on the high ground near the old village green is the pre-Reformation church of St. Mary the Virgin (a complete medieval church) said to have been founded or endowed by Bishop Richard de Marisco sometime before 1222, probably on the site of an earlier Saxon building. A Norman tower - used of old as a landmark for sailors - and much of the rest of the church in the Early English style reminds us of our ancestors in the Faith who worshipped here. At the foot of the tower is placed a Saxon Cross probably a relic of the earlier building.

It appears there were two chantries to Our Lady in the church where Mass was said regularly by chaplains for the souls of benefactors. Not long before chantries were abolished by the Reformation changes, one was endowed in 1526, believed to be dedicated to Our Lady of Pity. By the terms of the endowment it was requested 'for one preeste to sing at the awlter of Our Ladye in the Church of Easington, for the saules of the said John Jakeson, Jenet his wife, his parents, Deane Henry Dalton ... and for all Christen saules ...'

A keen observer wandering around the ancient village of Easington with its green almost surrounded by houses will notice to the north of the church an old house with buttressed walls. This was the old rectory built in the mid-13th century; behind this are some further architectural remains in a building which may have been an oratory and also a tithe barn.

Most people are aware of the changes in religion following the Reformation in the 16th century and Easington did not remain untroubled by them. As late as 1545 the Radcliffe family owned land in the nearby village of Hawthorn. When the Northern Rising occurred in 1569 one if its leaders was the Earl of Westmorland (a Radcliffe) who had in his contingent six men from Easington. Having failed in its attempt to restore the Faith of old, severe punishments were inflicted on the insurgents. Many villages in Durham County witnessed executions, among them 20 men from the Easington ward, two of whom suffered on the village green.

So how did those fare who wished to preserve their Catholic beliefs in the years of persecution? That there were faithful souls who persevered in their beliefs we can be certain, although it was done unobtrusively and sometimes at great personal cost. To the south of Easington were the strong Catholic enclaves of the Maires at Hardwick Hall and the Trollopes at Thornley. Richard Holtby, the Jesuit, who resided in the North and was never apprehended, did much heroic work here building up a network of secret places of worship in the houses of the gentry. To these houses, where there was often a resident priest, local Catholics would have recourse to the Mass and the sacraments. East of Easington was Horden Hall where the recusant family of Conyers lived - here, too, was a pocket of Catholicism. Sir John Conyers, who died in 1664, was buried at Easington and a memorial tablet of the Conyers can be seen on the south wall of the old church. When adult males over 18 were obliged to make public protestations in 1642, which virtually meant a denial of their Catholic Faith, among about 550 listed in the County of Durham who refused were four from Easington, ten from Thornley and six from Monk Hesleden.

As the 18th century progressed there was an increasing toleration towards those who dissented from the Anglican Church. Persecution lessened and eventually, due to a number of factors, Catholics were able to practise their Faith more openly. The Papist Returns of 1767 show there were 23 recusants in the Easington parish and about 23 at Monk Hesleden, including the priest, the Rev. Clavering.

It was not so much the rapid rise in the Catholic population in the Easington area in the second half of the 19th century which led to a small chapel being built here, but rather the generosity of the Crowe family in the person of Father Thomas Crowe who was ordained at Ushaw in 1820, dying at Formby in 1862. His family had resided in the Easington area for many years and are mentioned in the Papist Returns of 1767; some of his ancestors lie buried in the old churchyard of St. Mary the Virgin. There used to be two small miniatures of Father Crowe and his mother in the old presbytery at Easington and a considerable number of books given to the parish by him. They left money also for the education of priests at Ushaw. His mother lived to the age of 90, being born in 1755 and dying in 1845. Her lifetime spanned the period of gradual change of the Catholic Church's fortunes. In her youth she would have witnessed small Catholic enclaves persevering resolutely in their Faith and hoping for better days which came later in her life with the removal of the penal legislation, the granting of Catholic Emancipation and the steady growth of Catholic congregations in their rural and urban settings.

Before the foundation of parishes in this area of south east Durham, Catholics from the small villages - which were later to expand as the pits were developed - travelled to Hardwick Hall and, after 1825 to Hutton House, or the priest from there said Mass locally for the people in a suitable house or building in their village. In the case of Easington we know that the priest said Mass in the front room of the Robinson home which later became the Brampton Club.

In an agreement, dated July 11th, 1861, and kept in the diocesan archives, Father Crowe is shown as the Founder of the Easington Mission, having arranged with Bishop Hogarth that a place of worship should be built near the old parish church. Bishop Hogarth was able to fulfil the intentions of the will by purchasing in 1863 'a house and premises in a close called Great Garth' once the Anglican curate's residence; one of the rooms was converted into a small chapel. Father Patrick Thomas Matthews who came in 1865 was the first resident priest here but stayed less than a year moving to north west Durham where he did pioneering work in founding the parishes at Sacriston, Byermoor, and Stanley.

The first purpose-built post-Reformation church to serve the Catholics of Easington for almost 100 years was built by Thomas Brown in 1875 or 1876 during the incumbency of Father Laurence Boland on the Chapelgate site purchased by Bishop Chadwick in 1870; the cost was just over £236.

Easington Colliery did not start producing coal until 1910; this development brought many people to the area necessitating the erection of 1,000 houses and the beginning of a new community east of the village including a considerable number of Catholics. Similar growth was experienced at Murton, Horden, Shotton and Wheatley Hill demanding a response by the church for spiritual ministry to the new inhabitants. In 1899 a school-chapel was opened at Murton and served by the Easington priests until 1912 when the parish was given a permanent pastor. Likewise at Horden priestly ministry was supplied from Easington until it became a separate parish in 1921.

As early as 1916 Mass was said for the Catholics in Shotton in the local council school but when Father Ord opened a church in 1921 at Fleming Field the situation was somewhat eased; it became an independent parish in 1940. Blackhall, served from Hutton House, had by 1924 a school-chapel at Hardwick and a new church and school were built for the Blackhall community in the village in 1945. Such is the brief description of how Catholicism developed in this area of the county in and around Easington. Fathers Ord (1918-30) and Leech (1930-45) parish priests of Easington were to play, along with the curates and parishioners, important roles in building up the Faith communities in this area.

It became obvious to Father Ord that a new church was necessary in the colliery. Plans were set in hand and a new church of artificial stone with accommodation for 300 souls was opened and blessed by Mgr. James Rooney in July, 1923, and named in honour of Our Lady's Assumption. Easington had for a number of years two churches and presbyteries catering for village and colliery communities.

Miners and their families have always had to live with the fear of injury and death as part of their hazardous occupation. On May 29th, 1951, the Easington community suffered one of the worst mining disasters of the century when 81 miners and two rescue workers lost their lives as a result of an underground explosion. This tightly-knit community, shattered by this experience, nevertheless supported and consoled each other throughout the days following the tragedy. Fathers Clifford and Corrigan remained at the pithead for 24 hours comforting the bereaved and assisting in the identification of the bodies. Ten of the deceased miners were from the parish and were buried in the local cemetery after Requiem Masses in the Our Lady of the Assumption Church. A memorial garden with sculptures in the Easington cemetery is a permanent reminder and tribute to the men whose lives were so tragically cut short. To further honour the mining dead, Memorial Avenue was laid out with trees on either side and a bronze plaque was placed on a piece of stone taken from the scene of the accident.

Not far away is the new town of Peterlee where it was hoped after the Second World War more modern housing, public amenities and new industries could be developed in this area of the County. There was, however, a fear that the old mining communities and their villages would suffer if too many people were attracted to the new town. In 1954 a new parish was established there by Father John Burns and the large commodious church of Our Lady of the Rosary was built.

With the introduction of comprehensive education Catholic children over 11 years of age were transferred from their all-age parish schools to the newly-built St. Bede's Comprehensive School in Peterlee. Many of the parish schools reverted to primary schools and still continue their good work to-day, although Easington children, in spite of efforts to obtain one, have never had their own school - their needs in the past and present being supplied by St. Bede's and the Catholic primary school at Horden.

As well as the desire for a new school the parishioners of Easington hoped to have a new church in a more central location. Their desire was realised during the incumbency of Father Patrick O'Connor, who arrived as a curate in 1971, succeeding as parish priest in 1975 and remaining here until 1987.

The last Mass in the old village chapel was celebrated in September, 1976. A year later on a plot of land acquired in Cemetery Lane the building of the new church was begun to a modern design of the architects Messrs. David Brown and Associates of Newcastle; the builder was Mr George Stephenson of Bishop Auckland. The presbytery adjoins the church which has a seating capacity for 250 worshippers.

On the right-hand side of the nave is a stained-glass screen, designed by Mr Ramm of the Gateshead firm of Reed Millican, which incorporates a colourful depiction of Our Lady with the Ave Maria scroll beneath (this section comes from a convent in Golders Green). The St. Luke window is a reminder of the earlier days of the parish having at one time been in the old village Catholic Church.

The social life of many parishes has changed somewhat from the days when, in addition to meeting people's spiritual needs, the parish was also the focus for much of the parishioners' community activities. Some of the older organisations are either depleted in membership or have disappeared altogether. However, priests and congregation attempt to meet the needs of these changing times and Our Lady's is no exception. From 1989 until May 1996 Father Paul McDermott, a Yorkshireman, educated at Ushaw, had been parish priest continuing the work of his predecessors (too many to list here). He was succeeded in the Spring of 1996 by Father Alban Walker who came from St. John Bosco parish in Sunderland.

Priests and committed lay people have worked together through the years and continue to do so. A finance group encourages the making of covenants to swell the parish income; there are 24 Lay Ministers of the Eucharist who through regular visitation enable the sick and housebound to receive communion frequently. A small care group visits the housebound bringing solace to them in their need. There are four teams working within the Children's Liturgy Group - a valuable contribution to evangelisation in making the Sunday readings meaningful to the young.

Our Lady's parishioners are encouraged to look beyond their parish to the needs of others in the Third World. The First Friday Self-Denial Group raises about £180 per month for eight months in the year; they also man a Traidcraft stall which sells Third World goods at a price which pays the producers a fair return for their labour. The profits from the coffee mornings held after the Saturday Mass are donated to the H.C.P.T., an organisation devoted to assisting the disabled to travel to Lourdes. Sixteen ladies from the Women's Guild meet on a Monday evening to provide some social life for older parishioners; they also organise the Christmas Fayre.

Our Lady's parish, in terms of population and area, is now much smaller than it was at the turn of the century but it can proudly boast distant links with our Catholic past, perhaps unbroken since Saxon days.

21. ESH LAUDE　　St. Michael　　*(January, February, 1998)*

Standing on a high ridge of land five miles west of Durham City and overlooking the Deerness valley to the south and the Browney to the north is the church of St. Michael opened in 1799. Surrounded by trees the isolated church, west of Esh Village, might leave the casual passer-by with the impression that it was no more than a set of farm buildings and this was what the priest and people of 200 years ago intended.

Although Catholics, by the end of the 18th century, could practise their Faith more openly, with memories of persecution and discrimination still fresh in their minds they deemed it advisable to remain inconspicuous as in the days of St. John Boste, a local martyr, who was apprehended in the home of the recusant Claxton family at Waterhouses not far from Esh.

John, a Fellow of Queen's College, Oxford, converted to Catholicism in 1576 then proceeded to the English College at Rheims where he was ordained in 1581. Such was his zeal and success as a missioner that the authorities named him 'The greatest stag in the forest'; he suffered martyrdom at Durham on July 24th, 1594.

Prominent, by the roadside, in Esh Village is the Anglican church - also named after St. Michael - which has virtually been re-built over the centuries but incorporating some reminders of its more ancient past, such as the St. Helen porch; it is believed to stand on the original site of the first chapel.

More than likely this was the Esh family chapel not far from which stood the original Esh Hall said to have been situated near the village green. Possibly of Norman origin, the Esh family were certainly in possession of the manor before 1313 and retained ownership until approximately 1530 when Anthony Esh died.

When Margaret, one of Anthony's two daughters, married William Smythe of Nunstainton, Co. Durham, the lands around Esh passed into his family's hands and were to remain in their possession for almost 300 years. William, who participated in the Northern Rising of 1569 and was attainted appears to have held on to his Esh estate. This retention was to bring inestimable benefits to those who wished to continue the practice of the Old Faith in and around Esh.

About 100 years later a descendant of William, Edward Smythe, came to own, through his wife Mary Lee and by his widowed mother's second marriage to Sir Robert Lee, the estate of Acton Burnell in Shropshire. This became their chief seat about 1714 but their contribution to the preservation of the Faith in the area of Esh was still considerable.

We believe it was Sir Edward Smythe of Esh, made a baronet in 1660, who was responsible for the building of the second Esh Hall sometime after this date, on the upper floor of which was a chapel with a priest's hiding hole incorporating an escape route onto the roof. Here, at the Hall, the local Catholics would have been welcomed by the family to receive spiritual sustenance from the chaplain or visiting priest.

When Henry Smith, a Yorkshire Catholic, who looked after the Esh estate demolished the old Hall in 1857 a hidden room was discovered (possibly the priest's hiding hole) containing an iron-bound box in which were found four vestments, a 14th century French ivory triptych, a missal owned by the martyr, Blessed Alexander Briant, and some 14th century embroideries which were later sewn onto vestments at Ushaw College; the old chapel altar was given to Ushaw in 1894.

This find has come to be known as the 'Taylor Treasure' after a local family into whose possession it came.

An earlier Edward Smythe who died in 1651 and his father George, who were probably not always resident in Esh, were concerned that permanent provision should be made for a priest to serve the area. In 1651 a Deed of Settlement was drawn up which provided that one priest of the Secular Clergy of England may for the comfort of our neighbours have a convenient lodging with provision for fire and meat for one horse and two kine in the most convenient place for the purpose with a stipend or annuity of ten pounds yearly to be paid unto him.

It was decided that the priest so endowed would reside at Newhouse, near Esh Winning, in the Deerness valley, a little over a mile downhill from Esh Hall. Why this place was chosen we can only hazard a guess. Maybe there were more Catholics there or it may have been more secluded and safer than the area immediately around Esh.

The names of the earliest priests at Newhouse we do not know; we do know, however, that 20 recusants of Esh, including Sir Edward Smythe, in 1673 were brought before the Durham court. The Rev. John Torbet (alias Simpson) is the first priest whose name is recorded. Born in Yorkshire, he trained at Valladolid and was ordained there. According to Anstruther he came to Newhouse in 1693. Little is known about his unobtrusive ministry; he went to live with the Batmansons near Ushaw where he died in 1727, leaving £550 to support the mission. He was buried in the Anglican graveyard at Esh as was his probable successor, Dr. Luke Gardiner (alias Carnaby), a Northumbrian; and it may have been during the latter's incumbency, sometime in the 1730s, that a small chapel was built next to the priest's house.

The development of the Newhouse mission is really another story, but one cannot leave it without mentioning one of its longest-serving priests, the Rev. Ferdinand Ashmall. Born at Amerston, in the parish of Sedgefield in 1695, he trained for the priesthood in Lisbon and was ordained in 1720. For four years he was chaplain to Mrs Mary Salvin at Old Elvet, Durham, until she died about 1727. He seems to have suffered a period of ill-health which caused him to retire to the family home until 1744 when his health improved and he went to the Newhouse mission.

In the *Catholic Magazine* of March, 1832, a description is given of the venerable missioner as he journeyed around 'his parish' serving his scattered flock: 'The old leather gaiters, drawn considerably above the knee, the left heel alone armed with a spur, the well-worn grey coat, the check cloak wrapped up and fixed behind the saddle, and the slouched hat drawn carefully over the flaxen wig. Mounted upon a pony, whose colour, age recounted, should have been white but whose rough and soiled coat wore the appearance of no great expense of grooming, and whom the loss of sight rendered at once unfashionable and unsafe. The salutation of the peasant, as going to his daily toil, of "Weel, I warrant ye are for the fair"; and the ready reply of "Aye, aye, I reckon see" has afforded many a joke to his friends.'

In Esh village is the old inn, the Cross Keys, which title may have some religious significance. In the Rev. Ashmall's days it would have had a thatched roof and whitewashed walls. It was for many years in the ownership of the Marley family, who were Catholics, and it has even been suggested that it may have been used on occasions as a meeting place where people could converse with their priest in safety.

Ferdinando (as he was sometimes known) was a tall, well-built man who was approached one day on the Esh road by a man who wished to arrest him for being a Catholic priest. The story may be apocryphal, but he is supposed to have dismounted grabbed the accuser by the scruff of the neck and breeches and deposited him on the far side of the road hedge.

As old age got the better of him he was given an assistant priest the last of which was the Rev. John Yates who succeeded to the mission when Ferdinand died. It is a great pity we have no detailed biography of a priest whose priestly life spanned 75 years, 54 of which were spent at Newhouse. He epitomises the dogged adherence to Faith and principle and the great sacrifices that many priests of his era made in order to comfort and sustain the beliefs of those Catholics who, against the odds, persevered in their religious observance. He lived to be 103, dying in 1798, and was buried in front of the altar rails at Newhouse; there is reason to suppose that he was later re-interred in the Catholic graveyard at Esh Laude. 'A most active kind missioner, a man of family and fortune and respected by everyone' is a fitting epitaph.

It fell to the Rev. John Yates to implement the change from Newhouse to Esh Laude. The buildings at the former were now dilapidated and the latter seemed to be a more appropriate place particularly as Sir Edward Smythe was happy to exchange the land at Newhouse for the ten acres of the Salutation Field in Esh; the transfer also coincided with the relaxation of the penal laws which allowed Catholics to build public chapels provided they were registered. It was, also, at this time that negotiations between Bishop William Gibson, vicar-apostolic, and Sir Edward were in progress for the sale of land on which Ushaw College was to be built. Mr John Taylor, land agent for the Smythes, signed the agreement of purchase on March 26th, 1799 for the college land; the final settlement was agreed in November at a cost of £4,626.

No time seems to have been wasted; the foundation stone of St. Michael's, Esh Laude, was laid by Mr Peter Holford, agent and father-in-law of Sir Edward in June, 1798. The last Mass at Newhouse was celebrated on the Sunday before New Year and the first Mass at Esh Laude on New Year's Day, 1799, although the Rev. Yates did not take up permanent residence there until 1804 when the presbytery was completed. The Newhouse mission was now closed but was to have a re-birth when pits were sunk at Waterhouses and Esh Winning (1866) bringing sufficient Catholics into the area to warrant the building of a new church which was opened in 1871, on land donated by the ever-generous Smythe family.

Of Lancashire stock, the Rev. John Yates, a Douai man ordained at York, served the parish of Esh Laude for over 27 years until his death. From February, 1819, every other Sunday he travelled to Brooms to minister to the growing congregation there. He was succeeded by the Rev. William Fletcher who continued to serve Brooms until he moved there in 1837. Described as an 'indefatigable missioner', he had to be; for when at Esh his territory covered more than 400 square miles.

When the Rev. Fletcher went to Brooms he was followed by the Rev. Roger Glassbrook who was at Esh for three years. The Rev. Thomas Edward Witham was here for a short time; the next two incumbents were between them to serve Esh Laude for 90 years.

The Rev. William Thompson, educated at Ampleforth and the English College, Rome, took over at Esh in 1841 having been an assistant there with the Rev. Witham. During his tenure he built new schools and improved and enlarged the church. He was a friend of Cardinal Wiseman and his literary executor which explains why the Esh altar is dedicated to this English prince of the church. Canon Thompson retired in 1880 to a farm at Stella left to him by his father, where he died in 1893.

His time at Esh was exceeded by his successor, Father (later Canon) Samuel Harris, who was parish priest here for over 50 years until his death in 1933. He further enlarged the church with the addition of the south aisle, saw Lanchester created a separate parish from Esh in 1926 and began the Mass centre at Langley Park in 1920.

Another priest who did devoted work here was Mgr. Cogan (1933-55) who had the stone-slabbed roof replaced with slates and the school buildings improved.

Father Philip Blandford, a Claretian Father, is the present parish priest of Esh Laude and Langley Park. He is helped in his ministry by Brother Denis Casey from Carrick-on-Suir. Also resident with the community, whilst pursuing their priestly studies at Ushaw and Durham University, are two Claretian students: Martin Stone and Dominic McDonagh.

This missionary order of Claretians was founded by Anthony Claret. Born in 1807 in Catalonia into a family who owned a textile mill, he became a master weaver and designer.

Although offered the position of head of a large corporation he was dissatisfied with worldly ambition and after trying his vocation as monk and Jesuit novice he was finally ordained for the diocesan priesthood.

He began to organise parish missions and after much thought and prayer, and with the assistance of six young men who joined him, the Claretian missionary order was formed in 1849; their aim was to live the gospel ideal in community and devote their lives to the ministry of preaching.

Appointed Archbishop of Santiago in Cuba he did much reforming work there amongst the clergy and people. On his return to Spain he became confessor to Queen Isabella II but insisted that his missionary work must take priority; he died near Narbonne in 1870 and was canonised in 1950. Claretian missionaries are to be found today in many parts of the world.

The parish of St. Michael's includes Langley Park, Quebec, and Cornsay Colliery - not the extensive parish it was in the time of Ferdinand Ashmall. Father Blandford and his committed parishioners continue the good work done in the past and are looking at ways of making it more effective. The oldest organisation continuing the charitable work begun in 1914 is the S.V.P. conference of 12 members (men and women). To enable those who wish to attend daily Mass provision is made in St. Joseph's church and Esh convent.

In spite of the scattered nature of the parish the Youth Club, led by Phil Eckermann, is so popular that two separate sessions are necessary to meet the demand.

A developing relationship with other denominations is prominent in the area, also; a joint Service of Remembrance is held every November and in July (1997) an inter-denominational 'Songs of Praise' took place in Langley Park. Father Philip meets regularly ministers of other faiths at clergy fraternals. An R.C.I.A. course has been running for some years in the parish giving an opportunity for Catholic and non-Catholic alike to learn more about our Faith.

It is only to be expected that in a parish staffed by missionary priests the Third World needs should figure prominently. As well as the usual assistance given to CAFOD and other charities the parishioners have been involved in fund-raising to help Claretians abroad - Guatemala is an example. Another is the financial help given by parishioners to help the poor in the Andes region of Peru; this was taken recently to them by Martin Stone, a Claretian student.

Much has been written in the past about Esh Laude but one must remember that Langley Park, where the majority of the parishioners live, is a vital and integral part of the parish with its own church of St. Joseph's which was built in Father Cain's time and opened on October 24th, 1968; it is a Swedish prefabricated building costing £36,000 which included demolition charges and site development.

Like many other areas in Durham County, it was the opening of the pit in 1875 which led to the creation of the community. The first Mass celebrated here was in 1910 in the local Church of England school through the kind permission of the local vicar - an early ecumenical gesture surely!

Canon Harris was responsible for the erection of the first church at Langley Park in 1920 where the present parish hall now stands. During Mgr. Cogan's time the Springwell presbytery was purchased for £1,000 providing accommodation for assistant secular priests to be near the people until the Claretians took over in 1978 with the arrival of Father Wareing; they removed to Esh Laude when the late Father Bryce retired in 1995.

It was with much sadness that the people of the parish heard of the death of Father Godfrey Bryce on October 19th, 1997, whilst attending the A.G.M. of the St. Vincent de Paul Society in Liverpool.

Father Bryce was parish priest of Esh Laude and Langley Park for 23 years during which time he endeared himself to old and young alike in his concern for their welfare. He participated in the ecumenical dialogue that was developing during his pastorate; his frequent visitation of St. Michael's School, St. Leonard's School in Durham, and the parish Youth Club assured his young parishioners of his support and interest in their lives.

One cannot fail to mention the great work the Catholic school at Esh has done since 1795 when it was first opened. Sister Anna, a Sister of Mercy from the Alnwick community who came here in September, 1979 - when after many dedicated years to the children the Sisters of St. Paul left - claims this is the oldest Catholic School in the diocese still currently used. Sister comments on the great supportive role Father Bryce gave to them all in his years here - he is much missed.

A small school with 140 children, who come from far and near, including some non-Catholics, it received recently an excellent OFSTED report 'giving good value for money.'

St. Michael's must be unique - it seems to have the oldest school and the oldest parish church in our diocese - a proud record of the continuity of Faith on which the priests and people of Langley Park and Esh Laude will want to build.

22. FELLING   St. Patrick   *(April, 1985)*

There are two reasons for writing this article on Felling: firstly, a parishioner Mr Edward Kennedy has written more than once to *Northern Cross* requesting an article and remarking that 'every parish in the Diocese should be aware of the glorious history of this, our parish of St. Patrick's'; and secondly, to pay a tribute to the present parish priest, Father Bernard Stronge, who - soon to retire - has spent his whole priestly life in the Felling and Gateshead area.

Felling and its surrounding area was once, in medieval days, a manor within the parish of Heworth and a document of 1214 testifies that a chapel was here too; both were the responsibility of the prior and monastery of Durham.

The coming of the Reformation brought many changes yet the old Faith was not completely extinguished; it was kept alive in the home of the Brandling Family at Felling Hall. One legend maintains that a monk was hanged from a mulberry tree in the grounds of the Hall. One source claims that the existing Mulberry Tree Inn is the original Felling Hall - an interesting coincidence of name, if nothing else.

A well-authenticated piece of evidence is the Felling Mass vestment, a chasuble, believed to be of the 15th century which is now in the library of Stonyhurst College, Lancashire, and as its name implies was probably used for many years by the chaplains at the hall. We know that the Brandlings were settled there in the reign of Edward VI (1547 - 1553) and that a Ralph Brandling was in residence in 1732 when the Dominicans acted as chaplains; the first one being Father Robert Pius O.P.

It was to Felling Hall that Father John Walshe S.J., who served the Gateshead Mission, fled after the burning of the Gateshead House in 1746. One source claims the chapel was closed in 1749 when Ralph Brandling died and the property passed to a non-Catholic branch of the family; another supports the view that Mass continued to be said there until 1776.

With the resurgence of Catholicism in the late 18th century pioneered by Father James Worswick along the banks of the Tyne, Felling was near enough to St. Andrew's to feel the benefit too. One of Father Worswick's assistants was Father William Riddell, a member of an old Northumberland recusant family, who in 1847 became Bishop and Vicar-Apostolic of the Northern District; unfortunately his reign was short for whilst visiting the sick, he fell victim to the typhus epidemic raging in Newcastle at the time.

This brave priest had provided the money for the first St. Patrick's church at Felling Shore, opened in 1842, which he served regularly for two years from his base at St. Andrew's. The first resident priest at St. Patrick's was a Father A. McDermott who after two years was succeeded by Father John Kelly from Kilkenny - a remarkable man who having spent some years in the joinery trade was ordained at Ushaw at the age of 43 and served the Felling parish for 35 years.

Tyneside in the 19th century was a bustling hive of industrial activity and drawn to it were many Catholics, particularly from Ireland, looking for work in the mines, factories and workshops dotted along the riverside. Father Kelly, to meet this need, extended the Gothic church in 1853 doubling the seating capacity but even this proved inadequate. Another major concern was the provision of Catholic education for the children in the area: to procure this end he purchased a field on a sloping site in the High Street area. Using his own expertise and the voluntary labour of his male parishioners, St. John's school soon arose on the site and was opened on January 17th, 1864. Three or four years later part of the upper storey was screened off and was used as a chapel for weekday masses.

By 1853 the present presbytery was ready for occupation and, alongside it and immediately above the level of the school, Father John and his volunteers began at an unknown date the preliminary work for the present church, the foundation stone of which was laid in 1873. Sadly a fire occurred in 1877 delaying the completion of the church for 15 years.

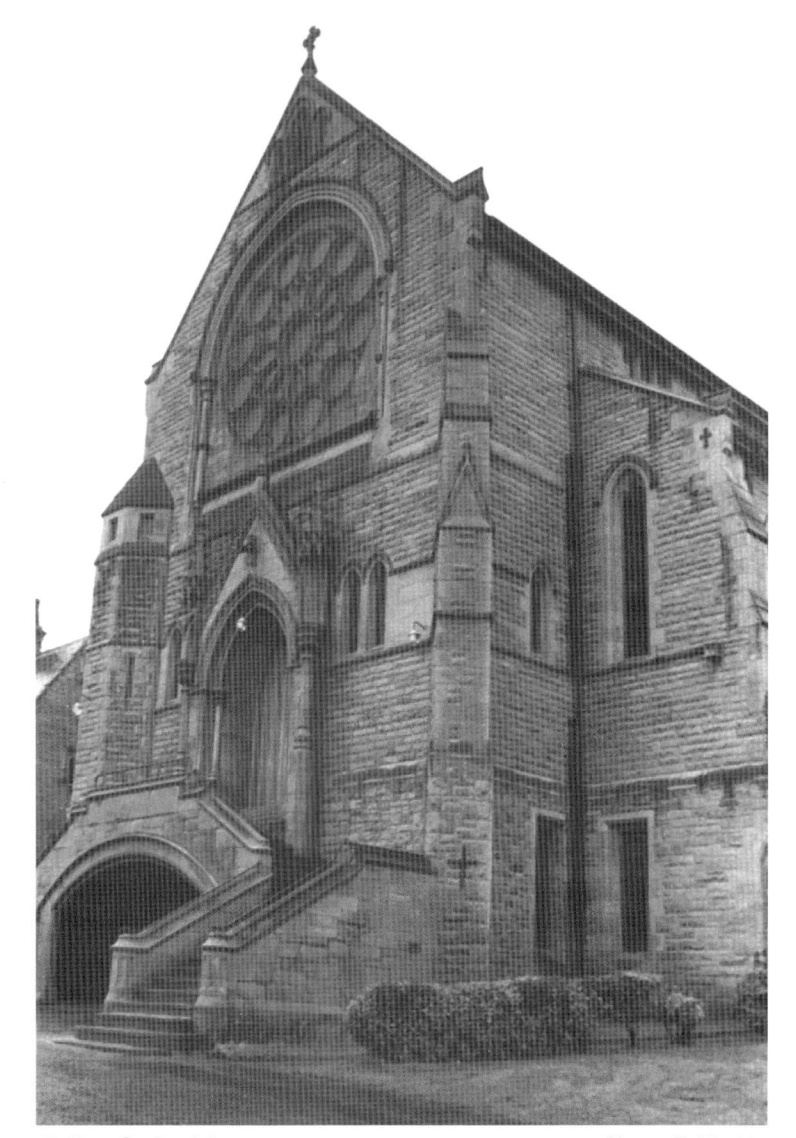

Felling, St. Patrick   *Photo: T. Mackin*

A remarkable story associated with Father Kelly and the secrecy of the confessional is worth quoting in some detail. Whilst hearing confessions on Christmas Day, 1859, a stolen silver watch was handed to him in the confessional. Father Kelly took it to the owner's house who was out at the time so he offered it to the owner's father who refused to accept it. Father Kelly stated he would hand it over to the police which he did. In the following March he was summoned as a witness to the Durham Assizes: 'called upon to take the oath, he objected to the form, because he could not swear to speak the 'whole' truth. The judge pointed out that a witness was not obliged to answer every question, but only those which might be legitimately put to him. After some demur Father Kelly ultimately took the oath in the usual form, and acknowledged to the prosecuting counsel that he had received a watch on Christmas Day. To the next question: "From whom did you receive the watch?" the witness replied, "I received it in connection with the confessional". The judge insistently repeated the question and the witness answered, "The reply to that question would implicate the person who gave it to me; therefore, I cannot answer it". The Judge remonstrated with the witness who replied, "If I answered that question I should be suspended for life. I should be violating the laws of the Church, and the natural law". To the judge's final demand, Father Kelly's reply was, "I really cannot answer, my Lord, whatever may be the consequences". "Then", said his lordship, Mr Justice Hill, "I adjudge you to be guilty of contempt of court, and order you to be committed to gaol". Father John Kelly was taken into custody, as a misdemeanant of the first division, on Monday afternoon and was released by order of the Judge on Wednesday morning, at 10 o'clock, after the question had been raised in the House of Commons.'

A collection was made by the parishioners to purchase a gold watch on which was inscribed: 'Presented to the Rev. John Kelly, by his parishioners, to commemorate his incarceration of forty hours in Durham gaol, for not revealing the secrets of the confessional'.

In his 68th year he was sprightly enough to climb and bless the steeple at St. Mary's Cathedral. When he reached the age of 77 he retired but continued to live in the parish until his death in 1883. He had achieved much but much still had to be done. His successor was his former curate since 1874, Father Thomas Carroll, who does not appear to have had his predecessor's robust constitution; he remained there 11 years dying at the age of 47 in 1892.

Father John Murphy who had gained a Doctorate of Divinity at the Gregorian University in Rome replaced Father Carroll in 1892 - the same year that the S.V.P. was started in the parish. Two major problems faced him immediately: extra school accommodation which he solved by buying the site and buildings of Lee's Factory Institute which became St. John the Baptist School in May, 1893; and the completion of the unfinished church.

Adjoining the presbytery was the daily reminder of a church to be completed where no progress had been made since the fire 15 years earlier. He engaged Mr Charles Walker of Newcastle to draw up plans incorporating the existing foundations with an extension. The builders were Messrs. Howe of West Hartlepool; the total cost was in the region of £13,500. Bishop Wilkinson opened the church on St. Patrick's Day 1895 and this was followed a few days later by a solemn opening performed by Archbishop Whiteside of Liverpool at which 50 priests and many parishioners were present.

'St. Patrick's Roman Catholic Church, the glory of Felling and the admiration of the visitor is a basilica of the Romanesque style' (Pevsner claims it is Early English) is a description given in the parish history which if anyone wishes to verify with a visit would not be disappointed. A separate article would be needed to describe adequately the solid exterior and the fascinating interior of this church with cathedral-like proportions capable of accommodating a seated congregation of 1000 people.

There is much beautiful craftsmanship to be seen here: the massive mullioned rose window above the entrance; the finely carved alabaster pulpit resting on a base of Frosterley marble; the marble-mounted communion rails with shining brass gates; the reredos behind the high altar intricately carved in Caen stone by Milburn of York; the stained-glass windows at the rear of the sanctuary donated by the people in memory of Father Kelly and showing St. Patrick receiving his mission to the Irish from Pope Celestine - all these and many more show the love past priests and people had for their parish church.

'Clarity and serenity are the dominant impressions of this noble edifice fit chamber for the contemplation of sublime truth' - quoted in the parish history.

A sad reminder of the effects of war is the brass memorial tablet listing 157 men of the parish who lost their lives in the Great War. However, Father Stronge informs us that a certain William Strother's name was put there by mistake when he was missing presumed killed; he survived and was anointed on his death bed about 15 years ago by Father Stronge.

Father Edward Costello followed Doctor Murphy and he set about reducing the large debt which hung over the parish. He, also, was responsible for the building of St. Alban's School at Pelaw, the foundation stone of which was laid by Bishop Thorman on April 18th, 1927.

The present parish priest, Father Bernard Stronge, who is to retire soon to a house in the parish has spent all his priestly life in the Gateshead area; after 18 years as a curate at Gateshead he moved down the road to Felling in 1946 to succeed Father Costello and there he has been ever since.

His long ministry has seen many changes: at one time there were four curates in the parish; now Father Michael Marr, is the only assistant in what is still a large parish of over 3,000 souls. In the post-war period of expansion during the 1950s Father Stronge and his curates had many demands made on them. Two

Masses were said every Sunday in the Black Bull at Wardley before St. Augustine's was built; he was, also, responsible for the building of the school there. Father Stronge was once approached by a person who felt a public house was not an appropriate place for the celebration of Mass. His reply was: 'If the innkeeper at Bethlehem had been as hospitable as John Wright at the Black Bull there would have been no need for Our Lord to have been born in a stable.'

When the original school had its upper storey removed - the remaining ground floor now serves as a parish hall - the stone and timber were transported for £50 to Otterburn and used in the construction in 1947 of the church and house.

The present primary school of St. John's - originally an all-age school - was erected in 1936 when Father Costello was parish priest.

A noteworthy honour was conferred on Father Stronge on June 10th, 1978, - the year of his Golden Jubilee - when he was made a Freeman of the Borough of Gateshead. This was mainly in recognition of his work for youth in the area over many years.

This work, of course, extended beyond the confines of his own parish when he was Diocesan Youth representative visiting and supporting parishes in their youth development work. He is, also, proud of the fact that he encouraged a considerable number of young priests from Ireland to work in our diocese - a kind of 'recruiting sergeant' is the description he uses.

Standing on a mantelpiece in the presbytery is a testimonial to his 50 years as a chaplain to the Knights of St. Columba. The Legion of Mary, started by him 30 years ago, still continues its valuable work along with the S.V.P. now in its 93rd year. He also claims the honour of being president of the Gateshead Historical Society for twenty years.

Everyone needs some form of relaxation and Father Stronge has found his in golf; this, perhaps, helps to explain his fitness and vitality over the years. Four times he has been champion at Heworth Golf Club - he has prayed and played with the fathers and grandfathers of some of his present parishioners.

For 36 years he has been fortunate in having the services of his housekeeper, Miss Monica Russell, who has played an important, if unassuming role, in the parish and she too hopes to retire soon.

St. Patrick's, 'the Glory of Felling', standing in a prominent position and offering a distant view across the Tyne is a daily reminder to all who see it of the Faith nurtured in these parts in times past and through many vicissitudes to the present day.

23. GATESHEAD   Corpus Christi   *(September, 1986)*

On April 14th, this year (1986), Corpus Christi church celebrated the Golden Jubilee of its opening with a special Mass concelebrated by Bishop Lindsay, Canon Patrick McKenna, the parish priest, and 20 other priests. Father William Nicholson of Whittingham was the preacher.

Not a long time in the history of the Catholic Church in Gateshead, but nevertheless for the diocese and the parish a story of 50 years steady growth in the Faith in this area which has been recently recorded in Mr. Vincent Carney's Parish History. The early history of Catholicism in Gateshead, of course, precedes, by many years, the foundation of Corpus Christi parish - a history too detailed to record here and perhaps, more appropriately told when an article on St. Joseph's, the mother church of Gateshead is written.

However, to understand the development of Corpus Christi parish within the Gateshead Catholic community a few links with the past need to be mentioned. The 14th century St. Mary's Church, near the river, and the 13th century chapel of St. Edmund, now part of Holy Trinity, are visible reminders of the ancient Faith in these parts. One cannot omit to mention Gateshead's own martyr, John Ingram, a native of Hereford, who was tried and sentenced to death along with St. John Boste and Blessed George Swallowell at Durham. He was executed for the Faith on the afternoon of July 26th, 1594, on a spot opposite Holy Trinity church. Nearby stood Gateshead House (now demolished) for many years the home of the Riddell family who harboured chaplains to minister to their spiritual needs and those of local Catholics. This mission was staffed by Jesuits one of whom was Fr William Riddell S.J. (son of the owner) who died there in 1711 and was buried in Gateshead.

When Bishop Williams O.P. made a visitation to Gateshead in 1729, 100 people were confirmed. The last Jesuit to reside in Gateshead was an Irish priest, Father John Walshe, who fled for safety to the Brandlings of Felling Hall - later continuing his mission from Newcastle - after a mob had attacked Gateshead House in 1746 during the Jacobite unrest.

Not far from Corpus Christi church is Saltwell Park and near the West Park Road entrance is a drinking fountain on which are inscribed the letters I.H.S. It seems reasonable to suppose that this religious inscription has some connection with the Dunn family of Saltwellside who were Catholics. Between 1816 and 1822 the chaplain there was a Benedictine, Father Jerome Digby, O.S.B. When Mrs Elizabeth Dunn of the same residence died in 1821 she left her books to start a Catholic circulating library. Another religious order, also, has historical links with Gateshead and Corpus Christi parish: this is the La Sagesse Order who arrived here in June 1906 and began a foundation at Summerfield House and seven months later they took possession of Ferndene House which became a day and boarding school. From here they moved to Jesmond in 1911. One of the French sisters who came in 1906 to Gateshead was Sister Roger de la Croix who died in 1971, aged 96, at the Jesmond convent.

Corpus Christi parish - originally called the Blessed Sacrament Parish - was established in April, 1927, with the appointment of its first parish priest, Father Ernest Wilkinson, who settled into the presbytery in Dunsmuir Grove recording his first baptism in May, 1927.

Eighteen years before Father Wilkinson's arrival, Mass had been said regularly in the Blessed Sacrament School - opened in 1909 - by priests from St. Joseph's. The north end of the upper floor of the present primary school is the place where Mass was offered until the church was built.

After three years here, Father Wilkinson was transferred as parish priest in 1930 to St. Joseph's, Gateshead, and later to St. Mary's Cathedral in Newcastle. He was succeeded at Corpus Christi by Father Nicholas Hodgson Brown who moved into a larger house in Dunsmuir Grove in order to accommodate the first curate Father Andrew Hannon (now parish priest of Immaculate Heart of Mary parish, Sunderland), a housekeeper, Miss Grieveson and a maid, Miss Ethel Burnyeat.

Housing developments in Bensham and Saltwell at the beginning of the century and later in the 1930s at Fern Dene, Field House and the Racecourse estate meant an increase in the number of Catholics in this part of Gateshead. The numbers at Easter Duties in 1926 and 1927 were in the region of 4,000 indicating the urgent need for a permanent place of worship.

This task fell to Father Brown who in November, 1930 requested a second silver collection for the church building fund the first of which realised £5.18.0. Other fund-raising efforts were begun: the children were asked to contribute to a weekly collection, the first of which realised £1.11.4; sixpence per week was asked from those over 17 years of age; a one million penny fund was initiated; and the first three-day Sale of Work raised the considerable sum of £200. A rather unusual source of income was the sale of garden produce from the parish allotment. By early June 1934 the building of the church had begun and on July 7th Bishop Thorman laid the foundation stone in the presence of many clergy and about 1,000 people.

In an age of high unemployment it is interesting to record that 50 years ago when unemployment was also high, the ordering by the church of natural stone from the Springwell Quarries enabled the firm to retain staff who otherwise may have become redundant.

Few parishes have suffered the shock and disappointment encountered during the building of their church as Corpus Christi did. After a period of favourable progress, two completed arches collapsed. The incident is remembered still by Father Bernard Stronge, then a curate at St Joseph's and now living in retirement in Felling: 'I was in the school yard (St. Joseph's) after tea one Thursday evening when I heard news that the arches of the new church had fallen after the men had finished work for the day'. Fortunately, the rubble from the two collapsed arches and tower near the sanctuary had fallen inside the partially completed building. It was probably the first church in the north east to have ferro-concrete arches - a relatively new construction process - but whatever the fault may have been, rigorous testing occurred over the ensuing months to meet the necessary safety standards.

For 27 years the parishioners of Corpus Christi worshipped in the school-chapel. We can imagine their delight when Bishop Thorman came on April 14th, 1936, to bless and open the church designed in the modern Gothic style by a Newcastle architect, Mr R. Burke, and built by Mr E. Thompson, also of Newcastle; the cost, including the presbytery, was £13,000.

During his sermon preached to a large congregation and 160 priests, the Rev. Dr. Cogan of Esh reminded everyone that 'the Catholic Church looms large in the world and this little church in Gateshead is a picture in miniature of what the Universal Church stands for.' A special Benediction was celebrated by the Bishop for the children followed by a tea-party. Still prominent in the church are the statues of St. John Fisher and St. Thomas More carved by a former Gateshead man, Mr A. Southwick, A.R.B.S.; these were blessed at a special evening ceremony two days after the opening.

Since its inception Corpus Christi parish has had five parish priests including the present one, Canon P. J. McKenna, who came here in 1965 and who last year celebrated the 40th anniversary of his ordination to the priesthood. Canon McKenna is assisted in the parish by Father Michael Griffiths. Father Griffiths who preached this year at the Blessed John Ingram Walk - held annually in July - is (like the martyr) Hereford born. This month Father Griffiths transferred to St. Joseph's, Sunderland, and will be replaced by Father Peter Carr. The parish has been fertile ground for vocations; it is thought that 23 priestly vocations have come from the parish with two parishioners, at present, studying at Ushaw and one with the Mill Hill Fathers.

Lay involvement in the church and co-operation between the priests and people in the spiritual and social activities of the parish are much in evidence here. A Parish Committee, consisting mainly of representatives of the various parish organizations, meets monthly to co-ordinate and initiate parish activities; nine lay ministers of the Eucharist are commissioned to distribute Holy Communion; the S.V.P. conference (founded, 1911) of 13 members continues its valuable work of helping those in need. The Youth Club meeting every Thursday evening in the school caters for the needs of the 7 to 14 age group whilst the Women's Confraternity gives an opportunity to those who so wish to meet socially and be involved in parish life.

Four other group activities have engendered much enthusiasm and interest in Corpus Christi parish. The Justice and Peace group undertakes an annual CAFOD project; this year the effort has been directed to Ethiopia. For the last three years they have organized a Summer Peace Camp which draws students from all over the world who are housed in parishioners' homes and who undertake voluntary social work in the local community. Last year Catholic and Protestant youngsters from Northern Ireland were amongst those participating in the Summer Peace Camp.

A prayer group of 15 to 20 people has met weekly over the last three years sharing prayer and scripture. It provides for all age groups from the quite young to an 85-year-old parishioner. Once a month people of other Faiths are invited to the inter-denominational prayer group meeting.

Very active and of a high standard is the music group comprising guitarists, singers, brass instrumentalists from the secondary school, a young non-Catholic organist, Stephen Office, and a veteran member of the choir, Mr Bob Hughes, who sang at the official opening of the church 50 years ago.

A more recent innovation is the Care Group which was established following a survey made by the Diocesan Rescue Society. After some discussion and working on the principle of See, Judge and Act, the group has supplemented the work of the existing parish societies by visiting the bereaved, the sick and the housebound.

The April celebrations in Corpus Christi were a time for looking back but also a chance to look forward and continue the work started by others. Canon McKenna makes the point in the foreword to the parish history: 'With confidence which springs from our Faith, we are now on our way towards the centenary of Corpus Christi parish.'

24. GATESHEAD   St. Joseph   *(November, December, 1997)*

When St. Joseph's, the mother-church of Gateshead, was opened on July 5th, 1859, it was yet another example of the prodigious growth of the Catholic Church in the North East in the second half of the 19th century.

It was also part of the continuing story of the Christian Faith in this area which began in Saxon times. The first written record is in Bede's History where he mentions Adda, who was brother of Utta, abbot of the monastery of Gateshead. Adda was instrumental with other priests in the evangelisation of the Midlands round about 653 A.D.

The period after the Norman Conquest reveals more about our Faith's development in this area as part of the medieval diocese of Durham. Much of the land was forested then and became a hunting ground for some of the prince-bishops of the Palatinate who had a manor house here; the monks of Durham also owned land in this area. Over the centuries much of the land was sold and developed as private estates.

Not far from the old Tyne Bridge was a small community of our ancestors who worshipped in the parish church of St. Mary's, a church of the 14th century with many alterations since. Still visible is stone work of the pre-Reformation era and on the north wall is an anchorite's cell restored in the 18th century.

Of much greater interest is the church of the Holy Trinity in High Street built in Victorian times but incorporating the 13th century chapel of St. Edmund in its south aisle. Here outside the ancient chapel was martyred Blessed John Ingram in 1594. John, after conversion to the Faith, through the example of some Oxford graduates who had embraced the old religion, proceeded to Rheims and later Rome where he was ordained in 1589. After a spell of missionary work in Scotland he came to northern England where he was captured; there followed spells of incarceration at Berwick, Newcastle, London, York and Durham.

Although tortured by the notorious Topcliffe in London he refused to divulge the whereabouts of his fellow-priests. Tried at Durham along with John Boste and George Swallowell he was sentenced to death and executed on July 26th, 1594.

His memory and sacrifice are celebrated annually in the John Ingram walk which takes place in July when pilgrims from the diocese and of other denominations process from Newgate Street, Newcastle, across the swing bridge to the site of the martyrdom. Frank Donovan, a Corpus Christi parishioner who has done much to publicise this event, was elected mayor of Gateshead this year (1997) and had the honour as chief citizen of welcoming the pilgrims, led by Bishop Ambrose Griffiths, at the borough boundary.

Near to St. Edmund's chapel was Gateshead House, the residence of the Riddell family, where the Faith was cherished and sustained for many years during the years of persecution. In the Presentment of the Churchwardens of the Parish of Gateshead made in 1609 they state: 'We have only one gentlewoman, Mrs Riddle (formerly Conyers) the wife of Thomas Riddle Esquire who refuses to come to Church and to communicate with us ... We have no recusants who have reformed themselves or who keep any popish schoolmasters, popish servants ...' A later presentment to the Durham Sessions in 1614 mentions Elizabeth Riddell and also Katherine, the wife of William Kennet of Saltwellside.

From Jesuit records we know that members of the Society were based intermittently in Gateshead towards the end of the 17th century and for much of the 18th century. It is thought that a Father Philip Leigh was here in 1704 and a Jesuit, Father William Riddell, resided at Gateshead House with his sister prior to his death in 1711.

Residing in Gateshead for a time, also, was Father George Brown S.J., friend and confessor of the Earl of Derwentwater whom he attended at his execution after the failure of the Jacobite rebellion of 1715. Perhaps the best known is Father (Daddy) John Walshe who left hurriedly to live with the Brandlings at Felling Hall when Gateshead House was attacked by a mob in 1746. When quieter times prevailed he moved across the river to continue his ministry in Newcastle.

Felling Hall, home of the recusant branch of the Brandling Family, was another haven for the local Catholics for a short period until 1749. In a note attached to the Felling Mass vestment - parts of which are said to be of the 15th century and now at Stonyhurst College - Hilda Brandling, who died in 1967 states:

'Felling vestment, drab velvet, bought by my great-grandmother Dunn from 'Daddy' Walshe who was smoked out of Gateshead by the Duke of Northumberland's (sic) troops. He got this with others from Felling Hall when the chapel was broken up'. It was, in fact, the Duke of Cumberland who was passing through at the time; the general opinion is that a mob sitting on the wall to watch this event and attacked by the gardener's dogs committed the arson as a reprisal and not Cumberland's men.

'The good protestants of Gateshead' were contrasted by a writer in 1575 with the people of Newcastle who were virtually 'all papists'. It is fair to assume, however, that the Faith was practised here by a few in secret receiving their spiritual nourishment from the priests at Gateshead House and across the Tyne. We know that in 1729 when Bishop Williams O.P., visited Gateshead 100 people were confirmed. In 1767, the Papist Returns list 58 recusants in the Gateshead area some of whom had resided here for over 40 years.

When Father James Worswick opened the first St. Andrew's church, Newcastle, in February 1798, Gateshead would have been included in his ministry, as would Felling where he opened a chapel in 1841.

Gateshead was part of the phenomenal growth of population and industry which occurred in many parts of Britain in the 19th century. In 1801 the inhabitants of Gateshead numbered 8,597 but by 1851 with the prospects of employment improving, this figure had increased to 25,570 of which it has been estimated 3,000 were Catholics and 1,554 were Irish born. The second half of the 19th century saw an even greater increase with an obvious proportionate increase in the Catholic population.

It is no surprise then to find the bishop sending Father Frederick Betham from St. Andrew's to take up residence at 13, St. Catherine's Terrace in 1851 as parish priest-elect. A small oratory was provided in the house for weekday services; for Sunday Mass a temporary chapel was used being no more than the top storey of a warehouse in Hillgate and was known as Our Lady and St. Wilfrid. When a fire occurred there in 1854 the Long Room of the Queen's Head Hotel, Mirk Lane, became the place of Sunday worship until the opening of the present St. Joseph's church in 1859. One source claims that the Long Room continued to be used for mission purposes under the name of All Saints.

Father Betham, realising that only a permanent stone church would meet the needs of his growing congregation, issued a circular (still extant in the parish archives) in 1850 sanctioned by Bishop William Hogarth 'to the faithful Catholics of the parish of Gateshead in the Diocese of Hexham'. In it he gives a brief account of how the Faith developed in the area telling his readers he hoped to build a wooden church until a 'Church of stone' could be constructed. He exhorted them to make regular contributions and hoped 'to solicit the alms of the faithful in the neighbouring cities and towns'.

Of Lincolnshire stock, Father Betham, a convert, was trained at the English College in Rome but left the diocese in 1854 to join the Jesuit Order. Until the appointment of Father Edward Consitt, the first parish priest, the Gateshead congregation was served from Newcastle. It was his main task to continue the Betham appeal which enabled the building of the church to be commenced on land purchased from Cuthbert Ellison, Lord of the Manor, in Father Betham's time.

The *Gateshead Observer's* reporter gives in great detail the official laying of the foundation stone. Here are a few extracts: 'the procession gained the church while the psalm was in progress... and the bishop was conducted to a chair with faldstool or prie-dieu in front of the foundation stone (the same chair by the way which was occupied by the Queen when Her Majesty opened the Central Railway Station of Newcastle)'. After psalms and sermon 'the stone was lowered to its bed - his Lordship laying it in the most approved fashion with mallet, plumb and rule. No coins were deposited but a parchment scroll was inserted, bearing a Latin inscription of the following purport:

THE FOUNDATION STONE OF THIS CHURCH
ERECTED IN HONOUR OF ALMIGHTY GOD UNDER THE INVOCATION
OF THE GLORIOUS ST. JOSEPH
SPOUSE OF THE BLESSED AND IMMACULATE MARY
EVER VIRGIN
IN THE PRESENCE OF A GREAT MULTITUDE OF THE FAITHFUL
WAS SOLEMNLY BLESSED AND LAID BY THE RIGHT REVEREND

WILLIAM, LORD BISHOP OF HEXHAM
ON THE THIRD DAY WITHIN THE OCTAVE OF PENTECOST
MAY 25, 1858.
PIUS IX, P.M. HAPPILY REIGNING
EDWARD CONSITT, M.A. PASTOR
ARCHIBALD M. DUNN, ARCHITECT
JAMES HOGG, BUILDER.

In just over a year after this event Bishop Hogarth was able to return for the solemn opening of the almost completed Gothic style church which was designed to accommodate a congregation of 1,000 and is estimated to have cost £3,000.

Again the reporter from the *Gateshead Observer* describes the red-letter day: 'Tuesday, July 5th, was the day of dedication; and flowers and evergreens, arches and banners were outward indications of the opening ceremony. Inhabitants of all churches were drawn together by the proceedings ... Between 10 and 11 the doors were opened and admission was granted at 10 shillings, 5s, 2s, 6d and 1s.6d according to locality. The church was not crowded, but the attendance was numerous. Many were admitted free...' Bishop Hogarth, in the presence of Bishop Briggs of Beverley, many priests and lay representatives (including the consular representatives of France and Spain) presided at High Mass and the sermon was given by the Rev. Father Furlong of the Order of Charity who in it praised 'the kindness of many Protestants'.

In the afternoon at a Luncheon in the Queen's Head Hotel at which Sir William Lawson, Bart., of Brough Hall presided - a descendant of the saintly Dorothy Lawson of Heaton who had helped to preserve the Faith on the banks of the Tyne in penal days - speeches were made and when Father Consitt spoke he emphasised that there had been some large donations but 'All the rest had been raised from small subscriptions, the highest of which was 10 shillings and the lowest a farthing a week ... and ... that there was nothing that gratified him so much as to witness round about the church the large crowd of poor who took exactly the same interest in it as himself'. Many parishioners were prepared to forego the privilege of being in the church that day so that those who could afford subscriptions for entry would by their presence reduce the church debt.

We no longer build these fine Gothic-style stone churches of the 19th century like St. Joseph's with the large nave and two side aisles leading to the side chapels. The chapel of the Sacred Heart contains (or used to contain) the old altar from Mirk Lane and an interesting seven sacraments window. Within the church, and particularly the sanctuary, are some fine stained-glass windows by Burnett of Newcastle depicting St. Patrick, St. Cuthbert, Our Lady, St. Joseph, St. Edward the Confessor and St. Henry. In 1982 when Father O'Brien was parish priest, the church was decorated and the sanctuary re-ordered; much of the original marble pulpit etc. was re-fashioned into the lectern and presidential chair. The decorative marble altar and pulpit were the gift of Alderman Costelloe who was mayor of Gateshead in 1910 and 1911.

The Church has always considered the provision of Catholic Schools, where the young can be nurtured in their Faith, to be of primary importance. St. Joseph's School was opened in 1864 on a site where the parish centre now stands and All Saints in 1928 - each had a pupil roll of 900! The present St. Joseph's Primary School under the headship of Mrs E. Donelly, was opened in 1972. Provision for private education began with the arrival of the La Sagesse Sisters in 1906; their first foundation was at Summerfield House on Durham Road for seven months, after which they occupied Ferndene House which became a day and boarding school, until the transfer to Jesmond in 1911 where their school continues to thrive. During their time in Gateshead they did provide some free education and did much work in and around the parish. One of the founding sisters, Sister Roger de La Croix, died at Jesmond in 1971, aged 96.

St. Joseph's parishioners were mainly of the working class and many with Irish origins; they lived in the crowded areas of Oakwellgate, Pipewellgate and Bottle Bank and laboured in the local industries many at the Allhusen's Chemical Works and with their small wages supported their church and schools.

Led by Alderman Costelloe and the priests they acquired a property in Ellison Street which became the C.Y.M.S. Men's Club and a focal point where the parish's spiritual and social life was enhanced. Here met regularly the S.V.P. (founded in 1859), the Men's Confraternity, the Women's Confraternity, the Children of Mary, the Legion of Mary, the Boys' Club and Cubs and Scouts. During the depression of the 1930s the club became a haven for the unemployed; they cut each other's hair, cobbled boots and shoes, repaired and pressed their suits filling the long days as best they could. It is claimed that in 1937 the population of the parish was about 5,000 souls cared for by a parish priest and five curates. A Mass attendance of 3,000 saw the need to use All Saints' School and the Men's Club for Sunday worship. St. Joseph's great years of expansion were from 1859 until the end of the Second World War but like similar town centre parishes the post-war building boom and re-development over the years were to have their effect. As new estates sprang up on the old town's perimeter - such as Leam Lane, Beacon Lough, Wrekenton and Lobley Hill - new parishes were created and with the demolition of old crowded streets the de-population of St. Joseph's quickened. Further decline was evidenced with the closures of the two old parish schools, the Men's Club and the parish hall.

During the incumbency of Father Lewis Landreth St. Joseph's centenary celebrations occurred on July 7th, 1959; there were now seven churches in Gateshead looking after the needs of about 20,000 Catholics.

Earlier in May of that same year the church had been consecrated by Bishop Cunningham and he was able to use the same trowel used by Bishop Hogarth at the laying of the foundation stone. Attending the July centenary celebrations - the highlight of which was the Pontifical High Mass celebrated by Bishop Cunningham - were many priests, and civic dignitaries led by the Mayor and Mayoress, Alderman and Mrs Pike. In his sermon Canon Wilkinson, a former parish priest, paid tribute to the people of the parish and thanked them 'for without their support this fine church of St. Joseph's would never have come into being and we would not be keeping this centenary'.

With a much reduced congregation St. Joseph's parishioners and their parish priest, Father Anthony Donaghue, who came here in 1990, continue to meet the spiritual and social needs of those remaining. Some of the older societies have ceased to exist such as the C.W.L., and the Legion of Mary but one society, the S.V.P., founded the year the church was opened, continues its ministrations to the needy. A pastoral care team of eight ladies supplements this work visiting the sick regularly. Thirty Lay Eucharistic Ministers ensure that the housebound are not deprived of the solace of communion. A devoted group of adults supervises the Children's Liturgy every other Sunday consolidating the work of the school in passing on the Faith. Baptismal courses, Engaged Couples' courses, and a Marriage Enrichment course are further ways in which the parish extends its ministry.

Mention must be made of the ecumenical dimension here in Gateshead: the participation by other Christian denominations in the John Ingram Walk, the bi-monthly ecumenical breakfasts, the joint Lenten services, the attendance at induction ceremonies and the Good Friday Procession of Witness are good examples of Christians reaching out to each other in the search for unity.

On the social side the Parish Centre, built in 1972 on the site of the first school, is the venue for such varied activities as a Senior Citizens' Club, line dancing, sequence dancing, the Mothers and Toddlers' group, the Blind Club, the Youth Club and the Sunday parish social. A rambling club provides an opportunity for those who are more energetic to enjoy the open spaces together and share each other's company.

St. Joseph's Centre also meets a wider need than just the parish; it is used by the local community, and as many readers will be aware, provides a venue for diocesan meetings and organisations. Jack Hirst, and John Mulgrew, caretaker and steward respectively, do great work in ensuring the smooth running of the centre.

Here the Diocesan Pastoral Council meets twice a year with Bishop Ambrose. The Council of Priests, the Church Music Association, the Diocesan C.W.L. and others, find it a convenient meeting place when people have to travel from various parts of the diocese.

Finally, great work is done by Catholic Care North East who provide six days a week respite care for Alzheimer's sufferers and carers using the ground floor of the large old presbytery.

As will be seen from the activities listed above St. Joseph's parish is meeting the challenges of changing times and doing it admirably. Although the area and parish has changed considerably in the last 140 years nevertheless the bond of Faith continues to be a source of inspiration to everyone here as they apply their beliefs to the demands of the age.

POSTSCRIPT   *(Fr. A. M. Donoghue, 1998)*

The building of a new Civic Centre and the Town Development in the 1980s meant the demolition of terraced houses around the church. Folk were rehoused in the Gateshead Borough. Numbers on the parish census decreased, as did Mass attendance. At the same time there was a growing indifference to organised religion and to the coming to church. The Metro Centre was described as the 'Cathedral of our times' when it was opened and the shopping malls are its aisles.

The redecoration of St. Joseph's began in September, 1997, and took Duncan Page 14 weeks to complete. It was a labour of love and undertaken to affirm the central place of Christ in our hearts and in our lives. It was to this end that Duncan painted a fresco of the Crucifixion on the centre apse; a full-size risen Christ beside the fourteenth station and a painting of a Lamb beneath the Tabernacle. The Greek letters for Christ and Alpha and Omega have been drawn on the Lectern. All of which has been undertaken to lift up our hearts in praise of the Lord.

The grounds beside the church were developed also in September, 1997. The Garden of Christian Mysteries reflects in its layout the themes of the mystery of the Rosary - Joyful, Sorrowful and Glorious mysteries. The Garden of Grace has the Lourdes Grotto at its centre. A dry stream from the Grotto links to the Diocesan Cross on the wall beneath - a stream of grace and healing. All these gardens are gardens of Remembrance for loved ones who have been placed in the Lord's hands; and they are gardens of thanksgiving for birth and achievement.

25. GOSFORTH   St. Charles   *(March, April 1997)*

The centenary celebration marking the foundation of St. Charles parish, Gosforth (mentioned briefly in the December issue of the *Northern Cross*) is one of a number that has occurred in the last few years reminding us that 100 years ago was an era of Diocesan expansion when new parishes were carved out of the old missions which had existed since the penal days.

This period of rapid growth in our diocese took place to meet the needs of a rising Catholic population, requiring priests, churches and schools where spiritual support could be provided to sustain and develop the Faith.

St. Charles' church stands a short distance to the east of the old A.1, off Gosforth High Street; an imposing sandstone edifice designed in the Gothic style by the Belgian architect, Charles Menart, who was living and working in the early part of this century in Glasgow. The foundation stone was laid by Bishop Collins on August 14th, 1910, on a site generously donated by George Dunn of Maidenhead, a descendant of an old Newcastle family. The builder, Mr William Cuthbert Fleck of Gosforth, completed its erection in just over a year, permitting the church to be officially opened by Bishop Collins with the celebration of a Pontifical High Mass on December 3rd, 1911, followed a few days later by a 'second opening' at which Bishop John Vaughan preached.

It was due to the persistence of Father Thomas Reilly, who was parish priest here from 1897 until 1932, that the parishioners could feel proud at what had been achieved. No doubt financial constraints limited the design to a significantly shorter nave than was originally intended, giving a square appearance rather than the elongated cruciform shape.

Nevertheless it has a fine interior much to be admired and enjoyed with its marbled walls and sanctuary, and side chapels and some very impressive stained glass windows donated over a period of years. An unusual feature of the church was a stately baldacchino, the gift of Elizabeth Potts in memory of her husband George, which was removed in 1986 when the re-ordering took place, although parts of it were incorporated into the new lectern, baptismal font and sanctuary.

One unusual aspect of life in the parish of Gosforth in its early days, for which the priests had some responsibility, were the two Industrial Schools established by the diocese to shelter deprived or orphaned children - a development in late Victorian times organised by the state and supplemented by voluntary bodies.

The Bishop Chadwick Memorial School for boys was founded in 1882 on Grandstand Road and did much valuable work here until it was transferred to Carlisle in 1905. A similar institution for girls, St. Elizabeth's, was established at Ashburton House in Gosforth closing in 1906 on its transfer to Darlington. There was also an industrial school at Elswick. The Sisters of Charity did much valuable work in staffing some of these schools whilst the Bishop Chadwick School was, for a period, staffed by the Presentation Brothers.

Set in suburban surroundings, this rather sumptuous church belies the fact that when the parish was founded in September, 1897, with the arrival of Father Reilly, its early history was one of struggle to meet the financial demands made on it to support a priest, school and chapel.

Parish roots, before the advent of Father Reilly, can be traced to the area of Coxlodge where a number of pits had been sunk in the early part of the 19th century. The village, situated at the north end of Kenton Road, was populated mainly by miners and their families and it was for these souls that Canon Charles Eyre, Rector of St. Mary's Cathedral (later Archbishop of Glasgow), decided to provide a school-chapel, and a presbytery completed in 1861, each building costing £400. Generous benefactors such as William Dunn, Matthew and John Liddell enabled what must have been a poor community to meet the cost of these buildings. Until the appointment of Father Birgen in 1875, as priest-in-charge, the small chapel had been served from the cathedral.

For short spells a number of priests served the Catholic congregation at Coxlodge but it was Father Aidan Wilkinson, appointed in October 1895, who, seeing a diminishing community as the local pit closed and their families move on, decided that the centre of the parish was more appropriately in the area of South Gosforth.

Accordingly, through the generosity of Mr George Dunn (mentioned earlier), Father Wilkinson was able to erect in 1896 a 'tin church' as a temporary measure. His successor, Father Reilly, tried unsuccessfully to have a stone one built, but with a parish debt of £1,975, his dream at that time was not realisable. He did, however, manage to erect the present presbytery in 1901 and turned his attention to enlarging the Catholic school at Coxlodge on the site of which now stands St. Cuthbert's Court, a sheltered housing complex.

Determined and undaunted he pressed ahead with his vision of a permanent church asking 28 parishioners to guarantee the payment of interest on a £5,000 loan which he sought. The diocesan administrators had reservations, and plans were put on hold until an old friend of Father Reilly, Canon Joseph Watson, Provost of the Cathedral Chapter (remembered in the black marble memorial in the Blessed Sacrament chapel), who had retired to Gosforth, offered anonymously £100 in April 1909 and three months later proffered a cheque for £1,000 for the building of St. Charles. The old 'tin church', once the new church was opened, became the parish hall - demolished long ago. The present parish centre was formerly St. Charles' School, which opened in 1928 costing £5,000, and it was at this time that the Sisters of Mercy from Sunderland came to teach in the school.

Father Reilly was to serve the parish of St. Charles for 35 years until his death in 1932, a long incumbency which much endeared him to Catholics and non-Catholics alike who sought his help on many occasions, particularly when husbands or sons were killed in the First World War. A poignant reminder of the 36 men who died in the war is a copy of the 'Sistine Madonna' presented to the parish by Mr Felix Lavery in 1923 as a war memorial to be seen today in the Blessed Sacrament Chapel. Father Reilly certainly was a priest who 'got things done'. Such was the esteem in which he was held in the Gosforth area that after the Solemn Requiem Mass traffic had to be held up - it happened to be Race Wednesday - on the Great North Road to allow the funeral cortege to pass on its way to Ashburton Cemetery

Father Bernard McElduff, his successor, was to encourage and shepherd the flock at St. Charles' during the economic depression, the Second World War and its aftermath, a long pastoral ministry of 30 years from 1932 until his death in 1962.

One of his major tasks was to try and reduce the parish debt of £7,750 - a large amount when we consider the average earnings of the 1930s. The organising of concerts, whist and bridge drives, lectures, evening parties, and sales of work, etc., achieved two objectives: one, reducing the parish debt, and two, providing opportunities - what we would call to-day collaborative ministry - for social cohesion in a parish whose population was reckoned in the mid 1930s to be approximately 1,880 members.

An increasing demand for pupil places saw the purchase of Salters Road Methodist Church as extra school accommodation, and it also served a useful purpose as a larger parish hall with greater scope for social activities.

Father McElduff, who died in October 1962 three days before the opening of the Second Vatican Council was, so the parish history suggests 'an arch-traditionalist in everything, (but) he had never failed the parish; it had grown and prospered in his care, and he had given it, above all, stability'. After a 30-year stay here as parish priest his influence was bound to be great, winning much affection from his parishioners, amongst whom there must have been some he had not only baptised but in their adulthood officiated at their weddings.

The parish history chronicles in some detail the changes and effects of the reforms initiated by Vatican II which Monsignor John J. Cunningham the Vicar General - a former professor at Ushaw College and for 20 years headmaster of St. Cuthbert's Grammar School - had to implement when he became parish priest of St. Charles' in February 1963. It was his 'firm leadership' and willingness to explain the changes, along with much prayer and special Masses for the success of the Council, that enabled his parishioners to absorb the changes, such as the English Mass, when they came.

At a more mundane level the church roof was repaired, new lighting was installed and a Parish Association formed, under the chairmanship of Mr Tony Gray, which contributed in no small way to enhance and stimulate life in the parish community. Shortly before his retirement to Darlington as chaplain to Clare Abbey, Mgr. Cunningham was involved in the consultation and organisation which was to lead to the establishment in the area of a Catholic Comprehensive education system.

Although only here for six years he had left his mark and had won 'a deep affectionate regard and there were many who realised just how excellent a job he had done in the days of transition when to be in a post of responsibility is far from easy, and can be acutely uncomfortable'. His own words when exhorting the parish to study and accept the liturgical changes are an apt expression of his own commitment: ' "Thy Kingdom Come" is the whole purpose of the renewal of the Liturgy'.

Father Joseph O'Neill, who followed Monsignor Cunningham at Gosforth in October 1969, was to build on the earlier changes and introduce others. After much patient consultation with parishioners, and with the help of his assistant, Father Michael Campion, he saw the long-delayed re-ordering of the sanctuary.

The latter was ably wrought to the designs of a parishioner, Mr Bill Stoner, the architect, and executed by Morris Marbleworks, assisted by the decorating firm of Charles McReavy. Though initially some of the parishioners may have had reservations, the changes came to be generally accepted and were, in fact, found pleasing. Father O'Neill, after the re-ordering, conveyed the general feeling of satisfaction: 'Our church is proof that the reforms of the Second Vatican Council, once understood and tastefully implemented, are worthwhile'.

On approaching the church one sees the large glass porch constructed in 1970 and also designed by Mr Bill Stoner. It cost one and a half times more than the original church, but one must bear in mind the relative value of the pound in 1911 and in 1970. Unfortunately vandalism, the scourge of our times, made it necessary to keep the church locked when not in use - a common necessity sadly in many places. However, more recently, Father Kevin Bolger, after an affirmation from 79% of those who replied to a questionnaire, decided that the church should remain open and encouraged parishioners to make visits to the Blessed Sacrament and thus indirectly to provide surveillance.

When Father O'Neill died suddenly on January 20th, 1978, he left behind 'a sense of sadness and emptiness (which was)... felt intensely by the parish'. A great parish visitor who will be remembered 'in his bustling devotion to his duties; he was visiting sick and sleepless parishioners at an early hour every morning, a pastor in the best tradition. A humble man who saw his duty clearly and did it without hesitation'. He was laid to rest in Ashburton Cemetery near to some of his priest predecessors.

When Father Kevin Bolger succeeded as parish priest in September 1987 he was able to build on and consolidate many of the good things that were happening in the parish. He had used his musical talents in his previous parishes and decided to form a choir at St. Charles which continues to thrive today. When the re-ordering occurred the seating capacity of the church was reduced. Father Bolger and parishioners decided on the addition of an upper West gallery with extra seats at a cost of £40,000 - £800 per seat! It was also Father Bolger's responsibility to see to the building of the new St. Charles' School which was opened and blessed by Bishop Lindsay, a former pupil, on November 24th, 1995. St. Oswald's, the second parish school, was opened on the northern boundary of the parish in 1962, and the deputy head of St. Charles' was appointed to the headship. This was the late and deeply lamented Gerry Miller, who launched St. Oswald's in fine style, though in the teeth of many initial difficulties.

There is much happening in this vibrant parish at Gosforth; long-established groups and activities continue, supplemented by new ideas as 'collaborative ministry' takes a hold - the parish now has four commissioned lay leaders for Eucharistic Services. Such are of great assistance to the new parish priest, Father Daniel Treacy, who was inducted here in the presence of a full congregation and 29 priests during the centenary celebration Mass on November 4th, 1996, at which Bishop Ambrose was the chief concelebrant.

If we mention only some of the activities that energise the parish like the Children's Liturgy of the Word each Sunday, the Playgroup and Toddler Group, the Ivy Club (for senior citizens), the Youth Club, the Prayer Group, the C.W.L., the S.V.P., the Justice and Peace Group, Mother Teresa's co-workers, the Brownies and Guides, plus many of the routine tasks such as church cleaning, we get some idea of how St. Charles' parish is a community where many people are involved in the day to day life of the parish. And further encouraging signs for the future are the many committed young families and the involvement of the youth; there are so many volunteers to serve on the altar that an age limit has had to be set.

Whilst this article has described the development of the parish under successive parish priests, the vital role of the many assistant priests must also be acknowledged. If we mention Father John O'Gorman now at Norton, Father Peter Carr and Father Thomas Burke at Seaham, Father Michael Campion at South Shields, Father William Jacks at Highfield, and Father Christopher Hughes at the Newcastle University Chaplaincy, they may be taken as typifying all the others who, by their efforts, along with parish priests and parishioners, made St. Charles' what it is today. Nor should we forget that Gosforth has been fertile ground where the seeds of a vocation to the priesthood and religious life were liberally sown.

The centenary has given everyone the opportunity to look back with gratitude on the achievements of the past and the confidence to build on it for the future.

**26. HARTLEPOOL   St. Joseph   *(February, March 1995)*

One hundred years ago this month on February 5th, St. Joseph's Church in West Hartlepool was opened. In this centenary year the priests and people of the parish have much to celebrate as they look back at what has already been achieved and look forward with hope and faith to the future.

A hundred years is but a short time span, of course, in the history of Christianity in the Hartlepool area. More than 1300 years ago Bede in his history informs us that 'Heiu, who is said to have been the first woman that in the province of the Northumbrians took upon her the habit and life of a nun, being consecrated by Bishop Aidan' established a monastery there in 640 A.D. - believed to have been sited on

Hartlepool, St. Joseph *Photo: E. Croghan*

the headland, near the sea. Six years later the more famous St. Hilda became the abbess of this foundation moving later to Whitby. Two ancient churches in the area remind us of the faithful who worshipped here centuries ago. Firstly, in the village of Hart is the church of St. Mary Magdalene of Saxon origin with its Norman tower and font and other reminders of its antiquity. Aptly named in the old part of Hartlepool is the ancient parish church of St. Hilda with its great west tower, built around 1250 A.D. Pevsner described it architecturally as 'one of the most important parish churches in the county.' The medieval Franciscan friary of the 13th century, which no longer exists, is a further reminder of Hartlepool's early Christian connections. Tradition has it that it was erected on or near the site of the first Saxon monastery.

The Reformation changes of the 16th century were to be felt in Hartlepool as elsewhere especially when the penal laws were enforced. It is a possibility - Hartlepool being Durham's major port until 1700 - that some seminary priests from the Catholic colleges on the continent may have landed here to disperse to the Catholic households where the Faith was secretly kept alive; the homes of the Trollopes at Thornley Hall and that of the Maires at Hardwick Hall, Castle Eden, were two places where priests lived in those difficult times.

Evidence is scanty on how Catholics survived during the days of persecution. One source suggests that some brave souls continued the practice of their Faith for in 1620 an objection was raised against Hartlepool being represented by an M.P. as it was 'so much given to Popery.'

Small pockets of Catholicism appear to have survived as the Papist Returns of 1767 show us that about 25 Catholics (including children) were living in the parish of Hart; in the township of Hartlepool there were approximately 16 faithful souls.

The nearest Mass centre for Hartlepool Catholics during the penal days was the previously mentioned Hardwick Hall (a secret hiding hole still exists in the roof of the Hall) where there was a resident chaplain provided by the Maire family. Here they were able to minister spiritually to the family and the neighbouring faithful until 1825 when Hutton Henry became the new mission.

At the end of the 18th century the population of Hartlepool was about 993 and that of West Hartlepool 325. One hundred years later the old town's population had increased to over 22,000 and West Hartlepool's to almost 64,000. Such a rise was due to the opportunities for employment provided by the expanding port, shipbuilding, the railways and other associated industries. Father Sharratt in his history - using the diocesan statistics of 1964 - estimated the Catholic community of West Hartlepool to be 1 in 7 of the population. Whether or not this was true of the 19th century there is, no doubt, that as the general population increased so proportionately did the Catholic congregation.

Aware of this trend and to fulfil the needs of Hartlepool Catholics the first post-Reformation chapel in Prissick Street was opened by Bishop Briggs in 1834; eight days later Father William Knight, who was to remain here for 40 years, was appointed the first resident priest. There is no evidence of Mass being said here before Father Knight's time, other than the pre-Reformation period, but we do know that the Silvertop family owned Dyke House Farm in the early 19th century where, one may speculate, Mass could have been said. By 1851, when it is estimated the Catholic numbers had grown to 1,500, Father Knight had erected the much bigger church of St. Mary's which was officially opened by Bishop Hogarth in the presence of Cardinal Wiseman, and Bishops Briggs, Brown and Morris.

'At the beginning of the nineteenth century West Hartlepool did not exist. In 1812 there was the drowsy little village of Stranton clustered round the old parish church. There were 50 stone dwellings painted white and a population of 350. The "green" is remembered now only by name.' This 'rural idyll' was, however, to change and eventually disappear as the need for housing Hartlepool's families increased. Father Knight's task became somewhat lighter in 1856 with the assistance of Father P.E. Harivel, who in a rented room over a warehouse in Princess Street, West Hartlepool, was able to instruct the people in the Faith and offer a service on a Sunday evening.

This, presumably, was a congregation who would become the founder - parishioners of St. Joseph's parish when the first parish priest, Father Robert Suffield was appointed in 1867. By this time a larger place for services was necessary and a lease had been taken on the Central Hall in Church Street. Any hopes the people and a succession of priests had of building their own church were dashed and remained unfulfilled for nearly 30 years. Although it has often been said that our churches were built with 'the pennies of the poor' most of the people, at that time - generous though they were - would not have been able to give much. A priority for the third parish priest, the Rev. James Shea, was the building of a school where the young people could be taught the Christian way of life. This was accomplished in 1873 when St. Joseph's School was opened in South Whitby Street at a cost of £1,500.

Father James Crolly (1878-83) must have, like his predecessors, wished to commence the building of a parish church but an increasing demand for school places diverted what money there was to the renting of the Halladown Hall in Park Road. A Church Bazaar which raised £650, a magnificent amount in those days, at least paid the debt off the school. Sometime between 1883 and 1884 it was decided to celebrate Mass in the school, but when Father Michael Green came to the parish in 1884 he hired the old skating rink (on which the Labour Hall stands today) and this was the principal place of worship for St. Joseph's parishioners for eleven years prior to the building of the church.

It was during the incumbency of the seventh parish priest, Father William Wickwar (1888 - 1933), later canon, that St. Joseph's parish finally got its present church. The necessity of building a new school near the old one had further delayed its erection and it was seven years after the arrival of Father Wickwar that the long desired church was opened in 1895.

An account of that great day, February 5th, 1895, is recorded in the annals of the Faithful Companions of Jesus, a religious order of sisters who came to the town in 1885 to assist in the education of the children:

> On Sunday, 3rd February, the snow was thick on the ground as we set out on our cold walk to Holy Mass, but we did not mind the falling flakes as we reflected that it was the last time that we would hear Mass in the miserable edifice in which, for eleven years, our dear Lord deigned to dwell.
>
> Tuesday 5th February, was a red letter day for the Catholic community of Hartlepool, for on that day was opened the magnificent church which is pronounced by one and all to be one of the finest in the North. The spacious sanctuary, beautiful oak carving and exquisite roof are the leading features of this noble church, the appointments of which testify to the refined taste of our zealous pastor, the Reverend William Wickwar. The ceremony began at

11.30 a.m.; our venerable Bishop (Thomas Wilkinson) himself sang Mass, whilst their Lordships the Bishops of Middlesbrough, Liverpool and Leeds assisted. The sanctuary and front seats were occupied by the numerous clergy from all parts who, notwithstanding the severe weather, had come to honour the grand occasion...

Basilica-like in its proportions, costing £13,000, and capable of accommodating a congregation of 1,000, St. Joseph's can only be appreciated by a personal visit. Of red brick construction with window frames and arches of stone in the Gothic style designed by the Newcastle firm of architects Dunn, Hansom and Fenwick, it is a 19th century gem of church architecture. Notable features inside the church are the fine hammer-beam roof, the formidable stone work of the arches supported on graceful pillars above which corbels of angels and saints look down into the wide nave; and, of course, the stained-glass windows in the sanctuary and side aisle walls. A recent visitor to the church working for English Heritage, Mr Neil Moat, stated that the two windows of St. Philip Neri and St. Gilbert of Sempringham in the aisle wall are the work of Arthur A. Orr whilst the remainder are that of the Hardman firm of Birmingham; a firm founded by A.W. Pugin and John Hardman.

Only a brief mention can be made in this article of all that happened in St. Joseph's parish from 1933 until the present day. Father Francis Dunne succeeded Canon Wickwar in that year and remained until 1961. Further school building was necessary and the coming of the Second World War not only disrupted the school life of the teachers and children but 'on the night of 19th June, 1940, at 12.20 a.m. six high-explosive bombs were dropped in the streets and on the houses in the neighbourhood of St. Joseph's School. The school was shattered, window panes blown in, etc. It was impossible to use the school.'

One of the chief concerns in the late 1940s of Father Dunne, Canon Burke and Father O'Sullivan, the three parish priests of Hartlepool, was the provision of a grammar school education for boys, and after protracted negotiations two large houses in Wooler Road and Grange Road were purchased eventually opening as St. Francis Grammar School in 1956 staffed by the Xaverian Brothers. The Faithful Companions of Jesus looked after much of the girls' education assisted by dedicated lay staff and the people of Hartlepool owe them a great debt of gratitude for their service in the area for more than 100 years.

Canon Patrick Lacey (1962 - 1980) 'a very well-loved parish priest' - who was also known as 'the building priest', having organised the building of St. Thomas More's church and St. John Vianney's as well as St. Peter's School - is still fondly remembered here. Many will still recall the rapturous applause he received at the end of his Golden Jubilee Mass in 1980. During his time here he continued his building activities adding a new church porch in 1966, a new presbytery in 1976 and the Parish Centre in 1979. He, also had the delicate task, after parish consultation, of re-ordering the sanctuary to meet the new liturgical requirements of Vatican II.

Also, remembered with affection is Canon John Bell (1980 - 91) who, having taught for a spell at Ushaw and been headmaster of St. Francis Grammar School since 1965, succeeded Canon Lacey 'transforming himself into a true pastor of the people and ... greatly mourned when he died.'

The present parish priest, Father Anthony Owens, came here in 1991 and has had the privilege of organising and celebrating with his parishioners the centenary of St. Joseph's Church.

The preparations for the centenary may be said to have begun in 1992 with a Mission preached by Fathers John Docherty and Michael Hickey, and the formation of the Centenary Committee of 12 parishioners under the chairmanship of Mr Phil Smith who, working alongside Father Owens and Father Campbell, planned the year-long celebrations.

The highlight, naturally, was the Mass on February 5th concelebrated by Bishop Ambrose Griffiths, Bishop Owen Swindlehurst and Bishop Leo McCartie of Northampton who was baptised in St. Joseph's. A full congregation, also saw, concelebrating with the bishops, 24 priests who had served here in the past and others from the various parts of the diocese. Readers of the *Northern Cross* were able to see the splendour of St. Joseph's when I.T.V.'s Morning Worship included the screening of the Sunday Mass on February 19th concelebrated by Father Owens and Father Campbell.

The centenary calendar includes many events of both a spiritual and social nature. A social evening was held in the Mayfair on January 27th. As the year progresses the variety of the celebration unfolds: a parish ceilidh on March 17th; two concerts in the church in April and June; a pilgrimage to Walsingham in May; a children's May procession and a Corpus Christi procession in June; a parish picnic and a visit to Ampleforth in July; and a Flower Festival from September 14th to the 17th with a recital by the Queen's organist, Mark Wardell on September 15th.

St. Joseph's (as Austin Brown's parish history records) was always a place where much was happening in and around the church as the spiritual, educational and social needs of young and old alike were met. How many older parishioners will remember the Children of Mary, the Blessed Sacrament Guild, the Grail, the Catholic Women's League, the S.V.P. the Youth Club and the Drama Group? Many parishes in the past had their own football teams and St. Joseph's can claim the proud record of being the only parish in the diocese to have won the Durham County Amateur Cup in 1913.

This long Christian tradition of community spirit is no less to-day. Opportunities abound for those who wish to be involved in parish life. The two primary schools of the Sacred Heart and St. Joseph provide a Catholic education for 670 children; the older children are educated at English Martyrs' Comprehensive School. Remaining with the young; the parish has an abundance of 24 altar boys - prepared and trained by Tony Carter - under the guidance of 83 year old Mr Clifford Hey who has been faithful to this ministry since his youth.

A team of dedicated ladies assists with the Children's Liturgy each Sunday at the 10.30 Mass. One interesting form of evangelisation to youth is the Junior R.C.I.A. course, held at the F.C.J. Convent, which has helped a number of interested young people follow a journey in Faith culminating in their reception into the Church; there is also a senior R.C.I.A. course from September to Pentecost.

One of the oldest organisations is the S.V.P. which has been in existence here for more than 70 years; a conference of 8 members continues this valuable work to the needy in the area. Forty-two members of the Women's Guild, who meet fortnightly, are ever-ready to assist where required with catering and other hospitable tasks. Three organists, Kathleen Monaghan, Angela Keenan and Sister Bernadette provide the musical accompaniment at church services.

To remind the parish to look outwards too, the Third World Group heightens the awareness of the needs of our brothers and sisters overseas. Profits from their Sunday Coffee Morning have been used to help the poor in India and sponsor the training of doctors, nurses and teachers. An S.V.P. monthly Disaster Fund Collection provides ready cash to be sent to stricken areas at home and abroad while there is always generous A.P.F. and mission support.

Helping the disadvantaged and those unable to speak for themselves are the H.C.P.T. and Life Group (both groups have St. Joseph's parishioners involved). The former organises a weekly club for the handicapped in the Sacred Heart School and raises funds to send members to Lourdes.

St. Joseph's is also blessed with an abundance of lay readers and lay ministers of the Eucharist who each week take Christ to the sick and housebound.

To complete the list of those involved in parish life one needs to mention the Finance and Social committees; the Brownies and an elderly Keep Fit group; and the parish bulletin team who each week provides vital information to all through 'The Word in Action' - a newsletter in its 19th year.

Here too, at the parish centre, is the *Northern Cross* Office where the editor, John Bailey (a St. Joseph's parishioner) and others, such as Ken Bradley who is there every Thursday, organise and plan the many tasks involved in producing the newspaper.

On the Feast of the Epiphany Father Owens blessed and installed a new centenary banner for the parish. It was made by Josie Harvey, a parishioner - also an enthusiastic flower arranger - and Pat Vaughan, an Anglican. On this striking piece of embroidery Christ is depicted as the Good Shepherd with his command to Peter: 'Feed my Lambs: Feed my Sheep.'

A fitting reminder to all in the centenary year and for the future as this is what the priests and people of St. Joseph's have tried to do in the past and will continue to do in the years to come.

POSTSCRIPT   *(Fr. David Coxon, 1998)*

Father David Coxon came to St. Joseph's in February, 1998, succeeding Father Tony Owens (1991-1998) who moved to Crook as Parish Priest. Father David Phillips has been assistant priest at St. Joseph's since 1995.

27. HARTLEPOOL   St. Mary   *(November, 1984)*

'This little walled fishing port twelve hundred years old' is one description of Hartlepool which few residents would recognise today. The transformation of this fishing port into a large town was a direct result of 19th century industrial expansion which attracted many people here seeking employment; among these were a considerable number of Catholics, many of whom were Irish. St. Mary's Parish - celebrating this year its 150th anniversary - was founded to meet the spiritual needs of those Catholics who flocked here to earn their livelihood.

Christianity's story in this area is, however, a much older one as St. Bede testifies in his *Ecclesiastical History* where he notes the foundation of a monastery here in 7th century by Heiu 'who is said to have been the first woman that in the province of the Northumbrians took upon her the habit and life of a nun, being consecrated by Bishop Aidan.'

Another source claims that Heiu, of Irish origin, was more commonly known as St. Bega who founded another monastery at St. Bees in Cumberland named after her; the parish primary school keeps the name alive today. Heiu was to leave Hartlepool and settle in Calcacestir (site unknown) to be replaced by the illustrious Saint Hilda whom St. Aidan recalled from East Anglia to the convent, first at Wearmouth, and later to Hartlepool where she became abbess.

Viking raids left little untouched along the north east coast and just as Lindisfarne and Tynemouth suffered so did the monastery at Hartlepool in 800 A.D. Nothing remains of this early Christian settlement although the Franciscan Friary founded in Hartlepool, sometime before 1258, is believed to have been built near the same spot; today the old hospital - recently vacated - is supposed to be on this holy site. If this is so, it is an interesting example of how

Hartlepool, St. Mary   *Photo: T. Mackin*

151

certain sites have continued through the centuries to be used to dispense the spiritual and corporal works of mercy.

Further confirmation of a Franciscan presence in Hartlepool is given in the will of John Trollope of Thornley made in 1476 and witnessed by Richard Vavasour, Mayor of Hartlepool. In it he committed his soul to Our Lady, St. John the Baptist and St. Cuthbert desiring that his body should be buried with the Friars Minor of Hartlepool; he also left ten shillings for Masses to be sung for his soul. The friary which had been inhabited by a prior and eighteen friars was dissolved in 1546.

Very near to the Catholic church of St. Mary's stands the church of St. Hilda - one of the most important parish churches architecturally in the county - reminding us, once again, of the Faith established here in Hartlepool many years ago. St. Hilda's incorporates into its structure a number of building styles, the earliest being the Norman porch. Before the Reformation there existed within the church several chantry chapels - one dedicated to St. Mary, one to St. Nicholas and one to St. Helen - where chaplains were engaged to offer Mass and pray for the living and the deceased members of families who had provided endowments; two chaplains whose names we know were Thomas Del Kyrke and John de Thornton.

It would appear that Hartlepool did not take kindly to the religious changes of the 16th century. Details of those penal times are scanty but the Faith appears to have been strong here in 1620 when objections were raised against the suggestion that Hartlepool should have an M.P. as it was 'much given to Popery'.

At the beginning of the 19th century it has been estimated that 20 to 30 Catholics resided in Hartlepool and they were served by priests resident at Hardwick Hall near Castle Eden. From 1825 Father Thomas Augustine Slater continued this work from the newly formed parish at Hutton Henry.

Hartlepool's first post-Reformation church in Prissick Street was opened by Bishop Briggs, Coadjutor - Vicar-Apostolic of the Northern District on January 10th, 1834; eight days later Father William Knight, a Lancastrian, came as the first parish priest and was to remain there for 40 years. Mr John Wells, whose wife Mary was probably a Catholic, provided the money for the building of the chapel; a few years later he was repaid the loan of £250.

Father Knight, realising the importance of a Catholic school as a nursery of the Faith, soon had one built in 1837 - with financial help from a Mrs Cayley of Scorton - in which about 20 pupils were enrolled by the first and only teacher, Mr Joseph Taylor; two years later a girl of 16, a Miss Hedley, was employed to teach the young girls in an upper room.

It was obvious to Father Knight by the mid-1840s that the present chapel was totally inadequate to meet the needs of a rapidly expanding congregation as they flooded into Hartlepool seeking work on the railways and the docks. Within 27 years - from 1824 when the parish had about 25 Catholics - the numbers had risen to 1,500. To raise the necessary funds a Mr Lawrenson was appointed to take charge of a group of weekly collectors; this gentleman paid personally for the peal of bells - the first to be installed in a Catholic church in northern England since the Reformation. Generous donations were also made by a number of Catholic gentry including the Salvins of Croxdale, the Withams of Lartington and the Silvertops of Minsteracres.

Costing £4,000 approximately the church - designed by Joseph Hansom and built by Mr John Galley - was officially opened by Bishop Hogarth on August 28th, 1851, in the presence of Cardinal Wiseman and Bishops Briggs, Brown and Morris. Bishop Hogarth had laid the foundation stone in the July of the previous year - something of a record, then, in the time taken to build a church. The cost included the site and presbytery also.

An increasing Catholic population also meant pressure on the existing school so in the early 1850s a room was hired in Chapman Street and Miss Alice Knight (Father Knight's sister) assisted by a Mrs Leonard began teaching the children in the northern part of the town; later an old building was bought and became St Bega's School and later still a Men's Club. In 1883, a Presbyterian chapel was purchased along with three cottages and after conversion was opened in February 1884 - the present school was built in the 1970s.

Since the parish was founded in 1834 St. Mary's has had only six parish priests, including the present one, Father Francis Ellis, who has been there since 1961.

Father Knight (later Canon) spent 40 years in the parish; the second parish priest was Father Francis Moverley who remained here for six years. He was succeeded by Father Gerard Van Hooff, a Dutchman, who was much involved in the public life of Hartlepool becoming chairman of the Board of Guardians as well as the School Board. On his retirement in 1899 he continued to live in Hartlepool until his death in 1915. Father Gerard Van Kippersluis followed him and during his time here the Golden Jubilee of the church occurred; the celebrations were attended by Cardinal Vaughan, the Archbishop of Westminster.

Saint Mary's longest serving parish priest was Father Laurence Burke (later Canon) who came as a boy from Tipperary to study at St. Cuthbert's Grammar School and afterwards at Ushaw College where he was ordained in 1899. He began his term of office at St. Mary's in 1907 and remained here until his death in 1961 having been parish priest for 54 years. Much was accomplished during his time here; he, too, was a member of the Board of Guardians and a governor of the Hartlepool Hospital; he served on the Hartlepool Education Committee and was chief examiner of the Catholic schools in the diocese. Public recognition of his involvement in town affairs was shown when he became a Freeman of the Borough in 1957. In Canon Burke's early days St. Mary's Primary School was opened, in 1913, and from 1938 until 1961 was used as a Mass centre. Post-war housing development at West View led to many of St. Mary's parishioners moving away from the Mother Church resulting in the formation of a new parish in 1950 called St. Thomas More's.

Hartlepool and West Hartlepool have provided over the years a considerable number of vocations to the priesthood and the religious life. For St. Mary's to have existed for 150 years is indeed a cause for celebration, but old parishes and churches are also a cause for concern where numbers have dwindled as inner urban areas are redeveloped - St. Mary's parish now numbers 500 souls. The crumbling spire, once a landmark for fishermen, was removed for safety reasons in 1946; the bells in the tower lay silent in case their vibrations brought it crashing to the ground. Father Bernard Sharratt in his book about the Hartlepool parishes, written 20 years ago, sums it up rather well: 'Anyone troubled with woodworm or dry rot or crumbling stone should ring Hartlepool 66080 and ask for Father Ellis.' Father Knight's achievements of 1851 are now Father Ellis's problems of 1984.

Since Father Ellis arrived in 1961 much has been done to stem the ravages of nature and time: woodworm has been eradicated, stonework has been repaired and the stained-glass windows renewed by Reed Milligan. What Father Ellis calls the 3 R's - re-wiring, re-lighting and re-heating - were all renewed in 1965; the rear of the church has been redesigned; the Lady Chapel and Baptistry were opened out in the Sixties and given a wrought-iron surround; a porch screen has been erected which serves to keep the heat in and provides a Crying Room for mothers, with young babies, who wish to use it. In 1967 the church was repainted; a year later railings were erected around the boundary and the church surrounds resurfaced with tarmac. Once again the bells ring out.

Father Ellis must, indeed, be an expert in the renovation of old churches and his task is not accomplished yet. A new roof is now required; gutterings need replacing and a damp course inserted at an estimated cost of £73,000. The worry is that in spite of the efforts of the parish priest and a hardworking parish committee, who have devised many ways of raising money, at the end of the year they can just manage to break even. No doubt, donations will be welcome from readers.

We have only been able to tell a little of the growth of Catholicism in Hartlepool - the story of St. Joseph's founded from St. Mary's in 1867 is another story. The mother church of Hartlepool and its immediate area has a history of which the diocese can be proud. Father Ellis, assisted by other priests of the Hartlepool Deanery, commemorated the 150th anniversary with a concelebrated Mass in St. Mary's on October 9th, 1984. A social gathering took place on Friday, October 12th, in the Borough Hall where priests and parishioners were able to get together to celebrate this historic occasion in the parish. Another milestone on the pilgrim road had been reached.

28. HEBBURN   St. Aloysius   *(November, 1988)*

In June of this year the priests and people of St Aloysius, Hebburn, had the joy of celebrating the centenary of their parish church which was officially opened and blessed by Bishop Wilkinson on June 3rd, 1888. This large imposing red-brick structure was designed, according to the Newcastle *Daily Journal* reporter, in the Early French style by Mr Charles Walker of Newcastle; the main contractor was Mr Lumsden and the cost was £5,000. The architect's original drawing of the church shows clearly a tower with a belfry and a semi-circular apse; these it was decided would be added later but, in fact, never were. Had they been, an even more impressive church would have adorned the site.

Anniversaries are times for reflection and in Father Michael Purtill's history of the parish, details of the community's Christian heritage are clearly delineated. Those familiar with the area of South Tyneside will know of the nearby St. Paul's monastery at Jarrow where lived the historian and scholar, St. Bede, who played a significant role in the flowering of culture during the Golden Age of Northumbria. To the south of Hebburn lies Monkton, reputedly the birthplace of this northern saint.

What may not be so well-known is that the Faith continued here, possibly without a break, during the post-Reformation period. The penal laws enacted in Elizabeth's reign, and later, did not bring about the demise of the Catholic Faith in these parts. The River Tyne provided a supply and lifeline to those Catholics who clung tenaciously to their religion when the state was against them. Ships returning from the continent carried secretly to our shores the priests who were to meet the spiritual needs of the diminishing faithful. Catholic houses were dotted along the banks of the Tyne providing refuge for the missionaries: Ursula Taylor's home in South Shields; Dorothy Lawson's at St. Anthony's, Walker; John Darell's centre at Jarrow, and finally the home of the Hodgsons at Hebburn Hall.

Richard Hodgson, an important Newcastle merchant, was known openly as a Catholic in those difficult times; this did not, however, prevent him from being elected Mayor of Newcastle on three occasions in 1555, 1566 and 1580. Robert, his son, married in 1588 Anne Langley whose father, Blessed Richard Langley of Grimthorpe, near Pocklington, was hanged at York in 1586 for harbouring priests. Her sister, Isobel, was to die for the Faith in York prison in 1597. Robert and Anne were, also, the proud parents of two priests - Fathers Edmund and John Hodgson. With such a staunch Catholic pedigree it is not surprising that when Robert's son, Sir Robert Hodgson, inherited his father's estates in 1625, Hebburn Hall should continue as a spiritual haven for neighbouring Catholics. Such activities led the Vicar of Newcastle, John March to write that 'Popery flourishes and the river is in danger of being blocked up...' Three of Sir Robert's ships were searched at Newcastle Quay and they had on board passengers who were suspected priests and 'many popish books, pictures and relics etc.' On one occasion when Hebburn Hall was raided Sir Robert was absent and his faithful servant, John Davel (could this be the same John Darell of Jarrow?), 'had fled across the Tyne into Northumberland.'

Certainly Father Richard Holtby S.J., who masterminded the Jesuit mission in the North East visited the Hodgsons and it is quite possible that martyrs such as St. Henry Morse, who stayed for a time at St. Anthony's, across the river, also stayed at Hebburn Hall.

Although Hebburn Hall seems to disappear from the scene as a Catholic mission centre in the mid-17th century, the Catholics along both banks of the Tyne were ministered to by the secular and Jesuit missions in Newcastle and also the Jesuit Mission in Gateshead. After 1821 when St. Cuthbert's at North Shields was opened it was possible for Hebburn Catholics to attend Mass there, until the opening of the chapel at Felling in 1842 which became more convenient. When St. Bede's, Jarrow, was opened in 1861 the parish priest, Father Meynell, was able eventually to establish a mission at Hebburn saying Mass regularly in what was probably, as yet, an unidentified inn. Later, Mass was said regularly in the Ellison Buildings.

The latter half of the 19th century saw a rapid expansion of industry in many areas of our diocese including Hebburn to which many families moved seeking employment in the local pit, the Hawthorn Leslie shipyards and other heavy industries. Hebburn's population more than doubled between 1871 and 1888 from 5,220 to 11,618; the Catholic population being estimated in 1882 at around 2,000. This concentration of Catholics made it necessary for Bishop Chadwick to create a separate parish here with the appointment of Father James Corboy as the first parish priest in December, 1871.

Catholics have always appreciated the value of Catholic education. So often priests starting a parish have been faced with the dilemma of building a church and school with limited financial resources. One solution which appears to have been quite common in the diocese was to build a school-chapel until the parish could afford to erect a separate church. This was the temporary solution decided in Hebburn when the school-chapel was opened in 1872. The first entry in the Log Book is as follows:

> 'The school was opened on January 8th by Fanny Wood, a certified teacher. 98 children present, the greater number of whom had never attended any school before. The Rev. J. Corboy, principal manager, visited in the morning and afterwards sent in Anne Carr to assist for a time as a paid monitress.'

By 1907 the school was providing education for 526 children at seven standards in five rooms! An absent colleague could mean a member of staff teaching over 100 children. The problem of overcrowding was somewhat eased when Father Edward Witty built and opened a new infant school in 1928 in Argyle Street.

One of the first tasks facing the present parish priest, on his arrival in Hebburn in 1955, was the building of the new secondary school which had already commenced on a site where the Civic Centre now stands. The local authority were keen to acquire this site and had offered alternative locations; it was eventually agreed to build the new school on land adjoining the Catholic grammar school in Mill Lane. Father Walsh was also able to build the church of St. James's nearby which was opened in 1967; its first parish priest was Father George Dolan now on the missions in Kenya. The grammar and secondary modern schools in Mill Lane were amalgamated in 1974 to form St. Joseph's Comprehensive School.

The original school which had served its purpose well for over 100 years was replaced in 1980 by a new junior school in Argyle Street next to the infant school. A modern parish centre, completed in 1984, stands on the spot where the first school-chapel was erected.

It was during the tenure of Dr. Matthew Toner as parish priest that the efforts to raise funds for a new church to accommodate a much larger congregation were multiplied: 'the excitement and gratitude of the Catholic people were intense as they saw their church slowly rise to its magnificent height' as churches and chapels of other denominations appeared during this period on the skyline. As to the name of the church there remains some uncertainty regarding the choice of a patron saint. Father Purtill suggests that in choosing St. Aloysius, a Jesuit saint, the parish and people may have been giving due recognition to an order which had kept the flame of Faith alight in earlier days.

Father Witty served as parish priest for 43 years at St. Aloysius witnessing and implementing many changes during his long incumbency. He was their spiritual father during the traumatic years of the First World War; the economic depression of the 1920s and 1930s and the equally upsetting years of the Second World War. He was responsible for the erection of the Lady Chapel as a memorial to those men of the parish who fell in the 1914-1918 War.

Father M. Purtill's parish history - published this year to celebrate the church's centenary - has many passages worth quoting. One in particular emphasises the fatherly care shown by the priests at Hebburn during the slump of the inter-war years. 'It was during this time that the priests of St. Aloysius identified with their flock and in so many practical and generous ways, helped them to cope with their difficulties and hardships. When many of the thousands who now composed the Catholic community had a shortage of necessities it was the church they turned to for help and it was from there that the practical help came. The priests serving St. Aloysius at this time formed a tremendous bond with their people.'

For a time, beginning on September 10th, 1939, 240 Catholic children from the area along with 13 teachers and 11 helpers were evacuated to the Sedgefield area for safety causing disruption to the home, school, and parish life in Hebburn.

Father Austin Forkin succeeded Father Witty in 1948 and remained there until Father James Walsh, the present parish priest, took over in 1955. During his 33 years at Hebburn Father Walsh, assisted by his curates - the present one is Father P. J. Morrissey - has achieved much in the spiritual and social development of the parish. He was responsible for the building of the Derwent Road Hall as a Mass centre in 1958 to meet the needs of parishioners on the new estates erected by the council in the post-war era.

The new parish centre is the focus of social life in the parish. Here the varying age groups can meet and enjoy the modern amenities provided. The Over 60's is a thriving group - so popular it has a waiting list. A Mother and Toddler Group is very much in evidence as are the Girl Guides and a 'Stroke' Club. The older parish societies such as the S.V.P. (founded in 1911), the Legion of Mary and the Ladies' Guild continue their efforts in making the parish a loving and caring community.

St. Aloysius' parish has much cause for jubilation this year; not only have they celebrated the centenary of the church, but the parishioners have also joined Father Walsh in celebrating the diamond jubilee of his priesthood. To honour his work and long association with the district Father Walsh was made a freeman of the borough by South Tyneside Borough Council in June.

A week of celebrations began in the parish on Tuesday, June 7th when Bishop Hugh Lindsay concelebrated a Mass of Thanksgiving with more than 50 priests. Before a congregation of 700 people, in a church bedecked with flowers for the occasion, Father M. Purtill preached, reminding those present of all the unnamed people of Hebburn who by allegiance to their beliefs in the last 100 years had kept the Faith alive in these parts; and he hoped that in the future it would be possible to praise those of today who continued to uphold that which had been passed on to them by their forefathers. Also in the congregation that evening were the Lord Mayor of South Tyneside, councillors, and representatives of other denominations. A Social Evening followed with a Buffet Meal to which all were invited.

The following evening, within the setting of the Mass, the people of the parish had the opportunity to renew their Baptismal and Marriage vows. Young people in the parish prepared the liturgy and music for the celebration of Mass on the Thursday evening - their special contribution to the anniversary week. At the social which followed they included a drama production in their programme.

Friday evening, June 10th, was special to Father Walsh who with more than 30 priests concelebrated a Mass of Thanksgiving for 60 years in the priesthood; his assistant, Father P. J. Morrissey, was celebrating on that same day his ten years as a priest. Father Tom Cass was the preacher at this Mass and presentations were made to both priests of the parish afterwards.

On the Saturday a Mass was celebrated for all the members of the parish living and dead and for former parishioners who had once been part of the parish community. The week of celebration concluded with a Dinner Dance - a week of great joy and happiness that will be remembered for many years by all those who participated in the festivities.

POSTSCRIPT   *(M. McNabola, 1998)*

Ten years on from the centenary of the official opening of their church and, once again, the parishioners of St. Aloysius Parish, Hebburn, are preparing for, and looking forward to, another exciting and important event. As was stated in the *'Down your Aisle'* article of 1988, the building plans for the church were never actually finished. Consequently, it has never been consecrated.

In April this year the parish, under the guidance and leadership of their parish priest, Father Michael Griffiths, celebrated a wonderful time of refreshment and renewal in the form of a mission. Led by two C.M.S. missioners, Father John O'Toole and Father John Loughlin, known affectionately to the parishioners as John Major and John Minor, the mission was a perfect beginning for a time of hard work and preparation needed for the long-awaited blessing and consecration by Bishop Ambrose Griffiths in time for the Millennium. The liturgies, which were mostly planned and implemented by parishioners, encompassed all aspects of parish life – ecumenism, youth, faith and the Church, healing and reconciliation, prayer and the needs of the sick and handicapped. It was a time when all the parish pulled together, providing excellent hospitality, transport, befriending and advertising. The masses and services were enhanced by the beautiful music provided by the choir under the leadership of Sister Mary Lees. It was very heartening to see that members of the sister-parish of St. James's supported the mission as well as members of churches of other denominations in Hebburn. The schools also helped by designing posters and banners and contributing to the parish exhibition which was on display in Hebburn library and also in the parish hall. The final mass of the mission was celebrated by Bishop Ambrose, who also joined the parishioners in the parish hall afterwards to celebrate the ending of the mission week.

Always a close community, the parish is already reaping the benefits of the mission, with people becoming even closer both spiritually and socially and parishioners coming forward to offer their time and skills in parish work. At a time when, because of the shortage of priests, the workload of the parish priest is quite phenomenal, this sharing of the workload is essential for the continuation of a close and caring community life.

Very soon there is to be an open meeting for parishioners to meet the architect, Mr. Waugh, where plans for the refurbishment of the church, including new flooring, replacement stained-glass windows, a new altar and many other exciting features, will be revealed. If all goes to plan the church will be ready by the end of 1999, in time for the New Millennium.

To conclude, St. Aloysius parish is thriving, alive and kicking, and it is certain that all the priests and parishioners who worked so hard for this community in the past would be very proud of the way the present priest and parishioners are keeping the faith alive in Hebburn.

29. HEXHAM   St. Mary   (October, November 1994)

The obvious place to begin a study of the Christian Faith in Hexham is surely the abbey of St. Andrew which stands overlooking the market square. Here on this site the first church of Hexham was built - a Saxon one by St. Wilfrid on land granted by Queen Etheldreda of Northumberland.

Below the abbey choir, access can be gained to the crypt where, it is believed, the remains of Wilfrid's church are extant and where his successor, St. Acca, is buried.

There is much to be seen in the abbey but what is of particular interest are the Saxon frithstool and a reputed Saxon chalice. The former is modelled in the style of a chair of early Christian Rome and may be connected with the right of sanctuary granted to the abbey; it may also have been the bishop's chair.

When the Danes raided Hexham in 875 A.D. much of the town, church and monastery were destroyed. The abbey was rebuilt round about 1180 and served by the Augustinian Canons until the 16th century dissolution. Invasion by the Scots in the 12th and 13th centuries added further to the difficulties experienced by the canons and the people: 'Its beautiful church was fired, its priceless relics wantonly thrown into the flames and the gold and gems that adorned its shrines were torn off and carried away by the triumphant invaders.'

Not everything was lost and among the pre-Reformation links is the fine wooden choir screen on which are paintings of several bishops of Hexham and Lindisfarne

After the failure of the Pilgrimage of Grace in 1536 to restore the ancient Faith and to reinstate the monks in their monasteries, the abbey of Hexham was forfeited to the crown and the Augustinian Canons expelled.

As the penal legislation of Elizabeth's reign was enacted and enforced it became increasingly difficult for those who wished to remain loyal to their Catholic Faith to do so.

In 1600, some 150 Northumbrians were convicted of recusancy and Francis Radcliffe of Dilston was imprisoned at York. Four of his daughters became Poor Clares at Gravelines; two granddaughters became Benedictines at Cambrai; and two great-granddaughters were Canonesses at Louvain. Roger Widdrington, who was reconciled to the church after witnessing the martyrdom of John Boste at Durham in 1594, was said by a contemporary to have 'poisoned with popery all Hexhamshire; spread dangerous books; dissuaded openly from religion.'

Priests trained in seminaries abroad, adopting aliases, were sheltered in the homes of the Catholic gentry where they ministered to those who wished to remain faithful. One, John Sicklemore, was captured at Corbridge and imprisoned in Newcastle and Durham. During his interrogation, 'he refused to confess any place of abode or any acquaintances or priesthood'. He was banished in 1606. The Venerable William Southerne, who was baptised at Aycliffe, Co. Durham and who was known to have served at Halton, near Hexham, received the ultimate penalty being martyred at Newcastle in 1618.

Such severity did not seem to deter those of strong convictions such as Robert Thompson, a native of Hexham - and later others - who entered the English College in Rome in 1634. Nor did it weaken the resolve of the Radcliffe family in their Catholic stronghold at Dilston, near Corbridge, where they built a Mass chapel - a rarity in those times when the chapel was usually a room in the house. Sir Edward, the second baronet, who died in 1663, was an early benefactor of the Northern Brethren's Fund.

Sir Francis, grandson of the first Sir Francis Radcliffe, was created the first Earl of Derwentwater by James II in 1688 and it was his two sisters who were Benedictine nuns.

During a short period of toleration Francis welcomed to his Dilston home in 1687, Bishop Leyburn - the first visit by a Catholic bishop since the Reformation - who confirmed 481 people, a goodly number being from Hexham.

The Radcliffes of Dilston were to suffer considerably when James, the third Earl of Derwentwater, was executed in 1716 for allying himself to the Jacobite cause which wished to restore the Stuarts to the English throne. The Dilston estates were eventually forfeited and for many years were in non-Catholic hands. By 1874, when the estates were sold again it was decided to exhume the bodies of the Radcliffes who were interred in the family vault. The body of the executed earl was taken to the chapel of the Petre family at Thorndon Hall, Essex. The earl's daughter had married into this family; and a Benjamin Petre, who had been a chaplain at Dilston, was to become in 1721 auxiliary bishop of the London District.

Within the grounds of St. Mary's, Hexham, is the Derwentwater memorial beneath which lie five Radcliffes who were re-interred here, also, in 1874.

Dilston was not the only missionary centre in the Hexham area. An equally important one was the farm at Stonecroft owned for many years by the Gibson family. Ursula Mountney was given in the will of her brother, John Widdrington, an estate which included Stonecroft. She expressed the wish in 1680 that 'my loving friend and Kinsman, William Lord Widdrington That Stonecroft and Nunbush with Appurtances may always be let to ffarme to some discrete Catholicke qualified to entertain a priest for the helpe of poor Catholicks in Hexham and Warden parishes and other places adjacent.' She, also, reiterated the wish of her deceased brother that the chaplain should be a Dominican or Franciscan and left a sum of £20 for this purpose.

Dominicans served the people of Tynedale for nearly 200 years and a number of them were local men. Three Armstrong brothers of Ordley became priests: John, a Jesuit; and Robert and Thomas Dominicans, who both served in Hexham for a time, the latter dying at Stonecroft in 1662.

Mrs Mountney's will, regarding the maintenance of a priest, allowed either order of friars to supply the mission so we see Franciscans serving at Stonecroft too; the first one was probably Peter Atkinson who died there in 1686. Another buried in Hexham in 1698, a Mr Goodyear, is described as 'a popish priest'. A tombstone in the abbey cemetery marks the burial place of Jasper Leadbitter the last Dominican to serve in Hexham; he was the sixth Leadbitter, of 'the order of St. Dominick', who died in 1830.

The Benedictines, also, served the Hexham area too - as early as 1632, according to one source. At different times they ministered at Dilston, Beaufront, Capheaton Hall and Swinburne Castle. Francis Porter, Durham born, was professed at Lambspring serving Beaufront for 21 years until his death in 1689. A later Benedictine, Dom James Higginson, was at Swinburne Castle from 1795 until 1828; he, also, served the Catholics of Corbridge.

Father Deegan, the present parish priest of St. Mary's, Hexham, continues this long tradition of the celebration of Mass in Corbridge and Swinburne. Since 1977 he has been able to say a weekly vigil Mass in the Anglican church of St. Andrew which has its origins in Saxon days; he was the first priest to say Mass there since the Reformation. A Sunday Mass is, also, celebrated weekly in the small intimate chapel, built in 1841, at Swinburne.

It would seem that the Catholics of Hexham town were served by the priests from some of the mission centres mentioned above until 1721 when Peter Antoninus Thompson O.P., moved from Stonecroft to lodge with a Mr Rymer, a merchant of Hexham; he ministered at the High Chapel on Battle Hill continuing to serve Stonecroft.

Jasper Leadbitter (previously mentioned) served this Dominican mission for 45 years and was responsible for the move to Hencotes in 1797 - the site on which the present church and schools stand.

Alongside the Dominican mission was the valuable service rendered to the Hexham Catholics by the Cockshaw Mission. We know that house masses were said in this area before 1721, one of the places being a cottage near Ladle-well in Cockshaw-Lonnen belonging to the Leadbitter family.

A Father George Gibson served Cockshaw from 1757 until 1778 building a chapel there with funds mainly subscribed by Lawrence Hall of Dilicote Hall. The old presbytery is still standing; the chapel to the rear was demolished some years ago. George was one of four priest brothers, sons of Jasper Gibson of Stonecroft whose wife Margaret was a Leadbitter. Two of them became bishops. Matthew was bishop of the Northern District from 1780 until 1790 when he was succeeded by his brother, William, who was president of Douai College and who was largely responsible for the establishing of Ushaw College after the French revolutionary upheaval made it impractical, if not impossible, to train clerical students in the college founded by Cardinal Allen in Elizabeth's reign.

In 1826 Father Michael Singleton - a Lancashire man trained at the English College in Lisbon - came to Cockshaw and the following year it was decided with the retirement of the Dominican priest, Father Leadbitter, to amalgamate the two existing missions.

He decided a new chapel was needed and in his appeal for funds he stated that: 'till last year there were in this town two Catholic chapels, but such have been our losses that these cannot any longer be supported... The old chapel has for many years threatened to bury its congregation in its ruins, and that which is called the new one is so circumscribed in its dimensions that it will neither admit of enlargement nor accommodate more than half the present members many of whom come from a distance of seven miles and some from a distance of twenty miles'.

Some of the cost was offset by the sale of the Cockshaw property which realised £600. The foundation stone was laid in April, 1828, but it was more than two years later, in September 1830, that Bishop Thomas Penswick was able to open it officially. There seems to be some uncertainty as to who the architect was. Bonomi submitted a design. However, Pevsner claims that John Green who designed the church at Stella, which has similarities to St. Mary's, was responsible. The parish history suggests that Father Singleton's plan was adopted.

Two years after the opening of the church the parish had its own school at a cost of £400; parents, who could afford it, were expected to contribute 9d. per week. By 1858 the Sisters of Mercy from Sunderland had established themselves here; they were housed initially by the Kirsopp family whose son was, at that time, a curate in Sunderland. Two of the pioneering Hexham sisters were Mother Gonzaga and Mother Joseph who had entered the Mercy community shortly after its arrival in Sunderland.

The second half of the 19th century was a rapid period of growth in the diocese including the Tyne Valley. Father Kirsopp, whose family hailed from the Spital in Hexham, was assigned to the care of the western part of St. Mary's which then comprised Haltwhistle and Haydon Bridge where chapels were built in 1864 and 1873 respectively.

It is not possible to mention all the priests and people who faithfully served the Hexham Mission up to the present day. Father Singleton spent his whole ministry here until his death in 1863 and his successor, the Rev. John Anderton Cooke, served the parish for 44 years dying in 1907, whilst in more recent times Father Francis Marley was here for 22 years.

To prepare for the 150th anniversary of the church opening the sanctuary was re-ordered using the reredos and other timber in the making of pulpit and presidential chair. On Friday, December 21st, 1979, Bishop Hugh Lindsay re-opened and consecrated the church and concelebrated a Mass with the deanery priests.

With such a long Christian history it is not surprising that the priests and people continue this long tradition of commitment to the Faith to-day which is nurtured by Father Martin Deegan, assistant priest Father Noel Carrigg, a Camillan Father, and all those who minister in the parish. The provision of Catholic schooling goes back over 160 years. Some 190 pupils are in the present First School under the headship of Sister Philip who continues the Mercy presence here started in 1858. Sister Joan, a Marist sister, is head of the Middle School; she is one of three from the order who came to work in the parish in 1985.

At the rear of the church is a large notice board with the title 'Called to Ministry' and it shows the many talents of the parishioners and how they each contribute to the development of the parish community.

There is much talk to-day of collaborative ministry and empowerment and it can be clearly seen here. Mr Alan Hodgson, chairman of the Pastoral Area Council, is initiating, with the help of a working party, a further extension of lay ministries.

Listed among the many groups are: the Parish Pastoral Council of 20 members representing the main organisations; the long serving S.V.P. and C.W.L.; the Focolare group encouraging support for families; a branch of the Society for the Protection of the Unborn Child; two P.T.A.s - one in each school - developing parent, pupil and teacher relations; a Scripture group led by Sister Joan and, of course, R.C.I.A. which runs from October to July.

We cannot fail to mention the large number of Lay Ministers of the Eucharist who assist Father Deegan and distribute communion to the sick and housebound; nor the Churches Together ecumenical work; nor the work for youth done by Mr John Nixon under the umbrella of the school. These are only some of the many activities done by the parishioners.

Three religious orders serve and are resident in the parish. The longest serving are the Sisters of Mercy, who live now in a small convent in Elvaston Terrace ministering in the parish, schools, and hospital. Their first convent was behind the church and is now the refurbished presbytery. Their second convent fronts the main street but has, in the last few years, been converted and extended to become the Carntyne Residential Home for the elderly supervised by Sister Elizabeth. More recently, the Marist Sisters have served the parish community for the last nine years.

The Order of St. Camillus, a nursing order of priests and brothers, arrived in Hexham in 1949. Their first hospital for the recuperation of patients was Swinburne Castle. They later moved to Oakwood where to-day - adapting to N.H.S. changes - they function as a care hospital for the rehabilitation of the long-term mentally ill.

Father Noel Carrigg, the superior, and three other Camillan brothers continue here the work of their founder. Father Carrigg, also, assists Father Deegan in visiting the sick and housebound and Hexham General Hospital.

In bringing this short account of St. Mary's Parish, Hexham, to a conclusion no words are more fitting than those of Father Bede Bailey, O.P. in the foreword to the parish history.

'What a story of loyalty Father Nicholson has to tell. What a constant succession of priests came from Hexhamshire families during difficult times. What pride today's parishioners of St. Mary's must have in the Armstrongs, Gibsons, the Leadbitters, the Kirsopps and others. There are few parishes in the country that can boast such a history. We thank God.'

POSTSCRIPT   *(Fr. M. Deegan, 1998)*

Following St. Mary's First School extension and the creation of a small play area of half an acre field - there remained a 200 year-old building. It was owned by the Diocese for many years and served as a dwelling house - upstairs and downstairs - for two families. In the late 1950s it became rented accommodation and was used as a Catholic Club.

With the recent school development, the club had to be closed as it became marooned in the school grounds. The Diocese sold it to the parish. We are presently developing this building to provide Nursery/Early Years Provision on the ground floor and, with separate access, the first floor will serve parish needs in a variety of ways. The parish with its own resources and no aid from the L.E.A. is doing this task and it should be ready for September, 1998.

Alnwick, St. Paul (Anglican church by Anthony Salvin, 1846, taken over in 1982)   Photo: E. Croghan

Amble, The Sacred Heart & St. Cuthbert   Photo: T. McQuillen

Bellingham, St. Oswald

Photo: E. Croghan

Birtley, St. Joseph   *Photo: J. Aiken*

Blyth, Our Lady and St. Wilfrid   *Photo: E. Croghan*

Bishop Auckland, St. Wilfrid *Photo: E. Croghan*

Blackhill, Our Blessed Lady Immaculate   Photo: E. Croghan

Brooms, Our Blessed Lady & St. Joseph Photo: E. Croghan

Byermoor, The Sacred Heart Photo: E. Croghan

Crawcrook, St. Agnes   *Photo: E. Croghan*

Darlington Carmel

Darlington, St. Augustine: residence of Bishop W. Hogarth

Easington Colliery, Our Lady   Photo: E. Croghan

Esh Laude, St. Michael   Photo: E. Croghan

Gateshead, Corpus Christi

Photo: J. Aiken

Gateshead, St. Joseph   *Photo: E. Croghan*

Gosforth, St. Charles — Photo: E. Croghan

Hexham, St. Mary — Photo: E. Croghan

Hebburn, St. Aloysius. Consecration of the altar by Bishop A. Griffiths, OSB, 28th October 1999 *Photo: G. Tufnell*

Highfield, St. Joseph — Watercolour by D. Rowley

Langley Moor, St. Patrick — Photo: E. Croghan

Jarrow, St. Bede, statue of the patron saint   *Photo: J. Aiken*

Minsteracres, St. Elizabeth of Hungary   Photo: E. Croghan

Morpeth, St. Robert of Newminster   Photo: E. Croghan

Murton, St. Joseph — Photo: E. Croghan

Newcastle, St. Andrew — Photo: P. Tucker

Newcastle, East Denton Hall, Bishop's House — Photo: J. Aiken

Newcastle, remains of the shrine of Our Lady of Jesmond — Photo: J. Aiken

North Gosforth, Sacred Heart. Sanctuary window designed by Sir Edward Burne-Jones   *Photo: E. Croghan*

North Shields, St. Cuthbert — Photo: E. Croghan

South Shields, St. Bede — Photo: J. Aiken

Sedgefield, St. John Fisher

Photo: E. Croghan

Stella, Sts. Mary and Thomas Aquinas; Presbytery Photo: J. Aiken

Sunderland, St. Anthony's Convent of Mercy (Memorial Cross)

Photo: J. Aiken

Sunderland, St. Benet

Photo: J. Aiken

Sunderland, St. Cecilia Photo: E. Croghan

Tudhoe, St. Charles   Photo: E. Croghan

Tynemouth, Our Lady & St. Oswin

Photo: E. Croghan

Ushaw College in 1828 (by Ramsay)

Whittingham, St. Mary Immaculate (Rev. Fr. David Tanner holding a chalice dating to recusant times.)   Photo: E. Croghan

Wooler, St. Ninian (statue of Saint Aidan on Holy Island)

Wooler, St. Ninian (statue of Saint Cuthbert on Holy Island)

30. HIGHFIELD   St Joseph   *(March, April 1998)*

The parish of St. Joseph's, Highfield, (Rowlands Gill), is situated a few miles south-west of Gateshead off the A694, Consett Road. It is a 20th century parish and does not appear to have in its immediate locality any detailed reference to early Christian roots.

Brief references inform us that when Bishop Hugh Pudsey was Bishop of Durham (1153-95) he exchanged some land in the Chopwell area with the Cistercian monks of Newminster Abbey, Morpeth, for land in Wolsingham; near Lintzford can be seen the ruins of the 14th century Friarside chapel, possibly a hermitage; and it is believed that a chapel dedicated to St. Anne at Winlaton was destroyed during the Northern Rising of 1569.

It is possible that Blessed Ralph Corby, the Jesuit martyr, may have ministered to the few Catholics in the scattered hamlets around here before his arrest in 1644 at Hamsterley Hall near Lintz Green, the home of the Catholic Swinburnes.

When local drift mines were exploited round about 1750 the population of the area began its slow growth. As the demand for coal and iron increased in the early 19th century deeper pits were sunk, and waggonways were built to carry the coal to the staithes on the Tyne; this was to lead to more people seeking employment in the area amongst whom would have been a number of Catholics. Provision to practise their Faith could be found at Stella, Byermoor, Crawcrook and Blaydon.

Before the appointment of a permanent priest at Highfield, Mass was said - maybe for the first time in 1912 - by a visiting priest in a room above a grocery shop in Ramsay Street, High Spen. In the Diocesan Finance Committee Minutes of March, 1913, it is recorded that Canon Wilson had submitted a plan for a church at Spen costing £1300 of which £700 was already in hand; in January, 1914, the Minutes state that no building work had commenced. The *Northern Catholic Calendar* of 1930 records that a church was built in 1914 at Highfield and St. Joseph's was created a new parish in 1929.

The brief parish history relates that the first parish priest was Father Thomas McManemy, a Durham man trained at Ushaw and ordained in 1912. With the assistance of willing parishioners he established the parish on a firm basis. The land obtained was on a sloping site and with the people's voluntary efforts it was made suitable for building. Miners of the parish agreed to a voluntary deduction of their wages to help finance the development; generous families made donations for some of the church furnishings.

With the expectation that the parish population would continue to rise, the commodious presbytery was built in the years 1928 and 1929 with accommodation for a housekeeper and hopefully two curates. The depression of the Thirties put paid to such expectations and a contraction rather than an expansion occurred, especially in the local Alloy Works.

However, there was still a need for a school which was blessed and dedicated by Bishop Joseph Thorman in December, 1932, and opened the following January, the first headmistress being Miss Carroll. She was succeeded by Sister Mary of the Sacred Heart assisted by Sister Mary of the Cross - both from the Ebchester Convent - and Miss Winifred Connolly, a parishioner. Those were the days of the all-age schools where children, unless they proceeded to a Grammar school, received their entire education.

Today, the same school, modernised and refurbished, provides a Christian education at primary level for 117 children in the care of Miss Teresa March and her dedicated staff; for their secondary education the children proceed to St. Thomas More's, Blaydon, whose first head was Mr Bill March, father of Teresa.

When Father McManemy left the parish in 1938 the parish had supply priests from St. Mary's Cathedral until the appointment of Father Hugh O'Connor, a larger-than-life character, in 1939. He reputedly arrived with housekeeper, dog and goat (to provide milk for his tea). He was assiduous in visiting the school to check on Mass attendance and the children's knowledge of their Faith. With his blackthorn walking stick, and accompanied by his black and white collie dog, he was a familiar and welcome sight as he made his visitation of the parish. Father O'Connor remained at Highfield during most of the war years experiencing a new influx of parishioners from the camp at High Spen of American soldiers and German and Italian P.O.Ws. Noted for their singing at the Sunday Masses some of the P.O.Ws, as a token of their thanks to the parish, presented a carved wooden canopy to surround the statue of the Holy Infant of Prague to which Father O'Connor had great devotion.

On moving to St. Cecilia's parish, Sunderland in 1944, where he built the modern church on Ryhope Road, he continued to encourage this devotion amongst the children as the writer well remembers. At St. Cecilia's the statue was placed in the sanctuary and adorned in various coloured capes according to the liturgical feast. To further this devotion he started the Little Army of the Little King to inspire the children's love of the Infant Jesus. Members were enrolled and encouraged to attend Mass, receive communion regularly and to pray for the lapsed and conversions. Enrolment forms were signed and lapel badges issued to publicise their devotion and commitment.

Father Crawford, who followed Father O'Connor was the first parish priest of Highfield to own a car; his popularity, it is recorded, was increased amongst the altar boys when he took them on trips to the seaside. Popular too in the community - with non-Catholics as well - was his successor, Father Edward Hodgson, who took over in 1951 and who had a 'cheerful word for anyone he met'. He appears to have been a Do-It-Yourself enthusiast ready to turn his hand to anything, thus saving the parish money on maintenance.

When Father Malachy Mulligan (now retired to Ireland) came in 1956 he had to deal with an uncertain situation. Houses were demolished at Lintzford and Victoria Garesfield; Thornley was affected too and High Spen designated as a Category 'D' village which allowed demolition but no new building. The population balance was somewhat restored when houses were built in Highfield and Rowlands Gill. Talk of a new town in the area would have meant a larger church or an additional church but such plans came to nothing.

Still remembered with affection is Father Hugh Lavery, a scholar noted for his writings, lectures and T.V. epilogues. These gifts were used in his pastoral work whose 'sermons were small gems of learning, logic and the love of God'. He was practical, too, overseeing the improving of the presbytery and church's central heating system and rewiring; and more, importantly, implementing the liturgical changes emanating from Vatican II.

Other priests who served St. Joseph's were Canon Landreth (1972-80) who celebrated his priestly golden jubilee here; and Father Michael McFadden who had a short dedicated ministry here and 'made an impression that was not to disappear from the minds of many'.

During the 1980s Father James Keane, who had been a curate at Highfield returned as parish priest. He had to deal with the social and financial effects of the reorganisation of Catholic secondary education; he, also, saw to the refurbishing of the parish school including a total re-roofing. When he celebrated his silver jubilee in 1989 he decided to use part of the gift he received to enhance the church precincts with paths, walls and flower-beds.

Father William Jacks, the present parish priest, was educated at Ampleforth and the College of Law in Guildford where he graduated in law before he entered Ushaw College to study for the priesthood. He was one of two priests who welcomed Bishop Ambrose on Newcastle Railway Station when he paid his first visit to the diocese as Bishop-elect - very appropriate as Father Jacks had been a former pupil of Father Ambrose when he taught at Ampleforth.

Many people who have attended St. Mary's Cathedral will have seen Father Jacks directing the music for special diocesan occasions. He is, also, chairman of the Diocesan Music Association which seeks to encourage and develop musical talent in worship. Extra - parochial duties include being secretary of the Northern Brethren's Fund and Catholic adviser to Channel 3, North East.

Within the existing parish boundaries of St. Joseph's are the communities at High Spen, Barlow, Hamsterley Mill, Lockhaugh, Rowlands Gill and Lintzford. Although a scattered congregation of about 778 souls, Father Jacks and committed parishioners attempt to bring vitality and dedication to the spiritual and social life of the area. Twenty five lay ministers of the Eucharist enable the sick and housebound to receive Communion regularly; some lay ministers are commissioned to hold Eucharistic Services when no priest is available.

The youth of the parish are encouraged to participate fully in the church's mission; they form the core of a Folk Group who sing each Sunday at the 10.30 Mass; they join with older members to form a choir for special occasions at Christmas and Easter; and 18 altar servers are a further visible sign of the commitment of the young.

On November 2nd, 1997, the young people of St. Joseph's organised a Youth Service with a 12-hour Exposition of the Blessed Sacrament which was attended by 60 young people; a covenant was signed committing the parish to greater involvement in helping the poor.

A finance committee and a social committee assist Father Jacks in the everyday running of the parish. The local village hall was the venue late last year for a successful ceilidh; the Summer Fayre held in the parish grounds realised a profit of £2,500; and a Race Night, a Christmas Flower Arranging Demonstration, coffee mornings, and the Ladies' Club provided opportunities for parishioners to enjoy themselves and to get to know each other better.

Ecumenical co-operation is strong in Highfield and the links with other denominations is doing much good. Combined services of prayer and hymn singing are held annually on the first Sunday in Lent and the first Sunday in October. A Churches Together Group holds meetings once every two months; and regular clergy fraternals, an ecumenical breakfast on the first Saturday of each month in the Methodist Hall are ways of bringing Christians together in the love and service of Christ and neighbour.

The Diocese and many parishes have already begun to think of ways in which the Millennium may be fittingly celebrated. St. Joseph's has its Millennium Committee already meeting and planning for this great event. At a local level they are working, with other Christians, on a project to improve care in the community under the title of 'Live at Home Scheme'; and it is hoped that a link will be established with a Third World community that will encourage the parish to fulfil its covenant to our poor brothers and sisters overseas.

It was feared not so long ago that the church may have deteriorated so much that it was beyond repair. Fortunately this was not the case and a new roof has saved the interior from the depredations of the weather allowing re-decoration to the sanctuary, facilities for open confession and re-siting of the organ near to the altar designed and constructed by Robin Clucas.

But as T.M. Conway states in the short history of the parish: 'A renovated building is only really appropriate to a re-vitalised parish' and this is what Father Jacks and his parishioners are attempting as we move towards the Third Millennium.

31. HOUGHTON - LE - SPRING   St Michael   *(June, 1983)*

The Catholic church of St Michael's stands today in a quiet backwater beside the old Sunderland to Durham road enjoying the peace and solitude it must have had when it was first opened almost 150 years ago. The church, built like so many of those days, in the Gothic style, was designed by that ubiquitous architect, Ignatius Bonomi, and opened by the Vicar-Apostolic of the Northern District, Bishop John Briggs on November 7th, 1837 - just seven years after the arrival of the first parish priest, Fr. James Augustine McEvoy. Like so many other priests sent to establish a new parish he had to find temporary accommodation for the celebration of Mass; this he was able to do in an upstairs room in Sunderland Street.

Fund raising, ever a necessity in order to build a church, was partly provided from the pockets of the local Catholics who were increasing in number, particularly from Ireland, as the new coal mines in the area were being sunk. Another source was to appeal to the general Catholic community in 1833 by means of the *Directory of Catholic Clergy and Chapels in England*: 'The Catholics of this large and populous village, and its neighbourhood, being totally destitute of religious instruction, an apartment has been taken and a temporary altar erected ... The obstacles, it is true, are many and serious, for this little flock being composed exclusively of the poor, it is with difficulty they meet the rent, and other incidental expenses ... The great

Houghton-le-Spring, St. Michael   *Photo: T. Mackin*

object of his ambition is to erect a temple for the worship of the living God on a site which still bears the impress of former respectability. The fine old Cruciform Church, which is still the chief ornament of the village, attests at once the Faith, the zeal, and religious magnificence of our Catholic ancestors'.

Outwardly the church has changed little in its appearance since it was built. It was originally a dual-purpose building; the ground floor being used as a school with accommodation for a master, and the upper floor being used as the chapel. For 70 years the building served as church and school until the upper floor became unsafe and had to be removed; the main nave windows were altered and are now much longer. The only apparent exterior addition is the modern porch which blends admirably with the rest of the church; it was designed by professional architects from an idea of a parishioner, Mr Tommy Docherty, and as Mr Don Lincoln says in his parish history: 'I am sure Mr Bonomi would have approved'. Mentioned earlier was the Cruciform Church which is, of course, the much older church of St. Michael's and All Angels still used today by the Anglicans.

Built originally in Norman times, much of the present building is of the 13th century with early 14th century windows in the Decorated style - apparently a rarity in Durham County. A local historian, C.A. Smith, regarded as not improbable the possibility that a Christian church of Saxon days may have existed here. Two legends, unverifiable, claim that St. Bede named a local spring 'Holywell' after visiting the area around Newbottle where he found the water so refreshing; and during the travels of St. Cuthbert's body around northern England it is reputed to have rested near Houghton, at Warden Law, and could not be moved for three days until, after seeking guidance and prayer, the monks were inspired to move in the direction of Durham. Historical evidence is available, however, telling us that during the 15th century there was a chapel of the Blessed Mary at West Herrington and that the Reverend Henry Gillow, Rector of

Houghton from 1470-1483, left funds for the building of a small church.

Houghton Feast which is celebrated on October 10th is another reminder of the ancient roots of Catholicity in the area. Fr. Dunne in his centenary history surmises that it may have originated in pre-Reformation days to celebrate the patronal feast of St. Michael which is on September 29th; the disparity in dates being due to the introduction of the Gregorian Calendar in England in 1752 when there was an omission of eleven days.

One could not write an article about Houghton without mentioning the English martyr, George Swallowell. Although his birthplace is uncertain, we do know his family owned land at Haswell and that he was brought up as a Protestant eventually receiving deacon's orders. He became Parish Clerk at Houghton and taught at the local Kepier School. Whilst on a visit to Durham Gaol he came into conversation with an imprisoned Catholic gentleman who convinced him of the rightness of the Catholic claim and was soon after converted; another source claims that the execution of four priests at Durham in 1590 which was instrumental in the conversion of Robert and Grace Maire of Hardwick Hall - mentioned in a previous article - was also an influential factor.

Filled with fervour, he was bold enough to recant publicly in the church at Houghton admitting the error of his beliefs. Arrested he was tried at Durham in 1593, but reprieved and returned to jail. The following year he was again brought to trial along with Fathers John Boste and John Ingram. St. John Boste and Blessed John Ingram bravely accepted the sentence of death, but Swallowell took fright and promised to reform. Father Boste turned to him and said, 'George Swallowell! What have you done?' Immediate repentance followed and plucking up courage he withdrew his statement at which the judge warned him of the consequences. Boldly he stated his profession of Faith and kneeling down in the court he received absolution from Father Boste who encouraged him with the words: 'Now keep to that, and I go shortly to offer up my soul for you.' Fathers Boste and Ingram were martyred at Durham and Gateshead respectively. Blessed George was taken on foot to Darlington where at the place of execution he asked the crowd to join with him in the recitation of the Our Father, the Hail Mary and the Creed, after which he was cruelly put to death.

A commemorative plaque inside the church porch lists the priests who have served the parish over the last century and a half. Three priests only can be mentioned here: Fr. Joseph Aloysius Browne (later Canon) served as parish priest from 1857 until 1889 and was responsible for the building of the Senior School in 1880; his ministry also took him regularly on horseback, crossing the Wear at Lambton, to say Mass at Washington. He was responsible for the building of the school and Mass centre there and it is also of interest to note that the first parish priest of Washington was a Frenchman, a Father Francis Cambours, who had served as a curate at Houghton prior to his move across the Wear. The longest serving parish priest in Houghton was Father Francis Tuohey who served here from 1931 to 1972. How different today, thankfully, are the relationships existing among the various denominations which have been developed and strengthened through ecumenical dialogue. Joint services are held during the Unity Octave Week and at the most recent one Fr. William O'Gorman, parish priest of St. Michael's was able to give a talk in the Anglican church hall on 'Celibacy and the Catholic Priesthood'. Fr. O'Gorman has also preached, on ecumenical occasions, in the Anglican Church and the Methodist Chapel.

In addition to the longstanding C.W.L. and S.V.P. which has two conferences in the parish, one of men and one of women, many other activities are in progress to deepen the parishioners' spiritual life. Ten Parish Renewal weekends have taken place over the last two years; for the uninitiated these are intensive spiritual formation sessions, held in the church beginning on a Friday evening (7.30 - 10.30 p.m.) and continuing on Saturday (9.30 a.m. - 9.30 p.m.) and Sunday (2 p.m. - 9.30 p.m.). Usually attended by 15 to 30 parishioners at a time, and under the direction of the parish priest, they explore together the meaning of being a Catholic today with great emphasis on prayer, scripture, and the sacraments.

A prayer group meets weekly on a Thursday evening and a further development in the prayer life of the parish is the daily recitation of the Morning and Evening Prayer of the Church; some parishioners are now meeting in small groups in their own homes to say the Divine Office; and to encourage the devotion to the Rosary a small band of people visit daily a different home in the parish.

Parental involvement in the religious education of children is nurtured by means of the Brusselmann's Course which enables mothers and fathers to participate more fully in preparing their children for the reception of the sacraments and in developing their spiritual commitment to their Faith.

With a parish population of over two and half thousand, the commissioning of 19 Lay Ministers of Communion has not only been a great help in the distribution of Communion at Sunday Masses, but also has made it possible for the sick and housebound to receive Communion every Sunday and more often if the individual wishes it.

Rich Man-Poor Man's Suppers and Famine Lunches have been held in the parish to bring home the problems and needs of the Third World. St. Michael's remedy is to encourage as many people as possible to join in the weekly Family Fast; the money saved is brought weekly to the church and such has been the response that it was possible recently to send £1,000 to Fr. Pat McKenna, a diocesan priest, working in Lima, Peru; last year £2,000 was sent to the Apurimac Valley Help Project in Peru which attempts to provide self-help for subsistence farmers in the area. Outpatient clinics, better farming methods, care of orphans, consumer co-operatives, a river transport system are examples of what is and will be provided in the future; and an S.V.P. Twinnage scheme brings material help to Indian families.

Some words of Fr. O'Gorman written in the foreword to the parish history summarize what this article has attempted to describe: 'But Christians are not limited to what is reasonable - their vision is broader, their insight deeper and their spirit is more daring. The Catholics of the past proved this by their deeds. We would be letting them down if we did not follow their example, relying just not on human effort but on the power and inspiration of the Holy Spirit in God's Church today.'

32. HUTTON HOUSE   Saints Peter and Paul   *(February, 1983)*

In a rural setting surrounded by fields yet only a short distance from the busy A.19 stands the red-brick church of Saints Peter and Paul adjacent to the presbytery - known locally as Hutton House. To reach it one needs to leave the dual carriageway at the signpost marked 'Hutton Henry', proceed along the road for approximately 100 yards and turn right into the long drive that leads up to the church. The enquiring visitor may ask himself the question why it stands outside the village; or familiar with its parochial boundaries, which encompass a wide area - including Hutton Henry, Wingate, Station Town, and Castle Eden - why it is not sited in one of the three last mentioned?

To attempt to answer this question it is necessary to know something of the history of the parish which has already celebrated its 150th anniversary. The Durham coastline is not lacking in its churches which can be dated from Norman times but the upheaval of the Reformation took these churches out of Catholic hands and in order to preserve the Faith the Church went underground. Not far from Hutton Henry stands Hardwick Hall which was purchased by the Maire Family in 1587. During this late Tudor period the persecution of Catholics continued unabated with heavy fines, imprisonment and even death for some who persisted in their recusancy. The Maire family home became a missionary centre in those troubled times and continued for over 200 years to be so, through the example of four missionary priests who were martyred in Durham in 1590.

This was a particularly difficult time for those who wished to spread the Faith and when Fathers John Holiday, John Hogg, Edmund Duke and Richard Hill landed on Tyneside in March they were captured almost immediately and executed at Durham on May 27th, 1590. Their heroism and constancy at the place of execution did not go unnoticed for in the crowd was a recently married Protestant couple, Robert and Grace Maire, who were so impressed by the martyrs' example they became Catholics in spite of the risks involved.

Robert's wife, Grace, was virtually disinherited by her Puritan father, who in his will agreed to her being paid £100 every Sunday she attended the State church until the amount bequeathed was paid. This she resolutely refused to do and thereby forfeited about £2,500 - a considerable sum in those days.

Hutton House (Hutton Henry), Sts. Peter and Paul   Photo: T. Mackin

    Because of the necessity for secrecy in their work sparse information is available of these heroes - both priest and lay - who were prepared to give all in the practice of their beliefs. One such priest, however, does occasionally appear in written sources from this dim, distant past and must have visited Hardwick Hall. His name was Fr. Richard Holtby, a Jesuit, who used Thornley Hall belonging to the Trollope family as one of his missionary centres. The strong Catholic connection between the two recusant families was further strengthened when Thomas Maire, the son of Robert, married a cousin of the Trollopes.

    Fr. Holtby was an ingenious builder of hiding holes - designed to hide priests when pursuivants might raid a suspected house at any time - and one example of his work can still be seen at Hardwick Hall today, concealed in the attic against the chimney breast. It is possible that priests were landed near Castle Eden Dene where tradition claims there was once an underground passage leading from the Dene to Hardwick Hall; also, it is said that in some part of the Dene was a Rock Chapel with a simple altar and the remains of a carved crucifix where Mass could be said.

    The last Jesuit chaplain at Hardwick was Fr. Christopher Rose who remained there 55 years dying at the Jesuit house in Durham in 1826. Four years before his death the Reverend Thomas Augustine Slater came from Ushaw College to help the old priest with his pastoral duties. In 1825, the Maire Family sold their house to a non-Catholic family but before leaving, and in the fine tradition of their ancestors, they purchased land at Hutton House and their young chaplain, Fr. Slater, became the first parish priest residing in the house which is still used today as the presbytery. An extract, in his own words, recorded in the parish history states briefly: 'I, Thomas Augustine Slater, went on the Mission on 10th day of January, 1822, to Hardwick Hall, near Castle Eden, Durham. In 1824, built the Chapel and Residence at Hutton House and removed to it the 5th day of April, 1825.'

    The church at Hutton House was one of the few Catholic places of worship in East Durham during those early days of Fr Slater (later Canon) who laboured manfully for over 50 years in south-east Durham, providing where possible the services of the church to increasing number of Catholics, including Hartlepool, which he looked after until the appointment of the first parish priest there in 1834.

    Standing on the site of the original church is the present red-bricked one opened in 1895 and consecrated by Bishop Collins in 1911. A pleasant interior is enhanced by the colourful semi-circular sanctuary around the walls of which are five wall paintings of Saints Peter and Paul, St Anne and Our Lady as a child, The Sacred Heart, and St Joseph with the child Jesus. The seating capacity is 240 and every Sunday and holyday transport by bus is provided free to bring the scattered parishioners to Mass.

In spite of the travelling problems common to a country area, Saints Peter and Paul's parish still manages to maintain a variety of activities. The Catholic Club based at Wingate provides a Social Centre three miles away; the S.V.P. (including a junior section of 15-20 boys and girls) and the Women's Guild along with other involved parishioners, continue their works of charity by regularly donating money and gifts of clothing to such diverse groups as the Little Sisters at Sunderland, St. Mungo's Community in London, the Durham Cyrenians, and the Pro-Life Group in Newcastle.

Originally there were two Catholic Schools in the parish: one at Castle Eden and the other at Chapel Chare in Wingate, opened in 1881, where the youth of the parish were nurtured in their Faith. This good work continues today in St. Mary's Primary School at Wingate and for older children at St. Bede's Comprehensive School in Peterlee.

There are many memories in a parish's past on which the priests and people may look back with satisfaction. Two in particular are a cause of pride and joy to the present parish priest, Fr. Edward Vincent Marron, who has now served the parish for over 20 years. The first is a memento of the past which has become a parish treasure: it is a pre-Reformation embroidered cross sewn onto a modern chasuble - a possible link with Hardwick Hall and the priests who served the area so courageously over the years. The second, remembered with affection by Fr. Marron, was the celebration held in July, 1982 which marked his 40 years in the priesthood. The highlight was the Mass at which 18 fellow-priests concelebrated. A festival atmosphere prevailed for three days in the field in front of Hutton House where two large marquees were erected in and around which the children and adults participated in various social events.

Although unable to carry out their missionary work, the four priests martyred at Durham in 1590 had by their example converted the Maire Family who were to use their position and influence in maintaining the Faith in various parts of County Durham; and the parish of Hutton Henry, in these more tolerant ecumenical days, stands as a fitting memorial to their fidelity and perseverance.

POSTSCRIPT *(Fr. S. Doyle, 1998)*

Celebrations marking Fr. Marron's Golden Jubilee in the Priesthood took place in July, 1992. Again, two marquees were erected and the parish community celebrated in its usual style, with a special mass, a huge cake and singing/dancing; the festival lasted 3 days.

In the early part of 1993, Father Marron announced his forthcoming retirement, on reaching his 75th birthday. This took effect in September and the parish gave him a great send-off. At the Wingate Community Centre, a shared meal was arranged. Members of the Anglican Community, Methodist and Salvation Army representatives and Trimdon Ladies presented him with gifts. The parish presented him with a cheque as well as other personal gifts.

The parish was then served for a time by Monsignor Kevin Nichols and Fr. Kevin Daley. Due to pressures of work in the field of education, at St. Vincent's Centre in Newcastle, Monsignor Nichols moved to a parish closer to this work.

St Peter and Paul's, Hutton House, is now served from Peterlee, by Fr. S. Doyle and Fr. G. Dodds. The parish house is looked after by a family in the parish as there is no longer a resident priest.

33. JARROW   St. Bede   *(January, February 1992)*

For a Christian the words Bede and Jarrow are synonymous; one cannot think of one without the other. Bede and Jarrow - saint and monastery - have their place in history not only here but in other parts of the world too and deservedly so.

It was only ten years after the opening of the monastery at Monkwearmouth that Benedict Biscop, the founder, was able to have a sister-monastery, St. Paul's, erected in what was then a quiet rural location where the small river Don entered the Tyne. About the same time as the dedication of the monastery a young boy of seven, named Bede and of obscure origin entered therein.

Here early Christianity flowered more than 1300 years ago; here the Venerable Bede spent his life in prayer, study and teaching - enjoying the simple life of the saintly scholar. Here he wrote his many books the most well-known being, *The Ecclesiastical History of the English Nation,* from which we learn about the early history of our country since Roman times. Dom. David Knowles writing of him says: 'Bede was loved and revered by those who knew him; he loved the men he wrote of - he wrote of them, that is, as men who were the children of God - and it is impossible for a reader not to feel behind his words the lover of truth and justice, the humane God-fearing monk who could sing on his deathbed the antiphon of the Ascension, 'O Rex Gloriae' and rejoice that he was about to see that King in his beauty.'

Few would dispute his eminence as the outstanding figure of that 'Golden Age', yet his unknown family background and reputed birthplace at Monkton are in sharp contrast to his later fame.

One can still visit the site and buildings where he spent his life from the age of seven. Much has been altered over the centuries but in the present chancel (formerly the nave) one can touch the stonework that was seen and touched by Bede those many years ago. Bede was buried originally in a porch on the north side of the church until the early 11th century when his remains were removed to Durham Cathedral where they now rest.

This idyllic rural setting was, however, to be shattered when the East coast became a victim to the depredations of the heathen Northmen. Lindisfarne was despoiled in 793 A.D. followed a year later by the Jarrow Monastery. Although monastic life may have continued after this, some attempt at a revival was made when a monk Aldwine settled there with others in 1074. In 1083 the Bishop of Durham, William de Carileph, reduced it to a cell of the Benedictine monastery at Durham. Thus it remained, inhabited by a few monks until its dissolution in 1537 when Henry VIII attempted to destroy monasticism in England.

With the onset of persecution in Tudor times there is limited evidence available regarding the practice of the ancient Faith in these parts. In spite of the dangers and risks involved loyal adherents continued to practise their Faith. The Hodgson family at Hebburn Hall were recusants and, no doubt, continued to offer the consolations of the Mass and the sacraments to this scattered flock. To the east Ursula Taylor of South Shields allowed her home to be used as a staging post for the clandestine shipping of priests and students to and from the Catholic colleges on the continent. A well-known recusant is listed at Jarrow in the early 17th century; he was John Darell who organised a Catholic centre here. So for those who were brave enough to cling to their beliefs there were opportunities to continue their practice. As the Church emerged from its enforced containment towards the end of the 18th century we have evidence from the Papist Returns of 1767 of 40 faithful Catholics in Jarrow and Hedworth chapelry and 29 in the South Shields area.

After the passing of the Relief Acts allowing Catholicism a public expression once again, Father James Worswick of St. Andrew's, Newcastle, filled with missionary zeal played an important part in revitalising the Faith along the banks of the Tyne. He journeyed on horseback once every three weeks to say Mass in North Shields until 1821 when the church of St. Cuthbert's was built there. Before this foundation, Jarrow Catholics like others on both sides of the river journeyed, often on foot, to St. Andrew's for Mass. They would then adjourn to a kindly widow's house in Gateshead for tea then back to the church for Vespers after which the journey home was started. Almost the whole of that day was spent attending to their religious duties.

With the opening of St. Cuthbert's across the river Catholics in this north east corner of County Durham were able to cross the Tyne by ferryboat. 'The fare for a single person was 2d and for more than one, one and a halfpence each. It was found too expensive for those with families to cross twice every Sunday and in order to remedy this, the Catholics of South Shields formed a committee of management. They hired a boat rowed by two men, the fare being a penny a week.' We know the names of four Catholics living in Jarrow at this time: a Mrs Russell (an Irish widow), a Mrs Rankin and a Mr & Mrs Curry. The lot of Jarrow Catholics was made easier when after 1849 they were able to travel to St. Bede's in South Shields.

Even more than a 1000 years after Bede's time the saint would have recognised the almost unchanged aspect of Jarrow and its surroundings; it still retained that somewhat, rural appearance of his day. But like so many other places it was to change dramatically in the 19th century with the onset of industrialisation. Industry needs workers and they came flocking in their thousands to areas where new employment was offered. Amongst them was a goodly proportion of Irish people and their spiritual needs were met when Father Edmund Kelly came in 1856 from South Shields to say Mass in a house (believed to be 175, High Street). A Mr Duggan relates in the parish history that his mother and grandmother heard Mass and received Holy Communion there and when the priest left and the house was occupied by his family his mother frequently remarked: 'You are very lucky to be sleeping in the room where Holy Mass was said'.

Father Kelly and his parishioners were obviously keen to have a church to be proud of and this hope became a reality when Bishop Hogarth laid the foundation stone on October 30th, 1860. The procession to the site was led by the South Shields Catholic Band and included priests from various parts of the Diocese. 'The Bishop vested in cope and mitre proceeded with the ceremony of laying the stone,' records the parish history and, 'he deposited in a cavity, a bottle containing a parchment, setting forth: on 30th October the Right Reverend Father in God, William, Lord Bishop of Hexham, laid and blessed the foundation stone of the Church of Jarrow-upon-Tyne, built in honour of the Most High and Blessed God, and under the invocation of St. Bede, Confessor.'

Much of the ensuing labour needed to complete the church was of a voluntary nature often done in the evenings and on Saturdays by enthusiastic parishioners under the supervision of Mr Thomas Lumsden and Mr McGlinshey who were both skilled craftsmen.

Before the church's completion Father George Meynell - a member of an old Yorkshire Catholic family from Crathorne who had preserved the Faith throughout the penal days - came to assist Father Kelly and he was not averse to lending a hand in the building process. There must have been great joy when after much labour the church, in the Gothic style, was officially opened on Sunday, December 27th, 1861. Father Kelly said the High Mass assisted by the deacon, Mgr. Eyre (later Archbishop of Glasgow). Amongst the congregation were a number of Protestants.

After the opening it appears Father Kelly, the founder of the mission, confined his activities to South Shields until his death in 1871. Father Meynell became the first parish priest of St. Bede's, Jarrow; his immediate task was the erection of a presbytery and the furnishing of the new church. The presbytery 'was commenced with as little delay as possible and in the manual labour Father Meynell took a man's share. He became a labourer in the full meaning of the word. He dug the foundations and took part in the excavations which provided the cellars beneath the presbytery and later the school. The parishioners continued to work on the buildings in the evenings, but Father Meynell occupied, as well, his spare time during the day furthering the work. On those occasions, school children assisted him by carrying bricks. It is said that he preferred girls as helpers because "boys were too rough".'

The increasing demand for workers in shipbuilding, chemicals and the ironworks brought more Irish people to the area, so much so that St. Bede's became an Irish parish and was referred to as 'Little Ireland.' Conscious of their obligations to their parents they brought increasing business to the local Post Office as they despatched some of their earnings home.

Financial provision in the large expanding urban parishes was always a problem when the majority of the congregation probably had little to give anyway; it has often been said that our churches were built through the generosity and the 'pennies of the poor.' Father Meynell was not the only parish priest who was prepared to stand outside the workgates on pay day and receive donations. On a later occasion he revealed that he knew who to ask, as the Catholic workmen showed him an individual mark of respect as they passed. This source of income was simplified when one of the largest employers, Palmers, arranged for those workers who wished to do so, to have the 'nimble sixpence' deducted weekly from their pay. Occasionally workers were asked for a 'day's pay'.

By the last quarter of the 19th century the congregation had expanded to 6,000 necessitating extensions to the existing structure. The outcome was the building of the 'new end' with the sanctuary re-sited where the original entrance had been. The first sanctuary stood where the present narthex is. The blessing and opening were performed by the Bishop of Galloway (the Rt. Rev. John McLachlan) in March, 1883.

Much was happening in the parish in those days to encourage greater participation of the people in the spiritual and social activities provided. Some parishes had their own brass band and St. Bede's was no exception. It provided the music for church services and developed a regular custom of playing *Adeste Fideles* in the nearby streets of Jarrow on Christmas morning at 4 a.m to arouse the 5 a.m. massgoers! A Confraternity of the Holy Family was established to deepen the Faith of its members. St. Bede's can boast one of the earliest S.V.P. conferences in the Diocese having been formed in 1862. In its report of 1869 it declared that 'through the exertions of the Brothers made one convert and had brought to their religious duties five persons who had been away for a long time, one in particular, eight years.'

Father Meynell served faithfully for 23 years the people of Jarrow until 1884 when he moved to Penrith (then part of our Diocese). Sometime later in his presentation address he praised his past parishioners saying 'he preferred the affection of his old congregation to anything else in the world.' His desire to be buried amongst them was fulfilled in 1897 when his remains were returned for burial there.

The provision of Catholic schools in Jarrow is a story too long to be told here. Suffice to record that the first school, adjacent to the church, was opened on October 19th, 1868, under the leadership of a Miss Maria White. Never was the word 'elementary' truer as we are told 'the furnishing of the school consisted of five groups of desks, a blackboard, an easel, with a few reading sheets, books and slates which had previously been used.' In 1872 the East Jarrow School was opened and four years later it came under the supervision of the Marist brothers who did solid educational work here for 30 years.

Father Martin Hayes who succeeded Father Meynell saw a need for a Catholic voice to be heard in local politics. Catholics were encouraged to put up as candidates in local elections and to participate more fully in public life. His work was to bear fruit as the *Centenary Brochure* of 1961 lists six Catholic mayors.

At the rear of the church to-day is a statue of St. Bede which was placed originally on the sanctuary shortly after Father Hayes' arrival; the dedication of the new High Altar by Bishop Wilkinson took place in April, 1885.

The matter of rate-aid for voluntary schools had been simmering since 1902 when the Education Act of that year had relieved the financial pressure on our Catholic schools with the assistance from local rates. 'Rome on the Rates' was the cry in some quarters and some Nonconformist supporters of the Liberals expected that when they came to power in 1906 neither Catholic nor Anglican schools would be financed locally. The Education Amendment Bill of that year proposed that voluntary schools should be transferred to local authorities unless they were self-supporting and that 'undenominational' teaching only should be allowed.

Catholic public opinion was quickly organised led by Cardinal Bourne who in his Lenten Pastoral stated that if necessary 'We shall be prepared, to the extent of our power to continue the struggle of the past rather than sacrifice our children'. A packed Albert Hall publicised nationally the Catholic case prompting *The Times* to comment that 'this remarkable protest could not be ignored'.

In support of this campaign the parish history records that 'The first Catholic procession in Jarrow on a large scale was held on Sunday, March 25th, 1906. At the time the Catholics of the country were 'up in arms' against the Education Act Amendment Bill introduced into Parliament by Augustine Birrell. The Jarrow demonstration was carried out with an enthusiasm and determination of purpose which had behind it the wholehearted encouragement of Father Hayes. It is worth-while recalling that procession through the streets of the town. A large school banner was carried in front of the Birtley League of the Cross Band. School children and parents made a gallant show and at the rear walked the Chadwick Memorial School Band. The spirit of the times may be gathered from the banner-scrolls which were carried by the older scholars and teachers: 'Peace Not Strife', 'Defence Not Defiance', 'Our Fathers Built Our Schools', 'We want Catholic Schools and Catholic Managers', 'Faith of Our Fathers', 'United We Stand', and 'God Bless

Our Pope'. At the close of the procession, Father Hayes gave Benediction in the Church. It was a great Catholic Day, and prepared the way for a crowded meeting in the Co-operative Hall on the following night. How far the Jarrow protest was typical of the rest of the Catholic community it is hard to say, but history records that the Bill was dropped and the voluntary sector kept its hard-won status.

In 1906 Father Mackin of Washington parish exchanged places with Father Hayes. During his incumbency spiritual groups proliferated: the Children of Mary Sodality, the Blessed Sacrament Confraternity, the Guilds of St. Agnes, St. Patrick and St. Bede, the Catholic Social Guild and the Catholic Women's League, who played an important role in the running of the Catholic Clinic for child welfare, were all part of the parish scene. Like his predecessor he made strenuous efforts on behalf of Catholic education and in particular the right to have County Council scholarships gained by Catholic children transferred to Catholic Secondary schools. He saw with satisfaction the opening of the new school in Harold Street in 1914, costing £10,000, and the new central school in Bede Burn Road staffed by the Daughters of the Cross.

The successor in 1931 to Father Mackin was Father Martin McDonnell who during his ministry here shared with his people the sufferings engendered by the economic slump culminating in the famous 'Jarrow March' of 1936, and the onset of the Second World War. During these difficult years the Faith sustained priests and people and in 1935 they were able to celebrate the 1200th anniversary of the death of their patron saint, Bede. Much preparation went into the organisation of this great occasion: 'All roads led to the town on Whit Tuesday, 11th June, 1935. By train, bus and ferry as well as on foot, earnest Catholics poured into the town. Over six hundred buses had been chartered for transport. The Jarrow and Howdon Ferry carried record loads of travellers from the north bank of the river. Hebburn pilgrims, led by Father Witty and the Drum and Fife Band, walked in procession to the point of assembly. It was estimated that between 50 to 60,000 people congregated on a field near Jarrow Hall to attend the Pontical High Mass celebrated by Archbishop (later Cardinal) Hinsley.'

Father McDonnell's health deteriorated from 1938 onwards and during an air-raid on Jarrow on April 10th, 1941, whilst the curates - as was their custom - were visiting casualties, Father McDonnell had a heart attack and died.

It is not possible to mention all the priests who served so faithfully in Jarrow. As a compliment to them all, the words of a parishioner quoted by Canon Wilfrid Blenkin in the centenary brochure on the night he arrived in 1941 and entered the darkened church show how much their ministry was appreciated: 'God bless you Father. Welcome to Jarrow. We haven't much to offer you but we've always loved our priests'.

Amongst the many responsibilities of Canon Blenkin during almost 30 years at St. Bede's were the implementation of the changes brought about by Vatican II; the establishment of the two parishes of St. Mary's (1952) and St. Joseph's (1962); and the organisation of the centenary celebrations of 1961.

His successor, Father Lawrence Tinnion, had the onerous task, along with neighbouring parishes, of re-organising Catholic secondary education into the present comprehensive system we know to-day. He had the honour of being parish priest at St. Bede's when the 13th centenary celebration of Bede's birth occurred in May, 1973, at which Cardinal Heenan was the principal guest.

Like so many of our older urban parishes St. Bede's, the mother church of Jarrow Catholics, has seen a contraction of its population when many of the older houses were demolished and their residents moved to new housing estates.

Re-ordering a large 19th century church to meet the liturgical changes of Vatican II is not always an easy task. A satisfactory blend of the old and the new has been achieved with the extended sanctuary, on which stands a colourful marble altar which came from the Catholic church in Alnwick and was erected by J. S. Lowery. The fine lectern, incorporating some of the pillars from the old altar, was donated by the Tinnion family in memory of the former parish priest.

Aware of a long Christian tradition here Father John Gibbons and his parishioners continue to maintain and develop a considerable number of spiritual and social activities. The oldest organisation is the S.V.P. consisting of six members whose ministry to the needy continues unabated. There are 45 Lay Ministers of the Eucharist who assist with the distribution of communion in church and in the homes of the sick and housebound. Every Tuesday evening a prayer group of about 24 people meets in the parish centre. An R.C.I.A. programme is a regular feature of the parish's pastoral strategy providing an introduction and deepening of the Faith for those who attend.

Involvement of families in the spiritual training of their own children is, also, encouraged here through the pre-baptismal and pre-communion courses. Marriage preparation for engaged couples has been a notable feature enabling those concerned to attend six weekly evening sessions where they are fully informed of their future responsibilities. Married people who have benefited from such a course often return as counsellors and links among participants are supported and maintained by the renewal of friendship at two annual socials.

The Daughters of the Cross who first came here over 70 years ago to fulfil an educational role are represented to-day by Sister Jane, a retired probation officer (her services are still in demand locally) who with Sister Teresa, a teacher, assists in the development and growth of the parish community. Also part of this community are Sr. Catherine McInnes, a Jarrovian, now retired and Sr. Agnes, a retired radiographer, who works as a parish sister in Saints Peter & Paul's Parish, Tyne Dock.

There have been many changes in Jarrow since the days of Bede and latterly since the erection of St. Bede's Church but the essentials remain: the Faith, the Mass, prayer and the sacraments, education and the sense of community - all of which Bede delighted in - are still in evidence to-day.

POSTSCRIPT *(Mgr. R. Brown, 1998)*

In 1996 the Grotto, which had been damaged by fire from the votive candles, was moved from the New End into the main body of the Church.

In 1997 the New End transept was converted into a parish hall and the sacristy was altered to provide a meeting room, kitchen and toilets, thus giving the parish community facilities on the same site. These facilities are now much used for coffee mornings, mothers and toddlers and group activities.

34. LANGLEY MOOR   St. Patrick   *(October, November 1995)*

St. Patrick's is a typical example of many Catholic parishes founded in the late 19th century, in the Durham and Northumberland coalfield, to meet the spiritual needs of a rising population seeking work here, amongst whom was a large number of Irish people escaping the harsh economic conditions of their homeland.

The story of the growth of St. Patrick's, three miles west of Durham City, is a late chapter in a much earlier Christian history of which the ancient parish of Brancepeth played an important part. Within the grounds of Brancepeth Castle is the church of St. Brandon - said to be one of only two churches in England so-named - who had founded a monastery at Clonfert in Ireland in the 6th century. More commonly known as Brendan, he is said in the course of his missionary journeys to have visited Scotland and Wales. One explanation why Brancepeth Church has as its patron a Celtic saint is that in Saxon days the land here was owned by the Bulmer family when the Celtic influence of Lindisfarne was strong in Northumbria and if, as some claim, there was a wooden Saxon Church here, before the present stone one, then it is not surprising, because of his popularity, that he became the patron saint of Brancepeth Church.

This fine stone medieval building of cruciform shape exhibits various architectural styles as alterations and additions have been made over the centuries; the earliest part of the tower is said to be of the 12th century. Inside there is much of interest such as the Lady Chapel, the tomb of the third Earl of Westmorland and his son, wooden effigies of the second earl and his wife, some fine wooden carving of the 17th century and amongst the stained-glass windows is one dedicated to St. Brandon.

The lands of Brancepeth were to pass into the hands of the famous family of Neville in the 13th century when Bertram Bulmer's daughter, Emma, married Geoffrey Neville, grandson of Gilbert de Neville who had come to England during the Norman Conquest. They were to be a powerful influence in this area until the Northern Rising of 1569, in Elizabeth's reign, when they sought to restore the Catholic Faith to England.

The rebellion against the religious changes of Edward VI's reign and of his half-sister Elizabeth, is said to have begun in the North at Brancepeth Castle when the Earl of Westmorland (Charles Neville) and the Earl of Northumberland (Thomas Percy), marched on Durham with their followers. On the feast of St. Andrew a High Mass was sung in the Cathedral and on December 4th there was a sung Mass at which the Reconciliation of Durham to the Church took place.

Although the rebellion had much popular support it was soon put down by the Queen's forces with great severity. Eighty were hanged in Durham City and many more in the county villages. One of the most prominent figures to die for the Faith was Blessed Thomas Plumtree, principal chaplain to the Earl of Northumberland, who was martyred in Durham market place in 1570 after refusing a pardon if he would renounce his Catholic beliefs - the first of the Durham martyrs.

Charles Neville managed, along with other leaders, to escape to the continent where he was to die in exile. Less fortunate was Thomas Percy who having escaped to Scotland was sold to the English for £2,000. Tried and executed at York in 1572, he was offered the opportunity to save his life if he conformed and swore the Oath of Supremacy. This he refused to do and the Church honours him to-day as Blessed Thomas Percy, a martyr for the Faith. There followed the confiscation of the Brancepeth estates which were to pass into non-Catholic hands.

Throughout the penal days, pockets of Catholicism survived in Durham usually centred around the homes of Catholic gentry who were able to supply and maintain a priest. Over the hill from Brandon is Waterhouses in the Deerness Valley where St. John Boste was apprehended. A less well-known personage of these parts was George Birket whose mother was of the ancient Catholic family of Salvin. Born in 1549 he received his early education at Douai University after which he was ordained at Cambrai in 1577. Described by a spy as 'about 40, short of stature, slender and lean, his face full of wrinkles, pale of colour, his beard black and thick, cut short', he held the important position of Archpriest (head of the secular clergy but without episcopal authority) from 1608 until his death in 1614. He was the uncle of the Venerable Joseph Lambton who suffered martyrdom in Newcastle in 1592.

In spite of the risks involved converts to the Faith were still forthcoming. Perhaps, one of the most remarkable, was John Cosin, born in 1633, and baptised at Brancepeth Church where his father, who after the Restoration became Bishop of Durham, was rector. Young John was ordained in 1658 after studying at the English College in Rome; he appears to have settled in London where he died. Another convert was Miles Pinckney of Brandon who was baptised at Brancepeth in 1599 and ordained at Cambrai. He was procurator at Douai and later chaplain to the Augustinian nuns in Paris where he died in 1674. Ordained as a priest, the year before Pinckney, was Ralph Salvin of Croxdale who entered the Jesuit order but died at the early age of 27.

Although the easing of penal legislation did not come until the latter part of the 18th century it is apparent from evidence available that the Catholics in and around Brancepeth and Brandon were able to receive the ministrations of a priest in such places as Croxdale Hall and even Durham City itself where there was a strong Jesuit presence. Amongst a list of popish chapels (some would be a room in a house) of 1705, one is named at Brandon in the home of Mr John Johnson. The Papist Returns of 1767 reveal three Catholics in Brancepeth and over 30 (including children) in the Brandon area as well as a considerable number in the city itself and in the Salvin household at Croxdale.

It has already been mentioned how the development of coalmining in the 19th century brought many migrant workers to the Brandon area many of whom were Irish. One only has to look at the frequency of Irish names occurring in our diocese to understand why so many Catholic schools and chapels were necessary. St. Brandon's and St. Patrick's Celtic influence was to return with these people.

The sinking of the collieries at Brandon, Croxdale, and Littleburn were all started before 1846 and the Browney Colliery sometime before 1880. Until the appointment of Father James Hanley to Langley Moor in 1876, Catholics of the area - then numbering about 1,000 - had been looked after by a priest from

Croxdale. Father Hanley, educated at Thurles and ordained at Ushaw, had to start from scratch to provide for the spiritual needs of a fairly extensive parish which included in those days Littleburn, Alum Waters, New Brancepeth. Meadowfield, Browney Colliery, Brandon Colliery and Brandon Village.

His first abode was a rented house in Langley Moor High Street and in the same street he said Mass in the home of a Catholic family. He moved to a bigger house and said Mass in a large room of the Littleburn Hotel. His first major task was to build a place of worship and if possible a school. A temporary solution was a galvanised iron structure which could be used as a chapel and a school on a site behind the present presbytery. With the help of men from the parish - two we know by name, Hugh McDermott and Lawrence Cummings - the building, capable of accommodating 350 people, was completed and formally opened on March 4th, 1878. The commitment of the people to their newly formed parish was evident when the men promised to give one day's pay per fortnight to help pay off the debt.

Obviously times were hard and a recurrent theme in the last quarter of the 19th century and beyond was of financial hardship occasioned by reductions in wages, slumps and strikes. Special events were organised to raise church funds, one example being a concert of sacred music in the Alhambra Theatre in 1878 at which Father Hanley presided.

One year later Bishop Chadwick paid his first visit to the parish and confirmed 130 people. By 1883 the temporary church was certified as a place of worship and licensed for the solemnisation of marriages. When Father Hanley returned to Ireland in 1880 he was succeeded by Father Richard Hannan whose 23-stone figure became a familiar sight in the area; it was during his stay here that the present presbytery was built in 1885. When Father Hannan died comparatively young at the age of 49 in Durham County Hospital he was followed as parish priest by Father Joseph Thorman, in 1899, who was later to become bishop of our diocese. Father Thorman during his seven years here 'made many friends' and was responsible for the new school of 1903 and a new altar and organ in the church.

For many years the Catholics of the Langley Moor parish had worshipped in their tin chapel desiring all the time to have a more fitting place of worship. Father John Parker, appointed in 1906, was within five years to see the parishioners' dream turned into a reality.

From the *Diocesan Council of Administration Minute Book (1906 - 1914)* we learn that in 1909 Father was submitting plans for a new church; he had £500 saved towards the estimated total cost of £3,000 but he was advised by the bishop to wait until one third of the amount had been subscribed, particularly as the parish income was likely to fluctuate if the impending coal strike took place. Overcrowding in the old chapel, it was also suggested, could be alleviated with a third Sunday Mass. Permission was granted in 1910 for the parish to borrow £1,200 and on October 1st of that year the foundation stone was laid by Bishop Collins. A novel way of increasing income was to charge sixpence to attend the ceremony and £170 was raised that day.

The stone church, officially opened with a Solemn High Mass on October 8th, 1911, was built to a Gothic design of Mr Edward Kay of Stockton-on-Tees with accommodation for 450 people. Apart from the changes to the sanctuary to conform to the new liturgical requirements of recent times, the church's appearance has probably changed little over the last 80 years.

There is much of interest to the eye inside St. Patrick's. Looking down the central aisle one notices the three stained-glass windows in the sanctuary wall portraying St. Cuthbert, the Holy Spirit and St. Aidan. The oblong windows in the side-aisle walls show various scenes from the life of Christ and the patron saint is depicted in the window above the organ gallery at the west end. Some unusual stations of the cross, in part mosaic, may be of Italian manufacture. Described by one travel writer as 'an attractive little R.C. church' both the exterior and interior certainly live up to this description.

When Father Parker died at the age of 65 in 1934, after 28 years in the parish, he and his parishioners had achieved much. One example we can give among many - of their mission not being exclusively to their own people but to anyone in need - is in 1926, the year of the General Strike, when a soup kitchen in St. Patrick's clubroom was set up; one of a number supported by the local churches: 'Gallant miners and their wives saw that the children attending the soup kitchens were provided with hot meals, their time and energy were given without stint.' The year before his death he could look back with pride and applaud the generosity of his parishioners when the church was consecrated on October 10th, the debt having been paid off.

The longest serving parish priest appears to have been Father Austin McShane (1938-1976) who had the privilege of saying Mass regularly at Brancepeth during the war years, the first probably since the Reformation. It was, also, during Father McShane's time that Father Dermot O'Sullivan served as a curate here. He is well-remembered in the parish for he was later to become Bishop of Kerry and in a letter of thanks to the parish he remarks: 'I have very fond and grateful memories of the people of Langley Moor and of Father Austin McShane who was one of nature's gentlemen', and as Bishop Thorman had been parish priest here at the turn of the century his description of the area as 'a fertile ground for bishops' is most apt. In fact, the late Bishop Owen Swindlehurst was a schoolboy at the parish school at the time his parents lived in Langley Moor.

Father Joseph Hughes, the present parish priest has been at Langley Moor since 1979 continuing the spiritual ministry so ably carried out by his predecessors. The refurbished school of Bishop Thorman's days provides a Catholic education for 115 pupils under the able direction of Mrs M. Spedding. The children's secondary education is completed at St Leonard's Comprehensive School in Durham City.

35. LONGHORSLEY   St. Thomas of Canterbury   *(January, 1984)*

In the extensive country parish of St. Thomas of Canterbury at Longhorsley in Northumberland, which includes medieval foundations, post-Reformation missions and recent 20th century re-adjustments, can be found clues which suggest that the Faith has continued here unbroken since possibly Saxon days.

One of the earliest Christian foundations in the area was Brinkburn Priory founded round about 1135 by William Bertram I of Mitford. Early records tell us that Osbert Colutaris (possibly a master-builder) was granted the place called Brinkburn in order that he might build there a monastery for Sir Ralph, the priest and other of his brethren of the monastery of St. Mary de Insula (probably the priory of Pentney in Norfolk). Over the years neighbouring landowners granted lands to the Augustinian Canons at Brinkburn and in 1386 there is evidence that Ralph, Lord Greystoke, gave the church of Longhorsley to them; this would be the Norman church nothing of which remains today. It is, also, of interest to note that during the 16th century the priest at Felton was a canon of Brinkburn Priory.

The upheaval of the Reformation and the problems which ensued, ushered in a period when the Faith was practised unobtrusively in the area, usually in the homes of the Catholic gentry who were able to procure a chaplain for the spiritual needs of their families and tenantry. Because of the necessity for secrecy, information is rather scarce on the state of Catholicism in the Longhorsley area until the end of the 17th century when we learn that Longhorsley was in the hands of Sir Thomas Horsley who entertained General Monk as he made his way south in 1660 to support the Stuart cause; the General describes Sir Thomas as being 'of the Romish religion.'

Edward Widdrington II, grandson of Sir Thomas, is believed to have resided at Longhorsley sometime after 1687, and in the will of his wife made in 1730 she left '£400 to keep a Jesuit at Horsley, in Northumberland', and '£20, to my spiritual director, Mr John Smith.' It is possible that Father Smith served at Longhorsley prior to 1730.

Other Jesuits who served the area were a Father Robert Widdrington who, we know, supplied in 1736 from Biddlestone and who may have lived at Longhorsley for a time; Fr. Thomas Clifton who came here from Callaly Castle and possibly remained during much of the 1740s; and Fr Joseph Howe, who in his report for 1750 had, 'about 125 customers to shop ... £30 from the factory (Jesuit funds) and £5 to pay house rent.' Father Howe extended his ministry to Bullers Green, Morpeth, where he was able to say Mass for the Catholics in that area.

Father Howe died in 1792 and about this time the ownership of Longhorsley passed into the hands of the Riddell family who were responsible for bringing the Benedictines to the area; the first being Father

John Dunstan Sharrock who remained in the mission for 37 years until his death in 1831. This well-known Northumbrian Catholic family, also, provided Benedictine priests for Felton, Swinburne and Morpeth. Longhorsley may, with some justification, claim to be the mother church of Morpeth (1779), Cowpen (1836), Blyth (1861), Bedlington (1876), Ashington (1893) and New Hartley (1895).

Before the present church of St. Thomas was built in 1841, the chapel was on the top floor of the 16th century pele tower (now a private residence standing next to the church) which continued to be used as a presbytery until the present one was built by Father James Wright. Within the old tower were two hiding holes one of which was reached from a first floor room and the other from a chimney in a small bedroom.

To the west of Longhorsley are two places of great Catholic interest - Netherwitton and Witton Shields, both of which were incorporated into the parish in 1833. Netherwitton had belonged for centuries to the old Catholic family of the Thorntons one of whose early ancestors, Roger Thornton, in the 15th century was a great benefactor of churches and charities in Newcastle and who was buried in All Saints Church there. Netherwitton remained a Catholic enclave after the Reformation and a stronghold of the Faith. A stone cross, dated 1698, now stands in a house garden, which was once part of the village green, and it was here on feastdays that the Catholic villagers would hold their public festivities. Two examples illustrate the firm faith that existed there: in 1687, Dr John Leyburn, Vicar-Apostolic of England visited the village and confirmed 243 souls; and in 1706 a report stated there were 35 Catholic householders living in Netherwitton.

Longhorsley, St. Thomas of Canterbury *Photo: T. Mackin*

At nearby Witton Shields there was another chaplaincy where for 22 years lived Father Hankin after he escaped from Sunderland when his Mass house was invaded by a bigoted mob in 1746. His successor was Father John Cotes whose life spanned most of the 18th century, being born in 1700 and dying in 1794. Educated at Douai, he taught philosophy there for some years returning to England in 1730 to become chaplain to the Maire Family at Hardwick Hall, Castle Eden. Seven years later he came to Netherwitton and served the Thornton family and local Catholics for 36 years.

Father Cotes who wrote a catechism, was elected canon and later became Archdeacon. He moved in 1773 to Witton Shields and lived in the tower, (built in 1608 by Nicholas Thornton and adjoining the modern farmstead) for 21 years using the second floor as a chapel which was in service as such until about 50 years ago.

One local martyr, not yet raised to the altar, was Father Thomas Wilkinson S.J., who served at Felton and Longhorsley during the latter half of the 17th century. He had on one occasion been tried and condemned to death about the same time as Blessed Thomas Thwing but had been reprieved. Whilst serving in the area he was betrayed, arrested and imprisoned in Morpeth Gaol where he fell ill and died in 1681.

Felton, to the north east of Longhorsley, is a village standing astride the old A1 and for many years was associated with yet another Northumbrian Catholic family, the Riddells. The church of St. Michael's (now Anglican) of the 13th and 14th centuries is a reminder of how deep the Faith runs here; the pre-Reformation bell, which can still be seen, must have called many of the local Catholics to Mass there before the changeover took place. The present Catholic chapel, which stands near the Hall in Felton Park, was opened by Bishop Hogarth and was built in 1857 to the Gothic design of Mr Gilbert Blount for the owner, Sir Thomas Riddell, who died in 1870 and lies buried in the church vault. A pre-Reformation vestment is kept here which is believed to have come from the chapel of the Riddell family in Gateshead. From 1792 to 1883 the Benedictines served Felton, the last being Father Charles Gregory Smith who went on to Amble to found a mission there.

Yet another Catholic family, the Widdringtons, over the years played its part in the continuance of the Faith; unfortunately they were to lose their lands in that area after the Jacobite rebellion of 1715. Widdrington, too had its pre-Reformation church and a mile away at Low Chibburn, it is claimed, was a 14th century preceptory of the Knights Hospitallers, who were given land, also, at nearby Ulgham in 1294; and Ulgham Grange, many years ago, belonged to the monks of Newminster. Jesuit and Benedictine priests served the area during the period when there were few Catholics living there. As the population increased during the 1930s Fr. Hugh O'Connor, then parish priest at Felton, said Mass regularly in the Widdrington Workmen's Club until a chapel was built and opened by Bishop McCormack in 1937; the present church of St. Joseph replaced the chapel in 1964.

Although there are no Catholic schools in the parish today a presentment of 1680 tells us that there was a school at Netherwitton where the teaching was done by a papist who had not been licensed by the authorities. One did exist at Longhorsley in the late 19th century; the parish notice book contains an entry regarding the closing of the school in May, 1897, due to an outbreak of measles. A school, also existed at Felton but was closed in 1922 having, at that time, 27 pupils. There was, obviously, a need for one in the area in the 1930s as it was re-opened in 1935 and was under the supervision of the Sisters of Mercy from Alnwick who managed without financial assistance from the Local Authority; the Riddell family helped with the maintenance of the building. In 1970 the school was closed and today the children of the parish must travel to Alnwick, Ashington, Morpeth or Bedlington in order to receive a Catholic education.

Father Joseph Lennon, the parish priest at Longhorsley - who, we must record, attended the inaugural meeting of the *Northern Cross* when a curate at St. Andrew's in Newcastle - is responsible for this widespread parish today which contains 300 parishioners. The focal point of their spiritual lives is the Mass which is celebrated every Sunday and Holyday at Longhorsley, Felton and Widdrington. Even though there are three Mass centres some parishioners have considerable journeys to make in order to attend; and the people of each area make it their responsibility to look after the church. Weekday Masses are usually said in Longhorsley but there are occasions when they are said at the other two chapels. First communions are always joyous occasions for family and parish, and no more so than here, where they are looked upon as a festival in which all can participate. House Masses, house meetings, and occasionally prayer meetings help further to strengthen the ties of religion and develop the sense of community.

A census of the parish has been done by the Legion of Mary from Ryhope St. Patrick's who have worked in the parish on four occasions doing house-to-house visitation of Catholic and non-Catholic alike. During Church Unity week the ecumenical aspect is not forgotten when Catholics and Anglicans meet together for a prayer service.

Still surviving in the presbytery is a printed pamphlet describing a pilgrimage to Holy Island by the parishioners in 1892, an extract from which ably illustrates the difficulties met then - and even now - in practising one's Faith in a country area and the determination to keep that Faith alive. Father Joseph

Stephenson, S.J. had come to the parish some days beforehand to prepare the people for the pilgrimage and whilst there made this observation: 'On the Sunday evening after the service (Benediction) I had some conversation with two young ladies who wished to ask me some questions. During the course of our talk I found that in spite of the rain and dirty roads they had come from Felton, a distance of five miles. To my surprise I saw them again in church on the Monday night; and then to my wondering admiration I found that upon these two occasions they had walked both ways, and they did not seem to consider this exploit as anything extraordinary. They have the respected name of Hedley'.

POSTSCRIPT   *(Fr. J. Lennon, 1998)*

As more people now possess motor cars the House Masses, meetings in people's homes, prayer meetings now take place in the church. There has not been a parish census since the Ryhope Legion of Mary carried one out some years ago.

36. MINSTERACRES   St. Elizabeth of Hungary   *(February, March, April 1996)*

The Passionist monastery and conference centre, situated off the A68, a few miles south of Riding Mill came into the hands of the order in 1949 when it was purchased from the Silvertop family who had owned the estate for more than 200 years.

It has not within its pastoral boundaries as many Christian reminders of our past that, perhaps, some parts of our diocese have; for this was for centuries a rather wild and desolate area with a sparse population.

There are two places that cannot go unmentioned because of their significance in the planting of Christianity in the area. The first is the village of Bywell with two churches of ancient origin (known as the black and white churches) within a short distance of each other. St. Andrew's (the white church) is believed to have derived its name from the 'White Canons' of Blanchland who, it is claimed, served the people here. Tradition has it that the first church was built by St. Wilfrid and in that same building Egbert was consecrated the 12th Bishop of Lindisfarne.

St. Peter's, of the 11th century, is known as the 'black church' as it was served by the 'black monks' (the Benedictines) of Durham. On one of two bells in the tower is the inscription '+ TU ES PETRUS +'; and, not often seen today, a leper squint where the sufferer could view the altar from outside and receive communion.

Blanchland, a few miles south west of Minsteracres, is named after the 'White Canons' of the Premonstratensian Order founded by Saint Norbert in 1120 at Premontre. In the second half of the 12th century they settled in the remote valley of the Derwent and remained here until the dissolution of the 16th century. To-day's village, much rebuilt over the years, still bears traces of its monastic past; the Lord Crewe Arms stands where once the abbot's quarters and guest house stood. Part of the parish church contains a portion of the monastic choir.

Two recusant families owned land in the area of Minsteracres; the Nevilles were to lose them after the failed Northern Rising of 1569. A well-known family, the Swinburnes, also owned land here late into the 17th century. One might think that the word Minsteracres has a religious derivation but etymologists tell us that it, perhaps, has a more mundane meaning: Millstonacres - a landmark for travellers in this thinly populated region.

Silvertop (earlier Slipertop) is an ancient Northumbrian name recorded as early as 1279. The Stella branch of the family, near Ryton, which later came to own the estate and build the mansion, rose to prominence and wealth through their involvement in the coal trade. Albert Silvertop, born 1667, may have been the first of the family to buy land in the Minsteracres area.

His son, George (1705-1789) '... a leading coal-owner in his day ... of strict honour and integrity ... (who) had been introduced to all the foreign courts of Europe ...' acquired most of the land which comprised this once large estate. He established the first mission here about 1765, appointing the first chaplain,

William Gibson, who acted as tutor to his young son, John. The Rev. William Gibson, a member of the staunch Catholic family of Stonecroft, near Hexham, was eventually to become president of the Douai seminary in Flanders and in 1790 Vicar-Apostolic of the Northern District. In this latter position he was responsible for the founding of Ushaw College after the French revolutionary armies had compelled the Douai students to return to England. His former pupil, John Silvertop, was to play a part in assisting the bishop to found the Northern seminary.

The first chapel serving the Minsteracres congregation is believed to have been in a blacksmith's house at Barley Hill and probably the chaplain lived here until 1808. Sometime between 1780 and 1800 John had the hall built on a new site using a large south-facing room as a chapel.

George Silvertop II (1774-1849) succeeded his father, John, on his death in 1801. Born at Benwell and educated at Douai, he returned to England during the French Wars and completed his education at Old Hall Green in the south of England. He was a much-travelled man who took a great interest in public affairs being appointed High Sheriff of Northumberland after the passing of the Catholic Emancipation Act in 1829. As a landowner he took seriously his responsibilities 'and put into practice the duties imposed upon him by his position ... He was an up-to-date agriculturist and as landlord had few equals in consideration for his tenantry.'

He transferred the house-chapel to outside buildings, collected a fine library, provided a school for the tenants' children on the Blanchland Road and encouraged and supported, John G. Lough, a local stonemason to follow a career as a well-known sculptor.

Approaching the monastery along the mile-long drive one cannot fail to be impressed by the rhododendrons which border it and provide a colourful spectacle in the months of early summer. Even more striking to the eye are the stately *Wellingtonia* pines that adorn certain sections of the roadway. George was responsible for the planting of the latter and many other species of plants brought from abroad to grace the parkland around the mansion from which, on a clear day, the Cheviot Hills are visible.

George Silvertop II died a bachelor in 1849, the estate passing to his grand-nephew, Henry Charles Englefield, who assumed the name of Silvertop. He was the son of Henry Englefield and Catherine Witham, whose father, Henry, was the late George's brother.

In the year he occupied Minsteracres he married the Hon. Eliza Stonor, daughter of Lord Camoys; they had three children: Henry Thomas who succeeded his father; George Edward who became a Benedictine priest at Fort Augustus Abbey, later transferring to our diocese; and Agnes Mary who became a nun.

The most significant event which occurred whilst Henry Charles owned Minsteracres was the erection of the beautiful small Gothic church dedicated to St. Elizabeth of Hungary, the patroness of his wife. Mr Joseph Hansom was chosen as the architect and given a commission which all architects long for. He was told to build 'Something nice; no matter the cost.'

Almost two years after the laying of the foundation stone the church was formally opened by Bishop Hogarth on August 24th, 1854. Amongst the congregation attending the Mass of Celebration were the Rev. Thomas Witham (an uncle) and the Hon. Edmund Stonor who was later to be made Archbishop of Trebizond. It is believed that at this time the Mission comprised more than 100 souls.

A comparatively small church measuring approximately 60 feet by 21 feet the interior has much of interest to the visitor. A number of wall plaques tell us a little about some members of the family but what is of particular interest are the stained-glass windows in the rear sanctuary wall depicting St. Henry (the founder's patron), Our Lady, St. Joseph, and the patroness, St. Elizabeth of Hungary. In the nave walls are other windows showing the patron saints of other members of the family. The Stations of the Cross executed in alabaster by Mr Boulton of Cheltenham are in memory of Francis Somerled Silvertop who was killed in Flanders in 1917. A more recent addition to the church is the painting of St. Paul of the Cross, the founder of the Passionists.

Henry Charles decided in 1875 to reside in his London home returning to his northern estate each year for a summer break; he died in 1887 and was buried in the family vault below the chapel. His son, Henry Thomas, whose mother was Eliza Stonor, inherited the estate and set about improving it after it had been somewhat neglected. By his wife, Rachel McDonnell of Co. Antrim, he had five children but he was to die prematurely at the age of 40. The eldest Francis Somerled Silvertop was also to die at the early age of 34 on the battlefield in the Great War leaving an heir of only three months old, Charles Arthur Joseph Oswald.

It was this Charles Silvertop who was to negotiate with the Passionist Order the sale of the mansion and 60 acres of land. The contract was signed in the presence of the provincial, the owner and the trustees on December 8th, 1949. Father Camillus Nolan came in 1951 to oversee the alterations necessary to house an expected community of 35 members; later that year Father Benignus Duffy was appointed the first superior.

The Order of Passionists was started by St. Paul of the Cross. Born at Ovada in Piedmont in 1694 he led an exemplary life as a youth. He experienced a series of visions, which prompted him to found the order, devoted to Christ's Passion, establishing his first house in 1737. He preached throughout Tuscany and the Papal States and as more young men joined him the Passionists were able to spread their gospel message abroad. Paul desired the conversion of England and prayed daily for that intention.

One of his followers, Dominic Barberi (later beatified) also had a similar wish for England and was the first Passionist to come to our country founding the first house at Aston in Staffordshire in 1842. Initially he met with much hostility but 'his goodness, zeal and concern for everyone irrespective of their religious denomination' soon won people over. It was he who received the famous Anglican convert, John Henry Newman, into the Catholic Church 150 years ago.

Dominic was also to receive into the Passionist Order in 1848 another illustrious English convert, George Spencer, son of the second Earl Spencer. Educated at Eton and Cambridge he became an Anglican clergyman in 1824. His theological difficulties eventually led to his conversion to Catholicism in 1830 followed by study in Rome where he was ordained two years later. As a Passionist he was to spend the remainder of his life giving missions, retreats and promoting ecumenism. He died in 1864 and was buried next to his beloved friend, Father Dominic, at St. Anne's Retreat, Sutton, in Lancashire.

As in its early days Minsteracres monastery continues to function as a novitiate for the English Province. But it is not cut off from the world: it reaches out through its missionary work and offers spiritual hospitality to all in the retreat and conference centre; it is, also, a parish catering for the needs of local Catholics numbering about 150.

What were once a coach-house and stables are now modern commodious buildings where retreatants are accommodated. Much of the refurbishment was done by volunteer workers whose contribution and the gratitude of the Passionists is commemorated on a wall plaque in the entrance hall.

Anyone is welcome to make a visit or retreat here either alone or in a group. Young people are encouraged to deepen their spiritual life and enjoy the open countryside at the Youth Centre, a short distance from the monastery.

Father Richard Appleyard is the present rector here assisted by Fathers Aelred Smith (Parish Priest), Luke Magee (Provincial), Mark Whelehan, Benedict McCaffrey, Frank Keevins, Brother Peter Aspin and Andrew O'Connor (Deacon).

Assisting them in their work are the Sisters of Charity of St. Paul (who came here in 1976): Sisters Dympna, Alice, Kathleen and Pauline are members of the Minsteracres' community currently contributing to the Passionist spiritual ministry.

In addition to the fine Gothic chapel already described is the monastery chapel (formerly the dining room) where the community of priests, brothers, sisters and visitors celebrate the daily liturgy.

This site and estate which has been in Catholic hands for more than 200 years has an atmosphere of peace and relaxation away from the strains and stresses of the outside world - a place where many have found comfort, consolation, strength, peace and joy on their spiritual journey.

37. MORPETH   St. Robert of Newminster   *(October, November 1987)*

Situated in Oldgate, the oldest part of Morpeth, and in a secluded position on the east bank of the River Wansbeck is the fine stone church of St. Robert's erected almost 140 years ago by the Benedictine monks who provided priests to minister here for nearly 200 years until their departure in 1969.

Morpeth's association with monasticism is, of course, much older than the present parish as are the roots of Faith here. About one mile west of the town are the partially restored ruins of Newminster Abbey founded in 1138 by Ranulph de Merlay, the lord of the manor, who invited the Cistercians of Fountains Abbey, near Ripon, to make a foundation in this part of Northumberland with St. Robert as its first abbot. He was born in the diocese of York and his studious disposition, allied to a love of prayer and the bible, enabled him to be ordained as a secular priest; he worked for a time in a parish until the call of God to the monastic life led him to join the Benedictine community of Our Lady of York. Wishing to follow the more strict observance of the Cistercian order, Richard, the abbot of the York monastery led a group of monks, including Robert, to a wild uncultivated area where the now famous Fountains Abbey was established. From here Robert was to journey north to Morpeth to found the Newminster monastery which was to last 400 years until its dissolution in the 16th century. Robert who was 'reported to have been of modest bearing, gentle in manner and kind to all men' was a close friend of St. Godric, the hermit of Finchale, whom he visited regularly.

The pre-Reformation church of St. Mary the Virgin, Morpeth - of mainly 14th century construction - furnishes us with more evidence of the antiquity of the Faith here. Of particular interest is the rare Jesse tree window (showing Christ's ancestry); a precious example of medieval glass.

As part of the Bicentenary celebrations of St. Robert's, Father Thomas Cunningham and Father Desmond Meagher were invited by the Anglican community to celebrate Mass in St. Mary's Church, the first since the Reformation. The church was crowded to capacity with Catholic and Anglican parishioners of Morpeth. The Anglican Rector, Geoffrey Bateson, preached the homily and presented a magnificent Jerusalem Bible to St. Robert's people, with the inscription: 'As a token of Christian affection from the Anglicans of Morpeth to their brothers and sisters in Christ at St. Robert's commemorating their 200th anniversary.'

Chantry chapels were also part of the town's Christian heritage: three in all - dedicated to Our Lady, All Saints and St. Mary Magdalene - could, before the Reformation, be located in a building still standing on the north side of the main road bridge. Later it was used as a grammar school; today the edifice - still showing a bell-tower and the pointed arch windows reminding us of its former religious purposes - is converted to a craft centre and a Tourist Board information office.

If one goes further afield in this scattered rural parish more evidence of our Catholic past is obvious. In 'a truly idyllic little spot in the midst of rural scenery' is Hartburn church, 'a beautiful and interesting specimen of Early English work'. One of its peculiarities is the inclination of the chancel to the North from its East-West axis. Many medieval churches had a ground plan in the shape of a cross - the inclined chancel at Hartburn is said, perhaps to indicate the drooping head of Christ on the cross.

Mitford's original Norman church - with Early English additions much restored in the 19th century - is yet another building proving the antiquity of the Faith in this area. Nor was it the only one; there once stood on a hill overlooking the village, St. Leonard's Hospital founded by Sir William Bertram in Henry I's reign; and it has also been proved by excavations in 1938-9 that there was a cruciform chapel of the 13th century within the walls of the ruined Mitford Castle.

The changes in religious practice brought about by the 16th century Reformation no longer allowed Catholics to worship in the churches of their ancestors. There remains to be told the detailed story of those who adhered to their Faith in these parts in those difficult times. In the late 17th century a Jesuit priest, Father Thomas Wilkinson, who laboured on the Northumberland and Durham Mission, was arrested after the Titus Oates' Plot (1678) - a fabrication to discredit Catholics - and condemned to death about the same time as Blessed Thomas Thwing. He was reprieved and continued his ministry until betrayed and re-arrested. His final place of incarceration was Morpeth where, according to one source, he died at the hands of a poisoner. Foley's *Records* go on to state, 'that nearly ten years later, on his body being dug up, it was found perfectly incorrupt and as white and flexible as that of a living person whilst the linen in which it was wrapped and the coffin were quite rotten...'

At some risk, Mary Coates was preserving her family's faith in 1681: 'a true bill was found against her for high treason for sending her son, John, overseas to school at St. Omer' in order that he could receive a Catholic education. The wife of the latter was Winifred Coates who was subsequently to provide a Masshouse in Alnwick before 1750. Another family noted for its recusancy were the Fenwicks of Morpeth. In 1793 the *Newcastle Chronicle* recorded the death in Morpeth of Widdrington Bourne who in a letter written by Archdeacon Sharp in 1762 to the Bishop of Durham is described as 'the popish schoolmaster in this town who has a great number of scholars and brings them on extremely well; he also teaches them the catechism and attends them to church when they come to say it ...'

Influenced by the above-mentioned and supported in their Faith by the Jesuits based at Longhorsley it is, perhaps, not surprising to find amongst a list of papists of 1767, 85 in Morpeth alone. They were not all from the gentry or middle class as the following random selection shows: Michael Holland, a weaver, his wife and their eight children; Garrett Heckles, a bricklayer and his wife Jane; Robert Chapman, a labourer, and wife Mary; Mary Pringle, a quilter; and John Smith, a shoemaker.

These staunch Catholics of Morpeth worshipped in a rented house in Buller's Green at the north end of Newgate Street.

When Elizabeth Riddell inherited her father's estates in Felton and Longhorsley in 1762 it enabled her husband, Thomas Riddell of Swinburne Castle, to provide eventually a church for the Morpeth Catholics. The Benedictines had been chaplains at Swinburne for many years and it had been customary to send the Riddell boys abroad to the Benedictine schools at Douai and Lambspring. Acting as a trustee of charitable funds left by Basil Forcer of Harbour House and Kelloe he was able to purchase in 1778 a house for £180 in Oldgate opposite where the present church now stands; there he built the chapel of St. Bede's and a priest's house for £850; he then created an endowment to provide an income for the mission.

In Oldgate today can be seen a plaque bearing the words 'St Bede's Place' reminding us of the first post-Reformation Catholic Church in Morpeth. It is important because Morpeth was the centre from which other Benedictine missions were to grow; Cowpen (1836), Blyth (1861), Bedlington (1876), Ashington (1893) and New Hartley (1895).

Father Charles Thomas Turner was the first Benedictine to serve St. Bede's (c.1788); he is described by one of his successors as 'a great musician who used to have concerts in the Town Hall. They say he was well-beloved'.

Recorded in some detail in the parish history is the dedicated work of all the priests from Ampleforth, Downside and Douai who served here for the last two hundred years. It is only possible to mention here a few and to highlight the major events over those years.

One cannot omit from the story the priest responsible for building the present church at Morpeth; he was Father George Augustine Lowe who served here for 33 years from 1836. Opened by Bishop Hogarth in 1850 the church, with its 115 feet spire, was designed by T. Gibson and cost £2,400.

Bishop Hedley of Newport, together with his brother and sister, donated the fine marble altar in memory of their mother, Mary Ann Hedley, who had lived in Collingwood House - once owned by Admiral Collingwood - which was bought to replace the old presbytery. Built at the same time as the church was the parish school situated on the right of the drive; it remains in use today as a first school but, it is hoped, a new one will be built within the next three years.

Father Kershaw, writing later of Father Lowe, records '... the old Catholics of Morpeth cherish and love his name and memory and some old inhabitants, non-Catholics, who might not perhaps be expected to appreciate his work have sometimes spoke to me of Father Lowe in words of highest praise and admiration'.

Expansion occurred during the incumbency of Father Ignatius Stuart (1891-1894) when a house was rented in Ashington to provide a Mass Centre for local Catholics. Father Aloysius O'Leary (1894-1905) typifies the care and concern shown to all regardless of their denomination by all the Benedictine priests who came to Morpeth.

Doctor Hugh Dickie in an obituary remarks that '... when an epidemic raged and the call for spiritual help and comfort arose, the barriers of sect and creed fell down and he had a cheering word, a loving smile or a helpful prayer for all ... Few knew the heroic side of his life when typhoid and smallpox scourged this town and members of all sects were sick and dying, no man proved himself so devoted and untiring as our friend who sleeps.'

Morpeth's longest-serving Benedictine was Father Robert Kershaw who served the Morpeth parish for 41 years from 1905 to 1946 celebrating his diamond jubilee here and eventually retiring at the age of 91 years - the oldest living Benedictine; he was to die in the 66th year of his priesthood.

Each Benedictine sent to Morpeth made his own individual contribution to the development of the parish and Father Ceolfrid Swarbrick (1952-65) was no exception. He noted in the Parish Log Book that at his first weekday Mass 'there was not a soul in church and I had no server until the housekeeper came and answered the Latin. I had been accustomed to rows of communicants.' There could be various explanations why this was so; the Sunday Masses, however, must have been well-attended as he introduced an 8 o'clock Mass to ease the overcrowding at the other two morning Masses. He was responsible for the purchase of a Methodist Chapel in 1957 at Pegswood which became the Church of Our Lady and St. Edmund - still served from Morpeth.

In scattered rural communities the provision of Catholic education for all children is more difficult usually than in urban areas. Senior children were transferred in 1953 to St. Wilfrid's Blyth; today the children at Morpeth attend the First School until the age of 7 when they transfer to St Benedict's Middle School, Ashington, and then on to St. Benet Biscop High School, Bedlington, to complete their secondary education.

The last Benedictine parish priest at Morpeth was Father Gerard Spencer who succeeded Father Swarbrick in 1965; he was assisted for a time by Father Swinhoe and finally, for the last two years of the Benedictine era by Father L Devine until 1969 when the Order handed over the parish to the diocese. Commenting on their departure in the *Northumberland Gazette* Father Spencer gave the reason: 'There is such a vast area to cover (including hospitals) that they really need some young men here, and we are so far from the abbey that it isn't possible to get someone here just for a day or two to help out. There is a general shortage of vocations these days, probably because we live in a material age and people do not want to give up their comforts.'

Father Edward Wilkinson was the first secular parish priest of Morpeth and he was assisted by Father Henry O'Reilly; it was their responsibility to implement the liturgical changes decreed by Vatican II.

When Father Wilkinson moved to a Newcastle parish, shortly before the Bicentenary celebrations in 1979, he was succeeded by the present parish priest, Father Thomas Cunningham, who today is assisted by Father Bernard Traynor.

Throughout the week of celebration for the Bicentenary, St. Robert's Church was given over to a festival of flowers. The themes and floral decorations were the work of all the various denominations in Morpeth, as well as parishioners of St. Robert's. For a week St. Robert's was the centre of attraction for visitors to the town.

The highlight of the celebrations was a High Mass held in the grounds of the Church which attracted 900 people. Bishop Lindsay was the principal celebrant along with priests of the Deanery and priests who had served at St. Robert's, both Benedictine and Secular. The Abbot of Douai preached the homily.

As St. Robert's moves into its third century a study of its history has given an added impetus to the desire in the parish to continue this proud record, which few parishes can claim, and to develop and enhance the life of the Church here.

Father Cunningham and Father Traynor, with the help and co-operation of many parishioners, maintain this continuity of service to the parish and wider community. Much of the priests' time is spent, in addition to parochial duties, visiting four hospitals in the locality.

One of the oldest lay groups is the S.V.P. Conference, established in 1931, with a present membership of 20 brothers who perform their works of charity begun more than 50 years ago by its founder members. The C.W.L., celebrating this year their silver jubilee, has 40 members; they presented to the parish recently pieces of embroidered church linen to mark this occasion; some of their members are very involved in helping out at the Summer Catechetical Camps held annually at Burn Hall.

For the younger members of the parish a play group is organised and run three days each week by parishioners in the small parish hall adjoining the presbytery. The Youth Club provides some social life in a Christian atmosphere every Thursday evening - over 70 youngsters attend in the summer period. A small Y.C.W. group, also, meets weekly on a Wednesday enabling the young people present to understand their role in the church and the world.

The commissioning of 30 lay ministers of the Eucharist has made it possible for communion to be distributed under both kinds whenever Mass is celebrated.

St. Robert's can boast two choirs; the 15 members of the parish choir sing every Sunday at the 11 o'clock Mass; whilst the Folk Choir customarily provide the music and sing the hymns at the evening Mass.

Mention has been made of the four hospitals within the parish boundaries. At two of them a Mass is said monthly and when this occurs at St. George's Hospital, ladies of the parish volunteer to transport the patients from the wards to the chapel.

Finally, a few words about the six young men of St. Robert's who on their own initiative, in August, organised and completed a sponsored walk from St. Bee's Head in Cumberland to Robin Hood's Bay in North Yorkshire; they covered the distance of 190 miles in 11 days - so far they have raised £550 which will be shared between CAFOD's Mozambique Appeal Fund and Catholic Care, North East. A nice gesture from the youth of the parish showing their care and concern for others.

One of Cardinal Hume's comments from the congratulatory letter he sent in 1979 will more than adequately conclude this article: 'A continuous history of two hundred years of celebrating Mass and the Sacraments and of serving the people of Morpeth is indeed a matter for rejoicing.'

38. MURTON St. Joseph *(December, 1989)*

Father Felix Daley and the parishioners of St. Joseph's, Murton, will be celebrating on December 17th, 1989, the 25th anniversary of the opening of their church. In the December 17th, 1964, edition of a local newspaper the headline reads: 'A GREAT DAY FOR R.C.'s OF MURTON ... the new £50,000 church of St. Joseph for which they have been striving for many years was blessed and opened by the Bishop of Hexham and Newcastle, the Rt. Rev. James Cunningham. More than 70 priests from all parts of the diocese were in the procession as the Bishop, watched by hundreds of parishioners, went round the whole exterior of the church, and then the interior giving it his blessing'.

St. Joseph's, a large church by any standards, with a seating capacity of 400, was designed by Mr. A. Rossi and built by Findlay of Ryhope during the incumbency of Father A. McShane. His predecessor, Father Daniel Keane, was responsible for the planning and preparation necessary for the building of the church. The marble altar in three colours cost £658. The church, built on a sloping site, enabled the architect to include in the design a crypt at the south end which is used as a parish centre. Twenty steps which lead to the main entrance have the unusual feature of being electrically heated to prevent the formation of ice in cold weather - a facility never used.

Before the building of the present church the Murton Catholics worshipped in a 'tin church' erected on the same piece of land where the new church stands. Two reminders from those days of the temporary chapel are the stained glass in the south window and the wooden altar in the Lady Chapel.

In retrospect there does not appear much evidence, within the present parochial boundaries, of any pre-Reformation church or religious foundation although a local historian, the late Mrs Helen Abbott, relates that part of a stone cross plinth unearthed in 1912, when the foundations of the Aged Miners' Homes were being laid, may be of Saxon origin. She mentions, also, an East Anglian font, possibly of the 14th century, which was discovered some time ago on the Murton to Hawthorn shaft road. Of course the few inhabitants of Murton, who lived in this area before the religious changes of the 16th century, would have been able to worship at the church of St. Andrew in Dalton-le-Dale (early 13th century) or at St. Mary's in Easington (Norman).

If the tradition of 19th century Murton Catholics was the continuance of an earlier one then the latter church seems to be the more likely place of worship as it was a common occurrence before the building of the school-chapel in 1899 for parishioners to journey through 'Lammy's fields' to Sunday Mass and confession in Father Boland's time at Easington.

Murton, like many other villages in the coalfields, owes its expansion into a much larger community to the opening of the colliery there in 1838. Among the many who flocked here in the second half of the 19th century was a considerable number of Irish from other pits; they would be a fair proportion of the total population of Murton which in 1851 numbered 1,387 increasing five-fold to 6,514 by 1901. This remarkable development is the reason why the priests from Easington expanded their mission to these parts. Information gleaned from the memories of older parishioners reveals that Communion was given regularly, for a time, at 12 Silver Street, and it explains the need to erect the school-chapel in Murton towards the close of the 19th century to which Fathers Gregson and Campbell journeyed on horseback to administer the sacraments and say a Sunday Mass.

Miss Kate Baker was the first headmistress of the school which was opened on March 15th, 1899, with an enrolment of 252 children; the first Mass was celebrated here on November 5th, 1899. It would appear that St. Joseph's was served from Easington until 1911 when it was formally established as a parish, in its own right, with the appointment of Father John Bull. His first place of residence was 9, Brooklyn Terrace; he remained in the parish for ten years and was responsible for the building of the fine stone presbytery in 1914.

Probably because of the lack of space in the school-chapel for Sunday services it was decided to erect a 'tin chapel' adjacent to the presbytery. It was duly opened in 1931 and in October of that year witnessed the attendance of over 100 priests and many parishioners at the funeral of Father Martin McDermott. It has been established that this rather grandiose 'tin church' came from Annitsford. For a temporary building it was a very imposing structure with side aisles and clerestories as the old photographs clearly show.

Today there are many varied opportunities in the parish encouraging the growth of the spiritual and social life of all.

The parish S.V.P - celebrating this year its 40th anniversary - continues the essential work of helping those with differing needs. The senior and junior praesidia of the Legion of Mary persevere in their apostolic work of prayer and spiritual support for parishioners. St. Joseph's, as with many other parishes today, has its Lay Ministers of Communion who take the sacrament after the Sunday Mass to the sick and housebound; a Journey in Faith group meets weekly every Tuesday; and every Friday after the evening Holy Hour of silent adoration a prayer group gathers to study and meditate on the scriptures.

In the social sphere there are a number of activities to satisfy the needs of the different parish groups: a Ladies' Club meeting weekly arranges outings, and speakers on a variety of topics; the Confraternity of the Sacred Heart provides another opportunity for the ladies to keep in touch with each other; there is Old Time Dancing every Thursday evening; and the Junior Crusaders' Club allows the under twelves to enjoy their recreation together.

Parental involvement in the life of the school is enhanced through the Friends of St. Joseph's who, together with the teachers, organise discos and social events, not purely as a fund raising exercise, but also as a means of enabling closer parent-teacher-pupil links to be forged.

Over and above the normal parish aid to the Third World, St. Joseph's has a special bond with the Malindi Mission in Kenya helping regularly with donations. This parish to parish co-operation was established when an old friend of Father Daley's, Father Joseph Cain of the Salford Diocese, did a spell of missionary work in this area of Africa.

Ecumenical co-operation is not neglected either; at present Father Daley is the current chairman of the steering committee for the Murton district churches. St. Joseph's community participates in the annual memorial service for the war dead at Holy Trinity church; they partake in the Harvest Festival held in the first week of September; they are involved each night in the denominational services of Unity Octave Week and the annual inter-church 'musicals' and a book display which encourages a wider Christian readership. At Wellfield House, a senior citizens' home, the various denominations take their turn in conducting a Sunday evening service which is well attended and much appreciated.

Anniversaries evoke memories of the past and if one looks carefully around St. Joseph's church there are ample reminders. Already mentioned are the stained-glass and wooden altar from the 'tin church'. On the front of the re-ordered altar is a brass Sacred Heart encircled with a crown of thorns; this object which once adorned a Divine Office book in the choir of Nunraw Abbey may awaken memories of the days when a considerable number of Murton men spent their annual holiday there helping the monks in the building of the abbey. To Father Daley it is a reminder of his late brother, Bro. Bede Daley, O.C.S.O., who was for many years a monk there; and the recently completed War Memorial plaque, by a parishioner, Mr. Kevin Bartley, recalls the names of those who gave their lives in two world wars. The beautiful oak lectern and wall pedestals are the work of Mr Sawley, a retired non-Catholic undertaker, who donated them to the church.

From the parish, too, have come three vocations to the priesthood: Father Wrigley O.P., Father B. Finan, a Salvatorian Father, and the late Father J. Loftus. Two nuns, Sister Mary Hilda of the Sisters of Mercy and Sister Anselm of the Little Sisters of the Poor, were also born in the parish. Nor should we forget two deceased sisters: Sister Ligouri and Sister Catherine of the Mercy Order.

As the 25th anniversary celebrations draw near much has already been done to mark this important occasion: the church has been recarpeted; men and women of the parish have set to and hand cleaned and varnished all the church benches; and the crypt has been refurbished.

Liturgical preparations are almost complete, the highlight, obviously, being the concelebrated Mass on December 13th to which all priests, who have served or were born here, have been invited to participate. The Dinner Dance in the Welfare Hall and other social events will enable the parishioners to enjoy together this milestone in their church's history - its silver jubilee.

POSTSCRIPT   (Fr. F. Daley, 1998)

Our own men, under the professional leadership of Kevin Dixon, and using stone, abundant in beautiful variety and size, unearthed by our volunteer grave diggers, built a splendid Grotto of Our Blessed Lady. The statue was donated by Bill and Pat Hudson with money from the savings of their daughter, Clare, tragically killed while acting as courier on the way to Lourdes. Under Our Lady's feet is a large rock brought by Bill from Lourdes. Other memorabilia are around, Honeysuckle from Nunraw, Berberis from Carfin and white Valerian from Walsingham.

The donation of a life-size picture of the Divine Mercy by the Sisters of St. John's Convent at Kiln Green inspired the setting up of a shrine in the Church. Our Lady's picture and candlestand have been moved into the Church and adorn the front wall and the Lady Altar is now dedicated to the Divine Mercy. For the first time this year Murton Churches shared the Stations of the Cross. Each Church took a turn carrying the Cross through the village and leading the meditation and traditional prayers at five stations led by the ever-willing Murton Brass Band. A large crowd took part with great interest.

Regular pilgrimages to Lourdes, Fatima, Medjugorje and Rome are organised by Bill Hudson. Audrey Willers organises the annual Walsingham pilgrimage.

St. Joseph's has hosted Masses for the Marian Priests' Movement, the Legion of Mary Acies and Celebrations, and many inter-Church Services with the other Churches of Murton.

St. Joseph's Junior School received a very good report from the Ofsted inspection in 1997. We are very happy to include this item.

The whole of the presbytery has been refitted with double glazing by the local firm Fahrenheit Thor of Easington Colliery.

39. NEWCASTLE   St. Andrew   *(November, 1983)*

In 1979 two priests from our Diocese were vesting for Mass in the sacristy of Westminster Cathedral when they were approached by Cardinal Hume. 'Where are you from, fathers?' 'Newcastle, Your Eminence,' replied Father McNamara. 'Which parish?' asked the Cardinal. 'St. Andrew's' was the reply. 'Ah, that's my parish,' said Cardinal Hume, the record of whose baptism can still be seen in the parish baptismal register. His family resided in the parish for a number of years and when home on holiday from Ampleforth Abbey he frequently said Mass in St. Andrew's Church.

Saint Andrew's seems to have been, over the years, a training ground for bishops. The first curate, Fr. William Riddell, a member of the well-known Northumberland family, during his time at St. Andrew's supplied at Felling and paid for the erection of a chapel there out of his own pocket; later, in 1844, he was consecrated Bishop, succeeding Bishop Mostyn as Vicar-Apostolic of the Northern District in 1847, a few months before his death from typhus fever. Four other priests who served the parish and were later raised to the episcopate were the Rev. George Errington who became Bishop of Plymouth and later Archbishop of Trebizond; the Rev. Charles Eyre who became Archbishop of Glasgow; and two bishops of our diocese, the Rev. Richard Collins and the Rev. Joseph Thorman.

The first parish priest was a Father James Worswick who, because of his outstanding contribution to the city of Newcastle, has the street in which the present church stands named after him. Born in Lancashire of an old Catholic family and following in the footsteps of two uncles and a brother, he crossed to Douai in Flanders to study for the priesthood. His studies were interrupted by the upset of the French Revolution and during the Reign of Terror of 1793 he managed to escape with four companions. Evading capture, they reached the allied army lines where they were kindly received by the Duke of York who furnished them with money and passports.

On reaching England he gathered with other Douai refugees at Crook Hall, where he received the diaconate; a year later he was ordained by Bishop William Gibson at York in April, 1795, and within two months of his ordination he was appointed to Newcastle where he spent the whole of his priestly life.

Before his coming, the Catholics of Newcastle had worshipped in two makeshift chapels in Newgate Street and Westgate Road. Father Worswick appears to have been a man of boundless faith and energy and the record of his 48 years as a priest bears testimony to his determination to make the Newcastle mission a success. He was soon able to purchase a site for a church at 73, Pilgrim Street, with a large garden at the rear, much of which today is occupied by the present Fire Station. Again, like so many impoverished missions of those days, it was necessary to make a public appeal: 'It has often been lamented that the Catholic inhabitants of Newcastle are not possessed of a spacious and convenient chapel, suitable to the dignity of divine worship ... The two chapels in present use ... are inconveniently situated, one of them also entirely excluded from the benefit of daylight ... it is impossible to accommodate the numerous Catholics of Shields, and those on the banks of the Tyne ... or the families not of our persuasion who have expressed a desire of being admitted into our chapels and of becoming more immediately acquainted with our religion ... the building is begun ... it has become necessary to solicit the benefactions of those whom the Almighty has placed in easier circumstances...' Over £900 was subscribed for the brick chapel which was opened in 1798 with High Mass celebrated by Father Worswick who was assisted by two French refugee priests.

His concern for the education of the parish children is shown in the opening of the two schools shortly after the church building was completed. As the church was built on a sloping piece of land, there was a large room available at the east end which he had converted into a girls' school; a boys' school was built further down in 1800 and the first master mentioned was a Mr. Robson.

With the industrial expansion of Tyneside, an influx of Irish immigrants and the closing of the Jesuit mission he found it necessary to extend the church in 1830 to accommodate a congregation of 1000. This extension was obviously badly needed as it is reckoned, at this time, Fr. Worswick was responsible for the spiritual welfare of half the 8,000 Catholics in Northumberland. In addition to these labours he was responsible for the building of St. Cuthbert's at North Shields, a chapel at Felling, and - although he did not live to see it finished - the building of St. Mary's Cathedral where he was interred in 1843.

Such was the respect and love in which he was held in Newcastle, by Catholic and non-Catholic alike, that it was decided in 1835 to honour publicly his 40 years residence with a presentation of a marble bust of himself and a silver tea and coffee service which are still preserved in the parish as a memento of this great priest. A eulogy printed in 1832 gives us an insight of his priestly qualities: 'As a preacher he is bold, eloquent, animated and impressive ... No severity of exertion, no fatigue, no want of time will induce him to omit the performance of this sacred and important duty. In the confessional till a late hour on Saturday night and again early on Sunday morning ... the children are catechised in public on Sunday afternoons ... and in private twice a week. At our public hospitals he is a daily visitant ...'

In 1860 at the invitation of Bishop Hogarth the Dominicans returned to Newcastle and ministered in the parish for 14 years until their own church was opened at Red Barns in 1873. During their stay here the Town Council planned re-development in the area desiring to build a new police court on the site of Fr. Worswick's original foundation. After protracted negotiations it was agreed that the land to the rear of the police court could be used for a new church and presbytery. Built in freestone in the Decorated Style and designed by a local architect, Mr. T.G. Leadbitter, it was opened on September 26th, 1875 by Bishop Chadwick; the only remaining reminder of Fr. Worswick's church being the stained glass in the mullion windows which face the visitor on entering the small courtyard.

It is not possible here to mention all the priests who served at St. Andrew's so faithfully over the years, but mention must be made of the Rev. Doctor Harriott, who received his early education in the parish school, and to whom the *Northern Cross* owes a debt of gratitude for his unstinting support during his 28 years as parish priest. He was, also, involved in the setting up of the University Catholic Chaplaincy, the formation of the Catholic Film Society, the Church Music Society, the Catholic Writers' Guild and the Catholic Stage Guild.

How different today is the parish compared with the years of growth in the 19th and early 20th century; it is typical of many inner city parishes that have been affected by urban re-development which has reduced the number of parishioners to 80. In spite of the small numbers, however, St. Andrew's - in the care of the present parish priest, Father Brian McNamara, assisted by Father Michael Corbett - continues to play an important part in the Catholic life of Newcastle. It is in some sense a 'commuters' church still very popular for those Catholics who like to pop in and say a prayer and light a candle. The re-organisation of the transport system and the coming of the Metro have reduced these numbers somewhat. On Sundays it can muster a congregation of 100 at each Mass and a goodly number at the Friday midday Mass. Holydays see the church packed to capacity for the midday Mass by those Catholics who work, but do not necessarily live, in the city.

Those who have not visited the church recently would be pleasantly surprised to see the exterior stonework restored to its former colour after the removal of much industrial grime. Interior renovations, recently completed, have enhanced the appearance without altering it radically; and the generosity of those who visit and worship here has enabled a debt of £45,000 spent on these improvements to be partially paid off, £10,000 of which was raised in 18 months by a special appeal.

Finding a conference room in the city has never been a problem for groups or societies, in and outside the area, who wish to meet here; St. Andrew's has always been available and open to all. Today the Catholic Scouts and Guides meet here regularly; the St. Camillus S.V.P. Hospital Conference - continuing the work of one of the oldest S.V.P conferences in the diocese - holds conference meetings regularly before visiting Hunters Moor Hospital; and the Third Order of St. Francis meets monthly under the direction of Father McNamara, their chaplain.

Father McNamara, who celebrated his silver jubilee this year, spends much of his time as a member of the Diocesan Marriage Tribunal and, along with Father Corbett, acts as chaplain to Nazareth House; the main responsibility for hospital visitation rests with Fr. Corbett who looks after the spiritual needs of the staff and the sick at the Royal Victoria Infirmary and Hunters Moor Hospital.

The Reverend Vincent Smith in his book *Catholic Tyneside* provides us with a fitting conclusion:

'When Mr. Worswick arrived in Newcastle, twenty years (sic) before the Emancipation Act of 1829, Catholics held their services in private chapels hidden away in dark alleys ... but before the end of his life they owned and openly used several public chapels and a large school, they had full civic liberty, and were held in such esteem by their fellow-citizens that a Catholic had been elected Lord Mayor of the city.'

And we might add that he could not have imagined that a future Cardinal Archbishop of Westminster would one day be baptised in Father Worswick's parish.

40. NEWCASTLE   St. Mary's Cathedral   *(November, 1991)*

A History and Guide of the Cathedral Church of St. Mary, Newcastle by Vincent A. Bartley - for many years M. C. at the Cathedral - is a mine of information for anyone interested in church architecture, stained-glass or the historical and spiritual development of our principal diocesan church.

Consisting of 219, A4, Spiro-bound pages (with illustrations) it deals in some detail with the construction, evolution and everyday happenings of a Pugin-designed building which has served the parishioners and the wider congregation of Hexham and Newcastle for almost 150 years.

Its ten chapters and eleven appendices will provide for most people more than enough facts to make a series of worthwhile visits to this spiritual haven set in the midst of busy streets noisy with traffic. In the first chapter dealing with the description of the church we are reminded of its primary purpose: 'In the second buttress up Bewick Street is a niche with a figure of Our Lord and this indicates the presence of the Blessed Sacrament Chapel in this part of the church.' A well-designed church is always a reminder of God and our Faith.

Chapter Two gives an account of the preliminary efforts made to build Newcastle's second post-Reformation Catholic church. A group of Catholics met on July 26th, 1838, under the chairmanship of the Rev. William Riddell and formulated a number of proposals. The first resolution was moved by George Thos. Dunn Esq., and seconded by the Rev. Thos. Witham of Stella: 'That the Catholic chapel in the town being quite inadequate to accommodate the present numerous congregation, it is highly expedient that another Edifice should be erected, in addition to the existing building.' Subscriptions were asked for and when £6,500 had been collected the site - part of the garden of Forth House - was purchased and the most noted Catholic architect of the day, a convert, Augustus Welby Pugin was invited to undertake the commission.

Pugin, an advocate of the Gothic revival, designed St. Mary's similar to the parish church at Grantham in Lincolnshire; the style was to be of the Decorated period of Edward III's reign. The committee favoured a church with side aisles and clerestory whilst the architect had in mind a church with a triple roof. How Pugin got his way can be read in Chapter 3.

The following chapter deals with some 'facts and figures' revealing that the contractors, Myers and Wilson of Hull, charged just over £7,500 for their work. Surprisingly, perhaps, Pugin claimed an architect's fee of only £370 plus £40 travelling expenses. George Myers is supposed to have executed the carvings on the main altar, reredos and Lady Altar (now the main altar since re-ordering) in Caen Stone. It's a good chapter to browse through as are Appendices I, II and III, perhaps more so, for in them Vincent Bartley has collected numerous extracts - some serious some amusing - from notice books and diaries kept in the archives. One gets a flavour of daily life in a busy urban parish as well as some enlightening facts about other happenings in our diocese.

On Low Sunday, April 23rd, 1854, it was announced that the Wednesday Mass at the request of the Bishop would be offered to allow the faithful to 'petition Almighty God to avert them from the calamities of war (Crimean War).'

An extract of August 26th, 1866, tells us that the 'Little Sisters of the Poor opened a house in 36, West Clayton Street.'

On October 29th, 1876, people were requested to inform the priests if their friends were taken to the

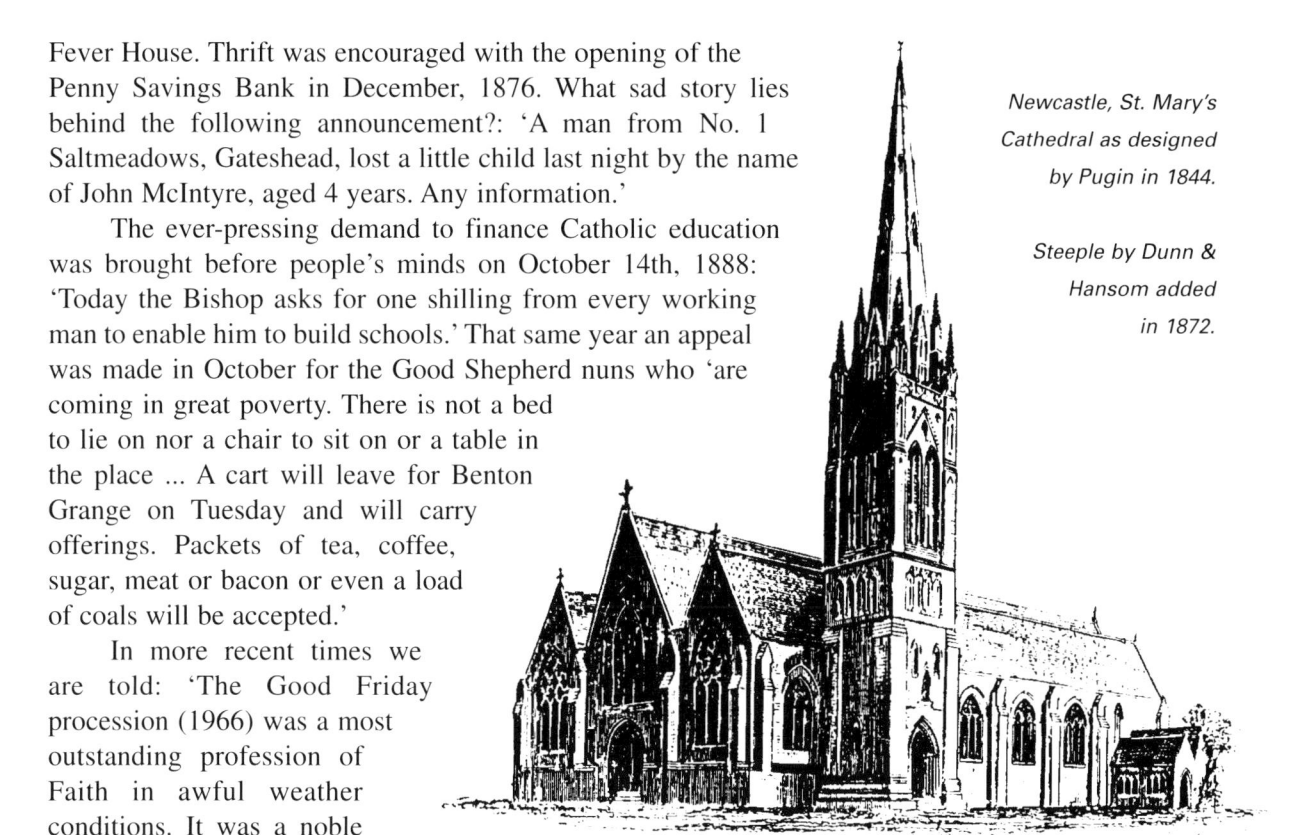

Fever House. Thrift was encouraged with the opening of the Penny Savings Bank in December, 1876. What sad story lies behind the following announcement?: 'A man from No. 1 Saltmeadows, Gateshead, lost a little child last night by the name of John McIntyre, aged 4 years. Any information.'

The ever-pressing demand to finance Catholic education was brought before people's minds on October 14th, 1888: 'Today the Bishop asks for one shilling from every working man to enable him to build schools.' That same year an appeal was made in October for the Good Shepherd nuns who 'are coming in great poverty. There is not a bed to lie on nor a chair to sit on or a table in the place ... A cart will leave for Benton Grange on Tuesday and will carry offerings. Packets of tea, coffee, sugar, meat or bacon or even a load of coals will be accepted.'

Newcastle, St. Mary's Cathedral as designed by Pugin in 1844.

Steeple by Dunn & Hansom added in 1872.

In more recent times we are told: 'The Good Friday procession (1966) was a most outstanding profession of Faith in awful weather conditions. It was a noble effort on everybody's part (and perhaps the greatest effort was by Fr. Lawrence Tinnion who delivered the homily in pouring rain)'.

News Bulletins, as in most parishes, have replaced pulpit notices. Again these documents chronicle the life of a cathedral parish with the occasional humorous reference to members of the clergy. In January, 1968, it mentioned Father Laydon who 'As usual at this time of the year was practically unapproachable because of a streaming cold, due to his anti-flu injection, which he takes religiously to ensure that he is the first in the house to have a cold'.

Stained-glass enthusiasts will delight in the detailed information contained in the book. The window at the rear of the sanctuary was designed by Pugin and executed by William Wailes, a well-known Newcastle stained-glass manufacturer, who had premises in Bath Lane. It is a 'Jesse' window portraying the genealogy of Christ as recorded in Matthew's Gospel.

At the rear of the church is a window the central light of which shows the crucifixion. At the bottom of this section of window can be seen a lady kneeling in front of the cathedral porch without tower or steeple. This is Elizabeth Dunn who left money for the addition of the tower and steeple which were designed by Hansom and Dunn and completed in 1872.

If you wish to find out more about this generous Catholic family Appendix X is the place.

In writing of its history one should remember the cathedral's principal function of prayer and worship and its role in serving the parish community and anyone who enters its threshold for spiritual nourishment or counselling. There is always a high attendance at the midday daily Mass after which the cathedral centre is open for light refreshments providing an opportunity for all who attend to mix informally. Throughout the day there is a regular visitation by many busy people who 'pop in' to the Blessed Sacrament Chapel for a period of quiet prayer and reflection. The priests are always available for consultation and advice.

Vincent Bartley has done a great service to the cathedral and the diocese in publishing this fine book. It will be of interest to everyone as it is written in a simple straightforward style and where it is necessary, when dealing with technical matters, explanations are given. Specialists interested in Catholic history will also find something new in its pages. Schools and colleges would find it an invaluable source book for religious and historical studies and a worthy addition to their reference library. Schools and groups contemplating visits to the cathedral would find it useful for background information before they came.

41. NEWCASTLE (BENWELL)   St. Joseph   *(June, 1986)*

'MAGISTER ADEST ET VOCAT TE - The master is here and calleth for thee' is the welcoming inscription greeting everyone who enters St. Joseph's, Benwell, Newcastle. In the tympanum, above the gold-lettered invitation, is a light blue mosaic depicting the host and chalice and reminding the worshipper why the church was built.

St. Joseph's, a church of unusual shape and appearance, was designed - it is claimed in the Romanesque style - by Steinlat and Maxwell who were also the architects of St. Edward's at Whitley Bay. Benwell Catholic Church was opened in October, 1931, by Bishop Joseph Thorman and consecrated seven years later by Bishop Joseph McCormack in March, 1938.

As a place of general historical interest Benwell has much to offer; it first appears in the pages of history when a Roman fort (Condercum) was built here - the third from the mouth of the Tyne - as part of Hadrian's Wall. The earliest mention we can find of the Christian Faith in the area is round about 1280 when the vicar of Benwell was a priest named Patrick (not, as far as we know, any relation of the present parish priest, Father Patrick O'Connell). During the later Middle Ages Benwell was in the parochial chapelry of the ancient parish of St. John's, Newcastle.

Various families held lands in Benwell throughout the centuries: Peter Scot, a member of a wealthy Newcastle merchant family, became Mayor of Newcastle in 1251; Richard Scot, in 1367, obtained permission to enclose his wood at Benwell to make a park of 200 acres - hence, it is believed the derivation of the name Scotswood, part of which is in St. Joseph's parish today.

Two religious orders held lands in the area too. Sir Hugh Delaval (living 1277 - 1302) gave a house and three acres of land in Benwell to the Augustinian Canons of Hexham Priory. As early as 1334 coal was being mined at Benwell and it is a well-known fact that the priory at Tynemouth had mines at Elswick and Benwell, the coals from which were shipped from the prior's wharves at North Shields. Between the years 1458 and 1539 Tynemouth Priory owned an estate in Benwell and Benwell Towers became the summer residence of the priors, the last of whom, Robert Blakeney, resided there after the dissolution of Tynemouth Priory until his death sometime before 1547.

Benwell Towers of pre-Reformation days no longer stands; it was demolished by a later owner, Thomas Crawford, and replaced in 1831 by the present building which became the residence of the Anglican Bishop of Newcastle in 1881 when the Newcastle Diocese was created.

What is of interest from a Catholic point of view is that there once stood a chapel in the grounds of Benwell Towers described as the domestic chapel of the priors of Tynemouth - evidence that Mass was celebrated here about four hundred and fifty years before St. Joseph's Catholic parish came into existence.

Benwell was incorporated into the city of Newcastle in 1904 and in the previous year St. Joseph's parish was established with the appointment of the first parish priest, Father J. Parker.

In retrospect it is not difficult to see why a new parish at Benwell was necessary. A glance at the population figures from 1851 to 1911 suggests an area of rapid industrial development and the resulting movement of people seeking employment; amongst this large increase there was bound to be a proportionate number of Catholics. In 1851 Benwell had a population of 1,272 which by 1891 had risen to 10,354. This latter figure was almost to double in ten years to 18,158 and by 1911 the number of people in Benwell had risen to 27,049.

Small wonder, then, that Father Parker and his successors had a formidable task meeting the spiritual and educational needs of their parishioners. St. Joseph's first church (opened in 1903) was a corrugated iron structure erected, it is said, where the playground of the present primary school is now situated. A house

Benwell, St. Joseph   *Photo: M. Morris*

was purchased in the parish and became a temporary presbytery. These early ventures in establishing parochial life - after donations and parochial efforts - left the priest and people with a debt of £2,000, a considerable sum at the beginning of the century. The worries and difficulties of those early years appear to have affected Father Parker's health and necessitated his leaving the parish in 1905. Father John Rowe followed him and remained probably until 1912.

He was succeeded by Father Richard Vaughan who remained here, as far as we can ascertain, until the arrival of Father J.W. Milroy in 1924. A parish year book notes that during the First World War German prisoners-of-war were housed in the school; another problem was the deterioration of the church fabric, due to lack of repairs during the war period. The parish continued to expand and when Father J.W. Milroy arrived he was faced with the daunting prospect of providing a permanent church and presbytery at a time when there was still much poverty and limited financial resources. Voluntary labour made it possible to concrete the playground and carry out necessary repairs to the tin church. Two years after his arrival a new infants' school had been built.

It is a remarkable fact that in spite of the depression years, when it was reckoned that 75 percent of the male parishioners were unemployed, the parish had cleared its debts soon after the opening of the new school and it was now possible to concentrate the energies of all on the proposed building of the new church. A sloping site was purchased in Armstrong Road and in October, 1931, the fine Romanesque brick church with the prominent dome - not a common feature of our churches - was blessed and opened by Bishop Thorman.

The long wide nave was built to accommodate a large congregation whose eyes must have been immediately focused on the sanctuary where marble and mosaic were to be seen in abundance. Much of the Italian marble work around the sanctuary - including the altar - was paid for by an anonymous benefactor; the cost of an imported marble baptismal font was met by contributions from the infants; and older schoolchildren's offerings helped to pay for the fine marble communion rail. In less than seven years the debt on the church was cleared and it was possible to have it consecrated on March 22nd, 1938. The Lady

Chapel, in honour of the Mother of God, was also the memorial to those who had died in the war.

Father Milroy, in the years immediately following the Second World War, had like many other priests the duty of ensuring sufficient capital was available for the expansion of Catholic education. A number of changes in the field of education have occurred in the intervening years, some of which became the responsibility of succeeding parish priests: Father J. Kenny (1961 - 1964), Father J. McKenny (1965 - 1970) and Father P. Smith (1971 - 1980), the predecessor of Father O'Connell. Today what was once the parish all-age school is now a primary school; the older boys go to St. Cuthbert's Comprehensive School and the girls to the Sacred Heart, Fenham.

Encouraging his parishioners to further efforts in 1959, Father Milroy commented: 'St. Joseph's parish, in spite of the absence of pools (presumably football pools), has not run dry' and he went on to exhort them to continue to fulfil their 'parochial duties.'

Of more recent interest to the people of St. Joseph's are the alterations which were made to the church in 1982 to update the church interior and, in particular, the sanctuary in order to conform to modern liturgical requirements.

Dietz-Lyons of Newcastle were the consultant architects engaged by the parish priest, Father Patrick O'Connell, and the main contractors were Bell and Ridley of Durham. The delicate task of re-ordering this sanctuary was entrusted to Morris Marble works who re-sited the altar forward, below the dome, and erected the presidential chair, ambo, tabernacle, pedestal and font using much of the original Italian marble.

A striking example of contemporary craftsmanship and design is the multi-coloured glass screen (25ft. wide and 30ft. high) which was built into the semi-circular sanctuary arch and which acts as a translucent partition separating the nave and main altar from the Day Chapel (now in the former sanctuary apse) which can accommodate up to 50 people for weekday Mass. The screen structure of aluminium was supplied and fixed by Durham Aluminium and N.E. Engineering Limited.

Much could be written about this unique glass screen but a visit to the church is necessary to appreciate its beauty. Mr. L. C. Evetts, A.R.C.A., was the design consultant and the 1,116 pieces of glass - paid for by individual parishioners - were supplied by the firm of Hartley Wood. Elders, Walker, Millican of Gateshead supplied and fixed the intricate glass leaded panel using five cwt. of lead. This entailed 200 hours of work for the Gateshead firm and most of the bench work was done by a Mr. Sid Hunt, an employee with 49 years of service. This modern tribute to God in stained glass - showing prominently the sanctuary cross, the motif of which is repeated in subsidiary panels - testifies that this ancient art still thrives on 20th century Tyneside.

Other changes in the church include: the lowering of the dome and nave ceilings which will cut heating costs; the re-erection of the organ from St. Mary's College, Fenham, in the south transept; the re-structuring of the confessional to provide open confession for those requiring it; and the re-siting of the baptismal font in the former Sacred Heart chapel which has allowed a spacious narthex to be constructed with a repository at the rear of the church; the total cost was approximately £70,000. When all was complete Bishop Hugh Lindsay came to the parish on May 25th, 1982 to concelebrate Mass and dedicate the new altar.

St. Joseph's parish has not escaped the effects of urban re-development and the consequent movement of parishioners. According to the *Northern Catholic Calendar* (1940) the parish population was over 3,000; today it is roughly 2,000. However, there is still much happening here in this parish community. Because of the sloping site it was possible to build the church over a crypt which is now the parish social centre and in which many parochial activities take place. The St. Vincent de Paul Society (founded in 1928) consisting of ten members meets weekly and continues its work of supporting the needy; the Legion of Mary does much good work, too; a Padre Pio Prayer Group has recently begun to meet in the parish and the Brownies and Guides are in evidence here, also, under the care of their leaders. Eight Lay Ministers have been commissioned to take Communion to the sick and housebound. A Parish Council of 15 members - some elected, others representing parish organisations - meets nine times a year and holds its A.G.M. in April.

An R.C.I.A. Course - A Journey in Faith - has been running in the parish since October and will continue every Thursday until Pentecost under the team leader, Sister Monica. About 40 people have attended regularly, 25 per cent of whom are non-Catholics. It is hoped to hold this course, annually.

Within the wider community of Benwell, St. Joseph's and other denominations are involved in offering help where needed. The Good Shepherd Project in Scotswood, funded partly by the Manpower Services Commission and the Catholic Church, is a Drop-In Centre supervised by a Good Shepherd nun, Sister Hilda, where local residents can call for advice, or just a cup of coffee and a chat. Last year Father O'Connell was the chairman of the Benwell Council of Churches. On March 14th, this year, this Council organised a tour of the community projects functioning in the area; Bishop Lindsay was one of the regional church leaders who participated in this event.

The welcoming inscription mentioned at the beginning of the article - spoken 2,000 years ago by Christ - and carved on the stone lintel of St. Joseph's church entrance is a perpetual and important invitation to the parish community to love and serve the Master in his local church and to render service to the wider community in the 20th century.

42. NEWCASTLE   Bishops' Residences   *(April, May 1994)*

Bishop's House, East Denton Hall, West Road, Newcastle, where Bishop Ambrose Griffiths resides has not always been a bishop's residence nor, indeed, the only one.

Before the restoration of the hierarchy in 1850, when Bishop William Hogarth became our first bishop, our part of England had been under the jurisdiction of vicars apostolic for much of the penal era.

In 1685, when Dr. John Leyburn, a Westmorland man, was appointed vicar apostolic he divided England and Wales into four districts each with its own vicar-general. Our present diocese was then part of the Northern District which comprised the counties of Northumberland, Cumberland, Westmorland, Durham, Lancashire, Cheshire and Yorkshire. The first vicar apostolic in the North was James Smith from 1688 until his death in 1711; he is buried at Cliffe.

The latter three counties became two separate districts each with its own bishop in 1840 so when William Hogarth was consecrated Bishop of Samosata in 1848 he ruled as vicar apostolic of a much smaller area which after the restoration of the hierarchy in 1850 was known as the See of Hexham of which he was the first bishop; the name was altered to Hexham & Newcastle in 1861.

Bishop Hogarth, of old Catholic farming stock, was born at Dodding Green, near Kendal, Westmorland. Along with his elder brother Robert he entered Crook Hall (the precursor of Ushaw) in 1796 to train for the priesthood. With the opening of Ushaw College he moved there and after ordination in 1809 remained as a professor and administrator until 1816 when he went as missioner to Cliffe Hall (vicars apostolic had resided here for a time, too), near Piercebridge, where he remained as chaplain to the Witham family until his move to Darlington in 1824.

Here he built the church of St. Augustine and later the extensions of 1865. Throughout his ministry, as priest and bishop, he continued to live in his house in Darlington which still stands to-day to the right of the entrance gate leading to the church.

His successor was Bishop James Chadwick who was born at Drogheda, in Ireland, studied at Ushaw and after teaching there for a period went on to do diocesan mission work for seven years returning there until raised to the episcopate in 1866. He was consecrated at Ushaw by Archbishop Manning (later cardinal) and resided at 11, Elswick Villas, Newcastle, and also in Rye Hill; he returned in 1877 to Ushaw as president for a year. He died in Newcastle in 1882.

He was followed by John William Bewick who was born at Minsteracres in the year 1824. Appointed vicar-general in 1868 he moved the following year to Tynemouth from North Shields to found the parish of Our Lady and St. Oswin. His residence was initially 48, Front Street, which he named 'Martyr's Peace'. After consecration as bishop of the diocese he continued to live here until his death in 1886 having been bishop for four years; he lies buried in Ashburton Cemetery, Gosforth. Altogether five bishops resided at one time or another at Tynemouth.

After a vacancy of 14 months the Vatican appointed Henry O'Callaghan in 1888 as bishop of our diocese. He was a friend of Cardinal Manning and a member of the Oblates of St. Charles as well as being rector of the Venerabile (The English College) in Rome for 21 years. Ill-health forced his resignation after six months. 'He had lived so long in Italy that the change of climate and the new way of life proved altogether too much for him.' Father Milburn remarks of him in his *History of Ushaw College*: 'The grey skies and his scrupulosity had so worn him down that he pleaded either a release from or assistance with his burden.' Perhaps Tynemouth's proximity to the cold North Sea was too great a contrast to the warmer weather of Italy.

Canon Thomas Wilkinson, a convert from Anglicanism, was at this time vicar-general; he was consecrated auxiliary bishop in May 1888, and became the fifth bishop of our diocese in 1889. The Wilkinson home was at Harperley Hall in County Durham and he was educated at Harrow and Durham University. His ability as an administrator set Ushaw College on a firm financial foundation. He was president of the college for almost 20 years as well as bishop of the diocese until his death in 1909. In his later years he was assisted by an auxiliary bishop, Richard Preston, who lived in Tynemouth, but he pre-deceased Bishop Wilkinson dying at the age of 49.

Richard Collins, who became the auxiliary bishop after Bishop Preston, succeeded Bishop Wilkinson and lived in Newcastle at the cathedral until he died in 1924: the same year that our present diocesan boundaries were defined by an Apostolic Constitution when the two counties of Cumberland and Westmorland were ceded to the Diocese of Lancaster.

When Bishop Joseph Thorman administered the Diocese from 1925 until 1936 he dwelt in Tynemouth as did Bishop Joseph McCormack (1937-58) until 1941 when he moved to Sandyford House, Newcastle. In 1943 he went to live at East Denton Hall, West Road, which has been the residence of our bishops ever since. Here Bishop Ambrose lives as did his two predecessors Bishop Hugh Lindsay (1974-1992) and Bishop James Cunningham (1958-1974). Bishop Owen Swindlehurst, our auxiliary bishop, resides at Oaklea, in Sunderland. He was born at Newburn, a few miles from Denton, educated at Ushaw, ordained priest in 1954 and consecrated auxiliary bishop in 1977.

East Denton Hall, Bishop's House, has a long and varied history. The present structure is said to date from 1622 when the owner, Anthony Errington, had it built in the Jacobean style. From a Christian perspective it would seem that the site had a much earlier occupation. Some of the land in the Denton area was once owned by the nunnery of St. Bartholomew in Newcastle. The Benedictine monastery of Tynemouth is also said to have owned the manor of Denton as early as 1380 and it is also claimed a pre-Reformation chapel once stood in the grounds.

An interesting thought - that some of our earlier bishops lived near the Tynemouth Priory and now we have a Benedictine bishop living at Denton.

Bishop's House has links too with recusant days. Various branches of the old Northumbrian family of Erringtons lived in different locations in the county. The Denton line appear to have established themselves here in the early 16th century. John Errington, a son of Lancelot Errington of Denton, was arrested in 1580 and questioned concerning a journey he had made to France. Part of the document regarding his interrogation still survives:

'An exa. taken of John Errington sonne to Lancelot Errington dwellyng at Denton within thre myles of Newcastell.'

'Being asked where he dyd embarke he saythe he tooke shipping at the Shells (Shields) in a frenche shipp bownde for Deape (Dieppe)...he admitted to have known "the seyd Errington not long"'.

This brief reference to the 'seyd Errington' is interesting because it possibly refers to the well-known recusant the Venerable George Errington, of Hirst, near Ashington who devoted his life to aiding students and priests to pass to and from the continental colleges, such as Douai, where these young men could receive a Catholic education and train for the priesthood.

A Mrs Ursula Taylor of South Shields was well-known for the risks she took in supporting Errington in his work. From here he would convey secretly the missionary priests to the homes of Catholics, who would harbour them, and assist them to sustain the faith of those around them. Probably John Errington had accompanied George on one of his voyages hence his interrogation by the state. George was eventually captured and put to death at York in 1596.

The ground floor of East Denton Hall originally had a large reception hall. When it became the residence of our bishops it was sub-divided to create a small intimate chapel where the Blessed Sacrament is reserved. To the right of the hall are the domestic quarters where three Sisters of Mercy - Sister Immaculata, Sister Vianney and Sister Fintan - together attend to the household and domestic duties.

On the first floor is the Bishop's office and the offices of his two secretaries and information officers: Father John Foley and Mrs Patricia Campbell.

Bishop Ambrose Griffiths, O.S.B. was born in Twickenham. His early education was at preparatory schools in Seaford and Gilling, the latter being the prep. school for Ampleforth to which he later proceeded. After completing his secondary education he went to Oxford University where he graduated in chemistry in 1950. After graduation he became a novice at Ampleforth and was professed in 1954. He continued with further studies at San Anselmo College in Rome and was ordained priest in 1957. He taught chemistry, R.E. and woodwork at Ampleforth College and Canon Law and Theology to the novices. He was appointed procurator in 1971 until he was elected abbot in 1976 succeeding Cardinal Hume who moved from Ampleforth to become Archbishop of Westminster. When his term as abbot ended in 1984 he became parish priest at St. Mary's, Leyland, in Lancashire, until he was appointed Bishop of Hexham and Newcastle in 1992.

43. NEWCASTLE   The Shrine of Our Lady (Jesmond)   *(June, 1987)*

'They came from their farms and homesteads and after spending the night at the Pilgrim's Inn in Pilgrim Street, on the following morning they attended Holy Mass and then assembled in Carliol Square, where they took their positions for the procession to the shrine - the young girls in white dresses, the clergy and religious in their habits, the soldiers, the parishes in groups carrying crosses, the various guilds and then any other pilgrims who had come along. Once outside the City gates the procession would cross the Barras Bridge, keeping well away from the leper colony on their left and go along by Sandyford and so to Jesmond Village and the shrine'.

The above extract is an imaginative account of a medieval pilgrimage to Jesmond from the late Father Daniel Costar's C.T.S. pamphlet entitled: *The Shrine of Our Lady of Jesmond.*

It would seem an appropriate occasion to look at our ancestors' devotion to Mary in our diocese at the beginning of a Marian Year inaugurated by Pope John Paul II on Pentecost Sunday, June 7th, 1987. The Rosary Rally held at Gosforth Park in late May was 'part of the preparation for the Marian Year', which has helped to put before the minds of all the important role of Our Lady in the Church.

Cardinal Dadaglio, Head of the Vatican Committee for the Marian Year said recently that such a celebration would promote, 'an understanding of the presence of the Blessed Virgin Mary and of her mission in the saving mystery of Christ and the Church'.

England was once known as the 'Dowry of Mary'; the many shrines in her honour were spread across the land to which the faithful journeyed over the centuries to show their devotion to the Mother of God.

Although Walsingham can claim to be the oldest Marian shrine in England, Our Lady's shrine at Jesmond is, also, steeped in antiquity. Pilgrim Street in Newcastle provides a clue to the popularity of the shrine in pre-Reformation days. Historians have disputed the origin of the name, some suggesting that it was so-called because of the pilgrims who came to the city to see the relics in the Franciscan Friary nearby. However, as there is architectural evidence that St. Mary's chapel in Jesmond was built before 1125 - long before the Franciscan order was founded - it may be that the Marian pilgrims gave the street its name; if not, it is generally agreed that they lodged in Pilgrim Street and set forth from there to the Jesmond shrine.

It was once thought that the word Jesmond was derived from 'Jesus Mount', possibly because of the shrine's location; however - so etymologists tell us - it has the more mundane meaning of 'the mouth of the Ouseburn', a tributary of the Tyne.

No less a person than Pope Martin V, in his papal rescript of 1428, provides us with written evidence of the importance of the shrine whereby he granted a partial indulgence on major feast days to pilgrims who having confessed their sins visited St. Mary's chapel and gave help for its repair and preservation:

'Martin ... to all the faithful who shall see this letter, health ... Since, therefore, as we have learned, the buildings and structure of the chapel of the Blessed Mary of Jesmond in the Diocese of Durham are in very ruinous condition to which out of remarkable devotion a great many of the Faithful are wont to congregate, on account of the various miracles the Most High has deigned to work there at the behest of the glorious Virgin and since the alms of the same Faithful will, it is evident, be in no small measure opportune for its repair and preservation, being desirous that the buildings and structure of this chapel be repaired and also preserved and that the Faithful should gather there the more gladly out of devotion ... ' This document is preserved in the Vatican archives.

Another piece of written evidence proving the antiquity of Mary's shrine at Jesmond is shown in the will of William Ecopp, parish priest of Heslarton in Yorkshire who wrote in 1472: 'Likewise I wish that a pilgrim or pilgrims set out immediately after my burial to one of the below mentioned Holy Places, viz ... St. Thomas of Canterbury, Blessed Mary of Walsingham ... Blessed Mary of Scarborough ... Blessed Mary of Gysborough ... Blessed Mary of Jesmownt, Blessed Mary of Carlisle ... and that the pilgrim or pilgrims offer at each of these Holy Places, 4d.' The above list does not include all the shrines he mentions.

St. Mary's chapel 'owes its erection to the piety of the Grenvilles who were at that time Lords of Jesmond'. The earliest structure - with Norman masonry still visible in the chancel arch - was probably built in the first quarter of the 12th century. Later alterations and extensions, including a chantry chapel, are still evident; three piscinas can be seen clearly set in the walls one of which, we noticed, held some flowers put there it would seem by some recent 20th century pilgrim. Little of the nave remains and it would be difficult, without excavation, to ascertain its length.

Near the chapel stood St. Mary's Well on the headstone of which could be seen - according to Father Costar, writing in 1959 - the carved letters, GRATIA. It has been suggested that the original inscription contained the angel's greeting to Mary - AVE GRATIA PLENA. Few pilgrims return from Lourdes without their Lourdes water and the water from St. Mary's Well seems to have been treasured too. Father Thaddeus O.S.F. records in his book, *Pilgrims May - Wreath,* the case of a young child from Manchester in May, 1878, 'who was after a protracted illness, almost given up by the doctors and medicine was of no avail. A few drops of water from the holy well of Our Lady of Jesmownt were given to the child; from that very moment a striking improvement was noticed, and in a short time the disease had entirely disappeared'. Father Thaddeus, of course, in his Foreword cautions, 'that the wonderful occurrences here recorded (throughout his book) and not recognised as miracles by ecclesiastical authority, are merely related as historical facts.'

It would be misleading to suggest that since its foundation the Jesmond shrine of Our Lady has had undiminished attention from pilgrims; there were periods when its popularity, for various reasons, waxed and waned.

During the reign of Edward VI, like many other shrines at the Reformation, it was suppressed (in 1548) and was sold for £144.13.4 to the Mayor and Burgesses of Newcastle who the same year sold it to John Brandling whose son, Sir Robert, dismantled part of the chapel buildings. Today it is maintained and cared for by the City of Newcastle who became the owners in 1883 when it was presented to the Mayor and Corporation by the then owner, Lord Armstrong.

To follow the pilgrim route today would be rather difficult: it began in Pilgrim Street crossing Barras Bridge, along part of Sandyford Road, continuing west of the old Jesmond Station, across Jesmond Road into what is now Fernwood Road, then left of the cricket ground turning right into Osborne Avenue and back onto Jesmond Road to the left turn before the Armstrong Bridge which brings one into the road leading to the shrine which can be visited at any time (parking is a problem). F.W. Dendy writing in 1904 made a plea for its preservation: 'weary pilgrims have travelled long distances to lay their offerings on its altar. Many generations of men have knelt and prayed within its narrow walls. This silent witness of all the changes we have chronicled is still worth preserving ... .' That request has been met for many years by the Newcastle City Council who have played their part in preserving a building older than the Newcastle Keep.

A revival of interest in the shrine occurred in the Marian Year of 1954 when many people from the diocese visited St. Mary's Chapel. Father Costar relates: 'The Diocesan Catholic Scouters and Guiders Guild have been the strongest and largest of these groups, coming each year in October'. The *Northern Cross*, too, assisted in the revival: 'April 29th, 1956, was a great day in the history of Jesmond because by permission of His Lordship, the Bishop of Hexham and Newcastle, the diocesan newspaper, The *Northern Cross*, issued an invitation to the people of Northumberland and Durham to visit Our Lady's Shrine at Jesmond. Some four thousand pilgrims came and gave back gloriously to Mary this ancient shrine of hers for at least one hour'.

We hope this article may engender further interest in this shrine of Our Lady during the Marian Year which has just started.

44. NEWCASTLE (North Gosforth)   The Sacred Heart   *(February, March 1987)*

Although no longer part of the Gosforth Park Estate, the imposing stone church of the Sacred Heart stands within the old boundary wall which runs alongside the eastern edge of the Great North Road. Most parishes date their foundations from the time when the Bishop formally appoints the parish priest who then, with the help of parishioners, raises funds and eventually builds a church for worship. Unusually, this North Gosforth parish had its church before the appointment of its first parish priest - being originally an Anglican church purchased by Bishop Collins in the early years of this century.

It would be difficult to find a Catholic church today in the diocese which cannot claim some link in its neighbourhood with a pre-Reformation foundation. The Sacred Heart church is no exception as various sources mention the chapel of St. Mary in the grounds of Low Gosforth; one of these sources is Mr. John Bell, a librarian, who in a letter to John Adamson Esq. in 1826 said he had surveyed the site and made some observations. It is recorded as being 67 feet long and 23 feet wide and may have been destroyed by fire (cause unknown) probably in the late 17th century. It is likely that it existed before the religious changes of the 16th century and therefore would have had Mass celebrated there and the sacraments administered to our ancestors in the Catholic Faith.

The Brandling family - some of whom remained Catholic - had held lands in the Newcastle area since about 1509 when the manors of North Gosforth and Felling passed to Sir Robert Brandling on marrying Ann Place who was related to the well-known Surtees family of Durham County; the Felling residence of the Brandlings, according to one source, is now the Mulberry Tree Inn near Felling railway station. One of his descendants, a Charles Brandling erected Gosforth House in 1760 from a design of Payne.

Associated with the Brandling family is the Felling Mass Vestment now in Stonyhurst College and believed to be of 15th century origin. This chasuble was, no doubt, used for many years in the Brandling's family residence in Felling. The first Catholic member of the family to live there after the Reformation appears to have been Ralph Brandling. A Mrs Brandling was recorded as a papist there in 1767 as was her son Charles living at Gosforth. When she died in 1776 Mass was no longer said at Felling. Henry Charles Brandling, who became a Catholic, was born at Low Gosforth House in 1823 and was the father of nine children. The vestment was passed on to him by 'S.C.' - as yet unidentified - but who may have been a member of the Caley family descended from the Dunn family.

In the year 1852 Gosforth House and estate were put up for auction and acquired by Mr Thomas Smith - a shipbuilder and ship repairer on the Tyne - for £25,100. One of the friends of Mr Smith was the famous artist, Edward Burne-Jones, who, it is said, suggested a church should be built on the estate to his design; the church of St. Mary was duly built and opened in 1865 providing a place of worship for the servants and estate workers of the Smith family. Designed in the Gothic style the building boasts a priceless stained-glass window - depicting the crucifixion and designed by Burne-Jones - on the rear wall of the sanctuary and below it the richly decorated pipe organ which previously was situated in the present Blessed Sacrament chapel; both were made by craftsmen in Paris.

With the retirement of the Smith family from the Dry Dock business and their move to London the Hall and land were bought by the High Gosforth Park Company, in 1880, becoming what it is today, the famous race course.

No longer needed as a place of worship the church fell into disuse and its ivy-covered walls echoed no more to the music of Matins and Evensong. Anxious to dispose of this fine but redundant building, the last surviving member of the previous owners, a Miss Smith, acting on the advice of her solicitors, journeyed North to see what could be done. Various denominations, including the Baptists and the Jewish community, were approached but none accepted. It was suggested to Miss Smith that she should approach the Bishop of Hexham and Newcastle which she did and the offer was promptly accepted by Bishop Collins who wrote out a cheque for £3,000. However, according to the *Northern Catholic Calendar of 1912*, there were long drawn out negotiations before the transaction was completed.

If the bishop did accept the offer so promptly, a traditional story circulating in the parish - but difficult to verify - may explain why he accepted without hesitation. Residing in the built-up area of Newcastle, Bishop Collins, a lover of the countryside, journeyed regularly by tram to North Gosforth and on alighting made his way to a nearby cottage where the occupier kindly allowed him to keep his bicycle. As he rode around the country lanes he was bound to notice the prominent tower of the deserted Anglican church visible through the trees. He is said to have visited 'the church in the Park' (a name it is commonly known by) placing a Sacred Heart badge behind one of the pillars and praying that one day the church would be purchased by the diocese for the use of the Catholics in North Gosforth, Dinnington, Seaton Burn, Brunton and Hazelrigg. His prayers were answered in 1912 when he had the privilege of performing the solemn opening; the sermon was preached by Canon Smith and the music was provided by the choir of St. Dominic's.

Since its foundation the Sacred Heart parish has had five parish priests: Father Hart (Senior), Father Bede Tuohy, Father James Phelan, Father Edward Ord and Father Tom Cass, the present parish priest. Father Ord and Father Phelan had been young curates together in 1932 at St. Joseph's in Sunderland. Their friendship was renewed during the Second World War when Father Ord, who was senior army chaplain with Northern Command based at York, visited occasionally Father Phelan who had been appointed officiating chaplain to the troops stationed at Sandy Lane Camp. It was to his church that the Catholic soldiers came to hear Mass.

Father Ord, after his retirement from the army, was appointed parish priest of North Gosforth in 1963 succeeding Father Phelan; he was to remain there for 20 years. During that period he was responsible for the building of the Sacred Heart Primary School at Brunswick Green, Wideopen, and the building of the new presbytery (1979) in the church grounds. The old presbytery, some distance away in Woodlands Park, is now a diocesan house occupied by a retired priest, Father Henry Higgins.

It was the responsibility of Father Tom Cass, shortly after his arrival, to initiate the re-ordering of this fine church so that it might conform to the requirements of the changed liturgy. The original deep chancel (sanctuary) area has been extended into the nave of the church allowing a new altar, ambo and presidential chair to be sited much nearer the congregation. The old Paris organ has been renovated and placed at the rear of the sanctuary beneath the valuable Burne-Jones stained-glass window. This has allowed the space vacated by the organ to become a small but impressive Blessed Sacrament chapel. The old stone altar rails have been refashioned and used as supports for the seating around the walls of the chapel.

The large vacant area at the rear of the church, below the tower, has been well-utilised incorporating a gallery above and a day chapel below with adjacent reconciliation room. Sliding glass screens enable the day chapel to be separated from the main body of the church creating a more intimate atmosphere for weekday Mass and small group services - as well as keeping down fuel costs. For major church occasions, such as Sunday Mass, the doors can be opened allowing the day chapel area to become part of the main body of the church. In the west wall of the tower two beautiful modern stained glass windows - one in the gallery above in traditional style and a striking modern representation of the risen Christ in the day chapel below - further enhance the tasteful blending of the old with the new. 'The whole effect especially in the evening light, is very powerful and the image of the risen Christ in the day chapel has created an extremely prayerful atmosphere' (J. Shepherd).

The architect responsible for the recent alterations at the Sacred Heart Church is Mr Ralph Pattison of Newcastle. His artist wife, Vicky, designed the modern day chapel window of Christ's resurrection using a type of glass called 'dalle de ver' set into 21 concrete panels made by the architect himself and placed in a new stone west window erected by the Grady brothers of M. Grady (Newcastle) Limited; the design and construction blend beautifully into the old building.

After 15 months of waiting and worshipping in the wooden hall at the rear of the presbytery, Father Cass and his parishioners were able, once again, to use their much admired church when Bishop Hugh Lindsay performed the re-dedication ceremony and concelebrated Mass with fifty priests on June 6th, 1986, in the presence of ministers of other denominations. On this occasion the church could not hold all those who wished to attend, so an overflow congregation of 150 people had the service relayed to them in the church hall. A reception followed in the hall and an adjacent marquee.

Parish activities are many and varied and reflect the commitment of many of the parishioners. The S.V.P. conference (founded 1931) has continued its charitable role fulfilling the request of the Society's founder, Frederic Ozanam - to assist all those who are in need. It is a mixed conference of 15 members who, in addition to their normal parish work, assist with the S.V.P. soup run on Newcastle quayside and are part of the 'wheelchair rota' at the Royal Victoria Infirmary which enables patients to attend the Sunday Mass there. A number of Sacred Heart parishioners are, also, members of the St. Nicholas S.V.P. Hospital Conference; this is a special S.V.P. work concentrating on the visitation of the sick in hospital.

A Youth Group of 20 members meets every Tuesday evening for recreation in the parish hall; part of the meeting is used for scripture reading and discussion and concludes with a visit to the church for prayer. The R.C.I.A. course, every Thursday evening, attracts about 40 people.

Thirty lay ministers of the Eucharist have been commissioned for the parish. Each Sunday after the 10.00 a.m. Mass they take communion to the sick and housebound. With their help it is possible at each Sunday and weekday Mass to have communion under both kinds and every sick person, if they so wish, may avail themselves of the opportunity of daily communion at home.

After evening Mass each Wednesday the lay ministers of the Eucharist, readers and anyone else interested meet for Eucharistic Devotions in the day chapel. Here the Blessed Sacrament is exposed and scripture is read with the emphasis on the readings of the forthcoming Sunday. A parish council of twelve members assists Father Cass in the organising of the parish's spiritual and social activities.

Father Tom Cass was in 1986 the chairman of the Local Council of Churches - a fitting response from the parish priest of a Catholic church which was once in Anglican ownership. Church Unity week is entered into fully, as is the Lenten ecumenical programme. A quarterly service is also supported when it is held in the various denominational churches.

A Justice and Peace Group - common in many parishes today - thrives here too, reminding all of the needs of our neighbours at home and abroad. Their prayer and deliberations are centred round the Eucharist when every Friday evening they meet before the Blessed Sacrament exposed.

Bishop Collins' fortuitous acquisition of the former Anglican church, in the early years of this century, provided the Catholics of the North Gosforth area with an outstanding building in which to celebrate the divine mysteries; and its recent re-ordering has successfully accomplished the changes necessary to continue to do so, in an appropriate setting, in the later years of the 20th century.

45. NORTH SHIELDS   St. Cuthbert   *(April, 1983)*

The new church of St. Cuthbert's in Albion Road West could easily leave the first-time visitor with an impression that here is a modern church in a new parish with little or no roots in history. The opposite, in fact, is true for St. Cuthbert's has a story to tell which is interesting and can, in part, be traced back over the last 200 years.

It would appear that in pre-Reformation days the spiritual needs of the people in this area were catered for by the monks of Tynemouth Priory; and in the penal days, which followed the dissolution of the monasteries, information on the activities of Catholics becomes scarce, but like older parishes, previously mentioned in these articles, Catholic practice appears once more in the open as the severity of the penal laws diminished towards the end of the eighteenth century.

Perhaps, July 15th, 1784, should be recorded as a red-letter day in the annals of North Shields Catholicism, for on that day Fr. James Johnson came over from Pontop Hall and said Mass in a room which had been engaged for the purpose in Milburn Place. He was able to do this once a month and early in the 19th century Fr. P. Wilcox from Sunderland is recorded as helping out occasionally.

The French Revolution of 1789 had far-reaching effects not only in France but throughout Europe. Many Catholics fled abroad when the Faith was persecuted and some sought refuge in England. Among these refugees were the student priests of the English College at Douai, in Flanders, some of whom settled at Pontop Hall then Crook Hall and lastly Ushaw College. It is believed that 8,000 French priests, nuns and laymen came to England and of these 295 landed at North Shields on October 5th, 1793. Many of them were later to return to their native land; three, however, died here and were buried in Tynemouth Cemetery; whilst two priests, the Rev. M Duboisson and the Rev. A Danneville ministered for a time in the area using a converted chapel in Norfolk Street.

Father James Worswick's name will be familiar to many north-east Catholics for the sterling work he did in Newcastle and surrounding districts; so much was he held in esteem by Catholic and non-Catholic alike that the town authorities honoured him by naming the street after him where St. Andrew's Church now stands. Like many more seminarians of that generation he escaped from the persecution in Flanders, came to England, and was ordained at York in 1795. An extract from his obituary in *The Tablet (1843)* describes the heroic qualities of the man.

'Regardless of his own personal safety he not only visited continuously the wretched abodes of disease in all parts of the town (Newcastle), but the workhouse, the prison, and above all the fever wards in the infirmary ... His manifold charities were only bounded by his means, and they were distributed to all in want, without regard to their religious opinions.'

His concern for the Gospel spread beyond the confines of Newcastle and by 1810 he was journeying to North Shields, on horseback, every third Tuesday to say Mass and give the sacraments at a chapel on the corner of Percy Street and Bedford Street. It is to this man that the foundation of the parish and the building of the church are to be credited.

Much of the early history of the parish is recorded in Canon Stark's History published in 1903. He was fortunate that an old lady, Miss Isabella Errington, who had lived in the parish most of her life wrote down an eyewitness account of its growth. She describes the efforts Catholics made to attend Mass before the opening of St. Cuthbert's Church. Travelling by coach to Newcastle was expensive and they found, by experience, that the journey by river invariably made them late: 'Therefore they resolved to follow Mr Pinkney's example and walk to Newcastle and back every Sunday and Holyday. They invited Mr Turpin's family to accompany them every week. After morning service they went over to Gateshead to the house of an old woman who kept a little shop. There was an agreement with her, always to have her room at liberty and to prepare tea for them. After which they returned to Pilgrim Street to Vespers at three o'clock; then after service, commenced their journey homewards, full of joy and gladness ... One particular part of the road was named the 'Prayer Walk', and no conversation was allowed, everyone keeping silence and meditating in that particular space'.

The church was officially opened on June 14th, 1821, by Bishop Thomas Smith, Vicar-Apostolic, the opening sermon being preached by the recently appointed parish priest, Fr. Thomas Gillow, who had been chaplain at Callay Castle in Northumberland and who was to remain at St. Cuthbert's for 36 years. In his sermon - a copy of which is still extant - Fr. Gillow thanked all those who had contributed to the building of the church and he emphasised the apparent good relations which existed with other denominations: 'But above all I wish to express my admiration of those gentlemen of other communions, who, regulating their conduct according to the broad principles of Christian charity and religious liberty, have generously added their names to the subscription, and expressed in the handsomest terms their good wishes for its prosperity and success'. Some of these gentlemen attended regularly the Sunday sermon - preached in those days before Mass - but, usually, left before the Mass began.

Catholics from many villages, north and south of the Tyne, were to use St. Cuthbert's until they had churches of their own. Those crossing the Tyne from South Shields and neighbouring areas found the cost prohibitive; undaunted they formed a committee of management and hired their own boat at a cheaper rate; this meant a considerable saving for those Catholic families who crossed twice a day to attend Mass and Evening Service.

Two other interesting features concerning the parish are worth mentioning: firstly, two past bishops of the Diocese, served in the parish - the Rev. James Chadwick (1853-4) and the Rev. William Bewick (1854-57); and secondly, St. Cuthbert's may claim to have one of the earliest St. Vincent de Paul Conferences in the North East, begun in 1846.

By 1847, 11 members were in the Conference and in 1873 the Brothers were teaching in the Sunday Schools, conducting the Catholic children in the workhouse to Mass on Sundays and attending to the religious instruction of the Catholic boys on board the *Wellesley* training ship.

On reading the parish handbook one is struck by the variety of activities available in the parish and all centring around the parish complex which incorporates the church, hall, presbytery, youth clubroom and two committee rooms - all very functional and modern. This building, opened in 1975, when the late Father Loftus was parish priest, replaces the old church which was in use for over 150 years.

The present parish priest, Fr. Leo Pyle, assisted by Fr. Gordon Ryan and Fr. Dominic McGivern minister to approximately 3,000 parishioners and all three see their role, alongside them, as an exercise in co-responsibility for the mission of the church. As a means of achieving this the elected Parish Council oversees and co-ordinates the various groups within the parish 'by which the congregation organises its part in the activities and responsibilities of the parish to the maximum effort, both in spiritual matters and practical ways'.

And what a variety exists: Action, Worship, and Formation Committees deal with the spiritual aspects, whilst the practical problems of running a parish are dealt with by the Finance, Building, Social and Management committees. Further enquiry would reveal other groups, new and old, such as the S.V.P., Justice and Peace, Bible and Prayer groups, Pro-Life, a Youth Club, Mothers and Toddlers, Guides and Brownies; and a recent innovation is the provision of altar wine by parochial home winemakers.

A further extract from Fr. Gillow's opening sermon of 162 years ago could now, as then, emphasise the importance of a caring parish in everyday life: 'Let us henceforward live in peace with all men, put the best construction upon their words and actions, excuse their failings, forgive all injuries from our hearts, soothe their sorrows, and above all, with kind and tender compassion, succour them in their necessities. Thus, my brethren, shall we promote the honour and glory of God ... '

46. PONTELAND   St. Matthew   *(October, 1984)*

July 16th, 1884, is an important date in the history of St. Matthew's, Ponteland, for on that date the Mass was once again celebrated there after a break of many years. The priest responsible for this was Father W.E. Barron who came fortnightly, by pony and trap from Cheeseburn Grange, to say Mass in a hired room of a house (now demolished) in Merton Way. It is another example showing the growth of the Catholic population in the diocese and, also, the emergence of the Faith into the open - much later than in some areas - from a quiet and secluded existence it had under the patronage of the Catholic gentry of Northumberland: in this case the Widdringtons and Riddells of Cheeseburn Grange, an estate situated five miles west of Ponteland

As in many other missions and parishes in the north east the story of the faith can be traced back to much earlier pre-Reformation times. In 1297 John de Normanville granted Nesbit and Cheeseburn to the prior and convent of Hexham and mention is made as early as 1379 of a chapel at Cheeseburn which probably belonged to the grange of Hexham Priory.

Cheeseburn remained in Catholic hands, as far as we know, throughout the penal days; one of its owners in 1593 was a Mrs Lawson who almost died in a brick oven where she had concealed herself during a house search. The Widdringtons also owned the grange for some years, the last being Ralph Widdrington who left the estate to his nephew, Ralph Riddell, whose father owned Swinburne Castle. By 1871 Cheesesburn Grange was owned by Francis Riddell who had married Ellen Blount of Mapledurham, Oxfordshire. Their son, Edward Francis Riddell, inherited the land and assumed the name of Riddell Blount. Today's owners are Philip Riddell and his sister, Miss Nell Riddell.

We do not know the names of all the priests who served at Cheeseburn; the earliest one who can be traced was there during Ralph Widdrington's occupation. Father Dominic Phillips, a Dominican, who died there in 1783 began the first register. It is likely that until 1820 - when the present chapel of St. Francis Xavier was built - the chapel was a room in the house. Situated on the west side of the Hall is the chapel where Father Vincent Melia, the present parish priest of St. Matthew's, celebrates a Sunday Mass continuing a tradition that has gone on for many, many years.

A stranger visiting the present Catholic church of St. Matthew's in

Ponteland, St. Matthew   *Photo: T. Mackin*

Ponteland may be misled into thinking that here is a modern parish with little history - but this is not so. Nor far away is the Anglican church of St. Mary's with its Norman tower bearing visible witness to the Catholic Faith practised here eight centuries ago. The earliest document relating to Ponteland church concerns the sharing of tithes at Horton Grange between the monks of Newminster (near Morpeth) and the parson of Eland and two other persons. Horton Grange was, apparently, given to the Cistercians of Newminster by the second Baron Mitford who died in 1190 and possibly it was he who ordered the building of the Norman church.

Within the present Anglican church, the *Northumberland County History* for the area tells us of the existence of a grave cover, near the organ, showing the figure of a 13th or 14th century priest in Mass vestments, and a font believed to be of the 14th century. It also mentions the presence of a pre-Reformation bell inscribed with the word, 'Maria'.

Near the famous Blackbird Inn - once a pele tower - stood the home of the Erringtons; Ralph and Nicholas Errington were recorded as still adhering to the Old Faith in the middle of the seventeenth century.

Another interesting centre of Catholicity of bygone years, within the parish of St. Matthew's, is Capheaton Hall - the home of the Swinburnes - now no longer in Catholic hands. It was served by Benedictine priests and one source claims it to have had seven hiding places. Perhaps the most interesting was the one reached by opening a picture on a pivot in the wall at the rear of the altar; this gave access to the timbered roof where it is believed another place of concealment was cunningly contrived alongside a chimney stack. Capheaton ceased to be a Catholic mission on the death of Sir Edward Swinburne in 1786.

By the turn of the century it was deemed necessary to provide a more commodious and purpose-built chapel for the celebration of Mass in Ponteland. This was done in 1906 by Father Henry Walmsley who built a wooden chapel on the present site capable of seating 50 people. This structure continued to be used until the building of a brick chapel and presbytery in 1947 by the then priest-in-charge, Father Leo Doyle. Miss Winnie Smith, who has lived most of her long life in the parish, recalls those post-war years when the new brick chapel was being built. Her family had owned, for many years, land and a large cafe opposite the church. They readily put at the disposal of Father Doyle their premises in which Holy Mass could be celebrated whilst the church was being completed. Their cafe was also used as a parish centre for whist drives and dances, thereby helping to raise funds for the parish. Miss Smith remembers in her younger days cycling from Ponteland to Cheeseburn for Midnight Mass.

Father Doyle's church - believed to be a replica of St. Teresa's at Annfield Plain - has been considerably enlarged recently since the arrival of the present parish priest, Father Vincent Melia. The original brick church is now the sanctuary reordered to meet the new liturgical requirements; the newly extended, well-lit, comfortable nave, capable of seating 260 people, was built by Cummins of Sunderland at a cost of £67,000. A new altar and lectern of Nebrascina marble were made by Brian Morris and designed by Kevin Thompson, both parishioners of St. Matthew's.

There is much happening in the parish: the Legion of Mary, the S.V.P., the C.W.L., a Ladies' Tea Club, the Y.C.W., a Mother and Toddler group, a prayer group and a choir provide plenty of opportunities for the people to participate in the life of the church. For the young, a Youth Club meets weekly in the parish centre at the rear of the church and in August the parish acted as hosts to 17 young people from various parts of the country who were attending a Zion week at St. Dominic's.

Ponteland and its surroundings have changed much in the 20th century - Newcastle Airport within the parish is a frequent reminder of this - but the faith of our ancestors continues in these parts, a celebration of which occurred on September 21st, the Feast of St. Matthew, when Bishop Lindsay, along with Father Melia and other priests, joined the parishioners in a Mass and a social gathering reminding those present of the purpose of the Faith and its practice.

47. SEAHAM HARBOUR   St. Mary Magdalen   *(April, May 1987)*

Within sight and sound of the sea, overlooking one of the many denes which intersect the Durham coastline, stands the ancient church of Seaham St. Mary - a good place to begin searching for the early Christian roots in this area, five miles south of Sunderland.

Pevsner describes it as 'one of the most worthwhile of the small churches in the county' because of the various styles that exist in its structure. The masonry of the nave is either Late Saxon or Early Norman indicating that the Mass was celebrated here and the Sacraments administered 900 years ago; and possibly even earlier if the present church was built on the site of an earlier Saxon foundation. The chancel and tower are Early English in style whilst in the south wall are two Perpendicular style windows near to the porch which is of the late 16th century.

A font, of probably the late Norman period, can still be seen evoking memories of the ceremony of Baptism which through the ages brought the young and older catechumens into the Seaham Christian community. Still, also, to be seen is the double piscina, with carved hand raised in blessing, where the sacred vessels were once cleansed. Fordyce in his *History and Antiquities of the County Palatine of Durham* mentions a stone coffin in the churchyard with the inscription: 'Hic Jacet Richardus ... Seahaiam,' supposedly the tomb of Richard de Overton who was rector there in the late 13th century.

Amongst a list of vicars of St. Mary's is a Thomas Wright who died in 1575; he may be the same person who during this period of religious transition 'acknowledged that he says Matins to Our Lady everyday, privately, in his room.' It would appear from such a statement that the religious changes of the 16th century may not have met with his approval.

Not far away from the present Catholic church of St. Mary Magdalen's is yet another fine old church - St. Andrew's in Dalton-le-Dale - which, also, can claim to have roots in pre-Reformation times. The Norman doorway reveals its antiquity, although the existing church building is mainly of the early 13th century. Perhaps unique is the sun-dial with the Roman numerals I to VII carved on the north wall which registered an approximate time when the sun shone on them through a window opposite. Resting within the church are two stone effigies which may be those of Sir William Bowes and his wife Matilda of Dalton

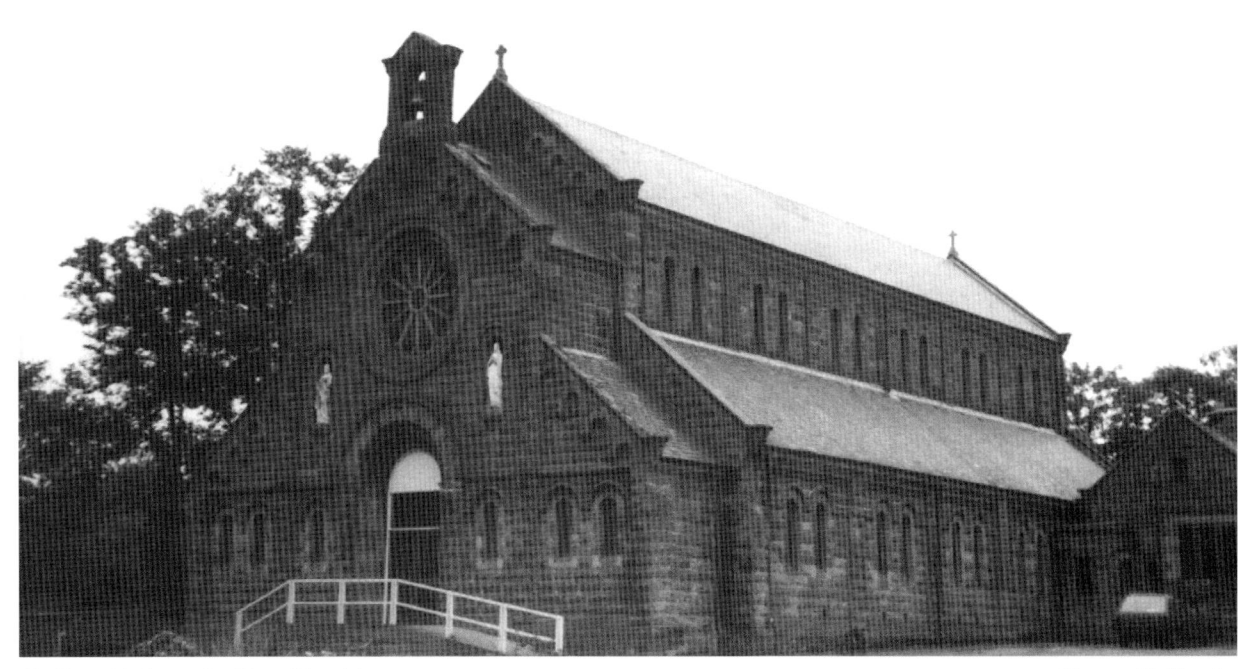

Seaham Harbour, St. Mary Magdalen   *Photo: M. Morris*

(Dalden) Tower, the ruins of which may be seen in the dene on the road east from St. Andrew's.

Very little remains of this once border fortress with square keep tower and walled enclosure for the protection of cattle. The Escolland family held Dalton (Dalden) Tower soon after the Norman Conquest and in 1325 Sir Jordan de Dalden was licensed to establish a chapel or oratory there. Later, through marriage, the manor was to pass to the Bowes family - ancestors of our present Queen Mother - and became their favourite seat for a considerable number of years.

Little, so far, is known about the immediate post-Reformation years and how those who wished to remain faithful to the ancient Faith fared. Some did persist, however, for in a list of papists for the year 1642, two are recorded at Seaham, three at Seaton and ten at Dalton-le-Dale.

In the latter place the following names occur: George Collingwood, William Wytham Collingwood, Robert Horsley, Adam Robinson, George (the schoolmaster), and Thomas and John Collingwood. The Collingwoods appear to have followed the Bowes as occupants of Dalden Tower and by the mid-17th century this may have been the only Mass centre between Sunderland and Hardwick Hall, near Castle Eden.

Industrial development, particularly in the coal trade, was to transform the face of Durham County in the 19th century and no more so than in this area of East Durham where a new town began to grow around the harbour at Seaham in 1828; this man-made harbour was the creation of the Londonderry family purposely built to facilitate the shipment of coal from their pits in the Rainton district.

Within this expanding 19th century town, situated about half a mile south from the old village of Seaham, a new community gathered including a considerable number of Catholics, many of whom were of Irish origin.

Their spiritual needs had to be met, but how? - since similar demands were arising elsewhere in the North East. A parish bazaar handbook of 1934 records that Mass was probably first said in Seaham Harbour in 1835 when a travelling priest (name unknown) celebrated the Holy Sacrifice in the presence of 30 Catholics on a simple kitchen table in a private house in John Street. A relic of such an important occasion is preserved in St. Mary Magdalen's today; part of this table forms the top of the pedestal on which rests the statue of St. Teresa.

No resident priest was yet available so in order to fulfil their Sunday obligation Seaham Catholics had to walk to St. Mary's in Sunderland, although by 1855 when the Londonderry private railway, between Sunderland and Seaham, was carrying passenger traffic the journey would, no doubt, have been less arduous.

By 1856 the priests of St. Mary's - Fathers Bamber, Kirsopp, Wrennall and others - regularly celebrated Mass in a loft behind the Lord Seaham Hotel in North Terrace and later in the house of a Mrs Ford at 9, William Street.

Seaham Harbour's first parish priest was the Rev. Robert Belaney, a Scotsman of wealthy parents who had studied at Edinburgh and Cambridge. Before his conversion to Catholicism in 1852 he had been a curate in Northumberland and later the vicar of a Sussex parish. His life and works were in many ways remarkable; he is said to have introduced the Jesuits to Glasgow and the Servites to London. His wealth he donated to the church - to one chapel alone he gave £1,000 - eventually dying impoverished in 1899 at the age of 95, reputedly the oldest priest, at that time, in England.

His stay in Seaham lasted about two years but during his short incumbency he endeavoured to obtain land for the building of a church and school. As much of the land in the district belonged to the Londonderrys he wrote in 1860 to the Dowager Marchioness of Londonderry. After dismissing his request he wrote again: 'I can hardly imagine your Ladyship to be aware of the misery and inconvenience which these persons - a large proportion of whom have been your Ladyship's faithful though poor workmen for many years - are at this time enduring from want of a proper place for Divine Worship and a school for their children ... But without a Church, and without a School, my aim, be it ever so good, can avail nothing ... '

In his letter when speaking of the good effect the Catholic Faith would have in raising moral standards in Seaham he appears to have upset her Ladyship by inferring that things were not as they should be in this town created by her family's munificence and patronage.

Father Belaney continued in his letter to support in his congregation 'the poor Irish brought over and settled ... by your Ladyship' and in a subtle plea remarked that they would not be 'better workmen if they became worse Catholics'.

Too long to relate here the complex details of what followed. Suffice to say that Lady Londonderry did promise, 'that when the Roman Catholic population shall have reached such a figure as will render it necessary, I shall be ready to grant a site for a church for 99 years on the same terms I grant leases to other denominations.' It is of interest that her daughter-in-law, Lady Elizabeth, wife of the Fourth Marquis, converted to the Catholic Faith in 1855. Earl Vane inherited the estate on the death of his mother, Lady Londonderry, in 1865 and it was he who granted the land in Londonderry Road for the building of a Catholic church in Seaham, the foundation stone being laid by Bishop Chadwick on July 22nd, 1869. A year later it was opened and could accommodate a congregation of 500. School and presbytery were erected by 1870 when Father Michael Greene was parish priest; the extended school building off Vane Terrace was opened in 1877, in Father J. C. Fawell's time.

The premier Catholic earl, the Duke of Norfolk, is said, also to have played a part in procuring a church site for the Catholics of Seaham Harbour. Whilst staying with the Londonderrys at Seaham Hall he visited the loft chapel in order to attend Mass and enquired why they had no proper church. He promised to use his influence to persuade the Londonderry family to grant the land the Catholics needed on which to build a church to hold the expanding congregation.

At the beginning of this century the Sisters of Mercy in Sunderland were able to extend their pastoral and educational mission further afield; and in 1904 they established themselves in Seaham at the invitation of Canon J. J. Hayes who seven years earlier had invited them to work in Ryhope.

The pioneering sisters in Seaham were Mother Magdalene English, Sister Mary Gonzaga Ryan and Sister Monica Flynn. Three years after the arrival of the nuns, in 1907, Canon Hayes had built the present fine church which now stands in Harbour Walk. This allowed the original site to be used exclusively for a convent and school.

Built in the Romanesque style, St. Mary Magdalen's is similar in construction and design to St. Joseph's, Millfield, Sunderland. Both parish priests, at the time, are said to have played their part in suggesting to their architect - a Mr Thomas Axman of Ryhope, engineer - the design they desired. The two churches are almost identical and the innovatory use of concrete blocks, cast on the site, instead of natural stone is supposed to have cut the cost by one-third. The foundation stone was laid by Bishop Collins in August, 1906, and the church was opened on September 19th, 1907, a month before the opening of Sunderland St. Joseph's - each church is estimated to have cost around £3,000.

Canon Hayes foreseeing the needs of an expanding parish, particularly in the western area, was also responsible for the building of an infant and junior school in New Seaham in 1911. His successor in 1914 was Father M. J. Haggarty who in 1929 was to purchase Park House, the manor house of the Brough family, from which chapel-of-ease developed the new parish of St. Cuthbert's, New Seaham, in 1934 with the appointment of Father John Gits as parish priest. A source at the time records: 'It is the nearest Mass House to Warden Law, a place recorded in the life of St. Cuthbert. The chapel is dedicated to that saint. It consists of a well-built mansion and close on an acre of land, surrounded by trees, a vinery and a shrine and statue of the Sacred Heart of Jesus'.

Much expansion and development had occurred between the years 1900 and 1935. Two bazaar brochures of 1927 and 1934, still extant in the parish, tell us something of the efforts made by priests and people to meet the increasing financial burden this expansion had caused. The brochure of 1927 states specifically that the Grand Bazaar of October, 1927, was to be held to reduce the debt of over £3,000 still outstanding on the new St. Joseph's School opened in February, 1926, at a cost to the parish of £7,815. The opening of the new school, in charge of a lay head, eased the accommodation problem in the original school by allowing the older boys and girls to move to the new site west of the railway crossing, thus leaving the old school accommodation for use as an infant and junior school still in the care of the Sisters of Mercy.

St. Joseph's continued as a Senior school - the last secondary head being Mr Gerald Cunningham assisted by his deputy, Mr Kevin Finn - until 1969 when with the coming of comprehensive education the children were transferred to St. Bede's at Peterlee. The building continued in use as a primary school until 1984 when the fairly modern Dene House Road Primary School was purchased from Durham County L.E.A. during the headship of Mr W. Hudson; his successor, of the re-named St. Mary Magdalen's Primary School, is Mr John Abbott.

Magdalen Court, a sheltered housing scheme, today occupies the site where once stood Seaham's first post-Reformation Catholic church, school and convent. From the latter the Sisters of Mercy moved when they acquired a new convent in Antrim Gardens remaining there until 1983 when it became the Diocesan Youth Centre under the care of its director, Father David Taylor, where much good pastoral work is being done for the youth who come here on residential courses from all parts of the diocese. The nuns' presence has not, however, gone entirely from this area as Sister Benedict, resident at Ryhope Convent, continues the great work of the Mercy Order as part-time parish sister preparing children and adults for the reception of the sacraments and visiting the homes of parishioners.

Many older parishioners will remember well Canon Avery who spent more than 25 years as parish priest here. Before he moved to Longhorsley in 1971 he commenced the alterations to the sanctuary to meet the requirements of the changed liturgy. This work was completed by his successor, Father Desmond Meagher, who remained here for ten years before moving to the Holy Rosary parish at Peterlee. Included in his many activities was the good work - with others - encouraging and publicising the Marriage Encounter Movement which supports and strengthens marriage and the family.

Father Meagher and the present parish priest, Father George Carey - who came in 1981 - were assisted between the years 1979 to 1986 by Father Hugh Lavery. Father Lavery, well-known in the diocese and beyond, as a lecturer, preacher, writer and broadcaster has not severed entirely his links with St. Mary Magdalen's; he returned recently to give a series of Lenten talks in the parish.

Father Carey, assisted by Father Patrick McMahon, continues with the parish community to keep alive the gospel message in this area where the seed of Faith was planted many centuries ago. Thirty lay ministers of the Eucharist have been commissioned in the parish providing the sick and housebound more frequently with communion after one of the parish Masses.

One of the oldest parish groups is the St. Vincent de Paul Society, founded in 1895, who continue their weekly ministrations to those in need. A variety of other groups seeks to meet the various needs within the parish community; the Women's Guild meets fortnightly for spiritual and social events; a Prayer Group prays together every Monday evening; and a choir and liturgy group, predominantly of young people, provides, amongst other things, the music for the Folk Mass each Sunday at 10.30 a.m.

Many of the parish's social activities take place in the parish hall built about seven years ago through the initiative of the parish council. Even the youngest parishioners are catered for in the pre-school playgroup. For those so inclined Sequence Dancing is popular every Tuesday evening. Social functions, over the years, have raised money for charitable appeals and emergencies - one recent example being aid to Poland after the Chernobyl disaster.

Renewal weekends (a form of parish retreat) have been provided in the parish for a number of years. They usually begin on a Friday evening and continue until Sunday evening at which about 20 parishioners, at a time, have the opportunity to 'come away for a while' to pray and deepen their spiritual lives. So far a considerable number of parishioners have used the opportunity of this valuable renewal experience.

A Third World Group helps to keep the needs of our poorer brethren abroad before the minds of the people. Their latest project has been to assist an area of the church in Kenya supervised by Mgr. Owara.

Ecumenical involvement is, also, encouraged especially during Unity Octave Week when priests and people participate in the programme with other denominations. Furthering this ecumenical work a bible study group meets in each others' homes to read the word of God and pray together at regular intervals.

When Father Belaney, the first parish priest, arrived in Seaham Harbour in June, 1860, to inaugurate a new Catholic parish he could hardly have foreseen how successful his efforts and those of his successors - in partnership with the Catholic community - would be 127 years later.

48. SEDGEFIELD   St. John Fisher   *(March, April 1986)*

Sedgefield is rural England, claims the *Shell Guide to County Durham* whilst a 19th century history of Durham County by W. Fordyce, states that a Doctor Askew called it the Montpellier of the North and sent his patients there to benefit from the air.

Sedgefield has today its former repose restored with the help of the modern by-pass; it enjoys the peace and tranquillity which it had before the coming of the motor car and the traffic jams. Although Sedgefield is a town, it has the appearance of a village with its green - intersected by roads and bordered by Georgian houses - an ideal location to view the exteriors of the Anglican church of St. Edmund and the Catholic one of St. John Fisher. The latter with its narrow unpretentious frontage, jammed between houses, is not noticeable immediately as is the old church of St. Edmund with its Perpendicular style tower - a rarity in County Durham - and its Early English style nave. It is likely that some of the Early English stonework was the work of a stonemason who had worked on the building of the Chapel of the Nine Altars at Durham Cathedral.

Written sources tell us that around 900 A.D. before St. Edmund's was built, the village of Sedgefield was in the care of Bishop Cutheard; and in 1085 Ulchild was the rector of an earlier church here probably on the same site where St. Edmund's stands today. Within the walls of St. Edmund's are more reminders of the antiquity of the Faith hereabouts: the south porch was formerly a chantry chapel dedicated to St. Thomas; in the north transept stood St. Catherine's chantry founded in 1379 by John de Henly, parson of the church; and it is thought there was one dedicated to St. Mary.

These chantry chapels were common in pre-Reformation days where priests said regular Masses for the repose of the souls of benefactors who usually left land or money for their support; some chantry priests were also engaged as schoolmasters. Two reclining stone figures in the south transept may be effigies of these chantry benefactors.

Religious changes brought about by the 16th century Reformation do not appear to have been welcomed by some residents of Sedgefield. When the Northern Rebellion of 1569 occurred, to restore the practices of the ancient Faith, it was joined by 19 men from Sedgefield, 7 from Fishburn, 4 from Shotton and one from Mordon. A priest, Richard Hartborn, is reputed to have re-erected the altar in Sedgefield church and celebrated the Holy Mass there for those wishing to remain faithful to their beliefs. After the failure of the rebellion five men from Sedgefield were executed, two from Fishburn, one from Foxton and one from Mordon. Tolerance and ecumenical dialogue were non-existent - it would appear in those days.

Today the parish boundaries of St. John Fisher include places such as Great Stainton, Fishburn, Bishop Middleham, Mainsforth, Bradbury and Mordon. Like Sedgefield their association with the Faith reaches back a long way into the past. Bishop Middleham, as the name implies, was an important residence of the Bishop of Durham from the late 11th century until, it is said, the close of the 14th century when Bishop Auckland assumed greater importance. The present church of St. Michael's was built in the 13th century. Two bishops died at Bishop Middleham castle: Richard de Insula in 1283 and Bishop Kellow in 1316. Bishop Richard de Bury, it is noted, distributed 100 shillings to the poor whenever he journeyed to Durham.

In 1349, it is recorded, that John Harpyn held land in Mordon and supported three chantry priests at the altar of St. Helen's of Kellawe (Kelloe?); a portion of land in Mordon was also owned, for a time, by the well-known recusant family, the Trollops of Thornley. The Neville family forfeited lands they owned in Bradbury after the Northern Rebellion; an old chapel (date unknown) named after St. Nicholas once stood in Bradbury.

At Butterwick a tenement was held for the support of St. Catherine's chantry whilst a little to the north east of Great Stainton is Cross Hill which suggests another site with Christian connections.

About three miles south of Sedgefield were two other estates with Catholic connections: Shotton and Foxdene (Foxton). The latter, before the mid-16th century dissolution, belonged to the Knights Templars and afterwards it was transferred to the Knights Hospitallers of St. John.

In 1685 the Shotton estate belonged to the old Catholic family of Salvins, who have lived for many years at Croxdale Hall; it is thought that a member of this family, Thomas Salvin, was the last Roman

Catholic priest to celebrate Mass in St. Edmund's at Sedgefield.

Howe Hills at Mordon is now the seat of the Right Hon. Simon Scott, son of Lord Eldon, both are parishioners of St. John Fisher's.

Sedgefield's Catholic history after the Reformation is scant, although such a strong adherence to the Faith in the area would indicate that it continued secretly to avoid the attention of the authorities. Father Tweedy's book *Popish Elvet* contains some evidence to suggest the continuance of the Faith in the Sedgefield area. A Jesuit priest, Father Francis Mason (1593-1681) who spent most of his ministry in the Durham district was the son of William Mason, a Sedgefield yeoman; he and his wife were both in prison at the time of Francis' birth.

In 1642 a survey showed that nine papists were living in the Sedgefield locality, one at Bishop Middleham and five at Great Stainton. A document written in 1705 by an unknown gentleman listing popish chapels and activities is quoted by Father Tweedy and contains two references to the area: 'Mr Jo. Hildridge at B.Midlam - and a public school or seminary there, in ye Bps Manor House, 26 boys taught openly. Several children lately baptised there publicly ... . The popish gentlemen have weekly meetings with many of ye Justices of peace at Hallywell and Sedgefield.' These quotations would seem to show that a spirit of toleration was being practised. However, it was not until the mid-19th century that the Faith appeared publicly and openly when a chapel dedicated to St. Joseph - the ruins of which are detectable in the garden separating the present church and presbytery - was built in Sedgefield.

A ten-day Mission was held in the parish, probably in the 1850s, and was given by a priest from the Diocesan Mission House of St. Ninian's in Wooler. The Reverend Markland appears to have been the first resident priest here since the religious turmoil of the 16th century. The last Mass was celebrated in St. Joseph's in 1871 and four years later the missions at Cornforth and Trimdon were established.

It was from the former Mission that Father Lucey re-established the Catholic parish at Sedgefield and built the church of St. John Fisher in 1935. The small brick-built church was erected on the site of Fred Kingston's saddler's shop and last year celebrated its Golden Jubilee. Father John Caden, the present parish priest, tells us that his church was the first church in the world to be named after the martyr-Bishop of Rochester, who died for the Faith in 1535.

St. John Fisher Parish - of approximately 700 souls - has had the following priests serving them since Father Lucey's time: Father William Costello, Father Vincent Sheehan, Father Frank Rice and Father James Scott. Father Caden, who succeeded Father Scott, came here in 1966 for an expected five-year term; he remains happily here today about to complete a period of 20 years as parish priest.

Like his predecessors, much of his work has been as chaplain to the Winterton Psychiatric Hospital and the Sedgefield Community Hospital - in all a total of 1,100 beds - making the former the largest psychiatric hospital in the north of England.

Since his arrival in Sedgefield, Father Caden has been much involved in the community life of the district; he has represented the Sedgefield area as a Durham County Councillor for 13 years and is an elected member of the Social Services and Education committees. As a member of the Education Committee he was very much involved in the struggle to keep open Carmel Comprehensive School, Darlington, and St. John's, Bishop Auckland, when there were proposals made recently to amalgamate them.

Father Caden is, also, the vice-chairman of the S.W. Durham Health Authority and chairman of the Winterton and Sedgefield Hospitals' League of Friends, the latter of which Bishop Hugh Lindsay is the president.

A considerable number of parishioners are involved in the parish and community too. The S.V.P. - in addition to their normal parochial visitations - assisted by lady members, visits regularly the local hospitals and by means of a fortnightly indoor games club brings the world closer to the lives of the patients. A Saturday evening Mass, celebrated by Father Caden in Winterton, provides the spiritual help and comfort for the patients there.

In the extensive rural parish of Sedgefield Lay Ministers of the Eucharist are of inestimable benefit in taking the sacrament to the housebound, the sick, the hospital, and local authority homes; two lay ministers from the parish assist, also, at Carmel School.

The ecumenical activities, bringing the Christians of various denominations closer together in the Lord, abound in this locality. Unity Week is celebrated in the Catholic, Anglican and Methodist Churches; a procession of witness on Good Friday morning, with the large processional cross carried by a St. John Fisher parishioner, visits in turn the three churches; and joint Harvest Festivals are now common practice - Bishop Lindsay has preached at one in St. Edmund's and Father Caden claims the honour of being the first Catholic priest of Sedgefield to preach there since Reformation days.

The Women's World Day of Prayer last month was held in St. John Fisher parish; and finally the present discussions among Christians, linked with local Radio broadcasts, are a new feature of the ecumenical dialogue occurring in the homes of the members from the various Christian denominations.

A pleasing and encouraging development in sharp contrast with the troublesome and sometimes acrimonious occurrences of the 16th century.

49. SILKSWORTH   St. Leonard   *(March, 1983)*

Whilst not the oldest Catholic church in Sunderland, and certainly not in our diocese, St. Leonard's, New Silksworth, can claim links with a Catholic past which reaches back into the Middle Ages. Approximately 100 yards east of the present church stands the modern village of Tunstall which is recorded in Bishop Hugh de Puiset's *Boldon Book - a Northern Doomsday Book* compiled in 1183 in order to assess the revenues of the Durham Bishopric. The account informs us that 800 years ago in the village and nearby Wearmouth 22 villeins (villagers), six cotmen, a smith, a carpenter and a pounder lived a simple rural life. As the survey did not include members of a household, nor those who were freemen, we are unable to estimate the population; but what can be assumed is that these inhabitants held the same Faith, attended Mass, and received the same sacraments as the parishioners of St. Leonard's do today.

Further evidence of a Christian presence can be found in a pre-Reformation charter (probably 13th century) which states: 'John, the soldier, son of Marmaduke, (wishes) good health in the Lord. You will know that I have given to John, the chaplain at Dalton, my relative, a piece (gift?) of land in the village of Silksworth lying to the west part of the same village next to the chapel of St. Leonard in the same place ...

Silksworth, St. Leonard   *Photo: T. Mackin*

Thus (it is expected) that the aforesaid John, the chaplain, throughout his whole life, serves the chapel of St. Leonard properly ... worshipping on my behalf and on behalf of the souls of my ancestors ...'
It is unusual for a parish to know the name of one of its priests so many hundreds of years ago.

When the present stone church was opened by Bishop Chadwick on September 16th, 1873, the priest and people had the rare joy of knowing that the church and presbytery were without debt due to the generosity of Lady Beckwith of Silksworth House whose ancestors had suffered for the Faith as recusants in early Stuart times; and in whose grounds tradition claims the original chapel of St. Leonard stood. Commemorative brasses at the foot of the sanctuary steps and around the sanctuary walls furnish more information about her immediate relatives. This generous lady was also responsible for the building of St. Leonard's School, opened in 1874; and to ensure the maintenance of church, school and presbytery provided generous endowments. Many churches built about this time to cater for an expanding Catholic population - moving into the new coalfields, principally from Ireland - were not so fortunate as to have such a magnanimous benefactress.

Lady Beckwith appears to have been a convert from the Oxford Movement of which Cardinal Newman is the most famous. A silver finger-bowl on which is inscribed the words: 'The gift of Very Rev. J. H. Newman D. D. to St. Leonard's Church' is a reminder of the famous Anglican convert's interest in Lady Beckwith's generosity to the parish. Hanging in the presbytery dining room is a pencil sketch of Cardinal Newman drawn by Lady Coleridge and dated 1873-4, which has been left to the parish by Fr. James Burke, the predecessor of the present priest, Fr. Gerard Monaghan.

Who is the patron saint of the present church? There is no doubt that the medieval chapel was named after St. Leonard of Noblac, a Frankish saint, who lived in the sixth century and whose popularity spread throughout Europe and eventually to England during the 11th century. It is this saint who is depicted in a stained-glass window in the present church. However, six years before the church was opened another St. Leonard was canonised - St. Leonard of Port Maurice of whom much more is known. He was born on the Italian Riviera in 1676 and baptised Paul Jerome. On entering the order of Franciscans he took the religious name of Leonard; the name of an uncle who had been very kind to him. The greater part of his life was spent preaching missions in Italy and in the course of his priestly work he helped to popularise The Way of the Cross, encouraged the erection of the Stations in the parishes he visited, and on one occasion had them erected in the Colosseum. He further encouraged devotion to the Exposition of the Blessed Sacrament, the Sacred Heart and to Our Lady's Immaculate Conception. For a time he was spiritual director to Clementina Sobieski, the wife of James III, the old Pretender. According to the parish history it is to this more recent saint, whose life is much better documented, that the present church is dedicated. However, tradition and the previously mentioned stained-glass window could suggest otherwise.

Standing in its own grounds, St. Leonard's Church, designed in the Early English style still preserves, when viewed from certain angles, a rural appearance with the cemetery to the west and the modern primary school to the north. It is not difficult to imagine what it must have looked like before all the surrounding houses were built - a village church set on high ground in peaceful isolation.

Like many more rural parishes which were at one time outside major towns, St. Leonard's parish has grown considerably as new housing estates have been developed around it. Fr. Monaghan, the present parish priest, speaks highly of the work done by previous priests who succeeded in developing and fostering the caring community so necessary in parishes today. To encourage this sense of belonging, a Sunday evening Mass is celebrated in Mill Hill Primary School thus enabling those who live some distance from the parish church to feel they are part of the Catholic community of St. Leonard's.

The monthly parish newsletter, the Social Club, the Youth Club, the S.V.P., the Women's Guild and the annual ecumenical carol service are just some ways in which the parish caters for the varied needs of its members today.

Conscious of their obligations to help the under-developed parts of the globe, the Third World Group meets every First Friday to pray for and support financially Aid to the Church in Need and the African Missions

In the world of cricket St. Leonard's Primary School is certainly making its mark. Recently they won the Town Primary Schools' Championship and followed this up by coming first in the Northumberland and Durham Primary Schools' Cricket Festival. Now, because of their prowess and the facilities, the school has become the official cricket centre for primary schools in the borough.

During the Middle Ages the name of St. Leonard spread across Europe and came eventually to Silksworth: this process, to some extent, is now reversed as the well-known St. Leonard's Irish Dance Group - started thirty three years ago by Mr Philip Conroy who now directs the Billingham Festival - has performed in at least nine European countries. Mr Conroy relates that in 1964 when the group visited France they were invited to perform in the town of St. Leonard de Noblat. Although this was not possible, he did visit the church where he was shown a map of Europe on which were marked the churches named after St. Leonard and Silksworth was indicated.

A quotation, written by Fr. James Burke in the preface to the parish history, puts into perspective the past, present and future of the parish: 'Here our great-grandparents, our grandparents, our mothers and fathers have confessed their sins, received their Lord, presented their babies for baptism, have married, and been buried. It is indeed a holy place. One hundred years is truly a mark in the march of time and our own Centenary (1973) an event which puts pride into our hearts. We are glad, and we rejoice. We are grateful to God for His many blessings in all that time and we thank Him for giving us this home wherein we have been allowed to practise our faith. Joyously, with the hope that He places in us, we move forward to the second Centenary.'

50. SOUTH SHIELDS   St. Bede   *(November, 1985)*

If one wishes to stand in the place where Christianity first flowered in South Shields one needs to go to the area called the Lawe Top which overlooks the entrance to the Tyne and also gives a view across the river to Tynemouth Priory in the distance.

Canon Fee, the present parish priest of St. Bede's, writing in his parish centenary booklet states that St. Aidan, who had been invited by St. Oswald to preach the gospel in Northumbria, may have carried out his missionary work, for a time, in this locality where the latter had a royal residence. Oswald's son, Oswin, was born at the Lawe Top which once was known as Oswin's Hill. It was Oswin who gave land for the founding of a community of nuns in South Shields by St. Hilda round about 647 A.D. The present-day Anglican church, erected in the 18th century, perhaps stands on this site of St. Hilda's Convent - unfortunately no evidence of these early days is visible.

The rivers along the north east coast afforded easy access to invaders from the continent from earliest times. South Shields, always in a prominent position, would hardly escape the Viking raids of the 8th and 9th centuries. According to one account the nuns took refuge in Tynemouth Priory which was itself raided; the nuns were massacred and '... they were translated by martyrdom to heaven.'

Through the intercession of St. Cuthbert, it was said, these pagan Northmen were driven from the area by Guthred who was invested as King of Northumbria on Oswin's Hill. Guthred's victory brought English rule, once more, to this area and in thanksgiving Guthred bequeathed lands in Tyne and Wear to the church to be governed for many years by the Bishops and Priors of Durham.

Westoe, in the southern part of the parish, once had a chapel - established from Jarrow in 1347 - dedicated to St. Lawrence and it is believed that the tower acted as a landmark for mariners leaving and entering the Tyne; the chapel house today in Westoe is possibly situated on this medieval site. Westoe Towers preserves a link with the Catholic past here through the Apostleship of the Sea Residential Club, now in the care of the port chaplain, Father Michael McKenna, who is also Diocesan Vocations Director.

Usually, in many areas of the Diocese, the post-Reformation period is not one where much information is available. However, South Shields is one of the exceptions. In order to keep the Faith alive it was vital to train priests abroad for the English Mission; they could no longer be trained at home and to send students abroad was also illegal. As a result the priests, supported by the Catholic laity, devised a clandestine network of refuges where priests could minister secretly to their flocks.

One such centre was established by a brave lady, Ursula Taylor, in her house on the Lawe Top which became a place of sanctuary for those who wished to study abroad in Catholic seminaries and return ordained to the mission field. It would have been easy from this house to convey the students and priests to and from the collier brigs which traded with the continent. A report sent to the government in 1589 shows that the Lawe Top refuge of Ursula Taylor had not escaped notice: 'South Shields was the chief landing place for Jesuits and seminary priests ... having for this purpose a house at South Shields belonging to one Ursula Taylor, a recusant, to receive and lodge there ... to furnish them with money and other needful provisions, and one George Errington, a tall gentleman, well horsed, to guide them and convey them to such gentlemen's houses and other places as they were assigned to...'

George Errington born at Hirst, near Ashington, round about 1554, was educated at Trinity College, Oxford, where he came into contact with students who were later reconciled to the church; some of them were ordained and later died for the Faith. He became a Catholic and devoted much of his life to the dangerous work of smuggling priests and students in and out of England and escorting them on landing to the homes of the old Catholic families in the vicinity - Thornley Hall, the home of the Trollopes was likely once such place.

In 1591 he and Ursula Taylor were arrested and imprisoned. George, after several years in gaol, was tried and executed for his Faith at York on November 29th, 1596 - he had deservedly gained the title of Venerable. Ursula was incarcerated in the Peter Prison at York and later transferred to York Castle where she suffered great hardships being put in solitary confinement 'in a dark cell without heating of any kind, without water and lacking even the bare necessities of life'. Father Christopher Grene wrote of her: 'She suffered all this for the love of Our Lord and for the sake of the Catholic Faith.' Refusing to conform she was sent to the South Blockhouse in Hull where she suffered further privations and the prospect of life imprisonment until her friends persuaded the authorities to release her on bail. South Shields today, then, may be justly proud of its adopted heroes.

One writer describes South Shields in 1743 as 'a large village in which are two hundred pans for boiling seawater into salt' No such description would fit it today as the last two hundred years have seen it grow into an industrial town absorbing the neighbouring villages. The relaxation of the penal laws in the late 18th century enabled Catholicism to show its public face, and the first visible evidence of this on Tyneside was St. Andrew's in Newcastle built in 1798 by Father James Worswick who journeyed regularly on horseback to North Shields to say Mass. The opening of St. Cuthbert's in 1821 enabled the South Shields Catholics to travel there twice on Sundays by boat for the services. Because of the expense the South Shields congregation eventually hired their own boat until 1829 when the ferry began its regular service. Through the efforts and generosity of Mr Temple, a convert, a cottage was bought at Mill Dam where a Sunday School, under the supervision of Mr Turpin, was opened in 1832.

The port and industry attracted workers to the area and by 1848 the Catholics of South Shields were petitioning the Bishop for a priest of their own. His reply was 'a church first, then a priest.' No time was wasted and after three fruitless attempts to acquire a site the chapel of the Bristol Brethren was purchased in old St. Cuthbert Street (now Western Approach), dedicated to St. Cuthbert, and opened by Bishop Hogarth on December 4th, 1849. The addition of a small school to the north of the chapel and a presbytery to the south - for the first parish priest, Father Richard Singleton - completed the first phase in the permanent restoration of the Faith here.

St. Cuthbert's chapel was, for more than 20 years, the place of worship of the South Shields congregation until the numbers became so large it was necessary to find a new site on which to build a bigger church. This was achieved by Canon Waterton with the opening on August 22nd, 1876, of the present church in Westoe Road at an estimated cost of £8,000 which rose to £11,000 when quicksand was discovered and deeper foundations were necessary. The original plan was to include a tower but the foundations' problem did not allow this - the photograph shows where it should have been.

St. Bede's today stands proudly in the town centre free from industrial grime and next to it a large presbytery which once accommodated five priests, but now only two: Canon Wilfrid Fee and Father Andrew Faley who devotes much of his time to diocesan catechetical work.

The Shields Gazette, in 1876, described the church as 'a splendid ornament to the locality' and this compliment still holds true today. The church interior still retains its original shape and form except for the re-ordered sanctuary completed in 1972. This re-ordering, with the altar facing the people, has managed to preserve much that is of traditional interest whilst fulfilling the latest liturgical requirements. Links with the past can be seen in the Sacred Heart chapel whose lancet windows came from the old St. Cuthbert's chapel; and probably those in the Lady Chapel, too. Seven stained-glass windows in the rear wall of the sanctuary portray Christ's giving of himself in the seven sacraments. Below them is a finely carved oak reredos in which the figures of saints are placed including the four northern saints: Wilfrid, Cuthbert, Aidan and Bede.

St. Bede's can boast a bishop amongst its former priests; he was Father George Burton (1895 -1902) who became Bishop of Clifton. Canon Joseph Byrne, parish priest from 1911 to 1942, with the help of the people, cleared the parish debt shortly before his death and was responsible for the building of the Derby Street School in 1913; he also had the honour of erecting St. Bede's Central School, one of the first of its kind in the North.

Behind the church is the continuing link with Catholic education through the ages and within the parish; the present primary school of St. Bede's was opened by Bishop Hugh Lindsay on January 12th, 1971, replacing the older one in Derby Street. That same year the parish acquired the former Marsden Miners' Hall which now serves as the parish social centre.

Like many other parishes in urban areas, St. Bede's has felt the effects of re-development and the drift of population to new estates and newer parishes. Many houses have been demolished to be replaced by factories, new roads, car parks and landscaped areas resulting in a fall of the Catholic population from 4,000 to 1,700.

Nevertheless the parish continues its mission today with the same enthusiasm of former days. Parishioners are active in the St. Vincent de Paul Society (first established in 1854), the Legion of Mary, a Justice and Peace Group, a Sewing Guild, the Senior Citizens, a Mother and Toddler Group as well as the normal everyday spiritual and social life that makes a parish a community. St. Bede's is also the centre for meetings of the South Shields branch of the Catholic Nurses' Guild.

Our thanks to Canon Wilfrid Fee who supplied the information which made this article possible and who has given us a prayer with which to conclude it:

> 'O God, through the intercession of our Blessed Lady, St. Bede, our patron, along with St. Oswald, St. Oswin, St. Hilda, St. Cuthbert and the Venerable George Errington, we thank you for all the blessings of past years and we pray that we may walk worthily in the footsteps of our Catholic forefathers to whom we are so greatly indebted.'

51. SOUTH SHIELDS (Tyne Dock)   Saints Peter and Paul   *(December, 1984)*

Situated on the south bank of the Tyne between Jarrow and South Shields is the parish of Saints Peter and Paul, Tyne Dock, preparing to celebrate - informally on December 14th - its centenary. The name Jarrow automatically brings to mind memories of St. Paul's Anglo-Saxon monastery where St. Bede spent most of his priestly life; whilst to the east is South Shields where during the penal days, when the Faith was proscribed, priests and seminarians sailed from here to reach the Catholic colleges on the continent for their training and on their return used the port as a starting point for their missionary work. A number of English Martyrs probably landed here including, we think, Fathers Hill, Hogg, Duke and Holiday who died for their beliefs at Durham in the year 1590. Records reveal that by 1642 the Catholic population was quite small -

South Shields, Tyne Dock, Sts. Peter and Paul Photo: T. Mackin

ten were listed residing in Jarrow.

Until the foundation of the South Shields Mission in 1849 at St. Bede's, Westoe Road, the area was served by the priests of the Newcastle Mission. Mention was made in a previous article of the establishing of the North Shields Mission in 1810 and after this date Catholics on the south bank hired a boat each Sunday to attend Mass and even, occasionally, Vespers in the new church of St. Cuthbert's.

Tyne Dock's growth can be directly attributed to the expansion of commerce and industry in that area in the latter half of the 19th century. The construction of a large dock at Jarrow Slake in 1858, the development of the glass-making industry, and the growth of shipbuilding and heavy engineering all helped to attract people to the area seeking employment. The church goes where the people are and it was soon evident to Bishop Bewick that a new parish was necessary to cater for the spiritual needs of those Catholics who had moved into the Tyne Dock area, including a number of Irish immigrants.

In a letter of October 17th, 1884, to Father Kirwan - then ministering at St. Bede's in Jarrow - the Bishop had this to say: 'I have hereby to direct and commission you to undertake the formation of a mission at Tyne Dock. The primary object of this is to give the inmates of the Poor House - that is children and adults, the fullest opportunity of attending to church and school ... it is work of an uphill character, without a solitary provision - without church; without school; without presbytery; without land; without money ... set down your roots "In Nomine Domine" - like an Apostle ... .'

How many priests over the years have received similar letters, yet undaunted have overcome with Faith in God and the help of loyal parishioners what seemed initially to be insurmountable obstacles. Father Kirwan's mission began on December 14th, 1884, in a cellar of the Exchange Buildings, Whitehead Street. On the following day the *South Shields Gazette* reported the occasion and emphasised the large congregation present at the services; the special preacher was Father O'Brien of St. Mary's Cathedral.

It is not uncommon when a new parish is started to build a school first, using part of it for Sunday Mass and other services. Through the generosity of his parishioners - many, no doubt, would be very poor - and the help of influential non-Catholics in South Shields (an ecumenical touch here!) Father Kirwan was able to build the school-chapel which was formally opened by Bishop Wilkinson on July 28th, 1889, with a Solemn High Mass sung by an excellent choir and accompanied by a full orchestra conducted by Mr. W.

J. Larkin. The total cost of the site and building was £4,000.

As there was no presbytery Father Kirwan resided in the Commercial Buildings, now part of the Perseverance Club. He remained in the parish for six years until 1890 when he returned to his birthplace in County Waterford as parish priest, being succeeded by Father Robert Taylerson who was responsible for the building of the present presbytery in 1893 and the opening of a Mass Centre at Boldon Colliery in 1896. After nine years here he moved to Stockton where he continued his ministry for many years.

His replacement was Father James Bradley who had been a curate at South Shields; he holds the record as the longest serving parish priest in Tyne Dock remaining here for 46 years. One of his first objectives was the erection of a church suitable for his increasing congregation who had subscribed £1,000 before its opening. Bishop Collins, then the auxiliary bishop, laid the foundation stone on September 23rd, 1905. The *South Shields Gazette* reported: 'The bishop was met at the Mechanics' Institute, in Hudson Street, where a procession was formed. At the head was a large number of the clergy of the diocese, who were followed by the bishop, in an open landau. Then came the school children and the laity, and accompanied by the Band of the Birtley League of the Cross they walked to the site ... . In the course of the service the Bishop duly performed the ceremony of solemnly blessing and laying the foundation stone, after which he went round the boundaries of the church, which he similarly blessed and sprinkled with holy water'.

The church, built reputedly in the Romanesque style, was 100 feet long and 52 feet wide and was opened on July 8th, 1906. Designed by the architects Messrs Broderick, Lowther and Walker of Hull, the church was completed in less than a year by the builder, Mr James Young of Tyne Dock; its seating capacity was 600.

Continual fund raising through parish collections, supplemented by voluntary deductions from miners' wages and Father Bradley's appeals at the Dock Gates on pay days, enabled the debt to be cleared in 25 years. On October 23rd, 1930, the church was consecrated by Bishop Thorman who, at the same ceremony, blesssed a new marble high altar in memory of the 80 parishioners who had lost their lives in the Great War. This fine altar in the Roman style contained 15 different kinds of marble and was the work of Almando Battelli of Toscana in Italy.

Fortunately, little damage was caused to the church when raids on the docks and shipyards occurred during the Second World War. Father Bradley, who had served the South Shields area for 51 years, died shortly after the war on July 14th, 1945. His ministry had been a long and fruitful one having sustained his people spiritually during the two World Wars and the years of economic depression in the 1930s.

He was followed as parish priest by Father Leo Landreth who was ordained in 1925. During the First World War he had served in the Royal Navy becoming a naval chaplain in the Second. Whilst Father Landreth was here the Golden Jubilee of the Church was celebrated in 1956. The choirmaster at this celebration was a Mr Charles Turner, aged 75, a member of the South Shields Orchestra who 50 years earlier had fulfilled the same role at the opening of the church in 1906. Surely, something of a record in faithful dedication to the church and its music. He was supported by a choir in which many of the choristers could claim over 30 years membership; among them Miss Mamie Birkett who had regularly accompanied the choir on the organ for over 33 years.

Since its foundation Saints Peter and Paul's parish has had six parish priests, including the present one Father Thomas Dollard, who came here in March, 1983. His predecessor had been Father Peter Starrs (now at St. Anne's, Sunderland) who had succeeded Father Landreth on his retirement in 1978.

Mr Paul Hoben has recorded in some detail in their parish history, the origins and development of the school since 1889 which then housed the chapel too; all we can do here is mention a few details.

The original building was divided into a large schoolroom and two classrooms capable of accommodating 200 pupils. Probably a large number of the first entrants was transferred from St. Bede's in South Shields supplemented by Catholic children moving from the local Board schools. An extension was added in 1923 to house an extra 150 pupils thus increasing the school roll to 350; some classes had 50 pupils in each! Round about 1930 this extension was converted into a senior school and it was this building which caught fire on April 20th, 1947, necessitating the use of temporary accommodation in the Youth Club and canteen until other classrooms were built. The contribution by the school (a new one was built in 1967) to the development of the Faith in the parish is neatly summarised in the words of Mr Hoben: 'The Catholic Faith in Tyne Dock has, in part, been sustained by a century of work by teachers, parents and pupils. Please God, let the Catholic Faith, Catholic values and Catholic education be living still in Tyne Dock in 2084 A.D. at the parish bi-centenary.'

On visiting the church one is struck by its simplicity and a harmonious blending of the new with the old; the original structure is retained with its wooden barrel-vaulted roof - an uncommon feature in our churches. One's eye is immediately attracted to the sanctuary where, since Father Dollard's arrival in 1983, the beautiful marble altar has been brought forward replacing the temporary wooden one; the reredos remains at the rear of the sanctuary and immediately above it is the central lancet window donated by Father Bradley in honour of his parents. Marble from the altar steps has been used in the construction of a new ambo and presidential chair completing the work necessary to meet the new liturgical requirements. The re-sited altar was blessed and dedicated by Bishop Lindsay on September 27th, this year. Statues of the two patron saints, on either side of the sanctuary, recall not only the two great apostles but also the fact that the twin Anglo-Saxon monasteries at Jarrow and Wearmouth were proud to have them as their patron saints too.

Lay involvement began in the parish in its earliest days; the Apostleship of Prayer was begun in 1890; the Society of St. Vincent de Paul in 1891 (still thriving today); and a Men's Club called the Catholic Institute started in army huts in Lemon Street in 1920. No less so today is the commitment of many of the parishioners: parish groups include the Justice and Peace Group, the C.W.L., the Legion of Mary and a parish committee. Much individual work is undertaken by other people in the parish too - recently a number of them were involved in re-varnishing all the pews, and painting the side chapels. The re-lacquering of the tabernacle and candlesticks was made possible through the generous donations of parishioners.

Centenary celebrations in Tyne Dock - spiritual and social - have already started: a Vocations Vigil took place on November 2nd; a Mass for the sick and housebound was celebrated on November 3rd; Father George Forster, was invited to preach at all the Sunday Masses on November 4th; and on the following day there was a reconciliation service with Mass in the evening. Bishop Lindsay was the chief concelebrant at a Mass of Thanksgiving said on November 8th. Thirty priests concelebrated with the Bishop and the preacher was Father John Tweedy. That same evening a centenary buffet dance was held where priests and people were able to meet informally and recall the past.

A centenary is an opportunity to look back and take stock; it is also an opportunity to look forward and plan for the future; and this is what Father Dollard has been emphasising - especially the spiritual aspect. Future plans are in the process of being implemented. It is hoped soon to start a Bible and Prayer Group. A narthex and screen - providing more space at the rear of the nave and enabling the church to be visited yet secure - should complete the alterations.

December 14th is the centenary day when the first Mass was said in Tyne Dock and plans are already made to mark this great occasion. In the morning there will be a children's Mass and a party has been arranged. An evening Mass will also be celebrated for adults followed by a social gathering. It is hoped, also, to mark the event with a special celebration for the senior children attending St. Wilfrid's School.

Father Dollard in his foreword to the centenary history tells his parishioners: 'It was Pope Pius XI who introduced the term "Catholic Action", but long before that, our ancestors lived it out. That is why you have a thriving parish today'. He goes on to quote an extract from the *Northern Catholic Calendar* of 1906 where the ministry of Saints Peter and Paul's parish included visiting the Floating Hospital on the Tyne, the workhouse and the smallpox hospital. Father Dollard continues this ministry to the sick at the nearby General Hospital. He concludes with an exhortation to his people: 'The world in which we live has changed so much - but we know that God who doesn't change has made you and me to know, love and serve Him, through our loyalty to the church that was planted here in our midst, 100 years ago. Please keep on dear fellow-parishioners the work started here a century ago... '

52. STELLA   St. Mary and St. Thomas Aquinas   *(February, March 1990)*

A parish which can boast that Mass has been celebrated here possibly without a break since before the penal days; that two bishops - one of whom was the founder of Ushaw College - resided here, as well as Ushaw's first president; that the Benedictines, a Franciscan and a Jesuit served as chaplains; and that the Stella Mission was the mother church of four daughter parishes along the banks of the Tyne is, indeed, a remarkable story worth relating.

The earliest record of a Catholic presence here is in 1149 when the Bishop of Durham, William de St. Barbara, granted the manor of Stella (originally Stellingley) to the Benedictine nuns of St. Bartholomew's convent in Newcastle. Used, perhaps, as a summer retreat it may have, also, provided an income from farm rents for the Newcastle convent. The property remained in the nuns' possession until their convent was suppressed in 1540 - one of the many casualties of Henry VIII's dissolution policy against religious houses. Fortunately the survival of the Faith here was guaranteed when Nicholas Tempest - related to the merchant banking family of Newcastle - purchased the Stella property sometime before 1600. He was created a baronet by James I in 1622 and it is assumed that it was he who was responsible for the erection of Stella Hall in the Elizabethan style on the convent site.

In spite of the persecutions and proscribing legislation of the period, Stella seems to have weathered the storms and continued steadfastly in the Ancient Faith. As early as 1598 Dr. Toby Matthews, the Bishop of Durham - whose son incidentally was ordained a Catholic priest by St. Robert Bellarmine - writing to Lord Burghley regarding papists in Durham listed among others '... Nicholas Tempest of Stella, that great recusant ... where at Stella, if I am rightly informed, they keep up a Popish spiritual service ...'

Nicholas's great grand-daughter, Lady Jane Widdrington, provides an interesting link with those far-off days. Like her forebears she was able to keep a priest in the Hall and in her will she made provision for the continued maintenance of a priest: 'This maintenance by the sum of £20 per year ... and (he shall) say Mass once every week for the soul of the said Lady Jane Widdrington.' Her wish is still fulfilled today with the celebration of a weekly Mass for the repose of her soul.

Two years after the death of her brother in 1698, when Lady Jane inherited his estates, she married the fourth Lord Widdrington of Blankney who had been friendly with Sir Francis Tempest at the Jesuit College in Paris. Jane, who bore him eight children, died in 1714 the year before her husband made the ill-fated decision to join the Earl of Derwentwater's rebellion to restore the Stuarts to the throne. William was captured at Preston, taken with the other leaders to London, put on trial and condemned to death. He was, however, reprieved and eventually granted a pardon, although he had to suffer forfeiture of his estates and property.

Another sad aspect of Lord Widdrington's action was the arrest and imprisonment at Durham of many of his innocent co-religionists including his chaplain - the first of whose name we know, Dom. John Benedict Wilson O.S.B. - who passed 'through Winlaton with his feet tied under the horse's belly'. On his release he returned to Stella dying there in 1725; his burial is recorded in the Ryton parish register: '1725, June 25, John Wilson, a Romish priest, Stella'. Other Benedictines served the mission the final one being Dom. William Bede Hutton whose last mission was Hesleyside where he died in 1756.

The Catholics of Stella must have breathed a sigh of relief when the Stella estates were restored to the Widdringtons in 1733 and were inherited by Henry Francis in 1743 on the death of his father. Henry Francis was said to have invited a Jesuit chaplain to minister at the hall; he was Father Taylor (Turner) S.J. who reported to his superiors in the veiled language of the penal days that he had 'about 170 customers (parishioners) to shop (church) on days required, though few patients of mine, as most make use of another gentleman maintained there for many years for that purpose ... salary from this place £28, from the factory (Durham Jesuit headquarters) £12.' 'Another gentleman' refers to Father Thomas Greenwell who served a congregation at Blaydon.

The strong faith kept alive in this area of our diocese throughout the years of persecution was undeniably due to the families who inhabited Stella Hall and who supplied, out of their own pockets, a chaplain not only for themselves but also for those in the neighbourhood who wished to continue the profession of their Catholicism. Numerically there was a strong enclave here as the papist returns for the Durham diocese of 1780 show that in Ryton parish (of which Stella was part) there were 334 Catholics; the only other area to exceed it being Durham City.

With the death of the last Lord Widdrington in 1774 the Stella and Stanley estates passed to his nephew, Thomas Eyre of Hassop in Derbyshire, who appointed a relation, also called Thomas Eyre, to the Stella chaplaincy in 1775. This priest remained at Stella until 1792 when he became responsible for the care of the Douai students fleeing from the French Revolutionary troops who had captured the Flanders college. Stella House the home of the Silvertop family - not to be confused with Stella Hall nearby - was a temporary home for a short time of some Douai students and French refugee priests. Father Eyre was spiritual father at Tudhoe, Crook Hall and finally at Ushaw, where he became its first president in 1808. A further link with Ushaw and Stella, which is not generally known, is the hymn, *'Hail Queen of Heaven'*, - the words of which were written by John Lingard, the Catholic historian and one of Ushaw's earliest professors. The tune to which it is usually sung - *Stella* - was reputedly composed by the composer H. F. Hemy one evening after playing the organ at Benediction in the Stella Church.

Another notable cleric who also resided at Stella was Dr. Matthew Gibson, Vicar-Apostolic of the Northern District. He came to the parish in 1784 and died there in 1790; he was buried near the ancestral home in Newborough churchyard near Hexham. He was succeeded as Bishop of the Northern District by his younger brother, William, a former president of Douai College from 1781 to 1790 whose energies, along with others, made possible the foundation of Ushaw College. The Gibsons of Stonecroft were a remarkable Catholic family, giving four sons to the Church, two of whom became bishops.

Father Eyre's successor was the Rev. William Hull who was in charge of the Stella Mission for 37 years and one of its generous benefactors; he had the joy of being present at the church's opening.

During his stay at Stella Father Eyre had collected a considerable sum of money for the building of a new church but it was not until Father Hull's successor, the Rev. Thomas Edward Witham - the son of Henry Silvertop and Elizabeth Witham of Headlam - took charge that the church was built. Father Witham's first Mission was here in Stella when he became chaplain at Stella Hall which had now become the residence of his sister, Mrs Bridget Dunn. He was to eventually inherit the family estates at Lartington where he died in 1897 at the age of 91.

The church of St. Mary and St. Thomas Aquinas was designed in the Gothic style by the Newcastle architect, Mr John Green, who with his son has left us a number of notable landmarks in the area among which are the Scotswood Suspension Bridge, the Grey's Monument, the Newcastle Theatre Royal and Penshaw Monument. He became official architect to the Duke of Northumberland and his son Benjamin - who trained under the elder Pugin and was later to join his father as a partner - has left us a detailed drawing of the original Stella church before the alterations of 1849.

Costing around £1,500 and capable of seating a congregation of 300 the parish church of Stella in 1831, '... was opened on Wednesday, October 12th, with all the solemnity, splendour and grandeur of effect so peculiar to the Catholic Church. The Pontifical High Mass was celebrated by the Right Rev. Thomas Penswick, D.D. Bishop of Europum, and Vicar-Apostolic of the Northern District, in his full episcopal robes, with mitre and crozier, assisted by the Rev. William Hogarth of Darlington as deacon and the Rev. Mr Dugdale of Stockton-upon-Tees as sub-deacon. The service commenced at half-past ten o'clock. Nearly all the clergy of the counties of Durham and Northumberland attended ... Webbes' three-part Mass was performed with full orchestral accompaniment preceded by the overture from the Messiah, and terminated with Handel's Hallelujah Chorus ... the vestments ... were presented to the chapel by Mrs Dunn of Stella Hall, who has surpassed on this occasion her ordinary munificence ... They were the workmanship of the nuns of Clare House, Scorton ... The chapel was crowded to excess, and several of the most respected individuals of both sexes and of all religious denominations were present, and left the place much impressed by the solemnity of the service on this occasion ...' *(Catholic Magazine, 1832)*.

Included in the subscription list were Lady Mary Eyre (£950), George Silvertop (£100), George Dunn

& family (£230), Mrs Dunn of Stella Hall (£100) and various smaller sums from 'liberal Protestant gentlemen of the neighbourhood'.

To the north of the church stands the unique presbytery built of ashlar stone with castellated turrets. Until 1849 access could be gained from it direct to the sanctuary; after this date, alterations - believed to have been the work of John Dobson - resited the sanctuary at the southern end of the church and a west door was added near the rear of the presbytery.

The priests who served here so faithfully over the centuries are too numerous to mention by name. One should, perhaps, mention Father Ralph Platt who mastered the Gaelic language so that he might better meet the spiritual needs of Irish immigrants who arrived in our diocese in the mid-19th century in substantial numbers. Nor can one omit to mention Father Henry Wrennall (later Canon) parish priest from 1865 to 1913, who with his faithful assistant, Father David Scott, saw the necessity of establishing new parishes along both banks of the Tyne.

The parish history records that: 'There was no bridge across the Tyne at Newburn at that time and the faithful used to cross the river for Sunday Mass by means of the local sculler' (rowing boat). Obviously there were occasions when because of ice, fog, or high winds the crossing was not possible resulting in them remaining 'on the river bank following the course of the 11 o'clock Mass by means of the church bell'. The summoning bell told them Mass had begun; the Elevation bell informed them that the Consecration had occurred; and the Angelus bell told them Mass was concluded at which 'the Newburn congregation turned from the river bank and made their way home'.

It must have been with some relief and considerable satisfaction when Canon Wrennall and Father Scott were able to open the church at Bell's Close in 1868 and two years later, with the assistance of the Liddell family, the parish of Prudhoe was started. By 1898 the parish of St. Joseph's, Blaydon, was founded followed in 1905 by St. Agnes' at Crawcrook.

Father Anthony Cocurullo was succeeded in 1970 by Father John Galletly who was parish priest here for almost 20 years until his recent death in November, 1989. Some months before his death he had been of great assistance in making possible the publication of this article. During his incumbency the parish celebrated its 150th anniversary and at the sesquicentennial Mass Bishop Hugh Lindsay was the chief concelebrant. Much updating and refurbishing were carried out under the eye of Father Galletly: the stonework was restored; the rear of the church altered with the addition of a screen, behind which were built an office and quiet room; and a new central heating system was installed in the anniversary year of 1981.

The church has also been furnished with modern pews which blend well with the older aspects of the building. Victorian stained-glass, made by the Barnett family of Newcastle, adorn both nave walls although one in the East wall may be of Pugin design. The four west windows depict the Crucifixion, the Assumption, the Resurrection and the Ascension. In the Assumption window a nice touch can be noticed of an angel holding a scroll with the words: 'Stella Matutina, ora pro nobis'

Stella has had a school for many years but when exactly it began is obscure; there is evidence that there was a school here in the 1840s. When the school was inspected in 1849 by a Mr T. W. Marshall there were 31 boys and 34 girls at school that day. He found 'the desks and furniture fair, books and apparatus good, organisation mixed, the master he found diligent and studious, not highly qualified but conducting his school in a creditable manner'. He also reported that 'it was impossible to keep the children at school in consequence of the great demand for their labour, which commences in the coal pits at 7 years of age.' He was similarly pleased with the girls' school remarking that, 'the mistress was intelligent, laborious and fully competent to guide and instruct her pupils.'

Since the early 1970s Stella children have been accommodated in a modern school with a later addition of a nursery unit; pupils come from a wide area and the school is popular with non-Catholics.

As other parishes have developed in the area - once the sole missionary responsibility of Stella priests - it was inevitable that the mother parish would become geographically and numerically smaller. This, however, has not diminished among the parishioners the desire to keep the Faith alive in this ancient enclave of our diocese. The parish council of six members assists the priest in the smooth running of parish affairs;

the S.V.P., in existence now for 76 years, continues the work of helping those in need; and the C.W.L. provides an opportunity for the ladies of the parish to make their spiritual and social contribution.

Stella along with other parishes has found it advantageous to participate in joint-parochial ventures on a deanery basis: examples of this have been deanery Masses for special occasions, a deanery mission, and the annual pilgrimage to Our Lady's Shrine at Osmotherley.

Sadly Stella Hall, which became a victim of the bulldozer in 1954, is now only a memory but one which has been preserved in the parish history and in the present parish church - a proud record which few parishes can equal.

53. STOCKTON   St. Mary   *(June, 1984)*

On December 3rd, 1983, Bishop Lindsay, along with 17 other priests, - including the parish priest Father Noel Colahan and Mgr. William Carroll, representing the Bishop of Middlesbrough - concelebrated a Bicentenary Mass in the recently re-ordered sanctuary of St. Mary's. They were celebrating 200 years of Catholic witness by the mother church of Teesside which many years ago was also responsible for the Middlesbrough area - hence the presence of Monsignor Carroll.

But 200 years is a relatively short span of time when one considers how long the Faith has existed in this area. In nearby Norton stands the church of St. Mary whose Anglo-Saxon crossing tower reminds us of how long ago the Faith was brought here by our Christian forefathers on the banks of the Tees. There was, also, a chapel-of-ease at Stockton during the medieval period which housed a shrine honouring St. Thomas a Becket. This chapel probably served the small population of Stockton who worked in and around the Bishop of Durham's castle which was the most prominent building in the vicinity for many years - nothing of it remains today. It is most likely that somewhere within the castle was a chapel for the use of the Bishop his chaplains and anyone else who wished to worship there.

During the penal days, as elsewhere, the Faith went underground and what we know of the period is sketchy. In 1697 we learn that a Father Robert Jefferson, a Douai man and, also, a Father John Booth resided at the house of Marmaduke Witham, M.P., at Preston-on-Tees. The Catholic population, gleaned from a declaration of property made in 1723, included at least a dozen Catholic property owners; yet there must have been more than this for dependants, servants and non-property owners would not have been included.

Mrs Elizabeth Grange, a widow, gave a sum of money in 1743 which allowed Bishop Dicconson to arrange for Mass to be said in Stockton on three Sundays of the month and three weekdays. A few years after this, in the 1750s, a titled priest, Father Sir William Anderson, was serving the area after spending two years unjustly confined in York Castle after the 1745 rebellion. Another priest, Father John Hawarden, a Lancastrian, came from Douai in 1754 and assisted at Stockton but is believed to have lived in Darlington. As mentioned in previous articles, the priests of those pre-Emancipation days led quiet but effective ministries leaving little to record of their achievements.

Fortunately more is known about the first parish priest, a Father John Daniel, who came to Stockton in 1783 and began raising funds for a chapel which was eventually built in the Playhouse Yard at the rear of the north side of Finkle Street. Within the present presbytery one can see two reminders of those days: a hand-written letter, signed by Father Daniel, dated October 5th, 1791, informing the Durham Sessions in accordance with the law of the time that a chapel had been built and was in use in Stockton; and a pen and ink sketch of the same chapel drawn by the Catholic artist, Peter Anson, which dates the opening in 1796.

It was Father Daniel who began the Baptismal Register now in the Public Record Office; it gives the first baptism as that of Ann Kipling of Darlington on July 10th, 1783; the first Stockton baptism of Mary Brack on April 28th, 1784; and the first in Middlesbrough of Mary Elliott. After 1822 baptismal entries for Darlington cease so one may presume that from then on there was a priest ministering there.

From 1803 until his death in 1822 the parish priest was Father Thomas Storey, a Notary Apostolic. Various priests served in the parish before and after his time; however, it was during the incumbency of

Stockton, St. Mary   *Photo: T. Mackin*

Father Joseph Dugdale, who arrived in 1830, that the original church in Major Street was built to the design of the famous Victorian architect, Augustus Welby Pugin. It was opened on July 7th, 1842, by Bishop Mostyn with a Mass sung by the combined choirs of Stockton and Hartlepool. The north aisle and lower part of the tower were added in 1866 at a cost of £1,300 and four years later the Baptistry Chancel, and the south aisle were completed at a cost of £4,000. Unfortunately the proposed steeple was never built onto the upper portion of the tower completed along with the presbytery in 1909. A stained-glass window near the Lady Chapel perpetuates the memory of Father Dugdale, the founder of the church, who died at the age of 41, in 1847, after catching a fever which was then sweeping the town. Father Dugdale can also claim to be the founder of the Mass centre in Middlesbrough which was later to develop into the cathedral parish.

    Father Robert Cornthwaite succeeded him and remained here for five years before his appointment to the rectorship of the English College in Rome; later he was to be made Bishop of Beverley and when the diocesan boundaries were altered, the first Bishop of Leeds.

    By 1836 it was reckoned that there were approximately 250 Catholics living in Stockton, but this number was to grow rapidly in the mid-19th century as Irish immigration to the area increased; this explains the necessary extensions outlined above.

    An interesting letter of 1869, preserved in the presbytery, from the Rev. J. Milner, the vicar of Elton, shows the cordial relations that existed when he supports the attempt of the priest at Stockton to obtain permission for Catholic children at the Workhouse to attend the parish school. The importance of Catholic education is further demonstrated by the efforts made by Father Carlile (later Canon) to have more schools built in and around Stockton. Born in Castlewellan, Co. Down, he appears to have spent some years in business in the north of England before training for the priesthood at Ushaw and finally Rome - being over

40 at his ordination. With the passing of the Forster Act in 1870 he was elected to the local School Board and set about extending Catholic education in the area.

In a letter of March 2nd, 1871, to Bishop Cornthwaite he requested his assistance with the proposed building of a school and politely asked the Bishop if he would preach in St. Mary's and encourage the people to give donations for this purpose. In another letter a few days later he informs the Bishop: ... 'I have seen some half doz. pieces of land which would answer for sites for a school in South Stockton today from 4/6d to 7/6d a square yard according to situation. I will get a sketch made as intelligible as possible and forward it for inspection to your Lordship as soon as I am able. My schoolmaster has unfortunately got the smallpox at present. It is raging with great virulence on both sides of the river and my school has been closed for the past fortnight in South Stockton ...'

The result of this correspondence, coupled with the Canon's efforts locally, was the building of St. Patrick's School at Thornaby in 1872 and the start of a new parish there which originally was named St. Joseph's. By 1880, the Canon had built in the parish St. Mary's School for Boys costing £2,000 and another at Portrack which was uncompleted before his death and became known as the Carlile Memorial School. In the southern part of the town, in the year 1884, he opened St. Cuthbert's School costing £3,000 which was used as a Mass Centre, served from St. Mary's, until it became a parish in its own right.

Many parishes in the diocese have been assisted in their growth with the help of various orders of nuns. In Stockton the Sisters of Charity of St. Paul came here, in 1872, to teach in St. Mary's and St. Cuthbert's Schools; their first home was a house at the Quayside.

When Canon Carlile died in 1899 he was followed by Father (later Canon) Robert Taylerson who built the Sacred Heart Church to serve the people of Portrack and Tilery. He was, also instrumental in the opening of a Mass Centre in a council school at Stillington and according to Mr Jim Docherty, Mgr. Campbell, our present Vicar General, will still remember 'the perils of cycling to Stillington on wintry Sunday mornings'. Canon Taylerson, with great foresight, purchased land in the Newtown area which became St. Bede's parish; he lived long enough to see St. Bede's Senior Boys' School open there too.

Having served St. Mary's for 39 years he was succeeded by Doctor John McCormack the brother of Bishop McCormack. He had the church refurbished and saw it consecrated in 1942. With the advice of Mr Lindsay (father of our present Bishop) he commissioned a new organ from Nelson's of Durham and had St. Bede's Church built - a gift from St. Mary's and free of debt. His contribution to the development of Catholic education was great in the post-war years as new parishes in the expanding areas needed schools. At his suggestion, the parishes in the Deanery were asked to contribute towards the new school building programme, according to population, and the accumulated fund was available to all parishes; this idea bore fruit with the erection of schools in the areas where they were most needed.

Just as the years of Dr. McCormack had been years of expansion, the era of his successor, Canon Cornelius O'Callaghan - who came in 1954 and moved to Wolsingham in 1981 - were years of contraction. Demolition and redevelopment around St. Mary's caused a drift of population to the outskirts. At its greatest the parish contained 7,000 souls; by 1954 this figure had fallen to about 4,500; today there are 700 parishioners.

Whilst the closing of the primary school ended another chapter in the parish history Canon O'Callaghan began a new one by having the building converted into a thriving Day Centre supervised by Sister Ann Swales of the Daughters of Charity. This centre provides a community service for anyone who wishes to use it and is funded by the Social Services and the Deanery. A driver-attendant, a cook and an assistant warden provide services, with which we are all familiar, for the old and lonely. It was featured in the *Northern Cross* in December, last year.

Although presently assisted by Ushaw acolyte, Peter Hannah, the present parish priest, Father Noel Colahan, who spent three years with the Catholic Missionary Society, now ministers alone in a parish which once had five priests and seven Sunday Masses. In spite of the much smaller population St. Mary's still plays an important role in the Catholic life of the town. Being the mother church, and the parish where many older Stockton Catholics grew up, a considerable number of ex-parishioners still like to attend the services there.

An interesting innovation takes place here at the main Sunday Mass; during the Liturgy of the Word the children withdraw to the presbytery where in appropriate age-groups the Readings are explained in simple terms to them by volunteer teachers.

For 60 years the S.V.P has continued its work of charity in the parish; a parish committee assists Father Colahan with parish functions; and a Bible Class, every Friday night, attracts about 30 people. Talks for non-Catholics in the parish are given between October and April when converts are welcomed into the Church during the Easter Vigil.

If the stones of St. Mary's Church could speak they would tell us much more than we have been able to record in this article.

54. SUNDERLAND   St. Anthony's Convent   *(October, 1993)*

In mid-October, 1843, five Sisters of Mercy left their convent in Cork to begin a new foundation in an English town they probably knew very little about and which must have seemed to them, at the time, to be on the other side of the world.

Undaunted by what lay ahead and with a strong faith in Christ and their mission, they arrived in Liverpool aboard the steam-packet *Ocean,* 'after an uneventful voyage of thirty-six hours'. Here, at Mt. Vernon Convent - another new foundation - they were welcomed and cared for by their sisters. Soon they were on their way to the North East arriving by train at Durham where they were met by Father Philip Kearney, of St. Mary's in Sunderland, who brought them safely by carriage to their new abode in Green Street.

A brief reference in the *Sunderland and Durham County Herald* on Friday, October 20th, 1843, records their beginnings: 'Sunderland Nunnery. The house lately occupied by Mrs Mesnard, Green Street, in the town has been appropriated by the Roman Catholics to the purpose of a nunnery for the order of Sisters of Charity (sic) Six Ladies from Cork have already taken the veil, four of whom are young, and the remaining two advanced in life. They engage themselves in visiting the sick and in serving the destitute. An accession of numbers is shortly expected.'

There were, in fact, five ladies chosen by Mother Josephine of the Cork Mercy Community, all of whom had volunteered when asked, to begin the Sunderland foundation. Their names deserve to be recorded: Sister Mary Vincent Deasy was appointed superior and the rest of that small band were Sister Mary Aloysius O'Connell; Sister Mary Xavier Warde, Sister Mary Joseph Murphy, both novices; and a lay postulant, Agnes Scollard.

To understand why the Sisters of Mercy came to Sunderland in 1843 it is necessary to know something about the development of the Catholic community of that time. Small chapels serving small congregations, secreted in back streets, had existed long before the Catholic Emancipation Act of 1829. Prior to this date and long after it, the number of Catholics increased steadily largely due to the influx of Irish people seeking employment in the local industries. With great foresight, Father Philip Kearney, educated at Maynooth in Ireland, rose to the challenge and by 1835 had built and opened the large Early English church of St. Mary's in Bridge Street.

From this centre of post-Emancipation Catholicism Father Kearney was to be the driving force in establishing the foundations of future Catholic growth in the town. He could not, however, do this on his own, hence his appeal for help with his plans. After the completion of the church his next priority was education for the children. His first success was to persuade Bro. Edmund Rice, founder of the Christian Brothers, to send two of its members in 1836 to teach the boys in the schoolroom in Pann Lane; they were to remain until 1848 returning 100 years later to take charge of St. Aidan's, which they still do today.

It was the need to provide education for the girls which prompted Father Kearney to ask for more 'Labourers in this part of the Lord's vineyard'. His request did not go unheeded (as has already been described) when he approached the newly established order of the Sisters of Mercy founded in 1831 by Catherine McAuley, a Dublin lady.

The sisters soon established themselves in their residence near St. Mary's Church. Later, with an endowment of £1,000 left by Lady Peat, the new convent of St. Bede's (today occupied by British Home Stores) was built in Green Street where the early sisters were able to continue the expansion of their apostolic work. It soon became a common sight to see the sisters tramping the narrow streets to visit the insanitary tenement buildings where they could offer succour and consolation to the poor and sick. Existing penal legislation forbade them to wear a religious habit in public, so they were commonly seen garbed in a black cloak and bonnet with a thick gossamer veil over their faces. Their example of dedication and selflessness soon encouraged local young women to join them; the first two we know by name were, Anne and Henrietta Thompson professed as Sister Mary Joseph and Sister Mary Gonzaga.

A further glimpse of the nuns at work is afforded us when we look at a description of the time found in an S.V.P. report for, we think, 1849: 'In addition to the depression of trade which the town felt in common with the Kingdom, it suffered greatly from the blockade of the German ports ... A great number of men were thrown out of employment, in consequence of the contracts for the excavation of the docks, being about completion. It was just about this time, whilst the poor were suffering most severely, that the cholera reached this town ... the brothers then determined to make an extraordinary collection for the cases of cholera ... The brothers also bought a quantity of clothing, proper for overalls, frocks etc., and the nuns made them up; and thus were clothed the poor naked children who had been attending the schools, many of them with hardly a rag to cover them; so that then there were between 60 or 70 children clothed and educated at the expense of the Brotherhood'.

As the town's industry and population expanded there was a commensurate increase in the Catholic congregation necessitating the building of more schools and churches. Fortunately, the Mercy community numbers also increased allowing the sisters to widen their apostolate in the town. By 1870 they were teaching 'over the water' in St. Benet's parish not far from that Saxon seat of learning, St. Peter's, Monkwearmouth, where Bede received his early education.

Beyond the borough boundaries requests came for their assistance. Convents and schools were established in Hexham (1858), Darlington (1862), Tow Law (1870), Wolsingham (1890), Ryhope (1891), Seaham (1904), Easington (1923), Gosforth (1928) and Gainford (1943).

When the 50th anniversary of their arrival was celebrated in 1893 the Sisters could look back with justifiable pride at an achievement well and truly consolidated - and look forward to even greater success. A local press report of October 16th stated that: 'The golden jubilee of the foundation of St. Bede's Convent, Sunderland, was celebrated in the Convent Chapel, Green Street, this morning. There was a crowded attendance, many Protestant friends being present, and the greatest interest was taken in the celebrations which lasted about three hours. Pontifical High Mass was celebrated by the Right Rev. Dr. Wilkinson, Bishop of Hexham and Newcastle, the Rev. Father Dr. Preston (Ushaw College) acting as deacon and Father Lonsdale (Ushaw College) was the sub-deacon ... The sermon was preached by the Rev. Father Smith of London. He referred to the origin of the convent and the great progress the religious orders of women had made during the past 50 years. At one time, he said, the Sisters of Mercy were looked upon with a certain amount of suspicion but they were now almost universally respected.'

The considerable contribution made by the Sisters of Mercy to the development of Catholic education in the town cannot be underestimated - St. Anthony's School stands as a witness to that fact. In addition to running the parish school for girls at St. Mary's, the nuns were also in charge of the boys' school. They, also, started a private school for girls whose parents could afford the fees. This was the origin of St. Anthony's School then known as St. Bede's; the name change occurred in 1902 when it became a secondary school and a pupil teachers' training centre thus avoiding confusion with Bede Collegiate School started by the Local Authority. Much of the organisation and responsibility rested on the shoulders of Mother de Sales. An expanding community and school produced accommodation problems on a constricted site with little room for development so the Sisters began to look elsewhere to meet their needs. One writer describes it thus: 'Though there was an indescribable charm about the quadrangle in Green Street with its grass plot and green foliage, set like an oasis in a bleak sandy desert, with the fine stone Gothic chapel at the top left-hand corner, yet the ever increasing numbers were calling out for more space'

The solution was to be found in the area bordering Tunstall Road where large houses were occasionally for sale. The first property to be purchased was Oaklea (re-named Padua) in 1909 where boarders were accommodated. There was sufficient land around this building so a decision was made to build a new convent and chapel which were occupied in 1915 by the community allowing the Green Street convent to be used for school extensions. With the acquisition over the years of various large houses in the vicinity of Oaklea the present school was much enlarged making it possible by 1939 to relinquish the site that had been in use for 96 years.

Amongst the many links between the original foundation and the present one is a large Celtic cross in the Oaklea grounds which once stood in the garden of St. Bede's convent. Another one is the old stained-glass window from the original chapel which has recently been restored and fitted to a landing window in St. Anthony's convent.

Perhaps, the most obvious and lasting monuments to the Sisters' work are the three schools of St. Anthony's, the Montessori and St. Anne's in Wolsingham, but it would not tell the whole story as much of the work done by the community is carried out quietly and unobtrusively.

The Sisters are very involved today, like their founders, in visiting homes, hospitals and residential homes bringing Christ to those in need; some members of the community spend much of their time on parish work.

New needs offer a challenge and here the Sisters of Mercy have been flexible and responsive to it. Some years ago in conjunction with Catholic Care they established a respite home for handicapped children. Their convent at Seaham Harbour became for a time the Diocesan Youth Centre; now it functions as the Antrim Gardens Prayer Centre where groups of all ages are invited to spend a few hours of recollection in peaceful surroundings.

A further response to changing times has been the conversion of the Hexham convent into the Carntyne Residential Home under the supervision of Sister Elizabeth; it was officially opened on December 11th, 1990.

All religious orders, imbued with the missionary spirit, seek to make foundations elsewhere in order to propagate the Gospel. In 1976 Mother Martina, Sister Wilfrid, Sister Aquin and Sister Michael journeyed to Kenya and founded a school at Narok for Masai girls; this thriving school is now run by African sisters assisted by lay teachers; some years later the nuns from Sunderland began a secondary school for Masai boys at Lemek. This is now well established and is directed by the Christian Brothers from New Zealand and two American sisters. Having achieved two successful foundations the Sisters returned to work in our diocese. However, the community still has a presence in Kenya in the person of Sister Dominica who is involved in administrative work at Bishop's House in Nairobi. Sister Maureen, who has spent some time teaching in the Kenyan schools, will be returning there soon to teach in Turkana, an undeveloped desert area in Northern Kenya.

As the Sunderland Mercy Community and their branch houses prepare for their anniversary celebration they can see that much has been achieved in the last 150 years. Quoting from the short history written recently by Sister Wilfrid the past, present and hopefully the future are encapsulated in these selected extracts:

'The Sisters as a community gave their most direct input of service to poor, sick and ignorant in the first 100 years of their presence in Sunderland. They were the unpaid teachers, nurses, social workers, welfare visitors and catechists. Many of them brought endowments to the Community and/or skills by which they subsisted ... By their unflagging application to education work primarily they acted in the spirit of their foundress Catherine McAuley ... Because of this, the women and men of Sunderland acquired the skills, the training, the professional competence which enabled them to raise themselves and their families to contribute to the moral, intellectual and social well being of Sunderland ... The Sisters seem not to be needed so much in traditional apostolates. Certainly, their numbers are falling, their members ageing.

But that is not to say they are a spent force. A Sister of Mercy is not fundamentally a teacher or a nurse.

If she is of the mould of her foundress Catherine McAuley she is moved by the spirit of the Gospels to bring the compassion, the healing, the support of Christ to whom she has committed her whole life, to the areas of need that meet her in the contemporary scene. She is a person for the poor, whether poor materially, mentally or spiritually. She has a *practical* faith ever ready, as St. James says, to show her faith by her Good Works. The future will see fewer Sisters running institutes but we may hope that the generosity of young women will ensure that there will be more Sisters meeting the needs of today and tomorrow.

Catherine could not bear to fail the poor for in them she truly saw Christ himself, not in any sentimental way but according to His own solemn statement that whatever is done to the least of mankind is done to Him. The Church, the World needs such faith, such dedication expressed in practical service. It needs Sisters of many kinds but they must be women of prayer, of faith, of hope and of charity'.

Those seeking more information about the Sisters of Mercy should contact the community at St. Anthony's Convent, Tunstall Road, Sunderland.

55. SUNDERLAND   St. Mary   (April, May 1984)

Next year St. Mary's Church in Sunderland will celebrate its 150th anniversary. But not far away across the River Wear on the north bank stands the much older church of St. Peter's at Monkwearmouth built by St. Benedict Biscop in 674 A.D. and in which as a young boy the Venerable Bede was educated.

In his *Lives of the Holy Abbots*, he gives a detailed description of the church and its interior furnished by the founder, Benedict, with holy objects and pictures which he brought back with him from his travels to the continent and Rome. Like many other places in our diocese we have evidence that the seed of Faith was sown many hundreds of years ago; and in this particular case over 1300 years ago in Saxon days.

Much of the land immediately on the south side of the Wear belonged in the Middle Ages to the Bishops of Durham - hence its name Bishopwearmouth. In Bishop Hugh de Puiset's Boldon Book of 1183 we learn there were 30 villagers living in the villages of Tunstall and Wearmouth; this number, of course, does not include their families or freemen, but even so the population must have been quite small. Their place of worship, and their descendants before the Reformation, would have probably been the church of St. Michael - about half a mile from the present St. Mary's - which was largely rebuilt in the 19th and 20th centuries on a 13th century foundation believed to have been erected on the site of an earlier Saxon church.

During the days of persecution following the Reformation, although information is scarce, we have evidence that Hylton Castle in the north west of the town was used as a Mass centre by Saint John Boste and probably Father Richard Holtby. A local historian, Garbutt, tells us that in 1689 there were four Catholics in Bishopwearmouth whilst in nearby Wearmouth Panns there were 23: Robert Hallyman, Nicholas Lossaw, Robert Swinney, Jane Copeland and Mary Cresswell are five names selected at random from the list of recusants.

Some priests' names flit briefly through the story of Catholicism in Sunderland in the early part of the 18th century. The details of their dedicated lives, their problems and trials, and their places of worship are unknown to us. Only a few can be mentioned here: Father Wilkinson was known to be in the area in 1704 and we know that about this time a Father Francis Hodgson came here and in his will of 1725 he left £800 to a Mr. Marmaduke Tunstall for the support of poor Catholics in the Sunderland and South Shields area. Round about 1726 a Father Girlington came to the town after being for a time a chaplain at Dilston, near Hexham. During his stay of about three years, Bishop William came to Sunderland and confirmed 40 people. Father Allen came in the early 1730s and both priests were buried in the old Bishopwearmouth Cemetery near Silksworth Row.

The age of tolerance had not yet arrived - occasionally there were anti-Catholic riots and the *Gentlemen's Magazine* records one in Sunderland in 1746: 'Yesterday a number of people consisting chiefly of sailors went about 10 o'clock in the morning to a Popish Mass-house in the town where they found several people at prayers and a couple to be married who with Mr. Hankin their priest all fled out, upon

Sunderland, St. Mary   Photo: T. Mackin

which the sailors immediately pulled down their altar and crucifix, together with all their seats, the priest's robes, all their books, the furniture ... and burnt them in a fire for that purpose ...' believed to be on waste ground nearby. This was the Catholic chapel situated on the third floor of the house of a Mr Francis Whytehead, a master mariner, in Warren Street - now part of St. Patrick's parish.

No regular place of worship appears to have been available until the arrival of Father Bamber in 1769, who moved from Durham to Sunderland and ministered to a small flock at a small chapel in Vine Street. The law, in those days, did not allow priests to own property; to circumvent the problem lay trustees usually held the ownership. Unfortunately in this case the trustee went bankrupt and the property was forfeited. Father Bamber died in 1780 and for a short period Father James Johnson from Pontop Hall helped out until the arrival of Father Richard Rimmer who was able to say Mass in a room loaned by a relative of the bankrupt trustee.

With the passing of the Relief Act in 1791 Catholics were allowed to build public chapels. Father William Fletcher, now in charge of the Sunderland Mission, obtained a building in Dunning Street and converted it into a chapel with accommodation for 400 people. He was succeeded by Father Peter Wilcock in 1809 who was able to open a school for girls in 1813; apparently organised the first collection in the town for the building of Ushaw College amounting to £6; and as a scholar became known for his translation of Bede's *Lives of the Abbots of Wearmouth and Jarrow.*

The passing of the Catholic Emancipation Act of 1829, the gradual movement of the Irish to the north east and the coming of Father Kearney all played their part in the development of the Catholic community and the building of St. Mary's Church. When Father Philip, a native of Kells in Ireland, came to Sunderland in 1829 his task was formidable. An anonymous writer describes what he found: 'a fast increasing congregation, cabin'd cribb'd and conf'd in a dreary loft.' The interior during services would have been more attractive. With great faith and zeal he set about improving the situation. Within six months he had negotiated the sale of a piece of land between Green Street and Bridge Street from the Earl of Durham.

Six years later he was to see the church opened on September 15th, 1835, by Bishop Briggs, Bishop of the Northern District: 'A procession was formed headed by a crucifix and acolytes, with a brass band, and followed by some thousand people many bearing banners, and twenty-four Catholic priests in cassocks and surplice with the Bishop ... It proceeded from the old chapel in Dunning Street to St. Mary's where Pontifical Mass was sung and the new church dedicated to God under the invocation of His Blessed Mother'.

The church was designed in the Early English style by the Catholic architect, Ignatius Bonomi, and was, at that time, the only Catholic church in an area bounded by Felling in the north, Durham to the west and Hutton Henry to the south.

Concerned with the education of the children Father Kearney next turned his attention to the provision of a school which he soon had built in Pann Lane behind the church; the building consisted of two schoolrooms one above the other, each measuring 60 feet by 33 feet. Obtaining teachers then was a problem overcome by Father Kearney's persistence who persuaded Brother Edmund Rice, the founder of the Irish Christian Brothers, to send two brothers to Sunderland in spite of the heavy demands being made elsewhere. Father Kearney's interview was remembered by a Brother Carroll and is recorded in Brother Gillespie's *History of the Christian Brothers in England*: 'The priest called on our founder for two brothers ... but our superior regretted he could not comply ... Father Philip pressed hard and said many things about his distressed mission where he had no one to take care of his scattered flock. Fr. Philip stood up and walked to the door and raising his voice looked at our superior and said: "Mr Rice, I will not leave this room till you promise me two brothers" Our Superior, when he saw he was determined, gave his promise.'

Brothers Francis Grace and Lewis Monaghan were the two pioneering brothers who arrived here in June, 1836. What was, perhaps, unique about this school initially, was that of the 300 boys attending 250 were Protestants willingly sent by their parents; this number fell in 1841 to 130 due, no doubt, to more Catholic children seeking admission. Brother Carroll records the tolerance of the Protestant parents: 'We told their parents we could not teach them Protestant prayers. No matter, Protestant parents would say, teach them what you please. I know you will teach them nothing but what is good'.

The Christian Brothers were to leave here in 1848 but were to return 100 years later to take over Corby School (St. Aidan's) from the Jesuits - a school they still run today. One early S.V.P. report would seem to indicate that the Presentation Brothers taught at St. Mary's for a time, also.

It was Father Kearney who invited the Sisters of Mercy to the town in 1843 and their stay here has remained unbroken since that date. Their first convent and chapel in Green Street were on the site of the present British Home Stores, to the rear of the church. Mother Aloysius O'Connell was their second Superior and along with the other sisters attended to the girls' education and, after the departure of the Brothers, the boys too. Later the nuns were to provide a private school which, with the passing of the Balfour Act in 1902, enabled them to expand secondary education for Catholic girls in the town. By 1915 the convent of Oaklea in Tunstall Road was built, although the Green Street School continued to function until 1939. Secondary education became available for Catholic boys in the town and area in 1927 when Canon William Smith purchased Bede Towers which was re-named St. Mary's Grammar School. Three years after the Jesuits arrived here in 1933, to open a Retreat House (Corby Hall), they purchased a house and more land in Ashbrooke Road and the secondary school was transferred there and named after Blessed Ralph Corby. It must be remembered that, for a number of years, St. Anthony's and Corby School provided the only secondary education for Catholic boys and girls in much of the Durham area and occasionally beyond. St. Mary's School moved to Chester Road in 1902 occupying a building that had begun its life as an Infirmary - the move to the present school was made in 1974.

Increased Irish immigration, particularly following the famine years, contributed greatly to the increase in the Catholic population. It has been estimated that by 1851 there were about 4,000 Irish-born immigrants living in Sunderland - a figure which does not include children born here of Irish parents: this would explain the addition of the two side chapels at St. Mary's in 1852.

Social deprivation and economic hardship were faced by many of the parishioners in the mid-19th century and Father Kearney, ably assisted by the Christian Brothers and the Sisters of Mercy, was also helped in his labours for the poor by the formation of an S.V.P. Conference - one of the earliest, not only in the Diocese, but in England. Various annual reports from the Sunderland S.V.P., fortunately, are still extant from those early days. In 1847 they reported that they were diligent in visiting the homes of the poor; they provided them with shoes to attend the school of the Christian Brothers and helped with the small fees; and where possible 'the members use their best endeavours to procure employment for the unemployed, interest themselves in procuring proper masters for apprentices and situations for servants'.

Their report of 1849 illustrates vividly the difficulties of the time as cholera struck the town and many breadwinners became unemployed when the work on the Sunderland Docks was completed: 'The Brothers (S.V.P) then determined to make an extraordinary collection for the cases of cholera and a lady kindly volunteered to make another for providing clothes for the children then attending the schools. These collections amounted to upwards of £17 ... The Brothers also bought a quantity of cloth, proper for overalls, frocks etc., and the Nuns of the Convent of Mercy (ever ready in any charitable work) made them up, and thus were clothed the poor naked children who had been attending the schools, many of them with hardly a rag to cover them'. Thus were the conference members able to help about 60 children. They were on occasions able to provide a needy person with self-employment: 'The members have also found it a good service, when they have met with a case where there is a widow, or a man unable to do hard work, to purchase a basket and fit it out with a miscellaneous stock of huckster's wares, and send them out to sell them; and several cases have been thus taken off the funds, and they are always found to do much better ...'

Since its foundation St. Mary's has had only seven parish priests, five of whom became canons: Canon Kearney was succeeded by Father John Bamber in 1856 during whose time a number of other Sunderland parishes were started; he was followed in 1878 by Father Charles Turnerelli, the son of a sculptor to Royal families, who participated fully in the life of the town being a member of ten public bodies, two of which were the Board of Guardians and the Infirmary Committee - a good example of the toleration now being extended to Catholics and their willingness to participate in public life. When he retired through ill-health in 1897 he was succeeded by Canon Thomas Smith, parish priest for 28 years. A namesake Canon William Smith succeeded him until 1938 when Father Daniel O'Donovan came and remained in the parish until his death in 1975. Canon O'Donovan guided the parish through the turbulent war years and saw the church consecrated by Bishop McCormack on September 24th, 1947.

Town centre re-development brought with it changes in the late 1960s and early 1970s. What may have been the old school, then serving as the parish hall, was pulled down and a new hall was built opposite the church in Bridge Street. Further re-development saw this disappear and premises were acquired adjacent to the presbytery which were altered to serve as the present commodious parish centre.

Numerically and geographically the mother church of Sunderland of 1,450 souls is today still a large parish serving the needs of the people from a much wider area than the boundaries suggest. Unlike some town centre parishes whose numbers have fallen as town plans are implemented, St. Mary's remains the centre of a parish community stretching out into the suburbs. Under Father Joseph Connolly's direction the church interior has been recently altered to meet the needs of the new liturgical directives and in spite of some reduction of seating it is able to accommodate about 1,000 people who regularly attend the Sunday Masses and almost 2,000 on holydays.

Father Connolly, the present parish priest - once a curate in the parish - and his two curates, Father Michael Lockey and Father Paul Marriott, spend a considerable amount of their time visiting the Royal Infirmary and the new General Hospital as well as acting as chaplains to the Sisters of Mercy and the Christian Brothers. Due to the shortage of priests their role has extended beyond the parish taking on additional Deanery responsibilities by saying Mass when needed at weekends in the neighbouring parishes of St. Patrick's and St. Cecilia's, both of which are under the care of one priest now, Father Michael Sweeney.

The Deanery concept of co-operation does, of course, work both ways as the priests of St. Mary's are relieved of a lot of hospital night calls by a team of eleven priests working a rota system.

A parish council exists to help the priests in the spiritual and social development of the parish. In the new parish hall - very convenient for meetings in the town - many activities take place; herein is housed a branch of the Diocesan Rescue Society. CASSOC - a Catholic students' group from the Polytechnic - have their chaplaincy here. The Catholic Marriage Advisory Council, which serves a large area of East Durham and whose chairman is the parish priest, also meet regularly in the hall. A section of the CWL has done much good work in the parish over many years and still continues to do so. S.V.P. meetings usually attended by eight brothers, who continue the fine work of their predecessors, meet on a Monday evening - the same day and approximately the same time and place as their confreres did over 100 years ago.

Finally, it is worthy of note that the first parish priest, Father Kearney - who was a native of Kells in Ireland where the famous 8th century illuminated manuscript of the Gospels was written - should play such an important role in the revival of the Faith in a town where the oldest complete Latin Bible, the *Codex Amiatinus*, was written. Such ancient books remind us why St. Mary's and all our churches exist.

POSTSCRIPT *(C. Marshall, 1998)*

Since the *'Down Your Aisle'* article first appeared in April/May 1984, changes have occurred at St. Mary's. Fr. Joseph Connolly was succeeded as parish priest by Fr. Leo Pyle (1986-1997) and in 1997 he in turn was replaced by Fr. Chris Jackson, formerly an Anglican clergyman.

Other developments in the Parish included the refurbishment of the church hall, now renamed St. Mary's Parish Centre. This is used for various parish events and by groups including the Youth Club, and several outside bodies.

Also in the late 1980s and early 1990s work progressed inside St. Mary's Church on a new organ console and piper which were installed and the parish now has one of the finest musical instruments in the City.

Finally a Parish Handbook was produced in 1997 which includes brief outlines of all the groups and organisations represented in the parish – some 50 in all! This shows that St. Mary's is continuing to grow and develop into the next Millennium.

56. SUNDERLAND   St. Benet   *(April, May 1989)*

Above the main entrance to St. Benet's Church, Monkwearmouth, is a small statue of St. Benedict Biscop holding in his hand a model of a small Saxon church, St. Peter's, which still stands today (much restored) a few hundred yards distant. The name Monkwearmouth is self-explanatory and the early Christian origins of this parish of St. Benet's are preserved for us in Bede's *Lives of the Holy Abbots*. There can be few parishes which can claim to have such a detailed account of its earliest days in the 7th century.

Bede, who entered the monastery of Wearmouth at the age of 7 years, writes with affection of his spiritual father, Abbot Benedict, of noble lineage, who having been granted land in this area by King Egfrid built the church of St. Peter on the banks of the Wear in 674 A.D. Benedict, who in his lifetime made six journeys to Rome, was determined that his church should be of the best in all that pertained to the glory and worship of God.

His faithfulness to the See of Peter is evident in much that he did. He named his church after the prince of the apostles and had it built in the Roman style by stonemasons from Gaul so that '... within a year from the time of the laying of the foundation you might have seen the roof on and the solemnity of the Mass celebrated there ... he sent messengers to Gaul to fetch makers of glass (more properly artificers) who were, at this time unknown, in Britain, that they might glaze the windows of his church'.

Wishing the monastic services to be of the highest standard and on the Roman model he persuaded Pope Agatho to allow John, the archchanter of St. Peter's, to return with him 'that he might teach in his monastery the method of singing throughout the year, as it was practised at St. Peter's at Rome'.

Monkwearmouth and Jarrow thrived as centres of Faith and learning in Northumbria until the Viking raids of the 8th century. The former ceased to function as a monastery after 870 A.D. although it continued its service as a parish church. After the Norman Conquest the former monastery became a cell of the Durham Benedictines until its dissolution in 1536. One of Wearmouth's greatest treasures is the *Codex Amiatinus* - an illuminated bible written at St. Peter's in Saxon days - now a treasure in the Laurentian library in Florence.

The penal days that followed the proscribing of the Catholic Faith in England in the 16th century have left us with scant records of how Catholics weathered the persecution. Two pieces of evidence suggest, however, that the Faith did not die out completely on the north bank of the Wear. In a report of 1593, it was stated that '...The ladie Hilton did much use Boste's services and has often been at Mass'. This was the famous St. John Boste who a year later was executed at Durham for being a priest. The report more than likely refers to the chapel at Hylton Castle which was then within the boundaries of the ancient parish of Monkwearmouth. A later record of 1642 lists four papists residing in Monkwearmouth: George Simpson, Cuthbert Wilkinson, John Coleson and Henry Dickinson.

Until the opening of St. Mary's Church in Bridge Street in 1835 the Catholics who may have resided near the north side of the river would have been able to attend Mass on the south side at one of the chapels that existed in the 18th and early 19th centuries.

The growth of industry in Sunderland in the last century, particularly in shipbuilding and coal mining, brought many families into the area with a commensurate increase in the Catholic population. St. Benet's Monkwearmouth, was the third post-Emancipation parish to be founded in Sunderland when Father Gibson was appointed its first parish priest. Bishop Hogarth, writing in 1865, had this to say to the people: 'On appointing Father Matthew Gibson to be your pastor we exhort you also to be united as one man in aiding him in his zealous endeavours to carry out his intention to erect a church sufficiently commodious to contain the very numerous congregation of Monkwearmouth and its vicinity'.

In the year previous to the appointment of Father Gibson, Canon Bamber of St. Mary's had announced the creation of the new parish of St. Benet's. A site behind Broad Street (now Roker Avenue) had been purchased, probably in 1861, by the Rev. George Dunn, chaplain to the Convent of Mercy in Green Street, from the late Sir Hedworth Williamson at a cost of £300. A number of architects submitted tenders for the building of the school; it was Mr. A. Dunn's of Newcastle which was finally accepted. The school was opened in 1865 and served also as a chapel until the building of the present church in 1889.

Fathers Macartney, Connolly and Davis served for short periods at St. Benet's until the appointment of Father Jules du Floer in 1873 who was responsible for the building of the present church. He was one among a number of Belgian and Dutch priests who served the diocese so well in the years of expansion. Born at Poperinghe, West Flanders, in 1840 he was ordained at the age of 25 and taught for five years in the College of Thiet, Flanders, before proceeding to his first parish in Jarrow. After a short spell at St. Mary's, Sunderland, he came to St. Benet's where he was to spend most of his priestly life. Through his exertions and the co-operation of his flock, in what was then a much more extensive parish of about 3,000 souls, he succeeded in building the fine church of St. Benet's.

The Sunderland Herald and Morning Post gives a detailed description of the opening of the Church on July 14th, 1889. 'The magnificent new Roman Catholic Church, lately completed at Monkwearmouth, and dedicated to St. Benet was opened for divine worship yesterday by the Right Rev. Dr. Wilkinson, Bishop of Hexham and Newcastle ... Pontifical High Mass was announced to take place at eleven o'clock, but the church was filled almost an hour before that time, the congregation including many non-Catholics who had come to witness the solemn function of the occasion ... Punctually at eleven o'clock the officiating clergy accompanying the Bishop entered the church ... The Bishop robed in full pontificals, with mitre and crozier imparted his blessing to the priests and people, the orchestra bursting forth in the grand Priest's march from Mendelssohn's Athalie'.

Among the large congregation were the Sisters of Mercy from the Green Street Convent and the Little Sisters of the Poor who when they first came to Wearside in 1882 set up their first home in the Causeway near the church of St. Benet.

At the Evening Benediction of July 14th the reporter described a procession of the Holy Sacrament in which 120 little girls who took part, dressed in white with veils crowned with silver wreaths, strewed the aisles with flowers. Forty boys in surplices and cottas and 70 Children of Mary participated also - the children alternating with the choir in the singing of the verses of 'Lauda Sion'.

At last the parishioners could worship in a large church (112 ft. x 42 ft.) capable of seating about 900 people. The architects were Dunn, Hansom and Dunn of Newcastle whose design in the Early Decorated Style was executed by the contractor, Mr Lumsden of Jarrow. There is extant a design for the church by a Mr Charles Walker (who was the architect of St. Aloysius, Hebburn opened in 1888) submitted in 1887 which suggests that more than one architect was asked to tender for the contract.

In Benedict Biscop's time craftsmen had come from Gaul to beautify his Saxon church; Father du Floer, in similar fashion, had Pierre Pieters of Antwerp design the altar which was erected by Belgian workmen on site. Much of the carving internally was done by a Mr Boulton of Cheltenham whilst the later addition of the fine baptismal font was the work of a Sunderland craftsman, Mr McMillan.

Father du Floer's achievements here were many and varied; he enlarged the schools, built a new wing to the presbytery and he returned the £250 he received at his Silver Jubilee presentation to the parish as a contribution to the new organ.

He encouraged lay participation through the Children of Mary (1876) the Apostleship of Prayer, the Society of St. Vincent de Paul (1895); and the Catholic Club 'with reading rooms, bagatelle and billiard tables and every comfort for the members'. An accomplished musician he produced an annual concert for 24 years and left behind a fine musical tradition in the parish which still continues today.

Due to ill-health and increasing parochial responsibilities Father du Floer retired from St. Benet's in 1897 to live with his sister at Poperinghe, his birthplace, where he died in 1904, aged 64.

About the time of his retirement the local press wrote movingly of him. He was said to have known every person in his parish, forever moving about amongst them and visiting them regularly ... 'Not only did he attend to their spiritual needs but he busied himself with their material interest proving ... to the poor, Catholic and Protestant alike, a guide philosopher and friend'. As one writer put it 'He had a wonderful way with him; all the young children were wild for to play with him; all the old people were wishful to pray with him'. As Father P. J. Haydon S.J. remarked at his Silver Jubilee celebration applying the inscription of Wren and St. Paul's to Father du Floer and St. Benet's: 'IF YOU WANT TO SEE A MONUMENT OF THIS MAN, LOOK ABOUT YOU.'

Canon Gillow, a member of an old Lancashire Catholic family succeeded Father du Floer and remained there until the arrival of the Redemptorist Fathers on September 20th, 1900.

The invitation to the Redemptorists - who had been giving Missions in the diocese using members of the Perth Community - to take over at Monkwearmouth came from Bishop Wilkinson, via his auxiliary, Richard Preston, in August, 1900. Father John Bennett, the Redemptorist provincial was informed and in some correspondence with Father Magnier C.S.S.R. he seemed to accept the offer remarking: 'there is a fine church and house - a garden retired from the street. It would be a magnificent mission centre and house of retreat for priests ... I do not think we could get anything to compare to it and I think it would be a fearful mistake not to take it. A religious house is awfully wanted at Sunderland and will do enormous good all over that thickly populated district ... the honour of God and the salvation of souls demand that we should not let such a chance slip from us ...'

There may have been earlier correspondence and deliberations about the move to St. Benet's but it appears from the available records that the decision was made extremely quickly for the Redemptorists to arrive the following month. Father Stebbing was the first rector assisted by Fathers Gaisford, McMullen and Taggart and three brothers: Brother Gerard from Clapham and Brothers Daniel and Mark from Bishop Eton.

By August 1902 the monastery building was completed and in that same year a school-chapel was erected in Southwick; it was handed over to the diocese in 1905 to form the separate parish of St. Hilda's.

This article has concentrated on the early history of the parish - a fuller treatment detailing the work of the Redemptorists and people here in the 20th century will be found in the parish history soon to be published. However, four important events are worthy of a brief mention. In 1924 Cardinal Bourne visited the parish to celebrate the 1250th anniversary of St. Peter's and addressed a congregation of 10,000 at the Bede Memorial in Cliff Park. Bishop McCormack officiated at the church's 50th Anniversary Mass where the congregation were reminded that Father du Floer in order to raise money for the building of the church 'used to stand outside Sunderland shipyards to collect from Catholic men and often he received from non-Catholics.'

Nearer to our own time, during the rectorship of Father Frank Dickinson (a great supporter of *Northern Cross*), the church was re-decorated and the sanctuary re-ordered 'in accordance with the Church's wishes, so that we, priests and people can be seen to be one worshipping community, offering one sacrifice of Our Lord and each of us playing his proper part ...' The new altar was consecrated when Bishop Swindlehurst concelebrated Mass here on March 24th, 1983.

Last year Father Timothy Buckley along with parishioners, the C.W.L. and the Cleadon Floral Arrangement Society, held a Festival of Flowers in St. Benet's Church to mark the Bicentenary of the death of the Redemptorist Order's founder, St. Alphonsus de Liguori. St. Benet's, on June 17th, joined other Redemptorist parishes and groups from all over Britain in Westminster Cathedral to celebrate with Cardinal Hume the Redemptorists' founder's anniversary.

Priests and people of St. Benet's now look forward to another anniversary - the centenary of their church on July 14th, 1989.

Many memories will be revived in the church and parish of St. Benet (the builder of St. Peter's) over the coming months: this house of the Lord where for 100 years the people of the parish have worshipped and praised God as a community contains this inscription below the Munich window: 'Pray for the good estate of the Rev. Jules du Floer, by whose untiring exertions the church has been increased and in your charity pray for the donor of this window A.D. 1888'. The donor of this window was a Miss Taylor of the Esplanade. There will be many other prayers offered too for all those who have made St. Benet's what it is today.

57. SUNDERLAND　　　St. Cecilia and St. Patrick　　　*(January, February 1999)*

Within the parish boundaries of the present St. Cecilia and St. Patrick's parish (amalgamated in 1982) the story of our Faith is deeply rooted in the past.

Across the river is St. Peter's, Monkwearmouth, where Bede began his life as a monk. The monastery received a later grant of land on the south side (in the present parish) and this may explain the origin of the town's name - the land sundered by the river. One source claims that there may have been a 13th century chapel dedicated to Our Lady on this piece of land. We know very little about how Catholics preserved their Faith after the 16th century Reformation; there is evidence that Mass was celebrated at Hylton Castle and Ralph Corby, the Jesuit martyr, was shipped from Sunderland to suffer martyrdom at Tyburn.

Before the relaxation of the penal laws the few Catholics in Sunderland worshipped quietly, in the 18th century, in the room of a house belonging to Mr Francis Whytehead, a master mariner of Warren Street. When the Jacobite rebellion failed to restore the Stuarts to the throne there were outbursts of anti-Catholic feeling one of which occurred in 1746 at the Warren Street chapel in the East End when a group of sailors raided the premises 'where they found several people at prayers and a couple to be married who with Mr Hankin, their priest, all fled out'. No one was harmed but the furniture, vestments and books were taken outside and burnt.

Catholic congregations were very small then; the Papist Returns of 1767 list about 150 in our town. In 1769 Father John Bamber moved from Durham and came to reside in a house in Vine Street (again in the East End and not far from Warren Street) where he opened a small chapel. Sometime after 1782, a chapel was opened in Dunning Street and served the Catholics of the area until St. Mary's was opened in 1835.

One hundred and forty years ago the East End of the town was a densely populated area in which lived many Irish people who had come to the town seeking a better life. In 1861 there were almost 5,000 Irish-born people living in Sunderland. Most of these would have been Catholic, so priests from St. Mary's came, we think, and said Mass in the old Arcade Hall until St. Patrick's was built - many Sunderland Catholics are descended from these families. Opened on December 8th, 1861, it was the second post-Emancipation church in the town; a year later Father A. Buckley was appointed as the first resident priest. Before the days of universal free education the church, seeing the paramount importance of educating children in the Faith, wherever possible, provided schooling. St. Patrick's began life as a school-chapel divided by a thick green curtain which was drawn aside for Mass and other services. The first teachers were Mr & Mrs Michael Crangle who lived in part of the adjoining presbytery.

More suitable school accommodation was provided when the Union Chapel and Session House was purchased on the corner of Coronation Street and Sussex Street (not far from where the present Catholic Youth Centre stands) in 1871 and was the main school until St. Patrick's All-Age School was built and opened nearby in 1906.

St. Patrick's continued to thrive as a community until well after the Second World War but re-development in the area, the demolition of old property and the building of new estates in the western part of the town led to a mass exodus. On December 6th, 1984, the last Mass in St. Patrick's church was concelebrated by Bishop Swindlehurst and 20 priests; some, like Father Mallaly who preached the sermon, had served here as curates. Many people attended and reminisced on their days in the school and the church. St. Cecilia's church has some of the stained-glass from St. Patrick's, the trowel used at the laying of the foundation stone and the brass memorial plaque commemorating the men who died in the First World War. The Stations of the Cross now adorn the walls of St. Mary's Cathedral and much of the slate has been used in the roof at St. Godric's, Durham, when it was repaired after the fire. So much more could be written about this old parish. Perhaps, if we list some of the priests who served here it may evoke memories for older people: Fathers Marley, Anthony, Bull, Stack, Mullaly, Kellett, Sharratt are but a few of many who gave much to the people here.

St. Cecilia's first place of worship was a 'tin church' in Corporation Road (still standing, now the property of the Maranatha community) opened in April, 1926, and served as a chapel-of-ease from St. Mary's.

It became a parish in its own right with the appointment of Father William Harris as the first parish priest who arrived here on December 18th, 1927, to live in the newly-acquired presbytery at 46, Percy Terrace. These were difficult economic times yet the parishioners, although having little to give, were most generous with their offerings and time in developing the life of this new parish. It has been estimated that in 1929 the parish's regular weekly income was about £9 per week supplemented by profits from Whist Drives, Bazaars, Garden Fetes, Raffles etc.

When Father Bernard Sharratt arrived as the first curate in September, 1929, he set about turning the 2 acre site (purchased from the Wearmouth Coal Company, and costing about £1,000 per acre) into a market garden assisted by some of the unemployed men of the parish who were only too willing to assist the church in any way they could.

Father Harris, who was not in good health, left St. Cecilia's in 1937 to be replaced by Father McManemy who like all the succeeding priests attempted to have a school built; he claimed, at that time, there were 400 children of school age in the parish. Like his predecessor he too did not have good health, so after almost two years here he moved to the quieter parish of Bellingham to be replaced in 1939 by Mgr. Jefferys, who had been headmaster at St. Cuthbert's Grammar School. His priority was the school which, it is said, would have cost £10,000. It is likely - had the war not intervened - that the church, school and presbytery would have been built on the Corporation Road site.

Those who lived through the War remember vividly the effect it had on their lives and the parish. The evacuation of children to the safety of the countryside, the call-up of men to the armed forces, the black-out, and the bombing were to disrupt the normal life of the parish. Air-raid shelters were built in the church grounds, the men of the parish formed a fire-watching rota in case incendiary bombs fell on the church and

Catholics wore lapel badges on which were the words: 'In case of injury call a Catholic priest'.

The night of October 11th, 1942, was a particularly bad one for the area and the parish. It was customary for Father Sharratt to go to the church for the Blessed Sacrament to take to the injured. That night as he approached the church door a 2,000lb bomb exploded 50 yards away near Villette Road. He flung himself to the ground and managed to escape serious injury. There was much devastation round about and the church was badly damaged. Until the church was repaired Sunday Mass was said in the hall (commonly known as the hut) and daily Mass in the presbytery. Shortly before this incident Mgr. Jefferys and Father Sharratt had been appointed to Thornley so one can imagine how the new parish priest, Father Vincent Duffy, felt when he arrived and saw an unusable temporary church.

Father Duffy, assisted from 1942 by Father John Gannon, helped to see the parish through these traumatic events. The latter was much interested in the youth, organising a Boys' Club and a parish football team.

When Father Hugh O'Connor came from Rowlands Gill to succeed Father Duffy the war was almost over and there was much rejoicing and thanksgiving at the conclusion. The lifting of the war-time building restrictions enabled Father O'Connor and the people to consider the building of a permanent church. However, the demolition of older property in the east of the parish and the building of new houses in the west meant that the original site was no longer central. Father O'Connor - assisted during his time here by Fathers Gannon, Meagher, Burns and O'Gorman - was determined to raise the necessary funds and find a new site.

On the land where Southmoor School now stands was a farmhouse belonging to the Scott-Briggs family. The two sisters living there had been approached by Father O'Connor and at the same time, the Local Authority were interested in building a technical school on this piece of land..

Father O'Connor decided to write to the nephew of the two ladies, a Captain Scott-Briggs of Cornhill, who, on April 15th, 1954, replied that if the parish could collect 1,200 signatures demanding that no changes be made to the Grand National he would give half an acre free. The signatures were forwarded and the land was obtained. It is believed that Father O'Connor made special visits to the church for this request and asked his deceased young relatives - 'his angels in heaven' - to pray for this intention. When Captain Scott-Briggs received an invitation to the opening his reply was: 'I look forward to seeing your church and hope you will make it a thing of beauty as well as a joy forever'.

On June 6th, 1955, building work was begun by the firm of D. & J. Ranken to a design of the architects, S.W. Milburn and Partners. Older parishioners still remember the sense of anticipation as the church neared completion. The last Sunday services were held in the old church on Sunday, February 24th, 1957; it had served the parish for 30 years and was for many an association of sad and happy memories.

Bishop Joseph McCormack opened and blessed the new church in the presence of a packed congregation, a fulfilled Father O'Connor and his assistant, Father William O'Gorman, who became a great source of strength and support when Father O'Connor suffered a broken femur. He made a partial recovery, dying in 1962, a much-loved priest whose persistence and enthusiasm gave the parish their church costing approximately £29,500; much of the amount being raised through the Football Trebles and parish bingo. He will be remembered for that, but also for his priestly example, particularly with the young people whom he led in the Faith. His Little Army of the Little King (the Holy Infant of Prague devotion) is just one example of how he encouraged the youth to follow Christ. His wish was to be buried among his parishioners in Sunderland Cemetery; a Celtic Cross marks his resting place.

His successor was Canon J.L.Vincent Smith - an ex-army chaplain and later administrator of the Diocesan Rescue Society - who was the nephew of Canon Smith of St. Mary's, the founder of St. Cecilia's parish. It was during his incumbency that Vatican II occurred and he and Father Michael Keoghan saw to the implementation of the changes in the liturgy. Until 1972 when the main altar was brought forward, a temporary wooden altar was used for what was then new in the Catholic church - a vernacular Mass, facing the people, begun in St. Cecilia's in 1966.

Other changes in Canon Smith's time were the conversion of the old tin church into a parish hall; the building in 1964 of a meeting room (now part of the extended parish hall); and the Lady Altar which used to be in a niche at the front of the church was brought forward. This altar was donated by Miss Mallon, a former teacher of St. Patrick's School. The reredos of this altar and Our Lady's statue were the gifts of anonymous donors.

It was Canon Smith who introduced Planned Giving which helped to put the parish finances on a firm footing. Before its introduction the average income was £70 per week; the new system raised it to £117.

Parishioners and many Sunderland people are aware of the erection every Good Friday of the cross on Tunstall Hill - a public witness, for over 30 years, to our Faith. The idea came from Our Lady's Sodality, started by Canon Smith. This group met weekly for Bible discussions and how to apply Christian principles to everyday life. When Canon Smith retired in 1974 the responsibility for the parish fell to the curate Father Keoghan, who was to leave in 1975 to become parish priest in North Shields when Father Gerard White was appointed to St. Cecilia's.

Father White's years here saw the introduction of the Sunday Bulletin, a revival of the choir, the beginning of Offertory Processions and the extension of the meeting room into the fine parish hall it is today. He was, also, here when the parish celebrated its Golden Jubilee in 1977 - a very joyful occasion for everyone.

The present parish priest, Father Michael Sweeney, replaced Father White on his retirement, coming from St. Patrick's where he was the last parish priest. He had the unenviable task of supervising the demolition of the church and school. Sadly, also, in 1999 the Joint Catholic-Anglican school of St. John and St. Patrick's will close due to falling rolls. This school became the first ecumenical school in the country when the Catholic children went there in 1981 at the closure of St. Patrick's.

There is much happening in St. Cecilia's today. Parish activities are many and varied catering for most age groups. The S.V.P., started in 1928, continues the work of helping those in need. The next oldest organisation is the C.W.L. (claiming to be one of the first sections in the diocese) founded in the early days of the parish - although going into abeyance for a number of years until revived by Canon Smith in 1964. The members do much valuable work in the parish and beyond.

Other groups have sprung up over the years to meet the needs of young and old. A Hall Committee ably organises much of the social life in the parish. Activities and groups such as the Children's Liturgy Group, the Mother and Toddlers, the Senior Citizens, a Care Group, the Journey in Faith, the Two-plus group (a kindergarten) and the Craft Group which meets socially and has raised £800 in the past few months for charity; Sequence Dancing, Carpet Bowls, parish lunches, the Autumn Fayre and Summer Barbecue, the Sunday Coffee morning are all means of providing the people of the parish with an opportunity to participate in the life of the parish family. Lay ministers of the Eucharist enable those confined to their homes or in residential care to receive Communion frequently. In December a Justice and Peace Group was formed and hopes to promote awareness of issues concerning human rights.

So many people are involved in the above-mentioned activities that it is not possible to name them all. The smooth running of the parish is dependent on a large number of parishioners who give so generously of their time, often unseen and unheralded, - it is much appreciated by all. But there are two people who, everyone would agree, are worthy of mention by name. The first is Frances (Dolly) Thompson, the housekeeper, who has been looking after priests for more than 50 years and is still very active and efficient in spite of her 85 years. Secondly, there is Sister Angela, the parish sister, who spends much of her time walking around the extensive parish visiting the sick, the housebound and elderly and whose smiling countenance is known by so many people, including non-Catholics, in the area. She continues a long tradition of service by the Sisters of Mercy to St. Patrick's and St. Cecilia's parishes.

Since March, 1994, the parish has been blessed with the presence of the Emmaus Community who reside in the former Anglican vicarage of St. John's, not far from where St. Patrick's Church once stood. The community is involved in a variety of ministries, working in the Catholic Youth Centre, with families, older people and the local community association. Retreats and spiritual direction are also part of their service to a wider community.

The words of Father White in the preface to the parish history, written in 1977, are a fitting way to conclude the article: 'These men and women in the parish, who give so willingly of their time are the best monuments to the past fifty years. They are the living evidence of the spirituality of the parish so well fostered by all the priests who have worked in the parish'.

58. THROPTON   All Saints   *(September, 1984)*

Coquetdale is rich in Catholic history - much of it yet unwritten - and the parish of All Saints, Thropton, is a witness of that tradition and demonstrates the strong adherence of its inhabitants past and present to it.

To trace the parish's early history one can begin in nearby Rothbury where today a modern Catholic chapel stands. Not far away is the Anglican church, largely rebuilt in 1850, but originally of the 13th century. Within can be found an early relic relating to our Christian past: it is an Anglo-Saxon cross-shaft of about 800 A.D. supporting the font bowl of 1664. The sculpture shows one of the earliest carved representations, in England, of Christ's Ascension; other parts of this ancient cross are now kept in the Black Gate Museum, Newcastle.

A few miles west of Thropton can be seen another reminder of the Ancient Faith at Holystone where it is claimed St. Paulinus baptised 3,000 Northumbrians, on Easter Day at St. Ninian's Well or as it became known later - Lady's Well. The name change occurred when a community of Augustinian nuns was founded there by the Umfraville family and dedicated to St. Mary the Virgin; a member of the family took holy orders and became chaplain to the Sisters.

Before the Reformation a chapel was known to exist, in the early 15th century, at Cartington Castle and during the penal days the centre of Catholic worship moved from Rothbury to this quieter spot, about one and a half miles from Thropton. It is probable that one of the early tenants of Cartington was a Ralph de Fresburn who whilst on the Crusades came into contact with a group of hermits on Mount Carmel. Some of the friars returned with him and established themselves at Hulne, near Alnwick; Ralph, himself, joined the community becoming prior and later provincial of the Carmelites before his death in 1254.

In 1408 a William Chesman is mentioned as tenant of Cartington and it was he who was granted a licence for Divine Service in his chapel; a William Chesman - possibly the same person - appears to have joined the Cistercian Community at Newminster, near Morpeth.

By the middle of the 15th century Cartington Castle and much of the land thereabouts was in the hands of a family of that name and remained so until the marriage of the heiress, Ann Cartington, to Sir Edward Radcliffe when it became part of the Radcliffe estates. A Sir Francis Radcliffe, born in 1563, was convicted of recusancy and imprisoned in 1592; and in that same year a search was made of the castle for priests, 'but there were such secret conveyances and close corners made in walls that unless they hungered them out they could do no good'. The family's piety and firmness of faith are well attested when we learn that four Radcliffe girls became Poor Clares in the convent at Gravelines in Flanders. A fifth daughter married Roger Widdrington into whose family the estates passed remaining with their descendants until the last of them, a Reverend Gilbert Talbot, passed away in 1747; he was one of the founders of the Thropton Mission.

Lady Mary Charlton, who had married Sir Edward Charlton of Hesleyside, lived at Cartington after her husband's death in 1674 and three years later, along with her mother, was listed as a recusant. Lady Mary was well-known for her strong faith and ability to make converts. She was responsible for the founding of almshouses for four poor widows of the Rothbury parish; the house today - once called by locals, the 'nunnery' - is now in private hands. With a lull in the persecution during the reign of James II, Bishop Leyburn, the Vicar-Apostolic, was able to visit the Thropton area, in 1687, confirming 146 people - among them familiar Northumbrian families with names such as Selby, Robson, Davison, Howey and Potts.

Various people can claim the honour of helping, in part, to establish the Thropton mission and parish.

A Mrs Clare Ord (a Widdrington) who died in 1697 left a fund, a ciborium and church plate for the resident priest in Rothbury parish 'to assist ye poor Catholicks'. The Reverend Roger Mitford, a native of the parish and a Douay man, who was tutor and chaplain to Francis, the first Earl of Derwentwater, left two funds: the first one to the Douay College to educate a young man - preferably a Northumbrian - to the priesthood and the second 'to assist ye people near Rothbury, to be supplyed by one educated on that left to Douay'. The Reverend Gilbert Talbot, who succeeded to the Cartington estates in 1733, left £800 to the Franciscans at Osmotherley in Yorkshire and it is believed that the fund eventually reverted to Thropton to support the mission.

John Warburton writing, sometime before 1715, about old buildings in Northumberland states: 'At Thropton is a house lately purchased by the executors of Madam Ord of Cartington for ye maintenance of and entertainment of a Popish priest'. Another source claims there was a Mass house at the Rev. Mitford's house in 1736. This was the Reverend James Mitford, a nephew of the one mentioned earlier; James followed the Rev. William Edisford - a Yorkshireman educated at the English College in Rome - believed to be the first resident priest here. The Rev. James Mitford came to Thropton before 1712 dying at the age of 80 in March, 1750. Another descendant of the Mitfords, a Rev. Luke Potts, succeeded him and remained here for 37 years until he died in 1787 'suddenly in the kitchen after he had just settled and paid off all his bills' - possibly meaning in the guarded language of the time a hidden reference to the reception of the Last Sacraments.

During his time here, we know of two returns of papists made by the Anglican clergy at Rothbury: in 1767 there were 17 Catholics at Thropton and a total of 64 within the Rothbury Anglican parish boundaries among them the four widows at the Cartington almshouses - Mary Turner, Mary Robson, Christian Gardiner and Mary Stuart. In 1780 it was estimated that there were 48 papists in the same area over 16 years of age.

In 1797 there arrived in Thropton from the chaplaincy at Callaly Castle the Rev. Thomas Stout. Like many other priests of that time he had been educated at Douay and was a contemporary of Father Worswick. Like him, he too had fled from the college when the French Revolutionary forces invaded Flanders and was imprisoned at Doullens. When the hasty evacuation occurred one concealed treasure they left behind was the body of Blessed John Southworth. Many years later, in 1927, some workmen came across human

Thropton, All Saints   Photo: T. Mackin

remains while clearing a site for a new road in the vicinity of the Douay College. Father Stout had made notes on where the body was hidden and from them it was possible to pinpoint the place of concealment and identify the remains now at rest in Westminster Cathedral.

Father Stout rebuilt the Thropton presbytery which included a small chapel in 1810; this was extended by Rev. George Corless in 1842 giving it its present day form. Remarkable, in this Lancet style church, is the screen of three arches with pendants, separating the chancel from the nave. Bridge building was considered a work of charity in the Middle Ages enabling travellers and pilgrims to journey more easily and directly between destinations. This tradition seems to have been continued, by the Rev. Stout who it is claimed was instrumental in the building of the present road bridges at Thropton and Snitter. An entry in the register of Thropton Catholic Chapel reads thus: 'Thropton Bridge was founded 24th May, 1810, finished May 30th, 1811 - built by George Robson, Catholic - cost £365.'

Some of the old baptismal registers are still preserved and they contain quite a number of conditional baptisms presumably due to the fact that baptism was administered very soon after birth and if a priest was not available, or travelling conditions were difficult, the parents would do it themselves taking the child at a later date to the priest for conditional baptism when an opportunity arose.

Again, we cannot mention here all the priests who laboured quietly and effectively in this area of Northumberland; the work of the present parish priest exemplifies this fine continuing tradition. Father Thomas Vincent Sheehan, who has been here for twenty-three years would describe his parish of 201 souls - including Biddlestone (now infrequently used as a chapel), Rothbury and a number of other villages - as a praying parish and one where there is a wonderful relationship with non-Catholics.

There are no Catholic schools in this scattered parish but the Faith of the young is strengthened at an early age by means of an 'Over to You' course which has been running for three years now under the supervision of Miss Kerr and Sister Beatrice. The course, quite simply, sets out to instruct mothers on how to pass on the Faith to their children. Sister Michael from Alnwick Convent comes every Saturday to give religious instruction to the children and about four times a year special children's Masses are celebrated and are looked forward to eagerly by parents and children.

For many years Catholics in Rothbury were able to hear Sunday Mass through the generosity of a Miss Livingstone of Front Street who made available an upstairs room of a converted stable block. Now Rothbury has a sturdy stone chapel of its own cared for by local parishioners and served by Father Sheehan every Sunday and certain weekdays; the Sunday Mass attendance averages 70, swelling in the summer to 200 with the influx of visitors. The chapel which was opened in 1959, costing £10,500, was paid for from a benefaction left in the will of Doctor Arthur Samuel Hedley. The architect of St. Agnes' at Rothbury was Edward Gunning of Newcastle and the builder was Willie Brown, a member of an old Catholic family of Thropton. Other activities pursued here for the strengthening of the Faith are a prayer group, regular House Masses (attended, also, by a few non-Catholics), May recitation of the Rosary at home, a weekly Bible Study class, the C.W.L. and, of course, the S.V.P. which has done excellent work in the area for a considerable number of years.

All Saints parish, then, is another good example of the living 'Faith of our Fathers' and typifies the efforts made yesterday and today - sometimes at considerable sacrifice - to keep it and pass it on.

59 TOW LAW, St. Joseph & WILLINGTON, Our Lady and St. Thomas   [July, August, 1994]

This year the people of Tow Law are celebrating 150 years of their town's history. The Catholics of St. Joseph's parish and their non-Catholic friends, along with Bishop Ambrose, commemorated the occasion with a special Mass in St. Joseph's Church on June 15th.

More than a century and a half ago, in 1841, Tow Law was no more than a hill-top hamlet with about 30 inhabitants whose quiet seclusion was to be considerably disturbed with the development of Charles Attwood's Weardale Iron and Coal Company. By 1846 six furnaces were producing iron in the vicinity and coal production was rising too. These two labour-intensive industries were demanding, as they expanded, more and more workers, a goodly proportion of whom (about 10% of the growing town's population) came from the north and west of Ireland landing at Whitehaven and journeying on foot across the Pennines to this new source of employment.

It has been estimated that in 1851 the town's population had grown to 2,000; by 1861 it was in excess of 3,000 reaching a peak in 1871 of around 5,000.

Such a large influx of newcomers meant - especially with the Irish migration - a commensurate rise in the Catholic population. Bishop William Hogarth saw the need for a mission here and in 1849 he sent the newly-ordained convert Anglican, Thomas Wilkinson, as pastor to the Weardale Catholics. Thomas deserves a biography to himself having played a major role in our rapidly developing diocese in the latter half of the 19th century as priest, canon, bishop and president of Ushaw. A native of Weardale he helped to establish four missions here at Wolsingham, Tow Law, Crook and Willington.

Although he was appointed to Tow Law he decided to reside initially in Wolsingham where he opened a chapel in 1849 and built the present church in 1854. His ministrations extended to Crook which he supplied from 1852 and a year later he had opened a new church there.

For a number of years it appears that the Catholics of Tow Law journeyed to Wolsingham for Sunday Mass until 1857 when Father Wilkinson began to make weekly visits there saying Mass in the house of a local Catholic. He was able to open a small school-chapel built on a piece of land given by the owner of the ironworks, Mr Attwood - this first building was probably on the site which was later to become the Mercy Convent.

Shortly after the opening of the chapel at Tow Law he moved from Wolsingham to Crook and was succeeded by Fr. George Caley who stayed for just over a year. Fr. Robert Orrell followed him and in 1865 he built and extended the school-chapel. In 1866 a new, young, 31 year-old priest, Father William Gillow, arrived who two years later was able to witness the laying of a memorial stone for a new school-chapel by Edward Taylor Smith of Colpike Hall. An extract from *The Tablet of 1868* notes: 'The School hitherto in

Willington, Our Lady & St. Thomas

use being much too small for use as a chapel, and not admitting of any enlargement, the erection of a new school-chapel was undertaken with the generous co-operation of Edward Taylor Smith and of his son Thomas Taylor Smith of Hedley Hope Colliery, the former having made a free grant of a valuable plot of ground and the latter having purchased the old school at a liberal valuation with a view to its conversion into cottages'.

It was completed and opened in June 1869 and named after St. Thomas of Canterbury (a favourite saint of Thomas Wilkinson) but later changed to St. Joseph, to avoid confusion with the Wolsingham church. It was used exclusively as a church after 1870 when St. Joseph's School was erected and stands today substantially as it was then with the additional north aisle of 1876.

Just as Thomas Wilkinson returned to minister in the area of his birth, the fifth priest to serve Tow Law, Father William Taylor Smith, whose forebears (mentioned above) had supported the Tow Law mission, was to do likewise. It was Father William who invited the Sisters of Mercy to come and teach in Tow Law; four sisters arrived with their superior on June 14th, 1870, and the Order was to remain here until 1928 doing valuable work in the parish and school. They still retain a presence in Weardale at their school in Wolsingham. Father Taylor Smith was able to reside at Tow Law when the presbytery was completed in 1872; he died at Wolsingham in 1891 but his memory is perpetuated in the church of Tow Law and the street named after him there.

Three mementoes of those pioneering days are still extant in the parish: 'The Book of Life' listing donors of the 1876 north aisle extension; a fine Calvary group by Mayer of Munich on the plinth of which is a brass plaque to the memory of Edward Taylor Smith; and a chalice with the inscription: 'Presented by congregation and other friends of St. Joseph's, Tow Law, 1874'.

It is not possible in a short article to recount the many happenings in Tow Law since its formation as a parish.

Perhaps, one can conclude by mentioning the new primary school where the Faith is taught to the descendants of those Catholic ancestors who built up the church community here over many years. The school is appropriately named after Blessed John Duckett who was arrested on the Tow Law - Wolsingham road after baptising two children in the area. A cross near the summit of Redgate Hill marks the spot where he was apprehended; he was taken to London, tried and martyred at Tyburn along with the Jesuit martyr, Blessed Ralph Corby on September 7th, 1644.

Father John Reid, who is the parish priest of Tow Law, also, serves and resides in the Willington parish. As early as 1868 in the Crook Visitation Return of that year it is stated, we think, by Fr. Wilkinson: 'A few old people in Willington may not be able to travel and a Mass is said there occasionally on a weekday for them... The room at Willington established by leave of the late Bishop where Mass is occasionally said by myself'. Fr. Wilkinson, we know, journeyed to Willington to say Mass, hear confessions and instruct the children.

The first parish priest to be appointed to Willington was from Belgium, Father Aloysius Hosten, who received part of his theological training at the English College in Bruges, being ordained at Ushaw in 1869. He was to spend most of his priestly life in Willington laying the firm spiritual foundations of the parish and building the church; he died in 1923 and lies buried near the entrance to the church.

On his arrival in 1877 he took lodgings in the town when after two years he was able to move into the newly-built presbytery adjacent to which was the school-chapel. This was the place of worship for Willington Catholics for 26 years until in 1905 the fine stone cruciform church of Our Lady of Perpetual Succour and St. Thomas was built by a Mr Hopper of Wolsingham to a design of a London architect, a Mr. Kelly. The wide round-arched windows allow plenty of natural light to enter the church and one's eye is immediately attracted to the three colourful murals, within arches, on the wall of the apse of biblical scenes, the New Testament ones being: The Feeding of the 5,000, the Crucifixion and the miracle of Cana - all the work of L. Beyaert of Bruges completed in 1912.

Father Hosten encouraged the people to participate fully in the spiritual and social life of the parish. He established a fine choir to enrich the Latin liturgy at sung Masses and Benediction on Sundays and holydays. He formed the Institute where parishioners could mix socially and avail themselves of a good library and even a snooker table! Before and after Father Holmes time (1925-1952) lay societies flourished such as the S.V.P., the C.Y.M.S., the Boy Scouts, a football team, the Children of Mary and the Women's Guild.

Willington parish can boast a number of priestly vocations too. Father Richard Crawford was the first diocesan priest from the parish to be ordained whilst Fathers Traynor, Finnigan and Minto joined the Mill Hill Fathers. Father Connolly became a Salesian, Father Giblin a Sacred Heart Father. The most recent ordination was that of Father Purvis, a priest in the Salford Diocese, who died at the early age of 38.

Within the extensive boundaries of these two rural parishes Father Reid and his parishioners, proud of their inheritance, continue the work of the Gospel begun by their predecessors. Willington, like Tow Law, has its own small primary school whose patrons are Our Lady and St. Thomas; rather different from the cramped school-chapels of old. Children from both schools proceed to St. John's, Bishop Auckland, for their secondary education. The S.V.P. continues its work of helping those in need. Each parish has its own pastoral council and a shared liturgy committee enabling the people to work with their priest for the benefit of all in the area.

Two Ladies' Groups meet regularly (one in each parish) where guest speakers are invited and the raising of funds for the parish is part of their on-going commitment.

Unfortunately, space does not allow us the opportunity to mention all the good priests who served Tow Law and Willington for more than a century, nor the many good souls, past and present, who have generously given their time and talents to the church in Weardale. The celebrations at Tow Law in June enabled them to be remembered and appreciated.

60. TUDHOE   St. Charles   *(October, November 1986)*

Tudhoe, one of the prettiest villages in Durham County, lies in tranquil seclusion undisturbed by the rush of traffic which uses the Durham - Spennymoor road a short distance away. A long village, with its green bordered by mainly period houses (two are of great Catholic interest), it has probably changed little over the centuries giving an air of permanence and stability - qualities which are also part of the story of the Faith in this stronghold of Catholicism. The church of St. Charles Borromeo, south of the village green, is the visible reminder of this past of which the parish priest and people are so proud.

The two earliest religious vocations recorded there were those of John de Tuddoe, who became Vicar of Hartburn in 1393 and later Rector of Boldon; and Agnes Tuddowe, who in 1437, became Prioress of Neasham, a Benedictine convent near Darlington.

Like so many other places in the county the religious changes of the early 16th century were resisted, culminating in the Rising of the North in 1569 to restore the ancient practices of the Faith. After its failure the repercussions were felt far and wide resulting in the sequestration of land, fines and the execution in Durham City of two men from Tudhoe.

Penal legislation made life extremely difficult for those who still wished to practise the old Faith; for a priest to say Mass or for anyone to harbour a priest the punishment could be death, or a lengthy period of imprisonment. In spite of the risks incurred it would appear that the Catholic Faith survived in Tudhoe during these hard times.

Almost at the far end of the village, some distance from the present church and to the left of the green, is Tudhoe Hall Farm which, it is claimed, was a Catholic residence in the time of Elizabeth I. Mr Coia in his fascinating history of the parish states that the Hall boasts a priest's hiding-hole still visible in an upstairs room at the rear of the house. He goes on to suggest that there may have been an underground passage from the Hall to Tudhoe House, on the opposite side of the green, which would afford priests and congregation a means of escape if the Mass Centre was surrounded. Further evidence of the continued presence of the Faith here is recalled by older Tudhoe residents who remember seeing years ago a raised dais fronted by oak altar rails in the granary loft - possibly part of the original building of Tudhoe Hall. It was probably used as a small chapel in the late 18th century and maybe earlier.

Not far from Tudhoe is the small village of Hett, home of the grandfather of the Jesuit martyr, Blessed Ralph Corby, martyred in 1644. From the Jesuit residence in Old Elvet, Durham, Ralph ministered to the local Catholics in the area, so it is not unreasonable to suppose that he may have celebrated Mass in the chapel of Tudhoe Hall. A remarkable family, the Corbys: Ralph's two brothers became Jesuit priests and two sisters became Benedictine nuns. Both parents eventually entered the religious life: the father was training as a Jesuit lay-brother when he died; the mother entered the Benedictine convent at Ghent and it was there that she received news of the 'glorious martyrdom' of her son, Ralph, at Tyburn. 'He was', said his friend Father Whitfield S.J., 'in his paradise when he was with the poor Catholics at Durham and in the villages'.

Much of the land in the Croxdale and Tudhoe areas had been for centuries in the ownership of the Salvin family who still inhabit Croxdale Hall. Their faith was strong and in spite of the penalties and heavy fines inflicted they played an important part in keeping the Faith alive in this area south of Durham City thus enabling many ordinary Catholics, as the recusant rolls show, to cling to their Faith.

A document of 1705 giving a list of popish chapels lists one at Mr Ralph Salvin's home at Tudhoe, one in the home of Mr Gerard Salvin at Croxdale Hall and one at the residence of Mr Henry Grey at Sunderland Bridge; a list of papists from Tudhoe in 1767 includes at least 66 people.

A considerable number of priests served in this area south of the city - too many to mention here. Two, however, are of particular interest: the Rev. John Dunn, a Tudhoe native, who served the Croxdale Mission for three years round about 1750 after relinquishing his post as a professor at Douai; and the Rev. Arthur Storey who came to Croxdale in 1771 later taking up residence at Tudhoe in 1778. He was, obviously, a learned man with a great interest in education as he had been offered and declined the presidency of St. Omer's College in France.

With the relaxation of the penal laws towards the end of the 18th century it was possible for Catholics to show a public presence even if it was a discreet one. Father Storey was responsible for starting Tudhoe Academy, a boarding school for boys, under the patronage of the Salvin family - one of the earliest post-Reformation Catholic schools in England. The prospectus for 1794 is worth quoting in full:

> 'The Rev. Mr. Storey, Tudhoe, near Durham
> Terms: Board, Washing, Reading, Writing, Arithmetic, English, French, Latin, Greek. Languages are taught and lessons are given in Geography and History for twenty-two pounds per annum, to be paid half-yearly. The first quarter is to be advanced at admission.
> Two guineas, entrance. Six hand towels, knife, fork and silver spoon.
> Dancing, half a guinea entrance, and half a guinea a quarter.
>
> Recreation is allowed on Tuesday and Thursday afternoons. On these days the students walk out, attended by the instructors and proper care is taken, that no injury is received from rain and intense cold.
>
> Parents who wish to place their children under the care of the president of this school, may depend upon attention being paid to their morals, behaviour, and mental improvement. Age for education from eight to fourteen.'

It would appear that the Academy also served as a Mass Centre. It served, certainly for a short period, as a seminary when English seminarians were forced by the French Revolutionary armies to vacate their old college at Douai. Some of these refugee students, including the famous historian Dr. Lingard, continued their studies here until their transfer to Pontop Hall and eventually Crook Hall which closed when Ushaw

College was opened in 1808. Tudhoe Academy closed that same year.

It is clear from the joint appeal made by the Vicars-Apostolic - Bishops Walmesly, Gibson and Douglas - that Tudhoe was intended as a permanent seminary until changing circumstances made it necessary to look elsewhere: 'The unhappy events which have taken place in a neighbouring country having deprived the English Catholics of the greater part of those places of education in which hereto the succession of their clergy has been preserved ... we feel it to be our duty, most earnestly, to exhort and solicit the body at large to concur with us in supplying the said deficiency, by setting on foot a proper place of education in this Kingdom from which the ecclesiastical Ministry may be supplied, and in which the Catholic Youth in general may receive a solid, pious and learned education.

An establishment for that purpose will be commenced immediately at Tudhoe, in the County of Durham ...'

Father Storey's school can boast of at least one famous pupil: Charles Waterton, the naturalist, explorer and writer who spent some time at Tudhoe before moving to the Jesuit college at Stonyhurst.

The formal establishing of St. Charles' Parish can be traced to the year 1858 when a permanent priest, Father Joseph Humble, was appointed to Tudhoe. Nearby Spennymoor was expanding as the developing coal industry brought newcomers to the area. Canon Humble died in 1865 at the early age of 44 after seven years ministry here laying a firm foundation of spirituality on which other priests would build.

Until the appointment of Father Joseph Watson in 1867, Tudhoe was served by two priests from Croxdale: the Rev. John Smith and the Rev. James Farrell. Within two years of his arrival Father Watson saw the foundation stone of the present church laid in 1869.

This Gothic-style church - designed by Dunn and Hansom - was built through the generosity of Mr Marmaduke Salvin of Burn Hall who gave the parish the land and provided the money necessary to build by selling Tudhoe Academy to the Diocese, the proceeds of the sale being returned to finance the building of the church which cost £5,000. On October 11th, 1870, the church of St. Charles 'with elaborate rose window ... and spacious and lofty interior' was opened by Bishop James Chadwick with 50 priests in attendance. Twelve years later the church was extended to include a bell tower and the structure today is substantially that of 1882.

Catholic Care - as it is known today - was established here when, as mentioned previously, the Diocese bought Tudhoe Academy converting it into an orphanage for 40 girls from various parts of the Diocese; it was originally staffed by the Sacred Heart Order from Rennes in France. Round about 1884 the old Academy buildings were demolished and replaced by a three-storey edifice which was named St. Mary's. In 1940 the girls were transferred elsewhere and it became an orphanage for boys under the care of the Sisters of Charity who had been in charge of the home for many years preceding its closure in 1963 when it was decided that these disadvantaged children should be placed in Group Homes under the care of houseparents rather than in large institutions. The Tudhoe Orphanage, in the care of the nuns, had provided over a long period a loving and caring atmosphere for the many boys and girls who needed it and is still remembered with great affection by its former residents.

Since its foundation the parish has had only six parish priests - including its present one, Father James Gunning - in its 128 years existence. The second one, Father (later Provost) Watson was responsible, also, for the building of the school on Durham Road, which was opened in January, 1873, with a pupil roll of 513 under the care of the first headmistress, Miss Margaret McNeill and five teachers - a formidable task if one compares the pupil-teacher ratio with that of today's. Extended and modernised over the years St. Charles Primary School today, which incorporates and utilises the original building, is a multi-parish school providing a Catholic education for children in this area of Durham and under the supervision of Mr Anthony Coia, the present headmaster and eight other teachers.

Father Watson, after 41 years of ministry here, was succeeded by Father George Gregson (1908-1949) whose incumbency was to equal that of his predecessor and to embrace the period of the two World Wars. Towards the end of his ministry in 1944, the church suffered some blast damage (still visible) when a stray V.I. rocket exploded in Tudhoe cricket ground. The Anglican vicarage suffered considerable damage, whilst

St. Charles church escaped comparatively lightly with broken windows and damage to slates and ceilings.

Every parish has its lay organisations to meet the spiritual and social needs of its people and Tudhoe parish has them in abundance. One of the older - if not the oldest - is the parish choir which was formed around 1870 and appears to have continued since those days providing the music for the liturgical services. Mr Jack Murray is the choir master and his wife, Florence, the senior organist - senior because here they can boast of six competent organists. One of the longest serving members of the choir was Mr Michael Murray who celebrated 50 years of service in 1957. Another early group - no longer in existence - was the Children of Mary started in Father Watson's time and encouraged and supervised by the Sisters of Charity.

Father Thomas Battle (1955-71) was responsible for the inauguration of the Legion of Mary and the St. Vincent de Paul Society in the parish. The latter continues its work of helping those in need at home and in hospital. Along with other helpers they transport the sick and housebound to a special monthly Mass for the infirm. Since 1925 the Tudhoe Council of the Knights of St. Columba has worked continuously in the charitable field at parish level and in the national sphere; the Columba Club in Spennymoor belonging to the Knights is also used, on occasions, for parish functions. Extremely active, too, is the C.W.L. started almost 50 years ago, some of whose founder-members are still involved in the life of the parish.

For the younger generation the Scouts, Guides, Cubs and Brownies provide an outlet for youthful enthusiasm and are supervised by older committed parishioners who give freely of their time.

Father James Gunning, T.D., - celebrating this year five years as parish priest and last year the 40th anniversary of his ordination - has been responsible for implementing many of the changes recommended by Vatican II. Assisting him in this and other parish concerns has been the Parish Pastoral Council, formed in 1976, who decided that the 125th anniversary celebrations should be remembered in a fitting manner by the planting of 14 young trees in the cemetery each bearing an oak plaque (appropriately numbered and with the cross of St. Cuthbert) carved by a parishioner, Mr Harold Hall. These new 'station' trees are a reminder, we are told, of the penal days when there were said to be fourteen 'station' trees in the village allowing the Catholic villagers to keep in mind the Passion of Christ as they suffered the injustices of persecution. A second reminder of the 1983 anniversary is the new grotto built by Mr Robert Clarke who has tended the church grounds for many years.

Changes in the liturgy have brought about alterations to many sanctuaries throughout the Diocese. The problem with older churches is blending the old with the new; the traditional appearance has been preserved at St. Charles with the retention of the Bavarian reredos now fronted by a circular stone altar, a lectern and a baptismal font on an extended sanctuary.

There is an excellent relationship here with the various denominations one example of which is the ecumenical Remembrance Service held annually at the War Memorial on the village green.

When three years ago (1983) Bishop Swindlehurst, Father Gunning and a number of other priests concelebrated a Mass of Thanksgiving for 125 years of parish life it was an event which will be remembered for many years to come; it was an opportunity also to look back at the long history of Catholicism in this part of County Durham - so well told in Mr Coia's parish history - and to look forward and develop that Faith which others had begun and maintained over the centuries.

POSTSCRIPT   *(Fr. D. Burke, 1998)*

As Sunday Mass is no longer celebrated at Croxdale, the parishioners of St. Herbert's, Croxdale, now worship at Tudhoe and form part of the parish of St. Charles.

In 1990, Mr Tony Kemp succeeded Mr Coia as Headteacher at St. Charles Primary School. At noon on Saturday 27 May, 1995, the Rt Rev Dom. Ambrose Griffiths OSB., Bishop of Hexham and Newcastle, officially opened the newly-built St. Charles School at Tudhoe. The new school cost £971,087 and replaced the original 1873 building. Also in 1995 the school published a booklet of its history *'Tudhoe St. Charles School, 1873 – 1995'*.

The Tudhoe Knights of St. Columba handed over the Columba Hall to the parish and the building in King Street is now the thriving 'St. Charles Parish Centre'.

On 22 July, 1995, Fr James Gunning TD, celebrated his Golden Sacerdotal Jubilee and retired as parish priest of Tudhoe in September of that year. He was succeeded in September 1995 by Fr Dermot Burke, the present incumbent, who held his Mass of Installation at St Charles Church on Thursday 23 November, 1995.

61. TYNEMOUTH   Our Lady & St. Oswin   *(March, April 1992)*

When the *Northern Cross* team visited Tynemouth last summer they could sympathise - especially Father Croghan who took the photographs - with the 12th century monk who writing to a friend in St. Alban's described how the mist rolled in from the sea presenting a most gloomy aspect - it was no different in July, 1991. His letter still preserved at St. Alban's tells us that the priory 'is confined to the top of a high rock and is surrounded by sea on every side but one ... Day and night the waves break and roar and undermine the cliff. Thick sea-frets roll in, wrapping everything in gloom. Dim eyes and hoarse voices are the consequences. Spring and summer never come here. The north wind is always blowing, and it brings with it cold and snow, or storms in which the wind tosses the salt-sea foam in masses over our buildings...In the spring the sea air blights the blossoms of the stunted fruit trees so that you will think yourself lucky to find a wizened apple, though it will set your teeth on edge should you try to eat it ...'

'But the church is of wondrous beauty. It has lately been completed. Within it lies the body of the blessed martyr Oswin in a silver shrine magnificently embellished with gold jewels ... The martyr's protection and the church's beauty furnish us with a bond of unity ...'

This was not, however, the earliest religious foundation as our own saintly scholar, Bede, provides us with evidence of a Saxon foundation here when he writes that his friend, Herewald, was abbot of the monastery at the mouth of the Tyne. Nor was King Oswin of Deira and friend of Aidan the only saint to be buried here; one source claims that in 1127 St. Henry, a Danish nobleman who became a hermit on Coquet Island, was buried near the remains of Oswin.

Situated on a headland, the priory was a prime target for Danish raiders of the 9th century whose assaults led eventually to its ruin and the loss of St. Oswin's body. Shortly before the Norman Conquest it is said to have been re-discovered by a novice priest, Edmund, who served the chapel of the Virgin Mary there. Tynemouth Priory ruins today remind us of its former Norman and Benedictine glory when, throughout the Middle Ages, it was a place of pilgrimage until its dissolution by Henry VIII on January 12th, 1539.

How the ancient Faith survived in these parts throughout the penal days we have little evidence. Tynemouth Priory - or what was left of it - must have been a welcome sight and a reassurance of their belief to missionary priests, trained on the continent, returning to their homeland via the Tyne to keep alive the Faith which the old monks had attested to in the past. The recusant households of Mrs Ursula Taylor at South Shields, the Hodgsons at Hebburn and the home of Mrs Lawson at St. Anthony's, where St. Henry Morse stayed for a time, were all possible places where Tynemouth Catholics could have found solace in those difficult days. Their numbers - in the old parish of Tynemouth, anyway - must have been fairly small for when we look at the Papist Returns for 1767 we find only 28 Catholics one of whom a Margaret Forster had resided there for 30 years.

The year 1784 was an important one for Catholics in this south-eastern part of Northumberland for in that year a Father Johnson came monthly from Pontop to North Shields to minister to a small congregation.

Nine years after this date saw an influx of French refugees to England fleeing the persecution against the Catholic Church there by revolutionary forces. It is believed that 8,000 priests, nuns and lay people made a temporary home in England (some permanent) and of this number 295 landed in North Shields on October 5th, 1793. The Rev. A. Danneville and the Rev. M. Duboisson ministered in the North Shields area for a time; we also know that three refugee priests died here and were buried in Tynemouth Cemetery.

Father James Worswick, whose name has often appeared in these articles, journeyed regularly from

St. Andrew's in Newcastle to North Shields as part of his ministry to what was then a very scattered flock; so it must have been a great consolation to the Catholics living on the north bank of the Tyne near its mouth when he was able to open St. Cuthbert's Church in 1821.

Mass was said for the first time in Tynemouth, since the Reformation, when the chaplain to the Maire Family of Lartington Hall, Barnard Castle, a Mr Rutter, accompanied them to their summer residence which it was claimed was 46, Front Street. In Anstruther's *Seminary Priests* Vol.IV a Father Henry Banister (alias Rutter) is named as the chaplain to the Silvertops of Minsteracres from 1785 until 1822. The Silvertops and the Maires were related through marriage.

There is another interesting connection between Minsteracres and Tynemouth as the first parish priest of Our Lady and St. Oswin's was Father John William Bewick who was born on the Silvertop Estate from where he was taken at the age of 14, by his father on horseback, to begin his priestly studies at Ushaw.

When he was appointed to Tynemouth in 1869 he was able to move into a house, No 48, Front Street, which had been purchased by Father John Rogerson who had known the young Bewick as a boy when he was chaplain at Minsteracres.

Almost three years after his arrival Fr. Bewick was able to announce the opening of a temporary chapel (the incised roof line can still be seen on the stone wall of the present presbytery) 'erected for the benefit of the Catholic residents in the villages of Tynemouth, Cullercoats and Whitley as well as for the convenience of visitors to the seaside. It will be dedicated to the service of Almighty God under the joint title of our Blessed Lady and St. Oswin who of old time were the patron saints of Tynemouth and its far-famed priory'. The chapel was formally opened by Bishop Chadwick on the Feast of Our Lady's Assumption, 1871.

To many people Bishop's House is associated with East Denton Hall, Newcastle, but this was not always the case as five bishops made their residence here in Tynemouth. They were Bishop John William Bewick (the first parish priest) who lived here as bishop from 1882 until 1886, Bishop Henry O'Callaghan (1888-89), Bishop Richard Preston (1900 - 1905), Bishop Joseph Thorman (1925-1926) and Bishop Joseph McCormack from 1937 until 1941 when air-raid damage in the latter year brought about the move to Newcastle.

On his elevation to the episcopate, Bishop Bewick appointed Father George Howe to succeed him as Tynemouth's parish priest and it was he who was responsible for the building of the present church, the foundation stone of which was laid on September 8th, 1889. Costing £2,500, the church in the Gothic style was designed by E. J. Hansom of Newcastle, whose child was the first to be baptised in St Oswin's; it was opened and blessed by Bishop Wilkinson on June 1st, 1890, with the choir of St. Michael's, Newcastle in attendance.

The growth of the Catholic population towards the end of the 19th century in the Whitley Bay area made Canon Howe see the need for a church there. By 1898 he had acquired a site for £250 and fortuitously, a year later, Jane Collen left in her will £3,000 'towards the support of a Roman Catholic priest at Whitley if and when, within a period of 21 years of her death, a Roman Catholic Mission should be instituted there.' By 1911 a small brick church had been built to hold a congregation of 250; the first priest was Father P. J. Kearney.

When Canon Howe died in 1916 he was succeeded by Canon John Rogers who some years before had erected St. Joseph's Church in Sunderland. Towards the end of his incumbency, which lasted 24 years, his plans for a secondary school for the area, due to be implemented on September 4th, 1939, had to be shelved with the onset of war.

Seven months after the appointment of Father Austin Bede Fee as the new parish priest an event was to occur which is described at some length in the Notice Book: 'On 16th April, 1941, Church and Presbytery damaged. At 4.10 a.m. a huge bomb (it was actually an erratic sea mine descending by parachute and intended for the entrance to the river) dropped by German aeroplane exploded in the moat near the power-house of the castle. The Church, Bishop's House and Presbytery were damaged'. In the church Father Fee details the damage: 'All the windows were blown out, the main door, sacristy door and door of boiler house were all blown off. Most of the slates too. One of the large longitudinal roof beams was snapped, the supports cracked, and the whole gospel side of the roof was lifted about six inches from the purlins'. Further damage occurred to the presbytery and Bishop's House, requiring Bishop McCormack to move to temporary accommodation at Nazareth House and Father Fee to seek lodgings at 3, Percy Gardens.

The damage to the presbytery No. 49 and to No. 50 Front Street was irreparable and after temporary repairs were made to No. 48, Bishop's House, Father Fee moved in there and it has been the presbytery ever since.

Father Fee, like his predecessors, worked hard to improve the spiritual and social life of the parish and developing the educational provision for the children. When the Marden Estate was built arrangements were made to transport the people to St. Oswin's for Sunday Mass. In 1959 he saw the completion of St. Anselm's School in North Shields which catered for senior pupils from the surrounding parishes. St. Mary's Primary School was about ready for opening before he died in March, 1964.

Father Aidan Pickering, who succeeded him, taught at Ushaw College for 20 years before taking up this appointment. In 1970 he and his parishioners had the pleasure of seeing the opening of St. Mary's Church and Hall on an adjacent site to the primary school in Cullercoats.

Seeing the plain brick building from the outside for the first time does not suggest it is a church. However, on entering one discovers a fine modern chapel comparable with any built in the diocese recently; the attached hall is functional and caters adequately for the social needs of the congregation.

Much still happens here in a parish which has its roots deep in the past. The S.V.P. and the Legion of Mary continue their caring role, as do many other people in the parish; a Prayer Group meets weekly in St. Mary's Cullercoats; a Youth Club, supervised by Mr Ray Calboutin and Mr Alan Muir, provides an opportunity weekly for the youth of the parish to mix socially; and at the other end of the age spectrum the senior citizens enjoy their weekly get-together on a Monday.

Two highlights of Father Pickering's stay here must be the two occasions when Mass was celebrated in the ruins of Tynemouth Priory. The first occasion was to celebrate the centenary of Our Lady and St. Oswin's church in 1971. This was the first Mass said in Tynemouth Priory since the Reformation

The second occasion when he returned to say Mass there was on June 28th, 1991. This was something of a surprise for him as it had been arranged by David Cairns and the Jubilee Committee to honour Father Pickering's 50 years in the priesthood.

In a leaflet published just after the celebrations Father Pickering describes the joy of this 'special day': 'Fifteen priests vested in the Percy Chantry and processed to the altar at the West door. We said the Mass of the day - the Vigil of Ss. Peter and Paul. About 15 invited vicars, ministers and their wives were at the front of the congregation of about 770. 480 went to Communion. Our hymns: O Lord, My God ... Gloria in excelsis Deo ... Now thank we all our God ... My soul Proclaims ... To God be the Glory... and the Salve Regina were sung with great joy'.

He was delighted to bring, once again, the statue of Our Lady and enthrone her in her own priory of St. Mary and St. Oswin. His altar boys were suitably robed in 'mini-monk' Benedictine habits. All present bid Goodnight to Our Lady, as monks still do at the end of their monastic day, with the singing of the '*Salve Regina*'.

The weather, too, was in sharp contrast to the description given at the beginning of this article: 'quite perfect weather all day. Really hot with not a cloud in the sky, not a breath of wind'.

POSTSCRIPT   *(Canon S. Cunningham, 1998)*

Fr. Aidan Pickering retired on 7th March 1998 when Canon Seamus Cunningham took over as parish priest.

62. USHAW COLLEGE   St. Cuthbert   *(August, 1997)*

The history of Ushaw College is a varied and interesting one that goes back more than four centuries. When the penal laws of the 16th century proscribed the Catholic Faith in our country, a certain William Allen founded a college at Douai in Flanders in 1568 where priests could be trained for the English Mission thereby ensuring that the ancient Faith would survive. It would also provide a Catholic education for Catholic laymen.

About 2,000 priests did full or part-time training here. Out of these 150 priests were executed and 19 of them are included in the Forty Martyrs canonised in 1970.

The outbreak of war between England and France in 1793 saw the college occupied by French troops and the students after many vicissitudes drifted back to England. The hope was cherished that they would be able to return to Douai. This hope, however, never materialised so two seminaries were founded in England: one for the southern students at Old Hall Green, Ware, Hertfordshire (now at Allen Hall in London) and for those in the North, Ushaw.

Ushaw was not the first site considered by Bishop William Gibson and his advisers: Gainford, Hazlewood Castle and Tudhoe were for a time possibilities. As a temporary measure Pontop Hall was used for a short time by the northern students until Crook Hall was acquired in 1794. This remained a small seminary for student priests of the Northern Province until Ushaw was opened in 1808 under its first president the Rev. Thomas Eyre.

As the Catholic population expanded in the 19th century their needs could only be met by more priests, so Ushaw expanded accordingly; the man mainly responsible for this was Mgr. Charles Newsham who was president from 1837 until 1863.

The large impressive Gothic chapel of St. Cuthbert, designed by the architects Dunn and Hansom, was opened in 1884 and consecrated in 1897 replacing the earlier chapel of Augustus Welby Pugin. Some of his work is retained in the present chapel: the eye-catching West window (formerly the East window), other stained-glass windows, a brass lectern and a Paschal candle stand (both the work of Hardman of Birmingham) the latter being exhibited at the Crystal Palace Exhibition of 1851. A typical example of Pugin's enthusiasm for the Gothic style can be seen in the small Lady Chapel. The ornate stone altar in the main church was the gift of Father W. Taylor-Smith in 1890 and was designed by Peter Paul Pugin, a younger son of Augustus. In 1982 the modern wrought-iron screen and altar were installed; the screen and brasswork are the work of a local craftsman, Ron Field of Langley Park.

Ushaw has amongst its mementoes and relics the following which are of particular interest: a white cassock worn by St. Pius X; a mid-17th century chalice, believed to be of the penal days; St. Cuthbert's ring worn by our bishop on special occasions; silver cruets (1756) from the Douai days; and a president's cup believed to have belonged to the Rev. Robert Witham of Cliffe Hall, near Darlington, who was Douai's president from 1715 until 1738.

Within the 'Big Library' designed by Joseph and Charles Hansom, again in the Gothic style and opened in 1851, are about 50,000 books many of which came from donated collections of former students. Amongst them are three reminders of the penal days: a book written by Cardinal Allen (printed in 1585) defending English Catholics against the charge of treason; a small missal of 1615 used by travelling missionaries containing an abbreviated selection of Masses; and a Douai Dictate of 1757, a student's dictation of a professor's lecture (no photo-copiers then!).

One cannot mention Ushaw without a brief reference to John Lingard (1771-1851) of whom two portraits hang in the college. As a young boy he proceeded to Douai and in 1790 was almost murdered by a revolutionary mob. He escaped to England in 1793 and was ordained at York in 1795. He assisted in the settlement and education at Crook Hall of the Douai students who fled Flanders during the French Wars. Here he taught and acted as vice-president and procurator; he was to retain these responsibilities at Ushaw until 1811 when he moved to the small mission of Hornby in Lancashire.

This small mission allowed him time to develop his career as a historian and apologist attempting through his writings to correct a distorted view of English history and thereby remove the ignorance and bigotry that persisted in some quarters in the nineteenth century. His *History of England* established his reputation as 'the pioneer scientific historian of England'. He composed the hymn to Our Lady, 'Hail Queen of Heaven', which is perhaps better known to most Catholics today rather than his historical works. His love of Ushaw continued throughout his life being a generous benefactor and leaving to it his library. At his own request he was buried at Ushaw.

Numbered amongst its alumni are five cardinals. Nicholas Wiseman was to become the first archbishop of Westminster in 1850 and Raphael Merry del Val became Cardinal Secretary of State to St. Pius X. Too long to list here the number of bishops educated at Ushaw but our retired Bishop Lindsay will serve as an example.

Today Ushaw College has approximately 150 students from different dioceses including a small group of mature lay students studying theology. Since its foundation Ushaw has trained more priests than its precursor Douai.

Whilst Ushaw is proud of its past it lives in the present and looks with confidence to the future. Not so long ago it was in many ways an enclosed institution, but just as William Allen met the challenge of his time so the college to-day looks at the challenge of our world and offers - in addition to its primary role as a seminary - its expertise and facilities to a wider world where people from many different walks of life and places may come and develop their talents for the spreading of the Gospel.

63. WHITTINGHAM   St. Mary Immaculate   *(March, April 1993)*

When W.W. Tomlinson in his *Comprehensive Guide to Northumberland* described in 1888 the village of Whittingham as 'beautifully situated on the flower-strewn banks of the Aln in the centre of the most fertile vale of Northumberland, with the richest meadows and cornfields around it ... (retaining) the quiet old-charm of rusticity' he might have been surprised that to-day's visitors, more than a hundred years later, would in essence agree with his portrayal.

This Northumbrian vale, bordering the Cheviot Hills, has much to offer those seeking evidence of our ancient Christian heritage - and the later penal days where the Catholic tradition appears to have survived unbroken over the centuries.

It has been claimed, although difficult to prove conclusively, that Whittingham is the Twyford near the river Aln where a synod assembled in 684 A.D., in the presence of King Egfrid, at which Cuthbert was chosen to be Bishop of Lindisfarne. Other authorities prefer a location nearer to Alnmouth.

The fine stone parish church in Whittingham village, St. Bartholomew's, stands on the site of an early Christian foundation dating back to the mid-8th century when a Saxon church was erected by Ceolwulph, a Northumbrian King. The interior is mainly of the Early English style and in the south transept, which was formerly a chantry chapel dedicated to St. Peter, can be seen a piscina probably of the late 13th century. Saxon stonework is still visible in the lower portion of the tower. During the reign of Henry I he granted the church to the Augustinian Canons of Carlisle and today the living is still the gift of the Dean and Chapter of Carlisle.

Within the ancient boundaries of Whittingham parish can be found strongholds of the Catholic religion where our ancestors kept the light of Faith alive during the days of persecution. Outstanding witness to this tradition were the Claverings of Callaly Castle.

This family, it has been suggested, were descended from Charlemagne and also had Norman connections. When Robert Fitz-Roger succeeded to the Lordship of Warkworth he, also, received the Barony of Clavering in Essex; it was this estate which was eventually to determine the family name. In the year 1271 the estates of Yetlington and Callaly came to be owned by this ancient family and some years later six sons of Baron Robert and Margery la Zouche all adopted the Clavering name, the oldest one being John de Clavering. Until 1877, when the family relinquished the Callaly estate, it is believed the Catholic Faith was kept alive here for almost 600 years.

The estate was sufficiently remote, at the foot of the Cheviots with moorland to the south, to allow the practice of the Faith in the days of post-Reformation persecution. Within the castle there were said to be three hiding holes for the concealment of priests should this be necessary; one hiding hole was entered from the chimney in the drawing room. The Claverings of course, were not alone in preserving Catholicism in this part of Northumberland; other recusant households were at Cartington Castle, Biddlestone, Eslington and Edlingham.

Father Matthew Culley, writing in the early part of this century, suggests the possibility that the martyrs John Boste and John Ingram said Mass at the two latter places 'and elsewhere in the vales of the Aln and the Coquet'. Another martyr, Father George Gervase O.S.B., executed in 1608, laboured in the Borders saying Mass at Ford Castle and Etal and possibly stayed at Callaly for a time.

Sir John Clavering served the Royalist cause, being Sheriff of Northumberland in 1623; he was captured and died in prison in 1647, converting to Catholicism before his death (according to Anstruther) which suggests a break in the Catholic tradition of the Claverings. His son, Thomas, after studying in Rome was ordained priest in 1654.

The practice of one's Faith and the political upheavals of the 17th century must have been the cause of much anxiety to those faithful to Rome. We know in 1683 that 70 Northumbrian Catholics were imprisoned for a short time for refusing the Oath of Allegiance which no Catholic felt in conscience he could swear at that time.

In order that the children of these staunch Catholics could receive a Catholic education it was necessary to send them to schools on the continent. Here a number of them in the early 18th century decided to stay and follow a vocation in the religious life. Two sisters-in-law of the Claverings were nuns and, also, their niece; two Widdringtons became Jesuits and served on the mission in Northumberland; three Haggerstons became Jesuits also; whilst two Collingwoods of Eslington became priests - Thomas, a Jesuit and Roger, a Benedictine. Some of the above-mentioned served on the Northumberland mission.

A visit by Bishop Leyburn, the Vicar-Apostolic of England, to Callaly in 1687 where he confirmed 282 people implies that, in spite of the difficulties of earlier years, the Faith was still comparatively strong in these parts.

To mention the names of all the priests who served the Callaly congregation would be a fitting tribute to their missionary endeavours but space does not allow this. Among them were seculars, Dominicans and Jesuits. The earliest chaplains' names we do not know; one of the first recorded was Father Arthur Salthouse who was here in 1647.

During the ministry of Father John Darell, S.J. the foundation stone of the Callaly chapel was laid by Ralph Clavering in 1750. In that same year Father Darell reporting to his superiors stated: 'My salary from this place is £10.10s per annum ... Mortuaries and perquisites £1. The number of my customers (congregation), including all ages is about two hundred and eighty. Of my own gaining (converts) about half a dozen.' A much bigger congregation than exists today!

One priest Father Andrew Macartney - a convert at the age of 30, after serving as an officer in the Peninsular War - is said to have hewn out of rock a small cave with a Gothic entrance where he could retire for periods of meditation and study; it was known for many years as Macartney's or the Priest's Cave.

Callaly Castle and estate passed out of Catholic ownership in 1877. Outside the present Catholic Church at Whittingham is a monument to the last Catholic squire of Callaly, Edward John Clavering, and his wife Jane erected by their daughter, Augusta Lady Bedingfield. Father James Stark was probably the last chaplain to serve the Claverings here. The Rev. William Gillow was asked to organise the move to Whittingham village where the congregation's needs could be met. He and his brother, Canon Henry Gillow, were the last priests to say Mass in Callaly chapel. Ill-health forced him to take sick leave but not before he had moved the furnishings from the castle to temporary premises in the village. During the three-year interval between the closure of the castle chapel and the opening of St. Mary's Whittingham, in 1881, it was not unknown for some parishioners to journey ten miles to Alnwick or Wooler to fulfil their Sunday obligation. It is believed that much of the money needed to build the new church was given by the

Claverings. A public appeal was also made by Bishop Chadwick:

> 'To supply the spiritual wants of the Catholics in the neighbourhood of Whittingham, Glanton, and the district until recently included in the Mission of Callay, which dated from the XIIth Century, it is proposed to build a small Church with a residence for a priest.
>
> A suitable site has been procured from the Earl of Ravensworth, midway between the villages of Whittingham and Glanton. The Buildings, from the designs of Messrs Dunn & Hansom of Newcastle-upon-Tyne, will be begun forthwith and pushed forward to completion as speedily as possible.
>
> Though the district to be served is extensive, the population is scanty, and the Catholics few and mostly of the labouring class. An appeal to the generosity of all interested in the locality, and in the welfare of the poor thus becomes a necessity, and is hereby made with every confidence of success.'

Father Charles Ickenroth was appointed to look after the mission here in March 1881, and during his incumbency the church was officially opened and blessed by Bishop Chadwick in September of that same year.

Designed in the Norman style by architects, Dunn and Hansom of Newcastle and built by Messrs. Carse of Morpeth and Amble, the church stands in isolation north of the village on a piece of land that was formerly owned by a Catholic family, the Collingwoods of Eslington.

The interior of the chapel, like all Norman style churches, is robust and simple. This simplicity is offset around the sanctuary by the carved reredos executed by Charles Beyaert of Bruges. The colourful left-hand panel shows Cuthbert elected Bishop at the Twyford Synod whilst the right hand one depicts Cuthbert's consecration by St. Theodore.

Above the reredos is a fine stained-glass window with three lights; it was erected in memory of Edward John Clavering, the last Catholic squire of Callay by his widow. Upper left of the window is the coat of arms of this ancient Northumbrian family.

When the *Northern Cross* team visited Whittingham last summer Father David Tanner, the present parish priest, was able to show us two chalices which appear to have links with the penal days. The first one, with six rays extending from the stem to the middle of the bowl can be dismantled, suggesting it was used by travelling missioners in the days of clandestine Catholicism. The second chalice has under its base the inscription: 'Memento Janae et Mariae Clavering, 1671.' A silver monstrance may, also, be of this same period. There is, also, an enamelled crucifix which is possibly of the 12th century and may have come from Whittingham parish church.

Too long to list here all the priests who served St. Mary's, Whittingham since its foundation. The memory of some of them is preserved in a set of portraits in the sacristy. Father Charles Hart, parish priest from 1930 to 1949, wrote a short history of the parish and was, we believe, responsible for the erection of the Lourdes Grotto in 1930, the expense being borne by Mr F. Beavans; a holy water stoup in the Grotto is said to have been found in Jesmond Dene and may date back to the days before the shrine was dissolved at the Reformation.

One cannot omit to mention another parish priest Father William Nicholson, who served here until his death in 1988, for 26 years. He devoted a lot of his spare time to researching the history of Catholicism in the North East, was a founder member and chairman for many years of the North East Catholic History Society and was most helpful to anyone, including the *Northern Cross*, when they required the fruits of his research.

The present day parish boundaries of St. Mary's Whittingham, as with all rural parishes, are extensive. Father David Tanner serves a small congregation here of about 86 souls. Much of his time is spent as Associate Judicial Vicar to the Diocesan Marriage Tribunal which is based in Newcastle. In addition to the above-mentioned duties Father Tanner is, also, chaplain to the Catholic Care Residential Home at Lemmington Hall for Girls and Ladies with learning difficulties where he says a daily Mass.

In spite of the difficulties faced by the nature of the parish, Father Tanner and his congregation work together to develop the spirit of community.

A coffee morning on the first Sunday of each month enables parishioners to meet and get to know each other socially. A special coffee morning was held last summer to raise funds for Catholic Care; a Cheese and Wine Evening helped to provide money donated to CAFOD.

The annual sale of work held in October in the village hall helps to supplement the parish income as well as providing an opportunity for Catholic and non-Catholic friends to work together for the good of all.

This co-operation amongst the local people extends into the ecumenical field when members of the various denominations meet together in shared prayer during Unity Octave Week and at the November Remembrance Service.

Much more could be written about Callaly and St. Mary's, Whittingham, and the people's adherence to the Faith over the centuries. In conclusion, one can only admire the fortitude and perseverance of our ancestors here, and the determination of today's small congregation at St. Mary's who continue to keep alight the torch of Faith which was lit here more than 1,300 years ago.

64. WOLSINGHAM   St. Thomas of Canterbury   *(November, December 1998)*

Wolsingham in Weardale, because of its remoteness and sparse population, does not loom large in the history of pre-Reformation Catholicism. The present Anglican church of Saints Mary and Stephen, largely re-built in 1848, still retains its 12th century west tower indicating an earlier structure where once the Mass was celebrated. At Chapel Wells there once stood a house belonging to the Bishop of Durham and two miles south-east of Wolsingham is Bradley Hall which existed before 1431; it is a possibility that the two latter dwellings may have had chapels within their walls. There is, also, a tradition that St. Godric, the hermit, lived in Weardale before moving to Finchale.

The advent of the Reformation and the changes it brought were to be felt even in the remotest of localities such as Wolsingham. When the Northern Rising occurred in 1569 to restore the Ancient Faith, 29 men from Wolsingham and thereabouts participated. Lionel and Nicholas Neville were two, we know of amongst others, from Wolsingham. After its failure seven men from Weardale were executed for their part in the rebellion.

Although Weardale does not appear to have had Catholic gentry households where a priest might have sought refuge and support there is evidence to show that some brave Catholics kept their Faith through the difficult penal days. Saint John Boste, St. Henry Morse and Blessed Ralph Corby may have all worked in this area of the county supporting the faithful. Because of the dangers, not only to themselves but also to those who harboured them, their efforts were often not recorded - thus we have little evidence of their labours.

There is, however, one well-attested piece of evidence which furnishes us with some details of how precarious life could be for practising Catholics. Blessed John Duckett, who may claim to be Wolsingham's martyr, was returning to Durham from Weardale after baptising two children when he was arrested on the Tow Law

St. Thomas of Canterbury, Wolsingham

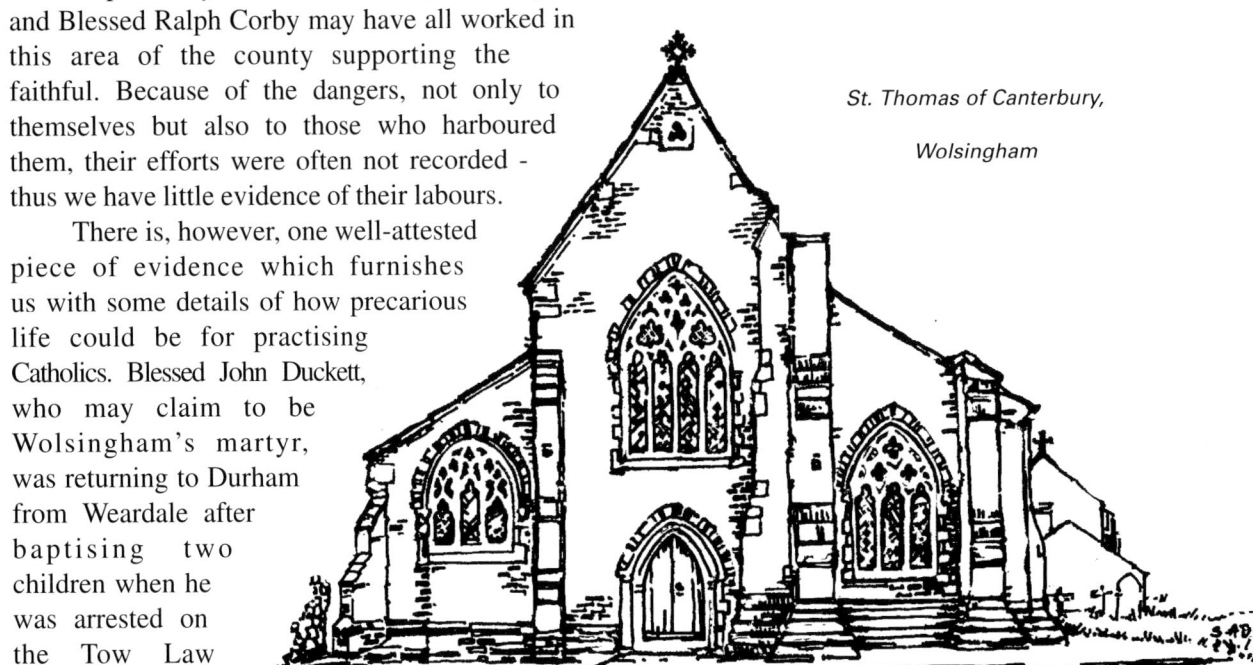

road. He bravely confessed his priesthood in order that his two companions could be set free. Taken to Sunderland, he was shipped, along with Blessed Ralph Corby, to London; they were both to die martyrs' deaths at Tyburn on September 7th, 1644. Today a commemorative stone cross, erected by the Sisters of Mercy, stands near the spot where the arrest occurred, replacing an earlier one put there by Father Thomas Wilkinson, Wolsingham's first parish priest, in the mid-19th century.

From recusant records one can see that a small number of Catholics kept the Faith in spite of the risk to life and property. It is well-known that non-attendance at the Anglican church in those days meant heavy fines resulting, in some cases, in impoverishment. Two examples from Weardale illustrate the point graphically. Michael Thompson of Stanhope who owed £480 resolutely refused to conform when brought before the Durham Court in 1636. Tunstall Toes, a Hamsterley man, had his farm confiscated in 1634 and it was only restored to him after he had paid the arrears.

Such punitive measures were bound to put an increasing strain on those who wished to continue in their beliefs. The Papist Returns of 1767 do not list any at Stanhope or St. John's Chapel; Wolsingham, however, retained a few elderly adherents:

'The postman aged 80, his wife aged 75. Their descendants converts to the Church of England. One woman aged 70. One woman aged 71. A farmer aged 55, his children (5)...' His wife and eldest daughter were Anglican. By 1780 only the five members of the Newton family were listed as papists.

Whilst this might have been the nadir of Catholicism in Weardale it was to have a revival in the mid-19th century as the coal and iron deposits of the area were exploited. Labour-intensive, these industries attracted workers and their families into the valley many of whom were Irish. Bishop William Hogarth saw similar developments in other parts of his diocese heralding an unprecedented growth in the Catholic population which required schools and churches. He wisely chose as missioner to Wolsingham and district the recently ordained Father Thomas Wilkinson, a convert Anglican clergyman, who had grown up at nearby Harperley Hall.

Born of wealthy parents, he was educated at Harrow and Durham University. Whilst completing his theological training at St. Saviour's in Leeds he came under the influence of the writings of Newman and the Tractarian Movement. His conversion to Catholicism was to influence not only his native surroundings, but was to extend throughout the diocese when he became bishop in 1889 and President of Ushaw a year later.

Thomas's father raised no objection to his son returning to his roots as a Catholic priest where his family still retained their Anglican identity. February 22nd, 1849, was a significant date for Weardale when the young Father Wilkinson, not quite 24-years-old, celebrated Mass in a rented house in Little Redgate, with a congregation of five which included a 12-year-old altar server, Thomas Wittenhall, who was to be the faithful servant of the new priest for many years.

The Wolsingham congregation was soon able to worship in more fitting surroundings when Father Wilkinson and the bishop purchased a plot of land on which stood a stone-built stable with a hayloft over it. The former became a small school and the latter a chapel capable - although hard to believe when one sees the building today - of accommodating 189 people; it has been estimated that the Mass attendance at this time numbered about 150. These temporary premises were to serve a widely scattered congregation until the present church was built in 1854. Many of them travelled down from Tow Law - a small town created by the iron and coal industry - to fulfil their religious duties. To meet their Sunday obligation considerable sacrifices had to be made; we know that Catholics in the Stanhope workhouse journeyed on foot to Wolsingham for Sunday Mass. And no doubt others in the dale did likewise.

Father Thomas's schedule was a busy one but he had the vitality of youth and the enthusiasm of one who had found his true vocation in the Universal Church. Each morning he said Mass and concluded the day with night prayers and the rosary; he kept a fatherly eye on the schoolchildren, catechising them on a Sunday; he instituted night classes for the adults; and his visitations of the sick required sometimes travelling great distances.

Perceiving the need to extend the Church's missionary role he began establishing new mission stations.

Crook became a regular mission station in 1851 where each Wednesday he said Mass in a house in Hope Street where he also instructed the children. His burden was somewhat eased when he obtained the valuable assistance of two of his former Anglican friends, Fathers Rooke and Ward who had, like himself, been ordained to the Catholic priesthood. Father Ward was to put the Crook mission on a firm foundation.

When Cardinal Wiseman visited Wolsingham in 1853, in the course of conversation Father Wilkinson intimated that he hoped a church would soon be built and, it is said, that the two of them paced out the boundaries of the proposed building. The church of St. Thomas of Canterbury - Father Wilkinson's patron saint on whose feastday he made his submission to Rome - was designed by the architect, Joseph Hansom, much of the cost of £1,600 being met by Fathers Rooke and Ward and likely Father Wilkinson too. It was solemnly opened on the morning of September 5th, 1854, by Bishop Hogarth in the presence of many clergy one of whom, Canon Platt, was the preacher.

It was not the nature of Father Tom (as he became affectionately known) to relax even though he had accomplished so much; his energy and sense of mission urged him on to establish further parishes at Tow Law and Willington. Provision for the Tow Law Catholics was made when he began to say a weekday Mass in the home of a local Catholic from 1857 onwards - probably earlier - until a chapel was erected there in 1860.

After consultation with the bishop, Father Wilkinson decided to settle at Crook to be replaced by Father George Caley who, also, had responsibility for Tow Law. Within a short time, from his base at Crook, he began weekly visits to Willington saying Mass in a rented room, hearing confessions and teaching the children the truths of the Faith.

To mention all the priests, who served Weardale over the years so faithfully, is not possible in such a short article. However, certain events that occurred during particular incumbencies must be mentioned. Father Taylor Smith's reign here was, like Father Wilkinson's, to have a great influence on the development of Catholicism in Weardale. He arrived in Wolsingham in 1870 but after two years decided to move to Tow Law where the majority of his parishioners resided; he returned to Wolsingham in 1890.

Father Taylor Smith belonged to an old Durham Catholic family of Colpike Hall and when his father died in 1889 leaving him £10,000 (a considerable sum in those days) he decided to use his inheritance for the development of Catholic Education. The parish school at Wolsingham was to benefit as well as Ushaw College but about £6,000 was used to purchase a building known as Bridge End which, after renovation, became a convent and boarding school of the Sunderland Sisters of Mercy; the foundation stone was laid by Mother Saviour. The sisters also taught in the parish school. St. Anne's School, Wolsingham, continues today as a day school under the headship of Sister Adrienne.

Father Wilkinson was not the only priest - having spent part of his early ministry in Wolsingham - to become bishop of our diocese; the second one to do so was Father Richard Collins who was here from 1886 until 1890 becoming auxiliary bishop to Bishop Wilkinson in 1905 and succeeding to the See in 1909 when the latter died. And it should also be recorded that during the pastorate of Father Adam Wilkinson (1898-1907) the golden jubilee of St. Thomas's was celebrated; it must have been with a great sense of joy and satisfaction that Bishop Wilkinson was able to attend the festivities on October 12th, 1904, in the place where his priestly ministry had begun and from which he had played a primary role in consolidating the Faith in this area of our diocese.

In St. Thomas's churchyard are buried a number of priests and nuns who served Weardale. Amongst them are Father Taylor Smith, Wolsingham's great benefactor, Father Hutchinson, one of the longest serving priests here from 1945 until 1964 and Father Francis Robinson from 1966 until his death in 1974.

Fathers Alban Walker, Sidney Riley and Philip Quinn served Wolsingham from the house in Tow Law but when the parishes were reorganised Tow Law was paired with Willington and Wolsingham with Crook; Wolsingham's spiritual needs are now met by Father Anthony Owens, parish priest at Crook.

Wolsingham's congregation to-day numbers about 50 at the Vigil Mass but in the summer months visitors sometimes treble this figure. They will have noticed the changes principally in the sanctuary occasioned by the needs of the liturgical reforms of Vatican II; such alterations are not always easy to accomplish but here there has been a successful blending of the old with the new.

The present altar facing the people has been re-modelled using the old altar and some of the wood from the former worm-ridden reredos. This old altar came originally from the first chapel at Ushaw designed by Pugin. Reduced in size the Gothic-style pulpit is now the ambo; the brass war memorial plate that was once incorporated into the pulpit is now affixed to the wall at the right of the sanctuary. The Ushaw tabernacle has recently been encased in Frosterley marble (a now rare local stone) and rests on a pedestal of sandstone. This piece of marble - peculiar to Weardale and once a memorial slab - was acquired from a Methodist chapel in Frosterley when it closed.

Three other religious items of interest, acquired in Father Walker's time, are worthy of note: the figure of Christ outside the south entrance; the rood cross above the sanctuary which came from the Sacred Heart church in Stockton; and the acrylic painting of St. Thomas of Canterbury executed by Sheila Mackie which portrays Thomas in his episcopal robes holding the pallium relic which is one of the parish's treasures now removed from the church for safe-keeping. A further reminder of our links with the past is the framed colour photograph of a painting of the local martyr, John Duckett, recently placed at the back of the church. Few people visiting the church to-day may be aware that the wooden frames of the Stations of the Cross were carved by German P.O.Ws. in the 1940s when along with other P.O.Ws. (including Italians) they inhabited three camps in Weardale from which the Catholics were marched under guard to attend Sunday Mass at the Wolsingham church. During a visit here in the 1970s a group of ex-P.O.Ws. were pleased to see that the frames were still there having been asked by the original carvers to check if they still existed.

Father Sydney Riley, who followed Father Walker had, along with the people of both parishes, to witness the closure of both primary schools. Fortunately the new school of Blessed John Duckett at Tow Law, opened in 1988, has solved the problem of providing a Catholic primary education for children in this area of Weardale.

Today in changing times and a shortage of priests Wolsingham Catholics, assisted by Father Owens, continue to keep the light of Faith alive here

The restoration work on the church, undertaken in the 1990s, has left the community with a debt which is being reduced by holding concerts and other fund-raising activities such as the Charity Shop which is open each Monday in the old primary school.

Next year the parish will celebrate its 150th anniversary - a time to celebrate its past and plan for the future.

65. WOOLER   St. Ninian   *(December 1990, January 1991)*

Stretching to the Scottish Border and flanked in the west by the Cheviots, our second most northerly parish, St. Ninian's in Wooler - whose present parish priest is Father John Timney - has within its boundaries a sacred place known to Christians world-wide, the Island of Lindisfarne. Here in the holiday season Father Timney says Mass for summer visitors in the chapel of St. Aidan not far from the monastic site where Aidan and Cuthbert offered the Holy Sacrifice many hundreds of years ago.

But even before Aidan and his brother monks settled here, St. Bede tells us in his *Ecclesiastical History* of the advent of an earlier Christian missionary - Paulinus, a co-worker with St. Augustine in the evangelisation of Kent and Southern England, who came to Northumbria as chaplain to the King of Kent's daughter, Ethelburga, who was to be married to Edwin, the pagan King of Northumbria. Edwin, influenced by the example of his wife and her chaplain, eventually accepted Christianity and was baptised by Paulinus at York in 627 A.D. Ever on the move in those troubled and unsettled times Edwin on one occasion went to his royal residence in the Cheviot Hills at Yeavering (near Kirknewton) and here according to Bede 'so great was then the fervour of the Faith, as is reported, and the desire of the washing of salvation among the nation of the Northumbrians, that Paulinus at a certain time coming with the king and queen to the royal country-seat which is called Adgefrin stayed there with them thirty-six days, fully occupied in catechising and baptising; during which days, from morning till night, he did nothing else but instruct the people resorting from all villages and places, in Christ's saving word; and when instructed he washed them with the water of absolution in the river Glen'.

A peaceful and joyous period in this new Christian community was to end when Edwin died defending his kingdom and Paulinus returned south. It was Oswald, Edwin's successor, who at last won sway in that part of Northumbria, north of the Tyne, and being much disturbed at the damage done to the Faith of his people he was determined to bring back the Christian message and who better, he thought, than the Celtic monks of Iona who had sheltered him in exile.

The man for the task was Aidan who founded the first monastery on Lindisfarne from which he and his monks journeyed around the villages and hamlets of the North and Midlands proclaiming the gospel message. During this 'Golden Age' Holy Island became a centre of culture and scholarship as the Lindisfarne Gospels testify. Here, too, the beloved patron of our diocese, St. Cuthbert, was schooled in sanctity and even today he has a special place in the hearts of the people of the North East.

Aidan died in 651 leaving behind the memory of a saintly priest and bishop evidence of which Bede had gathered from those who had known him: 'his love of peace and charity, his continence and humility; his mind superior to anger and avarice and despising pride and vain glory; his industry in keeping and teaching the heavenly commandments; his diligence in reading and watching; his authority, becoming a priest, in reproving the haughty and powerful and at the same time his tenderness in comforting the afflicted and relieving or defending the poor.'

He was buried in the monks' cemetery and after Finan, his successor, had completed his new church the remains of their holy founder were interred near the high altar. The present priory ruins date back to the 12th century when the monks of Durham re-built the monastery which had been forsaken when the Lindisfarne community had to flee with the body of St. Cuthbert from the Viking invaders of the late 9th century.

Dotted around within the confines of the present Wooler parish boundaries are many other stone witnesses of our earlier Christian heritage: pre-Reformation churches or their remains at Branxton, Chillingham, Doddington, Kirknewton and Etal are obvious examples. Such testimony reminds us of the firm foundations in the Faith laid by the monks of Lindisfarne and their successors.

Although the religious changes of the 16th century made life difficult and often dangerous for those who wished to continue the practice of the Faith it did not die out completely in this area for there were always those who were prepared, regardless of the cost, to remain loyal to their beliefs; such a family were the Haggerstons of Haggerston Castle situated on the mainland opposite Holy Island. Here they had their own private chapel dedicated to Our Lady and St. Cuthbert.

A Henry Haggerston is named in the first recusant roll and in 1597 he was 'imprisoned at Berwick and standeth indyted ...' He was convicted on three further occasions and in 1605 he sheltered the priest (later martyr) George Gervase, who was arrested at Haggerston and taken to Durham where in a statement he claimed that 'his first going overseas was with Sir Francis Drake in his last voyage to the Indies before he had any purpose to profess religion ... next spring went overseas to Douai where he remained five years and about three years since was priested at Cambrai by the Archbishop'. On this occasion he was banished returning to Douai. However, still wishing to serve the English Mission with its attendant risks he was soon apprehended and died a martyr at Tyburn on April 11th, 1608. The Benedictines claim that he took the Benedictine habit before his last return to England with the intention of full profession when the opportunity occurred.

Still strong in the Faith a hundred years later, a Sir Thomas Haggerston, who died round about 1710, was reported to have had nine sons three of whom were priests: Henry and John were Jesuits and Francis, a Franciscan. Ellingham was another residence of the Haggerston family after 1698, the chaplaincy there being staffed by Jesuits until 1805.

It would be wrong to assume, however, that the Haggerstons were the sole guardians of the Ancient Faith in this area. We know, among others, that some of the Greys of Chillingham were recusants. Thomas

Collingwood of Eslington, who was married to Anne Grey of Chillingham, was sentenced to prison in 1592 but escaped on his way there; his wife, Anne, was also convicted.

Often the tenants and servants of the Catholic landowners were of the same faith. In the Papist Returns of 1767 for the area, one sees listed 13 on Holy Island, 50 in Ancroft (Haggerston area), 36 at Lowick, and two at Wooler. Caution was obviously still needed as when the Haggerston return is looked at more closely we notice a Mr Charles Hann resident there for ten years and described as 'a domestic in Sir Thos. Haggerston's house and a reputed popish priest'.

Haggerston Castle ceased to be a mission centre about 1857 on the death of Lady Stanley of Cheshire, the heiress of Sir Carnaby Haggerston. The following year the estate passed into non-Catholic hands making it necessary for the priest at Wooler, Father William Carlile, to make other arrangements for the Catholics in the area; this he did by utilizing the school-chapel built at Lowick on land provided by the Haggerstons of Ellingham. The transfer appears to have gone smoothly assisted by Mr Stanley who writing to Father Eyre comments: 'I beg to inform you that if the bishop thinks it proper to close the chapel at Haggerston and open one at Lowick everything in the chapel and the priest's house may be removed to Lowick.'

Father Carlile was responsible for the conversion of the school-chapel into a church opened in April, 1861. Until the appointment of the first parish priest in 1864, Fr. Charles Dunn, who built the new school and presbytery, Father Carlile travelled fortnightly to Lowick to say Mass. For many years Lowick was a parish in its own right serving Holy Island and district. Father Timney was the last parish priest at Lowick moving to Wooler in 1987; he continues to say Mass weekly in Lowick in the Anglican church of St. John the Baptist since the sale of the land and property there. The last Mass in the church of St. Edward the Confessor at Lowick was said on February 9th, 1989 concelebrated by deanery priests; Father Cuthbert Rand, a native of Lowick, preached the closing sermon.

The foundation of the parish of St. Ninian's, Wooler, was due to the determination of one woman, Mrs Jane Silvertop, who on the death of her third husband, George Silvertop - with estates at Stella and Minsteracres - decided to return in 1792 to the place of her youth being the daughter of Charles Selby of Earle, near Wooler. She brought with her the Rev. Thomas Eyre, the chaplain at Stella, thus making him the first resident priest at Wooler. For two years he remained here until he undertook the responsibility of looking after the Douai students who fled to England as a result of the French revolutionary wars; he was to become Ushaw's first president.

Another effect of the French Revolution was the enforced exodus of many priests from their native land. Many came for a time to the North East where they were well received; four of them were looked after by Mrs Silvertop at St. Ninian's: Fathers Gilbert, Maquet, Gicquel and Bigot of the St. Malo Diocese. In 1802 - apart from Father Gilbert who went on to establish a mission at Whitby - they returned to France.

With the departure of the French emigre priests the Rev. William Hurst took over, moving to Berwick in 1803, to be succeeded by a Franciscan, the Rev. Richard Whalley, until 1810. After this date the Wooler Mission was served by various priests including the Rev. Thomas Gillow, chaplain at Callaly Castle, Whittingham, who has recorded that he came here 'for prayers once in three weeks which I never omitted during my attendance.' The Rev. Thomas Birdsall based at Ellingham (a Haggerston residence with its own chapel and served usually by Jesuits) and later at Berwick served the Wooler Mission for over twenty years. On one occasion he writes: 'What a dismal storm we had and I had to walk to Wooler in the middle of it. I went over snow perhaps 20 feet deep. I was very much fatigued.' For some reason he did not say Mass in St. Ninian's house (the chapel was on the top floor) but in cottages in Corby Knowe and later Tenterhill House.

It is not possible to mention all the priests who served Wooler so faithfully. However, it is of interest to know that the Rev. Charles Eyre recuperated at Wooler after succumbing to the Newcastle typhus epidemic of 1847 which carried off Bishop Riddell, the Vicar-Apostolic. A further period of convalescence at Haggerston made him sufficiently strong to accept the Archbishopric of Glasgow where he was to do great work for the church there.

Bishop Hogarth in 1850 was making plans to use St. Ninian's as a Diocesan Missionary Centre from which priests could offer retreats and missions to Northern England. Fathers Consitt, Suffield, Clavering and Chadwick were assigned to this work; the latter was to succeed Bishop Hogarth in 1866 as the second Bishop of our diocese.

During this period of missionary endeavour the church of St. Ninian's was built and opened costing £1,305. It was designed by George Goldie of the Sheffield firm of Weighman, Hadfield and Goldie.

The Tablet of 1856 records the official opening by Bishop Hogarth in the presence of 23 priests: 'Admission to the church was by tickets given the previous week gratuitously to all who applied for them, thus the poor were admitted as freely as the rich, and yet at the offertory at the High Mass £61.10s. was put into the plate and at the evening service £7.16s, an amount showing the liberality of Catholic and Protestant visitors.' (This we are told was more than could be expected in a year from the local congregation.) 'The church itself is a severely simple building in harmony with the wild scenery about it. The style is Early English (transitional) ... the East window representing S.S. Ninian, Cuthbert, Paulinus and Aidan is reckoned by many Wailes' most successful work ... . Mr Wailes has presented two lights in the Lady Chapel between which is to be placed a painting of Our Blessed Lady Immaculate, the work of a young artist who has devoted his pencil to religious art, C. Goldie Esq., the brother of the architect of the church ... a beautiful window in the Lady aisle - represents Our Lady in glory and Our Lady of sorrows ... it is an offering from George Goldie, Esq ... on the day of the opening Protestants seem to vie with Catholics in the generosity of their offerings'.

There was, however, a sad side to this day of celebration as shortly before the opening the old presbytery had been gutted by fire. Whether this was the ultimate cause of the end of St. Ninian's as a missionary centre, we cannot be sure; maybe its remoteness from the densely populated areas of the diocese was an additional factor which led to its closure.

Some time before the opening of the church a small school was started and named the Catholic Academy; its first teacher was John B. McSweeney. A statue of St. Aloysius donated by the children when the church was opened can still be seen in St. Ninian's.

After the demise of the Mission, St. Ninian's was from 1858 in the care of the Rev. John William Carlile (mentioned earlier) who removed the top floor of the house where the old chapel had been and made the building once more habitable. His major worry was the parish debt and a reduced income due to a small congregation made even smaller when the poor migrant agricultural workers were obliged to move elsewhere seeking employment. He describes these unfortunate workers as 'truly wanderers "super faciem terrae".' He bemoaned the thought of, perhaps, having to close the school as 'out of 80 children only 30 can pay anything this year (1859) so far'.

The longest serving parish priest at Wooler was Father Denis O'Kelly who ministered here for 35 years from 1903 to 1938. Although there is little recorded in the parish history of this period Father O'Kelly, like all the priests who served here, kept alive the Catholic Faith and through the Mass, the sacraments and prayer enriched the spiritual life of all his people.

Second in length of service was Father Arthur Vernon Wills who arrived at Wooler in 1938; in 1967 he celebrated his Golden Jubilee but due to failing health he retired from the parish in 1970 to become chaplain to the Mercy Convent in Alnwick where he died in 1983 at the age of 92.

He recorded assiduously many of the highlights of parish life particularly during the war years. He asks on September 10th, 1939: 'Will you kindly send your children to church tomorrow as usual for religious instructions at 9. Grateful to know of any Catholic refugees or evacuees who have come to the parish.'

He notes on May 16th, 1943, the recent appointment of Fr. Michael McCleary who spoke Italian and said Mass at the camp for Italian prisoners of war; Fr. Coakley C.F. said Mass at Lilburn Towers for the soldiers; Fr. Thomas O'Brien C.F. said Mass at Ewart Park for the soldiers too, and Father Wills said Mass at the aerodrome and St. Ninian's. Mass had been said on that Sunday at five different locations within the parish.

Between January 1943 and November 1944 he lists the nationalities who lived for a time in his parish:

English, Scots, Irish, Welsh, French, Belgian, Czech, Poles, Chinese, Italians, Maltese, Germans, Americans, Canadians, New Zealanders, Burmese (Latvians as well in 1948) - truly an example of the Catholicity of the church.

Further examples of the universality of the church were when Father Frederico Favorin (Italian chaplain) played the organ and the Italians sang the Mass - a *Missa Cantata* on December 9th, 1945 in St. Ninian's; the Rev. Hans Annas sang Mass for 150 German P.O.Ws. on Whit Monday, 1946; and in September of that year the Rev. Boleslaw Martinelis sang a Mass accompanied by a Polish choir.

Organising the spiritual and social life of a rural parish is not always easy where parishioners are scattered over a wide region. However in 1949, Mr C. Forster of Berwick established a conference of the S.V.P. at Wooler with Mr Thomas Dunne as its first president. Father Wills was a man of many and varied interests including photography; he became chairman of the Wooler and District Camera Club which met regularly in the presbytery basement. Father James McKenny succeeded Father Wills from 1970 to 1974 and since the latter date Father Timney has been parish priest here taking on the responsibility for two parishes. Within this extensive parish Fr. Timney and his parishioners attempt to meet the spiritual and community needs of the area. As there is no Catholic school near at hand children are given catechetical instructions on a Saturday morning and booklets are being prepared to enable parents to do this for their children in isolated areas.

St. Ninian's participate in the ecumenical services in the district such as the Unity Octave Week and the Remembrance Day Service at which the Catholics, United Reform, and the Anglicans lead the service in turn.

Over the August Bank Holiday weekend a Flower and Musical Festival was held at St. Ninian's in which many members of the Wooler community took part; organ recitals were also part of the three-day attraction.

To assist the parishioners to meet socially, four coffee mornings are held every year and recently three parishioners Mrs Howe of Amersidelaw, Mrs Wardlaw of Kirknewton and Lady Goodson have hosted parish lunches in their own homes enabling distant parishioners to get to know each other better on an informal basis. Recently, a half-day of recollection was given by a priest from Kelso at the home of Lady Goodson, Kilham, where about 18 people attended.

Today the parish of St. Ninian's continues to keep alive the Faith preached here, probably without a break, for 1,300 years since the days of St. Paulinus - indeed, a remarkable achievement.

66. WREKENTON   St. Oswald   *(February, 1985)*

Various orders of priests, over many years, have contributed to the spread of the Faith in our diocese; one of the earliest must be the Benedictines whose rule may have been followed in the Anglo-Saxon monasteries of Wearmouth and Jarrow and later in Norman times by the monks of Finchale and Durham. The dissolution of the monasteries in the reign of Henry VIII reduced their numbers considerably in this area but they continued to follow their monastic ideals in continental monasteries and their missionary work secretly in England, usually as chaplains to the Catholic families and their servants who could give them a home and support in their difficult task. Unfortunately, today the number of Benedictines in our diocese is reduced to two: Father Gibbons at Cowpen and Father Cunningham at New Hartley.

Birtley is, perhaps, the best known of the Benedictine parish missions in the north-east being staffed over a long period by priests from Douai Abbey, near Reading, which was founded in 1903 from a much earlier foundation in Flanders.

Wrekenton, St. Oswald's, owes its beginning to this order of monks who, we believe, first came to Birtley in 1696. By 1882, the parish priest of Birtley, Father Charles Henry Oswald O'Neill O.S.B., seeing an increase in the Catholic population in and around Wrekenton purchased a piece of land costing £824 and built a school-chapel behind where the present church now stands; it remains there today having been modernised for use as the parish social centre.

Wrekenton, St. Oswald *Photo: T. Mackin*

Father Oswald O'Neill, whose patron saint became the parish's too, appears to have left Birtley in 1882 to eventually become prior at St. Edmund's, Douai. Who his immediate successor was we are not sure, but we do know that Father Wilfrid Phillipson O.S.B. came to Birtley in January, 1884, and three months after his arrival the Wrekenton school-chapel was officially opened. Father Phillipson left behind in the Douai archives his own personal account of the beginning of the Wrekenton Mission. Perhaps, his arrival in January did not dispose him well towards our northern climate for he has this to say about our weather: 'The winters on the coast of N. E. Durham were very trying. During my seven years there I do not remember one winter when the cold was not almost Arctic in severity. In no part of England have I known such heavy falls of snow. Sometimes six weeks elapsed before it entirely disappeared on the road from Birtley to Wrekenton. Under such conditions it was by no means easy to make my rounds and attend the sick'.

According to his account a link with penal days was established in his time with the rediscovery of an altar stone: 'When I went to Birtley in January, 1884, with the approval and encouragement of Father Aidan Hickey, the recently elected Provincial, I undertook to complete what had been begun. Within a month I had the school completely furnished for use as a school-chapel, but one thing I had not got - an altar-stone. I was just getting ready to go to Ushaw for one when the late Miss Anne Humble called at the presbytery. "Father" she said, "you will need an altar stone". "Yes", I replied, "but you have not got one". "Yes, I have", she said, and she went on to tell me that before the previous church (Birtley) was built she used to hear Mass in the chapel (of which part remains) a few yards from her house; that she remembered the priest being taken ill, after the elevation, and being unable to finish the Mass, and how 48 hours after, a priest came from Newcastle and completed the sacrifice, and she added "when he was leaving - broken down in health - he brought the stone to me telling me I must never touch it. And it is in the drawer" she said "wrapped in paper just as he left it". I went to her house and having found it as she said took it to Wrekenton, where I used it on the opening day, that relic of the days of persecution.'

A protracted period of correspondence and negotiation lasting seven years was necessary before a school grant was obtained. During this time of financial hardship Father Phillipson was deeply grateful to the first headmistress, Miss Elizabeth Neville, an exemplary Catholic teacher, who lived on a salary of £40 per year - lower than the salary earned by an unqualified teacher in a state school.

'Since she never relaxed her efforts to ensure efficiency; and above all, to thoroughly instruct the children in the truths, and practice of their religion, I have in the long years of my missionary life employed many excellent teachers but not one equalled her in devotion to duty, in patience under hardships and adversity, in zeal for the spiritual good of those under her charge; and in generosity and self-sacrifice.'

Father Phillipson had laboured in Birtley and Wrekenton for seven years - without a holiday - and after recovering from meningitis, which almost killed him, he left to recuperate. Father Chambers was appointed in his place and in that year of 1891 the school qualified for the annual state grant. The following year a stone presbytery was built at a cost of £700 and allowed the first parish priest of Wrekenton to take up residence there; he was Father Austin Kershaw O.S.B. who left in 1901 for Cowpen where he remained 27 years, dying there in May 1928. *The Morpeth Herald* paid tribute to his Christian character: 'Catholics and Protestants alike recognised in the late priest one of nature's gentlemen. He was a man of deep piety and broad sympathies and was beloved by people of all creeds. Always wearing a smile he had a good word to offer when he met anyone, and there was a boyish ring in his hearty laughter.'

His successor at Wrekenton was Father Wulstan Fossato O.S.B. who was responsible for the building of the present church, designed by J. C. Parsons of Newcastle and costing £3,000. The foundation stone was laid by Bishop Preston, the auxiliary bishop, on May 31st, 1902 and it was officially opened on February 21st, 1903. Father Fossato had spent part of his life teaching at Douai and was for a time sub-prior there; he was an accomplished musician, who could speak fluently in German, French and Italian and was a scholar of Greek, Hebrew and Latin.

When he left Wrekenton in 1905 he was succeeded by Father Oswald James Hall O.S.B. - the longest serving parish priest - who apart from the period 1916 to 1921 when he was at Birtley, remained as parish priest at Wrekenton until 1951 when the parish was handed over to the diocese.

Father Hall can claim a record for longevity; he retired to Blyth and had the distinction of celebrating Mass on June 9th, 1966, his hundredth birthday. A writer in the Douai magazine claims he was the longest living member of the Douai community and possibly the English Benedictine community too. In his youth he had been a good footballer and he continued to play golf even in his advancing years; he was a founder member of the Wrekenton Golf Club where a cup was named after him.

The first diocesan priest to take charge at Wrekenton was Father Samuel Dickinson who had spent 12 years teaching at Ushaw followed by a period as assistant priest at St. Mary's Cathedral. Father Dickinson was responsible for the building of the new school to meet the needs of an increasing number of pupils; he pursued the matter as far as a personal visit to the Ministry of Education to expedite its erection.

Father Dickinson, who moved to Easington Lane in 1965, was succeeded by Father Joseph Lavery who remained in the parish until his death in November 1980. In January of the same year, Father Denis Kellett - the present parish priest - came here to assist Father Lavery who was not in good health and succeeded him on his death.

Two important recent dates in the parish were August 18th, 1983 when Bishop Owen Swindlehurst concelebrated Mass and consecrated the church on completion of the recent alterations; and March 2nd, 1984, when a special anniversary Mass was celebrated - with Father Gibbons O.S.B. representing the Benedictine Douai community - to commemorate the centenary of the first Mass centre at Wrekenton.

Many churches in the diocese have seen considerable alterations and refurbishing carried out in recent years. Richard Dietz Lyons Associates were the consultants for St. Oswald's and the reconstruction was carried out by Harry Nagel who was also responsible for the building of the new stone porch which connects the church to the presbytery.

The stonework and the altar were refashioned by Morris Marble works. Dietz Lyons were, also, responsible for the redesigning of the old school-chapel now the parish community centre; the alterations here were carried out by a Community Task Force funded by the Manpower Services Commission - an example of the church today co-operating in the provision of employment for those who, otherwise, may not have a job. The total cost of all these changes to the church and original chapel amounts to approximately £75,000.

A parish council, elected by the parishioners, assists Father Kellett in the administration of the parish. Other organisations which play a valuable role are: the S.V.P. which, as in every parish, continues the charitable work to those in need; the St. Oswald's Parish Ladies' Organisation; and a Monday Club for senior citizens.

In addition to the daily Masses celebrated in the church, St. Oswald's have special Masses regularly: one is celebrated every Friday prepared previously by the school children, and to which their parents and other parishioners are invited. On the first Saturday of every month the sick and elderly are transported by parishioners to a special Mass after which a cooked breakfast is provided by the ladies of the parish. Father Kellett hopes soon to have Lay Ministers of the Eucharist commissioned who will enable the sick to receive communion more frequently.

Two relics of those olden days at St. Oswald's - the altar stone and the old school-chapel - remain to remind us of the continuity of the Faith through the ages.

INDEX TO PART 2

References are to article numbers, not to pages. Main articles are indexed in **bold**

Abbott, Helen 38
Abbott, J. 47
Acklington, H.M. Prison 2
Adamson, John 44
Agnes, Sister 33
Aherne, Fr. 15
Aidan, St. 6, 26, 27, 50, 61, 65
Aimuller, Max 1
Alice, Sister 36
Allen, William Cardinal 4, 29, 55, 62
Alnmouth Priory, 1, 63
Alnwick, **1**, 2, 12, 16, 33
Alwinton 7
Amble **2**, 35
Ampleforth, 5, 7, 21, 30, 37, 39, 42
Amundeville Family, 16
Ancroft 6
Anderson, Sir William, 12, 53
Angela, Sister 57
Anlaby, Bl. William 4
Anna, Sister 21
Annas, Hans 65
Anne Family 5
Anne of Jesus, Ven. 19
Anne of St. Bartholomew, St. 19
Annfield Plain 13
Annitsford **3**, 38
Anselm, Sister (Little Sisters of the Poor) 38
Anson, Peter 53
Anthony, Father 57
Apostleship of Prayer 15, 56
Appleyard, Richard 36
Apurimac Valley Help Project 31
Aquin, Sister 54
Arcade Hall 57
Arcot Hall 3
Armstrong, Lord 43
Armstrong, John (S.J), Robert & Thomas (OSB) 29
Arras, 16
Arthurs, Austin (CSP) 11
Ashburton House 25
Ashington 35, 37
Ashmall, Ferdinand 21
Askew, Dr. 48

Aspin, Peter 36
Association for the Propagation of the Faith (APF), 11
Atkinson, Peter 29
Attwood, Charles 59
Augustinians 12, 29, 35, 41, 58, 63
Austin Friars 4
Avery, Canon 47
Axman, Thomas 47
Backhouse, Jonathan 18
Backworth 3
Bailey, Bede (O.P.) 29
Baker, Kate 38
Balfour Act 13, 55
Baliol, College, Oxford, 4; William, Barnard, Guy, John 4
Bamber, Canon John 47, 55-7
Banister (alias Rutter), Henry 61
Barker, Anthony 4
Barker, G.W., Councillor, (J.P.) 12
Barley Hill 36
Barnard Castle **4**
Barnett Family of Newcastle 52
Barrington, Shute, Bishop of Durham 10, 19
Barron, W.E. Fr. 46
Bartley, Kevin 38; Vincent 40
Bateson, Geoffrey 37
Battle, Thomas 60
Beatrice, Sister 58
Beaulieu 8
Bebside 12
Becket, St. Thomas a 53
Beckwith, Lady of Silksworth House 49
Bede, St. 10, 17, 24, 26-8, 31, 33, 51, 54-7, 61, 65
Bedingfield, Edmund & Sir Henry 19
Bedlington 12, 35, 37
Beech, Edward 15
Beith, Alan M.P. 6
Belaney, Robert 47
Belassis, Miles O.S.B. 5
Belgium 15
Bell and Ridley of Durham 41
Bell, Canon John 13, 26, 44
Bellarmine, Robert, St. 52

Bellingham **5**
Benedict, Abbot 56; Mother 13; St. 55
Benedictine(s) (OSB) 5, 7, 12/13, 16, 35-7, 42, 46, 52, 61, 65/66
Bennett, John 56
Bensham 23
Bentley, John Francis 16
Benton 11
Benwell 36, **41**
Bernard, Mother Mary Anne, 19
Berrington 6
Bertram, William I of Mitford 35, 37
Berwick **6**
Besnier, Philip 6
Betham, Frederick 24
Bewick, Bishop John William, 42, 45, 51, 61
Bewley 8
Biddlestone, **7**, 35
Bigot, Father M., 6, 65
Billingham, **8**, 49
Birdsall, Thomas 65; William 6
Birgen, Father 25
Birket, George 34
Birkett, Mamie 51
Birkley, Joseph, Elizabeth 15
Birrell, Augustine 33
Birtley, **9**
Biscop, Benedict, 33
Bishop Auckland **10**, 19
Bishop Chadwick Memorial School 25
Bishop Middleham 48
Bishop's House **42**
Black Bull at Wardley 22
Blackbird Inn 46
Blackhill 1, **11**, 13
Blagdon 12
Blakeney, Robert 41
Blanchland 1, 16, 36
Blandford, Philip 21
Blaydon, 15
Blenkin, Canon Wilfrid, 33
Blount, Gilbert 35
Blyth, **12**,35,37
Boland, Fr. Laurence 20, 38
Bolger, Kevin 25
Bolton, John Anselm (O.S.B.) 7, 9
Bolus, Thomas Anselm (O.S.B.) 5
Bonomi, Ignatius 5, 18, 31, 55
Booth, John 53

Boste, St. John 6, 13, 21, 23/4, 29, 31, 55/6, 63/4
Boulmer 1
Bourke, Michael 8
Bourne, Cardinal 33, 56,
Bowes, Bowes-Lyon Family, Earls of Strathmore; Museum, 4, 14, 47
Buller's Green 12
Boyle, Br. Mark 11
Brack, Mary 53
Bradbury 48
Bradford, Lancelot 10
Bradley Hall 64
Bradley, James 51
Brady, Eoghan 8
Brandling Family of Felling Hall 9, 22-4, 43/4
Brannigan, Owen 3
Brewer, H. (O.S.B.) 9
Briant, Bl. Alexander, 21
Briggs, Bishop John (Vicar Apostolic Northern District) 5, 24, 26/7, 31, 55
Brinkburn 12, 35
Brizlee Hill 1
Broderick, Lowther & Walker, Messrs. (architects) 51
Brompton Oratory 10
Broomhill Colliery 2
Brooms, 11, **13**
Brough Family 47; Brough Hall 19, 24
Brown, Bishop 26, 27
Brown, D. & Associates of Newcastle (architects) 20
Brown, Edda, Nicholas 5; George (S.J.) 24; Nicholas Hodgson 23; Thomas 20
Browne, Canon Joseph Aloysius, 31
Bruce, Robert 7
Brusselmann's course 31
Bryce, Godfrey 21
Buckley, Father A., 57; Timothy 56
Bull, Father 57; John 38
Bulmer Family 34; Edward (O.S.B.) 9
Burghley, Lord 13, 52
Burke, Dermot 60; James 49; Canon Laurence 26, 27; R. (architect) 23; Thomas 25
Burn Hall 18, 37
Burne-Jones, Edward 44
Burns, Father 57; Gerard (S.M.) 8; John 20
Burnyeat, Ethel 23
Burton, Bishop George 50

Bury, Richard de 48; Charles 19; Mary 1
Bute, Marquess of, 14
Butterwick 48
Buxton, Mgr. Wilfrid, 17
Byermoor, **14**
Byker 11
Byrne, Joseph 50
Bywell 36
Caden, John 48
Cain, Father 21; Joseph of Salford 38
Cairns, David 61
Calboutin, Ray 61
Caley, George Rev. 4, 59, 64
Callaghan, Peter 15
Callaly Castle 35, 45, 58, 65
Cambois 12
Cambours, Francis 31
Cambrai 34
Cambridge, Duke of 19, University 4
Camillus, Order of St. 29
Camoys, Lord 36
Campbell, Fr. 26, Mgr. 53; Patricia 42
Campion, Michael 25
Cannon, Paul 2
Capheaton Hall 46
Carew, John 6
Carey, George 47
Carileph, Bishop William 33
Caritas Folk Group 11
Carlile, Father (Canon) 53; John William 65
Carlisle 6
Carmelites 10, 18, 58; Carmel Convent **19**
Carr Family 19; Peter 23/5; Anne 28
Carroll, Brother 55; Philip 14; Thomas 22; William 53
Carter, Tony 26
Cartington 5, 58
Casey, Denis 21
Cass, Tom 44
Castington, H.M. Youth Custody Centre 2
Castle Eden 4, 32, 35
Cater, Mrs. 19
Catholic Care North East 4, 54
Catholic Emancipation Act (1829) 18, 36, 54, 55
Catholic Film Society 39
Catholic Fund for Overseas Development (CAFOD) 11, 15, 23, 63
Catholic Missionary Society (CMS) 2, 9, 12, 15, 53

Catholic Nurses Guild 50
Catholic Scouts & Guides 39
Catholic Social Guild 33
Catholic Stage Guild 39
Catholic Women's Guild 13, 20, 32, 59
Catholic Women's League (CWL) 8/9,12, 15/16, 25/26, 29, 31, 33, 37, 46, 51/2, 55-8, 60
Catholic Writers Guild 39
Catholic Young Men's Society (CYMS) 15, 24, 59
Cayley, Mrs. of Scorton 27
Chadwick, Alfred 14; Bishop James, 2, 11, 13/14, 16, 20, 28, 34, 39, 42, 45, 47, 49, 60/1, 63, 65
Chambers, Father 66
Chandler, Bishop (of Durham) 7
Chapel Wells 64
Chapman, Fr. 3; Robert 37
Charity of St. Paul, Sisters of 11, 16
Charity, Sisters of, 18, 25
Charlemagne 63
Charles II 5
Charlton Family 5, 15, 58
Cheeseburn Grange 46
Chesman, William 58
Chester-le-Street 13
Cheswick 6
Children of Mary 14/5, 24, 26, 33, 56, 59, 60
Chopwell 13
Christian Brothers 54
Church Music Society 39
Cistercians 12, 37, 46, 58 12
Clare Abbey, Darlington 6
Clare of Jesus, Sister 19
Claret, Anthony (Archbishop of Santiago);
Claretians 21
Clarke, Robert 60
Clavering Family of Callaly Castle, 20, 63, 65
Claxton Family 21
Cleveland, Duke of 4
Cliff House 2
Cliffe Hall 4, 42
Clifford, Father 20
Clifton, Thomas (S.J.) 35
Clopton, Family, Cuthbert 4
Coakley, Father (C.F.) 65
Coates (Cotes) Family 1; Mary, John & Winifred 37
Cocken Hall 10, 19
Cockerton Field House 19

Cockshaw Mission 29
Cocurullo, Anthony 52
Cogan, Mgr. 21; Cogan, Rev. Dr. of Esh 23
Coia, Anthony 60
Colahan, Noel 53
Coleridge, Lady 49
Coleson, John 56
Collen, Jane 61
Collierly 13
Collingwood, Family of Eslington 63; George
    & William, Thomas & John 47, 65
Collins, Bishop Richard, 15, 25, 32, 34, 39,
    42, 44, 47, 51, 64
Cologne 16
Colpike Hall 64
Colutaris, Osbert 35
Commons, House of, 22
Compiegne 14, 19
Condercum 41
Connolly, Father Joseph 55/6, 59
Conroy, Philip 49
Consett 11, 13
Consitt, Edward 24; Father 65
Conway, James 14; T.M. 30
Conyer Family of Horden Hall 20; John 13
Cooke, Rev. John Anderton, 29
Coquet Island 2, 61
Corbett, Michael 39
Corboy, James 28
Corby Hall 55
Corby, Bl. Ralph (S.J.) 16, 30, 55, 57, 59, 60, 64
Cork, Mercy Community 54
Corless, George 58
Cornforth 48
Cornthwaite, Bishop Robert 53
Corrigan, Father 20
Cosin, John 34
Costar, Fr. 43
Costello, James 5; Edward 22; William 48
Costelloe, Alderman 24
Cotes, John, Archdeacon 35
Countess de Montalbo, 4
Cowpen 8, 12, 35, 37
Coxlodge 25
Coxon, Basil 6; David 8, 26
Cramlington 3, 12
Crangle, Michael 57
Crathorne 33

Crawcrook, **15**
Crawford & Spenser of Middlesbrough 8
Crawford, Fr. 30; Richard 59; Thomas 8, 41
Crimea 1
Croghan, Father 61
Croix, Sister Roger de la 23
Crolly, James 26
Crook Hall 13, 39, 42, 45, 52, 60, 62
Crook, **16**
Crowe Family, Father Thomas 20
Croxdale, **17**; Croxdale Hall 34
Culley, Matthew 63
Cumberland, St. Bees 27; Duke of 24
Cummings, Lawrence 34
Cummins of Sunderland (builder) 46; Kevin 2
Cunningham, Anthony 10; Father 66;
    Gerald 47; Bishop James 8, 15, 24, 38, 42;
    Mgr. John J. 11, 25;
    Canon Seamus, 60; Thomas 37
Curry, Luke 10; Mr. & Mrs. 33; Osmund 6
Cuthbert, St. 2, 6, 13, 17, 31, 50, 63, 65
Cuthbert's Well, St. 6
Daley, Bede (O.C.S.O.); Felix, 38; Kevin 32
Dalton-le-Dale 38, 47
Daniel, Brother 56; John 18, 53
Danneville, A. Rev. 45, 61
Darell, John (S.J.) 63; John of Jarrow 28, 33
Darley, Bernard 4
Darlington 4, 13, **18**, 19, 31
Daughters of the Cross 33
Davel, John 28
Davis, Father 56; Vincent 2
Deasy, Sister Mary Vincent 54
Deegan, Father Martin 29; Lawrence 8
Delaney, Dr. Rev. 5
Delaval, Sir John 12; Sir Hugh 41
Dendy, F.W. 43
Derwent Valley 11
Derwentwater 17; Earl of (James Radcliffe)
    2, 24, 52, 58
Devine, L. Father (O.S.B.) 37
Devlin, Michael 17
Dicconson, Bishop 53
Dickie, Dr. Hugh 37
Dickinson, Frank; Henry 56; Samuel 66
Dietz-Lyons of Newcastle 41
Dieulouard 7, 9
Digby, Jerome (O.S.B.) 23

Diocesan: Marriage Tribunal 39;
    Religious Education Centre 14;
    Rescue Society 3, 23, 55, 57;
    Schools Commission 13; Youth Service 2
Dipton 13
Divine Mercy Shrine 38
Dixon, Kevin, 38
Dobson, John 9, 52
Docherty, John 26; Tommy 31; Jim 53
Dodds, G. 32
Dolan, George 28
Dollan, Jim 14
Dollard, Thomas 51
Dominica, Sister 54
Dominicans (O.P.) 7, 16, 22, 39, 63
Donaghue, Anthony 24
Donelly, E. 24
Donnelly, James 11
Donohough, John, Rev. 5
Donovan, Frank 24
Douai/Douay (College, France) 4, 5, 9,13,16, 21, 29, 34-7, 39, 42, 45, 52/3 58, 60, 62, 65/6;
Douai Abbey (Berks.) 12, 66
Dowfold 16
Downside Abbey 37
Doyle, Leo 46; Fr. S. 32
Drake, Sir Francis, 65
Dromgoole, Wilfrid (O.S.B.) 12
Duboisson, Rev. M. 45, 61
Duckett, Bl. John, 14, 16, 64
Duffy, Anthony, Gervase 11; Benignus 36; Tony 9; Vincent 57
Dugdale, Rev. Mr. 52; Joseph 53
Duggan, Mr. 33
Duke, Edmund 32, 51
Dunderdale, John 4
Dunn & Hansom (architects) 4, 14, 24, 27, 36, 40, 56, 60-4
Dunn Family of Castle Hill 15
Dunn Family of Saltwellside 23, 52; Bridget 52; Charles 65; Elizabeth 40; George 56; George William 25; George Thos., A.M. Commander 11/12, 15; John 60
Dunne, Father 31; Francis 26; Thomas 65
Dunstanburgh Castle 1
Durham 8, 13, 16-8, 21/2, 24, 31-3, 50
Durham, Thomas (alias Collingwood) 7, 12, 37
Durnin, Fr. 16
Dyce, William 1

Dyke House Farm 26
Easington Colliery, **20**, 38
Ebchester 13
Eckermann, Phil 21
Eckersley, John O.S.B. 12
Ecopp, William 43
Edisford, William 58
Edward King I 7; II 6; VI 5, 22, 34, 43
Edwin, King 65
Egbert, Bishop of Lindisfarne 36
Egfrid, King 56, 63
Egglestone 4
Egred, Bishop of Lindisfarne 4, 6
Eldon, Lord 48
Elizabeth I 1, 4, 5, 28, 29, 43, 60
Elizabeth, Sister 54
Ellingham 6
Elliott, Mary 53
Ellis, Michael Rev. 4, Francis 27
Ellison, Cuthbert (Lord of the Manor) 24
Elswick 41
Emmaus Community 57
England, 'Dowry of Mary' 43
Englefield, Henry Charles 36
English Martyrs 51
Errington Family 42, 46;
    George, Archbishop 5, 12, 39, 50;
    Isabella 45
Escolland Family 47
Escomb 10
Esh 13 **21**
Esp Green 13
Etal 63
Ethelburga, Queen 65
Etheldreda, Queen of Northumberland 29
Evetts, L.C. 41
Eyre, Family 52; Charles Archbishop 25, 33, 39, 65; Thomas 13, 62, 65
Eyrum, John, Sir 14
Faber, William Frederick 10
Fairfax, Anne, Lady 7
Faithful Companions of Jesus 26
Faley, Andrew 14, 50
Falkland Islands 11
Falstone 5
Farnacres 14
Farrell, James 60
Favorin, Frederico 65
Fawell, J.C. 47

Fee, Austin Bede 61; Canon Wilfrid 50
Felling **22**, 23, 28, 39, 44
Felton 2, 35, 37
Fenham, Sacred Heart School, St. Mary's College 41
Fenwick Family 37; Sir William 2
Ferndene House 23
Field House 23
Finan, B. (Salvatorian Father) 38
Finchale Abbey 16, 19, 37
Findlay of Ryhope 38
Finn, Kevin 47
Finnigan, Father 59
Fintan, Sister 42
Fishburn 48
Fishwick, John 1
Fitzgerald, Fr. 15
Fitz-Roger, Robert 63
Flambard Bishop 2
Flanders 45
Fleck, William Cuthbert (builder) 25
Fletcher, William 2, 13, 21, 55
Flint, John George 5
Floer, Jules du 56
Foes, John 15
Foley, John 42
Foran, James & Robert 11
Forcer, Basil 37
Ford Castle 63
Ford, Mrs. 47
Fordyce, W. 47, 48
Forkin, Austin 28
Forster, Fr. 3; George 51; Margaret 61
Forth House 40
Fortune, Maurice 15
Fossato, Wulstan (O.S.B.) 66
Fountains Abbey 37
Francis, Colonel 17
Franciscan(s) 27, 43, 58, 52, 65
Frazer, James 11
French Revolution 13, 39, 65
Fresburn, Ralph de 1, 58
Friars Minor of Hartlepool 27
Friarside 14
Frickley 5
Furlong, Rev. Father (Order of Charity) 24
Gainford 4, 6
Gaisford, Father 56
Galletly, John 52

Galley, John 27
Gannon, John 57
Gardiner, Christine 58; Dr Luke, 21
Gateshead: Corpus Christi 22, **23**, 31, 33, 35, 45; Historical Society 22; House 22-4; St. Joseph, **24**; Holy Trinity 23
George III 2
Gerard, Brother 56
Gervase, George (O.S.B.) 63, 65
Gibbons, Father (O.S.B.) 66; John 33, John O.S.B. 12
Giblin, Father 59
Gibside Chapel 4; Hall 14
Gibson Family 29; Family of Stonecroft 52; Bishop, Vicar-Apostolic Northern District 13; James 10; George, Jasper, Joseph, Bishop Matthew & William 1, 2, 29, 52, 56; Thomas (architect) 10, 37; Bishop William 19, 21, 36, 39, 62
Gicquel, Father 65
Gilbert, Father 65
Gillespie, Brother 55
Gilling Castle 7
Gillow, Fr. 6
Gillow, Canon Henry 11, 56, 63; Rev. Henry 31; Richard 10; Thomas 45, 65; William 59, 63
Girl Guides 28
Girlington, Father 55
Gits, John 47
Glassbrook, Roger 21
Godric, St. 14, 37, 64
Good Shepherd (order of nuns) 40; Project 41
Goodyear, Mr 29
Gordon, Genevieve 11
Gort, Lord, of Hamsterley 14
Gosforth, St. Charles **25**; Park 43
Grace, Francis, Brother 55
Grady, M. (Newcastle) Ltd. 44
Grange, Elizabeth, Mrs. 53
Grant, Gerard Brother O.P. 11
Gray, Tony 25
Gready, L. 18
Great Stainton 48
Green John (architect) 1, 52; Michael 26
Greencroft 13
Greene, Michael 47
Greenhall, Alan, of Ryton 15
Greenwell, Thomas 52
Gregorian, Calendar 31; University (Rome) 22

Gregory XVI, Pope 5
Gregson, Father 38; George 60
Grene, Christopher 50
Grenville Family (Lords of Jesmond) 3, 43
Grey Family of Chillingham 65; Henry 60
Greystoke, Ralph Lord 35
Grieve, James 6
Grieveson, Miss 23
Griffiths, Bishop Ambrose (O.S.B.) 9/10, 15, 24-6,
    28, 30, 42, 59, 60; Michael 23
Guilds, of St. Agnes, St. Patrick and St. Bede 33;
    Ladies 28
Gunning, James TD 60
Guthred, King of Northumbria 50
Habell, Mark 15
Hagan, James, Bishop of Makurdi, Nigeria 13
Haggarty, J. 47
Haggerston Family 6, 63, 65;
Hall, Harold 60; Lawrence of Dilicote Hall 29;
    Mrs. 13; Oswald, James (O.S.B.) 12, 66
Hampeth 1
Hamsterley Hall 14
Handicapped Children's Pilgrimage Trust
    (HCPT), 20
Hankin, Father 35; Mr 55
Hanley, James 34
Hann, Charles 65
Hannah, Peter 53
Hannan, Richard 34
Hanne, Mr. 6
Hannigan, Fr. 11
Hannon, Andrew 23
Hansom, Joseph (architect) see Dunn & Hansom
Harborn, Nicholas, Rector of Simonburn 5
Harbotel Family, Guiscard, Sir (Lord of Beamish)
Harden 7
Hardman, John 26
Hardwick Hall 20, 27, 32
Harivel, P.E. 26
Harperley Hall 16
Harpyn, John 48
Harriott, Rev. Dr 39
Harris, Samuel, Canon 21; William 57
Harrison, Aidan 15
Harrow 16
Hart 26; Charles 63; Fr. 44; Leo 2
Hartborn, Fr. 8
Hartburn 37

Hartlepool, Education Committee 27;
    Hospital 27; St. Joseph **26**, 32; St. Mary **27**;
St. Thomas More 27
Hartley Wood, Elders, Walker, Millican of
    Gateshead 41
Harvey, Mr. 4; Thomas 19
Hassock Hall, Derbys. 2
Haswell 31
Haverton Hill 8
Hawarden, John 53
Hawkins, Samuel & Margaret 1
Hawthorn Leslie 28
Haydon Bridge 12
Haydon, P.J. (S.J.) 56
Hayes, Fr. 16; Martin 33; Canon J.J. 47
Head, David 8
Hebburn, 15, **28**; Hall 28, 33
Heckles, Garrett 37
Hedley, Dr. Arthur Samuel, (O.S.B.) 58; Bishop of
    Newport & Menevia 9,12, 37;
    Mary Ann of Collingwood House 37;
    Miss 27
Hedworth 33
Heenan, Cardinal 33
Helen, Sister (S.N.D.) 14
Hemy, H.F. 52
Henly, John de 48
Henry I 37, 63
Henry III 2
Henry VIII 5, 15, 33, 52, 61, 66
Henry, Fr. 15; St. 2, 61
Herewald 61
Herswell, Yorkshire 17
Hesleyside 5
Hewitt, David 11
Heworth 22
Hexham, St. Mary 5, **29**, 46
Heyrick, T., Vicar of Gainford 4
Hickey, Aidan 66; Michael 26
Higgins, Henry 44
Higginson, James (O.S.B.) 29
High Woodifield 16
Highfield, St. Joseph 13, **30**
Hilda, Sr. 41; St. 26, 27, 50
Hildridge, Joseph 10
Hill, Fr. 51; Justice 22; Richard 32
Hillas, Thomas 11
Hinsley, Cardinal 33

Hodgson Family 5,13, 14, 33, 61; Alan 29; Edward 30; Francis 55; Richard 28; Robert, Edmund & John 28
Hogarth, Bp. William, 4, 10-12, 16, 18-20, 24, 26/7, 33, 35-7, 39, 42, 50, 52, 56, 59, 64/5
Hogg, Fr. 51; James 24; John 32
Holford, Peter 21
Holiday, Fr. 51; John 11, 32
Holland 15; Michael 37
Hollis, Canon Lawrence 14
Holmes, Fr. 59; Francis 15
Holmside 13
Holtby, Richard (S.J.) 20, 28, 32, 55
Holy Island 35
Holystone 58
Holywell 31
Hooff, Gerard Van 27
Hope Farm 2
Hopper, Paul (CSP) 11
Horsley 35; Robert 47; Sir Thomas 35;
Horton Grange 46; St. Mary 12
Hosten, Aloysius 59
Houghton-le-Spring, St. Michael 18, 19, **31**; Kepier School 31
Howard Fr. Dr. 1, 4
Howe Hills, Mordon 48
Howe, Fr. (S.J.) 13; Canon George 61; Joseph (S.J.) 35; Messrs. of West Hartlepool 22
Huddleston, chalice 5; Richard, John (OSB) 5
Hudson Bros. of Middlesbrough 8; Family, 38; W. 47
Hughes, Bob 23; Christopher 25; Joseph 34
Hull, William 52
Hulne Priory 1, 19, 58
Humble Family 9; Canon Joseph 60
Hume, Basil Cardinal 37, 39, 42
Hunt, Sid 41
Hunters Moor Hospital 39
Hurley, D. 9
Hurst, William 65
Hutchinson, Fr. 64; Francis 7
Hutton House, 20, 32; Sts. Peter & Paul 27, **32**; William Bede, (O.S.B.) 5, 52
Hylton Castle 55-7
I.C.I. 8
Ickenroth, Charles 63
Industrial Revolution 11, 13

Ingram, John of Hereford 23; Bl. John, 6, 24, 31, 63
Insula, Richard de 48
Iona 6
Ireland 2, 15, 22
Irish Christian Brothers 55
Iveston 13
Jacks, William 25, 30
Jackson, Chris 55; Leo 3
Jacobite 29, 57; rebellion 24
James I 52
James II 4, 58
Jane, Sister 33
Jarrow, St. Bede **33**, 50/1; St. Paul's monastery 28, 33
Jefferson, Robert 53
Jefferys, Mgr. 57
Jerningham, Sir Hugh and Lady 6
Jesmond 23; Holy Name 15; St. Mary's Chapel **43**
Jesson, Francis Xavier, Mother 19
Jesuits (S.J.) 1, 6/7, 10, 13/4, 21, 23, 28, 35, 37, 39, 50, 52, 55, 63, 65
Joan, Sister (Marist) 29
John of the Cross, St. 19
John Paul II, Pope 43
John XXIII, Pope 13, 19
Johnson, Fr. 13, 61; James 45, 55; John 34
Jones, John 13
Joseph, Marie (M.H.M.) 11
Jubb, Edward & Philip 12
Justice and Peace Group 13, 23, 25, 44
Kathleen, Sister 36
Kay, Edward 34; Fr. 11
Keane, Daniel 38; James 30
Kearney, Canon Francis (1825-1890) 11,13; Canon Francis 15; Father (Canon) Philip 1,54,55; P.J. 61
Keelan, Frank 8
Keenan, Angela 26
Keevins, Frank 36
Kellaw, (Kellow) Bishop 14, 48
Kellett, Denis 66; Fr. 57
Kelly, Edmund 33; John 22; Verna 4
Kemp, Tony 60
Kennedy, John 11; Edward 22
Kennet, William & Katherine 24
Kenny, Anthony (CSP) 11; J. 41

Keoghan, Michael 8, 57
Kerr, Miss 58
Kershaw, Austin (O.S.B.) 66; Robert (O.S.B.) 37
Kerwick, Patrick 8
Keswick, Our Lady and St. Charles 17
Kielder Forest 5
Kipling, Ann of Darlington 18, 53
Kippersluis, Gerard Van 27
Kirkham, Bishop of Durham 4
Kirsopp Family 29; Fr. 29, 47
Kirwan, Fr. 51
Knight, Canon William 26/7; Alice 27
Knights, Hospitallers 35;
    of St. Columba 14, 22, 60
Knowles, David (O.S.B.) 33
Kuyte, Francis James Arcadius 10, 15
Kyrke, Thomas Del 27
La Croix, Roger de, Sister 24
La Sagesse Order 23/4
Lacey, Canon Patrick 26
Lady's Well (St. Ninian's) 58
Lamb, Blanche 14; Fr. 16, Martha 4;
    Robert & Richard 3
Lambspring 37
Lambton 31; Ven. Joseph 34
Lancashire 5
Lanchester 13
Landreth, Canon Leo 30, 51; Lewis 24
Langley, Bl. Richard, Anne & Isobel 28
Langley Moor, St. Patrick **34**
Lanherne Carmel 19
Larkin, H.L. 9
Lartington 4
Lavery, Felix 25; Hugh 30, 47; Joseph 66
Lawe Top 50
Lawrenson, Mr. 27
Lawson Family of Brough Hall 13;
    Dorothy of St. Anthony's, Walker 3, 24, 28;
    Fenwick 18; Grace, John 19;
    Mrs. 46, 61; Sir John 3; Sir William 24
Laydon, Fr. 40
Leadbitter, Jasper (O.S.B.) 29; T.G. 39
Leadgate 13
League of the Cross 9, 13
Leckonby, Thomas (S.J.) 13
Lee, Sir Robert 21
Lee's Factory Institute 22
Leech, Fr. 20
Leeds, St. Saviour's Community 16

Legion of Mary 2, 8, 11, 13, 22, 24, 28, 35, 38, 41,
    46, 50/1, 60/1
Leigh, Philip 24
Lemek 54
Lennon, James 12, Joseph 35
Leo XIII, Pope 10
Leonard, Mrs. 27
Leslie, Lt. Col. Charles 2
Leyburn, Bishop John 29, 35, 42, 58, 63
Liddel Castle 7
Liddell Family 52; Matthew & John 25;
Liddell-Grainger family 6
Lierre Convent 19
Lincoln, Don 31
Lincolnshire 4
Lindisfarne 2, 6, 27, 33, 65
Lindsay, Bp. Hugh 1/2, 5/6, 12, 23, 25, 28/9, 37,
    41/2, 44, 46, 48, 50-53, 62
Lingard, Rev. Dr. 13, 52, 60, 62
Lintz Green Hall 13, 14
Little Sisters' Homes, Sunderland, Newcastle,
    13, 15, 40, 56
Little Way Association 13
Livingstone, Miss 58
Lockey, Michael 55
Lofthouse 13
Loftus, J 38, 45
London, St. Mungo's Community 32
Londonderry Family 47
Long Newton 4, 8
Longhorsley, St. Thomas of Canterbury 2, 12,
    15, **35**, 37, 47
Longhoughton 1
Longridge Towers 6
Longstaff, Owen 4
Lonsdale, Fr. 54
Lough, John G. 36
Loughlin, John (CMS) 28
Lourdes 12
Louvain, Convent of St. Monica 4
Lovel, Lady 19
Low Chibburn 35
Low Countries 15
Low Gosforth, 44
Lowe, George Augustine (O.S.B.) 12 37
Lowery, J.S. 33
Lowrie, William 16
Lowry, J. & W. of Newcastle 11, 15
Lucey, Fr. 48

Lugubalia, Cumberland 17
Lumley Family 9
Lumsden, Mr. 28, Thomas 33
Lynch, Malachy, Prior of Aylesford 1
Lynn, Jack 11
Macartney, Andrew 63
Mackie, Sheila 64
Mackin, Fr. 33
Maday, Leo 1
Maddison Family 9
Magee, Luke 36
Magill, Canon Augustine 13
Magnier, Father (C.S.S.R.) 56
Mainsforth 48
Maire, Family of Hardwick and Lartington 4, 20, 26, 31/2, 35, 61;
    William, Bishop of Cinna 4
Malia, Brian 2
Malindi Mission, Kenya 38
Mallaley, Fr. 57
Mallon, Miss 57
Malone, William 10
Manfield 4
Manning, Cardinal 42
Maquet, Fr. 65
March, John (Vicar of Newcastle) 28
Margaret of St. Francis, Sister 19
Marian, Priests Movement 38; Year 43
Marist Brothers 33
Mark, Brother 56
Markland, Rev. 48
Marley Family 21; Francis 29, Father 57
Marr, Michael 22
Marren, Joseph 1
Marriott, Paul 55
Marron, Fr. 3; Marron, J.V. 8;
    Edward Vincent 32
Marshall, T.W. 52
Marston Moor 14, 17
Martin V, Pope 43
Martinelis, Boleslaw 65
Mary Bridget of the Passion, Sister 19
Mary I 1, 5
Mason, Francis (S.J.) 48
Mathews, Patrick Thomas 14, 20
Matthews, Toby, Bishop of Durham 13, 52
McAuley, Catherine 54
McBrien, Philip 3
McCaffrey, Fr Benedict 36

McCartan, Canon Hugh 11
McCartie, Bp. Leo 26
McCartney, Fr. 56
McCleary, Michael 65
McConnell, Wilfrid 18
McCormack, Bp. Joseph, 5, 15, 35, 41/2, 53, 55-7, 61; Thomas 8
McDermott, A. 22; Hugh 34; Martin 38; Paul 20
McCullagh, Fr. F. 6
McDonagh, Dominic 21
McDonnell, Ciaran 10; Martin 33; Rachel 36
McElduff, Bernard 25
McElhone, John 11
McEvoy, James Augustine 31
McFadden, Michael 30
McGivern, Dominic 45
McGlinshey, Mr. 33
McInnes, Catherine 33
McKenna, Michael 50; Pat 31; Patrick 23
McKenny, James 41, 65
McKinlay, Boniface (O.S.B.) 12
McLachlan, John (Bishop of Galloway) 33
McLean, Fox, Plant & Co. 8
McMahon, Patrick 47
McManemy, Father 57; Thomas 30
McMullen, Father 56
McNamara, Brian 39
McNeill, Margaret 60
McShane, Austin 34, 38
McSweeney, John B. 65
Meaborne Family 13
Meagher, Desmond 37, 47; Fr. 57
Medomsley 13
Melia, Michael 6; Vincent 46
Menart, Charles 25
Mercy, Sisters of 1/2, 6, 10/11, 16, 25, 29, 35, 38, 42, 47, 54/5, 57-9, 64
Merlay, Ranulph de 37
Merry del Val, Cardinal Raphael 62
Mesnard, Mrs. 54
Mewburn, Francis 18
Meynell, Fr. 4; George 28, 33
Middleton-in-Teesdale, 4
Milburn, David 16, 42; of York 22;
    S.W. & Partners (architects) 57
Mill Dam 50
Mill Hill Fathers 23, 59
Miller, Gerry 25
Million Penny Fund 15

Milroy, J.W. 41
Minsteracres, St. Elizabeth 11, 12, **36**, 61
Minto, Fr. 59
Missouri, St. Louis Priory 5
Mitford, Mitford, Baron 46; Castle 37;
    Roger & James 58
Monaghan, Austin (M.H.M.) 11; Gerard 49;
    Kathleen 26; Br. Lewis 55
Monica, Sr. 41
Monk, General, 35
Monkridge Farm 5
Monkton 28, 33
Monkwearmouth 33
Morpeth, Bullers Green 35; St. Robert of
    Newminster 12, **37**
Morris, Bishop 26, 27; Brian 8, 46
Morrissey, P.J. 28
Morse, Henry, St. 19, 61, 64
Mostyn, Bishop, 9, 39, 53; Family 19
Mountney, Ursula 29
Moverley, Francis 27
Mowbray, Robert de 2
Muir, Alan 61
Mullarkey, P. (O.S.B.) 9
Mulligan, Malachy 30
Murphy, Rev. Dr. J. 5, 22; John 2
Murray, Family 60
Murton, St. Joseph **38**
Myers and Wilson of Hull 40
Narok 54
Nazareth House 39, 61
Netherton 7, 12
Netherwitton 35
Neville Family 34, 36, 64; Elizabeth 66;
    Lady Katherine 13
New Hartley 12, 35, 37
New Tunstall 15
Newbottle 31
Newbrough Earl and Countess of 2
Newcastle 2, 3, 11, 13, 15, 23, 43;
    St. Cuthbert's Grammar School 13, 15, 27;
    St. Andrew's 11, 22, 24, 33, **39** ;
    St. Mary's 15, 22, 23, **40**; All Saints 35
Newgate 4
Newhouse 21
Newman, Cardinal 10, 49
Newminster Abbey 12, 35, 37, 46
Newsham 12; Mgr. Charles 62

Newton Family 64; Elizabeth 10; William 7
Nichols, Mgr. Kevin 4, 32
Nicholson, William 23, 63
Nigeria 19
Nixon, John 29
Nolan, Camillus 36
Norbert, St. 36
Norbertines 1
Norham 6,
Norman 1, 20, 21, 24, 26, 35, 43, 47, 61, 63
North Gosforth, The Sacred Heart **44**
North Shields 11, 13; St. Cuthbert 28, 33, 39, **45**
Northallerton 17
Northern Brethren's Fund 30
Northern Ireland 23
Northern Province 62
Northumberland, Duke of 1; Earl of 8
Norton 53
Nunraw Abbey 38
O'Brien, Fr. 24, 51; Thomas (C.F.) 65
O'Callaghan, Canon Cornelius 53;
    Bishop Henry 42, 61
O'Connell, Mother Aloysius, 55; Patrick 41
O'Connor, Andrew 36; Hugh 30, 35, 57;
    Patrick 20
O'Donoghue, Canon 11
O'Donovan, Canon Daniel 55
O'Dwyer, Fr. 3
O'Gorman, Father William 31, 57; John 25
O'Kelly, Denis 65
O'Leary, Aloysius 37
O'Neill, Charles Henry Oswald (O.S.B.) 66;
    Joseph 25;
O'Neill, W. 11
O'Reilly, Henry 37
O'Sullivan, Dermot 34; Fr. 26
O'Toole, John (C.M.S.) 28
Office, Stephen 23
Olsen, Canon Henry 9
Oratorians 10
Ord Family 1; Edward 44; Fr. 20
Orr, Arthur A. 26
Orrell, Robert 59
Oscott 16
Oswald, King 6, 65; St. 6, 50
Oswin, King 61; Oswin's Hill 50; St. 2, 61
Otterburn 5, 22
Ouston 9

Owens, Anthony 24, 26, 64
Oxford 4, 10, 13; Oxford Movement 16;
    University 6, 21, 42, 50
Padre Pio 6, 11, 13, 41
Page, Brendan, Sister 11; Duncan 24
Palestine 1
Palmers 33
Papist's Cross 5
Paris 14, 16
Parker, John 34; John (George) 1, 34, 41
Parkous, Mr. of Newcastle 3
Pascal, J. Steinlet and Son 15
Passionist(s), monastery 7, 36
Paton, Alice 6
Pattison, Ralph of Newcastle (architect) 44
Paulinus, St. 58, 65
Peacock, Thomas 10
Peat, Lady 54
Pegswood 37
Pelaw 22
Pellechet, Jules 4
Penrith 33
Penswick, Bishop Thomas 29, 52
Pepper, William (O.S.B.) 6
Percy Family; Bl. Thomas 1, 2, 14, 34
Peter of Alcantara, St. 19
Peter, St. 6
Peterlee 32, 47
Petre Family 29
Pevsner, N. 47
Peyton, Fr. 16
Phelan, James 44
Philip, Father 55
Phillips, David 26; Dominic (O.P.) 46
Phillipson, Wilfrid (O.S.B.) 9, 66
Pickering, Aidan 61; Austin 14; Lancelot 4;
    Fr. 14
Piercebridge 4
Pieters, Pierre 56
Pilgrimage of Grace 1, 5, 29
Pinckney, Miles 34, 45
Pippet, Fr. 16
Pius IX, Pope 16
Pius, Robert (O.P.) 22
Plashett's Moor 5
Platt, Canon Ralph 52, 64
Plowman, Ernest 4
Plumtree, Bl. Thomas 34
Pocklington 28
Ponteland, **46**

Pontoise 6
Pontop Hall 13, 45, 55, 60, 62
Poor Clares 18, 58
Pope, J.A. (O.S.B.) 5
Port Clarence 8, 16
Porter, Francis 29
Potts, Elizabeth 25; Luke 58
Power, Thomas 12
Premonstratensian 1, 16; Order 36
Presentation Brothers 25
Preston, Bishop Richard, 8, 42, 54, 56, 61, 66
Pringle, Mary 37; & Co. of Gateshead 4
Pudsey, (de Puiset) Bishop Hugh 6, 30, 49, 55
Pugin, Augustus Welby, 8, 13, 16, 26, 40, 52/3,
    62, 64; Peter Paul 62
Purtill, Michael 28
Purvis, Fr. 59
Pyle, Leo 45, 55
Quinn, Philip 64
Raby Castle 4
Radcliffe (Ratcliffe) Family, 2, 5, 12, 20, 29, 58
Raffa, Leander 9
Rainton 47
Ramm, Mr. 20
Rand, Cuthbert 65
Rankin, Mrs. 33
Ravensdowne 6
Ravensworth, Earl of 14
Rawlins, Bl. Alexander 4
Reay, Mary 15
Red Barns 39
Red Row 2
Redemptorists 56
Reed Milligan 27
Reformation 20, 22, 26/7, 35, 64
Regan, John 14
Reginald of Durham 5
Reid, Fr. John 13, 59
Reilly, Thomas 25
Relief Acts 33, 55
Returns of Papists 15
Rheims 5, 21
Rice, Br. Edmund 54/5; Frank 48
Richmond, Ronald 13
Rickaby, W. 13
Rickard, Mary 3
Riddell Family 9, 24, 35, 37, 46;
    Bishop William 9, 10, 22-4, 39, 40, 65
Riding Mill 11
Ridsdale Family 18

Rievaulx Abbey 4
Riley, Henry 14; Sidney 64
Rimmer, Richard 55
Rising of the northern Earls 1, 17, 34, 36, 60, 64
Rite of Christian Initiation for Adults (R.C.I.A.) 9, 11/12, 21, 26, 29, 33, 41, 44
Rivonia, Johannesburg 19
Robert, Fr. 1; Edward 2
Robinson, Adam 47
Robson, Mary 58; Mr. 39
Roby, Father 19; James 10
Rogers, Canon John 61
Rogerson, John 61
Romaldkirk 4
Roman Wall 13, 41
Rome 5, 16, 21
Rooke, Fr. 16, 64
Rooney, Canon & Mgr. James 18, 20
Rose, Christopher (S.J.) 32
Rosminians 11
Rossi, A. 38
Rothbury 58
Routhbury, Walter de 17
Rowbotham, Ronnie 9
Rowe, John 41
Rowlands Gill 4
Rowley, J.M. 6
Rufus, William 4
Runic Cross 5
Russell, Monica 22; Mrs. 33
Rutter, Dominic 4
Ryan, Gordon 45; Michael 11
Ryhope 35
Rymer, Mr. 29
Ryton 15, 52
Sadgrove, Rev. 1
Sales, Mother de 54
Salkeld, Margaret 5
Salthouse, Arthur 63
Saltwell Park 23
Salvin Family of Croxdale Hall 17, 27, 34, 48, 60; Anthony 1
Sandhoe 5
Sandy Lane Camp 44
Sawley, Mr. 38
Saxon 1, 2, 4, 6, 10, 13, 20, 24, 26, 29, 31, 35, 38, 47, 55/6, 61, 63
Scannell, Benedict 9
Scarre, William Horner 4

Scollard, Agnes 54
Scot, Peter, Richard 41
Scotswood 41
Scott, David 52; Fr. 3 ; Geoffrey (O.S.B.) 9: James 48; Rt. Hon. Simon 48; Sir Walter 4
Scott-Briggs, Captain 57
Seaham Hall 47
Seaham Harbour **47**
Seaton Burn 3
Sedburgh, Westmorland 16
Sedgefield 8, 28, **48**
Sedgley Park School 13
Seghill 3
Selby Family 7, 65
Sharp, Archdeacon 37
Sharratt, Bernard 27, 57
Sharrock, John Dunstan (O.S.B.) 5, 35
Shaw, Norman 6
Shawe-Storey, Mrs. 3
Shea, James 26
Sheehan, Fr. 7; Thomas Vincent 48, 58
Sheep Hill (The Ridings) 15
Sheldon, Henry (S.J.) 1
Sherburn Hospital 11
Sheridan, James 9
Shilbottle 1
Shotley Bridge 11, 13
Shotton 48
Sicklemore, John 29
Sidney Arms 12
Sidney, Family of Cowpen Hall 12
Silksworth **49**
Silvertop Family of Minsteracres 4, 7, 12, 13, 26/7, 36, 52, 61, 65
Simm, Andy 2
Simonburn 5
Simpson, George 56
Singleton, Michael 29; Richard 50
Skivington, John 1
Slater, John 9; Canon Thomas Augustine 27, 32
Sledwich Hall 4
Smith, Aelred 36; Canon 57; C.A. 31; Charles Gregory (O.S.B.) 2, 35; Fr. 11, 54; Henry (S.J.) 6, 21; Bishop James 4, 42; John 60; John (S.J.) 13, 35, 37; P. 41; Phil 26; Thos. (shipbuilder) 44; Canon Vincent 6, 39, 44, 57; Winnie 46; Bishop Thomas 11, 13, 45; Canon Thomas 55; Canon William 55

Smythe, Family 21
Society of Jesus (see Jesuits)
Society of the Sacred Heart, Fenham 12
Soissons 4
Somerset House 4
South Shields **50**, 51
Southerne, Ven. William 29
Southgate, Paul 18
Southwick, A. (A.R.B.S.) 23
Southworth, Bl. John 58
Spedding, Mrs. M. 34
Spence, Canon Robert 10, 18
Spencer, Gerard (O.S.B.) 37; Michael 5
Spittal 6
Spraggon, Mgr. David (M.H.M.) 11
St. Agnes, (Guild of) 15
St. Bede's Place 37
St. Helen Hall 19
St. John of God, Brothers of 18
St. Omer 6, 14, 37
Stack, Father 57
Stafferton, Fr. 13
Staindrop 4
Stainton 4
Stanley 11, 13, 14, 16, 52; Lady Mary 6
Stark, Canon 45; James 63
Starrs, Peter 51
Station Town 32
Stebbing, Father 56
Steinlat and Maxwell 41
Stella 13, 15, **52**
Stephenson, George 20; Joseph (S.J.) 35
Stockton 4, 6, 18, **53**
Stone, Martin 21
Stonecroft 29, 36
Stoner, Bill (architect) 25
Stonor, Hon. Edmund (Archbishop of Trebizond) 36
Stonyhurst College, Lancs. 1, 22, 24, 44
Storey, Arthur 60; Thomas 53
Stout, Thomas 58
Stranton 26
Streatlam Castle 4
Strickland, W. Rev. 1
Stronge, Bernard 22
Strother, Edward 1; William 22
Stuart, Ignatius 37; Mary 58
Stuarts 29, 52, 57
Sturton Grange 1

Suffield, Fr. Robt. 26, 65
Summerfield House 23
Sunderland 13, 15-17, 35, 47; Little Sisters 32; St. Anthony's Convent **54** St.Benet **56**; St. Cecilia **57**; St. Mary 1, 18, **55**
Surtees Family 14, 44
S.V.P. (Society of St. Vincent de Paul) 2, 3, 6, 8-16, 19, 21, 22, 24-6, 28, 29, 31-3, 37, 38, 41, 44-53, 55-61, 65, 66
Swale, Sir John Bede Bt. (O.S.B.) 9
Swales John 4; Ann (Daughter of Charity) 53
Swallowell, Bl. George 18, 23/4, 31
Swarbrick, Ceolfrid (O.S.B.) 37
Sweeney, Michael 55, 57
Swinburne, Castle 29, 35, 46; Family 5, 14, 30, 36, 46
Swindlehurst, Bishop Owen 11, 26, 34, 42, 56/7, 60, 66
Swinhoe, Fr. (O.S.B.) 37
Taggart, Fr. 56; John 14
Tailboys, Mr. 13
Talbot, John & Gilbert 5; Gilbert 58
Tanfield 13, 14
Tanner, David 63
Taylerson, Canon Robert 51, 53
Taylor, David 47; John 21; Joseph 27; Miss 56; Ursula 12, 28, 33, 42, 50, 61
Taylor-Smith, Family 59, 62
Taylor Treasure 21
Teesdale 4
Tempest, Family 6, 9, 13, 15, 50, 52
Teresa of Avila, St. 19
Teresa of Jesus, Mother 19
Thaddeus, Fr. (O.S.F.) 43
Third Order of St. Francis 39
Thompson, E. 23; Frances (Dolly) 57; Kevin 46; Michael 64; Peter Antoninus (O.P.) 29; Robert 29; Canon William 21
Thorman, Bishop Joseph 4, 11, 22/3, 30, 34, 39, 41/2, 51
Thorngate 4
Thornley Hall 26, 32
Thornton Family, John 6, 27, 35
Thropton 7, 5, **58**
Thurlwell, Norman 8
Thwing, Bl. Thomas 35, 37
Tidyman, Fr. 6
Tigar, Clement (S.J.) 1
Timney, Father John 65

Tinn, Elizabeth 14
Tinnion, Lawrence 33, 40
Titus Oates' Plot 37
Toes, Tunstall 64
Tomaney, Austin 3
Tone Hall 5
Toner, Dr. Matthew 28
Topcliffe 24
Torbet, John 21
Tow Law 16, **59**
Towers, Denis 5
Townend 5
Traynor, Bernard 37, 59
Treacy, Daniel 25
Trimdon 48
Trollope, Family of Thornley Hall 20, 26/7, 32, 48, 50
Tuddoe, John de; Agnes (Prioress of Neasham) 60
Tudhoe 13, 52 **60**
Tunstall Family of Wycliffe 4; Marmaduke 55
Tuohey, Bede 10, 44; Francis 31
Turner, Charles Thomas (O.S.B.) 37, 51; Fr. (S.J.) 52; Fr. 5; Mary 58
Turnerelli, Charles 55
Turpin Family 45, 50
Tweedmouth 6
Tweedy, Fr. 48; John 51
Tyburn 16
Tyne Dock **51**
Tynemouth, 2, 12, 27, 41/2, 45, 50, **61**
Ulgham 35
Umfraville, Family 58
Umfrevill, Robert, Sir 14
Underwinter 16
University Catholic Chaplaincy 39
Ursulines 6
Ushaw (& College) **62**, 4, 5, 11, 13-16, 18-23, 26/7, 29, 30, 32, 36, 42, 45, 52, 54, 55, 59-61, 64, 66
Valka, John 1
Valladolid 6, 14, 21
Vatican Councils 13-15, 33, 57, 60, 64
Vaughan, Cardinal Archbishop of Westminster 27; Bishop John 25; Richard 41
Vavasour, Richard 27
Vesci, William de, Baron of Alnwick 1
Viking 27, 50
Voerde, St. Paul's 1
Wailes, William 40

Walker 11; Alban 20, 64; Charles 22, 28, 56; George Augustine (O.S.B.) 14; Robert 6
Walkergate 1
Wallsend 11
Walmsley, J. 2; Henry 3, 46
Walsh, James 28
Walshe, Edward (S.J.) 10; John (S.J.) 22-4
Walsingham 43; Francis 6
Warburton, John 58
Warcop, Family 4
Ward, Fr. 16, 64
Warde, Sr. Mary Xavier 54
Wardell, Mark 26
Warden Law 31, 47
Warkworth 2
Washington 31, 33
Waterton, Canon 50; Charles (S.J.) 10; Charles (explorer) 60
Watson, Provost Joseph 25, 60; Thomas 8
Waugh Mr. (architect) 28
Wawton, John 4
Wearmouth 27
Webster, William 4
Weldon, Fr. (O.S.B.) 3
Wellesley training ship 45
Wellfield House 8, 38
Wells, John & Mary 27
West Hartlepool 26/27
West Herrington 31
West Indian Mission 1
West View 27
Westminster Cathedral 16
Westmorland, Earl of 8, 20
Westoe Towers 50
Westwood 13
Whalley, Richard (O.F.M.) 65
Whalton, Robert de 17
Wheatley, Dr. 15
Whelehan, Mark 36
White Canons (of Blanchland) 1, 16; 11
White, Gerard 57; Matthew 12; Maria 33
Whiteside, Archbishop 22
Whitfield, Fr. (S.J.) 60; Thomas 14
Whitley Bay 41
Whitson, Luke 18
Whittingham, **63**
Whorlton 4
Whytehead, Francis 55, 57
Wickwar, William 26

281

Widdrington Castle & Family 1, 7, 15, 29, 35, 46, 52, 58; Widdrington 35, 37
Wilcock, Peter 55
Wilcox, P. Fr. 45
Wild, Gerry 18
Wilfrid, St. 5, 10, 29
Wilfridians 10
Wilkinson, Aidan 25; Cuthbert 56; George Hutton 16; Edward 37; Ernest 23; Fr., Canon & Bishop 3, 10, 16, 22, 24, 26, 28, 33, 35, 37, 42, 54-6, 59, 61, 64
William the Conqueror 4
William, Bishop 55
Williams, Bishop (O.P.) 23/4
Williamson, Sir Hedworth 56
Willers, Audrey 38
Willington 16; **59**
Wills, Arthur Vernon 65
Wilson, Canon John 14, 30; John Benedict (O.S.B.) 52
Wingate 32
Winterton 48
Wiseman, Nicholas, Cardinal 11, 21, 26/7, 62, 64
Witham Family of Cliffe & Lartington, 4, 21, 27, 36, 40, 42, 52/3, 62;
Wittenhall, Thomas 64
Witton 16
Witton Shields 35
Witty, Edward 28, Father 33
Wolsingham 7, 13, 16, **64**
Wolviston 8
Wood, Fanny 28
Wooler **65**
Woollett, Joseph Sydney (S.J.) Pro-Vicar Apostolic 1
Worcester 5
Worsley, Anne 19
Worswick, James 13, 22, 24, 33, 39, 45, 50, 58, 61
Wrekenton 12, **66**
Wrennall, Canon Henry 15, 47, 52
Wright, John 22; James 35; Thomas 47
Wrigley, Father (O.P.) 38
Wylam 15
Wynberg, Capetown 19
Xaverian Brothers 26
Yates, John 21
Y.C.W. 9, 37
York 1, 4, 5, 6, 13, 28, 37, 45; Duke of 19, 39
Young, James 51

SELECT BIBLIOGRAPHY

The archives of the Diocese of Hexham and Newcastle and published material in the *Records Series* of the Catholic Record Society, *Northern Catholic History, Northern Catholic Calendar, Northern Cross, The Tablet* and *Ushaw Magazine* have been used extensively in the writing of the outline history of the diocese and/or the individual articles. The following books, articles and pamphlets have also been consulted.

GENERAL WORKS

Addleshaw, G.W.O., *Blanchland - A Short History* (1951)
Anstruther, G., *The Seminary Priests* (4 vols. 1968-77)
Archer, A., *The Two Catholic Churches: A Study in Oppression* (1986)
Arthur, J., *The Ebbing Tide: Policy and Principles of Catholic Education* (1995)
Beck, G. (ed.), *The English Catholics 1850-1950* (1950)
Bede, The Venerable, *Ecclesiastical History of the English Nation* (Everyman 1723, Rev. 1847)
Bossy, J., *The English Catholic Community 1570-1850* (1975)
Caraman, P., *Henry Morse* (1957)
Cleary, J., *Catholic Social Action in Britain 1909-59 (1961)*
Coman, P., *Catholics and the Welfare State* (1977)
Cooter, R.J., 'Lady Londonderry and the Irish Catholics of Seaham Harbour: 'No-Popery' out of context' (*Recusant History* vol. 13 1976)
Corfe, T., *History of Sunderland* (1973)
Costar, D., *The Shrine of Our Lady of Jesmond* (1930)
Crangle, L.P., 'The Roman Catholic Community in Sunderland from the 16th Century' (Sunderland Antiquarian Society 1959)
Crichton, J., et al, *English Catholic Worship: Liturgical Renewal in England Since 1900* (1979)
d'Andrea, W., *A Martyr of Durham* (Bl. Ralph Corby) (1956)
Dictionary of National Biography
Dixon, D.D., *Whittingham Vale* (1895, rev. 1979)
Emery, N., 'Esh Hall' (*Durham Archaeological Journal*, No. 3, 1987)
Fee, W., *Martyrs of Northumberland and Durham* (1979)
Fitzgerald-Lombard C., *English and Welsh Priests 1801-1914* (1993)
Fordyce, W., *The History and Antiquities of the County Palatine of Durham* (2 vols. 1857)
Forster, A.M.C., 'The Maire Family of County Durham' (*Recusant History* vol. 10 1970)
Gillespie, W., *The Christian Brothers in England 1825-1880* (1975)
Gillow, J., *A Bibliographical Dictionary of the English Catholics* (5 vols. 1885-1902)
Gillow, H., *The Chapels at Ushaw* (1890)
Gooch, L., *The Durham Catholics & Industrial Development (1560-1850)* (unpub. York MA thesis 1984)
Graham, F., *The Old Halls, Houses and Inns of Northumberland* (1977)
Grierson, E., *The Companion Guide to Northumbria* (1976)
Heimann, M., *Catholic Devotion in Victorian England* (1995)
Hadcock, R.N., *Tynemouth Priory and Castle*
Hart, C., *The Early Story of St Cuthbert's Grammar School Newcastle on Tyne* (1941)
Haward, W.I., *Hide or Hang: Priest Holes of North East England* (1966)
Hornsby-Smith, M.P., *Roman Catholics in England: Studies in Social Structure since the Second World War* (1987)
Hornsby-Smith, M.P., *Roman Catholic Beliefs in England: Customary Catholicism and Transformations of Religious Authority* (1991)

Horton, M.C., *The Story of Cleveland* (1979)

Hutchinson, W., *The History and Antiquities of the County Palatine of Durham* (4 vols. 1816-40)

Johnstone, T., & Hagerty, J., *The Cross on the Sword: Catholic Chaplains in the Forces* (1996)

Kelly, B.W., *Historical Notes on English Catholic Missions* (1907)

Little, B., *Catholic Churches since 1623* (1966)

Mackenzie, E. & Ross, M., *The County Palatine of Durham* (2 vols. 1834)

MacRaild, D.M., *Irish Migrants in Modern Britain, 1750-1922* (1999)

McAndrews, T.L., *Amble and District*

McClelland V.A. & Hodgetts, M. (eds.) *From Without the Flaminian Gate: 150 Years of Roman Catholicism in England & Wales 1850-2000* (1999)

McNee, T., & Angus, D., *Seaham Harbour: The First Hundred Years 1828-1928* (1985)

Manders, F.W.D., *A History of Gateshead*

Mee, A., *Durham* (1953)

Mercy, Sisters of, *Trees of Mercy: Sisters of Mercy of Great Britain from 1839* (1993)

Merrington, J.P. & M.P., *Brancepeth 900* (1985)

Middlebrook, S., *Newcastle upon Tyne* (1950)

Milburn, D., *A History of Ushaw College* (1964)

Moyes, W.A., *Mostly Mining* (1969)

Myerscough, J.A., *The Martyrs of Durham and the North East* (1956)

Neal, F., 'English-Irish Conflict in the North-East of England' in P. Buckland & J. Belchem, *The Irish in British Labour History*, (1992)

Norman, E., *The English Catholic Church in the 19th Century* (1984)

Northumberland County History Committee, *History of Northumberland* (15 vols. 1893-1940)

Pevsner, N., *County Durham* (Penguin Buildings of England No. 9, 1953)

Reynolds, E.E., *The Roman Catholic Church in England & Wales* (1973)

Ridley, N., *Portrait of Northumberland* (1965)

Rowland, T.H., *Anglo-Saxon Northumberland*

Scott, G., *Gothic Rage Undone* (1992)

Smith, W.V., *Catholic Tyneside* (1930)

Surtees. R., *The History and Antiquities of the County Palatine of Durham* (4,vols. 1816-40)

Taylor, W.T., *Hexham Abbey* (1959)

Thorold, H., *County Durham* (1980)

Tigar, C., *Forty Martyrs of England and Wales* (1961)

Tomlinson, W.W., *Denton Hall and its Associations*

Tomlinson, W.W., *Comprehensive Guide to Northumberland* (1888)

Treble, J.H., 'The Attitude of the Roman Catholic Church towards Trade Unionism in the North of England 1833-42' (*Northern History* vol. 5 1970)

Tweedy, J. M., *Popish Elvet* Pts. I & II (1981)

Walsh E. & Forster, A.M.C., 'The Recusancy of the Brandlings' (*Recusant History* vol. 10 1969)

Wiggen, W.R., *Esh Leaves*

Worrall, E.S. (ed.), *Returns of Papists, 1767* vol. II, (C.R.S. 1989)

PARISH HISTORIES

Alnwick	Canon A. Chadwick, *St. Mary's Church, Alnwick* (1936)
	Guide to St. Paul's R.C. Church
Amble	*Parish Centenary Booklet* (Sacred Heart & St. Cuthbert) (1987)
Barnard Castle	Church Trustees, *St. Mary's Church, Barnard Castle*
	V. Chapman, *Lartington* (1985)
Benwell	*St. Joseph's Parish Handbook* (1959)
Berwick-upon-Tweed	J.M. Rowley, *A History of the Church of Our Lady and St. Cuthbert* (1992)
Bellingham	Rev. W. Nicholson, *St. Oswald's Church (1839-1989)*
Billingham	M. Morris, *Holy Rosary (1960-1985)*
Birtley	*Chronicles of St. Joseph's Mission*
Bishop Auckland	F. Hickey, *St. Wilfrid's (1846-1996)*
Blackhill	*St. Mary's Centenary Booklet* (1957)
	St. Mary's Re-opening Booklet (1986)
Brooms	T. Matthews, *History of Brooms Parish (1802-1969)*
Byermoor	S. McGahon, *The History of The Sacred Heart Parish, Byermoor*
Crawcrook	A. Harrison, *A History of St. Agnes Parish*
Crook	Parish History (typed sheets)
Darlington	The Community, *A History of Darlington Carmel 1619-1982* (1982)
	G. Wild, *The Darlington Catholics. A History up to 1866* (1983)
	St. Augustine's (1827-1977)
Easington Colliery	*Our Lady's, Easington (1865-1978)*
Esh Laude	W. Beavis, *Newhouse and Esh Laude (A short history)*
Esh Winning	*St. John Boste and the Continuity of Catholicism in the Deerness Valley* (1993)
Felling	J. Geraghty, *Parish History* (St. Patrick's)
Gateshead	V. Carney, *Corpus Christi Parish History 1936-1986*
	St. Joseph's Church Centenary Booklet
Gosforth	F. McCombie, *St. Charles's Parish History*
Hartlepool	A.E. Brown, *St. Joseph's Church (1895-1995)*
	Rev. B. Sharratt, *The Catholic Church in Hartlepool and West Hartlepool 1834 1964* (1965)
Hebburn	Rev. M. Purtill, *St. Aloysius (1888-1988)*
Hexham	Rev. W. Nicholson, *St. Mary's (1830-1980)*
Highfield	T.M. Conway, *St. Joseph's Parish History*
Houghton le Spring	D. Lincoln, *St. Michael's Parish History*
Hutton House	*Sts. Peter and Paul (1825-1975)*
Jarrow	M.J. Young, *A History of Catholic Jarrow*
Langley Moor	*St. Patrick's (Historical Sketch)* (1933)
	M. Purdom, unpub. dissertation on education
Minsteracres	Rev. J. Lenders, *Minsteracres* (1932)
Morpeth	K. Stewart and N. Cassidy, *A Short History of St. Robert's Church* (1969)
Murton	H. Abbott, *History of Murton* and parish notes
Newcastle	*St. Andrew's Parish History*
	Rev. D. Costar, *The Shrine of Our Lady of Jesmond.* (See also *Archaeologia Aeliana* 3rd series, vol. 1 1904)
	V. Bartley, *A History and Guide of the Cathedral Church of St. Mary*
North Gosforth	T. McQueen, Parish History Notes
North Shields	Canon Stark, *Parish History of St. Cuthbert's* (1903)

Silksworth	*St. Leonard's, New Silksworth, A Centenary History*
South Shields	Rev. W. Fee, *The Story of the Catholic Church in South Shields* (1976)
Stella	Rev. J. Galletly and Dr. T. Yellowley, *St. Mary and St. Thomas Aquinas* (1981)
Stockton-on-Tees	*St. Mary's (1842-1992)* and parish history notes
Sunderland	Sisters M. Wilfrid & M. Michael, *The Story of the Sunderland Sisters of Mercy 1843-1993*
	Sr. M. Stanislaus, *St. Anthony's, Sunderland* (1883-1983)
	M. Morris, *St. Cecilia's Parish (1927-1977)*
	St. Mary's, (Centenary Booklet)
	K. Devlin, et al, *St. Mary's Jubilee (1835-1985)*
	St. Benet's: parish history notes
	St. Patrick's: parish history notes
Tow Law	L. Gooch, *A Hilltop Parish* (St Joseph) (1994)
Tudhoe	A.J. Coia, *St. Charles's Parish (1858-1983)*
Tyne Dock	*Sts. Peter and Paul's Centenary (1884-1984)*
Tynemouth	Rev. A. Pickering, *The Story of Our Parish* (Our Lady and St. Oswin)
Willington	J. Conlon, Parish History Notes
Whittingham	Rev. C. Hart, *St. Mary's Church*
Wolsingham	L. Gooch et al, *Catholicism in Weardale* (1984)
Wooler	Rev. W. Nicholson, *St. Ninian's Parish History*
Wrekenton	J.P. Mallan, *History of St. Oswald's Parish and School*